Expert Oracle Database Architecture

9*i* and 10*g* Programming Techniques and Solutions

Thomas Kyte

To
Sudhir
Our resident Unix Expert

Tanmay

Apress®

**Thomas Kyte: Oracle Database Architecture: 9i and 10g
Programming Techniques and Solutions**

© 2006 Apress, Berkeley, CA, USA.

First Indian Reprint 2006
Fourth Indian Reprint 2007

ISBN 978-81-8128-425-9

This edition is manufactured in India for sale only in India, Pakistan, Bangladesh, Nepal and Sri Lanka and any other country as authorized by the publisher.

This edition is published by Springer (India) Private Limited,
A part of Springer Science+Business Media, Registered Office: 906-907, Akash Deep Building, Barakhamba Road, New Delhi – 110 001, India.

Printed in India by Rashtriya Printers, Delhi, India.

Contents

Foreword

"**T**HINK." In 1914, Thomas J. Watson, Sr. joined the company that was to become IBM, and he brought with him this simple one-word motto. It was an exhortation to all IBM employees, no matter their role, to take care in decision-making and do their jobs with intelligence. "THINK" soon became an icon, appearing on publications, calendars, and plaques in the offices of many IT and business managers within and outside IBM, and even in *The New Yorker* magazine cartoons. "THINK" was a good idea in 1914, and it is a good idea now.

"Think different." More recently, Apple Computer used this slogan in a long-running advertising campaign to revitalize the company's brand, and even more important, to revolutionize how people think of technology in their daily lives. Instead of saying "think differently," suggesting *how* to think, Apple's slogan used the word "different" as the object of the verb "think," suggesting *what* to think (as in, "think big"). The advertising campaign emphasized creativity and creative people, with the implication that Apple's computers uniquely enable innovative solutions and artistic achievements.

When I joined Oracle Corporation (then Relational Software Incorporated) back in 1981, database systems incorporating the relational model were a new, emerging technology. Developers, programmers, and a growing group of database administrators were learning the discipline of database design using the methodology of normalization. The then unfamiliar, nonprocedural SQL language impressed people with its power to manipulate data in ways that previously took painstaking procedural programming. There was a lot to think about then—and there still is. These new technologies challenged people not only to learn new ideas and approaches, but also to think in new ways. Those who did, and those who do, were and are the most successful in creating innovative, effective solutions to business problems using database technology to its best advantage.

Consider the SQL database language that was first introduced commercially by Oracle. SQL permits application designers to manipulate sets of rows with a nonprocedural (or "declarative") language, rather than writing iterative loops in conventional languages that process records one at a time. When I was first introduced to SQL, I found it required me to "think at 45 degrees" to figure out how to use set processing operations like joins and subqueries to achieve the result I wanted. Not only was the idea of set processing new to most people, but so also was the idea of a nonprocedural language, where you specified the result you wanted, not how to derive it. This new technology really did require me to "think differently" and also gave me an opportunity to "think different."

Set processing is far more efficient than one-at-a-time processing, so applications that fully exploit SQL in this way perform much better than those that do not. Yet, it is surprising how often applications deliver suboptimal performance. In fact, in most cases, it is application design, rather than Oracle parameter settings or other configuration choices, that most directly determines overall performance. Thus, application developers must learn not only details about database features and programming interfaces, but also new ways to think about and use these features and interfaces in their applications.

Much "conventional wisdom" exists in the Oracle community about how to tune the system for best performance or the best way to use various Oracle features. Such "wisdom" sometimes becomes "folklore" or even "mythology," with developers and database administrators adopting these ideas uncritically or extending these ideas without reasoning about them.

One example is the idea that "if one is good, more—lots more—is better." This idea is popular, but only rarely true. Take Oracle's array interface, for example, which allows the developer to insert or retrieve multiple rows in a single system call. Clearly, reducing the number of network messages between the application and the database is a good thing. But, if you think about it, there is a point of diminishing returns. While fetching 100 rows at once is far better than one at a time, fetching 1,000 rows at once instead of 100 is generally not really any more efficient overall, especially when you consider memory requirements.

Another example of uncritical thinking is to focus on the wrong aspects of system design or configuration, rather than those most likely to improve performance (or, for that matter, reliability, availability, or security). Consider the "conventional wisdom" of tuning the system to maximize the buffer hit ratio. For some applications, it's true that maximizing the chance that required data is in memory will maximize performance. However, for most applications it's better to focus attention on performance bottlenecks (what we call "wait states") than it is to focus on specific system-level metrics. Eliminate those aspects of the application design that are causing delays, and you'll get the best performance.

I've found that breaking down a problem into smaller parts and solving each part separately is a great way to think about application design. In this way, you can often find elegant and creative uses of SQL to address application requirements. Often, it is possible to do things in a single SQL statement that at first seem to require complex procedural programming. When you can leverage the power of SQL to process sets of rows at a time, perhaps in parallel, not only are you more productive as an application developer, but the application runs faster as well!

Sometimes, best practices that were based, even in part, on some degree of truth become no longer applicable as the facts change. Consider the old adage, "Put indexes and data in separate tablespaces for best performance." I've often seen database administrators express strong opinions over the merits of this idea, without taking into account changes in disk speeds and capacities over time, or the specifics of given workloads. In evaluating this particular "rule," you should think about the *fact* that the Oracle database caches frequently and recently used database blocks (often blocks belonging to an index) in memory, and the *fact* that it uses index and data blocks sequentially, not simultaneously, for any given request. The implication is that I/O operations for both index and data really should be spread across all simultaneous users, and across as many disk drives as you have. You might choose to separate index and data blocks for administrative reasons or for personal preference, but not for performance. (Tom Kyte provides valuable insights on this topic on the Ask Tom web site, http://asktom.oracle.com, where you can search for articles on "index data tablespace".) The lesson here is to base your decisions on facts, and a complete set of current facts at that.

No matter how fast our computers or how sophisticated the database becomes, and regardless of the power of our programming tools, there simply is no substitute for human intelligence coupled with a "thinking discipline." So, while it's important to learn the intricacies of the technologies we use in our applications, it's even more important to know how to think about using them appropriately.

Tom Kyte is one of the most intelligent people I know, and one of the most knowledgeable about the Oracle database, SQL, performance tuning, and application design. I'm pretty sure

Tom is an aficionado of the "THINK" and "Think different" slogans. Tom quite obviously also believes in that anonymous wise saying, "Give a man a fish and you feed him for a day. Teach a man to fish and you feed him for a lifetime." Tom enjoys sharing his knowledge about Oracle, to the great benefit of our community, but rather than simply dispensing answers to questions, he helps others learn to think and reason.

On his web site (http://asktom.oracle.com), in his public speaking engagements, and in this book, Tom implicitly challenges people to "think differently" too, as they design database applications with the Oracle database. He rejects conventional wisdom and speculation, instead insisting on relying on facts proven through examples. Tom takes a very pragmatic and simple approach to problem solving, and by following his advice and methodology, you can be more productive and develop better, faster applications.

Not only will Tom's book teach you about features of Oracle and how to use them, but it also reflects many of these simple thoughts:

- Don't believe in myths—reason for yourself.

- Don't follow "conventional wisdom"—often the things everybody knows are simply wrong!

- Don't trust rumors or opinions—test things for yourself and base decisions on proven examples.

- Break apart a problem into simpler questions, and assemble the answers to each step into an elegant, efficient solution.

- Don't do things in your programs when the database can do them better and faster.

- Understand the differences between the ideal and the real.

- Ask questions about and be skeptical of unjustified "company policies" for technical standards.

- Consider the big picture of what's best overall for the requirements at hand.

- Take the time to THINK.

Tom encourages you to treat Oracle as much more than a black box. Instead of you just putting data into and taking data out of Oracle, Tom will help you understand how Oracle works and how to exploit its power. By learning how to apply Oracle technology creatively and thoughtfully, you will be able to solve most application design problems quickly and elegantly.

As you read and enjoy this book, I know you'll learn a lot of new facts about Oracle database technology and important concepts about application design. As you do, I'm confident that you'll also start to "think differently" about the challenges you face.

IBM's Watson once said, "Thought has been the father of every advance since time began. 'I didn't think' has cost the world millions of dollars." This is a thought with which both Tom and I agree. Armed with the knowledge and techniques you'll learn in this book, I hope you'll be able to save the world (or at least your enterprise) millions of dollars, and enjoy the satisfaction of a job well done.

Ken Jacobs
Vice President of Product Strategy (Server Technologies)
Oracle Corporation

About the Author

I am **TOM KYTE**. I have been working for Oracle since version 7.0.9 (that's 1993 for people who don't mark time by Oracle versions). However, I've been working *with* Oracle since about version 5.1.5c (the $99 single-user version for DOS on 360KB floppy disks). Before coming to work at Oracle, I worked for more than six years as a systems integrator, building large-scale, heterogeneous databases and applications, mostly for military and government customers. These days, I spend a great deal of my time working with the Oracle database and, more specifically, helping people who are using the Oracle database. I work directly with customers, either in specifying and building their systems or, more frequently, in helping them rebuild or tune them ("tuning" frequently being a synonym for rebuilding). In addition, I am the Tom behind the "Ask Tom" column in *Oracle Magazine*, where I answer people's questions about the Oracle database and tools. On a typical day, I receive and answer dozens of questions at http://asktom.oracle.com. Every two months, I publish a "best of" in the magazine (all of the questions asked are available on the Web—stored in an Oracle database, of course). Additionally, I give technical seminars covering much of the material you'll find in this book. Basically, I spend a lot of my time helping people be successful with the Oracle database. Oh yes, in my spare time, I build applications and develop software within Oracle Corporation itself.

This book is a reflection of what I do every day. The material within covers topics and questions that I see people struggling with every day. These issues are covered from a perspective of "When *I* use this, *I* do it this way." It is the culmination of many years of experience using the product in myriad situations.

About the Technical Reviewers

JONATHAN LEWIS has been involved in database work for more than 19 years, specializing in Oracle for the last 16 years, and working as a consultant for the last 12 years. Jonathan is currently a director of the UK Oracle User Group (UKOUG) and is well known for his many presentations at the UKOUG conferences and SIGs. He is also renowned for his tutorials and seminars about the Oracle database engine, which he has held in various countries around the world.

Jonathan authored the acclaimed book *Practical Oracle 8*i (Addison-Wesley, ISBN: 0201715848), and he writes regularly for the UKOUG magazine and occasionally for other publications, including *OTN* and *DBAZine*. He also finds time to publish Oracle-related material on his web site, http://www.jlcomp.demon.co.uk.

RODERICK MANALAC graduated from the University of California, Berkeley in 1989 with a bachelor's degree in electrical engineering and computer science. He's been an employee of Oracle Support Services ever since. Practically all of that time has been spent in assisting external customers and internal employees (around the globe) gain a better understanding of the subtleties involved with running the Oracle database product on UNIX platforms. Other than that, he spends way too much time playing video games, watching TV, eating snacks, and willing the San Francisco Giants to win the World Series.

MICHAEL MÖLLER has been interested in computers since his tenth birthday, approximately 40 years ago. He's been involved in pretty much everything related to building and running software systems, as a programmer, design engineer, project manager, and quality assurance manager. He worked in the computer business in the United States, England, and Denmark before joining Oracle Denmark ten years ago, where he worked in Support and later in Premium Support. He has often taught in Oracle Education, even taking the "Oracle Internals" seminar on a whistle-stop tour of Europe. He spent the last two years of his time with Oracle working in development in the United States, creating the course materials for advanced courses, including "Internals on NLS" and "RAC." Nowadays, Möller is gainfully employed at Miracle A/S in Denmark with consultancy and education.

GABE ROMANESCU has a bachelor's degree in mathematics and works as an independent Oracle consultant. He discovered relational theory and technologies in 1992 and has found comfort ever since in the promise of applied logic in the software industry. He mostly benefits from, and occasionally contributes to, the Ask Tom and OTN forums. He lives in Toronto, Canada, with his wife, Arina, and their two daughters, Alexandra and Sophia.

Acknowledgments

I would like to thank many people for helping me complete this book.

First, I would like to thank Tony Davis for his work making my work read well. If you enjoy the flow of the sections, the number of section breaks, and the clarity, then that is probably in some part due to him. I have worked with Tony writing technical material since the year 2000 and have watched his knowledge of Oracle grow over that time. He now has the ability to not only "edit" the material, but in many cases "tech edit" it as well. Many of the examples in this book are there because of him (pointing out that the casual reader was not going to "get it" without them). This book would not be what it is without him.

Without a technical review team of the caliber I had during the writing of this book, I would be nervous about the content. Jonathan Lewis, Roderick Manalac, Michael Möller, and Gabe Romanescu spent many hours poring over the material and verifying it was technically accurate as well as useful in the real world. I firmly believe a technical book should be judged not only by who wrote it, but also by who reviewed it.

At Oracle, I work with the best and brightest people I have ever known, and they all have contributed in one way or another. I would like to thank Ken Jacobs in particular for his support and enthusiasm.

I would also like to thank everyone I work with for their support during this book-writing ordeal. It took a lot more time and energy than I ever imagined, and I appreciate everyone's flexibility in that regard. In particular, I would like to thank Tim Hoechst and Mike Hichwa, whom I've worked with and known for over 12 years now. Their constant questioning and pushing helped me to discover things that I would never have even thought of investigating on my own.

I would also like to acknowledge the people who use the Oracle software and ask so many good questions. Without them, I would never even have thought of writing this book. Much of what is included here is a direct result of someone asking me "how" or "why" at one time or another.

Lastly, but most important, I would like to acknowledge the unceasing support I've received from my family. You know you must be important to someone when you try to do something that takes a lot of "outside of work hours" and someone lets you know about it. Without the continual support of my wife Lori, son Alan, and daughter Megan, I don't see how I could have finished this book.

Introduction

The inspiration for the material contained in this book comes from my experiences developing Oracle software, and from working with fellow Oracle developers and helping them build reliable and robust applications based on the Oracle database. The book is basically a reflection of what I do every day and of the issues I see people encountering each and every day.

I covered what I felt was most relevant, namely the Oracle database and its architecture. I could have written a similarly titled book explaining how to develop an application using a specific language and architecture—for example, one using JavaServer Pages that speaks to Enterprise JavaBeans, which in turn uses JDBC to communicate with Oracle. However, at the end of the day, you really do need to understand the topics covered in this book in order to build such an application successfully. This book deals with what I believe needs to be universally known to develop successfully with Oracle, whether you are a Visual Basic programmer using ODBC, a Java programmer using EJBs and JDBC, or a Perl programmer using DBI Perl. This book does not promote any specific application architecture; it does not compare three-tier to client/server. Rather, it covers what the database can do and what you must understand about the way it works. Since the database is at the heart of any application architecture, the book should have a broad audience.

In writing this book, I completely revised an updated the architecture sections from *Expert One-on-One Oracle* and added substantial new material. There have been three database releases since Oracle 8.1.7, the release upon which the original book was based: two Oracle9*i* releases and Oracle Database 10*g* Release 1, which is the current production release of Oracle at the time of this writing. As such, there was a lot of new functionality and many new features to cover.

The sheer volume of new material required in updating *Expert One-on-One Oracle* for 9*i* and 10*g* was at the heart of the decision to split it into two books—an already large book was getting unmanageable. The second book will be called *Expert Oracle Programming*.

As the title suggests, *Expert Oracle Database Architecture* concentrates on the database architecture and how the database itself works. I cover the Oracle database architecture in depth—the files, memory structures, and processes that comprise an Oracle database and instance. I then move on to discuss important database topics such as locking, concurrency controls, how transactions work, and redo and undo, and why it is important for you to know about these things. Lastly, I examine the physical structures in the database such as tables, indexes, and datatypes, covering techniques for making optimal use of them.

What This Book Is About

One of the problems with having plenty of development options is that it's sometimes hard to figure out which one might be the best choice for your particular needs. Everyone wants as much flexibility as possible (as many choices as they can possibly have), but they also want things to be very cut and dried—in other words, easy. Oracle presents developers with almost unlimited choice. No one ever says, "You can't do that in Oracle"; rather, they say, "How many different ways would you like to do that in Oracle?" I hope that this book will help you make the correct choice.

This book is aimed at those people who appreciate the choice but would also like some guidelines and practical implementation details on Oracle features and functions. For example, Oracle has a really neat feature called *parallel execution*. The Oracle documentation tells you how to use this feature and what it does. Oracle documentation does not, however, tell you *when* you should use this feature and, perhaps even more important, *when you should not* use this feature. It doesn't always tell you the implementation details of this feature, and if you're not aware of them, this can come back to haunt you (I'm not referring to bugs, but the way the feature is supposed to work and what it was really designed to do).

In this book I strove to not only describe how things work, but also explain when and why you would consider using a particular feature or implementation. I feel it is important to understand not only the "how" behind things, but also the "when" and "why"—as well as the "when not" and "why not"!

Who Should Read This Book

The target audience for this book is anyone who develops applications with Oracle as the database back end. It is a book for professional Oracle developers who need to know how to get things done in the database. The practical nature of the book means that many sections should also be very interesting to the DBA. Most of the examples in the book use SQL*Plus to demonstrate the key features, so you won't find out how to develop a really cool GUI—but you will find out how the Oracle database works, what its key features can do, and when they should (and should not) be used.

This book is for anyone who wants to get more out of Oracle with less work. It is for anyone who wants to see new ways to use existing features. It is for anyone who wants to see how these features can be applied in the real world (not just examples of how to use the feature, but why the feature is relevant in the first place). Another category of people who would find this book of interest is technical managers in charge of the developers who work on Oracle projects. In some respects, it is just as important that they understand why knowing the database is crucial to success. This book can provide ammunition for managers who would like to get their personnel trained in the correct technologies or ensure that personnel already know what they need to know.

To get the most out of this book, the reader should have

- *Knowledge of SQL.* You don't have to be the best SQL coder ever, but a good working knowledge will help.

- *An understanding of PL/SQL.* This isn't a prerequisite, but it will help you to "absorb" the examples. This book will not, for example, teach you how to program a FOR loop or declare a record type—the Oracle documentation and numerous books cover this well. However, that's not to say that you won't learn a lot about PL/SQL by reading this book. You will. You'll become very intimate with many features of PL/SQL and you'll see new ways to do things, and you'll become aware of packages/features that perhaps you didn't know existed.

- *Exposure to some third-generation language (3GL), such as C or Java.* I believe that anyone who can read and write code in a 3GL language will be able to successfully read and understand the examples in this book.

- *Familiarity with the* Oracle Concepts *manual.*

A few words on that last point: due to the Oracle documentation set's vast size, many people find it to be somewhat intimidating. If you're just starting out or haven't read any of it as yet, I can tell you that the *Oracle Concepts* manual is exactly the right place to start. It's about 700 pages long and touches on many of the major Oracle concepts that you need to know about. It may not give you each and every technical detail (that's what the other 10,000 to 20,000 pages of documentation are for), but it will educate you on all the important concepts. This manual touches the following topics (to name a few):

- The structures in the database, and how data is organized and stored

- Distributed processing

- Oracle's memory architecture

- Oracle's process architecture

- Schema objects you will be using (tables, indexes, clusters, and so on)

- Built-in datatypes and user-defined datatypes

- SQL stored procedures

- How transactions work

- The optimizer

- Data integrity

- Concurrency control

I will come back to these topics myself time and time again. These are the fundamentals—without knowledge of them, you will create Oracle applications that are prone to failure. I encourage you to read through the manual and get an understanding of some of these topics.

How This Book Is Structured

To help you use this book, most chapters are organized into four general sections (described in the list that follows). These aren't rigid divisions, but they will help you navigate quickly to the area you need more information on. This book has 15 chapters, and each is like a "mini-book"—a virtually stand-alone component. Occasionally, I refer to examples or features in other chapters, but you could pretty much pick a chapter out of the book and read it on its own. For example, you don't have to read Chapter 10 on database tables to understand or make use of Chapter 14 on parallelism.

The format and style of many of the chapters is virtually identical:

- An introduction to the feature or capability.

- Why you might want to use the feature or capability (or not). I outline when you would consider using this feature and when you would not want to use it.

- How to use this feature. The information here isn't just a copy of the material in the SQL reference; rather, it's presented in step-by-step manner: here is what you need, here is what you have to do, and these are the switches you need to go through to get started. Topics covered in this section will include

  - How to implement the feature

  - Examples, examples, examples

  - How to debug this feature

  - Caveats of using this feature

  - How to handle errors (proactively)

- A summary to bring it all together.

There will be lots of examples, and lots of code, all of which is available for download from the Source Code area of http://www.apress.com. The following sections present a detailed breakdown of the content of each chapter.

Chapter 1: Developing Successful Oracle Applications

This chapter sets out my essential approach to database programming. All databases are *not* created equal, and in order to develop database-driven applications successfully and on time, you need to understand exactly *what* your particular database can do and *how* it does it. If you do not know what your database can do, you run the risk of continually reinventing the wheel—developing functionality that the database already provides. If you do not know how your database works, you are likely to develop applications that perform poorly and do not behave in a predictable manner.

The chapter takes an empirical look at some applications where a lack of basic under-standing of the database has led to project failure. With this example-driven approach, the chapter discusses the basic features and functions of the database that you, the developer, need to understand. The bottom line is that you cannot afford to treat the database as a black box that will simply churn out the answers and take care of scalability and performance by itself.

Chapter 2: Architecture Overview

This chapter covers the basics of Oracle architecture. We start with some clear definitions of two terms that are very misunderstood by many in the Oracle world, namely "instance" and "database." We also take a quick look at the System Global Area (SGA) and the processes behind the Oracle instance, and examine how the simple act of "connecting to Oracle" takes place.

Chapter 3: Files

This chapter covers in depth the eight types of files that make up an Oracle database and instance. From the simple parameter file to the data and redo log files, we explore what they are, why they are there, and how we use them.

Chapter 4: Memory Structures

This chapter covers how Oracle uses memory, both in the individual processes (Process Global Area, or PGA, memory) and shared memory (SGA). We explore the differences between manual and automatic PGA and, in Oracle 10g, SGA memory management, and see when each is appropriate. After reading this chapter, you will have an understanding of exactly how Oracle uses and manages memory.

Chapter 5: Oracle Processes

This chapter offers an overview of the types of Oracle processes (server processes versus background processes). It also goes into much more depth on the differences in connecting to the database via a shared server or dedicated server process. We'll also take a look, process by process, at most of the background processes (such as LGWR, DBWR, PMON, and SMON) that we'll see when starting an Oracle instance and discuss the functions of each.

Chapter 6: Locking and Latching

Different databases have different ways of doing things (what works well in SQL Server may not work as well in Oracle), and understanding how Oracle implements locking and concurrency control is absolutely vital to the success of your application. This chapter discusses Oracle's basic approach to these issues, the types of locks that can be applied (DML, DDL, and latches) and the problems that can arise if locking is not implemented carefully (deadlocking, blocking, and escalation).

Chapter 7: Concurrency and Multi-Versioning

In this chapter, we'll explore my favorite Oracle feature, multi-versioning, and how it affects concurrency controls and the very design of an application. Here we will see that all databases are *not* created equal and that their very implementation can have an impact on the design of our applications. We'll start by reviewing the various transaction isolation levels as defined by the ANSI SQL standard and see how they map to the Oracle implementation (as well as how the other databases map to this standard). Then we'll take a look at what implications multi-versioning, the feature that allows Oracle to provide non-blocking reads in the database, might have for us.

Chapter 8: Transactions

Transactions are a fundamental feature of all databases—they are part of what distinguishes a database from a file system. And yet, they are often misunderstood and many developers do not even know that they are accidentally not using them. This chapter examines how transactions should be used in Oracle and also exposes some "bad habits" that may have been picked up when developing with other databases. In particular, we look at the implications of atomicity and how it affects statements in Oracle. We also discuss transaction control statements (COMMIT, SAVEPOINT, and ROLLBACK), integrity constraints, distributed transactions (the two-phase commit, or 2PC), and finally autonomous transactions.

Chapter 9: Redo and Undo

It can be said that developers do not need to understand the detail of redo and undo as much as DBAs, but developers do need to know the role they play in the database. After first defining redo, we examine what exactly a COMMIT does. We discuss how to find out how much redo is being generated and how to significantly reduce the amount of redo generated by certain operations using the NOLOGGING clause. We also investigate redo generation in relation to issues such as block cleanout and log contention.

In the undo section of the chapter, we examine the role of undo data and the operations that generate the most/least undo. Finally, we investigate the infamous ORA-01555: snapshot too old error, its possible causes, and how to avoid it.

Chapter 10: Database Tables

Oracle now supports numerous table types. This chapter looks at each different type—heap organized (i.e., the default, "normal" table), index organized, index clustered, hash clustered, nested, temporary, and object—and discusses when, how, and why you should use them. Most of time, the heap organized table is sufficient, but this chapter will help you recognize when one of the other types might be more appropriate.

Chapter 11: Indexes

Indexes are a crucial aspect of your application design. Correct implementation requires an in-depth knowledge of the data, how it is distributed, and how it will be used. Too often, indexes are treated as an afterthought in application development, and performance suffers as a consequence.

This chapter examines in detail the different types of indexes, including B*Tree, bitmap, function-based, and application domain indexes, and discusses where they should and should not be used. I'll also answer some common queries in the "Frequently Asked Questions and Myths About Indexes" section, such as "Do indexes work on views?" and "Why isn't my index getting used?"

Chapter 12: Datatypes

There are a lot of datatypes to choose from. This chapter explores each of the 22 built-in datatypes, explaining how they are implemented, and how and when to use each one. First up is a brief overview of National Language Support (NLS), a basic knowledge of which is necessary to fully understand the simple string types in Oracle. We then move on to the ubiquitous NUMBER type and look at the new Oracle 10g options for storage of numbers in the database. The LONG and LONG RAW types are covered, mostly from a historical perspective. The main objective here is to show how to deal with legacy LONG columns in applications and migrate them to the LOB type. Next, we delve into the various datatypes for storing dates and time, investigating how to manipulate the various datatypes to get what we need from them. The ins and outs of time zone support are also covered.

Next up are the LOB datatypes. We'll cover how they are stored and what each of the many settings such as IN ROW, CHUNK, RETENTION, CACHE, and so on mean to us. When dealing with LOBs, it is important to understand how they are implemented and how they are stored by default—especially when it comes to tuning their retrieval and storage. We close the chapter by looking at the ROWID and UROWID types. These are special types, proprietary to Oracle, that represent the address of a row. We'll cover when to use them as a column datatype in a table (which is almost never!).

Chapter 13: Partitioning

Partitioning is designed to facilitate the management of very large tables and indexes, by implementing a "divide and conquer" logic—basically breaking up a table or index into many smaller and more manageable pieces. It is an area where the DBA and developer must work together to maximize application availability and performance. This chapter covers both table and index partitioning. We look at partitioning using local indexes (common in data warehouses) and global indexes (common in OLTP systems).

Chapter 14: Parallel Execution

This chapter introduces the concept of and uses for parallel execution in Oracle. We'll start by looking at when parallel processing is useful and should be considered, as well as when it should not be considered. After gaining that understanding, we move on to the mechanics of parallel query, the feature most people associate with parallel execution. Next we cover parallel DML (PDML), which allows us to perform modifications using parallel execution. We'll see how PDML is physically implemented and why that implementation leads to a series of restrictions regarding PDML.

We then move on to parallel DDL. This, in my opinion, is where parallel execution really shines. Typically, DBAs have small maintenance windows in which to perform large operations. Parallel DDL gives DBAs the ability to fully exploit the machine resources they have available, permitting them to finish large, complex operations in a fraction of the time it would take to do them serially.

The chapter closes on procedural parallelism, the means by which we can execute application code in parallel. We cover two techniques here. The first is parallel pipelined functions, or the ability of Oracle to execute stored functions in parallel dynamically. The second is do-it-yourself (DIY) parallelism, whereby we design the application to run concurrently.

Chapter 15: Data Loading and Unloading

This first half of this chapter focuses on SQL*Loader (SQLLDR) and covers the various ways in which we can use this tool to load and modify data in the database. Issues discussed include loading delimited data, updating existing rows and inserting new ones, unloading data, and calling SQLLDR from a stored procedure. Again, SQLLDR is a well-established and crucial tool, but it is the source of many questions with regard to its practical use. The second half of the chapter focuses on external tables, an alternative and highly efficient means by which to bulk load and unload data.

Source Code and Updates

As you work through the examples in this book, you may decide that you prefer to type in all the code by hand. Many readers choose to do this because it is a good way to get familiar with the coding techniques that are being used.

Whether you want to type the code in or not, all the source code for this book is available in the Source Code section of the Apress web site (http://www.apress.com). If you like to type in the code, you can use the source code files to check the results you should be getting—they should be your first stop if you think you might have typed in an error. If you don't like typing, then downloading the source code from the Apress web site is a must! Either way, the code files will help you with updates and debugging.

Errata

Apress makes every effort to make sure that there are no errors in the text or the code. However, to err is human, and as such we recognize the need to keep you informed of any mistakes as they're discovered and corrected. Errata sheets are available for all our books at http://www.apress.com. If you find an error that hasn't already been reported, please let us know.

The Apress web site acts as a focus for other information and support, including the code from all Apress books, sample chapters, previews of forthcoming titles, and articles on related topics.

Setting Up Your Environment

In this section, I cover how to set up an environment capable of executing the examples in this book, specifically with regard to the following topics:

- How to set up the SCOTT/TIGER demonstration schema properly

- The environment you need to have up and running

- How to configure AUTOTRACE, a SQL*Plus facility

- How to install Statspack

- How to install and run runstats and other custom utilities used throughout the book

- The coding conventions used in this book

All of the non-Oracle-supplied scripts are available for download from the Source Code section of the Apress web site (http://www.apress.com).

Setting Up the SCOTT/TIGER Schema

The SCOTT/TIGER schema may already exist in your database. It is generally included during a typical installation, but it is not a mandatory component of the database. You may install the SCOTT example schema into any database account—there is nothing magic about using the SCOTT account. You could install the EMP/DEPT tables directly into your own database account if you wish.

Many of the examples in this book draw on the tables in the SCOTT schema. If you would like to be able to work along with them, you will need these tables as well. If you are working on a shared database, it is advisable to install your own copy of these tables in some account other than SCOTT to avoid side effects caused by other users using the same data.

To create the SCOTT demonstration tables, simply

1. cd [ORACLE_HOME]/sqlplus/demo.

2. Run demobld.sql when connected as any user.

Note In Oracle 10g and later, you must install the demonstration subdirectories from the companion CD. I have reproduced the necessary components of demobld.sql later as well.

---

demobld.sql will create and populate five tables for you. When it is complete, it exits SQL*Plus automatically, so don't be surprised when SQL*Plus disappears after running the script—it is supposed to do that.

The standard demo tables do not have any referential integrity defined on them. Some of my examples rely on them having referential integrity. After you run demobld.sql, it is recommended that you also execute the following:

```
alter table emp add constraint emp_pk primary key(empno);
alter table dept add constraint dept_pk primary key(deptno);
alter table emp add constraint emp_fk_dept
                              foreign key(deptno) references dept;
alter table emp add constraint emp_fk_emp foreign key(mgr) references emp;
```

This finishes off the installation of the demonstration schema. If you would like to drop this schema at any time to clean up, you can simply execute [ORACLE_HOME]/sqlplus/demo/demodrop.sql. This will drop the five tables and exit SQL*Plus.

In the event you do not have access to demobld.sql, the following is sufficient to run the examples in this book:

```
CREATE TABLE EMP
(EMPNO NUMBER(4) NOT NULL,
 ENAME VARCHAR2(10),
 JOB VARCHAR2(9),
 MGR NUMBER(4),
 HIREDATE DATE,
 SAL NUMBER(7, 2),
 COMM NUMBER(7, 2),
 DEPTNO NUMBER(2)
);

INSERT INTO EMP VALUES (7369, 'SMITH',  'CLERK',     7902,
TO_DATE('17-DEC-1980', 'DD-MON-YYYY'),  800, NULL, 20);
INSERT INTO EMP VALUES (7499, 'ALLEN',  'SALESMAN', 7698,
TO_DATE('20-FEB-1981', 'DD-MON-YYYY'), 1600,  300, 30);
INSERT INTO EMP VALUES (7521, 'WARD',   'SALESMAN', 7698,
TO_DATE('22-FEB-1981', 'DD-MON-YYYY'), 1250,  500, 30);
INSERT INTO EMP VALUES (7566, 'JONES',  'MANAGER',   7839,
TO_DATE('2-APR-1981', 'DD-MON-YYYY'),  2975, NULL, 20);
INSERT INTO EMP VALUES (7654, 'MARTIN', 'SALESMAN', 7698,
TO_DATE('28-SEP-1981', 'DD-MON-YYYY'), 1250, 1400, 30);
INSERT INTO EMP VALUES (7698, 'BLAKE',  'MANAGER',   7839,
TO_DATE('1-MAY-1981', 'DD-MON-YYYY'),  2850, NULL, 30);
INSERT INTO EMP VALUES (7782, 'CLARK',  'MANAGER',   7839,
TO_DATE('9-JUN-1981', 'DD-MON-YYYY'),  2450, NULL, 10);
INSERT INTO EMP VALUES (7788, 'SCOTT',  'ANALYST',   7566,
TO_DATE('09-DEC-1982', 'DD-MON-YYYY'), 3000, NULL, 20);
INSERT INTO EMP VALUES (7839, 'KING',   'PRESIDENT', NULL,
TO_DATE('17-NOV-1981', 'DD-MON-YYYY'), 5000, NULL, 10);
INSERT INTO EMP VALUES (7844, 'TURNER', 'SALESMAN', 7698,
```

```
TO_DATE('8-SEP-1981', 'DD-MON-YYYY'),  1500,    0, 30);
INSERT INTO EMP VALUES (7876, 'ADAMS',  'CLERK',    7788,
TO_DATE('12-JAN-1983', 'DD-MON-YYYY'), 1100, NULL, 20);
INSERT INTO EMP VALUES (7900, 'JAMES',  'CLERK',    7698,
TO_DATE('3-DEC-1981', 'DD-MON-YYYY'),   950, NULL, 30);
INSERT INTO EMP VALUES (7902, 'FORD',   'ANALYST',  7566,
TO_DATE('3-DEC-1981', 'DD-MON-YYYY'),  3000, NULL, 20);
INSERT INTO EMP VALUES (7934, 'MILLER', 'CLERK',    7782,
TO_DATE('23-JAN-1982', 'DD-MON-YYYY'), 1300, NULL, 10);

CREATE TABLE DEPT
(DEPTNO NUMBER(2),
 DNAME VARCHAR2(14),
 LOC VARCHAR2(13)
);

INSERT INTO DEPT VALUES (10, 'ACCOUNTING', 'NEW YORK');
INSERT INTO DEPT VALUES (20, 'RESEARCH',  'DALLAS');
INSERT INTO DEPT VALUES (30, 'SALES',     'CHICAGO');
INSERT INTO DEPT VALUES (40, 'OPERATIONS', 'BOSTON');
```

The Environment

Most of the examples in this book are designed to run 100 percent in the SQL*Plus environment. Other than SQL*Plus, there is nothing else to set up and configure. I can make a suggestion, however, on using SQL*Plus. Almost all the examples in this book use DBMS_OUTPUT in some fashion. For DBMS_OUTPUT to work, the following SQL*Plus command must be issued:

```
SQL> set serveroutput on
```

If you are like me, typing in this command each and every time will quickly get tiresome. Fortunately, SQL*Plus allows us to set up a login.sql file—a script that is executed each and every time we start SQL*Plus. Further, it allows us to set an environment variable, SQLPATH, so that it can find this login.sql script, no matter what directory it is in.

The login.sql I use for all examples in this book is as follows:

```
define _editor=vi
set serveroutput on size 1000000
set trimspool on
set long 5000
set linesize 100
set pagesize 9999
column plan_plus_exp format a80
column global_name new_value gname
set termout off
define gname=idle
column global_name new_value gname
```

```
select lower(user) || '@' || substr( global_name, 1,
   decode( dot, 0, length(global_name), dot-1) ) global_name
  from (select global_name, instr(global_name,'.') dot from global_name );
set sqlprompt '&gname> '
set termout on
```

An annotated version of this is as follows:

- DEFINE _EDITOR=VI: This sets up the default editor SQL*Plus will use. You may set the default editor to be your favorite text editor (not a word processor) such as Notepad or emacs.

- SET SERVEROUTPUT ON SIZE 1000000: This enables DBMS_OUTPUT to be on by default (hence, you don't have to type it in each and every time). It also sets the default buffer size as large as possible.

- SET TRIMSPOOL ON: When spooling text, lines will be blank-trimmed and not fixed width. If this is set to OFF (the default), spooled lines will be as wide as your LINESIZE setting.

- SET LONG 5000: This sets the default number of bytes displayed when selecting LONG and CLOB columns.

- SET LINESIZE 100: This sets the width of the lines displayed by SQL*Plus to be 100 characters.

- SET PAGESIZE 9999: This sets the PAGESIZE, which controls how frequently SQL*Plus prints out headings, to a large number (you get one set of headings per page).

- COLUMN PLAN_PLUS_EXP FORMAT A80: This sets the default width of the explain plan output you receive with AUTOTRACE. A80 is generally wide enough to hold the full plan.

The next bit in login.sql sets up the SQL*Plus prompt:

```
define gname=idle
column global_name new_value gname
select lower(user) || '@' || substr( global_name,1,
   decode( dot, 0, length(global_name), dot-1) ) global_name
  from (select global_name, instr(global_name,'.') dot from global_name );
set sqlprompt '&gname> '
```

The directive COLUMN GLOBAL_NAME NEW_VALUE GNAME tells SQL*Plus to take the last value it retrieves for any column named GLOBAL_NAME and place it into the substitution variable GNAME. I then select the GLOBAL_NAME out of the database and concatenate this with the username I am logged in with. That makes my prompt look like this:

```
ops$tkyte@ora10g>
```

so I know who I am as well as where I am.

Setting Up AUTOTRACE in SQL*Plus

AUTOTRACE is a facility within SQL*Plus that shows you the explain plan of the queries you've executed and the resources they used. This book makes extensive use of the AUTOTRACE facility.

There is more than one way to get AUTOTRACE configured. This is what I like to do to get AUTOTRACE working:

1. `cd [ORACLE_HOME]/rdbms/admin`

2. `log into SQL*Plus as SYSTEM`

3. Run `@utlxplan`

4. Run `CREATE PUBLIC SYNONYM PLAN_TABLE FOR PLAN_TABLE;`

5. Run `GRANT ALL ON PLAN_TABLE TO PUBLIC;`

You can replace the `GRANT TO PUBLIC` with some user if you want. By making the `PLAN_TABLE` public, you let anyone trace using SQL*Plus (not a bad thing, in my opinion). This prevents each and every user from having to install his or her own plan table. The alternative is for you to run `@utlxplan` in every schema from which you want to use AUTOTRACE.

The next step is creating and granting the `PLUSTRACE` role:

1. `cd [ORACLE_HOME]/sqlplus/admin`

2. Log in to SQL*Plus as SYS or as SYSDBA

3. Run `@plustrce`

4. Run `GRANT PLUSTRACE TO PUBLIC;`

Again, you can replace `PUBLIC` in the `GRANT` command with some user if you want.

About AUTOTRACE

You can automatically get a report on the execution path used by the SQL optimizer and the statement execution statistics. The report is generated after successful SQL DML (i.e., SELECT, DELETE, UPDATE, MERGE, and INSERT) statements. It is useful for monitoring and tuning the performance of these statements.

Controlling the Report

You can control the report by setting the AUTOTRACE system variable:

- `SET AUTOTRACE OFF`: No AUTOTRACE report is generated. This is the default.

- `SET AUTOTRACE ON EXPLAIN`: The AUTOTRACE report shows only the optimizer execution path.

- `SET AUTOTRACE ON STATISTICS`: The AUTOTRACE report shows only the SQL statement execution statistics.

- SET AUTOTRACE ON: The AUTOTRACE report includes both the optimizer execution path and the SQL statement execution statistics.

- SET AUTOTRACE TRACEONLY: This is like SET AUTOTRACE ON, but it suppresses the printing of the user's query output, if any.

Setting Up Statspack

Statspack is designed to be installed when connected as SYSDBA (CONNECT / AS SYSDBA). To install it, you must be able to perform that operation. In many installations, this will be a task that you must ask the DBA or administrators to perform.

Once you have the ability to connect, installing Statspack is trivial. You simply run @spcreate.sql. You can find that script in [ORACLE_HOME]\rdbms\admin, and you should execute it when connected as SYSDBA via SQL*Plus. It looks something like this:

```
[tkyte@desktop admin]$ sqlplus / as sysdba
SQL*Plus: Release 10.1.0.4.0 - Production on Sat Jul 23 16:26:17 2005
Copyright (c) 1982, 2005, Oracle.  All rights reserved.
Connected to:
Oracle Database 10g Enterprise Edition Release 10.1.0.4.0 - Production
With the Partitioning, OLAP and Data Mining options

sys@ORA10G> @spcreate
... Installing Required Packages
... <output omitted for brevity> ...
```

You'll need to know three pieces of information before running the spcreate.sql script:

- The password you would like to use for the PERFSTAT schema that will be created

- The default tablespace you would like to use for PERFSTAT

- The temporary tablespace you would like to use for PERFSTAT

The script will prompt you for this information as it executes. In the event you make a typo or inadvertently cancel the installation, you should use spdrop.sql to remove the user and installed views prior to attempting another installation of Statspack. The Statspack installation will create a file called spcpkg.lis. You should review this file for any errors that might have occurred. The Statspack packages should install cleanly, however, as long as you supplied valid tablespace names (and didn't already have a PERFSTAT user).

Custom Scripts

In this section, I describe the requirements (if any) needed by various scripts used throughout this book. As well, we investigate the code behind the scripts.

Runstats

Runstats is a tool I developed to compare two different methods of doing the same thing and show which one is superior. You supply the two different methods and runstats does the rest. Runstats simply measures three key things:

- *Wall clock or elapsed time*: This is useful to know, but it isn't the most important piece of information.

- *System statistics*: This shows, side by side, how many times each approach did something (e.g., a parse call) and the difference between the two.

- *Latching*: This is the key output of this report.

As you'll see in this book, latches are a type of lightweight lock. Locks are serialization devices. Serialization devices inhibit concurrency. Applications that inhibit concurrency are less scalable, can support fewer users, and require more resources. Our goal is always to build applications that have the potential to scale—ones that can service 1 user as well as 1,000 or 10,000 users. The less latching we incur in our approaches, the better off we will be. I might choose an approach that takes longer to run on the wall clock but that uses 10 percent of the latches. I know that the approach that uses fewer latches will scale substantially better than the approach that uses more latches.

Runstats is best used in isolation—that is, on a single-user database. We will be measuring statistics and latching (locking) activity that result from our approaches. We do not want other sessions to contribute to the system's load or latching while this is going on. A small test database is perfect for these sorts of tests. I frequently use my desktop PC or laptop, for example.

Note I believe all developers should have a test bed database they control to try ideas on, without needing to ask a DBA to do something all of the time. Developers definitely should have a database on their desktop, given that the licensing for the personal developer version is simply "Use it to develop and test with, do not deploy, and you can just have it." This way, there is nothing to lose! Also, I've taken some informal polls at conferences and seminars and discovered that virtually every DBA out there started as a developer. The experience and training developers could get by having their own database—being able to see how it really works—pays large dividends in the long run.

To use runstats, you need to set up access to several V$ views, create a table to hold the statistics, and create the runstats package. You will need access to three V$ tables (those magic dynamic performance tables): V$STATNAME, V$MYSTAT, and V$LATCH. Here is a view I use:

```
create or replace view stats
as select 'STAT...' || a.name name, b.value
    from v$statname a, v$mystat b
   where a.statistic# = b.statistic#
  union all
  select 'LATCH.' || name,  gets
    from v$latch;
```

Either you can have SELECT on V$STATNAME, V$MYSTAT, and V$LATCH granted directly to you (that way you can create the view yourself), or you can have someone that does have SELECT on those objects create the view for you and grant SELECT privileges to you.

Once you have that set up, all you need is a small table to collect the statistics:

```
create global temporary table run_stats
( runid varchar2(15),
  name varchar2(80),
  value int )
on commit preserve rows;
```

Last, you need to create the package that is runstats. It contains three simple API calls:

- RS_START (runstats start) to be called at the beginning of a runstats test

- RS_MIDDLE to be called in the middle, as you might have guessed

- RS_STOP to finish off and print the report

The specification is as follows:

```
ops$tkyte@ORA920> create or replace package runstats_pkg
  2  as
  3      procedure rs_start;
  4      procedure rs_middle;
  5      procedure rs_stop( p_difference_threshold in number default 0 );
  6  end;
  7  /
Package created.
```

The parameter P_DIFFERENCE_THRESHOLD is used to control the amount of data printed at the end. Runstats collects statistics and latching information for each run, and then prints a report of how much of a resource each test (each approach) used and the difference between them. You can use this input parameter to see only the statistics and latches that had a difference greater than this number. By default this is zero, and you see all of the outputs.

Next, we'll look at the package body procedure by procedure. The package begins with some global variables. These will be used to record the elapsed times for our runs:

```
ops$tkyte@ORA920> create or replace package body runstats_pkg
  2  as
  3
  4  g_start number;
  5  g_run1    number;
  6  g_run2    number;
  7
```

Next is the RS_START routine. This will simply clear out our statistics-holding table and then populate it with the "before" statistics and latches. It will then capture the current timer value, a clock of sorts that we can use to compute elapsed times in hundredths of seconds:

```
 8   procedure rs_start
 9   is
10   begin
11       delete from run_stats;
12
13       insert into run_stats
14       select 'before', stats.* from stats;
15
16       g_start := dbms_utility.get_time;
17   end;
18
```

Next is the RS_MIDDLE routine. This procedure simply records the elapsed time for the first run of our test in G_RUN1. Then it inserts the current set of statistics and latches. If we were to subtract these values from the ones we saved previously in RS_START, we could discover how many latches the first method used, how many cursors (a statistic) it used, and so on.

Last, it records the start time for our next run:

```
19   procedure rs_middle
20   is
21   begin
22       g_run1 := (dbms_utility.get_time-g_start);
23
24       insert into run_stats
25       select 'after 1', stats.* from stats;
26       g_start := dbms_utility.get_time;
27
28   end;
29
30   procedure rs_stop(p_difference_threshold in number default 0)
31   is
32   begin
33       g_run2 := (dbms_utility.get_time-g_start);
34
35       dbms_output.put_line
36           ( 'Run1 ran in ' || g_run1 || ' hsecs' );
37       dbms_output.put_line
38           ( 'Run2 ran in ' || g_run2 || ' hsecs' );
39       dbms_output.put_line
40       ( 'run 1 ran in ' || round(g_run1/g_run2*100,2) ||
41         '% of the time' );
42           dbms_output.put_line( chr(9) );
43
44       insert into run_stats
45       select 'after 2', stats.* from stats;
46
47       dbms_output.put_line
48       ( rpad( 'Name', 30 ) || lpad( 'Run1', 10 ) ||
```

```
49           lpad( 'Run2', 10 ) || lpad( 'Diff', 10 ) );
50
51       for x in
52       ( select rpad( a.name, 30 ) ||
53          to_char( b.value-a.value, '9,999,999' ) ||
54          to_char( c.value-b.value, '9,999,999' ) ||
55          to_char( ( (c.value-b.value)-(b.value-a.value)), '9,999,999' ) data
56          from run_stats a, run_stats b, run_stats c
57         where a.name = b.name
58           and b.name = c.name
59           and a.runid = 'before'
60           and b.runid = 'after 1'
61           and c.runid = 'after 2'
62           and (c.value-a.value) > 0
63           and abs( (c.value-b.value) - (b.value-a.value) )
64                  > p_difference_threshold
65         order by abs( (c.value-b.value)-(b.value-a.value))
66       ) loop
67           dbms_output.put_line( x.data );
68       end loop;
69
70           dbms_output.put_line( chr(9) );
71       dbms_output.put_line
72       ( 'Run1 latches total versus runs -- difference and pct' );
73       dbms_output.put_line
74       ( lpad( 'Run1', 10 ) || lpad( 'Run2', 10 ) ||
75         lpad( 'Diff', 10 ) || lpad( 'Pct', 8 ) );
76
77       for x in
78       ( select to_char( run1, '9,999,999' ) ||
79              to_char( run2, '9,999,999' ) ||
80              to_char( diff, '9,999,999' ) ||
81              to_char( round( run1/run2*100,2 ), '999.99' ) || '%' data
82         from ( select sum(b.value-a.value) run1, sum(c.value-b.value) run2,
83                     sum( (c.value-b.value)-(b.value-a.value)) diff
84                 from run_stats a, run_stats b, run_stats c
85                where a.name = b.name
86                  and b.name = c.name
87                  and a.runid = 'before'
88                  and b.runid = 'after 1'
89                  and c.runid = 'after 2'
90                  and a.name like 'LATCH%'
91               )
92       ) loop
93           dbms_output.put_line( x.data );
94       end loop;
95   end;
```

```
96
97  end;
98  /
Package body created.
```

And now we are ready to use runstats. By way of example, we'll demonstrate how to use runstats to see which is more efficient, a single bulk INSERT or row-by-row processing. We'll start by setting up two tables into which to insert 1,000,000 rows:

```
ops$tkyte@ORA10GR1> create table t1
  2  as
  3  select * from big_table.big_table
  4  where 1=0;
Table created.

ops$tkyte@ORA10GR1> create table t2
  2  as
  3  select * from big_table.big_table
  4  where 1=0;
Table created.
```

Next, we perform the first method of inserting the records: using a single SQL statement. We start by calling RUNSTATS_PKG.RS_START:

```
ops$tkyte@ORA10GR1> exec runstats_pkg.rs_start;
PL/SQL procedure successfully completed.

ops$tkyte@ORA10GR1> insert into t1 select * from big_table.big_table;
1000000 rows created.

ops$tkyte@ORA10GR1> commit;
Commit complete.
```

Now we are ready to perform the second method, which is row-by-row insertion of data:

```
ops$tkyte@ORA10GR1> exec runstats_pkg.rs_middle;

PL/SQL procedure successfully completed.

ops$tkyte@ORA10GR1> begin
  2          for x in ( select * from big_table.big_table )
  3          loop
  4                  insert into t2 values X;
  5          end loop;
  6          commit;
  7  end;
  8  /

PL/SQL procedure successfully completed.
```

and finally, we generate the report:

```
ops$tkyte@ORA10GR1> exec runstats_pkg.rs_stop(1000000)
Run1 ran in 5810 hsecs
Run2 ran in 14712 hsecs
run 1 ran in 39.49% of the time

Name                             Run1        Run2        Diff
STAT...recursive calls          8,089   1,015,451   1,007,362
STAT...db block changes       109,355   2,085,099   1,975,744
LATCH.library cache             9,914   2,006,563   1,996,649
LATCH.library cache pin         5,609   2,003,762   1,998,153
LATCH.cache buffers chains    575,819   5,565,489   4,989,670
STAT...undo change vector size 3,884,940  67,978,932  64,093,992
STAT...redo size          118,854,004 378,741,168 259,887,164

Run1 latches total versus runs -- difference and pct
Run1       Run2        Diff      Pct
825,530  11,018,773  10,193,243     7.49%

PL/SQL procedure successfully completed.
```

Mystat

mystat.sql and its companion, mystat2.sql, are used to show the increase in some Oracle "statistic" before and after some operation. mystat.sql simply captures the begin value of some statistic:

```
set echo off
set verify off
column value new_val V
define S="&1"

set autotrace off
select a.name, b.value
from v$statname a, v$mystat b
where a.statistic# = b.statistic#
and lower(a.name) like '%' || lower('&S')||'%'
/
set echo on
```

and mystat2.sql reports the difference for us:

```
set echo off
set verify off
select a.name, b.value V, to_char(b.value-&V,'999,999,999,999') diff
from v$statname a, v$mystat b
```

```
where a.statistic# = b.statistic#
and lower(a.name) like '%' || lower('&S')||'%'
/
set echo on
```

For example, to see how much redo is generated by some UPDATE, we can do the following:

```
big_table@ORA10G> @mystat "redo size"
big_table@ORA10G> set echo off


NAME                                      VALUE
------------------------------   ----------
redo size                                   496

big_table@ORA10G> update big_table set owner = lower(owner)
  2  where rownum <= 1000;

1000 rows updated.

big_table@ORA10G> @mystat2
big_table@ORA10G> set echo off


NAME                                      V DIFF
------------------------------   ----------   ----------------
redo size                                 89592         89,096
```

That shows our UPDATE of 1,000 rows generated 89,096 bytes of redo.

SHOW_SPACE

The SHOW_SPACE routine prints detailed space utilization information for database segments. Here is the interface to it:

```
ops$tkyte@ORA10G> desc show_space
PROCEDURE show_space
 Argument Name                  Type                    In/Out Default?
------------------------------   -----------------------   ------  --------
 P_SEGNAME                       VARCHAR2                 IN
 P_OWNER                         VARCHAR2                 IN     DEFAULT
 P_TYPE                          VARCHAR2                 IN     DEFAULT
 P_PARTITION                     VARCHAR2                 IN     DEFAULT
```

The arguments are as follows:

- P_SEGNAME: Name of the segment (e.g., the table or index name).

- P_OWNER: Defaults to the current user, but you can use this routine to look at some other schema.

- P_TYPE: Defaults to TABLE and represents the type of object you are looking at. For example, SELECT DISTINCT SEGMENT_TYPE FROM DBA_SEGMENTS lists valid segment types.

- P_PARTITION: Name of the partition when you show the space for a partitioned object. SHOW_SPACE shows space for only one partition at a time.

The output of this routine looks as follows, when the segment resides in an Automatic Segment Space Management (ASSM) tablespace:

```
big_table@ORA10G> exec show_space('BIG_TABLE');
Unformatted Blocks .....................        0
FS1 Blocks (0-25) .....................        0
FS2 Blocks (25-50) .....................        0
FS3 Blocks (50-75) .....................        0
FS4 Blocks (75-100).....................        0
Full Blocks        .....................   14,469
Total Blocks............................   15,360
Total Bytes............................. 125,829,120
Total MBytes............................      120
Unused Blocks...........................      728
Unused Bytes............................  5,963,776
Last Used Ext FileId....................        4
Last Used Ext BlockId...................   43,145
Last Used Block.........................      296

PL/SQL procedure successfully completed.
```

The items reported are as follows:

- Unformatted Blocks: The number of blocks that are allocated to the table and are below the high-water mark (HWM), but have not been used. Add unformatted and unused blocks together to get a total count of blocks allocated to the table but never u ed to hold data in an ASSM object.

- FS1 Blocks–FS4 Blocks: Formatted blocks with data. The ranges of numbers after their name represent the "emptiness" of each block. For example, (0–25) is the count of blocks that are between 0 and 25 percent empty.

- Full Blocks: The number of blocks so full that they are no longer candidates for future inserts.

- Total Blocks, Total Bytes, Total MBytes: The total amount of space allocated to the segment measured in database blocks, bytes, and megabytes.

- Unused Blocks, Unused Bytes: These represent a portion of the amount of space never used. These blocks are allocated to the segment but are currently above the HWM of the segment.

- Last Used Ext FileId: The file ID of the file that contains the last extent that contains data.

- `Last Used Ext BlockId`: The block ID of the beginning of the last extent; the block ID within the last used file.

- `Last Used Block`: The offset of the last block used in the last extent.

When you use `SHOW_SPACE` to look at objects in user space managed tablespaces, the output resembles this:

```
big_table@ORA10G> exec show_space( 'BIG_TABLE' )
Free Blocks.............................              1
Total Blocks...........................        147,456
Total Bytes............................  1,207,959,552
Total MBytes...........................          1,152
Unused Blocks..........................          1,616
Unused Bytes...........................     13,238,272
Last Used Ext FileId...................              7
Last Used Ext BlockId..................        139,273
Last Used Block........................          6,576

PL/SQL procedure successfully completed.
```

The only difference is the `Free Blocks` item at the beginning of the report. This is a count of the blocks in the first freelist group of the segment. My script reports only on this freelist group. You would need to modify the script to accommodate multiple freelist groups.

The commented code follows. This utility is a simple layer on top of the `DBMS_SPACE` API in the database.

```
create or replace procedure show_space
( p_segname in varchar2,
  p_owner   in varchar2 default user,
  p_type    in varchar2 default 'TABLE',
  p_partition in varchar2 default NULL )
-- this procedure uses authid current user so it can query DBA_*
-- views using privileges from a ROLE, and so it can be installed
-- once per database, instead of once per user who wanted to use it
authid current_user
as
    l_free_blks             number;
    l_total_blocks          number;
    l_total_bytes           number;
    l_unused_blocks         number;
    l_unused_bytes          number;
    l_LastUsedExtFileId     number;
    l_LastUsedExtBlockId    number;
    l_LAST_USED_BLOCK       number;
    l_segment_space_mgmt    varchar2(255);
    l_unformatted_blocks number;
    l_unformatted_bytes number;
    l_fs1_blocks number; l_fs1_bytes number;
```

```
    l_fs2_blocks number; l_fs2_bytes number;
    l_fs3_blocks number; l_fs3_bytes number;
    l_fs4_blocks number; l_fs4_bytes number;
    l_full_blocks number; l_full_bytes number;

    -- inline procedure to print out numbers nicely formatted
    -- with a simple label
    procedure p( p_label in varchar2, p_num in number )
    is
    begin
        dbms_output.put_line( rpad(p_label,40,'.') ||
                             to_char(p_num,'999,999,999,999') );
    end;
begin
    -- this query is executed dynamically in order to allow this procedure
    -- to be created by a user who has access to DBA_SEGMENTS/TABLESPACES
    -- via a role as is customary.
    -- NOTE: at runtime, the invoker MUST have access to these two
    -- views!
    -- this query determines if the object is an ASSM object or not
    begin
        execute immediate
            'select ts.segment_space_management
               from dba_segments seg, dba_tablespaces ts
              where seg.segment_name      = :p_segname
                and (:p_partition is null or
                     seg.partition_name = :p_partition)
                and seg.owner = :p_owner
                and seg.tablespace_name = ts.tablespace_name'
              into l_segment_space_mgmt
             using p_segname, p_partition, p_partition, p_owner;
    exception
        when too_many_rows then
           dbms_output.put_line
           ( 'This must be a partitioned table, use p_partition => ');
           return;
    end;

    -- if the object is in an ASSM tablespace, we must use this API
    -- call to get space information, otherwise we use the FREE_BLOCKS
    -- API for the user-managed segments
    if l_segment_space_mgmt = 'AUTO'
    then
      dbms_space.space_usage
      ( p_owner, p_segname, p_type, l_unformatted_blocks,
        l_unformatted_bytes, l_fs1_blocks, l_fs1_bytes,
```

```
        l_fs2_blocks, l_fs2_bytes, l_fs3_blocks, l_fs3_bytes,
        l_fs4_blocks, l_fs4_bytes, l_full_blocks, l_full_bytes, p_partition);

    p( 'Unformatted Blocks ', l_unformatted_blocks );
    p( 'FS1 Blocks (0-25)  ', l_fs1_blocks );
    p( 'FS2 Blocks (25-50) ', l_fs2_blocks );
    p( 'FS3 Blocks (50-75) ', l_fs3_blocks );
    p( 'FS4 Blocks (75-100)', l_fs4_blocks );
    p( 'Full Blocks        ', l_full_blocks );
else
    dbms_space.free_blocks(
        segment_owner     => p_owner,
        segment_name      => p_segname,
        segment_type      => p_type,
        freelist_group_id => 0,
        free_blks         => l_free_blks);

    p( 'Free Blocks', l_free_blks );
end if;


-- and then the unused space API call to get the rest of the
-- information
dbms_space.unused_space
( segment_owner       => p_owner,
  segment_name        => p_segname,
  segment_type        => p_type,
  partition_name      => p_partition,
  total_blocks        => l_total_blocks,
  total_bytes         => l_total_bytes,
  unused_blocks       => l_unused_blocks,
  unused_bytes        => l_unused_bytes,
  LAST_USED_EXTENT_FILE_ID => l_LastUsedExtFileId,
  LAST_USED_EXTENT_BLOCK_ID => l_LastUsedExtBlockId,
  LAST_USED_BLOCK => l_LAST_USED_BLOCK );

    p( 'Total Blocks', l_total_blocks );
    p( 'Total Bytes', l_total_bytes );
    p( 'Total MBytes', trunc(l_total_bytes/1024/1024) );
    p( 'Unused Blocks', l_unused_blocks );
    p( 'Unused Bytes', l_unused_bytes );
    p( 'Last Used Ext FileId', l_LastUsedExtFileId );
    p( 'Last Used Ext BlockId', l_LastUsedExtBlockId );
    p( 'Last Used Block', l_LAST_USED_BLOCK );
end;
/
```

BIG_TABLE

For examples throughout this book, I use a table called BIG_TABLE. Depending on which system I use, this table has between 1 record and 4 million records, and varies in size from 200MB to 800MB. In all cases, the table structure is the same.

To create BIG_TABLE, I wrote a script that does the following:

- Creates an empty table based on ALL_OBJECTS. This dictionary view is used to populate BIG_TABLE.

- Makes this table NOLOGGING. This is optional. I did it for performance. Using NOLOGGING mode for a test table is safe; you won't use it in a production system, so features like Oracle Data Guard won't be enabled.

- Populates the table by seeding it with the contents of ALL_OBJECTS and then iteratively inserting into itself, approximately doubling its size on each iteration.

- Creates a primary key constraint on the table.

- Gathers statistics.

- Displays the number of rows in the table.

To build the BIG_TABLE table, you can run the following script at the SQL*Plus prompt and pass in the number of rows you want in the table. The script will stop when it hits that number of rows.

```
create table big_table
as
select rownum id, a.*
  from all_objects a
 where 1=0
/
alter table big_table nologging;

declare
    l_cnt number;
    l_rows number := &1;
begin
    insert /*+ append */
    into big_table
    select rownum, a.*
      from all_objects a;

    l_cnt := sql%rowcount;

    commit;

    while (l_cnt < l_rows)
    loop
        insert /*+ APPEND */ into big_table
        select rownum+l_cnt,
```

```
            OWNER, OBJECT_NAME, SUBOBJECT_NAME,
            OBJECT_ID, DATA_OBJECT_ID,
            OBJECT_TYPE, CREATED, LAST_DDL_TIME,
            TIMESTAMP, STATUS, TEMPORARY,
            GENERATED, SECONDARY
        from big_table
       where rownum <= l_rows-l_cnt;
      l_cnt := l_cnt + sql%rowcount;
      commit;
    end loop;
end;
/

alter table big_table add constraint
big_table_pk primary key(id)
/

begin
  dbms_stats.gather_table_stats
  ( ownname    => user,
    tabname    => 'BIG_TABLE',
    method_opt => 'for all indexed columns',
    cascade    => TRUE );
end;
/
select count(*) from big_table;
```

I gathered baseline statistics on the table and the index associated with the primary key. Additionally, I gathered histograms on the indexed column (something I typically do). Histograms may be gathered on other columns as well, but for this table, it just isn't necessary.

Coding Conventions

The one coding convention I use in this book that I would like to point out is how I name variables in PL/SQL code. For example, consider a package body like this:

```
create or replace package body my_pkg
as
   g_variable varchar2(25);

   procedure p( p_variable in varchar2 )
   is
      l_variable varchar2(25);
   begin
      null;
   end;
end;
/
```

Here I have three variables: a global package variable, G_VARIABLE; a formal parameter to the procedure, P_VARIABLE; and finally a local variable, L_VARIABLE. I name my variables after the scope they are contained in. All globals begin with G_, parameters with P_, and local variables with L_. The main reason for this is to distinguish PL/SQL variables from columns in a database table. For example, a procedure such as the following:

```
create procedure p( ENAME in varchar2 )
as
begin
   for x in ( select * from emp where ename = ENAME ) loop
      Dbms_output.put_line( x.empno );
   end loop;
end;
```

will always print out every row in the EMP table, where ENAME is not null. SQL sees ename = ENAME, and compares the ENAME column to itself (of course). We could use ename = P.ENAME—that is, qualify the reference to the PL/SQL variable with the procedure name—but this is too easy to forget and leads to errors.

I just always name my variables after the scope. That way, I can easily distinguish parameters from local variables and globals, in addition to removing any ambiguity with respect to column names and variable names.

CHAPTER 1

∎ ∎ ∎

Developing Successful
Oracle Applications

I spend the bulk of my time working with Oracle database software and, more to the point, with people who use this software. Over the last 18 years, I've worked on many projects—successful ones as well as complete failures—and if I were to encapsulate my experiences into a few broad statements, they would be

- An application built around the database—dependent on the database—will succeed or fail based on how it uses the database. Additionally, in my experience, all applications are built around databases. I cannot think of a single useful application that does not store data persistently somewhere.

- Applications come, applications go. The *data*, however, lives forever. In the long term, the goal is not about building applications; it really is about using the data underneath these applications.

- A development team needs at its heart a core of database-savvy developers who are responsible for ensuring the database logic is sound and the system is built to perform from day one. Tuning after the fact (tuning after deployment) typically means you did not give serious thought to these concerns during development.

These may seem like surprisingly obvious statements, but I have found that too many people approach the database as if it were a *black box*—something that they don't need to know about. Maybe they have a SQL generator that they figure will save them from the hardship of having to learn the SQL language. Maybe they figure they will just use the database like a flat file and do keyed reads. Whatever they figure, I can tell you that thinking along these lines is most certainly misguided: you simply cannot get away with not understanding the database. This chapter will discuss *why* you need to know about the database, specifically why you need to understand

- The database architecture, how it works, and what it looks like.

- What concurrency controls are, and what they mean to you.

- That performance, scalability, and security are requirements to be designed into your development efforts, not something to hope you achieve by accident.

- How features are implemented in the database. The way in which a specific database feature is actually implemented may not be the way you might envision. You have to design for how the database works, not how you think it should work.

- What features your database already provides for you and why it is generally better to use a provided feature than to build your own.

- Why you might want more than a cursory knowledge of SQL.

- That the DBA and developer staff members are fighting for the same cause; they're not two enemy camps trying to outsmart each other at every turn.

This may initially seem like a long list of things to learn, but consider this analogy for a second: If you were developing a highly scalable, enterprise application on a brand-new operating system (OS), what would be the first thing you would do? Hopefully, your answer is, "Find out how this new OS works, how things will run on it, and so on." If you did not do this, your development effort would fail.

Consider, for example, Windows versus Linux. Both are operating systems. Each provides largely the same set of services to developers, such as file management, memory management, process management, security, and so on. However, they are very different architecturally. Consequently, if you're a longtime Windows programmer and you're asked to develop a new application on the Linux platform, you would have to relearn a couple of things. Memory management is done differently. The way in which you build a server process is considerably different. Under Windows, you develop a single process, a single executable, with many threads. Under Linux, you do not develop a single stand-alone executable; instead, you have many processes working together. In summary, much of what you learned in the Windows environment doesn't apply to Linux (and vice versa, to be fair). You have to unlearn some old habits to be successful on the new platform.

What is true of applications running natively on operating systems is also true of applications that will run on a database: you need to understand that the database is crucial to your success. If you do not understand what your particular database does or how it does it, then your application is likely to fail. If you assume that because your application ran fine on SQL Server, it will necessarily run fine on Oracle then, again, your application is likely to fail. And to be fair, the opposite is true: a scalable, well-developed Oracle application will not necessarily run on SQL Server as is without major architectural changes. Just as Windows and Linux are both operating systems, but fundamentally different, so Oracle and SQL Server (pretty much any database could be noted here) are both databases, but fundamentally different.

My Approach

Before you read further, I feel I should explain my approach to development. I tend to take a database-centric approach to problems. If I can do it in the database, I will. There are a couple of reasons for this, the first and foremost being that I know if I build functionality in the database, I can *deploy* it anywhere. I am not aware of any popular server operating system on which Oracle is not available; from Windows, to dozens of UNIX/Linux systems, to the OS/390 mainframe, the same exact Oracle software and options are available. I frequently build and test solutions on my laptop running Oracle9*i*, Oracle 10*g* under Linux, or Windows XP using VMware to emulate either environment. I am able to then deploy these solutions on a variety

CHAPTER 1 ■ DEVELOPING SUCCESSFUL ORACLE APPLICATIONS

of servers running the same database software but different operating systems. When I have to implement a feature outside of the database, I find it extremely hard to deploy that feature anywhere I want. One of the main features that makes the Java language appealing to many people is the fact that their programs are always compiled in the same virtual environment, the Java Virtual Machine (JVM), making those programs highly portable. Ironically, this is the same feature that makes the database appealing to me. The database is *my* "virtual machine"; it is *my* "virtual operating system."

As just mentioned, my approach is to do everything I can in the database. If my requirements go beyond what the database environment can offer, I'll work in Java or C outside of the database. In this way, almost every OS intricacy will be hidden from me. I still have to understand how *my* "virtual machines" work (Oracle and occasionally a JVM)—you need to know the tools you are using—but they, in turn, worry for me about how best to do things on a given OS.

Thus, simply by knowing the intricacies of this one "virtual operating system," I can build applications that will perform and scale well on many operating systems. I do not intend to imply that you can be totally ignorant of your underlying OS. However, as a software developer who builds database applications, you can be fairly well insulated from it, and you will not have to deal with many of its nuances. Your DBA, who is responsible for running the Oracle software, will be infinitely more in tune with the OS (if he or she is not, please get a new DBA!). If you develop client/server software, and the bulk of your code is outside of the database and outside of a virtual machine (VM; JVMs perhaps being the most popular VM), you will have to be concerned about your OS once again.

I have a pretty simple philosophy when it comes to developing database software, and it is one that has not changed over many years:

- You should do it in a single SQL statement if at all possible.

- If you cannot do it in a single SQL statement, then do it in PL/SQL (but as little PL/SQL as possible!).

- If you cannot do it in PL/SQL (due to some missing feature like listing the files in a directory), try a Java stored procedure. This is an extremely rare need today with Oracle9*i* and above.

- If you cannot do it in Java, do it in a C external procedure. This is most frequently the approach when raw speed or the use of a third-party API written in C is needed.

- If you cannot do it in a C external routine, you might want to think seriously about why exactly you need to do it.

Throughout this book, you will see the preceding philosophy implemented. We'll use SQL whenever possible, exploiting powerful new capabilities, such as analytic functions to solve reasonably sophisticated problems without recourse to procedural code. When needed, we'll use PL/SQL and object types in PL/SQL to do things that SQL itself cannot do. PL/SQL has been around for a very long time—over 18 years of tuning has gone into it. In fact, the Oracle10*g* compiler itself was rewritten to be, for the first time, an optimizing compiler. You will find no other language so tightly coupled with SQL or any as optimized to interact with SQL. Working with SQL in PL/SQL is a very natural thing, whereas in virtually every other language—from Visual Basic to Java—using SQL can feel cumbersome. It never quite feels "natural"; it is not an extension of the language itself. When PL/SQL runs out of steam, which is exceedingly rare in

Oracle9*i* or 10*g*, we'll use Java. Occasionally, we'll do something in C, but typically as a last resort, when C is the only choice or when the raw speed offered by C is required. With the advent of native Java compilation (the ability to convert your Java bytecode into OS-specific object code on your platform), you will find that Java runs just as fast as C in many cases. Therefore, the need to resort to C is becoming rare.

The Black Box Approach

I have an idea, borne out by first-hand personal experience (meaning I made the mistake myself as I was learning software development), as to why database-backed software development efforts so frequently fail. Let me be clear that I'm including here those projects that may not be documented as failures, but take much longer to roll out and deploy than originally planned because of the need to perform a major rewrite, re-architecture, or tuning effort. Personally, I call these delayed projects "failures," as more often than not they could have been completed on schedule (or even faster).

The single most common reason for database project failure is insufficient practical knowledge of the database—a basic lack of understanding of the fundamental tool that is being used. The black box approach involves a conscious decision to protect the developers from the database—they are actually encouraged to not learn anything about it! In many cases, they are prevented from exploiting it. The reasons for this approach appear to be related to FUD (fear, uncertainty, and doubt). The accepted wisdom is that databases are "hard," and that SQL, transactions, and data integrity are "hard." The solution: don't make anyone do anything "hard." They treat the database as a black box and have some software tool generate all of the code. They try to insulate themselves with many layers of protection so that they do not have to touch this "hard" database.

This is an approach to database development that I've never been able to understand, for a couple of reasons. One of the reasons I have difficulty grasping this approach is that, for me, learning Java and C was a lot harder than learning the concepts behind the database. I'm now pretty good at Java and C, but it took a lot more hands-on experience for me to become competent using them than it did to become competent using the database. With the database, you need to be aware of how it works, but you don't have to know everything inside and out. When programming in C or Java, you do need to know everything inside and out, and these are *huge* languages.

Another reason I don't understand this approach is that when building a database application, then *the most important piece of software is the database*. A successful development team will appreciate this and will want its people to know about it and to concentrate on it. Many times I've walked into a project where almost the complete opposite was true. For example, a typical scenario would be as follows:

- The developers were fully trained in the GUI tool or the language they were using to build the front end (such as Java). In many cases, they had had weeks if not months of training in it.

- The developers had zero hours of Oracle training and zero hours of Oracle experience. Most had no database experience whatsoever and so had no real understanding of how to use core database constructs, such as the various indexes and table structures available.

- The developers were following a mandate to be "database independent"—a mandate they could not hope to follow for many reasons, the most obvious being that they didn't know enough about what databases are and how they might differ. This team would not be able to know what features of the database to avoid in an attempt to remain database independent.

- The developers encountered massive performance problems, data integrity problems, hanging issues, and the like (but they had very pretty screens).

As a result of the inevitable performance problems, I was called in to help solve the difficulties. Since I started my career attempting to build database-independent applications (to the extent that I wrote my own ODBC drivers before ODBC existed), I know where the mistakes will be made because at one time or another I have made them myself. I always look for inefficient SQL, lots of procedural code where a single SQL statement would suffice, no feature invented after 1995 being used (to remain database independent), and so on.

I can recall one particular occasion when I'd been called in to help and could not fully remember the syntax of a new command that we needed to use. I asked for the *SQL Reference* manual and was handed an Oracle 6.0 document. The development was taking place on version 7.3, five years after the release of version 6.0! It was all the developers had to work with, but this did not seem to concern them at all. Never mind the fact that the tool they really needed to know about for tracing and tuning didn't even exist back then. Never mind the fact that features such as triggers, stored procedures, and hundreds of others had been added in the five years since the documentation to which they had access was written. It was very easy to determine why they needed help—fixing their problems was another issue altogether.

Note Even today, in 2005, I often find that database application developers have not spent any time reading the documentation. On my web site (http://asktom.oracle.com), I frequently get questions along the lines of "What is the syntax for . . ." coupled with "We don't have the documentation, so please just tell us." I refuse to directly answer many of those questions, but rather point questioners to the online documentation, which is freely available to anyone, anywhere in the world. In the last ten years, the excuse of "We don't have documentation" or "We don't have access to resources" has been rendered obsolete. The introduction of the Web and sites such as http://otn.oracle.com (Oracle Technology Network) and http://groups.google.com (Google Groups Usenet discussion forums) make it inexcusable to not have a full set of documentation at your fingertips!

The very idea that developers building a *database application* should be shielded from the database is amazing to me, but this approach persists. Many people still believe that developers cannot afford the time to get trained in the database and that basically they should not have to know anything about the database. Why? Well, more than once I've heard "Oracle is the most scalable database in the world, so my people don't have to learn about it—it will just do X, Y, and Z." It is true that Oracle is the most scalable database in the world. However, it is just as easy (if not easier) to write bad, nonscalable code in Oracle as it is to write good, scaleable code. You can replace the word "Oracle" in the last sentence with the name of any other technology and the statement will remain true. This is a fact: it is easier to write applications that perform poorly than it is to write applications that perform well. If you don't know what you're doing, you may find that you've managed to build a single-user system in the world's most scalable database!

The database is a tool, and the improper use of any tool can lead to disaster. Would you use a nutcracker as if it were a hammer to smash walnuts? You could, but it would not be a proper use of that tool, and the result would be messy (and probably involve some seriously damaged fingers). Similar effects can be achieved by remaining ignorant of your database.

For example, I was called into a project recently. The developers were experiencing massive performance issues—it seemed that their system was serializing many transactions. Instead of many people working concurrently, everyone was getting into a really long line and waiting for those in front of them to complete before they could proceed. The application architects walked me through the architecture of their system—the classic three-tier approach. They would have a web browser talk to a middle-tier application server running JavaServer Pages (JSP). The JSPs would in turn use another layer, Enterprise JavaBeans (EJB), that did all of the SQL. The SQL in the EJBs was generated by some third-party tool and was done in a database-independent fashion.

Now, in this system it was very hard to diagnose anything, because none of the code was instrumented or traceable. *Instrumenting* code is the fine art of making every other line of developed code be debug code, something that allows you to trace the execution of your application so that when you are faced with performance, capacity, or even logic issues, you can track down exactly where the problem is. In this case, we could only say for sure that the problem was "somewhere in between the browser and the database." In other words, the entire system was suspect. Fortunately, the Oracle database is heavily instrumented, but unfortunately, the application needs to be able to turn the instrumentation on and off at appropriate points—an ability that this application did not have.

So, we were faced with trying to diagnose a performance issue with not too many details, just what we could glean from the database itself. Normally, an application-level trace would be preferred for investigating an application performance issue. Fortunately, however, in this case the solution was fairly easy. A review of some of the Oracle V$ tables (the V$ tables are one way Oracle exposes its instrumentation—its statistics) revealed that the major contention was around a single table, a queue table of sorts. We could see this based on the V$LOCK view, which would show us the blocked sessions, and V$SQL, which would show us the SQL that these blocked sessions were trying to execute. The application would place records into this table, and another set of processes would pull the records out of this table and process them. Digging deeper, we found a bitmap index on the PROCESSED_FLAG column in this table.

■**Note** Chapter 12 provides detailed information on bitmapped indexes, including a discussion of why they are not just for low-cardinality values and why they are not appropriate for update-intensive columns.

The reasoning was that this column, the PROCESSED_FLAG column, had only two values: Y and N. Records inserted into the table would have a value of N (for not processed). As the other processes read and processed the record, they would update the value from N to Y. These processes needed to be able to find the N records rapidly, hence the developers knew that they wanted to index that column. They had read somewhere that bitmap indexes are for *low-cardinality* columns (columns that have only a few distinct values) so it seemed a natural fit.

Nevertheless, that bitmap index was the cause of all of their problems. In a *bitmap index*, a single key entry points to many rows—hundreds or more of them. If you update a bitmap index key, the hundreds of records to which that key points are effectively locked as well as the single row you are actually updating.

So, someone inserting a new N record would lock an N key in the bitmap index, effectively locking hundreds of other N records as well. Meanwhile, the process trying to read this table and process the records would be prevented from modifying some N record to be a Y (processed) record, because in order for it to update this column from N to Y, it would need to lock that same bitmap index key. In fact, other sessions just trying to insert a new record into this table would be blocked as well, as they would be attempting to lock this same bitmap key entry. In short, the developers had implemented a set of structures that at most one person would be able to insert or update against at a time!

I can demonstrate this scenario easily with a simple example. Here, I use two sessions to demonstrate the blocking that can easily happen:

```
ops$tkyte@ORA10G> create table t ( processed_flag varchar2(1) );
Table created.
ops$tkyte@ORA10G> create bitmap index t_idx on t(processed_flag);
Index created.
ops$tkyte@ORA10G> insert into t values ( 'N' );
1 row created.
```

Now, in another SQL*Plus session, if I execute

```
ops$tkyte@ORA10G> insert into t values ( 'N' );
```

that statement will "hang" until I issue a COMMIT in the first blocking session.

So here we had an issue whereby a lack of understanding of the database feature (bitmap indexes), of what it did and how it worked, meant that the database was doomed to poor scalability from the start. Once this issue was discovered, correcting it was easy. We needed an index on the processed flag column, but not a bitmap index. We needed a conventional B*Tree index here. This took a bit of convincing because no one wanted to believe that use of a conventional index on a column with two distinct values was a "good idea." But after setting up a simulation (I am very much into simulations, testing, and experimenting), we were able to prove that it was the correct approach. There were two ways to approach the indexing of this particular column:

- Just create an index on the processed flag column.

- Create an index only on the processed flag column when the processed flag is N—that is, only index the values of interest. Typically, we do not want to use an index where the processed flag is Y, since the vast majority of the records in the table would have the value Y. Notice that I did not say "We never want to use"—if you need to frequently count the number of processed records for some reason, then an index on the processed records may well prove useful.

We ended up creating a very small index on just the records where the processed flag was N, which provided quick access to the records of interest.

Was that the end of the story? No, not at all. The developers still had a less than optimal solution on their hands. We fixed their major problem, caused by their not fully understanding the tools they were using, and found only after lots of study that the system was not nicely instrumented. We didn't yet address the following issues:

- The application was built without a single consideration for scalability. Scalability is something you have to design for.

- The application itself could not be tuned or touched. Experience has shown that 80 to 90 percent of *all* tuning is done at the application level, not at the database level.

- The application was performing functionality (the queue table) that the database *already supplied in a highly concurrent and scalable fashion*. I'm referring to the Advanced Queuing (AQ) software that is burned into the database, functionality they were trying to reinvent.

- The developers had no idea what the beans did in the database or where to look for potential problems.

That was hardly the end of the problems on this project. We then had to figure out

- How to tune SQL without changing the SQL. Oracle 10*g* actually does permit us to accomplish this magical feat for the first time to a large degree.

- How to measure performance.

- How to see where the bottlenecks are.

- How and what to index.

- And so on.

At the end of the week, the developers, who had been insulated from the database, were amazed at what the database could actually provide for them, how easy it was to get that information and, most important, how big a difference it could make to the performance of their application. In the end they were successful—just behind schedule by a couple of weeks.

This example is not meant to be a criticism of tools or technologies like EJBs and container-managed persistence. Rather, it is a criticism of purposely remaining ignorant of the database, how it works, and how to use it. The technologies used in this case worked well—after the developers gained some insight into the database itself.

The bottom line is that the database is typically the cornerstone of your application. If it does not work well, nothing else really matters. If you have a black box and it does not work well, what are you going to do about it? About the only thing you can do is look at it and wonder why it is not doing so well. You cannot fix it; you cannot tune it. You quite simply do not understand how it works—and you made the decision to be in this position. The alternative is the approach that I advocate: understand your database, know how it works, know what it can do for you, and use it to its fullest potential.

How (and How Not) to Develop Database Applications

So far, I've described the importance of understanding the database in a fairly anecdotal manner. In the remainder of this chapter, I'll take a more empirical approach, discussing specifically *why* knowledge of the database and its workings will definitely go a long way toward a successful implementation (without having to write the application twice!). Some problems are simple to fix as long as you understand how to find them. Others require drastic rewrites. One of the goals of this book is to help you avoid problems in the first place.

Note In the following sections, I discuss certain core Oracle features without delving into exactly what these features are and all of the ramifications of using them. I will refer you either to a subsequent chapter in this book or to the relevant Oracle documentation for more information.

Understanding Oracle Architecture

Recently, I was working with a customer running a large production application. This application had been "ported" from SQL Server to Oracle. I enclose the term "ported" in quotes simply because most ports I see are of the "what is the minimal change we can make to have our SQL Server code compile and execute on Oracle" variety. To port an application from one database to another is a major undertaking. The algorithms should be examined in detail to see if they work correctly in the target database; features such as concurrency controls and locking mechanisms work differently in different databases, and this in turn affects the way the application will function in different databases. The algorithms should also be looked at to see if there is a sensible way to implement them in the target database. The applications that result from a minimal "port" are, frankly, the ones I see most often because they are the ones that need the most help. Of course, the opposite is equally true: taking an Oracle application and just plopping it on top of SQL Server with as few changes as possible will result in a problematic and poorly performing application.

In any event, the goal of this "port" was to scale up the application to support a larger installed base of users. However, the customer wanted to achieve this aim with as little work as humanly possible. So, the customer kept the architecture basically the same in the client and database layers, the data was moved over from SQL Server to Oracle, and as few code changes as possible were made. The decision to impose on Oracle the same application design as was used on SQL Server had grave consequences. The two most critical ramifications of this decision were as follows:

- The connection architecture to the database was the same in Oracle as it was in SQL Server.

- The developers used literal (nonbound) SQL.

These two ramifications resulted in a system that could not support the required user load (the database server simply ran out of available memory), and abysmal performance for the set of users that could log in and use the application.

Use a Single Connection in Oracle

Now, in SQL Server it is a very common practice to open a connection to the database for each concurrent statement you want to execute. If you are going to do five queries, you might well see five connections in SQL Server. SQL Server was designed that way—much like Windows was designed for multithreading, not multiprocessing. In Oracle, whether you want to do five queries or five hundred queries, the maximum number of connections you want to open is one. Oracle was designed that way. So, what is a common practice in SQL Server is something that is actively discouraged in Oracle; having multiple connections to the database is something that you just don't want to do.

But do it they did. A simple web-based application would open 5, 10, 15, or more connections per web page, meaning that the server could support only 1/5, 1/10, 1/15, or an even fewer number of concurrent users that it should have been able to. Additionally, they were attempting to run the database on the Windows platform itself—just a plain Windows XP server without access to the Datacenter version of Windows. This meant that the Windows single-process architecture limited the Oracle database server to about 1.75GB of RAM in total. Since each Oracle connection was designed to handle multiple statements simultaneously, a single connection to Oracle typically takes more RAM than a single connection to SQL Server (but it can do a whole lot more). The developer's ability to scale was severely limited on this hardware. They had 8GB of RAM on the server but could use only about 2GB of it.

■**Note** There are ways to get much more RAM used in a Windows environment, such as with the /AWE switch, but this requires versions of the operating system that were not in use in this situation, such as Windows Server Datacenter Edition.

There were three possible solutions to this problem, and all three entailed quite a bit of work (and remember, this was after the "port" was supposedly complete!). Our options were as follows:

- Re-architect the application, to allow it to take advantage of the fact it was running "on" Oracle and use a single connection to generate a page, not somewhere between 5 to 15 connections. This was the only solution that would actually solve the problem.

- Upgrade the OS (no small chore) and use the larger memory model of the Windows Datacenter version (itself not a small chore either, as this process involves a rather involved database setup with indirect data buffers and other nonstandard settings).

- Migrate the database from a Windows-based OS to some other OS where multiple processes are used, effectively allowing the database to use all installed RAM (again, a nontrivial task).

As you can see, none of the presented options is the sort of solution that would have you thinking, "OK, we'll do that this afternoon." Each was a complex solution to a problem that would have most easily been corrected during the database "port" phase, while you were in the code poking around and changing things in the first place. Furthermore, a simple test to "scale" prior to rolling out a production would have caught such issues prior to the end users feeling the pain.

Use Bind Variables

If I were to write a book about how to build *nonscalable* Oracle applications, then "Don't Use Bind Variables" would be the title of the first and last chapters. This is a major cause of performance issues and a major inhibitor of scalability. The Oracle *shared pool* (a very important shared memory structure, found in the System Global Area [SGA]) is where Oracle stores parsed, compiled SQL among other things. We cover the shared pool in detail in Chapter 4. This structure's smooth operation is predicated on developers using bind variables in most cases. If you want to make Oracle run slowly—even grind to a total halt—just refuse to use bind variables.

A *bind variable* is a placeholder in a query. For example, to retrieve the record for employee 123, I can use this query:

```
select * from emp where empno = 123;
```

Alternatively, I can set the bind variable :empno to 123 and execute the following query:

```
select * from emp where empno = :empno;
```

In a typical system, you would query up employee 123 maybe once and then never again. Later, you would query employee 456, then 789, and so on. If you use literals (constants) in the query, then each and every query is a brand-new query, never before seen by the database. It will have to be parsed, qualified (names resolved), security checked, optimized, and so on—in short, each and every unique statement you execute will have to be compiled every time it is executed.

The second query uses a bind variable, :empno, the value of which is supplied at query execution time. This query is compiled once, and then the query plan is stored in a shared pool (the library cache), from which it can be retrieved and reused. The difference between the two in terms of performance and scalability is huge—dramatic, even.

From the previous description, it should be fairly obvious that parsing a statement with hard-coded variables (called a *hard parse*) will take longer and consume many more resources than reusing an already parsed query plan (called a *soft parse*). What may not be so obvious is the extent to which the former will reduce the number of users your system can support. This is due in part to the increased resource consumption, but an even larger factor arises due to the latching mechanisms for the library cache. When you hard-parse a query, the database will spend more time holding certain low-level serialization devices called *latches* (see Chapter 6 for more details). These latches protect the data structures in the shared memory of Oracle from concurrent modifications by two sessions (otherwise Oracle would end up with corrupt data structures) and from someone reading a data structure while it is being modified. The longer and more frequently you have to latch these data structures, the longer the queue to get these latches will become. You will start to monopolize scarce resources. Your machine may appear to be underutilized at times, and yet everything in the database is running very slowly. The likelihood is that someone is holding one of these serialization mechanisms and a line is forming—you are not able to run at top speed. It only takes one ill-behaved application in your database to dramatically affect the performance of every other application. A single, small application that does not use bind variables will cause the SQL of other well-designed applications to get discarded from the shared pool over time. That will cause the well-designed applications to have to hard-parse their SQL all over again as well. You only need one bad apple to spoil the entire barrel.

If you use bind variables, then everyone who submits the same exact query that references the same object will use the compiled plan from the pool. You will compile your subroutine once and use it over and over again. This is very efficient and is the way the database intends you to work. Not only will you use fewer resources (a soft parse is much less resource intensive), but also you will hold latches for less time and need them less frequently. This increases your applications' performance and scalability.

To give you an inkling of how huge a difference the use of bind variables can make performance-wise, we only need to run a very small test. In this test, we'll insert some rows into a table. The simple table we'll use is as follows:

```
ops$tkyte@ORA9IR2> drop table t;
Table dropped.

ops$tkyte@ORA9IR2> create table t ( x int );
Table created.
```

Now we'll create two very simple stored procedures. They both will insert the numbers 1 through 10,000 into this table; however, the first procedure uses a single SQL statement with a bind variable:

```
ops$tkyte@ORA9IR2> create or replace procedure proc1
  2  as
  3  begin
  4      for i in 1 .. 10000
  5      loop
  6          execute immediate
  7          'insert into t values ( :x )' using i;
  8      end loop;
  9  end;
 10  /
Procedure created.
```

The second procedure constructs a unique SQL statement for each and every row to be inserted:

```
ops$tkyte@ORA9IR2> create or replace procedure proc2
  2  as
  3  begin
  4      for i in 1 .. 10000
  5      loop
  6          execute immediate
  7          'insert into t values ( '||i||')';
  8      end loop;
  9  end;
 10  /
Procedure created.
```

Now, the only difference between the two is that one uses a bind variable and the other does not. Both are using dynamic SQL (i.e., SQL that is not known until runtime) and the logic in both is identical. The only change is the use or nonuse of a bind variable.

Let's now compare the two approaches in detail with *runstats*, a simple tool I've developed:

■**Note** For details on setting up runstats and other utilities, please see the "Setting Up" section at the beginning of this book.

```
ops$tkyte@ORA9IR2> exec runstats_pkg.rs_start
PL/SQL procedure successfully completed.

ops$tkyte@ORA9IR2> exec proc1
PL/SQL procedure successfully completed.

ops$tkyte@ORA9IR2> exec runstats_pkg.rs_middle
PL/SQL procedure successfully completed.

ops$tkyte@ORA9IR2> exec proc2
PL/SQL procedure successfully completed.

ops$tkyte@ORA9IR2> exec runstats_pkg.rs_stop(1000)
Run1 ran in 159 hsecs
Run2 ran in 516 hsecs
run 1 ran in 30.81% of the time
```

Now, that result clearly shows that by the wall clock, proc2, which did not use a bind variable, took significantly longer to insert 10,000 rows than proc1, which did. In fact, proc2 took three times longer, meaning that, in this case, for every "non-bind-variable" INSERT, we spent two-thirds of the time to execute the statement simply *parsing* the statement!

■**Note** If you like, you can run the example in this section without runstats by issuing SET TIMING ON in SQL*Plus and running proc1 and proc2 as well.

But the news gets even worse for proc2. The runstats utility produces a report that shows the actual values and calculates the differences in latch utilization, as well as statistics such as number of parses. Here I asked runstats to print out anything with a difference greater than 1,000 (that is the meaning of the 1000 in the rs_stop call). When we look at this information, we can see a significant difference in the resources used by each approach:

Name	Run1	Run2	Diff
STAT...parse count (hard)	4	10,003	9,999
LATCH.library cache pin	80,222	110,221	29,999
LATCH.library cache pin alloca	40,161	80,153	39,992
LATCH.row cache enqueue latch	78	40,082	40,004
LATCH.row cache objects	98	40,102	40,004

```
LATCH.child cursor hash table         35      80,023      79,988
LATCH.shared pool                 50,455     162,577     112,122
LATCH.library cache              110,524     250,510     139,986

Run1 latches total versus runs -- difference and pct
Run1        Run2        Diff       Pct
407,973     889,287     481,314     45.88%

PL/SQL procedure successfully completed.
```

■Note It is to be expected that you see somewhat different values in your testing. I would be surprised if you got exactly the same values for all numbers, especially the latching numbers. You should, however, see *similar* numbers, assuming you are using Oracle9*i* Release 2 on Linux, as I was here. In all releases, I would expect the number of latches used to hard parse to be higher than those for soft parsing each insert, or parsing the insert once and executing it over and over. Running the preceding test in Oracle 10*g* Release 1 on the same machine produced results such that the elapsed time of the bind variable approach was one-tenth of the non–bind variable approach, and the amount of latches taken was 17 percent. This was due to two factors, one being that 10*g* is a new release and some internal algorithms changed. The other was due to an improved way dynamic SQL is processed in PL/SQL in 10*g*.

You can see that there were only four hard parses with the bind variable approach, but over 10,000 hard parses without bind variables (once for each of the inserts). But that is just the tip of the iceberg. You can see here that twice as many "latches" were used in the non–bind variable approach than when using bind variables. This is because in order to modify this shared structure, Oracle must take care to allow only one process in at a time (it is very bad if two processes or threads attempt to update the same in-memory data structure simultaneously—corruption would abound). So, Oracle employs a latching mechanism, a lightweight locking device, to serialize access. Don't be fooled by the word "lightweight"—these are serialization devices, allowing one-at-a-time, short duration access to a data structure. The latches overused by the hard-parsing implementation are among the most used latches out there. The latch into the shared pool and the latch for the library cache are big-time latches; they're the ones that people compete for frequently. What that means is that as we increase the number of users attempting to hard-parse statements simultaneously, our performance problem will get progressively worse over time. The more people parsing, the more people fighting for the right to latch the shared pool, the longer the queues, the longer the wait.

■Note In 9*i* and above on machines with more than one processor, the shared pool may be divided into multiple subpools, each protected by its own latch. This permits increased scalability for applications that do not use bind variables, but it does not make the latching problem go away by any means.

Executing SQL statements without bind variables is very much like compiling a subroutine before each and every method call. Imagine shipping Java source code to your customers where, before calling a method in a class, they had to invoke the Java compiler, compile the class, run the method, and then throw away the bytecode. The next time they wanted to execute the exact same method, they would do the same thing: compile it, run it, and throw it away. You would never consider doing this in your application. You should never consider doing this in your database, either.

As it was, on this particular project, reworking the existing code to use bind variables was the best course of action. The resulting code ran orders of magnitude faster and increased many times the number of simultaneous users that the system could support. However, it came at a high price in terms of time and effort. It is not that using bind variables is difficult or error-prone, it's just that the developers did not do it initially and thus were forced to go back and revisit virtually *all* of the code and change it. They would not have paid this high price if they had understood that it was vital to use bind variables in their application from day one.

Understanding Concurrency Control

Concurrency control is one area where databases differentiate themselves. It is an area that sets a database apart from a file system and databases apart from each other. It is vital that your database application work correctly under concurrent access conditions, and yet this is something people fail to test time and time again. Techniques that work well if everything happens consecutively do not work so well when everyone does them simultaneously. If you don't have a good grasp of how your particular database implements concurrency control mechanisms, then you will

- Corrupt the integrity of your data.

- Have applications run slower than they should with a small number of users.

- Decrease your ability to scale to a large number of users.

Notice I don't say, "You might . . ." or "You run the risk of . . ." Rather, you *will* invariably do these things without proper concurrency control without even realizing it. Without correct concurrency control, you will corrupt the integrity of your database because something that works in isolation will not work as you expect in a multiuser situation. Your application will run slower than it should because it will end up waiting for resources. You'll lose your ability to scale because of locking and contention issues. As the queues to access a resource get longer, the wait times get longer and longer.

An analogy here would be a backup at a tollbooth. If cars arrive in an orderly, predictable fashion, one after the other, there will never be a backup. If many cars arrive simultaneously, lines start to form. Furthermore, the waiting time does not increase in line with the number of cars at the booth. After a certain point, considerable additional time is spent "managing" the people that are waiting in line, as well as servicing them (the parallel in the database is context switching).

Concurrency issues are the hardest to track down; the problem is similar to debugging a multithreaded program. The program may work fine in the controlled, artificial environment of the debugger but crashes horribly in the real world. For example, under race conditions, you find that two threads can end up modifying the same data structure simultaneously.

These kinds of bugs are terribly difficult to track down and fix. If you only test your application in isolation and then deploy it to dozens of concurrent users, you are likely to be (painfully) exposed to an undetected concurrency issue.

Over the next two sections, I'll relate two small examples of how the lack of understanding concurrency control can ruin your data or inhibit performance and scalability.

Implementing Locking

The database uses *locks* to ensure that, at most, one transaction is modifying a given piece of data at any given time. Basically, locks are the mechanism that allows for concurrency—without some locking model to prevent concurrent updates to the same row, for example, multiuser access would not be possible in a database. However, if overused or used improperly, locks can actually inhibit concurrency. If you or the database itself locks data unnecessarily, then fewer people will be able to concurrently perform operations. Thus, understanding what locking is and how it works in your database is vital if you are to develop a scalable, correct application.

What is also vital is that you understand that each database implements locking differently. Some have page-level locking, others have row-level locking; some implementations escalate locks from row level to page level, whereas others do not; some use read locks, others do not; and some implement serializable transactions via locking and others via read-consistent views of data (no locks). These small differences can balloon into huge performance issues or downright bugs in your application if you do not understand how they work.

The following points sum up Oracle's locking policy:

- Oracle locks data at the row level on modification only. There is no lock escalation to a block or table level under normal circumstances (there is a short period of time during a two-phase commit, a not common operation, where this is not true).

- Oracle never locks data just to read it. There are no locks placed on rows of data by simple reads.

- A writer of data does not block a reader of data. Let me repeat: *reads* are not blocked by *writes*. This is fundamentally different from almost every other database, where reads are blocked by writes. While this sounds like an extremely positive attribute (it generally is), if you do not understand this idea thoroughly, and you attempt to enforce integrity constraints in your application via application logic, *you are most likely doing it incorrectly.* We will explore this topic in Chapter 7 on concurrency control in much more detail.

- A writer of data is blocked only when another writer of data has already locked the row it was going after. A reader of data never blocks a writer of data.

You must take these facts into consideration when developing your application, and you must also realize that this policy is unique to Oracle—every database has subtle differences in its approach to locking. Even if you go with lowest common denominator SQL in your applications, the locking and concurrency control models employed by each database's vendor dictates that something about how your application behaves will be different. A developer who does not understand how his or her database handles concurrency will certainly encounter data integrity issues. (This is particularly common when developers move from another database to Oracle, or vice versa, and neglect to take the differing concurrency mechanisms into account in their application.)

Preventing Lost Updates

One of the side effects of Oracle's non-blocking approach is that if you actually want to ensure that no more than one user has access to a row at once, then you, the developer, need to do a little work yourself.

Consider the following example. A developer was demonstrating to me a resource-scheduling program (for conference rooms, projectors, etc.) that he had just developed and was in the process of deploying. The application implemented a business rule to prevent the allocation of a resource to more than one person, for any given period of time. That is, the application contained code that specifically checked that no other user had previously allocated the time slot (as least, the developer thought it did). This code queried the SCHEDULES table and, if no rows existed that overlapped that time slot, inserted the new row. So, the developer was basically concerned with two tables:

```
create table resources ( resource_name varchar2(25) primary key, ... );
create table schedules
(  resource_name references resources,
   start_time     date not null,
   end_time       date not null,
   check (start_time < end_time ),
   primary key(resource_name,start_time)
);
```

And, before making, say, a room reservation, the application would query:

```
select count(*)
  from schedules
 where resource_name = :room_name
   and (start_time <= :new_end_time)
   AND (end_time >= :new_start_time)
```

It looked simple and bulletproof (to the developer anyway): if the count came back as zero, the room was yours. If it came back as nonzero, you could not reserve the room for that period. Once I knew what his logic was, I set up a very simple test to show him the error that would occur when the application went live—an error that would be incredibly hard to track down and diagnose after the fact. Someone would be convinced it *must* be a database bug.

All I did was get someone else to use the terminal next to him. Both he and the other person navigated to the same screen and, on the count of three, each clicked the Go button and tried to reserve the same room for about the same time—one from 3:00 pm to 4:00 pm and the other from 3:30 pm to 4:00 pm. Both people got the reservation. The logic that worked perfectly in isolation failed in a multiuser environment. The problem in this case was caused in part by Oracle's non-blocking reads. Neither session ever blocked the other session. Both sessions simply ran the query and then performed the logic to schedule the room. They could both run the query to look for a reservation, even if the other session had already started to modify the SCHEDULES table (the change wouldn't be visible to the other session until commit, by which time it would be too late). Since they were never attempting to modify the same row in the SCHEDULES table, they would never block each other and, thus, the business rule could not enforce what it was intended to enforce.

The developer needed a method of enforcing the business rule in a multiuser environment—a way to ensure that exactly one person at a time made a reservation on a given resource. In this case, the solution was to impose a little serialization of his own. What he did was lock the parent row in the RESOURCES table prior to making a modification in the SCHEDULES table. That way, all modifications to the SCHEDULES table for a given RESOURCE_NAME value would be done one at a time. That is, to reserve a block of time for resource X, he locked the single row in the RESOURCES table for X and then modified the SCHEDULES table. So, in addition to performing the preceding count(*), the developer first performed the following:

```
select * from resources where resource_name = :room_name FOR UPDATE;
```

What he did here was to lock the resource (the room) to be scheduled immediately *before* scheduling it—in other words, before he queries the SCHEDULES table for that resource. By locking the resource he is trying to schedule, the developer ensures that no one else is modifying the schedule for this resource simultaneously. Everyone else must wait until he commits his transaction, at which point they will be able to see his schedule. The chance of overlapping schedules is removed.

Developers must understand that, in the multiuser environment, they must at times employ techniques similar to those used in multithreaded programming. The FOR UPDATE clause is working like a semaphore in this case. It serializes access to the RESOURCES tables for that particular row—ensuring no two people can schedule it simultaneously. My suggestion was to make this logic a *transaction API*—that is, bundle all of the logic into a stored procedure and only permit applications to modify the data via this API. The code could look like this:

```
create or replace procedure schedule_resource
( p_resource_name in varchar2,
  p_start_time    in date,
  p_end_time      in date
)
as
    l_resource_name  resources.resource_name%type;
    l_cnt            number;
begin
```

We start by locking the single row in the RESOURCES table for the resource we want to schedule. If anyone else has this row locked, we block and wait for it:

```
select resource_name into l_resource_name
  from resources
 where resource_name = p_resource_name
   FOR UPDATE;
```

Now that we are the only ones inserting into this SCHEDULES table for this resource name, it is safe to look at this table:

```
select count(*)
  into l_cnt
  from schedules
 where resource_name = p_resource_name
   and (start_time <= p_end_time)
   and (end_time >= p_start_time);
if ( l_cnt <> 0 )
then
    raise_application_error
    (-20001, 'Room is already booked!' );
end if;
```

If we get to this point in the code without raising an error, we can safely insert rows for our resource into the SCHEDULES table without any overlaps:

```
insert into schedules
( resource_name, start_time, end_time )
values
( p_resource_name, p_start_time, p_end_time );
end schedule_resources;
```

This solution is still highly concurrent, as there are potentially thousands of resources to be reserved. What we have done is ensure that only one person modifies a resource at any time. This is a rare case where the manual locking of data we are not going to actually update is called for. We need to be able to recognize where we need to do this and, perhaps as important, where we do not need to do this (I present an example of when not to shortly). Additionally, this does not lock the resource from other people reading the data as it might in other databases, hence this solution will scale very well.

Issues such as the one described in this section have massive implications when you're attempting to port an application from database to database (I return to this theme a little later in the chapter), and this trips people up time and time again. For example, if you are experienced in other databases where writers block readers and vice versa, then you may have grown reliant on that fact to protect you from data integrity issues. The *lack* of concurrency is one way to protect yourself from this—that is how it works in many non-Oracle databases. In Oracle, concurrency rules supreme and you must be aware that, as a result, things will happen differently (or suffer the consequences).

■**Note** We will revisit this example again in Chapter 7. The code as provided works under the assumption the transaction isolation level is READ COMMITTED. The logic will not work properly in SERIALIZABLE transaction isolations. Rather than complicate this chapter with the differences between those two modes, I defer that discussion until later.

Ninety-nine percent of the time, locking is totally transparent and you need not concern yourself with it. It is that other 1 percent that you must be trained to recognize. There is no simple checklist of "If you do this, you need to do this" for this issue. It is a matter of understanding how your application will behave in a multiuser environment and how it will behave in your database.

Chapter 7 delves into this topic in much more depth. There you will learn that integrity constraint enforcement of the type presented in this section, where we must enforce a rule that crosses multiple rows in a single table or is between two or more tables (like a referential integrity constraint), are cases where we must always pay special attention and will most likely have to resort to manual locking or some other technique to ensure integrity in a multiuser environment.

Multi-Versioning

This topic is very closely related to concurrency control, as it forms the foundation for Oracle's concurrency control mechanism—Oracle operates a multi-version, read-consistent concurrency model. Again, in Chapter 7, we'll cover the technical aspects of this in more detail but, essentially, it is the mechanism by which Oracle provides for the following:

- *Read-consistent queries*: Queries that produce consistent results with respect to a point in time.

- *Non-blocking queries*: Queries are never blocked by writers of data, as they would be in other databases.

These are two very important concepts in the Oracle database. The term *multi-versioning* basically describes Oracle's ability to simultaneously materialize multiple versions of the data from the database. If you understand how multi-versioning works, you will always understand the answers you get from the database. Before we explore in a little more detail how Oracle implements multi-versioning, here is the simplest way I know to *demonstrate* multi-versioning in Oracle:

```
ops$tkyte@ORA10G> create table t
  2  as
  3  select *
  4    from all_users;
Table created.

ops$tkyte@ORA10G> variable x refcursor

ops$tkyte@ORA10G> begin
  2      open :x for select * from t;
  3  end;
  4  /
PL/SQL procedure successfully completed.

ops$tkyte@ORA10G> delete from t;
28 rows deleted.

ops$tkyte@ORA10G> commit;
Commit complete.
```

```
ops$tkyte@ORA10G> print x

USERNAME                        USER_ID CREATED
------------------------------  ------- ---------
BIG_TABLE                           411 14-NOV-04
OPS$TKYTE                            410 14-NOV-04
DIY                                  69 26-SEP-04
...
OUTLN                                11 21-JAN-04
SYSTEM                                5 21-JAN-04
SYS                                   0 21-JAN-04

28 rows selected.
```

In the preceding example, we created a test table, T, and loaded it with some data from the ALL_USERS table. We opened a cursor on that table. We fetched *no data* from that cursor; we just opened it.

Note Bear in mind that Oracle does not "answer" the query. It does not copy the data anywhere when you open a cursor—imagine how long it would take to open a cursor on a 1-billion-row table if it did. The cursor opens instantly and it answers the query as it goes along. In other words, it just reads data from the table as you fetch from it.

In the same session (or maybe another session would do this; it would work as well), we then proceed to delete all data from that table. We even go as far as to COMMIT work on that delete. The rows are gone—but are they really? In fact, they are retrievable via the cursor. The fact is that the resultset returned to us by the OPEN command was preordained at the point in time we opened it. We had touched not a single block of data in that table during the open, but the answer was already fixed in stone. We have no way of knowing what the answer will be until we fetch the data; however, the result is immutable from our cursor's perspective. It is not that Oracle copied all of the data to some other location when we opened the cursor; it was actually the DELETE command that preserved our data for us by placing it into a data area called *undo segments*, also known as *rollback segments*.

This is what read-consistency and multi-versioning is all about. If you do not understand how Oracle's multi-versioning scheme works and what it implies, you will not be able to take full advantage of Oracle, and you will not be able to write correct applications (i.e., ones that ensure data integrity) in Oracle.

Multi-Versioning and Flashback

In the past, Oracle always made the decision as to the point in time from which our queries would be made consistent. That is, Oracle made it such that any resultset we opened would be current with respect to one of two points in time:

- *The point in time at which the cursor was opened.* This is the default behavior in READ COMMITTED isolation mode, which is the default transactional mode (we'll examine the differences between READ COMMITTED, READ ONLY, and SERIALIZABLE transaction levels in Chapter 7).

- *The point in time at which the transaction to which the query belongs began.* This is the default behavior in READ ONLY and SERIALIZABLE isolation levels.

Starting with Oracle9*i*, however, we have a lot more flexibility than this. In fact, we can instruct Oracle to present query results "as of" any specified time (with certain reasonable limitations on the length of time you can go back in to the past; of course, your DBA has control over this), by using a feature called *flashback query*.

Consider the following example. We start by getting an SCN (System Change or System Commit Number; the terms are interchangeable). This SCN is Oracle's internal clock: every time a commit occurs, this clock ticks upward (increments). We could use a date or timestamp as well, but here the SCN is readily available and very precise:

```
scot@ORA10G> variable SCN number
scott@ORA10G> exec :scn := dbms_flashback.get_system_change_number
PL/SQL procedure successfully completed.
scott@ORA10G> print scn
       SCN
----------
  33295399
```

We can now instruct Oracle to present data "as of" the point in time represented by the SCN value. We can query Oracle later and see what was in this table at this precise moment in time. First, let's see what is in the EMP table right now:

```
scott@ORA10G> select count(*) from emp;

  COUNT(*)
----------
        14
```

Now let's delete all of this information and verify that it is "gone":

```
scott@ORA10G> delete from emp;
14 rows deleted.

scott@ORA10G> select count(*) from emp;

  COUNT(*)
----------
         0
```

Also, using the flashback query (namely the AS OF SCN or AS OF TIMESTAMP clause) we can ask Oracle to reveal to us what was in the table as of the point in time represented by the SCN value of 33295399:

```
scott@ORA10G> select count(*) from emp AS OF SCN :scn;

  COUNT(*)
----------
        14
```

Further, this capability works across transactional boundaries. We can even query the same object "as of two points in time" in the same query! That opens some interesting opportunities indeed:

```
scott@ORA10G> commit;
Commit complete.

scott@ORA10G> select *
  2    from (select count(*) from emp),
  3         (select count(*) from emp as of scn :scn)
  4  /

  COUNT(*)   COUNT(*)
---------- ----------
        0         14
```

If you are using Oracle 10g and above, you have a command called "flashback" that uses this underlying multi-versioning technology to allow you to return objects to the state they were in at some prior point in time. In this example, we can put EMP back the way it was before we deleted all of the information:

```
scott@ORA10G> flashback table emp to scn :scn;
Flashback complete.

scott@ORA10G> select *
  2    from (select count(*) from emp),
  3         (select count(*) from emp as of scn :scn)
  4  /

  COUNT(*)   COUNT(*)
---------- ----------
14         14
```

■**Note** If you receive the error "ORA-08189: cannot flashback the table because row movement is not enabled using the FLASHBACK command," you must issue ALTER TABLE EMP ENABLE ROW MOVEMENT. This, in effect, gives Oracle the permission to change the rowid assigned to a row. In Oracle, when you insert a row, a rowid is assigned to it and that row will forever have that rowid. The flashback table process will perform a DELETE against EMP and reinsert the rows, hence assigning them a new rowid. You must allow Oracle to do this operation in order to flash back.

Read Consistency and Non-Blocking Reads

Let's now look at the implications of multi-versioning, read-consistent queries, and non-blocking reads. If you are not familiar with multi-versioning, what you see in the following code might be surprising. For the sake of simplicity, assume that the table we are reading stores one row per database block (the smallest unit of storage in the database) and that we are full-scanning the table in this example.

The table we will query is a simple ACCOUNTS table. It holds balances in accounts for a bank. It has a very simple structure:

```
create table accounts
( account_number number primary key,
  account_balance number
);
```

In reality, the ACCOUNTS table would have hundreds of thousands of rows in it, but for simplicity's sake we're just going to consider a table with four rows (we'll revisit this example in more detail in Chapter 7), as shown in Table 1-1.

Table 1-1. ACCOUNTS *Table Contents*

Row	Account Number	Account Balance
1	123	$500.00
2	234	$250.00
3	345	$400.00
4	456	$100.00

We would like to run an end-of-day report that tells us how much money is in the bank. That is an extremely simple query:

```
select sum(account_balance) from accounts;
```

And, of course, in this example the answer is obvious: $1,250.00. However, what happens if we read row 1, and while we're reading rows 2 and 3, an automated teller machine (ATM) generates transactions against this table and moves $400.00 from account 123 to account 456? Our query counts $500.00 in row 4 and comes up with the answer of $1,650.00, doesn't it? Well, of course, this is to be avoided, as it would be an error—at no time did this sum of money exist in the account balance column. Read consistency is the way in which Oracle avoids such occurrences, and you need to understand how Oracle's methods differ from those of most every other database.

In practically every other database, if you want to get a "consistent" and "correct" answer to this query, you either have to lock the whole table while the sum is calculated *or* you have to lock the rows as you read them. This prevents people from changing the answer as you are getting it. If you lock the table up front, you'll get the answer that was in the database at the time the query began. If you lock the data as you read it (commonly referred to as a *shared read lock*, which prevents updates but not other readers from accessing the data), you'll get the answer that was in the database at the point the query finished. Both methods inhibit concurrency a great deal. The table lock prevents any updates from taking place against the entire table for the duration of your query (for a table of four rows, this would be only a very short period, but for tables with hundred of thousands of rows, this could be several minutes). The "lock as you go" method prevents updates on data you have read and already processed, and could actually cause deadlocks between your query and other updates.

Now, I said earlier that you are not able to take full advantage of Oracle if you don't understand the concept of multi-versioning. Here is one reason why that is true. Oracle uses multi-versioning to get the answer, as it existed at the point in time the query began, and the query will take place *without locking a single thing* (while our account transfer transaction updates rows 1 and 4, these rows will be locked to other writers but not locked to other readers, such as our SELECT SUM... query). In fact, Oracle doesn't have a "shared read" lock (a type of lock that is common in other databases) because it doesn't need it. Everything inhibiting concurrency that can be removed has been removed.

I have seen actual cases where a report written by a developer who did not understand Oracle's multi-versioning capabilities would lock up an entire system as tight as could be. The reason: the developer wanted to have read-consistent (i.e., correct) results from his queries. In every other database the developer had used, this required locking the tables, or using a SELECT ... WITH HOLDLOCK (a SQL Server mechanism for locking rows in a shared mode as you go along). So the developer would either lock the tables prior to running the report or use SELECT ... FOR UPDATE (the closest they could find with holdlock). This would cause the system to basically stop processing transactions—needlessly.

So, how does Oracle get the correct, consistent answer ($1,250.00) during a read without locking any data? In other words, without decreasing concurrency? The secret lies in the transactional mechanisms that Oracle uses. Whenever you modify data, Oracle creates undo entries. These entries are written to *undo segments*. If your transaction fails and needs to be undone, Oracle will read the "before" image from the rollback segment and restore the data. In addition to using this rollback segment data to undo transactions, Oracle uses it to undo changes to blocks as it is reading them to restore the block to the point in time your query began. This gives you the ability to read right through a lock and to get consistent, correct answers without locking any data yourself.

So, as far as our example is concerned, Oracle arrives at its answer as shown in Table 1-2.

Table 1-2. *Multi-versioning in Action*

Time	Query	Account Transfer Transaction
T1	Reads row 1; sum = $500 so far.	
T2		Updates row 1; puts an exclusive lock on row 1, preventing other updates. Row 1 now has $100.
T3	Reads row 2; sum = $750 so far.	
T4	Reads row 3; sum = $1,150 so far.	
T5		Updates row 4; puts an exclusive lock on row 4, preventing other updates (but not reads). Row 4 now has $500.
T6	Reads row 4; discovers that row 4 has been modified. It will actually roll back the block to make it appear as it did at time = T1. The query will read the value $100 from this block.	
T7	Presents $1,250 as the answer.	

At time T6, Oracle is effectively "reading through" the lock placed on row 4 by our transaction. This is how non-blocking reads are implemented: Oracle only looks to see if the data changed, and it does not care if the data is currently locked (which implies that the data has changed). Oracle will simply retrieve the old value from the rollback segment and proceed on to the next block of data.

This is another clear demonstration of multi-versioning. Multiple versions of the same piece of information, all at different points in time, are available in the database. Oracle is able to make use of these snapshots of data at different points in time to provide us with read-consistent queries and non-blocking queries.

This read-consistent view of data is always performed at the SQL statement level. The results of any single SQL statement are consistent with respect to the point in time they began. This quality is what makes a statement like the following insert a predictable set of data:

```
Begin
    for x in (select * from t)
    loop
        insert into t values (x.username, x.user_id, x.created);
    end loop;
end;
```

The result of the SELECT * FROM T is preordained when the query begins execution. The SELECT will not see any of the new data generated by the INSERT. Imagine if it did—this statement might be a never-ending loop. If, as the INSERT generated more rows in T, the SELECT could "see" those newly inserted rows, the preceding code would create some unknown number of rows. If the table T started out with 10 rows, we might end up with 20, 21, 23, or an infinite number of rows in T when we finished. It would be totally unpredictable. This consistent read is provided to all statements so that an INSERT such as the following is predicable as well:

```
insert into t select * from t;
```

The INSERT statement will be provided with a read-consistent view of T. It will not see the rows that it itself just inserted; rather, it will only insert the rows that existed at the time the INSERT began. Many databases won't even permit recursive statements such as the preceding due to the fact that they cannot tell how many rows might actually be inserted.

So, if you are used to the way other databases work with respect to query consistency and concurrency, or you have never had to grapple with such concepts (i.e., you have no real database experience), you can now see how understanding how this works will be important to you. To maximize Oracle's potential, and to implement correct code, you *need* to understand these issues as they pertain to Oracle—not how they are implemented in other databases.

Database Independence?

By now, you might be able to see where I'm going in this section. I have made references to other databases and how features are implemented differently in each. With the exception of some read-only applications, it is my contention that building a wholly database-independent application that is highly scalable is extremely hard—it is, in fact, quite impossible unless you know exactly how each database works in great detail. And, if you knew how each database worked in great detail, you would understand that database independence is not something you really want to achieve (a very circular argument!).

For example, let's revisit our initial resource scheduler example (prior to adding the FOR UPDATE clause). Let's say this application had been developed on a database with an entirely different locking/concurrency model from Oracle. What I'll show here is that if we migrate our application from one database to another database, we will have to verify that it still works correctly in these different environments and substantially change it as we do!

Let's assume that we had deployed the initial resource scheduler application in a database that employed blocking reads (reads are blocked by writes). Also consider that the business rule was implemented via a database trigger (*after* the INSERT had occurred but before the transaction committed, we would verify that only our row existed in the table for that time slot). In a blocking read system, due to this newly inserted data, it would be true that insertions into this table would serialize. The first person would insert his or her request for "room A" from 2:00 pm to 3:00 pm on Friday and then run a query looking for overlaps. The next person would try to insert an overlapping request and, upon looking for overlaps, that request would become blocked (while waiting for the newly inserted data that it had found to become available for reading). In that blocking read database our application would be apparently well behaved (well, sort of—we could just as easily *deadlock,* a concept covered in Chapter 6, as well if we both inserted our rows and then attempted to read each other's data)—our checks on overlapping resource allocations would have happened one after the other—never concurrently.

If we migrated this application to Oracle and simply assumed that it would behave in the same way, we would be in for a shock. On Oracle, which does row-level locking and supplies non-blocking reads, it appears to be ill behaved. As shown previously, we had to use the FOR UPDATE clause to serialize access. Without this clause, two users could schedule the same resource for the same times. This is a direct consequence of our not understanding how the database we have works in a multiuser environment.

I have encountered issues such as this many times when an application is being moved from database A to database B. When an application that worked flawlessly in database A does not work, or works in an apparently bizarre fashion, on database B, the first thought is that database B is a "bad" database. The simple truth is that database B just *works differently.* Neither database is wrong or "bad"; they are just different. Knowing and understanding how they both work will help you immensely in dealing with these issues. Taking an application from Oracle to SQL Server exposes SQL Server's blocking reads and deadlock issues—in other words, it goes both ways.

For example, I was asked to help convert some Transact-SQL (T-SQL, the stored procedure language for SQL Server) into PL/SQL. The developer doing the conversion was complaining that the SQL queries in Oracle returned the "wrong" answer. The queries looked like this:

```
declare
    l_some_variable   varchar2(25);
begin
    if ( some_condition )
    then
        l_some_variable := f( ... );
    end if;
```

```
for C in ( select * from T where x = l_some_variable )
loop
    ...
```

The goal here was to find all of the rows in T where X was NULL if some condition was not met or where x equaled a specific value if some condition was met.

The complaint was that, in Oracle, this query would return no data when L_SOME_VARIABLE was not set to a specific value (when it was left as NULL). In Sybase or SQL Server, this was not the case—the query would find the rows where X was set to a NULL value. I see this on almost every conversion from Sybase or SQL Server to Oracle. SQL is supposed to operate under trivalued logic, and Oracle implements NULL values the way ANSI SQL requires them to be implemented. Under those rules, comparing X to a NULL is neither true nor false—it is, in fact, *unknown*. The following snippet shows what I mean:

```
ops$tkyte@ORA10G> select * from dual where null=null;
no rows selected

ops$tkyte@ORA10G> select * from dual where null <> null;
no rows selected

ops$tkyte@ORA10G> select * from dual where null is null;

D
-
X
```

This can be confusing the first time you see it. It proves that, in Oracle, NULL is neither equal to nor not equal to NULL. SQL Server, by default, does not do it that way: in SQL Server and Sybase, NULL is equal to NULL. Neither Oracle's, nor Sybase or SQL Server's SQL processing is *wrong*—it is just *different*. All these databases are, in fact, ANSI compliant, but they still work differently. There are ambiguities, backward compatibility issues, and so on to be overcome. For example, SQL Server supports the ANSI method of NULL comparison, just not by default (it would break thousands of existing legacy applications built on that database).

In this case, one solution to the problem is to write the query like this instead:

```
select *
  from t
 where ( x = l_some_variable OR (x is null and l_some_variable is NULL ))
```

However, this leads to another problem. In SQL Server, this query would use an index on x. This is not the case in Oracle, since a B*Tree index will not index an entirely NULL entry (we'll examine indexing techniques in Chapter 12). Hence, if you need to find NULL values, B*Tree indexes are not very useful.

What we did in this case to minimize impact on the code was to assign X some value that it could never in reality assume. Here, X, by definition, was a positive number, so we chose the number –1. Thus, the query became

```
select * from t where nvl(x,-1) = nvl(l_some_variable,-1)
```

and we created a function-based index:

```
create index t_idx on t( nvl(x,-1) );
```

With minimal change, we achieved the same end result. The important points to recognize from this example are as follows:

- Databases are different. Experience with one will, in part, carry over to another, but you must be ready for some *fundamental* differences as well as some very minor differences.

- Minor differences (such as treatment of NULLs) can have as big an impact as fundamental differences (such as concurrency control mechanism).

- Being aware of the database, how it works, and how its features are implemented is the only way to overcome these issues.

Developers frequently ask me (usually more than once a day) how to do something specific in the database, for example, "How do I create a temporary table in a stored procedure?" I do not answer such questions directly; instead, I respond with a question: "*Why* do you want to do that?" Many times, the answer that comes back is "In SQL Server we created temporary tables in our stored procedures and we need to do this in Oracle." That is what I expected to hear. My response, then, is easy: "You do not want to create temporary tables in a stored procedure in Oracle—you only think you do." That would, in fact, be a very bad thing to do in Oracle. If you created the tables in a stored procedure in Oracle, you would find that

- Doing DDL is a scalability inhibitor.

- Doing DDL constantly is not fast.

- Doing DDL commits your transaction.

- You would have to use dynamic SQL in all of your stored procedures to access this table—no static SQL.

- Dynamic SQL in PL/SQL is not as fast or as optimized as static SQL.

The bottom line is that you don't want to create the temp table in a procedure exactly as you did in SQL Server (if you even need the temporary table in Oracle at all). You want to do things as they are best done in Oracle. Just as if you were going the other way, from Oracle to SQL Server, you would not want to create a single table for all users to share for temporary data (as you would in Oracle). That would limit scalability and concurrency in SQL Server. All databases are not created equal—they are all very different.

The Impact of Standards

If all databases are SQL99 compliant, then they must be the same. At least that is the assumption made many times. In this section, I would like to dispel that myth.

SQL99 is an ANSI/ISO standard for databases. It is the successor to the SQL92 ANSI/ISO standard, which in turn superceded the SQL89 ANSI/ISO standard. It defines a language (SQL) and behavior (transactions, isolation levels, etc.) that tell you how a database will behave. Did you know that many commercially available databases are SQL99 compliant to at least some degree? Did you also know that it means very little as far as query and application portability goes?

The SQL92 standard had four levels:

- *Entry level*: This is the level to which most vendors have complied. This level is a minor enhancement of the predecessor standard, SQL89. No database vendors have been certified higher and, in fact, the National Institute of Standards and Technology (NIST), the agency that used to certify for SQL compliance, does not even certify anymore. I was part of the team that got Oracle 7.0 NIST-certified for SQL92 entry-level compliance in 1993. An entry level–compliant database has a feature set that is a subset of Oracle 7.0's capabilities.

- *Transitional*: This level is approximately halfway between entry level and intermediate level as far as a feature set goes.

- *Intermediate*: This level adds many features, including (this is not by any means an exhaustive list)

  - Dynamic SQL
  - Cascade DELETE for referential integrity
  - DATE and TIME datatypes
  - Domains
  - Variable-length character strings
  - A CASE expression
  - CAST functions between datatypes

- *Full*: Adds provisions for (again, this list is not exhaustive)

  - Connection management
  - A BIT string datatype
  - Deferrable integrity constraints
  - Derived tables in the FROM clause
  - Subqueries in CHECK clauses
  - Temporary tables

The entry-level standard does not include features such as outer joins, the new inner join syntax, and so on. Transitional does specify outer join syntax and inner join syntax. Intermediate adds more, and full is, of course, all of SQL92. Most books on SQL92 do not differentiate between the various levels, which leads to confusion on the subject. They demonstrate what a theoretical database implementing SQL92 full would look like. It makes it impossible to pick up a SQL92 book and apply what you see in the book to just any SQL92 database. The bottom line is that SQL92 will not go very far at entry level and, if you use any of the features of intermediate or higher, you risk not being able to "port" your application.

SQL99 defines only two levels of conformance: Core and Enhanced. SQL99 attempts to go far beyond traditional "SQL" and introduces object-relational constructs (arrays, collections, etc.). It covers a SQL MM (multimedia) type, object-relational types, and so on. No vendor is certifying databases to be SQL99 Core or Enhanced "compliant" and, in fact, I know of no vendor who is even *claiming* that their product is fully compliant with either level of conformance.

In addition to SQL syntactic differences, implementation differences, and differences in performance of the same query in different databases, there are the issues of concurrency controls, isolation levels, query consistency, and so on. We'll cover these items in some detail in Chapter 7 and see how their differences may affect you.

SQL92/SQL99 attempts to give a straightforward definition of how a transaction should work and how isolation levels are to be implemented, but in the end, you'll get different results from different databases. It is all due to the implementation. In one database, an application will deadlock and block all over the place. In another database, the same exact application will not do any of these things—it will run smoothly. In one database, the fact that you did block (physically serialize) was used to your advantage, and when you go to deploy on another database, and it does not block, you get the wrong answer. Picking an application up and dropping it on another database takes a lot of hard work and effort, even if you followed the standard 100 percent.

The bottom line is that you should not be afraid to make use of vendor-specific features—after all, you are paying a lot of money for them. Every database has its own bag of tricks, and we can always find a way to perform the operation in each database. Use what is best for your current database, and reimplement components as you go to other databases. Use good programming techniques to isolate yourself from these changes. I call this *defensive programming*.

Defensive Programming

The same defensive programming techniques that I advocate for building truly portable database applications are, in essence the same as those employed by people writing OS-portable applications. The goal is to fully utilize the facilities available to you, but ensure you can change the implementation on a case-by-case basis.

As an analogy, Oracle is a portable application. It runs on many operating systems. However, on Windows it runs in the Windows way: using threads and other Windows-specific facilities. On UNIX, Oracle runs as a multiprocess server, using individual processes to do what threads did on Windows—that is the UNIX way. The "core Oracle" functionality is available on both platforms, but it is implemented in very different ways under the covers. Your database applications that must function on multiple databases will be the same.

For example, a common function of many database applications is the generation of a unique key for each row. When you insert the row, the system should automatically generate a key for you. Oracle has implemented the database object called a SEQUENCE for this. Informix has a SERIAL datatype. Sybase and SQL Server have an IDENTITY type. Each database has a way to do this. However, the methods are different, both in how you do it and the possible outcomes. So, for the knowledgeable developer, there are two paths that can be pursued:

- Develop a totally database-independent method of generating a unique key.

- Accommodate the different implementations and use different techniques when implementing keys in each database.

The theoretical advantage of the first approach is that to move from database to database you need not change anything. I call it a "theoretical" advantage because the downside of this implementation is so huge that it makes this solution totally infeasible. What you would have to do to develop a totally database-independent process is to create a table such as

```
ops$tkyte@ORA10G> create table id_table
  2  ( id_name  varchar2(30) primary key,
  3    id_value number );
Table created.

ops$tkyte@ORA10G> insert into id_table values ( 'MY_KEY', 0 );
1 row created.

ops$tkyte@ORA10G> commit;
Commit complete.
```

Then, in order to get a new key, you would have to execute the following code:

```
ops$tkyte@ORA10G> update id_table
  2     set id_value = id_value+1
  3   where id_name = 'MY_KEY';
1 row updated.

ops$tkyte@ORA10G> select id_value
  2    from id_table
  3   where id_name = 'MY_KEY';

 ID_VALUE
----------
        1
```

Looks simple enough, but the outcomes (notice plural) are as follows:

- Only one user at a time may process a transaction row. You need to update that row to increment a counter, and this will cause your program to serialize on that operation. At best, one person at a time will generate a new value for this key.

- In Oracle (and the behavior might be different in other databases), all but the first user to attempt to concurrently perform this operation would receive the error "ORA-08177: can't serialize access for this transaction" in the SERIALIZABLE isolation level.

For example, using a serializable transaction (which is more common in the J2EE environment, where many tools automatically use this as the default mode of isolation, often unbeknownst to the developers), you would observe the following behavior. Notice that the SQL prompt (using the SET SQLPROMPT SQL*Plus command) contains information about which session is active in this example:

```
OPS$TKYTE session(261,2586)> set transaction isolation level serializable;
Transaction set.

OPS$TKYTE session(261,2586)> update id_table
  2      set id_value = id_value+1
  3    where id_name = 'MY_KEY';
1 row updated.

OPS$TKYTE session(261,2586)> select id_value
  2     from id_table
  3    where id_name = 'MY_KEY';


  ID_VALUE
----------
         1
```

Now, we'll go to another SQL*Plus session and perform the same operation, a concurrent request for a unique ID:

```
OPS$TKYTE session(271,1231)> set transaction isolation level serializable;
Transaction set.

OPS$TKYTE session(271,1231)> update id_table
  2      set id_value = id_value+1
  3    where id_name = 'MY_KEY';
```

This will block at this point, as only one transaction at a time can update the row. This demonstrates the first possible outcome, namely that we would block and wait for the row. But since we're using SERIALIZABLE in Oracle, we'll observe the following behavior as we commit the first session's transaction:

```
 OPS$TKYTE session(261,2586)> commit;
Commit complete.
```

The second session will immediately display the following error:

```
OPS$TKYTE session(271,1231)> update id_table
  2      set id_value = id_value+1
  3    where id_name = 'MY_KEY';
update id_table
       *
ERROR at line 1:
ORA-08177: can't serialize access for this transaction
```

So, that database-independent piece of logic really isn't database independent at all. Depending on the isolation level, it may not even perform reliably in a single database, let alone across any database! Sometimes we block and wait; sometimes we get an error message. To say the end user would be upset given either case (wait a long time, or wait a long time to get an error) is putting it mildly.

This issue is compounded by the fact that our transaction is much larger than just outlined. The UPDATE and SELECT in the example are only two statements of potentially many other statements that make up our transaction. We have yet to insert the row into the table with this key we just generated and do whatever other work it takes to complete this transaction. This serialization will be a huge limiting factor in scaling. Think of the ramifications if this technique were used on web sites that process orders, and this was how we generated order numbers. There would be no multiuser concurrency, so we would be forced to do everything sequentially.

The correct approach to this problem is to use the best code for each database. In Oracle, this would be (assuming the table that needs the generated primary key is T) as follows:

```
create table t ( pk number primary key, ... );
create sequence t_seq;
create trigger t_trigger before insert on t for each row
begin
    select t_seq.nextval into :new.pk from dual;
end;
```

This will have the effect of automatically—and transparently—assigning a unique key to each row inserted. A more performance driven approach would be simply

```
Insert into t ( pk, ... ) values ( t_seq.NEXTVAL, ... );
```

That is, skip the overhead of the trigger altogether (this is my preferred approach).

In the first example, we've gone out of our way to use each database's feature to generate a *non-blocking*, highly concurrent unique key, and we've introduced no real changes to the application code—all of the logic is contained in this case in the DDL.

■**Tip** The same effect can be achieved in the other databases using their built-in features or generating unique numbers. The CREATE TABLE syntax may be different, but the net results will be the same.

Once you understand that each database *will implement features in a different way*, another example of defensive programming to allow for portability is to *layer* your access to the database when necessary. For example, say you are programming using JDBC. If all you use is straight SQL SELECTs, INSERTs, UPDATEs, and DELETEs, you probably do not need a layer of abstraction. You may very well be able to code the SQL directly in your application, as long as you limit the constructs you use to those supported by each of the databases you intend to support—and that you have verified work exactly the same (remember the NULL=NULL discussion!). Another approach that is both more portable and offers better performance is to use stored procedures to return resultsets. You will discover that every vendor's database can return resultsets from stored procedures, but how they are returned is different. The actual source code you must write is different for different databases.

Your two choices here are either to not use stored procedures to return resultsets or to implement different code for different databases. I would definitely follow the different code for different vendors method and use stored procedures heavily. This apparently seems to increase the amount of time it would take to implement on a different database. However, you will find it is actually easier to implement on multiple databases with this approach. Instead of having to find the perfect SQL that works on *all* databases (perhaps better on some than on others), you implement the SQL that works best on that database. You can do this outside of the application itself, giving you more flexibility in tuning the application. You can fix a poorly performing query in the database itself, and deploy that fix immediately, without having to patch the application. Additionally, you can take advantage of vendor extensions to SQL using this method freely. For example, Oracle supports hierarchical queries via the CONNECT BY operation in its SQL. This unique feature is great for resolving recursive queries. In Oracle, you are free to use this extension to SQL since it is "outside" of the application (i.e., hidden in the database). In other databases, you would use a temporary table and procedural code in a stored procedure to achieve the same results, perhaps. You paid for these features, so you might as well use them.

This technique of developing a specialized layer of code for the database on which you will deploy is the same as that used by developers who implement multiplatform code. Oracle Corporation, for example, uses these techniques in the development of its own database. There is a large amount of code (but a small percentage of the database code overall), called operating system–dependent (OSD) code, that is implemented specifically for each platform. Using this layer of abstraction, Oracle is able to make use of many native OS features for performance and integration, without having to rewrite the large majority of the database itself. The fact that Oracle can run as a multithreaded application on Windows and a multiprocess application on UNIX attests to this feature. The mechanisms for interprocess communication are abstracted to such a level that they can be reimplemented on an OS-by-OS basis, allowing for radically different implementations that perform as well as an application written directly, and specifically, for that platform.

Another argument for this approach is that finding a single developer (let alone a team of developers) who is savvy enough to understand the nuances of the differences between Oracle, SQL Server, and DB2 (let's limit the discussion to three databases in this case) is virtually impossible. I've worked mostly with Oracle for the last 11 years (mostly, not exclusively). I learn something new about Oracle *every single day I use it*. To suggest that I could be expert in three databases simultaneously and understand what the differences between all three are and how those differences will affect the "generic code" layer I would have to build is highly questionable. I doubt I would be able to do that accurately or efficiently. Also consider the fact that we are talking about individuals here—how many developers actually fully understand or use the database they currently have, let alone three of them? Seeking to find the unique individual who can develop bulletproof, scalable, database-independent routines is a Holy Grail quest. Building a team of developers that can do this is impossible. Finding an Oracle expert, a DB2 expert, and a SQL Server expert, and telling them "We need a transaction to do X, Y and Z"—that's relatively easy. They are told, "Here are your inputs, these are the outputs we need, and this is what this business process entails," and from there it is relatively simple to produce transactional APIs (stored procedures) that fit the bill. Each will be implemented in the best manner for that particular database, according to that database's unique set of capabilities. These developers are free to use the full power (or lack thereof, as the case may be) of the underlying database platform.

Features and Functions

A natural extension of the argument that you shouldn't necessarily strive for database independence is the idea that you should understand exactly what your specific database has to offer and make full use of it. This section does not outline all of the features that Oracle 10*g* has to offer—that would be an extremely large book in itself. The new features of Oracle 9*i* Release 1, 9*i* Release 2, and 10g Release 1 themselves fill a book in the Oracle documentation set. With about 10,000 pages of documentation provided by Oracle, covering each and every feature and function would be quite an undertaking. Rather, this section explores the benefits of getting at least a cursory knowledge of what is provided.

As I've said before, I answer questions about Oracle on `http://asktom.oracle.com`. I'd say that 80 percent of my answers are simply URLs to the documentation (for every question you see that I've published—many of which are pointers into the documentation—there are two more questions I chose not to publish, almost all of which are "read this" answers). People ask how they might go about writing some complex piece of functionality in the database (or outside of it), and I just point them to the place in the documentation that tells them how Oracle has already implemented it and how to use it. Replication comes up this way frequently. I'll receive the following question: "I would like to keep a copy of my data elsewhere. I would like this to be a read-only copy. I need it to update only once a day at midnight. How can I write the code to do that?" The answer is as simple as a `CREATE MATERIALIZED VIEW` command. This is built-in functionality in the database. Actually, there are many ways to implement replication, from read-only materialized views, to updateable materialized views, to peer-to-peer replication, to streams-based replication.

It is true that you can write your own replication—it might even be fun to do so—but at the end of the day, it would not be the smartest thing to do. The database does a lot of stuff. In general, the database can do it better than we can ourselves. Replication, for example, is internalized in the kernel, written in C. It's fast, it's fairly easy, and it's robust. It works across versions and across platforms. It is supported, so if you hit a problem, Oracle's support team will be glad to help. If you upgrade, replication will be supported there as well, probably with some new features. Now, consider if you were to develop your own. You would have to provide support for all of the versions you wanted to support. Interoperability between old and new releases? This would be your job. If it "breaks," you won't be calling support—at least not until you can get a test case that is small enough to demonstrate your basic issue. When the new release of Oracle comes out, it will be up to you to migrate your replication code to that release.

Not having a full understanding of what is available to you can come back to haunt you in the long run. I was working with some developers with years of experience developing database applications—on other databases. They built analysis software (trending, reporting, and visualization software). It was to work on clinical data (healthcare related). They were not aware of SQL syntactical features such as inline views, analytic functions, and scalar subqueries. Their major problem was they needed to analyze data from a single parent table to two child tables. An entity-relationship diagram (ERD) might look like Figure 1-1.

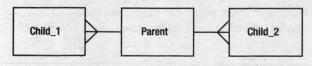

Figure 1-1. *Simple ERD*

They needed to be able to report on the parent record with aggregates from each of the child tables. The databases they worked with in the past did not support subquery factoring (WITH clause), nor did they support inline views, the ability to "query a query" instead of query a table. Not knowing these features existed, the developers wrote their own database of sorts in the middle tier. They would query the parent table and for each row returned run an aggregate query against each of the child tables. This resulted in their running thousands of queries for each single query the end user wanted to run. Or, they would fetch the entire aggregated child tables into their middle tier into hash tables in memory—and do a hash join.

In short, they were reinventing the database, performing the functional equivalent of a nested loops join or a hash join, without the benefit of temporary tablespaces, sophisticated query optimizers, and the like. They were spending their time developing, designing, fine-tuning, and enhancing software that was trying to do the same thing the database they already bought did! Meanwhile, end users were asking for new features but not getting them, because the bulk of the development time was in this reporting "engine," which really was a database engine in disguise.

I showed them that they could do things such as join two aggregations together, in order to compare data that was stored at different levels of detail in many different ways (see Listings 1-1 through 1-3).

Listing 1-1. *Inline Views: Query from a "Query"*

```
select p.id, c1_sum1, c2_sum2
  from p,
      (select id, sum(q1) c1_sum1
         from c1
        group by id) c1,
      (select id, sum(q2) c2_sum2
         from c2
        group by id) c2
 where p.id = c1.id
   and p.id = c2.id
/
```

Listing 1-2. *Scalar Subqueries: Run Another Query per Row*

```
select p.id,
       (select sum(q1) from c1 where c1.id = p.id) c1_sum1,
       (select sum(q2) from c2 where c2.id = p.id) c2_sum2
  from p
 where p.name = '1234'
/
```

Listing 1-3. *WITH Subquery Factoring*

```
with c1_vw as
(select id, sum(q1) c1_sum1
   from c1
```

```
 group by id),
c2_vw as
(select id, sum(q2) c2_sum2
  from c2
  group by id),
c1_c2 as
(select c1.id, c1.c1_sum1, c2.c2_sum2
  from c1_vw c1, c2_vw c2
 where c1.id = c2.id )
select p.id, c1_sum1, c2_sum2
  from p, c1_c2
 where p.id = c1_c2.id
/
```

Not to mention what they can do with analytic functions like LAG, LEAD, ROW_NUMBER; the ranking functions; and so much more. Well, rather than spending the rest of the day trying to figure out how to tune their middle-tier database engine, we spent the day with the *SQL Reference Guide* projected on the screen (coupled with SQL*Plus to create ad hoc demonstrations of how things worked). The end goal was no longer tuning the middle tier; now it was turning off the middle tier as quickly as possible.

I have seen people set up daemon processes in an Oracle database that read messages off of pipes (a database IPC mechanism). These daemon processes execute the SQL contained within the pipe message and commit the work. They did this so that they could execute auditing in a transaction that would not get rolled back if the bigger transaction did. Usually, if a trigger or something were used to audit an access to some data, but a statement failed later on, all of the work would be rolled back. So, by sending a message to another process, they could have a separate transaction do the work and commit it. The audit record would stay around, even if the parent transaction rolled back. In versions of Oracle before Oracle8*i*, this was an appropriate (and pretty much the only) way to implement this functionality. When I told them of the database feature called *autonomous transactions*, they were quite upset with themselves. Autonomous transactions, implemented with a single line of code, do exactly what they were doing. On the bright side, this meant they could discard a lot of code and not have to maintain it. In addition, the system ran faster overall and was easier to understand. Still, they were upset at the amount of time they had wasted reinventing the wheel. In particular, the developer who wrote the daemon processes was quite upset at having just written a bunch of shelfware.

This is something I see repeated time and time again—large, complex solutions to problems that are already solved by the database itself. *I've been guilty of this myself.* I still remember the day when my Oracle sales consultant (I was the customer at the time) walked in and saw me surrounded by a ton of Oracle documentation. I looked up at him and just asked "Is this all true?" I spent the next couple of days just digging and reading. I had fallen into the trap of thinking "I know all about databases," because I had worked with SQL/DS, DB2, Ingress, Sybase, Informix, SQLBase, Oracle, and others. Rather than take the time to see what each had to offer, I would just apply what I knew from the others to whatever I was working on. (Moving to Sybase/SQL Server was the biggest shock to me—it worked nothing like the others at all.) Upon actually discovering what Oracle could do (and the others, to be fair), I started taking advantage of it and was able to move faster, with less code. This was in 1993. Imagine what you can do with the software today, over a decade later.

Unless you take the time to learn what is available, you are doomed to do the same thing at some point. In this book, we are going to take an in-depth look at a *handful* of functionality provided by the database. I picked and chose the features and functions that I see people using frequently or functionality that should be used more often but is not. The material covered here is only the tip of the iceberg, however. There is so much more to Oracle than can be presented in a single book.

I'll say it again: I learn something new about Oracle pretty much *every single day*. It requires some keeping up with. I myself read the documentation (still). Even so, every day someone points out something to me that I didn't know.

Solving Problems Simply

There are always two ways to solve everything: the easy way and the hard way. Time and time again, I see people choosing the hard way. It is not always done consciously. More often, it is done out of ignorance. They never expected the database to be able to do "that." I, on the other hand, expect the database to be capable of anything and only do it the hard way (by writing it myself) when I discover it cannot do something.

For example, I am frequently asked, "How can I make sure the end user has only one session in the database?" (There are hundreds of other examples I could have used here.) This must be a requirement of many applications, but none that I've ever worked on—I've not found a good reason for limiting people in this way. However, people want to do it, and when they do, they usually do it the hard way. For example, they'll have a batch job run by the OS that will look at the V$SESSION table and arbitrarily kill sessions of users who have more than one session. Alternatively, they will create their own tables and have the application insert a row when a user logs in and remove the row when the user logs out. This implementation invariably leads to lots of calls to the help desk, because when the application "crashes," the row never gets removed. I've seen lots of other "creative" ways to do this, but none is as easy as this:

```
ops$tkyte@ORA10G> create profile one_session limit sessions_per_user 1;
Profile created.

ops$tkyte@ORA10G> alter user scott profile one_session;
User altered.

ops$tkyte@ORA10G> alter system set resource_limit=true;
System altered.

ops$tkyte@ORA10G> connect scott/tiger
Connected.
scott@ORA10G> host sqlplus scott/tiger

SQL*Plus: Release 10.1.0.2.0 - Production on Sun Nov 28 12:49:49 2004
Copyright (c) 1982, 2004, Oracle.  All rights reserved.
ERROR:
ORA-02391: exceeded simultaneous SESSIONS_PER_USER limit

Enter user-name:
```

That's it—now any user with the ONE_SESSION profile can log on only once. When I bring up this solution, I can usually hear the smacking of a hand on the forehead followed by the statement "I never knew it could do that!" Taking the time to familiarize yourself with what the tools you have to work with are capable of doing can save you lots of time and energy in your development efforts.

The same "keep it simple" argument applies at the broader architecture level. I urge people to think carefully before adopting very complex implementations. The more moving parts you have in your system, the more things you have that can go wrong, and tracking down exactly where that error is occurring in an overly complex architecture is not easy. It may be really "cool" to implement umpteen tiers, but it is not the right choice if a simple stored procedure can do it better, faster, and with fewer resources.

I've seen projects where application development has been going on for months, with no end in sight. The developers are using the latest and greatest technologies and languages, but still the development is not going very fast. It wasn't that big of an application—and perhaps that was the problem. If you are building a doghouse (a small woodworking job), you would not bring in the heavy machinery. You would use a few small power tools, but you wouldn't have use for the big stuff. On the other hand, if you were building an apartment complex, you would have a cast of hundreds working on the project and you would use the big machines— you would use totally different tools to approach this problem. The same is true of application development. There is not a single "perfect architecture." There is not a single "perfect language." There is not a single "perfect approach."

For example, to build my web site, I used HTML DB. It was a smallish application, and there was a single developer (or two) working on it. It has maybe 20 screens. Using PL/SQL and HTML DB was the correct choice for this implementation—it did not need a cast of dozens, coding in Java, making EJBs, and so on. It was a simple problem, solved simply. There are few complex, large-scale, huge applications (we buy most of those today: our HR systems, our ERP systems, etc.), but there are thousands of small applications. We need to use the proper approach and tools for the job.

I will always go with the simplest architecture that solves the problem completely over a complex one any day. The payback can be enormous. Every technology has its place. Not every problem is a nail, so we can use more than a hammer in our toolbox.

Openness

I frequently see people doing things the hard way for another reason, and again it relates to the idea that we should strive for openness and database independence at all costs. The developers wish to avoid using closed, proprietary database features—even things as simple as stored procedures or sequences—because doing so will lock them into a database system. Well, let me put forth the idea that the instant you develop a read/write application, you are already somewhat locked in. You will find subtle (and sometimes not-so-subtle) differences between the databases as soon as you start running queries and modifications. For example, in one database you might find that your SELECT COUNT(*) FROM T deadlocks with a simple update of two rows. In Oracle, you'll find that the SELECT COUNT(*) never blocks for a writer. You've seen the case where a business rule appears to get enforced on one database, due to side effects of the database's locking model, and does not get enforced in another database. You'll find that, given the same exact transaction mix, reports come out with different answers in different databases, all because of fundamental implementation differences. You'll discover that it is a very rare application that can simply be picked up and moved from one database to another. Differences in the way the SQL is interpreted (e.g., the NULL=NULL example) and processed will always be there.

On a recent project I was involved in, the developers were building a web-based product using Visual Basic, ActiveX controls, IIS server, and the Oracle database. I was told that the development folks had expressed concern that since the business logic had been written in PL/SQL, the product had become database dependent. I was asked, "How can we correct this?"

I was a little taken aback by this question. In looking at the list of chosen technologies, I could not figure out how being database dependent was a "bad" thing:

- The developers had chosen a language that locked them into a single OS supplied by a single vendor (they could have opted for Java).

- They had chosen a component technology that locked them into a single OS and vendor (they could have opted for J2EE).

- They had chosen a web server that locked them into a single vendor and a single platform (why not Apache?).

Every other technology choice they made locked them into a very specific configuration—in fact, the only technology that offered them any choice as far as operating systems went was the database.

Regardless of this (they must have had good reasons to choose the technologies they did), we still have a group of developers making a conscious decision to not use the functionality of a critical component in their architecture, and doing so in the name of openness. It is my belief that you pick your technologies carefully, and then you exploit them to the fullest possible extent. You have paid a lot for these technologies—would it not be in your best interest to exploit them fully? I had to assume that they were looking forward to using the full potential of the other technologies, so why was the database an exception? This was an even harder question to answer in light of the fact that it was crucial to their success.

We can put a slightly different spin on this argument if we consider it from the perspective of openness. You put all of your data into the database. The database is a very open tool. It supports data access via a large variety of open systems protocols and access mechanisms. Sounds great so far—the most open thing in the world.

Then, you put all of your application logic and, more important, your *security*, outside of the database. Perhaps in your beans that access the data. Perhaps in the JSPs that access the data. Perhaps in your Visual Basic code running under Microsoft Transaction Server (MTS). The end result is that you have just closed off your database—you have made it "nonopen." No longer can people hook in existing technologies to make use of this data; they *must* use your access methods (or bypass security altogether). This sounds all well and good today, but what you must remember is that the whiz-bang technology of today—EJBs for example—is yesterday's concept and tomorrow's old, tired technology. What has persevered for over 25 years in the relational world (and probably most of the object implementations as well) is the database itself. The front ends to the data change almost yearly, and as they do, the applications that have all of the security built inside themselves, not in the database, become obstacles—roadblocks to future progress.

The Oracle database provides a feature called *fine-grained access control* (*FGAC*). In a nutshell, this technology allows developers to embed procedures in the database that can modify queries as they are submitted to the database. This query modification is used to restrict the rows the client will receive or modify. The procedure can look at who is running the query, when they are running the query, what terminal they are running the query from, and so on, and it can constrain access to the data as appropriate. With FGAC, we can enforce security such that, for example

- Any query executed outside of normal business hours by a certain class of users returns zero records.

- Any data can be returned to a terminal in a secure facility, but only nonsensitive information can be returned to a remote client terminal.

Basically, FGAC allows us to locate access control in the database, *right next to the data*. It no longer matters if the user comes at the data from a bean, a JSP, a Visual Basic application using ODBC, or SQL*Plus—the same security protocols are enforced. You are well situated for the next technology that comes along.

Now I ask you, which implementation is more "open"? The one that makes all access to the data possible only through calls to the Visual Basic code and ActiveX controls (replace Visual Basic with Java and ActiveX with EJB, if you like—I'm not picking on a particular technology but an implementation here) or the solution that allows access from anything that can talk to the database, over protocols as diverse as SSL, HTTP, and Oracle Net (and others) or using APIs such as ODBC, JDBC, OCI, and so on? I have yet to see an ad hoc reporting tool that will "query" Visual Basic code. I know of dozens that can do SQL, though.

The decision to strive for database independence and total openness is one that people are absolutely free to take, and many try, but I believe that it is the wrong decision. No matter what database you are using, you should exploit it fully, squeezing every last bit of functionality you can out of that product. You'll find yourself doing that in the tuning phase (which again always seems to happen right after deployment) anyway. It is amazing how quickly the database independence requirement can be dropped when you can make the application run five times faster just by exploiting the software's capabilities.

"How Do I Make It Run Faster?"

I am asked the question in the heading all the time. Everyone is looking for the "fast = true" switch, assuming "database tuning" means that you tune the database. In fact, it is my experience that more than 80 percent (frequently 100 percent) of all performance gains are to be realized at the design and implementation level—not the database level. I have often achieved orders of magnitude increases in performance via application changes. It would be rare to be able to say that of a database-level change. You cannot tune a database until you have tuned the applications that run on the database.

As time goes on, there are some switches we can throw at the database level to help lessen the impact of egregious programming blunders. For example, Oracle 8.1.6 adds a new parameter, CURSOR_SHARING=FORCE. This feature implements an *auto-binder*, if you will. It will silently take a query written as SELECT * FROM EMP WHERE EMPNO = 1234 and rewrite it for us as SELECT * FROM EMP WHERE EMPNO = :x. This *can* dramatically decrease the number of hard parses and decrease the library latch waits we discussed earlier—*but* (there is always a "but") it can have some side effects. A common side effect with cursor sharing is something like this:

```
ops$tkyte@ORA10G> select /* TAG */ substr( username, 1, 1 )
  2    from all_users au1
  3    where rownum = 1;

S
-
B


ops$tkyte@ORA10G> alter session set cursor_sharing=force;
Session altered.

ops$tkyte@ORA10G> select /* TAG */ substr( username, 1, 1 )
  2    from all_users au2
  3    where rownum = 1;

SUBSTR(USERNAME,1,1)
-------------------------------
B
```

What happened there? Why is the column reported by SQL*Plus suddenly so large for the second query, which is arguably the same query? If we look at what the cursor sharing setting did for us, it (and something else) will become obvious:

```
ops$tkyte@ORA10G> select sql_text from v$sql
  2       where sql_text like 'select /* TAG */ %';

SQL_TEXT
--------------------------------------------------------------------------------
select /* TAG */ substr( username, 1, 1 )   from all_users au1  where rownum =
1

select /* TAG */ substr( username, :"SYS_B_0", :"SYS_B_1" )   from all_users au
2  where rownum = :"SYS_B_2"
```

The cursor sharing removed information from the query. It found *every* literal, including the parameters to the built-in substring function, which were constants we were using. It removed them from the query and replaced them with bind variables. The SQL engine no longer knows that the column is a substring of length 1—it is of indeterminate length. Also, you can see that where rownum = 1 is now bound as well. That seems like a good idea; however, the optimizer has just had some important information removed. It no longer knows that "this query will retrieve a single row"; it now believes "this query will return the first N rows and N could be any number at all." In fact, if you run these queries with SQL_TRACE=TRUE, you will find the query plans used by each query and the amount of work they perform to be very different. Consider the following:

```
select /* TAG */ substr( username, 1, 1 )
  from all_users au1
 where rownum = 1
```

call	count	cpu	elapsed	disk	query	current	rows
Parse	1	0.00	0.00	0	0	0	0
Execute	1	0.00	0.00	0	0	0	0
Fetch	2	0.00	0.00	0	77	0	1
total	4	0.00	0.00	0	77	0	1

Misses in library cache during parse: 0
Optimizer mode: ALL_ROWS
Parsing user id: 412

```
Rows     Row Source Operation
-------  ---------------------------------------------------------
      1  COUNT STOPKEY (cr=77 pr=0 pw=0 time=5767 us)
      1   HASH JOIN  (cr=77 pr=0 pw=0 time=5756 us)
   1028    HASH JOIN  (cr=70 pr=0 pw=0 time=8692 us)
      9     TABLE ACCESS FULL TS$ (cr=15 pr=0 pw=0 time=335 us)
   1028     TABLE ACCESS FULL USER$ (cr=55 pr=0 pw=0 time=2140 us)
      4     TABLE ACCESS FULL TS$ (cr=7 pr=0 pw=0 time=56 us)
**************************************************************************
```

```
select /* TAG */ substr( username, :"SYS_B_0", :"SYS_B_1" )
  from all_users au2
 where rownum = :"SYS_B_2"
```

call	count	cpu	elapsed	disk	query	current	rows
Parse	1	0.00	0.00	0	0	0	0
Execute	1	0.00	0.00	0	0	0	0
Fetch	2	0.00	0.00	0	85	0	1
total	4	0.00	0.00	0	85	0	1

Misses in library cache during parse: 0
Optimizer mode: ALL_ROWS
Parsing user id: 412

```
Rows     Row Source Operation
-------  ---------------------------------------------------------
      1  COUNT  (cr=85 pr=0 pw=0 time=3309 us)
      1   FILTER  (cr=85 pr=0 pw=0 time=3301 us)
   1028    HASH JOIN  (cr=85 pr=0 pw=0 time=5343 us)
   1028     HASH JOIN  (cr=70 pr=0 pw=0 time=7398 us)
      9      TABLE ACCESS FULL TS$ (cr=15 pr=0 pw=0 time=148 us)
   1028      TABLE ACCESS FULL USER$ (cr=55 pr=0 pw=0 time=1079 us)
      9     TABLE ACCESS FULL TS$ (cr=15 pr=0 pw=0 time=90 us)
```

The plans were subtly different (sometimes you'll find them to be radically different); they did different amounts of work. So, just turning on cursor sharing is something to do with great trepidation (well, testing really—you need to test this). It will potentially change the behavior of your application (e.g., the column widths) and because it removes *all* literals from SQL, even those that never really change, it can have a negative impact on your query plans.

Additionally, I have proven that while CURSOR_SHARING = FORCE runs much faster than parsing and optimizing lots of unique queries, I have also found it to be slower than using queries where the developer did the binding. This arises not from any inefficiency in the cursor sharing code, but rather in inefficiencies in the program itself. In many cases, an application that does not use bind variables is not efficiently parsing and reusing cursors either. Since the application believes each query is unique (it built them as unique statements), it will never use a cursor more than once. The fact is that if the programmer had used bind variables in the first place, he or she could have parsed a query once and reused it many times. It is this overhead of parsing that decreases the overall potential performance.

Basically, it is important to keep in mind that simply turning on CURSOR_SHARING = FORCE will not necessarily fix your problems. It may well introduce new ones. CURSOR_SHARING is, in some cases, a very useful tool, but it is not a silver bullet. A well-developed application would never need it. In the long term, using bind variables where appropriate, and constants when needed, is the correct approach.

■**Note** There are no silver bullets—*none*. If there were, they would be the default behavior and you would never hear about them.

Even if there are some switches that can be thrown at the database level—and they are truly few and far between—problems relating to concurrency issues and poorly executing queries (due to poorly written queries or poorly structured data) cannot be fixed with a switch. These situations require rewrites (and frequently a re-architecture). Moving data files around, changing the multiblock read count, and other database-level switches frequently have a minor impact on the overall performance of an application. Definitely not anywhere near the two, three, . . . *n* times increase in performance you need to achieve to make the application acceptable. How many times has your application been 10 percent too slow? No one complains about 10 percent too slow. *Five times* too slow, and people get upset. I repeat: you will not get a five times increase in performance by moving data files around. You will only achieve this by fixing the application, perhaps by making it do significantly less I/O.

Performance is something you have to design for, to build to, and to test for continuously throughout the development phase. It should never be something considered after the fact. I am amazed at how often people wait until the application has been shipped to their customer, put in place, and actually running before they even start to tune it. I've seen implementations where applications are shipped with nothing more than primary keys—no other indexes whatsoever. The queries have never been tuned or stress-tested. The application has never been tried out with more than a handful of users. Tuning is considered to be part of the installation of the product. To me, that is an unacceptable approach. Your end users should be presented with a responsive, fully tuned system from day one. There will be enough "product issues" to deal with without having poor performance be the first thing users experience. Users are expecting a few bugs from a new application, but don't make users wait a painfully long time for them to appear onscreen.

The DBA–Developer Relationship

It's certainly true that the most successful information systems are based on a symbiotic relationship between the DBA and the application developer. In this section, I want to give a developer's perspective on the division of work between developer and DBA (assuming that every serious development effort has a DBA team).

As a developer, you should not necessarily have to know how to install and configure the software. That should be the role of the DBA and perhaps the system administrator (SA). Setting up Oracle Net, getting the listener going, configuring the shared server, enabling connection pooling, installing the database, creating the database, and so on—these are functions I place in the hands of the DBA/SA.

In general, a developer should not have to know how to tune the OS. I myself generally leave this task to the SAs for the system. As a software developer for database applications, you will need to be competent in use of your OS of choice, but you shouldn't expect to have to tune it.

The single largest DBA responsibility is database recovery. Note I did not say "backup," I said "recovery," and I would claim that this is the sole responsibility of the DBA. Understanding how rollback and redo work—yes, that is something a developer has to know. Knowing how to perform a tablespace point-in-time recovery is something a developer can skip over. Knowing that you can do it might come in handy, but actually having to do it—no.

Tuning at the database instance level and figuring out what the optimum PGA_AGGREGATE_TARGET should be is typically the job of the DBA (and the database is quite willing and able to assist them in determining the correct figure). There are exceptional cases where a developer might need to change some setting for a session, but at the database level, the DBA is responsible for that. A typical database supports more than just a single developer's application. Only the DBA who supports all of the applications can make the right decision.

Allocating space and managing the files is the job of the DBA. Developers will contribute their estimations for space (how much they feel they will need), but the DBA/SA will take care of the rest.

Basically, developers do not need to know how to run the database. They need to know how to run *in* the database. The developer and the DBA will work together on different pieces of the same puzzle. The DBA will be visiting you, the developer, when your queries are consuming too many resources, and you'll be visiting the DBA when you cannot figure out how to make the system go any faster (that's when instance tuning can be done, when the application is fully tuned).

These tasks will all vary by environment, but I would like to think that there is a division of labor. A good developer is usually a very bad DBA, and vice versa. They are two different skill sets, two different mind-sets, and two different personalities, in my opinion. People naturally gravitate toward the job they enjoy doing most, and subsequently get better and better at it. It is not that they are necessarily bad at one of the jobs as much as they are better at the other because they enjoy it more. As for me, I consider myself more of a developer with lots of DBA opinions. I enjoy the development aspects of the job, but I also like to work "in the server" (which has sharpened my application-tuning capabilities, where the low-hanging fruit is always to be found).

Summary

In this chapter, we have taken a somewhat anecdotal look at why you need to know the database. The examples I gave throughout are not isolated—they happen every day, day in and day out. I observe a continuous cycle of these sorts of issues happening.

Let's quickly recap the key points. If you are developing with Oracle,

- You need to understand the Oracle architecture. You don't have to know it so well that you are able to rewrite the server if you want, but you should know it well enough that you are aware of the implications of using a particular feature.

- You need to understand the locking and concurrency control features, and that every database implements them *differently*. If you don't, your database will give "wrong" answers and you will have large contention issues, leading to poor performance.

- Do not treat the database as a black box—that is, something you need not understand. The database is the most critical piece of most applications. Trying to ignore it would be fatal.

- Solve problems as simply as possible, using as much of Oracle's built-in functionality as possible. You paid a lot for it.

- Software projects come and go, and programming languages and frameworks come and go. We developers are expected to have systems up and running in weeks, maybe months, and then move on to the next problem. If you reinvent the wheel, you will never come close to keeping up with the frantic pace of development. Just as you would never build your own hash table class in Java—since Java comes with one—you should use the database functionality you have at your disposal. The first step to being able to do that, of course, is to understand what it is you have at your disposal. I've seen more than one development team get in trouble, not only technically but also on a personal level, due to a lack of awareness of what Oracle provides for free.

- And building on that last point—software projects come and go, programming languages come and go—but the *data* is here forever. We build applications that use data, and that data will be used by many applications over time. It is not about the application—it is about the data. Use techniques and implementations that permit the data to be used and reused. If you use the database as a bit bucket, making it so that all access to any data must come through your application, you have missed the point. You cannot ad hoc query your application. You cannot build a new application on top of your old application. But if you use the database, you'll find adding new applications, reports, or whatever to be much easier over time.

So, with those points in mind, let's continue.

CHAPTER 2

■ ■ ■

Architecture Overview

Oracle is designed to be a very portable database; it is available on every platform of relevance, from Windows to UNIX to mainframes. For this reason, the physical architecture of Oracle looks different on different operating systems. For example, on a UNIX operating system, you will see Oracle implemented as many different operating system processes, with virtually a process per major function. On UNIX, this is the correct implementation, as it works on a multiprocess foundation. On Windows, however, this architecture would be inappropriate and would not work very well (it would be slow and nonscaleable). On the Windows platform, Oracle is implemented as a single, threaded process. On IBM mainframe systems, running OS/390 and z/OS, the Oracle operating system–specific architecture exploits multiple OS/390 address spaces, all operating as a single Oracle instance. Up to 255 address spaces can be configured for a single database instance. Moreover, Oracle works together with OS/390 Workload Manager (WLM) to establish execution priority of specific Oracle workloads relative to each other and relative to all other work in the OS/390 system. Even though the physical mechanisms used to implement Oracle from platform to platform vary, the architecture is sufficiently generalized so that you can get a good understanding of how Oracle works on all platforms.

In this chapter, I present a broad picture of this architecture. We'll examine the Oracle server and define some terms such as "database" and "instance" (terms that always seem to cause confusion). We'll take a look at what happens when we "connect" to Oracle and, at a high level, how the server manages memory. In the subsequent three chapters, we'll look in detail at the three major components of the Oracle architecture:

- Chapter 3 covers *files*. In this chapter, we'll look at the set of five general categories of files that make up the database: parameter, data, temp, control, and redo log files. We'll also cover other types of files, including trace, alert, dump (DMP), data pump, and simple flat files. We'll look at the Oracle 10g new file area called the Flashback Recovery Area, and we'll also discuss the impact that Automatic Storage Management (ASM) has on our file storage.

- Chapter 4 covers the Oracle *memory structures* referred to as the System Global Area (SGA), Process Global Area (PGA), and User Global Area (UGA). We'll examine the relationships between these structures, and we'll also discuss the shared pool, large pool, Java pool, and various other SGA components.

- Chapter 5 covers Oracle's *physical processes or threads*. We'll look at the three different types of processes that will be running on the database: server processes, background processes, and slave processes.

It was hard to decide which of these components to cover first. The processes use the SGA, so discussing the SGA before the processes might not make sense. On the other hand, when discussing the processes and what they do, I'll need to make references to the SGA. These two components are closely tied: the files are acted on by the processes and would not make sense without first understanding what the processes do.

What I will do, then, in this chapter is define some terms and give a general overview of what Oracle looks like (if you were to draw it on a whiteboard). You'll then be ready to delve into some of the details.

Defining Database and Instance

There are two terms that, when used in an Oracle context, seem to cause a great deal of confusion: "instance" and "database." In Oracle terminology, the definitions of these terms are as follows:

- *Database*: A collection of physical operating system files or *disk*. When using Oracle 10*g* Automatic Storage Management (ASM) or RAW partitions, the database may not appear as individual separate files in the operating system, but the definition remains the same.

- *Instance*: A set of Oracle background processes/threads and a shared memory area, which is memory that is shared across those threads/processes running on a single computer. This is the place to maintain volatile, nonpersistent stuff (some of which gets flushed to disk). A database instance can exist without any disk storage whatsoever. It might not be the most useful thing in the world, but thinking about it that way will definitely help draw the line between the *instance* and the *database*.

The two terms are sometimes used interchangeably, but they embrace very different concepts. The relationship between them is that a database may be *mounted* and *opened* by many instances. An instance may *mount* and *open* a single database at any point in time. In fact, it is true to say that an instance will mount and open at most a single database in its entire lifetime! We'll look at an example of that in a moment.

Confused even more? Some further explanation should help clear up these concepts. An instance is simply a set of operating system processes, or a single process with many threads, and some memory. These processes can operate on a database; a database is just a collection of files (data files, temporary files, redo log files, and control files). At any time, an instance will have only one set of files (one *database*) associated with it. In most cases, the opposite is true as well: a database will have only one instance working on it. However, in the special case of Oracle *Real Application Clusters* (*RAC*), an option of Oracle that allows it to function on many computers in a clustered environment, we may have many instances simultaneously mounting and opening this one database, which resides on a set of shared physical disks. This gives us access to this single database from many different computers at the same time. Oracle RAC provides for extremely highly available systems and has the potential to architect extremely scalable solutions.

Let's take a look at a simple example. Say we've just installed Oracle 10*g* version 10.1.0.3. We did a software-only installation. No starter databases, nothing—just the software.

The pwd command shows the current working directory (this example was performed on a Linux-based computer). We're in the dbs directory (on Windows, this would be the database directory) and the `ls -l` command shows it is "empty." There is no `init.ora` file and no SPFILEs (*stored parameter files*; these will be discussed in detail in Chapter 3).

```
[ora10g@localhost dbs]$ pwd
/home/ora10g/dbs
[ora10g@localhost dbs]$ ls -l
total 0
```

Using the `ps` (process status) command, we can see all processes being run by the user ora10g (the Oracle software owner in this case). There are no Oracle database processes whatsoever at this point.

```
[ora10g@localhost dbs]$ ps -aef | grep ora10g
ora10g    4173  4151  0 13:33 pts/0    00:00:00 -su
ora10g    4365  4173  0 14:09 pts/0    00:00:00 ps -aef
ora10g    4366  4173  0 14:09 pts/0    00:00:00 grep ora10g
```

We then use the `ipcs` command, a UNIX command that is used to show interprocess communication devices such as shared memory, semaphores, and the like. Currently there are none in use on this system at all.

```
[ora10g@localhost dbs]$ ipcs -a

------ Shared Memory Segments --------
key        shmid      owner      perms      bytes      nattch     status

------ Semaphore Arrays --------
key        semid      owner      perms      nsems

------ Message Queues --------
key        msqid      owner      perms      used-bytes   messages
```

We then start up SQL*Plus (Oracle's command-line interface) and connect AS SYSDBA (the account that is allowed to do virtually anything in the database). The connection is successful and SQL*Plus reports we are connected to an idle instance:

```
[ora10g@localhost dbs]$ sqlplus "/ as sysdba"

SQL*Plus: Release 10.1.0.3.0 - Production on Sun Dec 19 14:09:44 2004
Copyright (c) 1982, 2004, Oracle.  All rights reserved.
Connected to an idle instance.
SQL>
```

Our "instance" right now consists solely of the Oracle server process shown in bold in the following output. There is no shared memory allocated yet and no other processes.

```
SQL> !ps -aef | grep ora10g
ora10g    4173  4151  0 13:33 pts/0    00:00:00 -su
ora10g    4368  4173  0 14:09 pts/0    00:00:00 sqlplus    as sysdba
ora10g    4370     1  0 14:09 ?        00:00:00 oracleora10g (...)
ora10g    4380  4368  0 14:14 pts/0    00:00:00 /bin/bash -c ps -aef | grep ora10g
```

```
ora10g    4381    4380    0 14:14 pts/0    00:00:00 ps -aef
ora10g    4382    4380    0 14:14 pts/0    00:00:00 grep ora10g

SQL> !ipcs -a

------ Shared Memory Segments --------
key        shmid      owner      perms      bytes      nattch      status

------ Semaphore Arrays --------
key        semid      owner      perms      nsems

------ Message Queues --------
key        msqid      owner      perms      used-bytes    messages

SQL>
```

Let's try to start the instance now:

```
SQL> startup
ORA-01078: failure in processing system parameters
LRM-00109: could not open parameter file '/home/ora10g/dbs/initora10g.ora'
SQL>
```

That is the sole file that must exist in order to start up an instance—we need either a parameter file (a simple flat file described in more detail shortly) or a stored parameter file. We'll create the parameter file now and put into it the minimal information we need to actually start a database instance (normally, many more parameters will be specified, such as the database block size, control file locations, and so on):

```
$ cat initora10g.ora
db_name = ora10g
```

and then once we get back into SQL*Plus:

```
SQL> startup nomount
ORACLE instance started.
```

We used the nomount option to the startup command since we don't actually have a database to "mount" yet (see the SQL*Plus documentation for all of the startup and shutdown options).

■**Note** On Windows, prior to running the startup command, you'll need to execute a service creation statement using the oradim.exe utility.

Now we have what I would call an "instance." The background processes needed to actually run a database are all there, such as process monitor (PMON), log writer (LGWR), and so on (these processes are covered in detail in Chapter 5).

```
Total System Global Area  113246208 bytes
Fixed Size                   777952 bytes
Variable Size              61874464 bytes
Database Buffers           50331648 bytes
Redo Buffers                 262144 bytes
SQL> !ps -aef | grep ora10g
ora10g    4173  4151  0 13:33 pts/0     00:00:00 -su
ora10g    4368  4173  0 14:09 pts/0     00:00:00 sqlplus    as sysdba
ora10g    4404     1  0 14:18 ?         00:00:00 ora_pmon_ora10g
ora10g    4406     1  0 14:18 ?         00:00:00 ora_mman_ora10g
ora10g    4408     1  0 14:18 ?         00:00:00 ora_dbw0_ora10g
ora10g    4410     1  0 14:18 ?         00:00:00 ora_lgwr_ora10g
ora10g    4412     1  0 14:18 ?         00:00:00 ora_ckpt_ora10g
ora10g    4414     1  0 14:18 ?         00:00:00 ora_smon_ora10g
ora10g    4416     1  0 14:18 ?         00:00:00 ora_reco_ora10g
ora10g    4418     1  0 14:18 ?         00:00:00 oracleora10g (...)
ora10g    4419  4368  0 14:18 pts/0     00:00:00 /bin/bash -c ps -aef | grep ora10g
ora10g    4420  4419  0 14:18 pts/0     00:00:00 ps -aef
ora10g    4421  4419  0 14:18 pts/0     00:00:00 grep ora10g
```

Additionally, ipcs is, for the first time, reporting the use of shared memory and semaphores—two important interprocess communication devices on UNIX:

```
SQL> !ipcs -a

------ Shared Memory Segments --------
key        shmid      owner      perms      bytes      nattch     status
0x99875060 458760     ora10g     660        115343360  8

------ Semaphore Arrays --------
key        semid      owner      perms      nsems
0xf182650c 884736     ora10g     660        34

------ Message Queues --------
key        msqid      owner      perms      used-bytes   messages

SQL>
```

Note that we have no "database" yet. We have a name of a database (in the parameter file we created), but no database whatsoever. If we tried to "mount" this database, then it would fail because it quite simply does not yet exist. Let's create it. I've been told that creating an Oracle database involves quite a few steps, but let's see:

```
SQL> create database;
Database created.
```

That is actually all there is to creating a database. In the real world, however, we would use a slightly more complicated form of the CREATE DATABASE command because we would need to tell Oracle where to put the log files, data files, control files, and so on. But here we now have a fully operational database. We would need to run the $ORACLE_HOME/rdbms/admin/catalog.sql script and other catalog scripts to build the rest of the data dictionary we use every day (the views we use such as ALL_OBJECTS are not yet present in this database), but we have a database here. We can use a simple query against some Oracle V$ views, specifically V$DATAFILE, V$LOGFILE, and V$CONTROLFILE, to list the files that make up this database:

```
SQL> select name from v$datafile;

NAME
--------------------------------------------------------------------------------
/home/ora10g/dbs/dbs1ora10g.dbf
/home/ora10g/dbs/dbx1ora10g.dbf

SQL> select member from v$logfile;

MEMBER
--------------------------------------------------------------------------------
/home/ora10g/dbs/log1ora10g.dbf
/home/ora10g/dbs/log2ora10g.dbf

SQL> select name from v$controlfile;

NAME
--------------------------------------------------------------------------------
/home/ora10g/dbs/cntrlora10g.dbf

SQL>
```

Oracle used defaults to put everything together and created a database as a set of persistent files. If we close this database and try to open it again, we'll discover that we can't:

```
SQL> alter database close;
Database altered.

SQL> alter database open;
alter database open
*
ERROR at line 1:
ORA-16196: database has been previously opened and closed
```

An instance can mount and open at most one database in its life. We must discard this instance and create a new one in order to open this or any other database.

To recap,

- An *instance* is a set of background processes and shared memory.

- A *database* is a collection of data stored on disk.

- An instance can mount and open only a single database, ever.

- A database may be mounted and opened by one or more instances (using RAC).

As noted earlier, there is, in most cases, a one-to-one relationship between an instance and a database. This is probably how the confusion surrounding the terms arises. In most peoples' experience, a database is an instance, and an instance is a database.

In many test environments, however, this is not the case. On my disk, I might have five separate databases. On the test machine, at any point in time there is only one instance of Oracle running, but the database it is accessing may be different from day to day or hour to hour, depending on my needs. By simply having many different configuration files, I can mount and open any one of these databases. Here, I have one "instance" at a time but many databases, only one of which is accessible at any point in time.

So now when someone talks about an instance, you'll know they mean the processes and memory of Oracle. When they mention the database, they are talking about the physical files that hold the data. A database may be accessible from many instances, but an instance will provide access to exactly one database at a time.

The SGA and Background Processes

You're probably ready now for an abstract picture of what an Oracle instance and database looks like (see Figure 2-1).

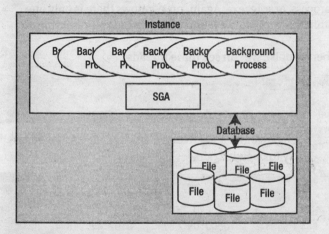

Figure 2-1. *Oracle instance and database*

Figure 2-1 is a depiction of an Oracle instance and database in their simplest form. Oracle has a large chunk of memory called the SGA where it will, for example, do the following:

- Maintain many internal data structures that all processes need access to.

- Cache data from disk; buffer redo data before writing it to disk.

- Hold parsed SQL plans.

- And so on.

Oracle has a set of processes that are "attached" to this SGA, and the mechanism by which they attach differs by operating system. In a UNIX environment, they will physically attach to a large *shared memory* segment, a chunk of memory allocated in the operating system that may be accessed by many processes concurrently (generally using shmget() and shmat()).

Under Windows, these processes simply use the C call malloc() to allocate the memory, since they are really threads in one big process and hence share the same virtual memory space. Oracle will also have a set of files that the database processes/threads read and write (and Oracle processes are the only ones allowed to read or write these files). These files hold all of our table data, indexes, temporary space, redo logs, and so on.

If you were to start up Oracle on a UNIX-based system and execute a ps command, you would see that many physical processes are running, with various names. You saw an example of that earlier when you observed the pmon, smon, and other processes. I cover what each of these processes are in Chapter 5, so just be aware for now that they are commonly referred to as the *Oracle background processes*. They are persistent processes that make up the instance, and you will see them from the time you start the instance until the time you shut it down.

It is interesting to note that these are processes, not individual programs. There is only one Oracle binary executable on UNIX; it has many "personalities" depending on what it was told to do when it starts up. The same binary executable that was run to get ora_pmon_ora10g was also used to get the process ora_ckpt_ora10g. There is only one binary executable program, named simply oracle. It is just executed many times with different names.

On Windows, using the pslist tool (http://www.sysinternals.com/ntw2k/freeware/pslist.shtml), we'll find only one process, oracle.exe. Again, on Windows there is only one binary executable (oracle.exe). Within this process, we'll find many threads representing the Oracle background processes.

Using pslist (or any of a number of tools), we can see these threads:

```
C:\Documents and Settings\tkyte>pslist oracle

PsList 1.26 - Process Information Lister
Copyright (C) 1999-2004 Mark Russinovich
Sysinternals - www.sysinternals.com

Process information for ORACLE-N15577HE:

Name          Pid Pri Thd  Hnd    Priv      CPU Time     Elapsed Time
oracle       1664   8  19  284  354684   0:00:05.687     0:02:42.218
```

Here we can see there are 19 threads (Thd in the display) contained in the single Oracle process. These threads represent what were processes on UNIX—they are the pmon, arch, lgwr, and so on bits of Oracle. We can use pslist to see more details about each:

```
C:\Documents and Settings\tkyte>pslist -d oracle

PsList 1.26 - Process Information Lister
Copyright (C) 1999-2004 Mark Russinovich
Sysinternals - www.sysinternals.com

Thread detail for ORACLE-N15577HE:

oracle 1664:
```

Tid	Pri	Cswtch	State	User Time	Kernel Time	Elapsed Time
1724	9	148	Wait:Executive	0:00:00.000	0:00:00.218	0:02:46.625
756	9	236	Wait:UserReq	0:00:00.000	0:00:00.046	0:02:45.984
1880	8	2	Wait:UserReq	0:00:00.000	0:00:00.000	0:02:45.953
1488	8	403	Wait:UserReq	0:00:00.000	0:00:00.109	0:02:10.593
1512	8	149	Wait:UserReq	0:00:00.000	0:00:00.046	0:02:09.171
1264	8	254	Wait:UserReq	0:00:00.000	0:00:00.062	0:02:09.140
960	9	425	Wait:UserReq	0:00:00.000	0:00:00.125	0:02:09.078
2008	9	341	Wait:UserReq	0:00:00.000	0:00:00.093	0:02:09.062
1504	8	1176	Wait:UserReq	0:00:00.046	0:00:00.218	0:02:09.015
1464	8	97	Wait:UserReq	0:00:00.000	0:00:00.031	0:02:09.000
1420	8	171	Wait:UserReq	0:00:00.015	0:00:00.093	0:02:08.984
1588	8	131	Wait:UserReq	0:00:00.000	0:00:00.046	0:02:08.890
1600	8	61	Wait:UserReq	0:00:00.000	0:00:00.046	0:02:08.796
1608	9	5	Wait:Queue	0:00:00.000	0:00:00.000	0:02:01.953
2080	8	84	Wait:UserReq	0:00:00.015	0:00:00.046	0:01:33.468
2088	8	127	Wait:UserReq	0:00:00.000	0:00:00.046	0:01:15.968
2092	8	110	Wait:UserReq	0:00:00.000	0:00:00.015	0:01:14.687
2144	8	115	Wait:UserReq	0:00:00.015	0:00:00.171	0:01:12.421
2148	9	803	Wait:UserReq	0:00:00.093	0:00:00.859	0:01:09.718

We cannot see the thread "names" like we could on UNIX (ora_pmon_ora10g and so on) but we can see the thread IDs (Tid), priorities (Pri), and other operating system accounting information about them.

Connecting to Oracle

In this section, we'll take a look at the mechanics behind the two most common ways to have requests serviced by an Oracle server: *dedicated server* and *shared server* connections. We'll see what happens on the client and the server in order to establish connections, so we can log in and actually do work in the database. Lastly, we'll take a brief look at how to establish TCP/IP connections—*TCP/IP* being the primary networking protocol used to connect over the network to Oracle—and at how the *listener* process on our server, which is responsible for establishing the physical connection to the server, works differently in the cases of dedicated and shared server connections.

Dedicated Server

Figure 2-1 and the pslist output presented a picture of what Oracle looks like immediately after starting. If we were now to log into this database using a dedicated server, we would see a new process get created just to service us:

```
C:\Documents and Settings\tkyte>sqlplus tkyte/tkyte

SQL*Plus: Release 10.1.0.3.0 - Production on Sun Dec 19 15:41:53 2004
Copyright (c) 1982, 2004, Oracle.  All rights reserved.
Connected to:
```

```
Oracle Database 10g Enterprise Edition Release 10.1.0.3.0 - Production
With the Partitioning, OLAP and Data Mining options

tkyte@ORA10G> host pslist oracle

PsList 1.26 - Process Information Lister
Copyright (C) 1999-2004 Mark Russinovich
Sysinternals - www.sysinternals.com

Process information for ORACLE-N15577HE:

Name              Pid Pri Thd  Hnd   Priv      CPU Time      Elapsed Time
oracle           1664   8  20  297 356020    0:00:05.906     0:03:21.546
tkyte@ORA10G>
```

Now you can see there are 20 threads instead of 19, the extra thread being our dedicated server process (more information on what exactly a dedicated server process is shortly). When we log out, the extra thread will go away. On UNIX, we would see another process get added to the list of Oracle processes running, and that would be our dedicated server.

This brings us to the next iteration of the previous diagram. Now, if we were to connect to Oracle in its most commonly used configuration, we would see something like Figure 2-2.

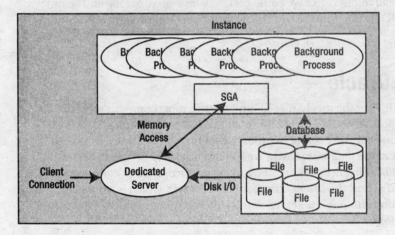

Figure 2-2. *Typical dedicated server configuration*

As noted, typically Oracle will create a new process for me when I log in. This is commonly referred to as the *dedicated server* configuration, since a server process will be dedicated to me for the life of my session. For each session, a new dedicated server will appear in a one-to-one mapping. This dedicated server process is not (by definition) part of the instance. My client process (whatever program is trying to connect to the database) will be in direct communication with this dedicated server over some networking conduit, such as a TCP/IP socket. It is this server process that will receive my SQL and execute it for me. It will read data files if necessary, and it will look in the database's cache for my data. It will perform my update statements. It will run my PL/SQL code. Its only goal is to respond to the SQL calls that I submit to it.

Shared Server

Oracle may also accept connections in a manner called *shared server* (formally known as Multi-Threaded Server, or MTS), in which we would *not* see an additional thread created or a new UNIX process appear for each user connection. In shared server, Oracle uses a pool of "shared processes" for a large community of users. Shared servers are simply a connection pooling mechanism. Instead of having 10,000 dedicated servers (that's a lot of processes or threads) for 10,000 database sessions, shared server allows us to have a small percentage of this number of processes/threads, which are (as the name implies) shared by all sessions. This allows Oracle to connect many more users to the database than would otherwise be possible. Our machine might crumble under the load of managing 10,000 processes, but managing 100 or 1,000 processes is doable. In shared server mode, the shared processes are generally started up with the database and just appear in the ps list.

A big difference between shared and dedicated server connections is that the client process connected to the database never talks directly to a shared server, as it would to a dedicated server. It cannot talk to a shared server because that process is, in fact, shared. To share these processes, we need another mechanism through which to "talk." Oracle employs a process (or set of processes) called *dispatchers* for this purpose. The client process will talk to a dispatcher process over the network. The dispatcher process will put the client's request into the request queue in the SGA (one of the many things the SGA is used for). The first shared server that is not busy will pick up this request and process it (e.g., the request could be UPDATE T SET X = X+5 WHERE Y = 2). Upon completion of this command, the shared server will place the response in the invoking dispatcher's response queue. The dispatcher process is monitoring this queue and, upon seeing a result, will transmit it to the client. Conceptually, the flow of a shared server request looks like Figure 2-3.

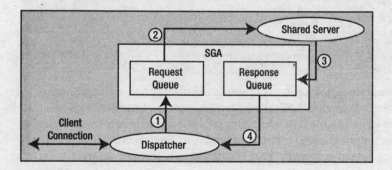

Figure 2-3. *Steps in a shared server request*

As shown in Figure 2-3, the client connection will send a request to the dispatcher. The dispatcher will first place this request onto the request queue in the SGA (1). The first available shared server will dequeue this request (2) and process it. When the shared server completes, the response (return codes, data, and so on) is placed into the response queue (3), subsequently picked up by the dispatcher (4), and transmitted back to the client.

As far as the developer is concerned, there is no difference between a shared server connection and a dedicated server connection.

Now that you understand what dedicated server and shared server connections are, you may have the following questions:

- How do I get connected in the first place?

- What would start this dedicated server?

- How might I get in touch with a dispatcher?

The answers depend on your specific platform, but the sections that follow outline the process in general terms.

Mechanics of Connecting over TCP/IP

We'll investigate the most common networking case: a network-based connection request over a TCP/IP connection. In this case, the client is situated on one machine and the server resides on another machine, with the two connected on a TCP/IP network. It all starts with the client. The client makes a request using the Oracle client software (a set of provided *application program interfaces*, or *APIs*) to connect to database. For example, the client issues the following:

```
[tkyte@localhost tkyte]$ sqlplus scott/tiger@ora10g.localdomain

SQL*Plus: Release 10.1.0.3.0 - Production on Sun Dec 19 16:16:41 2004
Copyright (c) 1982, 2004, Oracle.  All rights reserved.
Connected to:
Oracle Database 10g Enterprise Edition Release 10.1.0.3.0 - Production
With the Partitioning, OLAP and Data Mining options

scott@ORA10G>
```

Here, the client is the program SQL*Plus, scott/tiger is the username/password, and ora10g.localdomain is a TNS service name. *TNS* stands for *Transparent Network Substrate* and is "foundation" software built into the Oracle client that handles our remote connections, allowing for peer-to-peer communication. The TNS connection string tells the Oracle software how to connect to the remote database. Generally, the client software running on your machine will read a file called tnsnames.ora. This is a plain-text configuration file commonly found in the [ORACLE_HOME]\network\admin directory ([ORACLE_HOME] represents the full path to your Oracle installation directory). It will have entries that look like this:

```
ORA10G.LOCALDOMAIN =
  (DESCRIPTION =
    (ADDRESS_LIST =
      (ADDRESS = (PROTOCOL = TCP)(HOST = localhost.localdomain)(PORT = 1521))
    )
    (CONNECT_DATA =
      (SERVICE_NAME = ora10g)
    )
  )
```

This configuration information allows the Oracle client software to map the TNS connection string we used, ora10g.localdomain, into something useful—namely, a hostname, a port on that host on which a "listener" process will accept connections, the *service name* of the database on the host to which we wish to connect, and so on. A service name represents groups of applications with common attributes, service level thresholds, and priorities. The number of instances offering the service is transparent to the application, and each database instance may register with the listener as willing to provide many services. So, services are mapped to physical database instances and allow the DBA to associate certain thresholds and priorities with them.

This string, ora10g.localdomain, could have been resolved in other ways. For example, it could have been resolved using Oracle Internet Directory (OID), which is a distributed Lightweight Directory Access Protocol (LDAP) server, similar in purpose to DNS for hostname resolution. However, use of the tnsnames.ora file is common in most small to medium installations where the number of copies of such a configuration file is manageable.

Now that the client software knows where to connect to, it will open a TCP/IP socket connection to the server with the hostname localhost.localdomain on port 1521. If the DBA for our server has installed and configured Oracle Net, and has the listener listening on port 1521 for connection requests, this connection may be accepted. In a network environment, we will be running a process called the *TNS listener* on our server. This listener process is what will get us physically connected to our database. When it receives the inbound connection request, it inspects the request and, using its own configuration files, either rejects the request (e.g., because there is no such database, or perhaps our IP address has been disallowed connections to this host) or accepts it and goes about getting us connected.

If we are making a dedicated server connection, the listener process will create a dedicated server for us. On UNIX, this is achieved via a fork() and exec() system call (the only way to create a new process after initialization in UNIX is via fork()). The new dedicated server process inherits the connection established by the listener, and we are now physically connected to the database. On Windows, the listener process requests the database process to create a new thread for a connection. Once this thread is created, the client is "redirected" to it, and we are physically connected. Diagrammatically in UNIX, it would look as shown in Figure 2-4.

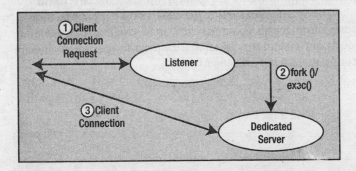

Figure 2-4. *The listener process and dedicated server connections*

On the other hand, the listener will behave differently if we are making a shared server connection request. This listener process knows the dispatcher(s) we have running in the instance. As connection requests are received, the listener will choose a dispatcher process from the pool of available dispatchers. The listener will either send back to the client the connection information describing how the client can connect to the dispatcher process or, if possible, "hand off" the connection to the dispatcher process (this is operating system– and database version–dependent, but the net effect is the same). When the listener sends back the connection information, it is done because the listener is running on a well-known hostname and port on that host, but the dispatchers will be accepting connections on randomly assigned ports on that server. The listener is made aware of these random port assignments by the dispatcher and will pick a dispatcher for us. The client then disconnects from the listener and connects directly to the dispatcher. We now have a physical connection to the database. Figure 2-5 illustrates this process.

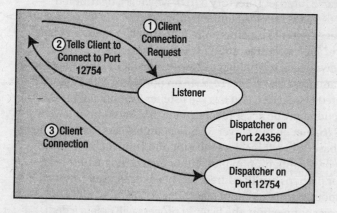

Figure 2-5. *The listener process and shared server connections*

Summary

That completes our overview of the Oracle architecture. In this chapter, we defined the terms "instance" and "database" and saw how to connect to the database through either a dedicated server connection or a shared server connection. Figure 2-6 sums up the material covered in the chapter and shows the interaction between a client using a shared server connection and a client using a dedicated server connection. It also shows that an Oracle instance may use both connection types simultaneously. (In fact, an Oracle database *always* supports dedicated server connections—even when configured for shared server.)

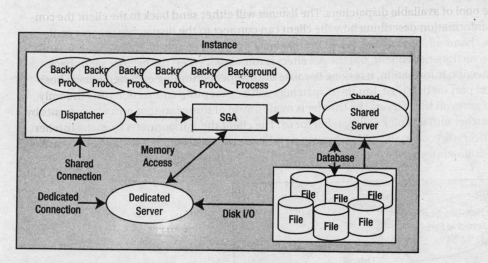

Figure 2-6. *Connection overview*

Now you're ready to take a more in-depth look at the processes behind the server, what they do, and how they interact with each other. You're also ready to look inside the SGA to see what it contains and what its purpose is. You'll start in the next chapter by looking at the types of files Oracle uses to manage the data and the role of each file type.

CHAPTER 3

■ ■ ■

Files

In this chapter, we will examine the eight file types that make up a database and instance. The files associated with an instance are simply

- *Parameter files*: These files tell the Oracle instance where to find the control files, and they also specify certain initialization parameters that define how big certain memory structures are, and so on. We will investigate the two options available for storing database parameter files.

- *Trace files*: These are diagnostic files created by a server process generally in response to some exceptional error condition.

- *Alert file*: This is similar to a trace file, but it contains information about "expected" events, and it also alerts the DBA in a single, centralized file of many database events.

The files that make up the database are

- *Data files*: These files are for the database; they hold your tables, indexes, and all other segments.

- *Temp files*: These files are used for disk-based sorts and temporary storage.

- *Control files*: These files tell you where the data files, temp files, and redo log files are, as well as other relevant metadata about their state.

- *Redo log files*: These are your transaction logs.

- *Password files*: These files are used to authenticate users performing administrative activities over the network. We will not discuss these files in any detail.

Starting in Oracle 10g, there are a couple of new optional file types that are used by Oracle to facilitate faster backup and faster recovery operations. These two new files are

- *Change tracking file*: This file facilitates a true incremental backup of Oracle data. It does not have to be located in the Flash Recovery Area, but as it relates purely to database backup and recovery we'll discuss it in the context of that area.

- *Flashback log files*: These files store "before images" of database blocks in order to facilitate the new FLASHBACK DATABASE command.

We'll also take a look at other types of files commonly associated with the database, such as

- *Dump (DMP) files*: These files are generated by the Export database utility and consumed by the Import database utility.

- *Data Pump files*: These files are generated by the new Oracle 10*g* Data Pump Export process and consumed by the Data Pump Import process. This file format may also be created and consumed by external tables.

- *Flat files*: These are plain old files you can view in a text editor. You normally use these for loading data into the database.

The most important files in the previous lists are the data files and the redo log files, because they contain the data you worked so hard to accumulate. I can lose any and all of the remaining files and still get to my data. If I lose my redo log files, I may start to lose *some* data. If I lose my data files and all of their backups, I've *definitely* lost that data forever.

We will now take a look at the types of files and what we might expect to find in them.

Parameter Files

There are many different parameter files associated with an Oracle database, from a `tnsnames.ora` file on a client workstation (used to "find" a server on the network), to a `listener.ora` file on the server (for the network listener startup), to the `sqlnet.ora`, `cman.ora`, and `ldap.ora` files, to name a few. The most important parameter file, however, is the database's parameter file—without this, we cannot even get a database started. The remaining files are important; all of them are related to networking and getting connected to the database. However, they are beyond the scope of our discussion. For information on their configuration and setup, I refer you to the *Net Services Administrator's Guide*. Typically as a developer, these files would be set up for you, not by you.

The parameter file for a database is commonly known as an *init file*, or an `init.ora` file. This is due to its historic default name, which is `init<ORACLE_SID>.ora`. I term it the "historic" default name because starting with Oracle9*i* Release 1, a vastly improved method of storing parameter settings for the database was introduced: the *server parameter file*, or simply *SPFILE*. This file has the default name of `spfile<ORACLE_SID>.ora`. We'll take a look at both kinds of parameter files in turn.

■**Note** If you're unfamiliar with the term SID or `ORACLE_SID`, a full definition is called for. The SID is a *site identifier*. It and `ORACLE_HOME` (where the Oracle software is installed) are hashed together in UNIX to create a unique key name for attaching an SGA. If your `ORACLE_SID` or `ORACLE_HOME` is not set correctly, you'll get the `ORACLE NOT AVAILABLE` error, since you can't attach to a shared memory segment that is identified by this unique key. On Windows, shared memory isn't used in the same fashion as UNIX, but the SID is still important. You can have more than one database on the same `ORACLE_HOME`, so you need a way to uniquely identify each one, along with their configuration files.

Without a parameter file, you cannot start an Oracle database. This makes the parameter file fairly important, and as of Oracle9*i* Release 2 (versions 9.2 and above), the backup and recovery tool *Recovery Manager* (*RMAN*) recognizes this file's importance and will allow you to include the server parameter file (but not the legacy init.ora parameter file type) in your backup set. However, since it is simply a plain text file, which you can create with any text editor, it is not a file you have to necessarily guard with your life. You can re-create it, as long as you know what was in it (e.g., you can retrieve that information from the database's alert log, if you have access to that).

We will now examine each type of parameter file (init.ora and SPFILE) in turn, but before we do that, let's see what a database parameter file looks like.

What Are Parameters?

In simple terms, a database parameter may be thought of as a "key" and "value" pair. You saw an important parameter, DB_NAME, in the preceding chapter. The DB_NAME parameter was stored simply as db_name = ora10g. The "key" here is DB_NAME and the "value" is ora10g—that is our key/value pair. In order to see the current value of an instance parameter, you can query the V$ view V$PARAMETER. Alternatively, in SQL*Plus you can use the SHOW PARAMETER command, for example:

```
sys@ORA10G> select value
  2  from v$parameter
  3  where name = 'pga_aggregate_target';

VALUE
--------------------------------------------------------------------------------
1073741824

sys@ORA10G> show parameter pga_agg

NAME                                 TYPE        VALUE
------------------------------------ ----------- ------------------------------
pga_aggregate_target                 big integer 1G
```

Both outputs show basically the same information, although you can get more information from V$PARAMETER (there are many more columns to choose from than displayed in this example). But SHOW PARAMETER wins for me in ease of use and the fact that it "wildcards" automatically. Notice that I typed in only pga_agg; SHOW PARAMETER adds % to the front and back.

■**Note** All V$ views and all dictionary views are fully documented in the *Oracle Database Reference* manual. Please regard that manual as the definitive source of what is available in a given view.

If you counted the number of documented parameters that you may set in each of the database versions 9.0.1, 9.2.0, and 10.1.0, you would probably find 251, 258, and 255 different parameters, respectively (I'm sure there could be additional parameters available on an operating system–by–operating system basis). In other words, the number of parameters (and their names) varies by release. Most parameters, like DB_BLOCK_SIZE, are very long lived (they won't go away from release to release), but over time many other parameters become obsolete as implementations change.

For example, in Oracle 9.0.1 there was a DISTRIBUTED_TRANSACTIONS parameter that could be set to some positive integer and that controlled the number of concurrent distributed transactions the database could perform. It was available in prior releases, but it is not found in any release subsequent to 9.0.1 and, in fact, attempting to use it with subsequent releases will raise an error:

```
ops$tkyte@ORA10G> alter system set distributed_transactions = 10;
alter system set distributed_transactions = 10
*
ERROR at line 1:
ORA-25138: DISTRIBUTED_TRANSACTIONS initialization parameter has been made
obsolete
```

If you would like to review these parameters and get a feeling for what is available and what each parameter does, you should refer to the *Oracle Database Reference* manual. The first chapter of this manual examines each and every documented parameter in detail. I would like to point out that in general, the default value assigned to these parameters (or the derived value for parameters that obtain their default settings from other parameters) is sufficient for most systems. In general, the values of parameters, such as the CONTROL_FILES parameter (which specifies the location of the control files on your system), DB_BLOCK_SIZE, and various memory-related parameters, need to be set uniquely for each database

Notice I used the term "documented" in the preceding paragraph. There are *undocu-mented* parameters as well. You can identify these by the fact that their names begin with an underscore (_). There is a great deal of speculation about these parameters. Since they are undocumented, some people believe they must be "magical," and many people assume that they are well known and used by Oracle "insiders." In fact, I find the opposite to be true. They are not well known and they are hardly ever used. Most of these undocumented parameters are rather boring, actually, as they represent deprecated functionality and backward-compatibility flags. Others help in the recovery of data, not of the database itself; for example, some of them enable the database to start up in certain extreme circumstances, but only long enough to get data *out*. You have to rebuild after that.

Unless you are so directed by Oracle Support, there is no reason to have an undocumented parameter in your configuration. Many have side effects that could be devastating. In my development database, I use only one undocumented setting, if any:

_TRACE_FILES_PUBLIC = TRUE

This parameter makes trace files readable by all, not just the DBA group. On my development database, I want my developers to use SQL_TRACE, TIMED_STATISTICS, and the TKPROF utility frequently (well, I demand it actually); hence they need to be able to read the trace files. With the advent of external tables in Oracle 9.0.1 and above, we'll see that we need not use even this parameter to permit access to trace files.

In my production database, I don't use any undocumented settings. In fact, the seemingly "safe" undocumented parameter just mentioned can have undesirable side effects in a live system. Think about the sensitive information that you might find in a trace file, such as SQL and even data values (see the upcoming section titled "Trace Files"), and ask yourself, "Do I really want any end user to have read access to that data?" The answer is most likely no.

■**Caution** Use undocumented parameters only at the request of Oracle Support. Their use can be damaging to a database, and their implementation can—and will—change from release to release.

You may set the various parameter values in one of two ways: either for the current instance or persistently. It is up to you make sure that the parameter files contain the values you want them to. When using legacy init.ora parameter files, this is a manual process. To change a parameter value persistently when using an init.ora file, to have that new setting be in place across server restarts, you must manually edit and modify the init.ora parameter file. With server parameter files, you'll see that this has been more or less fully automated for you in a single command.

Legacy init.ora Parameter Files

The legacy Oracle init.ora file is a very simple file in terms of its construction. It is a series of variable key/value pairs. A sample init.ora file might look like this:

```
db_name = "ora9ir2"
db_block_size = 8192
control_files = ("C:\oradata\control01.ctl", "C:\oradata\control02.ctl")
```

In fact, this is pretty close to the most basic init.ora file that you could get away with in real life. If I had a block size that was the default on my platform (the default block size varies by platform), I could remove that. The parameter file is used at the very least to get the name of the database and the location of the control files. The control files tell Oracle the location of every other file, so they are very important to the "bootstrap" process of starting the instance.

Now that you know what these legacy database parameter files are and where to get more details about the valid parameters that you can set, the last thing you need to know is where to find them on disk. The naming convention for this file by default is

```
init$ORACLE_SID.ora     (Unix environment variable)
init%ORACLE_SID%.ora    (Windows environment variable)
```

and by default it will be found in

```
$ORACLE_HOME/dbs        (Unix)
%ORACLE_HOME%\DATABASE  (Windows)
```

It is interesting to note that, in many cases, you will find the entire contents of this parameter file to be something like

```
IFILE='C:\oracle\admin\ora10g\pfile\init.ora'
```

The IFILE directive works in a similar fashion to an #include in C. It includes in the current file the contents of the named file. The preceding directive includes an init.ora file from a nondefault location.

It should be noted that the parameter file does not have to be in any particular location. When starting an instance, you may use the pfile=filename option to the startup command. This is most useful when you would like to try out different init.ora parameters on your database to see the effects of having different settings.

Legacy parameter files can be maintained by using any plain text editor. For example, on UNIX/Linux, I would use vi; on the many Windows operating system versions, I would use Notepad; and on a mainframe, I would perhaps use Xedit. It is important to note that you are fully responsible for editing and maintaining this file. There are no commands within the Oracle database itself that you can use to maintain the values contained in the init.ora file. For example, when you use the init.ora parameter file, the issue of an ALTER SYSTEM command to change the size of an SGA component would not be reflected as a permanent change in the init.ora file. If you would like that change to be made permanent—in other words, if you would like it to be the default for subsequent restarts of the database—it is up to you to make sure all init.ora parameter files that might be used to start this database are manually updated.

The last interesting point of note is that the legacy parameter file is not necessarily located on the database server. One of the reasons the stored parameter that we'll discuss shortly was introduced was to remedy this situation. The legacy parameter file must be present on the client machine attempting to start the database, meaning that if you run a UNIX server, but administer it using SQL*Plus installed on your Windows desktop machine over the network, then you would need the parameter file for the database on your desktop.

I still remember how I made the painful discovery that the parameter files are not stored on the server. This goes back many years to when a brand-new tool called SQL*DBA was introduced. This tool allowed us to perform remote operations (specifically, remote administrative operations). From my server (running SunOS at the time), I was able to connect remotely to a mainframe database server. I was also able to issue the "shutdown" command. However, it was at that point I realized that I was in a bit of a jam—when I tried to start up the instance, SQL*DBA would complain about not being able to find the parameter file. I learned that these parameter files—the init.ora plain text files—were located on the machine with the client, not on the server. SQL*DBA was looking for a parameter file on my local system with which to start the mainframe database. Not only did I have no such file, but I also had no idea what to put into one to get the system started up again! I didn't know the db_name or control file locations (even just getting the correct naming convention for the mainframe files would have been a bit of a stretch), and I didn't have access to log into the mainframe system itself. I've not made that same mistake since; it was a painful lesson to learn.

When DBAs realized that the init.ora parameter file had to reside on the client's machine that starts the database, it led to a proliferation of these files. Every DBA wanted to run the administrative tools from his desktop, and so every DBA needed a copy of the parameter file on his desktop machine. Tools such as Oracle Enterprise Manager (OEM) would add yet another parameter file to the mix. These tools would attempt to centralize the administration of all databases in an enterprise on a single machine, sometimes referred to as a "management server." This single machine would run software that would be used by all DBAs to start up, shut down, back up, and otherwise administer a database. That sounds like a perfect solution: centralize all parameters files in one location and use the GUI tools to perform all operations. But the reality is that sometimes it was much more convenient to issue the administrative startup command from within SQL*Plus on the database server machine itself during the course of some administrative task, so we ended up with multiple parameter files again: one on the management server and one on the database server. These parameter files would then proceed to get out of sync with each other, and people would wonder why the parameter change they made last month "disappeared," but seemingly randomly made a reappearance.

Enter the server parameter file (SPFILE), which can now be a single source of truth for the database.

Server Parameter Files (SPFILEs)

SPFILEs represent a fundamental change in the way Oracle accesses and now maintains parameter settings for the instance. An SPFILE removes the two serious issues associated with legacy parameter files:

- *It removes the proliferation of parameter files*. An SPFILE is always stored on the database server; the SPFILE must exist on the server machine itself and cannot be located on the client machine. This makes it practical to have a single source of "truth" with regard to parameter settings.

- *It removes the need (in fact, it removes the ability) to manually maintain parameter files using text editors outside of the database*. The ALTER SYSTEM command allows you to write values directly into the SPFILE. Administrators no longer have to find and maintain all of the parameter files by hand.

The naming convention for this file by default is

```
spfile$ORACLE_SID.ora      (Unix environment variable)
spfile%ORACLE_SID%.ora     (Windows environment variable)
```

I strongly recommend using the default location; doing otherwise defeats the simplicity SPFILEs represent. When an SPFILE is in its default location, everything is more or less done for you. Moving the SPFILE to a nondefault location involves you having to tell Oracle where to find the SPFILE, leading to the original problems of legacy parameter files all over again!

Converting to SPFILEs

Suppose we have a database that is using a legacy parameter file described previously. The move to an SPFILE is quite simple; we use the CREATE SPFILE command.

■**Note** You can also use a "reverse" command to create a parameter file (PFILE) from an SPFILE. (I'll explain shortly why you might want to do that.)

So, assuming we are using an init.ora parameter file, and that init.ora parameter file is in fact in the default location on the server, we simply issue the CREATE SPFILE command and restart our server instance:

```
sys@ORA10G> show parameter spfile;

NAME                                 TYPE        VALUE
------------------------------------ ----------- --------------------------------
spfile                               string
sys@ORA10G> create spfile from pfile;
File created.

sys@ORA10G> startup force;
ORACLE instance started.

Total System Global Area  603979776 bytes
Fixed Size                   780300 bytes
Variable Size             166729716 bytes
Database Buffers          436207616 bytes
Redo Buffers                 262144 bytes
Database mounted.
Database opened.
sys@ORA10G> show parameter spfile;

NAME                                 TYPE        VALUE
------------------------------------ ----------- --------------------------------
spfile                               string      /home/ora10g/dbs/spfileora10g.ora
```

The SHOW PARAMETER command was used here to show that initially we were not using an SPFILE, but after we created one and restarted the instance, we were in fact using one and it had the default name.

■**Note** In a clustered environment, using Oracle RAC, all instances share the same SPFILE, so this process of converting over to an SPFILE from a PFILE should be done in a controlled fashion. The single SPFILE can contain all of the parameter settings, even instance-specific settings in the single SPFILE, but you will have to merge all of the necessary parameter files into a single PFILE using the format that follows.

In a clustered environment, in order to convert from using individual PFILEs to a common SPFILE shared by all, you would merge your individual PFILEs into a single file resembling this:

```
*.cluster_database_instances=2
*.cluster_database=TRUE
*.cluster_interconnects='10.10.10.0'
*.compatible='10.1.0.2.0'
*.control_files='/ocfs/O10G/control01.ctl','/ocfs/O10G/control02.ctl'
*.db_name='O10G'
...
*.processes=150
*.undo_management='AUTO'
O10G1.instance_number=1
O10G2.instance_number=2
O10G1.local_listener='LISTENER_O10G1'
O10G2.local_listener='LISTENER_O10G2'
O10G1.remote_listener='LISTENER_O10G2'
O10G2.remote_listener='LISTENER_O10G1'
O10G1.thread=1
O10G2.thread=2
O10G1.undo_tablespace='UNDOTBS1'
O10G2.undo_tablespace='UNDOTBS2'
```

That is, parameter settings that are common to all instances in the cluster would start with *.. Parameter settings that are specific to a single instance, such as the INSTANCE_NUMBER and the THREAD of redo to be used, are prefixed with the instance name (the Oracle SID). In the preceding example,

- The PFILE would be for a two-node cluster with instances named O10G1 and O10G2.

- The *.db_name = 'O10G' assignment indicates that all instances using this SPFILE will be mounting a database named O10G.

- O10G1.undo_tablespace='UNDOTBS1' indicates that the instance named O10G1 will use that specific undo tablespace, and so on.

Setting Values in SPFILEs

Once our database is up and running on the SPFILE, the next question relates to how we set and change values contained therein. Remember, SPFILEs are binary files and we cannot just edit them using a text editor. The answer is to use the ALTER SYSTEM command, which has the following syntax (portions in <> are optional, and the presence of the pipe symbol indicates "one of the list"):

```
Alter system set parameter=value <comment='text'> <deferred>
              <scope=memory|spfile|both> <sid='sid'|*'>
```

The ALTER SYSTEM SET command, by default, will update the currently running instance *and* make the change to the SPFILE for you, greatly easing administration and removing the problems that arose when parameter settings were made via the ALTER SYSTEM command, but you forgot to update or missed an init.ora parameter file.

With that in mind, let's take a look at each element of the command:

- The parameter=value assignment supplies the parameter name and the new value for the parameter. For example, pga_aggregate_target = 1024m would set the PGA_AGGREGATE_TARGET parameter to a value of 1,024MB (1GB).

- comment='text' is an optional comment we may associate with this setting of the parameter. The comment will appear in the UPDATE_COMMENT field of the V$PARAMETER view. If we use the options to also save the change to the SPFILE, the comment will be written into the SPFILE and preserved across server restarts as well, so future restarts of the database will see the comment.

- deferred specifies whether the system change takes place for subsequent sessions only (not currently established sessions, including the one making the change). By default, the ALTER SYSTEM command will take effect immediately, but some parameters cannot be changed "immediately"—they can be changed only for newly established sessions. We can use the following query to see what parameters mandate the use of deferred:

```
ops$tkyte@ORA10G> select name
  2  from v$parameter
  3  where ISSYS_MODIFIABLE = 'DEFERRED';

NAME
-------------------------------
backup_tape_io_slaves
audit_file_dest
object_cache_optimal_size
object_cache_max_size_percent
sort_area_size
sort_area_retained_size
olap_page_pool_size

7 rows selected.
```

The code shows that SORT_AREA_SIZE is modifiable at the system level, but only in a deferred manner. The following code shows what happens if we try to modify its value with and without the deferred option:

```
ops$tkyte@ORA10G> alter system set sort_area_size = 65536;
alter system set sort_area_size = 65536
                                  *
ERROR at line 1:
ORA-02096: specified initialization parameter is not modifiable with this
option
```

```
ops$tkyte@ORA10G> alter system set sort_area_size = 65536 deferred;
System altered.
```

- `SCOPE=MEMORY|SPFILE|BOTH` indicates the "scope" of this parameter setting. We have the choice of setting the parameter value with the following:

  - `SCOPE=MEMORY` changes it in the instance(s) only; it will not survive a database restart. The next time you restart the database, the setting will be whatever it was before the change.

  - `SCOPE=SPFILE` changes the value in the SPFILE only. The change will not take place until the database is restarted and the SPFILE is processed again. Some parameters may only be changed using this option—for example, the processes parameter must use `SCOPE=SPFILE`, as we cannot change the active instance value.

  - `SCOPE=BOTH` means the parameter change takes place both in memory and in the SPFILE. The change will be reflected in the current instance and, the next time you restart, this change will still be in effect. *This is the default value for scope when using an SPFILE*. When using an `init.ora` parameter file, the default and only valid value is `SCOPE=MEMORY`.

- `sid='sid|*'` is mostly useful in a clustered environment; `sid='*'` is the default. This allows you to specify a parameter setting uniquely for any given instance in the cluster. Unless you are using Oracle RAC, you will not need to specify the `sid=` setting.

A typical use of this command is simply

```
ops$tkyte@ORA10G> alter system set pga_aggregate_target=1024m;
System altered.
```

or, better yet, perhaps, using the `COMMENT=` assignment to document when and why a particular change was made:

```
ops$tkyte@ORA10G> alter system set pga_aggregate_target=1024m
  2  comment = 'changed 01-jan-2005 as per recommendation of George';

System altered.

ops$tkyte@ORA10G> select value, update_comment
  2  from v$parameter
  3  where name = 'pga_aggregate_target';

VALUE
-----------------------------------------------------------------------
UPDATE_COMMENT
-----------------------------------------------------------------------
1073741824
changed 01-jan-2005 as per recommendation of George
```

Unsetting Values in SPFILEs

The next question that arises is, "OK, so we set a value, but we would now like to 'unset' it—in other words, we don't want that parameter setting in our SPFILE at all, and we would like it removed. Since we cannot edit the file using a text editor, how do we accomplish that?" This, too, is done via the ALTER SYSTEM command, but using the RESET clause:

```
Alter system reset parameter <scope=memory|spfile|both> sid='sid|*'
```

Here the SCOPE/SID settings have the same meaning as before, but the SID= component is not optional. The documentation in the *Oracle SQL Reference* manual is a bit misleading on this particular command, as it seems to indicate that it is only valid for RAC (clustered) databases. In fact, it states the following:

> The alter_system_reset_clause *is for use in a Real Application Clusters environment.*

Later, it does go on to state

> *In a non-RAC environment, you can specify SID=* '*' *for this clause.*

But this is a bit confusing. Nonetheless, this is the command we would use to "remove" a parameter setting from the SPFILE, allowing it to default. So, for example, if we wanted to remove the SORT_AREA_SIZE, to allow it to assume the default value we specified previously, we could do so as follows:

```
sys@ORA10G> alter system reset sort_area_size scope=spfile sid='*';
System altered.
```

The SORT_AREA_SIZE is removed from the SPFILE, a fact you can verify by issuing the following:

```
sys@ORA10G> create pfile='/tmp/pfile.tst' from spfile;
File created.
```

You can then review the contents of /tmp/pfile.tst, which will be generated on the database server. You will find the SORT_AREA_SIZE parameter does not exist in the parameter files anymore.

Creating PFILEs from SPFILEs

The CREATE PFILE...FROM SPFILE command from the previous section is the opposite of CREATE SPFILE. It takes the binary SPFILE and creates a plain text file from it—one that can be edited in any text editor and subsequently used to start up the database. You might use this command for at least two things on a regular basis:

- *To create a "one-time" parameter file used to start up the database for maintenance, with some special settings.* So, you would issue CREATE PFILE...FROM SPFILE and edit the resulting text PFILE, modifying the required settings. You would then start up the database, using the PFILE=<FILENAME> option to specify use of your PFILE instead of the SPFILE. After you are finished, you would just start up normally, and the database would use the SPFILE.

- *To maintain a history of commented changes.* In the past, many DBAs heavily commented their parameter files with a change history. If they changed the size of the buffer cache 20 times over the period of a year, for example, they would have 20 comments in front of the db_cache_size init.ora parameter setting, stating the date and reason for making the change. The SPFILE does not support this, but you can achieve the same effect if you get into the habit of doing the following:

```
sys@ORA10G> create pfile='init_01_jan_2005_ora10g.ora' from spfile;
File created.

sys@ORA10G> !ls -l $ORACLE_HOME/dbs/init_*
-rw-rw-r-- 1 ora10g ora10g   871 Jan  1 17:04 init_01_jan_2005_ora10g.ora
sys@ORA10G> alter system set pga_aggregate_target=1024m
2  comment = 'changed 01-jan-2005 as per recommendation of George';
```

In this way, your history will be saved in the series of parameter files over time.

Fixing Corrupted SPFILEs

The last question that comes up with regard to SPFILEs is, "SPFILEs are binary files, so what happens if one gets corrupted and the database won't start? At least the init.ora file was just text, so we could edit it and fix it." Well, SPFILEs shouldn't go corrupt any more than should a data file, redo log file, control file, and so forth. However, in the event that one does, you have a couple of options.

First, the amount of binary data in the SPFILE is very small. If you are on a UNIX platform, a simple strings command will extract all of your settings:

```
[tkyte@localhost dbs]$ strings spfile$ORACLE_SID.ora
*.compatible='10.1.0.2.0'
*.control_files='/home/ora10g/oradata/ora10g/control01.ctl','/home/ora10g/oradata/or
a10g/control02.ctl','/home/ora10g/oradata/ora10g/control03.ctl'
...
*.user_dump_dest='/home/ora10g/admin/ora10g/udump'
```

On Windows, simply open the file with write.exe (WordPad). WordPad will display for you all of the clear text in the file, and a simple cut and paste into init<ORACLE_SID>.ora will allow you to create a PFILE you can use to start your instance.

In the event that the SPFILE has just "gone missing" (for whatever reason—not that I have seen an SPFILE disappear), you can also resurrect the information for your parameter file from the database's alert log (more information on the alert log shortly). Every time you start the database, the alert log will contain a section like this:

```
System parameters with non-default values:
  processes               = 150
  timed_statistics        = TRUE
  shared_pool_size        = 67108864
  large_pool_size         = 8388608
  java_pool_size          = 33554432
  control_files           = C:\oracle\oradata\ora9ir2w\CONTROL01.CTL,
```

```
                        C:\oracle\oradata\ora9ir2w\CONTROL02.CTL,
                        C:\oracle\oradata\ora9ir2w\CONTROL03.CTL
....
  pga_aggregate_target      = 25165824
  aq_tm_processes           = 1
PMON started with pid=2
DBW0 started with pid=3
```

From this section, you can easily create a PFILE to be converted into a new SPFILE using the CREATE SPFILE command.

Parameter File Wrap-Up

In this section, we covered all of the basics of managing Oracle initialization parameters and parameter files. We looked at how to set parameters, view parameter values, and have those settings persist across database restarts. We explored the two types of database parameter files: legacy PFILEs (simple text files) and SPFILEs. For all existing databases, using SPFILEs is recommended for the ease of administration and clarity they bring to the table. The ability to have a single source of parameter "truth" for the database, coupled with the ability of the ALTER SYSTEM command to persist the parameter values, make SPFILEs a compelling feature. I started using them the instant they became available and haven't looked back.

Trace Files

Trace files are a source of debugging information. When the server encounters a problem, it generates a trace file full of diagnostic information. When a developer sets SQL_TRACE=TRUE, the server generates a trace file full of performance-related information. Trace files are available to us because Oracle is a heavily instrumented piece of software. By "instrumented," I mean that the programmers who wrote the database kernel put in debugging code—lots and lots of it. And they left it in, on purpose.

I've met many developers who consider debugging code to be overhead—something that must be ripped out before it goes into production in a vain attempt to squeeze every ounce of performance out of the code. Later, of course, they discover that their code has "a bug" or it "isn't running as fast as it should" (which end users tend to call "a bug" as well. To an end user, poor performance is a bug!). At that point, they are really wishing that the debug code was still in there (or had been in there if it never was), especially since they cannot drop debug code into the production system—that is an environment where new code must be tested first, not something you do at the drop of a hat.

The Oracle database (and Application Server and Oracle applications) is *heavily* instrumented. Signs of this instrumentation in the database are

- *V$ views*: Most V$ views contain "debug" information. V$WAITSTAT, V$SESSION_EVENT, and many others are there solely to let us know what is going on in the bowels of the kernel.

- *The auditing command*: This command allows you to specify what events the database should record for later analysis.

- *Resource Manager* (DBMS_RESOURCE_MANAGER): This feature allows you to micromanage resources (CPU, I/O, and the like) within the database. What makes a Resource Manager in the database a possibility is the fact that it has access to all of the runtime statistics describing how the resources are being used.

- *Oracle "events"*: These provide the ability for you to ask Oracle to produce trace or diagnostic information as needed.

- DBMS_TRACE: This facility within the PL/SQL engine exhaustively records the call tree of stored procedures, exceptions raised, and errors encountered.

- *Database event triggers*: These triggers, such as ON SERVERERROR, allow you to monitor and log any condition you feel is "exceptional" or out of the ordinary. For example, you can log the SQL that was running when an "out of temp space" error was raised.

- SQL_TRACE: The SQL Trace facility is also available in an extended fashion via the 10046 Oracle event.

. . . among others. Instrumentation is vital in application design and development, and the Oracle database becomes better instrumented with each release. In fact, the amount of additional instrumentation in the database between Oracle9*i* Release 2 and Oracle 10*g* Release 1 itself is phenomenal. Oracle 10*g* took code instrumentation in the kernel to a whole new level.

In this section we're going to focus on the information that can be found in various types of *trace files*. We'll cover what they are, where they are stored, and what we can do with them.

There are generally two types of trace file, and what we do with each kind is very different:

- *Trace files you expected and want*: For example, these are the result of enabling SQL_TRACE=TRUE. They contain diagnostic information about your session and will help you tune your application to optimize its performance and diagnose what bottlenecks it is experiencing.

- *Trace files you were not expecting to receive but the server generated as the result of an ORA-00600 "Internal Error", ORA-03113 "End of file on communication channel", or ORA-07445 "Exception Encountered" error*: These traces contain diagnostic information that is most useful to an Oracle Support analyst and, beyond showing us *where* in our application the internal error was raised, are of limited use to us.

Requested Trace Files

The trace files you expect to be most commonly generated as the result of setting SQL_TRACE=TRUE, or using the extended trace facility via the 10046 event, are as follows:

```
ops$tkyte@ORA10G> alter session set events
  2  '10046 trace name context forever, level 12';
Session altered.
```

File Locations

Whether you use SQL_TRACE or the extended trace facility, Oracle will start generating a trace file on the database server machine in one of two locations:

- If you are using a dedicated server connection, the trace file will be generated in the directory specified by the USER_DUMP_DEST parameter.

- If you are using a shared server connection, the trace file will be generated in the directory specified by the BACKGROUND_DUMP_DEST parameter.

To see where the trace files will go, you may either issue SHOW PARAMETER DUMP_DEST from SQL*Plus or query the V$PARAMETER view directly:

```
ops$tkyte@ORA10G> select name, value
  2  from v$parameter
  3  where name like '%dump_dest%'
  4  /

NAME                                VALUE
----------------------------------- ---------------------------------
background_dump_dest                /home/ora10g/admin/ora10g/bdump
user_dump_dest                      /home/ora10g/admin/ora10g/udump
core_dump_dest                      /home/ora10g/admin/ora10g/cdump
```

This shows the three dump (trace) destinations. Background dump destination is used by any "server" process (see Chapter 5 for a comprehensive list of Oracle background processes and their functions).

If you are using a shared server connection to Oracle, you are using a background process; hence the location of your trace files is defined by BACKGROUND_DUMP_DEST. If you are using a dedicated server connection, you are using a user or foreground process to interact with Oracle; hence your trace files will go in the directory specified by the USER_DUMP_DEST parameter. The CORE_DUMP_DEST parameter defines where a "core" file would be generated in the event of a serious Oracle internal error (such as a segmentation fault on UNIX) or if Oracle Support were to have to you generate one for additional debug information. In general, the two destinations of interest are the background and user dump destinations. As a note, unless otherwise stated, we will be using dedicated server connections in the course of this book.

In the event you do not have access to the V$PARAMETER view, you may use DBMS_UTILITY to access the values of most (but not all) parameters. The following example demonstrates that all you need is the CREATE SESSION privilege in order to, at the very least, see this information:

```
ops$tkyte@ORA10G> create user least_privs identified by least_privs;
User created.

ops$tkyte@ORA10G> grant create session to least_privs;
Grant succeeded.

ops$tkyte@ORA10G> connect least_privs/least_privs
Connected.
least_privs@ORA10G> declare
  2     l_string varchar2(255);
```

```
 3    l_dummy   number;
 4  begin
 5     l_dummy := dbms_utility.get_parameter_value
 6     ( 'background_dump_dest', l_dummy, l_string );
 7     dbms_output.put_line( 'background: ' || l_string );
 8     l_dummy := dbms_utility.get_parameter_value
 9     ( 'user_dump_dest', l_dummy, l_string );
10     dbms_output.put_line( 'user:        ' || l_string );
11  end;
12  /
background: /home/ora10g/admin/ora10g/bdump
user:        /home/ora10g/admin/ora10g/udump

PL/SQL procedure successfully completed.
```

Naming Convention

The trace file naming convention changes from time to time in Oracle, but if you have an example of a trace file name from your system, it is easy to see the template in use. For example, on my various servers, a trace file name looks as shown in Table 3-1.

Table 3-1. *Sample Trace File Names*

Trace File Name	Platform	Database Version
*ora10g*_ora_24574.trc	Linux	10*g* Release 1
*ora9ir2*_ora_24628.trc	Linux	9*i* Release 2
ora_10583.trc	Linux	9*i* Release 1
*ora9ir2w*_ora_688.trc	Windows	9*i* Release 2
*ora10g*_ora_1256.trc	Windows	10*g* Release 1

On my servers, the trace file name can be broken down as follows:

- The first part of the file name is the ORACLE_SID (with the exception of Oracle9*i* Release 1, where Oracle decided to leave that off).

- The next bit of the file name is just *ora*.

- The number in the trace file name is the process ID of your dedicated server, available to you from the V$PROCESS view.

Therefore, in practice (assuming dedicated server mode), you need access to four views:

- V$PARAMETER: To locate the trace file for USER_DUMP_DEST

- V$PROCESS: To find the process ID

- V$SESSION: To correctly identify your session's information in the other views

- V$INSTANCE: To get the ORACLE_SID

As noted earlier, you can use DBMS_UTILITY to find the location, and often you simply "know" the ORACLE_SID, so technically you need access to V$SESSION and V$PROCESS only, but for ease of use you would want access to all four.

A query, then, to generate your trace file name would be

```
ops$tkyte@ORA10G> alter session set sql_trace=true;
Session altered.

ops$tkyte@ORA10G> select c.value || '/' || d.instance_name ||
  2                       '_ora_' || a.spid || '.trc' trace
  3    from v$process a, v$session b, v$parameter c, v$instance d
  4   where a.addr = b.paddr
  5     and b.audsid = userenv('sessionid')
  6     and c.name = 'user_dump_dest'
  7  /

TRACE
--------------------------------------------------------------------------------
/home/ora10g/admin/ora10g/udump/ora10g_ora_24667.trc

ops$tkyte@ORA10G>
```

It should be obvious that on Windows you would replace the / with \. If you are using 9*i* Release 1, you would simply issue the following, instead of adding the instance name into the trace file name:

```
select c.value || 'ora_' || a.spid || '.trc'
```

Tagging Trace Files

There is a way to "tag" your trace file so that you can find it even if you are not permitted access to V$PROCESS and V$SESSION. Assuming you had access to read the USER_DUMP_DEST directory, you can use the session parameter TRACEFILE_IDENTIFIER. Using this, you may add a uniquely identifiable string to the trace file name, for example:

```
ops$tkyte@ORA10G> alter session set tracefile_identifier = 'Look_For_Me';
Session altered.

ops$tkyte@ORA10G> alter session set sql_trace=true;
Session altered.

ops$tkyte@ORA10G> !ls /home/ora10g/admin/ora10g/udump/*Look_For_Me*
/home/ora10g/admin/ora10g/udump/ora10g_ora_24676_Look_For_Me.trc

ops$tkyte@ORA10G>
```

As you can see, the trace file is now named in the standard <ORACLE_SID>_ora_ <PROCESS_ID> format, but it also has the unique string we specified associated with it, making it rather easy to find "our" trace file name.

Trace Files Generated in Response to Internal Errors

I'd like to close this section with a discussion about those *other* kinds of trace files—the ones we did not expect that were generated as a result of an ORA-00600 or some other internal error. Is there anything we can do with them?

The short answer is that in general, they are not for you and me. They are useful to Oracle Support. However, they can be useful when we are filing an iTAR with Oracle Support. That point is crucial: if you are getting internal errors, then the only way they will ever be corrected is if you file an iTAR. If you just ignore them, they will not get fixed by themselves, except by accident.

For example, in Oracle 10g Release 1, if you create the following table and run the query, you may well get an internal error (or not—it was filed as a bug and is corrected in later patch releases):

```
ops$tkyte@ORA10G> create table t ( x int primary key );
Table created.

ops$tkyte@ORA10G> insert into t values ( 1 );
1 row created.

ops$tkyte@ORA10G> exec dbms_stats.gather_table_stats( user, 'T' );
PL/SQL procedure successfully completed.

ops$tkyte@ORA10G> select count(x) over ()
  2    from t;
  from t
       *
ERROR at line 2:
ORA-00600: internal error code, arguments: [12410], [], [], [], [], [], [], []
```

Now, you are the DBA and all of a sudden this trace file pops up in the user dump destination. Or you are the developer and your application raises an ORA-00600 error and you want to find out what happened. There is a lot of information in that trace file (some 35,000 lines more in fact), but in general it is not useful to you and me. We would generally just compress the trace file and upload it as part of our iTAR processing.

However, there is some information in there that can help you track down the "who," "what," and "where" of the error, and also help you find out if the problem is something others have experienced—many times, the "why"—on http://metalink.oracle.com. A quick inspection of the very top of the trace file will provide you with some useful information, such as

```
Dump file c:\oracle\admin\ora10g\udump\ora10g_ora_1256.trc
Sun Jan 02 14:21:29 2005
ORACLE V10.1.0.3.0 - Production vsnsta=0
vsnsql=13 vsnxtr=3
Oracle Database 10g Enterprise Edition Release 10.1.0.3.0 - Production
With the Partitioning, OLAP and Data Mining options
Windows XP Version V5.1 Service Pack 2
CPU             : 1 - type 586
Process Affinity: 0x00000000
```

```
Memory (A/P)    : PH:11M/255M, PG:295M/1002M, VA:1605M/2047M
Instance name: ora10g
Redo thread mounted by this instance: 1
Oracle process number: 21
Windows thread id: 1256, image: ORACLE.EXE (SHAD)
```

The database information is important to have when you go to http://metalink.oracle.com to file the iTAR, of course, but it is also useful when you go to search http://metalink.oracle.com to see if this is a known problem. In addition, you can see the Oracle instance on which this error occurred. It is quite common to have many instances running concurrently, so isolating the problem to a single instance is useful.

```
*** 2005-01-02 14:21:29.062
*** ACTION NAME:() 2005-01-02 14:21:28.999
*** MODULE NAME:(SQL*Plus) 2005-01-02 14:21:28.999
*** SERVICE NAME:(SYS$USERS) 2005-01-02 14:21:28.999
```

This part of the trace file is new with Oracle 10*g* and won't be there in Oracle9*i*. It shows the session information available in the columns ACTION and MODULE from V$SESSION. Here we can see that it was a SQL*Plus session that caused the error to be raised (you and your developers can and should set the ACTION and MODULE information; some environments such as Oracle Forms and HTML DB do this already for you).

Additionally, we have the SERVICE NAME. This is the actual service name used to connect to the database—SYS$USERS, in this case—indicating we didn't connect via a TNS service. If we logged in using user/pass@ora10g.localdomain, we might see

```
*** SERVICE NAME:(ora10g) 2005-01-02 15:15:59.041
```

where ora10g is the service name (not the TNS connect string; rather, it's the ultimate service registered in a TNS listener to which it connected). This is also useful in tracking down which process/module is affected by this error.

Lastly, before we get to the actual error, we can see the session ID and related date/time information (all releases) as further identifying information:

```
*** SESSION ID:(146.2) 2005-01-02 14:21:28.999
```

Now we are ready to get into the error itself:

```
ksedmp: internal or fatal error
ORA-00600: internal error code, arguments: [12410], [], [], [], [], [], [], []
Current SQL statement for this session:
select count(x) over ()
  from t
----- Call Stack Trace -----
_ksedmp+524
_ksfdmp.160+14
_kgeriv+139
_kgesiv+78
_ksesic0+59
```

```
_qerixAllocate+4155
_qknRwsAllocateTree+281
_qknRwsAllocateTree+252
_qknRwsAllocateTree+252
_qknRwsAllocateTree+252
_qknDoRwsAllocate+9
...
```

Here we see a couple of important pieces of information. First, we find the SQL statement that was executing when the internal error was raised, which is very useful for tracking down what application(s) was affected. Also, since we see the SQL here, we can possibly start investigating possible work-arounds—trying different ways to code the SQL to see if we can quickly work around the issue while working the bug. Furthermore, we can cut and paste the offending SQL into SQL*Plus and see if we have a nicely reproducible test case for Oracle Support (these are the best kinds of test cases, of course).

The other important pieces of information are the error code (typically 600, 3113, or 7445) and other arguments associated with the error code. Using these, along with some of the stack trace information that shows the set of Oracle internal subroutines that were called in order, we might be able to find an existing bug (and work-arounds, patches, and so on). For example, we might use the search string

```
ora-00600 12410 ksesic0 qerixAllocate qknRwsAllocateTree
```

Using MetaLink's advanced search (using all of the words, search the bug database), we immediately find the bug 3800614, "ORA-600 [12410] ON SIMPLE QUERY WITH ANALYTIC FUNCTION". If we go to http://metalink.oracle.com and search using that text, we will discover this bug, see that it is fixed in the next release, and note that patches are available—all of that information is available to us. I find many times, the error I receive is an error that has happened before and there are in fact fixes or work-arounds for it.

Trace File Wrap-Up

You now know the two types of general trace files, where they are located, and how to find them. Hopefully, you'll use trace files mostly for tuning and increasing the performance of your application, rather than for filing iTARs. As a last note, Oracle Support does have access to many undocumented "events" that are very useful for dumping out tons of diagnostic information whenever the database hits any error. For example, if you believe you are getting an ORA-01555 when you absolutely feel you should not be, Oracle Support can guide you through the process of setting such diagnostic events in order to help you track down precisely why that error is getting raised, by creating a trace file every time that error is encountered.

Alert File

The alert file (also known as the *alert log*) is the diary of the database. It is a simple text file written to from the day the database is "born" (created) to the end of time (until you erase it). In this file, you will find a chronological history of your database—the log switches; the internal errors that might be raised; when tablespaces were created, taken offline, put back online;

and so on. It is an incredibly useful file for seeing the history of a database. I like to let mine grow fairly large before "rolling" (archiving) them. The more information the better, I believe, for this file.

I will not describe everything that goes into an alert log—that is a fairly broad topic. I encourage you to take a look at yours, however, and see the wealth of information that is in there. Instead, in this section we'll take a look at a specific example of how to mine information from this alert log, in this case to create an uptime report.

I recently used the alert log file for the http://asktom.oracle.com website and to generate an uptime report for my database. Instead of poking through the file and figuring that out manually (the shutdown and startup times are in there), I decided to take advantage of the database and SQL to automate this, thus creating a technique for creating a dynamic uptime report straight from the alert log.

Using an EXTERNAL TABLE (which is covered in much more detail Chapter 10), we can actually query our alert log and see what is in there. I discovered that a pair of records was produced in my alert log every time I started the database:

```
Thu May  6 14:24:42 2004
Starting ORACLE instance (normal)
```

That is, a timestamp record, in that constant fixed width format, coupled with the message Starting ORACLE instance. I also noticed that before these records there would either be an ALTER DATABASE CLOSE message (during a clean shutdown) or a shutdown abort message, or "nothing"—no message, indicating a system crash. But any message would have some timestamp associated with it as well. So, as long as the system didn't "crash," some meaningful timestamp would be recorded in the alert log (and in the event of a system crash, some timestamp would be recorded shortly before the crash, as the alert log is written to quite frequently).

I noticed that I could easily generate an uptime report if I

- Collected all of the records like Starting ORACLE instance %

- Collected all of the records that matched the date format (that were in fact dates)

- Associated with each Starting ORACLE instance record the prior two records (which would be dates)

The following code creates an external table to make it possible to query the alert log. (Note: replace /background/dump/dest/ with your actual background dump destination and use your alert log name in the CREATE TABLE statement.)

```
ops$tkyte@ORA10G> create or replace directory data_dir as '/background/dump/dest/'
  2  /
Directory created.

ops$tkyte@ORA10G> CREATE TABLE alert_log
  2  (
  3      text_line varchar2(255)
  4  )
  5  ORGANIZATION EXTERNAL
```

```
 6  (
 7      TYPE ORACLE_LOADER
 8      DEFAULT DIRECTORY data_dir
 9      ACCESS PARAMETERS
10      (
11          records delimited by newline
12          fields
13          REJECT ROWS WITH ALL NULL FIELDS
14      )
15      LOCATION
16      (
17          'alert_AskUs.log'
18      )
19  )
20  REJECT LIMIT unlimited
21  /
Table created.
```

We can now query that information anytime:

```
ops$tkyte@ORA10G> select to_char(last_time,'dd-mon-yyyy hh24:mi') shutdown,
  2          to_char(start_time,'dd-mon-yyyy hh24:mi') startup,
  3          round((start_time-last_time)*24*60,2) mins_down,
  4          round((last_time-lag(start_time) over (order by r)),2) days_up,
  5          case when (lead(r) over (order by r) is null )
  6              then round((sysdate-start_time),2)
  7          end days_still_up
  8    from (
  9  select r,
 10          to_date(last_time, 'Dy Mon DD HH24:MI:SS YYYY') last_time,
 11          to_date(start_time,'Dy Mon DD HH24:MI:SS YYYY') start_time
 12    from (
 13  select r,
 14          text_line,
 15          lag(text_line,1) over (order by r) start_time,
 16          lag(text_line,2) over (order by r) last_time
 17    from (
 18  select rownum r, text_line
 19    from alert_log
 20   where text_line like '__ ___ __ __:__:__ 20__'
 21      or text_line like 'Starting ORACLE instance %'
 22          )
 23          )
 24   where text_line like 'Starting ORACLE instance %'
 25          )
 26  /
```

SHUTDOWN	STARTUP	MINS_DOWN	DAYS_UP	DAYS_STILL_UP
	06-may-2004 14:00			
06-may-2004 14:24	06-may-2004 14:24	.25	.02	
10-may-2004 17:18	10-may-2004 17:19	.93	4.12	
26-jun-2004 13:10	26-jun-2004 13:10	.65	46.83	
07-sep-2004 20:13	07-sep-2004 20:20	7.27	73.29	116.83

I won't go into the nuances of the SQL query here, but the innermost query from lines 18 through 21 collect the "Starting" and date lines (remember, when using a LIKE clause, _ matches precisely one character—at least one and at most one). It also "numbers" the lines using ROWNUM. Then, the next level of query uses the built-in LAG() analytic function to reach back one and two rows for each row, and slide that data up so the third row of this query has the data from rows 1, 2, and 3. Row 4 has the data from rows 2, 3, and 4, and so on. We end up keeping just the rows that were like Starting ORACLE instance %, which now have the two preceding timestamps associated with them. From there, computing downtime is easy: we just subtract the two dates. Computing the uptime is not much harder (now that you've seen the LAG() function): we just reach back to the prior row, get its startup time, and subtract that from this line's shutdown time.

My Oracle 10g database came into existence on May 6 and it has been shut down four times (and as of this writing it has been up for 116.83 days in a row). The average uptime is getting better and better over time (and hey, it is SQL—we could easily compute that now, too).

If you are interested in seeing another example of mining the alert log for useful information, go to http://asktom.oracle.com/~tkyte/alert_arch.html. This page shows a demonstration of how to compute the average time it took to archive a given online redo log file. Once you understand what is in the alert log, generating these queries on your own becomes easy.

Data Files

Data files, along with redo log files, are the most important set of files in the database. This is where all of your data will ultimately be stored. Every database has at least one data file associated with it, and typically it will have many more than one. Only the most simple "test" database will have one file. In fact, in Chapter 2 we saw the most simple CREATE DATABASE command by default created a database with two data files: one for the SYSTEM tablespace (the true Oracle data dictionary) and one for the SYSAUX tablespace (where other nondictionary objects are stored in version 10g and above). Any real database, however, will have at least three data files: one for the SYSTEM data, one for SYSAUX data, and one for USER data.

After a brief review of file system types, we'll discuss how Oracle organizes these files and how data is organized within them. To understand this, you need to know what a tablespace, segment, extent, and block are. These are the units of allocation that Oracle uses to hold objects in the database, and I describe them in detail shortly.

A Brief Review of File System Mechanisms

There are four file system mechanisms in which to store *your* data in Oracle. By *your* data, I mean your data dictionary, redo, undo, tables, indexes, LOBs, and so on—the data you personally care about at the end of the day. Briefly, they are

- *"Cooked" operating system (OS) file systems*: These are files that appear in the file system just like your word processing documents do. You can see them in Windows Explorer; you can see them in UNIX as the result of an ls command. You can use simple OS utilities such as xcopy on Windows or cp on UNIX to move them around. Cooked OS files are historically the "most popular" method for storing data in Oracle, but I personally expect to see that change with the introduction of ASM (more on that in a moment). Cooked file systems are typically *buffered* as well, meaning that the OS will cache information for you as you read and, in some cases, write to disk.

- *Raw partitions*: These are not files—these are raw disks. You do not ls them; you do not review their contents in Windows Explorer. They are just big sections of disk without any sort of file system on them. The entire raw partition appears to Oracle as a single large file. This is in contrast to a cooked file system, where you might have many dozens or even hundreds of database data files. Currently, only a small percentage of Oracle installations use raw partitions due to their perceived administrative overhead. Raw partitions are not buffered devices—all I/O performed on them is a direct I/O, without any OS buffering of data (which, for a database, is generally a positive attribute).

- *Automatic Storage Management (ASM)*: This is a new feature of Oracle 10g Release 1 (for both Standard and Enterprise editions). ASM is a file system designed exclusively for use by the database. An easy way to think about it is as a database file system. You won't store your shopping list in a text file on this file system—you'll store only database-related information here: your tables, indexes, backups, control files, parameter files, redo logs, archives, and more. But even in ASM, the equivalent of a data file exists; conceptually, data is still stored in files, but the file system is ASM. ASM is designed to work in either a single machine or clustered environment.

- *Clustered file system*: This is specifically for a RAC (clustered) environment and provides for the appearance of a cooked file system that is shared by many nodes (computers) in a clustered environment. A traditional cooked file system is usable by only one computer is a clustered environment. So, while it is true that you could NFS mount or Samba share (a method of sharing disks in a Windows/UNIX environment similar to NFS) a cooked file system among many nodes in a cluster, it represents a single point of failure. In the event that the node owning the file system and performing the sharing was to fail, then that file system would be unavailable. The Oracle Cluster File System (OCFS) is Oracle's offering in this area and is currently available for Windows and Linux only. Other third-party vendors do provide certified clustered file systems that work with Oracle as well. The clustered file system brings the comfort of a cooked file system to a clustered environment.

The interesting thing is that a database might consist of files from any and all of the preceding file systems—you don't need to pick just one. You could have a database whereby portions of the data were stored in conventional cooked file systems, some on raw partitions, others in ASM, and yet other components in a clustered file system. This makes it rather easy to move from technology to technology, or to just get your feet wet in a new file system type without moving the entire database into it. Now, since a full discussion of file systems and all of their detailed attributes is beyond the scope of this particular book, we'll dive back into the Oracle file types. Regardless of whether the file is stored on cooked file systems, in raw partitions, within ASM, or on a clustered file system, the following concepts always apply.

The Storage Hierarchy in an Oracle Database

A database is made up of one or more tablespaces. A *tablespace* is a logical storage container in Oracle that comes at the top of the storage hierarchy and is made up of one or more data files. These files might be cooked files in a file system, raw partitions, ASM-managed database files, or files on a clustered file system. A tablespace contains segments, as described next.

Segments

We will start our examination of the storage hierarchy by looking at segments, which are the major organizational structure within a tablespace. *Segments* are simply your database objects that consume storage—objects such as tables, indexes, rollback segments, and so on. When you create a table, you create a table segment. When you create a partitioned table, you create a segment per partition. When you create an index, you create an index segment, and so on. Every object that consumes storage is ultimately stored in a single segment. There are rollback segments, temporary segments, cluster segments, index segments, and so on.

■Note It might be confusing to read "Every object that consumes storage is ultimately stored in a single segment." You will find many CREATE statements that create mulitsegment objects. The confusion lies in the fact that a single CREATE statement may ultimately create objects that consist of zero, one, or *more* segments! For example, CREATE TABLE T (x int primary key, y clob) will create four segments: one for the TABLE T, one for the index that will be created in support of the primary key, and two for the CLOB (one segment for the CLOB is the LOB index and the other segment is the LOB data itself). On the other hand, CREATE TABLE T (x int, y date) cluster MY_CLUSTER, will create no segments. We'll explore this concept further in Chapter 10.

Extents

Segments themselves consist of one or more extent. An *extent* is a logically contiguous allocation of space in a file (files themselves, in general, are not contiguous on disk; otherwise, we would never need a disk defragmentation tool!). Also, with disk technologies such as

Redundant Array of Independent Disks (RAID), you might find a single file is not only not contiguous on a single disk, but also spans many physical disks. Every segment starts with at least one extent, and some objects may require at least two (rollback segments are an example of a segment that require at least two extents). For an object to grow beyond its initial extent, it will request another extent be allocated to it. This second extent will not necessarily be located right next to the first extent on disk—it may very well not even be allocated in the same file as the first extent. The second extent may be located very far away from the first extent, but the space within an extent is always logically contiguous in a file. Extents vary in size from one Oracle data block to 2GB.

Blocks

Extents, in turn, consist of blocks. A *block* is the smallest unit of space allocation in Oracle. Blocks are where your rows of data, or index entries, or temporary sort results will be stored. A block is what Oracle generally reads from and writes to disk. Blocks in Oracle are generally one of four common sizes: 2KB, 4KB, 8KB, or 16KB (although 32KB is also permissible in some cases; there are restrictions in place as to the maximum size by operating system).

■**Note** Here's a little-known fact: the default block size for a database does not have to be a power of two. Powers of two are just a convention commonly used. You can, in fact, create a database with a 5KB, 7KB, or *n*KB block size, where *n* is between 2KB and 32KB. I do not advise making use of this fact in real life, though— stick with 2KB, 4KB, 8KB, or 16KB as your block size.

The relationship between segments, extents, and blocks is shown in Figure 3-1.

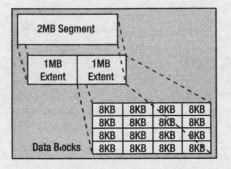

Figure 3-1. *Segments, extents, and blocks*

A segment is made up of one or more extents, and an extent is a contiguous allocation of blocks. Starting with Oracle9*i* Release 1, a database may have up to six different block sizes in it.

> **Note** This feature of multiple block sizes was introduced for the purpose of making transportable table-spaces usable in more cases. The ability to transport a tablespace allows a DBA to move or copy the already formatted data files from one database and attach them to another—for example, to immediately copy all of the tables and indexes from an Online Transaction Processing (OLTP) database to a Data Warehouse (DW). However, in many cases, the OLTP database might be using a small block size, such as 2KB or 4KB, whereas the DW would be using a much larger one (8KB or 16KB). Without support for multiple block sizes in a single database, you would not be able to transport this information. Tablespaces with multiple block sizes should be used to facilitate transporting tablespaces and are not generally used for anything else.

There will be the database default block size, which is the size that was specified in the initialization file during the CREATE DATABASE command. The SYSTEM tablespace will have this default block size always, but you can then create other tablespaces with nondefault block sizes of 2KB, 4KB, 8KB, 16KB and, depending on the operating system, 32KB. The total number of block sizes is six if and only if you specified a nonstandard block size (not a power of two) during database creation. Hence, for all practical purposes, a database will have at most five block sizes: the default size and then four other nondefault sizes.

Any given tablespace will have a *consistent block size*, meaning that every block in that tablespace will be the same size. A multisegment object, such as a table with a LOB column, may have each segment in a tablespace with a different block size, but any given segment (which is contained in a tablespace) will consist of blocks of exactly the same size. All blocks, regardless of their size, have the same general format, which looks something like Figure 3-2.

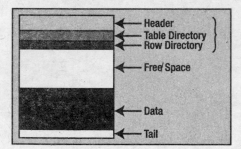

Figure 3-2. *The structure of a block*

The *block header* contains information about the type of block (table block, index block, and so on), transaction information when relevant (only blocks that are transaction managed have this information—a temporary sort block would not, for example) regarding active and past transactions on the block, and the address (location) of the block on the disk. The next two block components, table directory and row directiry, are found on the most common types of database blocks, those of HEAP organized tables. We'll cover database table types in much more detail in Chapter 10, but suffice it to say that most tables are of this type. The *table directory*, if present, contains information about the tables that store rows in this block (data from more than one table may be stored on the same block). The *row directory* contains information describing the rows that are to be found on the block. This is an array of pointers to where the rows are to be found in the data portion of the block. These three pieces of the block are collectively known as the *block overhead*, which is space used on the block that is not available for your data, but rather is used by Oracle to manage the block itself. The remaining two pieces of the block are straightforward: there will possibly be *free* space on a block, and then there will generally be *used* space that is currently storing data.

Now that you have a cursory understanding of segments, which consist of extents, which consist of blocks, let's take a closer look at tablespaces and then at exactly how files fit into the big picture.

Tablespaces

As noted earlier, a tablespace is a container—it holds segments. Each and every segment belongs to exactly one tablespace. A tablespace may have many segments within it. All of the extents for a given segment will be found in the tablespace associated with that segment. Segments never cross tablespace boundaries. A tablespace itself has one or more data files associated with it. An extent for any given segment in a tablespace will be contained entirely within one data file. However, a segment may have extents from many different data files. Graphically, a tablespace might look like Figure 3-3.

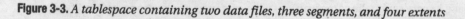

Figure 3-3. *A tablespace containing two data files, three segments, and four extents*

Figure 3-3 shows a tablespace named USER_DATA. It consists of two data files, user_data01 and user_data02. It has three segments allocated it: T1, T2, and I1 (probably two tables and an index). The tablespace has four extents allocated in it, and each extent is depicted as a logically contiguous set of database blocks. Segment T1 consists of two extents, one extent in each file. Segments T2 and I1 each have one extent depicted. If we need more space in this tablespace, we could either resize the data files already allocated to the tablespace or we could add a third data file to it.

Tablespaces are a logical storage container in Oracle. As developers, we will create segments in tablespaces. We will never get down to the raw "file level"—we do not specify that we want our extents to be allocated in a specific file (we can, but we do not in general). Rather, we create objects in tablespaces, and Oracle takes care of the rest. If at some point in the future, the DBA decides to move our data files around on disk to more evenly distribute I/O, that is OK with us. It will not affect our processing at all.

Storage Hierarchy Summary

In summary, the hierarchy of storage in Oracle is as follows:

1. A *database* is made up of one or more tablespaces.

2. A *tablespace* is made up of one or more data files. These files might be cooked files in a file system, raw partitions, ASM managed database files, or a file on a clustered file system. A tablespace contains segments.

3. A *segment* (TABLE, INDEX, and so on) is made up of one or more extents. A segment exists in a tablespace, but may have data in many data files within that tablespace.

4. An *extent* is a logically contiguous set of blocks on disk. An extent is in a single tablespace and, furthermore, is always in a single file within that tablespace.

5. A *block* is the smallest unit of allocation in the database. A block is the smallest unit of I/O used by a database.

Dictionary-Managed and Locally-Managed Tablespaces

Before we move on, we will look at one more topic related to tablespaces: how extents are managed in a tablespace. Prior to Oracle 8.1.5, there was only one method to manage the allocation of extents within a tablespace: a *dictionary-managed tablespace*. That is, the space within a tablespace was managed in data dictionary tables, in much the same way you would manage accounting data, perhaps with a DEBIT and CREDIT table. On the debit side, we have all of the extents allocated to objects. On the credit side, we have all of the free extents available for use. When an object needed another extent, it would ask the system to get one. Oracle would then go to its data dictionary tables, run some queries, find the space (or not), and then update a row in one table (or remove it all together) and insert a row into another. Oracle managed space in very much the same way you will write your applications: by modifying data and moving it around.

This SQL, executed on your behalf in the background to get the additional space, is referred to as *recursive SQL*. Your SQL INSERT statement caused other recursive SQL to be executed to get more space. This recursive SQL can be quite expensive if it is done frequently. Such updates to the data dictionary must be serialized; they cannot be done simultaneously. They are something to be avoided.

In earlier releases of Oracle, we would see this space management issue—this recursive SQL overhead—most often occurring in temporary tablespaces (this was before the introduction of "real" temporary tablespaces created via the CREATE TEMPORARY TABLESPACE command). Space would frequently be allocated (we would have to delete from one dictionary table and insert into another) and de-allocated (we would put the rows we just moved back where they were initially). These operations would tend to serialize, dramatically decreasing concurrency and increasing wait times. In version 7.3, Oracle introduced the concept of a *true temporary tablespace*, a new tablespace type dedicated to just storing temporary data, to help alleviate this issue. Prior to this special tablespace type, temporary data was managed in the same tablespaces as persistent data and treated in much the same way as permanent data was.

A temporary tablespace was one in which you could create no permanent objects of your own. This was fundamentally the only difference; the space was still managed in the data dictionary tables. However, once an extent was allocated in a temporary tablespace, the system would hold on to it (i.e., it would not give the space back). The next time someone requested space in the temporary tablespace for any purpose, Oracle would look for an already allocated extent in its internal list of allocated extents. If it found one there, it would simply reuse it, or else it would allocate one the old-fashioned way. In this manner, once the database had been up and running for a while, the temporary segment would appear full but would actually just be "allocated." The free extents were all there; they were just being managed differently. When someone needed temporary space, Oracle would look for that space in an in-memory data structure, instead of executing expensive, recursive SQL.

In Oracle 8.1.5 and later, Oracle goes a step further in reducing this space management overhead. It introduced the concept of a *locally-managed tablespace* as opposed to a *dictionary-managed* one. Local management of space effectively did for all tablespaces what Oracle 7.3 did for temporary tablespaces: it removed the need to use the data dictionary to manage space in a tablespace. With a locally-managed tablespace, a bitmap stored in each data file is used to manage the extents. Now to get an extent, all the system needs to do is set a bit to 1 in the bitmap. To free space, the system sets a bit back to 0. Compared to using dictionary-managed tablespaces, this is incredibly fast. We no longer serialize for a long-running operation at the database level for space requests across all tablespaces. Rather, we serialize at the tablespace level for a very fast operation. Locally-managed tablespaces have other nice attributes as well, such as the enforcement of a uniform extent size, but that is starting to get heavily into the role of the DBA.

Going forward, the only storage management method you should be using is a locally-managed tablespace. In fact, in Oracle9*i* and above, if you create a database using the database configuration assistant (DBCA), it will create SYSTEM as a locally-managed tablespace, and if SYSTEM is locally managed, *all other tablespaces in that database will be locally managed as well, and the legacy dictionary-managed method will not work.* It is not that dictionary-managed tablespaces are not supported in a database where SYSTEM is locally managed, it is that they simply cannot be created:

```
ops$tkyte@ORA10G> create tablespace dmt
  2   datafile '/tmp/dmt.dbf' size 2m
  3   extent management dictionary;
create tablespace dmt
*
ERROR at line 1:
ORA-12913: Cannot create dictionary managed tablespace

ops$tkyte@ORA10G> !oerr ora 12913
12913, 00000, "Cannot create dictionary managed tablespace"
// *Cause: Attempt to create dictionary managed tablespace in database
//         which has system tablespace as locally managed
// *Action: Create a locally managed tablespace.
```

This is a positive side effect, as it prohibits you from using the legacy storage mechanism, which was less efficient and dangerously prone to fragmentation. Locally-managed tablespaces, in addition to being more efficient in space allocation *and* de-allocation, also prevent tablespace fragmentation from occurring. This is a side effect of the way space is allocated and managed in locally-managed tablespaces. We'll take an in-depth look at this in Chapter 10.

Temp Files

Temporary data files (*temp files*) in Oracle are a special type of data file. Oracle will use temporary files to store the intermediate results of a large sort operation and hash operations, as well as to store global temporary table data, or result set data, when there is insufficient memory to hold it all in RAM. Permanent data objects, such as a table or an index, will never be stored in a temp file, but the contents of a temporary table and its indexes would be. So, you'll never create your application tables in a temp file, but you might store data there when you use a temporary table.

Temp files are treated in a special way by Oracle. Normally, each and every change you make to an object will be recorded in the redo logs; these transaction logs can be replayed at a later date in order to "redo a transaction," which you might do during recovery from failure, for example. Temp files are excluded from this process. Temp files never have redo generated for them, although they can have undo generated. Thus, there will be redo generated working with temporary tables since UNDO is always protected by redo, as you will see in detail in Chapter 9. The undo generated for global temporary tables is in order to support rolling back some work you have done in your session, either due to an error processing data or because of some general transaction failure. A DBA never needs to back up a temporary data file, and in fact to attempt to do so would be a waste of time, as you can never restore a temporary data file.

It is recommended that your database be configured with locally-managed temporary tablespaces. You'll want to make sure that as a DBA, you use a CREATE TEMPORARY TABLESPACE command. You do not want to just alter a permanent tablespace to a temporary one, as you do not get the benefits of temp files that way.

One of the nuances of true temp files is that if the OS permits it, the temporary files will be created *sparse*—that is, they will not actually consume disk storage until they need to. You can see that easily in this example (on Red Hat Linux in this case):

```
ops$tkyte@ORA10G> !df
Filesystem           1K-blocks     Used Available Use% Mounted on
/dev/hda2            74807888  41999488  29008368  60% /
/dev/hda1              102454     14931     82233  16% /boot
none                 1030804         0   1030804   0% /dev/shm

ops$tkyte@ORA10G> create temporary tablespace temp_huge
  2  tempfile '/d01/temp/temp_huge' size 2048m
  3  /

Tablespace created.

ops$tkyte@ORA10G> !df
Filesystem           1K-blocks     Used Available Use% Mounted on
/dev/hda2            74807888  41999616  29008240  60% /
/dev/hda1              102454     14931     82233  16% /boot
none                 1030804         0   1030804   0% /dev/shm
```

■Note df is a Unix command to show "disk free." This command showed that I have 29,008,368KB free in the file system containing /d01/temp before I added a 2GB temp file to the database. After I added that file, I had 29,008,240KB free in the file system.

Apparently it took only 128KB of storage to hold that file. But if we ls it

```
ops$tkyte@ORA10G> !ls -l /d01/temp/temp_huge
-rw-rw----   1 ora10g   ora10g   2147491840 Jan  2 16:34 /d01/temp/temp_huge
```

it appears to be a normal 2GB file, but it is in fact only consuming some 128KB of storage. The reason I point this out is because we would be able to actually create hundreds of these 2GB temporary files, even though we have roughly 29GB of disk space free. Sounds great—free storage for all! The problem is as we start to use these temp files and they start expanding out, we would rapidly hit errors stating "no more space." Since the space is allocated or physically assigned to the file as needed by the OS, we stand a definite chance of running out of room (especially if after we create the temp files someone else fills up the file system with other stuff).

How to solve this differs from OS to OS. On Linux, some of the options are to use dd to fill the file with data, causing the OS to physically assign disk storage to the file, or use cp to create a nonsparse file, for example:

```
ops$tkyte@ORA10G> !cp --sparse=never /d01/temp/temp_huge /d01/temp/temp_huge2

ops$tkyte@ORA10G> !df
Filesystem           1K-blocks     Used Available Use% Mounted on
/dev/hda2            74807888 44099336  26908520  63% /
/dev/hda1              102454    14931     82233  16% /boot
none                 1030804        0   1030804   0% /dev/shm

ops$tkyte@ORA10G> drop tablespace temp_huge;

Tablespace dropped.

ops$tkyte@ORA10G> create temporary tablespace temp_huge
  2  tempfile '/d01/temp/temp_huge2' reuse;

Tablespace created.

ops$tkyte@ORA10G> !df
Filesystem           1K-blocks     Used Available Use% Mounted on
/dev/hda2            74807888 44099396  26908460  63% /
/dev/hda1              102454    14931     82233  16% /boot
none                 1030804        0   1030804   0% /dev/shm
```

After copying the sparse 2GB file to /d01/temp/temp_huge2 and creating the temporary tablespace using that temp file with the REUSE option, we are assured that temp file has allocated all of its file system space and our database actually has 2GB of temporary space to work with.

■**Note** In my experience, Windows NTFS does not do sparse files, and this applies to UNIX/Linux variants. On the plus side, if you have to create a 15GB temporary tablespace on UNIX/Linux and have temp file support, you'll find it goes very fast (instantaneous), but just make sure you have 15GB free and reserve it in your mind.

Control Files

The *control file* is a fairly small file (it can grow up to 64MB or so in extreme cases) that contains a directory of the other files Oracle needs. The parameter file tells the instance where the control files are, and the control files tell the instance where the database and online redo log files are.

The control files also tell Oracle other things, such as information about checkpoints that have taken place, the name of the database (which should match the DB_NAME parameter), the timestamp of the database as it was created, an archive redo log history (this can make a control file large in some cases), RMAN information, and so on.

Control files should be multiplexed either by hardware (RAID) or by Oracle when RAID or mirroring is not available. More than one copy of them should exist, and they should be stored on separate disks, to avoid losing them in the event you have a disk failure. It is not fatal to lose your control files—it just makes recovery that much harder.

Control files are something a developer will probably never have to actually deal with. To a DBA they are an important part of the database, but to a software developer they are not extremely relevant.

Redo Log Files

Redo log files are crucial to the Oracle database. These are the transaction logs for the database. They are generally used only for recovery purposes, but they can be used for the following as well:

- Instance recovery after a system crash

- Media recovery after a data file restore from backup

- Standby database processing

- Input into Streams, a redo log mining process for information sharing (a fancy way of saying replication)

Their *main* purpose in life is to be used in the event of an instance or media failure, or as a method of maintaining a standby database for failover. If the power goes off on your database machine, causing an instance failure, Oracle will use the online redo logs to restore the system to exactly the point it was at immediately prior to the power outage. If your disk drive containing your data file fails permanently, Oracle will use archived redo logs, as well as online redo logs, to recover a backup of that drive to the correct point in time. Additionally, if you "accidentally" drop a table or remove some critical information and commit that operation, you can restore a backup and have Oracle restore it to the point immediately prior to the accident using these online and archive redo log files.

Virtually every operation you perform in Oracle generates some amount of redo to be written to the online redo log files. When you insert a row into a table, the end result of that insert is written to the redo logs. When you delete a row, the fact that you deleted that row is written. When you drop a table, the effects of that drop are written to the redo log. The data from the table you dropped is not written; however, the recursive SQL that Oracle performs to drop the table does generate redo. For example, Oracle will delete a row from the SYS.OBJ$ table (and other internal dictionary objects), and this will generate redo, and if various modes of *supplemental logging* are enabled, the actual DROP TABLE statement will be written into the redo log stream.

Some operations may be performed in a mode that generates as little redo as possible. For example, I can create an index with the NOLOGGING attribute. This means that the initial creation of the index data will not be logged, but any recursive SQL Oracle performed on my behalf will be. For example, the insert of a row into SYS.OBJ$ representing the existence of the index will be logged, as will all subsequent modifications of the index using SQL inserts, updates, and deletes. But the initial writing of the index structure to disk will not be logged.

I've referred to two types of redo log file: *online* and *archived*. We'll take a look at each in the sections that follow. In Chapter 9, we'll take another look at redo in conjunction with rollback segments, to see what impact they have on you as the developer. For now, we'll just concentrate on what they are and what their purpose is.

Online Redo Log

Every Oracle database has at least two online redo log file groups. Each redo log group consists of one or more redo log members (redo is managed in groups of members). The individual redo log file members of these groups are true mirror images of each other. These online redo log files are fixed in size and are used in a circular fashion. Oracle will write to log file group 1, and when it gets to the end of this set of files, it will switch to log file group 2 and rewrite the contents of those files from start to end. When it has filled log file group 2, it will switch back to log file group 1 (assuming we have only two redo log file groups; if we have three, it would, of course, proceed to the third group). This is shown in Figure 3-4.

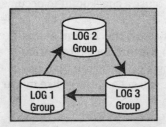

Figure 3-4. *Log file groups*

The act of switching from one log file group to the other is called a *log switch*. It is important to note that a log switch may cause a temporary "pause" in a poorly configured database. Since the redo logs are used to recover transactions in the event of a failure, we must assure ourselves that we won't need the contents of a redo log file in the event of a failure before we reuse it. If Oracle isn't sure that it won't need the contents of a log file, it will suspend operations in the database momentarily and make sure that the data in the cache that this redo "protects" is safely written (checkpointed) onto disk itself. Once Oracle is sure of that, processing will resume and the redo file will be reused.

We've just started to talk about a key database concept: *checkpointing.* To understand how online redo logs are used, you'll need to know something about checkpointing, how the database buffer cache works, and what a process called *data block writer* (DBWn) does. The database buffer cache and DBWn are covered in more detail a little later on, but we'll skip ahead a little anyway and touch on them now.

The *database buffer cache* is where database blocks are stored temporarily. This is a structure in the SGA of Oracle. As blocks are read, they are stored in this cache, hopefully to allow us to not have to physically reread them later. The buffer cache is first and foremost a performance-tuning device. It exists solely to make the very slow process of physical I/O appear to be much faster than it is. When we modify a block by updating a row on it, these modifications are done in memory, to the blocks in the buffer cache. Enough information to redo this modification is stored in the redo log buffer, another SGA data structure. When we COMMIT our modifications, making them permanent, Oracle does not go to all of the blocks we modified in the SGA and write them to disk. Rather, it just writes the contents of the redo log buffer out to the online redo logs. As long as that modified block is in the buffer cache and is not on disk, we need the contents of that online redo log in the event the database fails. If at the instant after we committed, the power was turned off, the database buffer cache would be wiped out.

If this happens, the only record of our change is in that redo log file. Upon restart of the database, Oracle will actually replay our transaction, modifying the block again in the same way we did and committing it for us. So, as long as that modified block is cached and not written to disk, we cannot reuse that redo log file.

This is where DBWn comes into play. This Oracle background process is responsible for making space in the buffer cache when it fills up and, more important, for performing *checkpoints*. A checkpoint is the writing of dirty (modified) blocks from the buffer cache to disk. Oracle does this in the background for us. Many things can cause a checkpoint to occur, the most common event being a redo log switch.

As we filled up log file 1 and switched to log file 2, Oracle initiated a checkpoint. At this point in time, DBWn started writing to disk all of the dirty blocks that are protected by log file group 1. Until DBWn flushes all of these blocks protected by that log file, Oracle cannot reuse it. If we attempt to use it before DBWn has finished its checkpoint, we will get a message like this in our database's ALERT log:

```
...
Thread 1 cannot allocate new log, sequence 66
Checkpoint not complete
  Current log# 2 seq# 65 mem# 0: C:\ORACLE\ORADATA\ORA10G\REDO02.LOG
...
```

So, at the point in time when this message appeared, processing was suspended in the database while DBWn hurriedly finished its checkpoint. Oracle gave all the processing power it could to DBWn at that point in the hope it would finish faster.

This is a message you never want to see in a nicely tuned database instance. If you do see it, you know for a fact that you have introduced artificial, unnecessary waits for your end users. This can always be avoided. The goal (and this is for the DBA, not the developer neces- sarily) is to have enough online redo log files allocated so that you never attempt to reuse a log file before the checkpoint initiated by it completes. If you see this message frequently, it means a DBA has not allocated sufficient online redo logs for the application, or that DBWn needs to be tuned to work more efficiently.

Different applications will generate different amounts of redo log. A Decision Support System (DSS, query only) or DW system will naturally generate significantly less online redo log than an OLTP (transaction processing) system would, day to day. A system that does a lot of image manipulation in Binary Large Objects (BLOBs) in the database may generate radi- cally more redo than a simple order-entry system. An order-entry system with 100 users will probably generate a tenth the amount of redo 1,000 users would generate. There is no "right" size for your redo logs, although you do want to ensure they are large enough for your unique workload.

You must take many things into consideration when setting both the size of and the num- ber of online redo logs. Many of them are beyond the scope of this particular book, but I'll list some of them to give you an idea:

- *Peak workloads*: You would like your system to not have to wait for checkpoint not-
  complete messages, to not get bottlenecked during your peak processing. You will be
  sizing your redo logs not for "average" hourly throughput, but rather for your peak processing. If you generate 24GB of log per day, but 10GB of that log is generated between
  9:00 am and 11:00 am, you'll want to size your redo logs large enough to carry you
  through that two-hour peak. Sizing them for an average of 1GB per hour would probably not be sufficient.

- *Lots of users modifying the same blocks*: Here you might want large redo log files. Since
  everyone is modifying the same blocks, you would like to update them as many times
  as possible before writing them out to disk. Each log switch will fire a checkpoint, so
  you would like to switch logs infrequently. This may, however, affect your recovery time.

- *Mean time to recover*: If you must ensure that a recovery takes as little time as possible,
  you may be swayed toward smaller redo log files, even if the previous point is true. It
  will take less time to process one or two small redo log files than a gargantuan one
  upon recovery. The overall system will run slower than it absolutely could day to day
  perhaps (due to excessive checkpointing), but the amount of time spent in recovery
  will be shorter. There are other database parameters that may also be used to reduce
  this recovery time, as an alternative to the use of small redo log files.

Archived Redo Log

The Oracle database can run in one of two modes: ARCHIVELOG mode and NOARCHIVELOG mode. The difference between these two modes is simply what happens to a redo log file when Oracle goes to reuse it. "Will we keep a copy of that redo or should Oracle just overwrite it, losing it forever?" is an important question to answer. Unless you keep this file, you cannot recover data from a backup to the current point in time.

Say you take a backup once a week on Saturday. Now, on Friday afternoon, after you have generated hundreds of redo logs over the week, your hard disk fails. If you have not been running in ARCHIVELOG mode, the only choices you have right now are as follows:

- Drop the tablespace(s) associated with the failed disk. Any tablespace that had a file on that disk must be dropped, including the contents of that tablespace. If the SYSTEM tablespace (Oracle's data dictionary) is affected, you cannot do this.

- Restore last Saturday's data and lose all of the work you did that week.

Neither option is very appealing. Both imply that you lose data. If you had been executing in ARCHIVELOG mode, on the other hand, you simply would have found another disk. You would have restored the affected files from Saturday's backup onto it. Lastly, you would have applied the archived redo logs and, ultimately, the online redo logs to them (in effect replaying the week's worth of transactions in fast-forward mode). You lose nothing. The data is restored to the point in time of the failure.

People frequently tell me they don't need ARCHIVELOG mode for their production systems. I have yet to meet anyone who was correct in that statement. I believe that a system is not a production system unless it is in ARCHIVELOG mode. A database that is not in ARCHIVELOG mode will, some day, *lose data*. It is inevitable; you will lose data if your database is not in ARCHIVELOG mode.

"We are using RAID-5, so we are totally protected" is a common excuse. I've seen cases where, due to a manufacturing error, all disks in a RAID set froze, all at about the same time. I've seen cases where the hardware controller introduced corruption into the data files, so they safely protected *corrupt* data with their RAID devices. RAID also does not do anything to protect you from operator error, one of the most common causes of data loss.

"If we had the backups from before the hardware or operator error and the archives were not affected, we could have recovered." The bottom line is that there is no excuse for not being in ARCHIVELOG mode on a system where the data is of any value. Performance is no excuse; properly configured archiving adds little to no overhead. This and the fact that a "fast system" that "loses data" is useless would make it so that even if archiving added 100 percent overhead, you would need to do it. A feature is overhead if you can remove it and lose nothing important; overhead is like icing on the cake. Preserving your data, and making sure you don't lose you data isn't overhead—it's the DBA's primary job!

Only a test or development system should execute in NOARCHIVELOG mode. Don't let anyone talk you out of being in ARCHIVELOG mode. You spent a long time developing your application, so you want people to trust it. Losing their data will not instill confidence in your system.

■Note There are some cases in which a large DW could justify being in NOARCHIVELOG mode if it made judicious use of READ ONLY tablespaces and was willing to fully rebuild any READ WRITE tablespace that suffered a failure by reloading the data.

Password Files

The *password file* is an optional file that permits remote SYSDBA or administrator access to the database.

When you attempt to start up Oracle, there is no database available that can be consulted to verify passwords. When you start up Oracle on the "local" system (i.e., not over the network, but from the machine the database instance will reside on), Oracle will use the OS to perform the authentication.

When Oracle was installed, the person performing the installation was asked to specify the "group" for the administrators. Normally on UNIX/Linux, this group will be DBA by default and OSDBA on Windows. It can be any legitimate group name on that platform, however. That group is "special," in that any user in that group can connect to Oracle "as SYSDBA" without specifying a username or password. For example, in my Oracle 10*g* Release 1 install, I specified an ora10g group. Anyone in the ora10g group may connect without a username/password:

```
[ora10g@localhost ora10g]$ sqlplus / as sysdba
SQL*Plus: Release 10.1.0.3.0 - Production on Sun Jan 2 20:13:04 2005
Copyright (c) 1982, 2004, Oracle.  All rights reserved.
Connected to:
Oracle Database 10g Enterprise Edition Release 10.1.0.3.0 - Production
With the Partitioning, OLAP and Data Mining options

SQL> show user
USER is "SYS"
```

That worked—I'm connected, and I could now start up this database, shut it down, or perform whatever administration I wanted to. However, suppose I wanted to perform these operations from another machine, over the network. In that case, I would attempt to connect using @tns-connect-string. However, this would fail:

```
[ora10g@localhost admin]$ sqlplus /@ora10g_admin.localdomain as sysdba
SQL*Plus: Release 10.1.0.3.0 - Production on Sun Jan 2 20:14:20 2005
Copyright (c) 1982, 2004, Oracle.  All rights reserved.
ERROR:
ORA-01031: insufficient privileges

Enter user-name:
```

OS authentication won't work over the network for SYSDBA, even if the very unsafe (for security reasons) parameter REMOTE_OS_AUTHENT is set to TRUE. So, OS authentication won't work and, as discussed earlier, if you're trying to start up an instance to mount and open a database, then there by definition is "no database" at the other end of the connection yet, in which to look up authentication details. It is the proverbial chicken and egg problem. Enter the *password file*. The password file stores a list of usernames and passwords that are allowed to remotely authenticate as SYSDBA over the network. Oracle must use this file to authenticate them and not the normal list of passwords stored in the database.

So, let's correct our situation. First, we'll start up the database locally so we can set the REMOTE_LOGIN_PASSWORDFILE. Its default value is NONE, meaning there is no password file; there are no "remote SYSDBA logins." It has two other settings: SHARED (more than one database can use the same password file) and EXCLUSIVE (only one database uses a given password file). We'll set ours to EXCLUSIVE, as we want to use it for only one database (i.e., the normal use):

```
SQL> alter system set remote_login_passwordfile=exclusive scope=spfile;
System altered.
```

This setting cannot be changed dynamically while the instance is up and running, so we'll have to restart for this to take effect. The next step is to use the command-line tool (on UNIX and Windows) named orapwd:

```
[ora10g@localhost dbs]$ orapwd
Usage: orapwd file=<fname> password=<password> entries=<users> force=<y/n>

  where
    file - name of password file (mand),
    password - password for SYS (mand),
    entries - maximum number of distinct DBA and  OPERs (opt),
    force - whether to overwrite existing file (opt),
There are no spaces around the equal-to (=) character.
```

to create and populate the initial password file. The command we'll use is

```
$ orapwd file=orapw$ORACLE_SID password=bar entries=20
```

That created a password file named orapwora10g in my case (my ORACLE_SID is ora10g). That is the naming convention for this file on most UNIX platforms (see your installation/OS admin guide for details on the naming of this file on your platform), and it resides in the $ORACLE_HOME/dbs directory. On Windows, this file is named PW%ORACLE_SID%.ora and is located in the %ORACLE_HOME%\database directory.

Now, currently the *only* user in that file is in fact the user SYS, even if there are other SYSDBA accounts on that database (they are not in the password file yet). Using that knowledge, however, we can for the first time connect as SYSDBA over the network:

```
[ora10g@localhost dbs]$ sqlplus sys/bar@ora10g_admin.localdomain as sysdba
SQL*Plus: Release 10.1.0.3.0 - Production on Sun Jan 2 20:49:15 2005
Copyright (c) 1982, 2004, Oracle.  All rights reserved.
Connected to an idle instance.
SQL>
```

We have been authenticated, so we are in—we can now successfully start up, shut down, and remotely administer this database using the SYSDBA account. Now, we have another user, OPS$TKYTE, who has been granted SYSDBA, but will not be able to connect remotely yet:

```
[ora10g@localhost dbs]$ sqlplus 'ops$tkyte/foo' as sysdba
SQL*Plus: Release 10.1.0.3.0 - Production on Sun Jan 2 20:51:07 2005
Copyright (c) 1982, 2004, Oracle.  All rights reserved.
Connected to:
Oracle Database 10g Enterprise Edition Release 10.1.0.3.0 - Production
With the Partitioning, OLAP and Data Mining options
SQL> show user
```

```
USER is "SYS"
SQL> exit
[ora10g@localhost dbs]$ sqlplus 'ops$tkyte/foo@ora10g_admin.localdomain' as sysdba
SQL*Plus: Release 10.1.0.3.0 - Production on Sun Jan 2 20:52:57 2005
Copyright (c) 1982, 2004, Oracle.  All rights reserved.
ERROR:
ORA-01031: insufficient privileges
Enter user-name:
```

The reason for that is that OPS$TKYTE is not yet in the password file. In order to get OPS$TKYTE into the password file, we need to "regrant" that account SYSDBA:

```
SQL> grant sysdba to ops$tkyte;
Grant succeeded.

Disconnected from Oracle Database 10g
Enterprise Edition Release 10.1.0.3.0 - Production
With the Partitioning, OLAP and Data Mining options
[ora10g@localhost dbs]$ sqlplus 'ops$tkyte/foo@ora10g_admin.localdomain' as sysdba
SQL*Plus: Release 10.1.0.3.0 - Production on Sun Jan 2 20:57:04 2005
Copyright (c) 1982, 2004, Oracle.  All rights reserved.
Connected to:
Oracle Database 10g Enterprise Edition Release 10.1.0.3.0 - Production
With the Partitioning, OLAP and Data Mining options
```

That created an entry in the password file for us, and Oracle will now keep the password "in sync." If OPS$TKYTE alters his password, the old one will cease working for remote SYSDBA connections and the new one will start:

```
SQL> alter user ops$tkyte identified by bar;
User altered.

[ora10g@localhost dbs]$ sqlplus 'ops$tkyte/foo@ora10g_admin.localdomain' as sysdba
SQL*Plus: Release 10.1.0.3.0 - Production on Sun Jan 2 20:58:36 2005
Copyright (c) 1982, 2004, Oracle.  All rights reserved.
ERROR:
ORA-01017: invalid username/password; logon denied

Enter user-name: ops$tkyte/bar@ora10g_admin.localdomain as sysdba
Connected to:
Oracle Database 10g Enterprise Edition Release 10.1.0.3.0 - Production
With the Partitioning, OLAP and Data Mining options
SQL> show user
USER is "SYS"
SQL>
```

The same process is repeated for any user that was a SYSDBA but is not yet in the password file.

Change Tracking File

The change tracking file is a new, optional file for use with Oracle 10g Enterprise Edition. The sole purpose of this file is to track what blocks have modified since the last incremental backup. In this fashion, the Recovery Manager (RMAN) tool can back up only the database blocks that have actually been modified without having to read the entire database.

In releases prior to Oracle 10g, an incremental backup would have had to read the entire set of database files to find blocks that had been modified since the last incremental backup. So, if you had a 1TB database to which you simply added 500MB of new data (e.g., a data warehouse load), the incremental backup would have read 1TB of data to find that 500MB of new information to backup. So, the incremental backup would have stored significantly less data in the backup, and it would have still read the entire database.

In Oracle 10g Enterprise Edition, that is no longer the case. As Oracle is running, and as blocks are modified, Oracle will optionally maintain a file that tells RMAN what blocks have been changed. The process of creating this change tracking file is rather simple and is accomplished via the ALTER DATABASE command:

```
ops$tkyte@ORA10GR1> alter database enable block change tracking
  2  using file
  3  '/home/ora10gr1/product/10.1.0/oradata/ora10gr1/ORA10GR1/changed_blocks.bct';
Database altered.
```

▪**Caution** I'll say this from time to time throughout the book: please bear in mind that commands that set parameters, change the database, and make fundamental changes should not be done lightly, and definitely should be tested prior to performing them on your "real" system. The preceding command will, in fact, cause the database to do more work. It will consume resources.

To turn off and remove the block change tracking file, you would use the ALTER DATABASE command once again:

```
ops$tkyte@ORA10GR1> alter database disable block change tracking;
Database altered.

ops$tkyte@ORA10GR1> !ls -l /home/ora10gr1/.../changed_blocks.bct
ls: /home/ora10gr1/.../changed_blocks.bct: No such file or directory
```

Note that that command *will in fact erase* the block change tracking file. It does not just disable the feature—it removes the file as well. You can enable this new block change tracking feature in either ARCHIVELOG or NOARCHIVELOG mode. But remember, a database in NOARCHIVELOG mode, where the redo log generated daily is not retained, cannot recover all changes in the event of a media (disk/device) failure! A NOARCHIVELOG mode database will lose data some day. We will cover these two database modes in more detail in Chapter 9.

Flashback Log Files

Flashback log files (or simply *flashback logs*) were introduced in Oracle 10*g* in support of the FLASHBACK DATABASE command, a new feature of the Enterprise Edition of the database. Flashback logs contain "before images" of modified database blocks that can be used to return the database to the way it was at some prior point in time.

Flashback Database

The FLASHBACK DATABASE command was introduced to speed up the otherwise slow process of a point in time database recovery. It can be used in place of a full database restore and a rolling forward using archive logs, and it is primarily designed to speed up the recovery from an "accident." For example, let's take a look at what a DBA might do to recover from an "accidentally" dropped schema, in which the right schema was dropped, just in the wrong database (it was meant to be dropped in the test environment). The DBA recognizes immediately the mistake he has made and immediately shuts down the database. Now what?

Prior to the flashback database capability, what would probably happen is this:

1. The DBA would shut down the database.

2. The DBA would restore the last full backup of database from tape (typically). This is generally a long process.

3. The DBA would restore all archive redo logs generated since the backup that were not available on the system.

4. The DBA would roll the database forward and stop rolling forward at a point in time just before the erroneous DROP USER command.

5. The database would be opened with the RESETLOGS option.

This was a nontrivial process with many steps and would generally consume a large piece of time (time where no one would be accessing the database, of course). The causes of a point in time recovery like this are many: an upgrade script gone awry, an upgrade gone bad, an inadvertent command issued by someone with the privilege to issue it (a mistake, probably the most frequent cause), or some process introducing data integrity issues into a large database (again, an accident; maybe it was run twice instead of just once, or maybe it had a bug). Whatever the reason, the net effect was a large period of downtime.

The steps to recover in Oracle 10*g* Enterprise Edition, assuming you configured the flashback database capability, would be as follows:

1. The DBA shuts down the database.

2. The DBA startup-mounts the database and issues the flashback database command, using either an SCN, the Oracle internal clock, or a timestamp (wall clock time), which would be accurate to within a couple of seconds.

3. The DBA opens the database with resetlogs.

To use this feature, the database must be in ARCHIVELOG mode and must have been set up to enable the FLASHBACK DATABASE command. What I'm trying to say is that you need to have set up this capability prior to having a need to use it. It is not something you can enable after the damage is done; you must make a conscious decision to use it.

Flash Recovery Area

The Flash Recovery Area is a new concept in Oracle 10g. For the first time in many years (over 25 years), the basic concept behind database backups has changed in Oracle. In the past, the design of backup and recovery in the database was built around the concept of a sequential medium, such as a tape device. That is, random access devices (disk drives) were always considered too expensive to waste for mere backups. You used relatively inexpensive tape devices with large storage capacities.

Today, however, you can buy terabytes of disk storage at a very low cost. In fact, by 2007, HP intends to ship *desktop computers with terabyte disk drives*. I remember my first hard drive on my personal computer: a whopping 40MB. I actually had to partition it into two logical disks because the OS I was using (MS-DOS at the time) could not recognize a disk larger than 32MB. Things have certainly changed in the last 20 years.

The Flash Recovery Area in Oracle 10g is a new location where Oracle will manage many of the files related to database backup and recovery. In this area (an *area* being a set-aside area of disk for this purpose; a directory, for example), you could find

- Copies of data files on disk

- Incremental backups of your database

- Redo logs (archived redo logs)

- Control files and backups of control files

- Flashback logs

This new area is used to allow Oracle to manage these files, for the server to have knowledge of what is on disk and what is not on disk (and perhaps on tape elsewhere). Using this information, the database can perform operations like a disk-to-disk restore of a damaged data file or the flashing back (a "rewind" operation) of the database to undo an operation that should not have taken place. For example, you could use the flashback database command to put the database back the way it was five minutes ago (without doing a full restore of the database and a point in time recovery). That would allow you to "undrop" that accidentally dropped user account.

The Flash Recovery Area is more of a "logical" concept. It is a holding area for the file types discussed in this chapter. Its use is optional—you do not need to use it—but if you want to use some advanced features such as the Flashback Database, you must use this area to store the information.

DMP Files (EXP/IMP Files)

Export and Import are venerable Oracle data extraction and load tools that have been around for many versions. Export's job is to create a platform-independent DMP file that contains all of the required metadata (in the form of CREATE and ALTER statements), and optionally the data itself to re-create tables, schemas, or even entire databases. Import's sole job in life is to read these DMP files, and execute the DDL statements and load any data it finds.

DMP files are designed to be *backward-compatible*, meaning that newer releases can read older releases' DMP files and process them successfully. I have heard of people exporting a version 5 database and successfully importing it into Oracle 10*g* (just as a test!). So Import can read older version DMP files and process the data therein. The converse, however, is most definitely not true: the Import process that comes with Oracle9*i* Release 1 cannot—will not—successfully read a DMP file created by Oracle9*i* Release 2 or Oracle 10*g* Release 1. For example, I exported a simple table from both Oracle 10*g* Release 1 and Oracle9*i* Release 2. Upon trying to use these DMP files in Oracle9*i* Release 1, I soon discovered Oracle9*i* Release 1 import will not even attempt to process the Oracle 10*g* Release 1 DMP file:

```
[tkyte@localhost tkyte]$ imp userid=/ full=y file=10g.dmp
Import: Release 9.0.1.0.0 - Production on Sun Jan 2 21:08:56 2005
(c) Copyright 2001 Oracle Corporation.  All rights reserved.
Connected to: Oracle9i Enterprise Edition Release 9.0.1.0.0 - Production
With the Partitioning option
JServer Release 9.0.1.0.0 - Production
IMP-00010: not a valid export file, header failed verification
IMP-00000: Import terminated unsuccessfully
```

When processing the Oracle9*i* Release 2 file, things are not that much better:

```
[tkyte@localhost tkyte]$ imp userid=/ full=y file=9ir2.dmp
Import: Release 9.0.1.0.0 - Production on Sun Jan 2 21:08:42 2005
(c) Copyright 2001 Oracle Corporation.  All rights reserved.
Connected to: Oracle9i Enterprise Edition Release 9.0.1.0.0 - Production
With the Partitioning option
JServer Release 9.0.1.0.0 - Production

Export file created by EXPORT:V09.02.00 via conventional path
import done in WE8ISO8859P1 character set and AL16UTF16 NCHAR character set
. importing OPS$TKYTE's objects into OPS$TKYTE
IMP-00017: following statement failed with ORACLE error 922:
 "CREATE TABLE "T" ("X" NUMBER(*,0))  PCTFREE 10 PCTUSED 40 INITRANS 1 MAXTRA"
 "NS 255 STORAGE(INITIAL 65536 FREELISTS 1 FREELIST GROUPS 1) TABLESPACE "USE"
 "RS" LOGGING NOCOMPRESS"
IMP-00003: ORACLE error 922 encountered
ORA-00922: missing or invalid option
Import terminated successfully with warnings.
```

While 9*i* Release 1 tried to read the file, it could not process the DDL contained therein. In Oracle9*i* Release 2 a new feature, *table compression*, was added. Hence Export in that version started adding NOCOMPRESS or COMPRESS as a keyword to each and every CREATE TABLE statement. The DDL from Oracle9*i* Release 2 does not work in Oracle9*i* Release 1.

If, however, I use the Oracle9*i* Release 1 Export tool against either Oracle9*i* Release 2 or Oracle 10*g* Release 1, I will get a valid DMP file that can be successfully imported into Oracle9*i* Release 1. So, the rule with DMP files is that they must be created by a version of Export that is *less than or equal to* the version of Import that will be used against them. To import data in Oracle9*i* Release 1, you must use Oracle9*i* Release 1's Export (or you could use a version 8*i* Export process as well; the DMP file must be created by a release of Export less than or equal to Oracle9*i* Release 1).

These DMP files are platform independent, so you can safely take an Export from any platform, transfer it to another, and import it (as long as the versions of Oracle permit). One caveat, however, with Windows and FTPing of files is that Windows will consider a DMP file a "text" file by default and will tend to convert linefeeds (the end-of-line marker on UNIX) into carriage return/linefeed pairs, thus totally corrupting the DMP file. When FTPing a DMP file in Windows, make sure you're doing a binary transfer, and if the import won't work, check the source and target file sizes to make sure they're the same. I can't recall how many times this issue has brought things to a screeching halt while the file has to be retransferred.

DMP files are binary files, meaning you won't be editing them to change them. You can extract a large amount of information from them—CREATE DDL, and more—but you won't be editing them in a text editor (or any sort of editor, actually). In the first edition of *Expert One-on-One Oracle* (which you as owner of the second edition have full access to in electronic form), I spent a great deal of time discussing the Import and Export utilities and working with DMP files. As these tools are falling out of favor, in place of the infinitely more flexible Data Pump utilities, I'll defer a full discussion of how to manipulate them, extract data from them, and use them in general to the online first edition.

Data Pump Files

Data Pump is a file format used by at least two tools in Oracle 10g. External tables can load and *unload* data in the Data Pump format, and the new import/export tools IMPDP and EXPDP use this file format much in the way IMP and EXP used the DMP file format.

■**Note** The Data Pump format is exclusive to Oracle 10*g* Release 1 and above—it did not exist in any Oracle9*i* release, nor can it be used with that release.

Pretty much all of the same caveats that applied to DMP files mentioned previously will apply over time to Data Pump files as well. They are cross-platform (portable) binary files that contain metadata (not stored in CREATE/ALTER statements, but rather in XML) and possibly data. That they use XML as a metadata representation structure is actually relevant to you and I as end users of the tools. IMPDP and EXPDP have some sophisticated filtering and translation capabilities never before seen in the IMP/EXP tools of old. This is in part due to the use of XML and the fact that a CREATE TABLE statement is not stored as a CREATE TABLE, but rather as a marked-up document. This permits easy implementation of a request like "Please replace all references to tablespace FOO with tablespace BAR." When the metadata was stored in the DMP file as CREATE/ALTER statements, the Import utility would have had to basically parse each SQL statement before executing it in order to accomplish this feat (something it does not do).

IMPDP, however, just has to apply a simple XML transformation to accomplish the same—FOO, when it refers to a TABLESPACE, would be surrounded by <TABLESPACE>FOO</TABLESPACE> tags (or some other representation).

The fact that XML is used has allowed the EXPDP and IMPDP tools to literally leapfrog the old EXP and IMP tools with regard to their capabilities. In Chapter 15, we'll take a closer look at these tools in general. Before we get there, however, let's see how we can use this Data Pump format to quickly extract some data from database A and move it to database B. We'll be using an "external table in reverse" here.

External tables, originally introduced in Oracle9*i* Release 1, gave us the ability to read flat files—plain old text files—as if they were database tables. We had the full power of SQL to process them. They were read-only and designed to get data from outside Oracle in. External tables in Oracle 10*g* Release 1 and above can go the other way: they can be used to get data out of the database in the Data Pump format to facilitate moving the data to another machine, another platform. To start this exercise, we'll need a DIRECTORY object, telling Oracle the location to unload to:

```
ops$tkyte@ORA10G> create or replace directory tmp as '/tmp'
  2  /
Directory created.
```

Next, we'll unload the data from the ALL_OBJECTS view. It could be from any arbitrary query, involving any set of tables or SQL constructs we want:

```
ops$tkyte@ORA10G> create table all_objects_unload
  2  organization external
  3  ( type oracle_datapump
  4    default directory TMP
  5    location( 'allobjects.dat' )
  6  )
  7  as
  8  select * from all_objects
  9  /
Table created.
```

And that literally is all there is to it: we have a file in /tmp named allobjects.dat that contains the contents of the query select * from all_objects. We can peek at this information:

```
ops$tkyte@ORA10G> !head /tmp/allobjects.dat
.........Linuxi386/Linux-2.0.34-8.1.0WE8ISO8859P1..........
<?xml version="1.0"?>
<ROWSET>
 <ROW>
  <STRMTABLE_T>
   <VERS_MAJOR>1</VERS_MAJOR>
   <VERS_MINOR>0 </VERS_MINOR>
   <VERS_DPAPI>3</VERS_DPAPI>
   <ENDIANNESS>0</ENDIANNESS>
   <CHARSET>WE8ISO8859P1</CHARSET>
```

That is just the *head*, or top, of the file; binary data is represented by the .... (don't be surprised if your terminal "beeps" at you when you look at this data). Now, using a binary FTP (same caveat as for a DMP file!), I moved this allobject.dat file to a Windows XP server and created a directory object to map to it:

```
tkyte@ORA10G> create or replace directory TMP as 'c:\temp\'
  2  /
Directory created.
```

Then I created a table that points to it:

```
tkyte@ORA10G> create table t
  2  ( OWNER          VARCHAR2(30),
  3    OBJECT_NAME    VARCHAR2(30),
  4    SUBOBJECT_NAME VARCHAR2(30),
  5    OBJECT_ID      NUMBER,
  6    DATA_OBJECT_ID NUMBER,
  7    OBJECT_TYPE    VARCHAR2(19),
  8    CREATED        DATE,
  9    LAST_DDL_TIME  DATE,
 10    TIMESTAMP      VARCHAR2(19),
 11    STATUS         VARCHAR2(7),
 12    TEMPORARY      VARCHAR2(1),
 13    GENERATED      VARCHAR2(1),
 14    SECONDARY      VARCHAR2(1)
 15  )
 16  organization external
 17  ( type oracle_datapump
 18    default directory TMP
 19    location( 'allobjects.dat' )
 20  )
 21  /
Table created.
```

And now I'm able to query the data unloaded from the other database immediately:

```
tkyte@ORA10G> select count(*) from t;

  COUNT(*)
----------
     48018
```

That is the power of the Data Pump file format: immediate transfer of data from system to system over "sneaker net" if need be. Think about that the next time you'd like to take a subset of data home to work with over the weekend while testing.

One thing that wasn't obvious here was that the character sets were different between these two databases. If you notice in the preceding head output, the character set of my Linux database WE8ISO8859P1 was encoded into the file. My Windows server has this:

```
tkyte@ORA10G> select *
  2  from nls_database_parameters
  3  where parameter = 'NLS_CHARACTERSET';

PARAMETER                        VALUE
-------------------------------- -----------------
NLS_CHARACTERSET                 WE8MSWIN1252
```

Oracle has the ability now to recognize the differing character sets due to the Data Pump file format and deal with them. Character-set conversion can be performed on the fly as needed to make the data "correct" in each database's representation.

Again, we'll come back to the Data Pump file format in Chapter 15, but this section should give you an overall feel for what it is about and what might be contained in the file.

Flat Files

Flat files have been around since the dawn of electronic data processing. We see them literally every day. The alert log described previously is a flat file.

I found these definitions for "flat file" on the Web and feel they pretty much wrap it up:

> *An electronic record that is stripped of all specific application (program) formats. This allows the data elements to be migrated into other applications for manipulation. This mode of stripping electronic data prevents data loss due to hardware and proprietary software obsolescence.*[1]

> *A computer file where all the information is run together in a signal character string.*[2]

A flat file is simply a file whereby each "line" is a "record," and each line has some text delimited, typically by a comma or pipe (vertical bar). Flat files are easily read by Oracle using either the legacy data-loading tool SQLLDR or external tables—in fact, I will cover this in detail in Chapter 15 (external tables are also covered in Chapter 10). Flat files, however, are not something produced so easily by Oracle—for whatever reason, there is no simple command-line tool to export information in a flat file. Tools such as HTMLDB and Enterprise Manager facilitate this process, but there are no official command-line tools that are easily usable in scripts and such to perform this operation.

That is one reason I decided to mention flat files in this chapter: to propose a set of tools that is capable of producing simple flat files. Over the years, I have developed three methods to accomplish this task, each appropriate in its own right. The first uses PL/SQL and UTL_FILE with dynamic SQL to accomplish the job. With small volumes of data (hundreds or thousands of rows), this tool is sufficiently flexible and fast enough to get the job done. However, it must

---

1. See http://osulibrary.oregonstate.edu/archives/handbook/definitions.
2. See http://www.oregoninnovation.org/pressroom/glossary.d-f.html.

create its files on the database server machine, which is sometimes not the location we'd like for them. To that end, I have a SQL*Plus utility that creates flat files on the machine that is running SQL*Plus. Since SQL*Plus can connect to an Oracle server anywhere on the network, this gives us the ability to unload to a flat file any data from any database on the network. Lastly, when the need for total speed is there, nothing but C will do (if you ask me). To that end, I also have a Pro*C command-line unloading tool to generate flat files. All of these tools are freely available at `http://asktom.oracle.com/~tkyte/flat/index.html`, and any new tools developed for unloading to flat files will appear there as well.

Summary

In this chapter, we explored the important types of files used by the Oracle database, from lowly parameter files (without which you won't even be able to get started) to the all important redo log and data files. We examined the storage structures of Oracle from tablespaces to segments, and then extents, and finally down to database blocks, the smallest unit of storage. We reviewed how checkpointing works in the database, and we even started to look ahead at what some of the physical processes or threads of Oracle do.

CHAPTER 4

███

Memory Structures

In this chapter, we'll look at Oracle's three major memory structures:

- *System Global Area (SGA)*: This is a large, shared memory segment that virtually all Oracle processes will access at one point or another.

- *Process Global Area (PGA)*: This is memory that is private to a single process or thread, and is not accessible from other processes/threads.

- *User Global Area (UGA)*: This is memory associated with your session. It will be found either in the SGA or the PGA depending on whether you are connected to the database using shared server (then it will be in the SGA), or dedicated server (it will be in the PGA, in the process memory).

█**Note** In earlier releases of Oracle, shared server was referred to as *Multi-Threaded Server* or *MTS*. In this book, we will always use the term "shared server."

We'll first discuss the PGA and UGA, and then we'll move on to examine the really big structure: the SGA.

The Process Global Area and User Global Area

The PGA is a process-specific piece of memory. In other words, it is memory specific to a single operating system process or thread. This memory is not accessible by any other process/thread in the system. It is typically allocated via either of the C runtime calls `malloc()` or `memmap()`, and it may grow (and shrink even) at runtime. The PGA is never allocated in Oracle's SGA—it is always allocated locally by the process or thread.

The UGA is, in effect, your session's state. It is memory that your session must always be able to get to. The location of the UGA is wholly dependent on how you connected to Oracle. If you connected via a shared server, then the UGA must be stored in a memory structure that every shared server process has access to—and that would be the SGA. In this way, your session can use any one of the shared servers, since any one of them can read and write your session's data. On the other hand, if you are using a dedicated server connection, this need for universal access to your session state goes away, and the UGA becomes virtually synonymous with the PGA; it will, in fact, be contained in the PGA of your dedicated server. When you look at the system statistics, you'll find the UGA reported in the PGA in dedicated server mode (the PGA will be greater than or equal to the UGA memory used; the PGA memory size will include the UGA size as well).

So, the PGA contains process memory and may include the UGA. The other areas of PGA memory are generally used for in-memory sorting, bitmap merging, and hashing. It would be safe to say that, besides the UGA memory, these are the largest contributors by far to the PGA.

Starting with Oracle9i Release 1 and above, there are two ways to manage this other non-UGA memory in the PGA:

- *Manual PGA memory management*, where you tell Oracle how much memory is it allowed to use to sort and hash any time it needs to sort or hash in a specific process

- *Automatic PGA memory management*, where you tell Oracle how much memory it should attempt to use *systemwide*

The manner in which memory is allocated and used differs greatly in each case and, as such, we'll discuss each in turn. It should be noted that in Oracle9i, when using a shared server connection, you can *only* use manual PGA memory management. This restriction was lifted with Oracle 10g Release 1 (and above). In that release, you can use either automatic or manual PGA memory management with shared server connections.

PGA memory management is controlled by the database initialization parameter WORKAREA_SIZE_POLICY and may be altered at the session level. This initialization parameter defaults to AUTO, for automatic PGA memory management when possible in Oracle9i Release 2 and above. In Oracle9i Release 1, the default setting was MANUAL.

In the sections that follow, we'll take a look at each approach.

Manual PGA Memory Management

In manual PGA memory management, the parameters that will have the largest impact on the size of your PGA, outside of the memory allocated by your session for PL/SQL tables and other variables, will be as follows:

- SORT_AREA_SIZE: The total amount of RAM that will be used to sort information before swapping out to disk.

- SORT_AREA_RETAINED_SIZE: The amount of memory that will be used to hold sorted data after the sort is complete. That is, if SORT_AREA_SIZE was 512KB and SORT_AREA_RETAINED_SIZE was 256KB, then your server process would use up to 512KB of memory to sort data during the initial processing of the query. When the sort was complete, the sorting area would be "shrunk" down to 256KB, and any sorted data that did not fit in that 256KB would be written out to the temporary tablespace.

- HASH_AREA_SIZE: The amount of memory your server process would use to store hash tables in memory. These structures are used during a hash join, typically when joining a large set with another set. The smaller of the two sets would be hashed into memory and anything that didn't fit in the hash area region of memory would be stored in the temporary tablespace by the join key.

These parameters control the amount of space Oracle will use to sort or hash data before writing (swapping) it to disk, and how much of that memory segment will be retained after the sort is done. The SORT_AREA_SIZE-SORT_AREA_RETAINED_SIZE is generally allocated out of your PGA, and the SORT_AREA_RETAINED_SIZE will be in your UGA. You can discover your current usage of PGA and UGA memory and monitor its size by querying special Oracle V$ views, also referred to as *dynamic performance views*.

For example, let's run a small test whereby in one session we'll sort lots of data and, from a second session, we'll monitor the UGA/PGA memory usage in that first session. To do this in a predicable manner, we'll make a copy of the ALL_OBJECTS table, with about 45,000 rows in this case, without any indexes (so we know a sort has to happen):

```
ops$tkyte@ORA10G> create table t as select * from all_objects;
Table created.

ops$tkyte@ORA10G> exec dbms_stats.gather_table_stats( user, 'T' );
PL/SQL procedure successfully completed.
```

To remove any side effects from the initial hard parsing of queries, we'll run the following script, but for now ignore its output. We'll run the script again in a fresh session so as to see the effects on memory usage in a controlled environment. We'll use the sort area sizes of 64KB, 1MB, and 1GB in turn:

```
create table t as select * from all_objects;
exec dbms_stats.gather_table_stats( user, 'T' );
alter session set workarea_size_policy=manual;
alter session set sort_area_size = 65536;
set termout off
select * from t order by 1, 2, 3, 4;
set termout on
alter session set sort_area_size=1048576;
set termout off
select * from t order by 1, 2, 3, 4;
set termout on
alter session set sort_area_size=1073741820;
set termout off
select * from t order by 1, 2, 3, 4;
set termout on
```

■Note When we process SQL in the database, we must first "parse" the SQL statement. There are two types of parses available. The first is a *hard parse*, which is what happens the first time a query is parsed by the database instance and includes query plan generation and optimization. The second is a *soft parse*, which can skip many of the steps a hard parse must do. We hard parse the previous queries so as to not measure the work performed by that operation in the following section.

Now, I would suggest logging out of that SQL*Plus session and logging back in before continuing, in order to get a *consistent* environment, or one in which no work has been done yet.

To ensure we're using manual memory management, we'll set it specifically and specify our rather small sort area size of 64KB. Also, we'll identify our session ID (SID) so we can monitor the memory usage for that session.

```
ops$tkyte@ORA10G> alter session set workarea_size_policy=manual;
Session altered.

ops$tkyte@ORA10G> select  sid from v$mystat where rownum = 1;

       SID
----------
       151
```

Now, we need to measure SID 151's memory from a second separate session. If we used the same session, then our query to see how much memory we are using for sorting might itself influence the very numbers we are looking at. To measure the memory from this second session, we'll use a small SQL*Plus script I developed for this. It is actually a pair of scripts. The one we want to watch that resets a small table and sets a SQL*Plus variable to the SID is called reset_stat.sql:

```
drop table sess_stats;

create table sess_stats
( name varchar2(64), value number, diff number );

variable sid number
exec :sid := &1
```

▪Note Before using this script (or any script, for that matter), make sure you understand what the script does. This script is dropping and re-creating a table called SESS_STATS. If your schema already has such a table, you'll probably want to use a different name!

The other script is called watch_stat.sql, and *for this case study*, it uses the MERGE SQL statement so we can initially INSERT the statistic values for a session and then later come back and update them—without needing a separate INSERT/UPDATE script:

```
merge into sess_stats
using
(
select a.name, b.value
  from v$statname a, v$sesstat b
 where a.statistic# = b.statistic#
   and b.sid = :sid
   and (a.name like '%ga %'
        or a.name like '%direct temp%')
) curr_stats
```

```
on (sess_stats.name = curr_stats.name)
when matched then
  update set diff = curr_stats.value - sess_stats.value,
            value = curr_stats.value
when not matched then
  insert ( name, value, diff )
  values
  ( curr_stats.name, curr_stats.value, null )
/

select *
  from sess_stats
 order by name;
```

I emphasized the phrase "for this case study" because of the lines in bold—the names of the statistics we're interested in looking at change from example to example. In this particular case, we're interested in anything with ga in it (pga and uga), or anything with direct temp, which in Oracle 10*g* will show us the direct reads and writes against temporary space (how much I/O we did reading and writing to temp).

Note In Oracle9*i*, direct I/O to temporary space was not labeled as such. We would use a WHERE clause that included and (a.name like '%ga %' or a.name like '%physical % direct%') in it.

When this watch_stat.sql script is run from the SQL*Plus command line, we'll see a listing of the PGA and UGA memory statistics for the session, as well as temporary I/O. Before we do anything in session 151, the session using manual PGA memory management, let's use this script to find out how much memory that session is currently using and how many temporary I/Os we have performed:

```
ops$tkyte@ORA10G> @watch_stat
6 rows merged.


NAME                                              VALUE       DIFF
------------------------------------------------- ----------- -----------
physical reads direct temporary tablespace              0
physical writes direct temporary tablespace             0
session pga memory                                 498252
session pga memory max                             498252
session uga memory                                 152176
session uga memory max                             152176
```

So, before we begin we can see that we have about 149KB (152,176/1,024) of data in the UGA and 487KB of data in the PGA. The first question is "How much memory are we using between the PGA and UGA?" That is, are we using 149KB + 487KB of memory, or are we using some other amount? This is a trick question, and one that you cannot answer unless you know whether the monitored session with SID 151 was connected to the database via a dedicated server or a shared server—and even then it might be hard to figure out. In dedicated server mode, the UGA is totally contained within the PGA, in which case we would be consuming 487KB of memory in our process or thread. In shared server, the UGA is allocated from the SGA, and the PGA is in the shared server. So, in shared server mode, by the time we get the last row from the preceding query, the shared server process may be in use by someone else. That PGA isn't "ours" anymore, so technically we are using 149KB of memory (except when we are actually running the query, at which point we are using 487KB of memory between the combined PGA and UGA). So, let's now run the first big query in session 151, which is using manual PGA memory management in dedicated server mode. Note that we are using the same script from earlier, so the SQL text matches exactly, thus avoiding the hard parse:

Note Since we haven't set a SORT_AREA_RETAINED_SIZE, its reported value will be zero, but its used value will match SORT_AREA_SIZE.

```
ops$tkyte@ORA10G> alter session set sort_area_size = 65536;
Session altered.

ops$tkyte@ORA10G>  set termout off;
query was executed here
ops$tkyte@ORA10G>  set termout on;
```

Now if we run our script again in the second session, we'll see something like this. Notice this time that the session xxx memory and session xxx memory max values do not match. The session xxx memory max value represents how much memory we are using right now. The session xxx memory max value represents the peak value we used at some time during our session while processing the query.

```
ops$tkyte@ORA10G> @watch_stat
6 rows merged.

NAME                                               VALUE      DIFF
-------------------------------------------- ---------- ----------
physical reads direct temporary tablespace         2906       2906
physical writes direct temporary tablespace        2906       2906
session pga memory                               498252          0
session pga memory max                           563788      65536
session uga memory                               152176          0
session uga memory max                           217640      65464

6 rows selected.
```

As you can see, our memory usage went up—we've done some sorting of data. Our UGA temporarily increased from 149KB to 213KB (64KB) during the processing of our query, and then it shrunk back down. To perform our query and the sorting, Oracle allocated a sort area for our session. Additionally, the PGA memory went from 487KB to 551KB, a jump of 64KB. Also, we can see that we did 2,906 writes and reads to and from temp.

By the time we finish our query and exhausted the resultset, we can see that our UGA memory went back down where it started (we released the sort areas from our UGA) and the PGA shrunk back somewhat (note that in Oracle8*i* and before, you would not expect to see the PGA shrink back at all; this is new with Oracle9*i* and later).

Let's retry that operation but play around with the size of our SORT_AREA_SIZE increasing it to 1MB. We'll log out of the session we're monitoring, log back in, and use the reset_stat.sql script to start over. As the beginning numbers are consistent, I don't display them here—only the final results:

```
ops$tkyte@ORA10G> alter session set sort_area_size=1048576;
Session altered.

ops$tkyte@ORA10G>  set termout off;
query was executed here
ops$tkyte@ORA10G>  set termout on
```

Now in the other session we can measure our memory usage again:

```
ops$tkyte@ORA10G> @watch_stat
6 rows merged.
```

NAME	VALUE	DIFF
physical reads direct temporary tablespace	684	684
physical writes direct temporary tablespace	684	684
session pga memory	498252	0
session pga memory max	2398796	1900544
session uga memory	152176	0
session uga memory max	1265064	1112888

```
6 rows selected.
```

As you can see, our PGA had grown considerably this time during the processing of our query. It temporarily grew by about 1,728KB, but the amount of physical I/O we had to do to sort this data dropped considerably as well (use more memory, swap to disk less often). We may have avoided a *multipass sort* as well, a condition that happens when there are so many little sets of sorted data to merge together that Oracle ends up writing the data to temp more than once. Now, let's go to an extreme here:

```
ops$tkyte@ORA10G> alter session set sort_area_size=1073741820;
Session altered.

ops$tkyte@ORA10G>  set termout off;
query was executed here
ops$tkyte@ORA10G>  set termout on
```

Measuring from the other session, we can see the memory used so far:

```
ops$tkyte@ORA10G> @watch_stat
6 rows merged.

NAME                                              VALUE        DIFF
-------------------------------------------  ----------  ----------
physical reads direct temporary tablespace            0           0
physical writes direct temporary tablespace           0           0
session pga memory                               498252           0
session pga memory max                          7445068     6946816
session uga memory                               152176           0
session uga memory max                          7091360     6939184

6 rows selected.
```

We can observe that even though we allowed for up to 1GB of memory to the SORT_AREA_ SIZE, we really only used about 6.6MB. This shows that the SORT_AREA_SIZE setting is an upper bound, not the default and only allocation size. Here notice also that we did only one sort again, but this time it was entirely in memory; there was no temporary space on disk used, as evidenced by the lack of physical I/O.

If you run this same test on various versions of Oracle, or perhaps even on different operating systems, you *might* see different behavior, and I would expect that your numbers in all cases would be a little different from mine. But the general behavior should be the same. In other words, as you increase the permitted sort area size and perform large sorts, the amount of memory used by your session will increase. You might notice the PGA memory going up and down, or it might remain constant over time, as just shown. For example, if you were to execute the previous test in Oracle8i, I am sure that you would notice that PGA memory does not shrink back in size (i.e., the SESSION PGA MEMORY equals the SESSION PGA MEMORY MAX in all cases). This is to be expected, as the PGA is managed as a heap in 8i releases and is created via malloc()-ed memory. In 9i and 10g, new methods attach and release work areas as needed using operating system–specific memory allocation calls.

The important things to remember about using the *_AREA_SIZE parameters are as follows:

- These parameters control the maximum amount of memory used by a SORT, HASH, and/or BITMAP MERGE operation.

- A single query may have many operations taking place that use this memory, and multiple sort/hash areas could be created. Remember that you may have many cursors opened simultaneously, each with their own SORT_AREA_RETAINED needs. So, if you set the sort area size to 10MB, you could use 10, 100, 1,000 or more megabytes of RAM in your session. These settings are not session limits; rather, they are limits on a single operation, and your session could have many sorts in a single query or many queries open that require a sort.

- The memory for these areas is allocated on an "as needed basis." If you set the sort area size to 1GB as we did, it does not mean you will allocate 1GB of RAM. It only means that you have given the Oracle process the permission to allocate that much memory for a sort/hash operation.

Automatic PGA Memory Management

Starting with Oracle9i Release 1, a new way to manage PGA memory was introduced that avoids using the SORT_AREA_SIZE, BITMAP_MERGE_AREA_SIZE, and HASH_AREA_SIZE parameters. It was introduced to attempt to address a few issues:

- *Ease of use*: Much confusion surrounded how to set the proper *_AREA_SIZE parameters. There was also much confusion over how those parameters actually worked and how memory was allocated.

- *Manual allocation was a "one-size-fits-all" method*: Typically as the number of users running similar applications against a database went up, the amount of memory used for sorting/hashing went up linearly as well. If 10 concurrent users with a sort area size of 1MB used 10MB of memory, 100 concurrent users would probably use 100MB, 1,000 would probably use 1000MB, and so on. Unless the DBA was sitting at the console continually adjusting the sort/hash area size settings, everyone would pretty much use the same values all day long. Consider the previous example, where you saw for yourself how the physical I/O to temp decreased as the amount of RAM we allowed ourselves to use went up. If you run that example for yourself, you will almost certainly see a decrease in response time as the amount of RAM available for sorting increases. Manual allocation fixes the amount of memory to be used for sorting at a more or less constant number, regardless of how much memory is actually available. Automatic memory management allows us to use the memory when it is available; it dynamically adjusts the amount of memory we use based on the workload.

- *Memory control*: As a result of the previous point, it was hard, if not impossible, to keep the Oracle instance inside a "box" memory-wise. You could not control the amount of memory the instance was going to use, as you had no real control over the number of simultaneous sorts/hashes taking place. It was far too easy to use more real memory (actual physical free memory) than was available on the machine.

Enter automatic PGA memory management. Here, you first simply set up and size the SGA. The SGA is a fixed-size piece of memory, so you can very accurately see how big it is, and that will be its total size (until and if you change that). You then tell Oracle, "This is how much memory you should try to limit yourself across all work areas—a new umbrella term for the sorting and hashing areas you use." Now, you could in theory take a machine with 2GB of physical memory and allocate 768MB of memory to the SGA and 768MB of memory to the PGA, leaving 512MB of memory for the OS and other processes. I say "in theory" because it doesn't work exactly that cleanly, but it's close. Before I discuss why that is true, we'll take a look at how to set up automatic PGA memory management and turn it on.

The process to set this up involves deciding on the proper values for two instance initialization parameters, namely

- WORKAREA_SIZE_POLICY: This parameter may be set to either MANUAL, which will use the sort area and hash area size parameters to control the amount of memory allocated, or AUTO, in which case the amount of memory allocated will vary based on the current workload present in the database. The default and recommended value is AUTO.

- PGA_AGGREGATE_TARGET: This parameter controls how much memory the instance should allocate, in total, for all work areas used to sort/hash data. Its default value varies by version and may be set by various tools such as the DBCA. In general, if you are using automatic PGA memory management, you should explicitly set this parameter.

So, assuming that WORKAREA_SIZE_POLICY is set to AUTO, and PGA_AGGREGATE_TARGET has a nonzero value, you will be using the new automatic PGA memory management. You can "turn it on" in your session via the ALTER SESSION command or at the system level via the ALTER SESSION command.

■**Note** Bear in mind the previously discussed caveat that in Oracle9*i*, shared server connections will *not* use automatic memory management; rather, they will use the SORT_AREA_SIZE and HASH_AREA_SIZE parameters to decide how much RAM to allocate for various operations. In Oracle 10*g* and up, automatic PGA memory management is available to both connection types. It is important to properly set the SORT_AREA_SIZE and HASH_AREA_SIZE parameters when using shared server connections with Oracle9*i*.

So, the entire goal of automatic PGA memory management is to maximize the use of RAM while at the same time not using more RAM than you want. Under manual memory management, this was virtually an impossible goal to achieve. If you set SORT_AREA_SIZE to 10MB, when one user was performing a sort operation that user would use up to 10MB for the sort work area. If 100 users were doing the same, they would use up to 1000MB of memory. If you had 500MB of free memory, the single user performing a sort by himself could have used much more memory, and the 100 users should have used much less. That is what automatic PGA memory management was designed to do. Under a light workload, memory usage could be maximized as the load increases on the system, and as more users perform sort or hash operations, the amount of memory allocated to them would decrease—to obtain the goal of using all available RAM, but not attempting to use more than physically exists.

Determining How the Memory Is Allocated

Questions that come up frequently are "How is this memory allocated?" and "What will be the amount of RAM used by my session?" These are hard questions to answer for the simple reason that the algorithms for serving out memory under the automatic scheme are not documented and can and will change from release to release. When using things that begin with "A"—for automatic—you lose a degree of control, as the underlying algorithms decide what to do and how to control things.

We can make some observations based on some information from MetaLink note 147806.1:

- The PGA_AGGREGATE_TARGET is a goal of an upper limit. It is not a value that is pre-allocated when the database is started up. You can observe this by setting the PGA_AGGREGATE_TARGET to a value much higher than the amount of physical memory you have available on your server. You will not see any large allocation of memory as a result.

- A serial (nonparallel query) session will use a small percentage of the PGA_AGGREGATE_TARGET, about 5 percent or less. So, if you have set the PGA_AGGREGATE_TARGET to 100MB, you would expect to use no more than about 5MB per work area (e.g., the sort or hash work area). You may well have multiple work areas in your session for multiple queries, or more than one sort/hash operation in a single query, but each work area will be about 5 percent or less of the PGA_AGGREGATE_TARGET.

- As the workload on you server goes up (more concurrent queries, concurrent users), the amount of PGA memory allocated to your work areas will go down. The database will try to keep the sum of all PGA allocations under the threshold set by PGA_AGGREGATE_TARGET. It would be analogous to having a DBA sit at a console all day, setting the SORT_AREA_SIZE and HASH_AREA_SIZE parameters based on the amount of work being performed in the database. We will directly observe this behavior shortly in a test.

- A parallel query may use up to 30 percent of the PGA_AGGREGATE_TARGET, with each parallel process getting its slice of that 30 percent. That is, each parallel process would be able to use about 0.3 * PGA_AGGREGATE_TARGET / (number of parallel processes).

OK, so how can we observe the different work area sizes being allocated to our session? By applying the same technique we used earlier in the manual memory management section, to observe the memory used by our session and the amount of I/O to temp we performed. The following test was performed on a Red Hat Advanced Server 3.0 Linux machine using Oracle 10.1.0.3 and dedicated server connections. This was a two-CPU Dell PowerEdge with hyper-threading enabled, so it was as if there were four CPUs available. Using reset_stat.sql and a slightly modified version of watch_stat.sql from earlier, I captured the session statistics for a session *as well as the total statistics for the instance*. The slightly modified watch_stat.sql script captured this information via the MERGE statement:

```
merge into sess_stats
using
(
select a.name, b.value
  from v$statname a, v$sesstat b
 where a.statistic# = b.statistic#
   and b.sid = &1
   and (a.name like '%ga %'
        or a.name like '%direct temp%')
 union all
select 'total: ' || a.name, sum(b.value)
  from v$statname a, v$sesstat b, v$session c
 where a.statistic# = b.statistic#
   and (a.name like '%ga %'
```

```
       or a.name like '%direct temp%')
  and b.sid = c.sid
  and c.username is not null
group by 'total: ' || a.name
) curr_stats
on (sess_stats.name = curr_stats.name)
when matched then
  update set diff = curr_stats.value - sess_stats.value,
            value = curr_stats.value
when not matched then
  insert ( name, value, diff )
  values
  ( curr_stats.name, curr_stats.value, null )
/
```

I simply added the UNION ALL section to capture the total PGA/UGA and sort writes by summing over all sessions, in addition to the statistics for a single session. I then ran the following SQL*Plus script in that particular session. The table BIG_TABLE had been created beforehand with 50,000 rows in it. I dropped the primary key from this table, so all that remained was the table itself (ensuring that a sort process would have to be performed):

```
set autotrace traceonly statistics;
select * from big_table order by 1, 2, 3, 4;
set autotrace off
```

■**Note** The BIG_TABLE table is created as a copy of ALL_OBJECTS with a primary key, and it can have as many or as few rows as you like. The big_table.sql script is documented in the "Setting Up" section at the beginning of this book.

Now, I ran that small query script against a database with a PGA_AGGREGATE_TARGET of 256MB, meaning I wanted Oracle to use up to about 256MB of PGA memory for sorting. I set up another script to be run in other sessions to generate a large sorting load on the machine. This script loops and uses a built-in package, DBMS_ALERT, to see if it should continue processing. If it should, it runs the same big query, sorting the entire BIG_TABLE table. When the simulation was over, a session could signal all of the sorting processes, the load generators, to "stop" and exit. The script used to perform the sort is as follows:

```
declare
    l_msg   long;
    l_status number;
begin
    dbms_alert.register( 'WAITING' );
    for i in 1 .. 999999 loop
        dbms_application_info.set_client_info( i );
        dbms_alert.waitone( 'WAITING', l_msg, l_status, 0 );
```

```
        exit when l_status = 0;
        for x in ( select * from big_table order by 1, 2, 3, 4 )
        loop
            null;
        end loop;
    end loop;
end;
/
exit
```

The script to stop these processes from running is as follows:

```
begin
    dbms_alert.signal( 'WAITING', '' );
    commit;
end;
```

To observe the differing amounts of RAM allocated to the session I was measuring, I initially ran the SELECT in isolation—as the only session. I captured the same six statistics and saved them into another table, along with the count of active sessions. Then I added 25 sessions to the system (i.e., I ran the preceding benchmark script with the loop in 25 new sessions). I waited a short period of time—one minute for the system to adjust to this new load—and then I created a new session, captured the statistics for it with reset_stat.sql, ran the query that would sort, and then ran watch_stat.sql to capture the differences. I did this repeatedly, for up to 500 concurrent users.

It should be noted that I asked the database instance to do an impossible thing here. As noted previously, based on the first time we ran watch_stat.sql, each connection to Oracle, before even doing a single sort, consumed almost .5MB of RAM. At 500 users, we would be very close to the PGA_AGGREGATE_TARGET setting just by having them all logged in, let alone actually doing any work! This drives home the point that the PGA_AGGREGATE_TARGET is just that: a target, not a directive. We can and will exceed this value for various reasons.

Table 4-1 summarizes my findings using approximately 25 user increments.

Table 4-1. *PGA Memory Allocation Behavior with Increasing Numbers of Active Sessions, with* PGA_AGGREGATE_TARGET *Set to 256MB*

Active Sessions	PGA Used by Single Session	PGA in Use by System	Writes to Temp by Single Session	Reads from Temp by Single Session
1	7.5	2	0	0
27	7.5	189	0	0
51	4.0	330	728	728
76	4.0	341	728	728
101	3.2	266	728	728
126	1.5	214	728	728
151	1.7	226	728	728
177	1.4	213	728	728

Continued

Table 4-1. *Continued*

Active Sessions	PGA Used by Single Session	PGA in Use by System	Writes to Temp by Single Session	Reads from Temp by Single Session
201	1.3	218	728	728
226	1.3	211	728	728
251	1.3	237	728	728
276	1.3	251	728	728
301	1.3	281	728	728
326	1.3	302	728	728
351	1.3	324	728	728
376	1.3	350	728	728
402	1.3	367	728	728
426	1.3	392	728	728
452	1.3	417	728	728
476	1.3	439	728	728
501	1.3	467	728	728

■**Note** You might wonder why only 2MB of RAM is reported in use by the system with one active user. It has to do with the way I measured. The simulation would snapshot the single session's of interest's statistics. Next, I would run the big query in the single session of interest and then snapshot that session's statistics again. Finally, I would measure how much PGA was used by the system. By the time I measured, the single session of interest would have already completed and given back some of the PGA it was using to sort. So, the number for PGA used by the system is an accurate measurement of the system's PGA memory at the time it was measured.

As you can see, when I had few active sessions, my sorts were performed entirely in memory. For an active session count of 1 to somewhere less than 50, I was allowed to sort entirely in memory. However, by the time I got 50 users logged in, actively sorting, the database started reining in the amount of memory I was allowed to use at a time. It took a couple of minutes before the amount of PGA being used fell back within acceptable limits (the 256MB request), but it eventually did. The amount of PGA memory allocated to the session dropped from 7.5MB to 4MB to 3.2MB, and eventually down to the area of 1.7 to 1.3MB (remember, parts of that PGA are not for sorting, but are for other operations—just the act of logging in created a .5MB PGA). The total PGA in use by the system remained within tolerable limits until somewhere around 300 to 351 users. There I started to exceed on a regular basis the PGA_AGGREGATE_TARGET and continued to do so until the end of the test. I gave the database instance in this case an impossible task—the very act of having 350 users, most executing a PL/SQL, plus the sort they were all requesting, just did not fit into the 256MB of RAM I had targeted. It simply could not be done. Each session, therefore used as little memory as possible, but had to allocate as much memory as it needed. By the time I finished this test, 500 active sessions were using a total of 467MB of PGA memory—as little as they could.

You should, however, consider what Table 4-1 would look like under a manual memory management situation. Suppose the SORT_AREA_SIZE had been set to 5MB. The math is very straightforward: each session would be able to perform the sort in RAM (or virtual memory as the machine ran out of real RAM), and thus would consume 6 to 7MB of RAM per session (the amount used without sorting to disk in the previous single-user case). I ran the preceding test again with SORT_AREA_SIZE set to 5MB, and as I went from 1 user to adding 25 at a time, the numbers remained consistent, as shown in Table 4-2.

Table 4-2. *PGA Memory Allocation Behavior with Increasing Numbers of Active Sessions, with* SORT_AREA_SIZE *Set to 5MB (Manual Memory Management)*

Active Sessions	PGA Used by Single Session	PGA in Use by System	Writes to Temp by Single Session	Reads from Temp by Single Session
1	6.4	5	728	728
26	6.4	137	728	728
51	6.4	283	728	728
76	6.4	391	728	728
102	6.4	574	728	728
126	6.4	674	728	728
151	6.4	758	728	728
176	6.4	987	728	728
202	6.4	995	728	728
226	6.4	1227	728	728
251	6.4	1383	728	728
277	6.4	1475	728	728
302	6.4	1548	728	728

Had I been able to complete the test (I have 2GB of real memory on this server and my SGA was 600MB; by the time I got to 325 users, the machine was paging and swapping to the point where it was impossible to continue), at 500 users I would have allocated around 2,750MB of RAM! So, the DBA would probably not set the SORT_AREA_SIZE to 5MB on this system, but rather to about 0.5MB, in an attempt to keep the maximum PGA usage at a bearable level at peak. Now at 500 users I would have had about 500MB of PGA allocated, perhaps similar to what we observed with automatic memory management—but at times when there were fewer users, we would have still written to temp rather than performing the sort in memory. In fact, when running the preceding test with a SORT_AREA_SIZE of .5MB, we would observe the data in Table 4-3.

Table 4-3. *PGA Memory Allocation Behavior with Increasing Numbers of Active Sessions, with* SORT_AREA_SIZE *Set to 0.5MB (Manual Memory Management)*

Active Sessions	PGA Used by Single Session	PGA in Use by System	Writes to Temp by Single Session	Reads from Temp by Single Session
1	1.2	1	728	728
26	1.2	29	728	728
51	1.2	57	728	728
76	1.2	84	728	728
101	1.2	112	728	728
126	1.2	140	728	728
151	1.2	167	728	728
176	1.2	194	728	728
201	1.2	222	728	728
226	1.2	250	728	728

This represents a very predicable—but suboptimal—use of memory as the workload increases or decreases over time. Automatic PGA memory management was designed exactly to allow the small community of users to use as much RAM as possible when it was available and back off on this allocation over time as the load increased, and increase the amount of RAM allocated for individual operations over time as the load decreased.

Using PGA_AGGREGATE_TARGET to Control Memory Allocation

Earlier, I wrote that "in theory" we can use the PGA_AGGREGATE_TARGET to control the overall amount of PGA memory used by the instance. We saw in the last example that this is not a hard limit, however. The instance will attempt to stay within the bounds of the PGA_AGGREGATE_TARGET, but if it cannot, it will not stop processing; rather, it will just be forced to exceed that threshold.

Another reason this limit is "in theory" is because the work areas, while a large contributor to PGA memory, are not the *only* contributor to PGA memory. Many things contribute to your PGA memory allocation, and only the work areas are under the control of the database instance. If you create and execute a PL/SQL block of code that fills in a large array with data in dedicated server mode where the UGA is in the PGA, Oracle cannot do anything but allow you to do it.

Consider the following quick example. We'll create a package that can hold some persistent (global) data in the server:

```
ops$tkyte@ORA10G> create or replace package demo_pkg
  2  as
  3          type array is table of char(2000) index by binary_integer;
  4          g_data array;
  5  end;
  6  /
Package created.
```

Now we'll measure the amount of memory our session is currently using in the PGA/UGA (I was using dedicated server in this example, so the UGA is a subset of the PGA memory):

```
ops$tkyte@ORA10G> select a.name, to_char(b.value, '999,999,999') value
  2    from v$statname a, v$mystat b
  3    where a.statistic# = b.statistic#
  4      and a.name like '%ga memory%';

NAME                                VALUE
------------------------------- ------------
session uga memory                  1,212,872
session uga memory max              1,212,872
session pga memory                  1,677,900
session pga memory max              1,677,900
```

So, initially we are using about 1.5MB of PGA memory in our session (as a result of compiling a PL/SQL package, running this query, etc.). Now, we'll run our query against BIG_TABLE again using the same 256MB PGA_AGGREGATE_TARGET (this was done in an otherwise idle instance; we are the only session requiring memory right now):

```
ops$tkyte@ORA10GR1> set autotrace traceonly statistics;
ops$tkyte@ORA10GR1> select * from big_table order by 1,2,3,4;
50000 rows selected.

Statistics
----------------------------------------------------------
          0  recursive calls
          0  db block gets
        721  consistent gets
          0  physical reads
          0  redo size
    2644246  bytes sent via SQL*Net to client
      37171  bytes received via SQL*Net from client
       3335  SQL*Net roundtrips to/from client
          1  sorts (memory)
          0  sorts (disk)
      50000  rows processed
ops$tkyte@ORA10GR1> set autotrace off
```

As you can see, the sort was done entirely in memory, and in fact if we peek at our session's PGA/UGA usage, we can see how much we used:

```
ops$tkyte@ORA10GR1> select a.name, to_char(b.value, '999,999,999') value
  2    from v$statname a, v$mystat b
  3    where a.statistic# = b.statistic#
  4      and a.name like '%ga memory%';
```

```
NAME                          VALUE
----------------------------- ------------
session uga memory            1,212,872
session uga memory max        7,418,680
session pga memory            1,612,364
session pga memory max        7,838,284
```

The same 7.5MB of RAM we observed earlier. Now, we will proceed to fill up that CHAR array we have in the package (a CHAR datatype is blank-padded so each of these array elements is exactly 2,000 characters in length):

```
ops$tkyte@ORA10G> begin
  2          for i in 1 .. 100000
  3          loop
  4                  demo_pkg.g_data(i) := 'x';
  5          end loop;
  6  end;
  7  /
PL/SQL procedure successfully completed.
```

Upon measuring our session's current PGA utilization after that, we find something similar to the following:

```
ops$tkyte@ORA10GR1> select a.name, to_char(b.value, '999,999,999') value
  2    from v$statname a, v$mystat b
  3    where a.statistic# = b.statistic#
  4      and a.name like '%ga memory%';

NAME                          VALUE
----------------------------- ------------
session uga memory            312,952,440
session uga memory max        312,952,440
session pga memory            313,694,796
session pga memory max        313,694,796
```

Now, that is memory allocated in the PGA that the database itself cannot control. We already exceeded the PGA_AGGREGATE_TARGET and there is quite simply nothing the database can do about it—it would have to fail our request if it did anything, and it will do that only when the OS reports back that there is no more memory to give. If we wanted, we could allocate more space in that array and place more data in it, and the database would just have to do it for us.

However, the database is aware of what we have done. It does not ignore the memory it cannot control; rather, it recognizes that the memory is being used and backs off the size of memory allocated for work areas accordingly. So if we rerun the same sort query, we see that this time we sorted to disk—the database did not give us the 7MB or so of RAM needed to do this in memory since we had already exceeded the PGA_AGGREGATE_TARGET:

```
ops$tkyte@ORA10GR1> set autotrace traceonly statistics;
ops$tkyte@ORA10GR1> select * from big_table order by 1,2,3,4;
50000 rows selected.
```

```
Statistics
----------------------------------------------------------
        6  recursive calls
        2  db block gets
      721  consistent gets
      728  physical reads
        0  redo size
  2644246  bytes sent via SQL*Net to client
    37171  bytes received via SQL*Net from client
     3335  SQL*Net roundtrips to/from client
        0  sorts (memory)
        1  sorts (disk)
    50000  rows processed
ops$tkyte@ORA10GR1> set autotrace off
```

So, because some PGA memory is outside of Oracle's control, it is easy for us to exceed the PGA_AGGREGATE_TARGET simply by allocating lots of really large data structures in our PL/SQL code. I am not *recommending* you do that by any means—I'm just pointing out that the PGA_AGGREGATE_TARGET is a more of a request than a hard limit.

Choosing Between Manual and Auto Memory Management

So, which method should you use: manual or automatic? My preference is to use the automatic PGA memory management by default.

■Caution I'll repeat this from time to time in the book: please do not make any changes to a production system—a live system—without first testing for any side effects. For example, please do not read this chapter, check your system, and find you are using manual memory management, and then just turn on automatic memory management. Query plans may change, and performance may be impacted. One of three things could happen:

- Things run exactly the same.

- Things run better than they did before.

- Things run much worse then they did before.

Exercise caution before making changes, test the proposed change first.

One of the most perplexing things for a DBA can be setting the individual parameters, especially parameters such as SORT|HASH_AREA_SIZE and so on. Many times, I see systems running with incredibly small values for these parameters—values so small that system performance is massively impacted in a negative way. This is probably a result of the fact that the default values are very small themselves: 64KB for sorting and 128KB for hashing. There is a lot of confusion over how big or small these values should be. Not only that, but the values you would like to use for them might vary over time, as the day goes by. At 8:00 am, with two users, a 50MB sort area size might be reasonable for the single user logged in. However, at 12:00 pm with 500 users, 50MB might not be appropriate. This is where the WORKAREA_SIZE_POLICY = AUTO setting and the corresponding PGA_AGGREGATE_TARGET come in handy. Setting the PGA_AGGREGATE_TARGET, the amount of memory you would like Oracle to feel free to use to sort and hash, is conceptually easier than trying to figure out the perfect SORT|HASH_AREA_SIZE, especially since there isn't a perfect value for these parameters; the perfect value varies by workload.

Historically, the DBA configured the amount of memory used by Oracle by setting the size of the SGA (the buffer cache; the log buffer; and the Shared, Large, and Java pools). The remaining memory on the machine would then be used by the dedicated or shared servers in the PGA region. The DBA had little control over how much of this memory would or would not be used. She could set the SORT_AREA_SIZE, but if there were 10 concurrent sorts, then Oracle could use as much as 10 * SORT_AREA_SIZE bytes of RAM. If there were 100 concurrent sorts, then Oracle would use 100 * SORT_AREA_SIZE bytes; for 1,000 concurrent sorts, 1,000 * SORT_AREA_SIZE; and so on. Couple that with the fact that other things go into the PGA, and you really don't have good control over the maximal use of PGA memory on the system.

What you would like to have happen is for this memory to be used differently as the memory demands on the system grow and shrink. The more users, the less RAM each should use. The fewer users, the more RAM each should use. Setting WORKAREA_SIZE_POLICY = AUTO is just such a way to achieve this. The DBA specifies a single size now, the PGA_AGGREGATE_TARGET or the maximum amount of PGA memory that the database should strive to use. Oracle will distribute this memory over the active sessions as it sees fit. Further, with Oracle9*i* Release 2 and up, there is even PGA advisory (part of Statspack, available via a V$ dynamic performance view and visible in Enterprise Manager), much like the buffer cache advisor. It will tell you over time what the optimal PGA_AGGREGATE_TARGET for your system is to minimize physical I/O to your temporary tablespaces. You can use this information to either dynamically change the PGA size online (if you have sufficient RAM) or decide whether you might need more RAM on your server to achieve optimal performance.

Are there times, however, when you won't want to use it? Absolutely, and fortunately they seem to be the exception and not the rule. The automatic memory management was designed to be multiuser "fair." In anticipation of additional users joining the system, the automatic memory management will limit the amount of memory allocated as a percentage of the PGA_AGGREGATE_TARGET. But what happens when you don't want to be fair, when you *know* that you should get all of the memory available? Well, that would be the time to use the ALTER SESSION command to disable automatic memory management in your session (leaving it in place for all others) and to manually set your SORT|HASH_AREA_SIZE as needed. For example, that large batch process that takes place at 2:00 am and does tremendously large hash joins, some index builds, and the like? It should be permitted to use all of the resources on the machine. It does not want to be "fair" about memory use—it wants it all, as it knows it is the only thing happening in the database right now. That batch job can certainly issue the ALTER SESSION commands and make use of all resources available.

So, in short, I prefer to use automatic PGA memory management for end user sessions—for the applications that run day to day against my database. Manual memory management makes sense for large batch jobs that run during time periods when they are the only activities in the database.

PGA and UGA Wrap-Up

So far, we have looked at two memory structures: the PGA and the UGA. You should under-stand now that the PGA is private to a process. It is the set of variables that an Oracle dedicated or shared server needs to have independent of a session. The PGA is a "heap" of memory in which other structures may be allocated. The UGA is also a heap of memory in which various session-specific structures may be defined. The UGA is allocated from the PGA when you use a dedicated server to connect to Oracle and from the SGA under a shared server connection. This implies that when using a shared server, you must size your SGA's Large pool to have enough space in it to cater for every possible user that will ever connect to your database con-currently. So, the SGA of a database supporting shared server connections is generally much larger than the SGA for a similarly configured, dedicated server mode–only database. We'll cover the SGA in more detail next.

The System Global Area

Every Oracle instance has one big memory structure referred to as the System Global Area (SGA). This is a large, shared memory structure that every Oracle process will access at one point or another. It will vary in size from a few of megabytes on small test systems, to hun-dreds of megabytes on medium to large systems, up to many gigabytes in size for really big systems.

On a UNIX operating system, the SGA is a physical entity that you can "see" from the OS command line. It is physically implemented as a shared memory segment—a stand-alone piece of memory to which processes may attach. It is possible to have an SGA on a system without having any Oracle processes; the memory stands alone. It should be noted, however, that if you have an SGA without any Oracle processes, this is an indication that the database crashed in some fashion. It is an unusual situation, but it can happen. This is what an SGA "looks like" on Red Hat Linux:

```
[tkyte@localhost tkyte]$ ipcs -m | grep ora
0x99875060 2031619     ora10g     660     538968064  15
0x0d998a20 1966088     ora9ir2    660     117440512  45
0x6b390abc 1998857     ora9ir1    660     130560000  50
```

Three SGAs are represented here: one owned by the OS user ora10g, another by the OS user ora9ir2, and the third by the OS user ora9ir1. They are about 512MB, 112MB, and 124MB, respectively.

On Windows, you really cannot see the SGA as a distinct entity the way you can in UNIX/Linux. Because on the Windows platform, Oracle executes as a single process with a single address space, the SGA is allocated as private memory to the oracle.exe process. If you use the Windows Task Manager or some other performance tool, you can see how much mem-ory oracle.exe has allocated, but you cannot see what is the SGA versus any other piece of allocated memory.

Within Oracle itself, you can see the SGA regardless of platform, using another magic V$ view called V$SGASTAT. It might look as follows (note that this code does not come from the preceding system; it's from a system with all features configured to enable viewing of all pools available):

```
ops$tkyte@ORA10G> compute sum of bytes on pool
ops$tkyte@ORA10G> break on pool skip 1
ops$tkyte@ORA10G> select pool, name, bytes
  2  from v$sgastat
  3  order by pool, name;

POOL            NAME                               BYTES
-------------   ----------------------------  ----------

java pool       free memory                     16777216
************                                  ----------
sum                                             16777216


large pool      PX msg pool                        64000
                free memory                     16713216
************                                  ----------
sum                                             16777216


shared pool     ASH buffers                      2097152
                FileOpenBlock                     746704
                KGLS heap                         777516
                KQR L SO                           29696
                KQR M PO                          599576
                KQR M SO                           42496
...
                sql area                         2664728
                table definiti                       280
                trigger defini                      1792
                trigger inform                      1944
                trigger source                       640
                type object de                    183804
************                                  ----------
sum                                            352321536


streams pool    free memory                     33554432
************                                  ----------
sum                                             33554432


                buffer_cache                  1157627904
                fixed_sga                         779316
                log_buffer                        262144
************                                  ----------
sum                                           1158669364


43 rows selected.
```

The SGA is broken up into various *pools*:

- *Java pool*: The Java pool is a fixed amount of memory allocated for the JVM running in the database. In Oracle10*g*, the Java pool may be resized online while the database is up and running.

- *Large pool*: The Large pool is used by shared server connections for session memory, by parallel execution features for message buffers, and by RMAN backup for disk I/O buffers. This pool is resizable online in both Oracle 10*g* and 9*i* Release 2.

- *Shared pool*: The Shared pool contains shared cursors, stored procedures, state objects, dictionary caches, and many dozens of other bits of data. This pool is resizable online in both Oracle 10*g* and 9*i*.

- *Streams pool*: This is a pool of memory used exclusively by *Oracle Streams*, a data-sharing tool within the database. This pool is new in Oracle 10*g* and is resizable online. In the event the Streams pool is not configured and you use the Streams functionality, Oracle will use up to 10 percent of the Shared pool for streams memory.

- *The "Null" pool*: This one doesn't really have a name. It is the memory dedicated to block buffers (cached database blocks), the redo log buffer, and a "fixed SGA" area.

A typical SGA might look as shown in Figure 4-1.

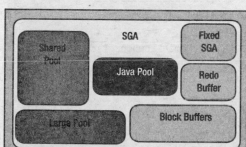

Figure 4-1. *Typical SGA*

The parameters that have the greatest effect on the overall size of the SGA are as follows:

- JAVA_POOL_SIZE: Controls the size of the Java pool.

- SHARED_POOL_SIZE: Controls the size of the Shared pool, to some degree.

- LARGE_POOL_SIZE: Controls the size of the Large pool.

- DB_*_CACHE_SIZE: Eight of these CACHE_SIZE parameters control the sizes of the various buffer caches available.

- LOG_BUFFER: Controls the size of the redo buffer, to some degree.

- SGA_TARGET: Used with automatic SGA memory management in Oracle 10*g* and above.

- SGA_MAX_SIZE: Used to control the maximum size to which the SGA can be resized while the database is up and running.

In Oracle9*i*, the various SGA components must be manually sized by the DBA but, starting in Oracle 10*g*, there is a new option to consider: automatic SGA memory management, whereby the database instance will allocate and reallocate the various SGA components at runtime, in response to workload conditions. When using the automatic memory management with Oracle 10*g*, it is a matter of simply setting the SGA_TARGET parameter to the desired SGA size, leaving out the other SGA-related parameters altogether. The database instance will take it from there, allocating memory to the various pools as needed and even taking memory away from one pool to give to another over time.

Regardless of whether you are using automatic or manual memory management, you will find that memory is allocated to the various pools in units called *granules*. A single granule is an area of memory either 4MB, 8MB, or 16MB in size. The granule is the smallest unit of allocation, so if you ask for a Java pool of 5MB and your granule size is 4MB, Oracle will actually allocate 8MB to the Java pool (8 being the smallest number greater than or equal to 5 that is a multiple of the granule size of 4). The size of a granule is determined by the size of your SGA (this sounds recursive to a degree, as the size of the SGA is dependent on the granule size). You can view the granule sizes used for each pool by querying V$SGA_DYNAMIC_COMPONENTS. In fact, we can use this view to see how the total SGA size might affect the size of the granules:

```
sys@ORA10G> show parameter sga_target

NAME                                 TYPE        VALUE
------------------------------------ ----------- ------------------------------
sga_target                           big integer 576M

sys@ORA10G> select component, granule_size from v$sga_dynamic_components;

COMPONENT                 GRANULE_SIZE
------------------------- ------------
shared pool                    4194304
large pool                     4194304
java pool                      4194304
streams pool                   4194304
DEFAULT buffer cache           4194304
KEEP buffer cache              4194304
RECYCLE buffer cache           4194304
DEFAULT 2K buffer cache        4194304
DEFAULT 4K buffer cache        4194304
DEFAULT 8K buffer cache        4194304
DEFAULT 16K buffer cache       4194304
DEFAULT 32K buffer cache       4194304
OSM Buffer Cache               4194304

13 rows selected.
```

In this example, I used automatic SGA memory management and controlled the size of the SGA via the single parameter SGA_TARGET. When my SGA size is under about 1GB, the granule is 4MB. When the SGA size is increased to some threshold over 1GB (it will vary slightly from operating system to operating system and even from release to release), I see an increased granule size:

```
sys@ORA10G> alter system set sga_target = 1512m scope=spfile;
System altered.

sys@ORA10G> startup force
ORACLE instance started.

Total System Global Area 1593835520 bytes
Fixed Size                  779316 bytes
Variable Size            401611724 bytes
Database Buffers        1191182336 bytes
Redo Buffers                262144 bytes
Database mounted.
Database opened.
sys@ORA10G> select component, granule_size from v$sga_dynamic_components;

COMPONENT                GRANULE_SIZE
------------------------ ------------
shared pool                  16777216
large pool                   16777216
java pool                    16777216
streams pool                 16777216
DEFAULT buffer cache         16777216
KEEP buffer cache            16777216
RECYCLE buffer cache         16777216
DEFAULT 2K buffer cache      16777216
DEFAULT 4K buffer cache      16777216
DEFAULT 8K buffer cache      16777216
DEFAULT 16K buffer cache     16777216
DEFAULT 32K buffer cache     16777216
OSM Buffer Cache             16777216

13 rows selected.
```

As you can see, at 1.5GB of SGA, my pools will be allocated using 16MB granules, so any given pool size will be some multiple of 16MB.

With this in mind, let's look at each of the major SGA components in turn.

Fixed SGA

The *fixed SGA* is a component of the SGA that varies in size from platform to platform and from release to release. It is "compiled" into the Oracle binary itself at installation time (hence the name "fixed"). The fixed SGA contains a set of variables that point to the other components of the SGA, and variables that contain the values of various parameters. The size of the fixed SGA is something with which we have no control over, and it is generally very small. Think of this area as a "bootstrap" section of the SGA—something Oracle uses internally to find the other bits and pieces of the SGA.

Redo Buffer

The *redo buffer* is where data that needs to be written to the online redo logs will be cached temporarily, before it is written to disk. Since a memory-to-memory transfer is much faster then a memory-to-disk transfer, use of the redo log buffer can speed up database operation. The data will not reside in the redo buffer for very long. In fact, LGWR initiates a flush of this area in one of the following scenarios:

- Every three seconds

- Whenever someone commits

- When LGWR is asked to switch log files

- When the redo buffer gets one-third full or contains 1MB of cached redo log data

For these reasons, it will be a very rare system that will benefit from a redo buffer of more than a couple of megabytes in size. A large system with lots of concurrent transactions could benefit somewhat from large redo log buffers because while LGWR (the process responsible for flushing the redo log buffer to disk) is writing a portion of the log buffer, other sessions could be filling it up. In general, a long-running transaction that generates a lot of redo log will benefit the most from a larger than normal log buffer, as it will be continuously filling up part of the redo log buffer while LGWR is busy writing out some of it. The larger and longer the transaction, the more benefit it could receive from a generous log buffer.

The default size of the redo buffer, as controlled by the LOG_BUFFER parameter, is whatever is the greater of 512KB and (128 * number of CPUs)KB. The minimum size of this area is OS dependent. If you would like to find out what that is, just set your LOG_BUFFER to 1 byte and restart your database. For example, on my Red Hat Linux instance I see the following:

```
sys@ORA10G> alter system set log_buffer=1 scope=spfile;
System altered.

sys@ORA10G> startup force
ORACLE instance started.

Total System Global Area 1593835520 bytes
Fixed Size                   779316 bytes
Variable Size             401611724 bytes
Database Buffers         1191182336 bytes
Redo Buffers                 262144 bytes
Database mounted.
Database opened.
sys@ORA10G> show parameter log_buffer

NAME                                 TYPE        VALUE
------------------------------------ ----------- ------------------------------
log_buffer                           integer     262144
```

The smallest log buffer I can really have, regardless of my settings, is going to be 256KB on this system.

Block Buffer Cache

So far, we have looked at relatively small components of the SGA. Now we are going to look at one that is possibly huge in size. The *block buffer cache* is where Oracle stores database blocks before writing them to disk and after reading them in from disk. This is a crucial area of the SGA for us. Make it too small and our queries will take forever to run. Make it too big and we'll starve other processes (e.g., we won't leave enough room for a dedicated server to create its PGA, and we won't even get started).

In earlier releases of Oracle, there was a single block buffer cache, and all blocks from any segment went into this single area. Starting with Oracle 8.0, we had three places to store cached blocks from individual segments in the SGA:

- *Default pool*: The location where all segment blocks are normally cached. This is the original—and previously only—buffer pool.

- *Keep pool*: An alternate buffer pool where by convention you would assign segments that were accessed fairly frequently, but still got aged out of the default buffer pool due to other segments needing space.

- *Recycle pool*: An alternate buffer pool where by convention you would assign large segments that you access very randomly, and which would therefore cause excessive buffer flushing but would offer no benefit, because by the time you wanted the block again it would have been aged out of the cache. You would separate these segments out from the segments in the Default and Keep pools so that they would not cause those blocks to age out of the cache.

Note that in the Keep and Recycle pool descriptions I used the phrase "by convention." There is nothing in place to ensure that you use neither the Keep pool nor the Recycle pool in the fashion described. In fact, the three pools manage blocks in a mostly identical fashion; they do not have radically different algorithms for aging or caching blocks. The goal here was to give the DBA the ability to segregate segments to *hot*, *warm*, and *do not care to cache* areas. The theory was that objects in the Default pool would be hot enough (i.e., used enough) to warrant staying in the cache all by themselves. The cache would keep them in memory since they were very popular blocks. You might have had some segments that were fairly popular, but not really hot; these would be considered the warm blocks. These segments' blocks could get flushed from the cache to make room for some blocks you used infrequently (the "do not care to cache" blocks). To keep these warm segments blocks cached, you could do one of the following:

- Assign these segments to the Keep pool, in an attempt to let the warm blocks stay in the buffer cache longer.

- Assign the "do not care to cache" segments to the Recycle pool, keeping the Recycle pool fairly small so as to let the blocks come into the cache and leave the cache rapidly (decrease the overhead of managing them all).

This increased the management work the DBA had to perform, as there were three caches to think about, size, and assign objects to. Remember also that there is no sharing between them, so if the Keep pool has lots of unused space, it won't give it to the overworked Default or Recycle pool. All in all, these pools were generally regarded as a very fine, low-level tuning device, only to be used after most all other tuning alternatives had been looked at (if I could rewrite a query to do one-tenth the I/O rather then set up multiple buffer pools, that would be my choice!).

Starting in Oracle9*i*, the DBA had up to four more optional caches, the db_Nk_caches, to consider in addition to the Default, Keep, and Recycle pools. These caches were added in support of multiple blocksizes in the database. Prior to Oracle9*i*, a database would have a single blocksize (typically 2KB, 4KB, 8KB, 16KB, or 32KB). Starting with Oracle9*i*, a database can have a default blocksize, which is the size of the blocks stored in the Default, Keep, or Recycle pool, as well as up to four nondefault blocksizes, as explained in Chapter 3.

The blocks in these buffer caches are managed in the same way as the blocks in the original Default pool—there are no special algorithm changes for them either. Let's now move on to cover how the blocks are managed in these pools.

Managing Blocks in the Buffer Cache

For simplicity, assume in this discussion that there is just a single Default pool. Because the other pools are managed in the same way, we need only discuss one of them.

The blocks in the buffer cache are basically managed in a single place with two different lists pointing at them:

- The *dirty* list of blocks that need to be written by the database block writer (DBWn; we'll take a look at that process a little later)

- A list of *nondirty* blocks

The list of nondirty blocks used to be a Least Recently Used (LRU) list in Oracle 8.0 and before. Blocks were listed in order of use. The algorithm has been modified slightly in Oracle8*i* and in later versions. Instead of maintaining the list of blocks in some physical order, Oracle employs a *touch count* algorithm, which effectively increments a counter associated with a block as you hit it in the cache. This count is not incremented every time you hit the block, but about once every three seconds—if you hit it continuously. You can see this algorithm at work in one of the truly magic sets of tables: the X$ tables. The X$ tables are wholly undocumented by Oracle, but information about them leaks out from time to time.

The X$BH table shows information about the blocks in the block buffer cache (which offers more information than the documented V$BH view). Here, we can see the touch count get incremented as we hit blocks. We can run the following query against that view to find the five "currently hottest blocks" and join that information to the DBA_OBJECTS view to see what segments they belong to. The query orders the rows in X$BH by the TCH (touch count) column and keeps the first five. Then we join the X$BH information to DBA_OBJECTS by X$BH.OBJ to DBA_OBJECTS.DATA_OBJECT_ID:

```
sys@ORA10G> select tch, file#, dbablk,
  2          case when obj = 4294967295
  3              then 'rbs/compat segment'
  4              else (select max( '('||object_type||') ' ||
  5                              owner || '.' || object_name  ) ||
  6                          decode( count(*), 1, '', ' maybe!' )
  7                     from dba_objects
```

```
 8                    where data_object_id = X.OBJ )
 9        end what
10    from (
11  select tch, file#, dbablk, obj
12    from x$bh
13   where state <> 0
14   order by tch desc
15        ) x
16   where rownum <= 5
17  /


     TCH      FILE#     DBABLK WHAT
---------- ---------- ---------- -----------------------------------------
   51099          1       1434 (TABLE) SYS.JOB$
   49780          1       1433 (TABLE) SYS.JOB$
   48526          1       1450 (INDEX) SYS.I_JOB_NEXT
   11632          2         57 rbs/compat segment
   10241          1       1442 (INDEX) SYS.I_JOB_JOB
```

■**Note** $(2^{32} - 1)$ or 4,294,967,295 is a magic number used to denote "special" blocks. If you would like to understand what the block is associated with, use the query `select * from dba_extents where file_id = FILE# and block_id <= <DBABLK and block_id+blocks-1 >= DBABLK`.

You might be asking what is meant by the 'maybe!' and the use of MAX() in the preceding scalar subquery. This is due to the fact that DATA_OBJECT_ID is not a "primary key" in the DBA_OBJECTS view as evidenced by the following:

```
sys@ORA10G> select data_object_id, count(*)
  2     from dba_objects
  3    where data_object_id is not null
  4    group by data_object_id
  5   having count(*) > 1;

DATA_OBJECT_ID  COUNT(*)
-------------- ----------
             2        17
             6         3
             8         3
            10         3
            29         3
           161         3
           200         3
           210         2
```

```
        294          7
        559          2

10 rows selected.
```

This is due to clusters (discussed in the Chapter 10), which may contain multiple tables. Therefore, when joining from X$BH to DBA_OBJECTS to print out a segment name, we would technically have to list all of the names of all of the objects in the cluster, as a database block does not belong to a single table all of the time.

We can even watch as Oracle increments the touch count on a block that we query repeatedly. We will use the magic table DUAL in this example—we know it is a one row, one column table. We need to find out the block information for that single row. The built-in DBMS_ROWID package is good for getting that. Additionally, since we query ROWID from DUAL, we are making Oracle actually read the real DUAL table from the buffer cache, not the "virtual" DUAL table enhancement of Oracle 10g.

■Note Prior to Oracle 10g, querying DUAL would incur a full table scan of a real table named DUAL stored in the data dictionary. If you set autotrace on and query SELECT DUMMY FROM DUAL, you will observe some I/O in all releases of Oracle (consistent gets). In 9i and before, if you query SELECT SYSDATE FROM DUAL or variable := SYSDATE in PL/SQL, you will also see real I/O occur. However, in Oracle 10g, that SELECT SYSDATE is recognized as not needing to actually query the DUAL table (since you are not asking for the column or rowid from dual) and is done in a manner similar to calling a function. Therefore, DUAL does not undergo a full table scan—just SYSDATE is returned to the application. This small change can dramatically decrease the amount of consistent gets a system that uses DUAL heavily performs.

So every time we run the following query, we should be hitting the real DUAL table:

```
sys@ORA9IR2> select tch, file#, dbablk, DUMMY
  2    from x$bh, (select dummy from dual)
  3   where obj = (select data_object_id
  4                  from dba_objects
  5                 where object_name = 'DUAL'
  6                   and data_object_id is not null)
  7  /

     TCH      FILE#     DBABLK D
---------- ---------- ---------- -
         1          1       1617 X
         0          1       1618 X

sys@ORA9IR2> exec dbms_lock.sleep(3.2);
PL/SQL procedure successfully completed.
```

```
sys@ORA9IR2> /

       TCH       FILE#     DBABLK D
---------- ---------- ---------- -
         2          1       1617 X
         0          1       1618 X

sys@ORA9IR2> exec dbms_lock.sleep(3.2);
PL/SQL procedure successfully completed.

sys@ORA9IR2> /

       TCH       FILE#     DBABLK D
---------- ---------- ---------- -
         3          1       1617 X
         0          1       1618 X

sys@ORA9IR2> exec dbms_lock.sleep(3.2);
PL/SQL procedure successfully completed.

sys@ORA9IR2> /

       TCH       FILE#     DBABLK D
---------- ---------- ---------- -
         4          1       1617 X
         0          1       1618 X
```

I expect output to vary by Oracle release—you may well see more than two rows returned. You might observe TCH not getting incremented every time. On a multiuser system, the results will be even more unpredictable. Oracle will attempt to increment the TCH once every three seconds (there is a TIM column that shows the last update time to the TCH column), but it is not considered important that the number be 100 percent accurate, as it is close. Also, Oracle will intentionally "cool" blocks and decrement the TCH count over time. So, if you run this query on your system, be prepared to see potentially different results.

So, in Oracle8*i* and above, a block buffer no longer moves to the head of the list as it used to; rather, it stays where it is in the list and has its touch count incremented. Blocks will naturally tend to "move" in the list over time, however. I put the word "move" in quotes because the block doesn't physically move; rather, multiple lists are maintained that point to the blocks and the block will "move" from list to list. For example, modified blocks are pointed to by a dirty list (to be written to disk by DBWn). Also, as they are reused over time, when the buffer cache is effectively full, and some block with a small touch count is freed, it will be "placed back" into approximately the middle of the list with the new data block.

The whole algorithm used to manage these lists is fairly complex and changes subtly from release to release of Oracle as improvements are made. The actual full details are not relevant to us as developers, beyond the fact that heavily used blocks will be cached, and blocks that are not used heavily will not be cached for long.

Multiple Blocksizes

Starting in Oracle9*i*, you can have multiple database blocksizes in the same database. Previously, all blocks in a single database were the same size and in order to have a different blocksize, you had to rebuild the entire database. Now you can have a mixture of the "default" blocksize (the blocksize you used when you initially created the database; the size that is used for the SYSTEM and all TEMPORARY tablespaces) and up to four other blocksizes. Each unique blocksize must have its own buffer cache area. The Default, Keep, and Recycle pools will only cache blocks of the default size. In order to have nondefault blocksizes in your database, you will need to have configured a buffer pool to hold them.

In this example, my default blocksize is 8KB. I will attempt to create a tablespace with a 16KB blocksize:

```
ops$tkyte@ORA10G> create tablespace ts_16k
  2  datafile size 5m
  3  blocksize 16k;
create tablespace ts_16k
*
ERROR at line 1:
ORA-29339: tablespace blocksize 16384 does not match configured blocksizes

ops$tkyte@ORA10G> show parameter 16k

NAME                                 TYPE        VALUE
------------------------------------ ----------- ------------------------------
db_16k_cache_size                    big integer 0
```

Right now, since I have not configured a 16KB cache, I cannot create such a tablespace. I could do one of a couple things right now to rectify this situation. I could set the DB_16K_CACHE_SIZE parameter and restart the database. I could shrink one of my other SGA components in order to make room for a 16KB cache in the existing SGA. Or, I might be able to just allocate a 16KB cache if the SGA_MAX_SIZE parameter was larger than my current SGA size.

■**Note** Starting in Oracle9*i*, you have the ability to resize various SGA components while the database is up and running. If you want the ability to "grow" the size of the SGA beyond its initial allocation, you must have set the SGA_MAX_SIZE parameter to some value larger than the allocated SGA. For example, if after startup your SGA size was 128MB and you wanted to add an additional 64MB to the buffer cache, you would have had to set the SGA_MAX_SIZE to 192MB or larger to allow for the growth.

In this example, I will shrink my DB_CACHE_SIZE since I currently have it set rather large:

```
ops$tkyte@ORA10G> show parameter db_cache_size

NAME                                 TYPE         VALUE
------------------------------------ ------------ ------------------------------
db_cache_size                        big integer  1G

ops$tkyte@ORA10G> alter system set db_cache_size = 768m;
System altered.

ops$tkyte@ORA10G> alter system set db_16k_cache_size = 256m;
System altered.

ops$tkyte@ORA10G> create tablespace ts_16k
  2    datafile size 5m
  3    blocksize 16k;
Tablespace created.
```

So, now I have another buffer cache set up: one to cache any blocks that are 16KB in size. The Default pool, controlled by the db_cache_size parameter, is 768MB in size and the 16KB cache, controlled by the db_16k_cache_size parameter, is 256MB in size. These two caches are mutually exclusive; if one "fills up," it cannot use space in the other. This gives the DBA a very fine degree of control over memory use, but it comes at a price. A price of complexity and management. These multiple blocksizes were not intended as a performance or tuning feature, but rather came about in support of transportable tablespaces—the ability to take formatted data files from one database and transport or attach them to another database. They were implemented in order to take data files from a transactional system that was using an 8KB blocksize and transport that information to a data warehouse using a 16KB or 32KB blocksize.

The multiple blocksizes do serve a good purpose, however, in testing theories. If you want to see how your database would operate with a different blocksize—how much space, for example, a certain table would consume if you used a 4KB block instead of an 8KB block— you can now test that easily without having to create an entirely new database instance.

You may also be able to use multiple blocksizes as a very finely focused tuning tool for a specific set of segments, by giving them their own private buffer pools. Or, in a hybrid system with transactional users, you could use one set of data and reporting/warehouse users could query a separate set of data. The transactional data would benefit from the smaller blocksizes due to less contention on the blocks (less data/rows per block means less people in general would go after the same block at the same time) as well as better buffer cache utilization (users read into the cache only the data they are interested in—the single row or small set of rows). The reporting/warehouse data, which might be based on the transactional data, would benefit from the larger blocksizes due in part to less block overhead (it takes less storage over-all), and larger logical I/O sizes perhaps. And since reporting/warehouse data does not have the same update contention issues, the fact that there are more rows per block is not a con-cern, but a benefit. Additionally, the transactional users get their own buffer cache in effect; they do not have to worry about the reporting queries overrunning their cache.

But in general, the Default, Keep, and Recycle pools should be sufficient for fine-tuning the block buffer cache, and multiple blocksizes would be used primarily for transporting data from database to database and perhaps for a hybrid reporting/transactional system.

Shared Pool

The Shared pool is one of the most critical pieces of memory in the SGA, especially with regard to performance and scalability. A Shared pool that is too small can kill performance to the point where the system appears to hang. A Shared pool that is too large can have the same effect. A Shared pool that is used incorrectly will be a disaster as well.

So, what exactly is the Shared pool? The Shared pool is where Oracle caches many bits of "program" data. When we parse a query, the parsed representation is cached there. Before we go through the job of parsing an entire query, Oracle searches the Shared pool to see if the work has already been done. PL/SQL code that you run is cached in the Shared pool, so the next time you run it, Oracle doesn't have to read it in from disk again. PL/SQL code is not only cached here, it is shared here as well. If you have 1,000 sessions all executing the same code, only one copy of the code is loaded and shared among all sessions. Oracle stores the system parameters in the Shared pool. The data dictionary cache (cached information about database objects) is stored here. In short, everything but the kitchen sink is stored in the Shared pool.

The Shared pool is characterized by lots of small (4KB or less in general) chunks of memory. Bear in mind that 4KB is not a hard limit—there will be allocations that exceed that size—but in general the goal is to use small chunks of memory to prevent the fragmentation that would occur if memory chunks were allocated in radically different sizes, from very small to very large. The memory in the Shared pool is managed on a LRU basis. It is similar to the buffer cache in that respect—if you don't use it, you'll lose it. A supplied package called DBMS_SHARED_POOL may be used to change this behavior—to forcibly pin objects in the Shared pool. You can use this procedure to load up your frequently used procedures and packages at database startup time, and make it so they are not subject to aging out. Normally, though, if over time a piece of memory in the Shared pool is not reused, it will become subject to aging out. Even PL/SQL code, which can be rather large, is managed in a paging mechanism so that when you execute code in a very large package, only the code that is needed is loaded into the Shared pool in small chunks. If you don't use it for an extended period of time, it will be aged out if the Shared pool fills up and space is needed for other objects.

The easiest way to break Oracle's Shared pool is to not use bind variables. As you saw in Chapter 1, not using bind variables can bring a system to its knees for two reasons:

- The system spends an exorbitant amount of CPU time parsing queries.

- The system uses large amounts of resources managing the objects in the Shared pool as a result of never reusing queries.

If every query submitted to Oracle is a unique query with the values hard-coded, the concept of the Shared pool is substantially defeated. The Shared pool was designed so that query plans would be used over and over again. If every query is a brand-new, never-before-seen query, then caching only adds overhead. The Shared pool becomes something that *inhibits performance*. A common but misguided technique that many use to try to solve this issue is adding more space to the Shared pool, which typically only makes things worse than before. As the Shared pool inevitably fills up once again, it gets to be even *more* of an overhead than the smaller Shared pool, for the simple reason that managing a big, full Shared pool takes more work than managing a smaller, full Shared pool.

The only true solution to this problem is to use shared SQL—to reuse queries. Earlier, in Chapter 1, we briefly looked at the parameter CURSOR_SHARING, which can work as a short-term crutch in this area. The only real way to solve this issue, however, is to use reusable SQL in the first place. Even on the largest of large systems, I find that there are typically at most 10,000 to 20,000 unique SQL statements. Most systems execute only a few hundred unique queries.

The following real-world example demonstrates just how bad things can get if you use the Shared pool poorly. I was asked to work on a system where the standard operating procedure was to shut down the database each and every night, to wipe out the SGA and restart it clean. The reason for doing this was that the system was having issues during the day whereby it was totally CPU-bound and, if the database were left to run for more than a day, performance would really start to decline. They were using a 1GB Shared pool inside of a 1.1GB SGA. This is true: 0.1GB dedicated to block buffer cache and other elements and 1GB dedicated to caching unique queries that would never be executed again. The reason for the cold start was that if they left the system running for more than a day, they would run out of free memory in the Shared pool. At that point, the overhead of aging structures out (especially from a structure so large) was such that it overwhelmed the system and performance was massively degraded (not that performance was that great anyway, since they were managing a 1GB Shared pool). Additionally, the people working on this system constantly wanted to add more and more CPUs to the machine, due to the fact that hard-parsing SQL is so CPU intensive. By correcting the application and allowing it to use bind variables, not only did the physical machine requirements drop (they then had many times more CPU power than they needed), but also the allocation of memory to the various pools was reversed. Instead of a 1GB Shared pool, they had less then 100MB allocated—and they never used it all over many weeks of continuous uptime.

One last comment about the Shared pool and the parameter SHARED_POOL_SIZE. In Oracle9*i* and before, there is no direct relationship between the outcome of the query

```
ops$tkyte@ORA9IR2> select sum(bytes) from v$sgastat where pool = 'shared pool';

SUM(BYTES)
----------
 100663296
```

and the SHARED_POOL_SIZE parameter

```
ops$tkyte@ORA9IR2> show parameter shared_pool_size

NAME                                 TYPE        VALUE
------------------------------------ ----------- ------------------------------
shared_pool_size                     big integer 83886080
```

other than the fact that the SUM(BYTES) FROM V$SGASTAT will always be larger than the SHARED_POOL_SIZE. The Shared pool holds many other structures that are outside the scope of the corresponding parameter. The SHARED_POOL_SIZE is typically the largest contributor to the Shared pool as reported by the SUM(BYTES), but it is not the only contributor. For example, the parameter CONTROL_FILES contributes 264 bytes per file to the "miscellaneous" section of the Shared pool. It is unfortunate that the "Shared pool" in V$SGASTAT and the parameter SHARED_POOL_SIZE are named as they are, since the parameter contributes to the size of the Shared pool, but it is not the *only* contributor.

In Oracle 10*g* and above, however, you should see a one-to-one correspondence between the two, assuming you are using manual SGA memory management (i.e., you have set the SHARED_POOL_SIZE parameter yourself):

```
ops$tkyte@ORA10G> select sum(bytes)/1024/1024 mbytes
  2  from v$sgastat where pool = 'shared pool';

   MBYTES
----------
      128

ops$tkyte@ORA10G> show parameter shared_pool_size;

NAME                                 TYPE        VALUE
------------------------------------ ----------- ------------------------------
shared_pool_size                     big integer 128M
```

This is a relatively important change as you go from Oracle9*i* and before to 10*g*. In Oracle 10*g*, the SHARED_POOL_SIZE parameter controls the size of the Shared pool, whereas in Oracle9*i* and before, it was just the largest contributor to the Shared pool. You would want to review your 9*i* and before actual Shared pool size (based on V$SGASTAT) and use that figure to set your SHARED_POOL_SIZE parameter in Oracle 10*g* and above. The various other components that used to add to the size of the Shared pool now expect that memory to have been allocated for them by you.

Large Pool

The *Large pool* is not so named because it is a "large" structure (although it may very well be large in size). It is so named because it is used for allocations of large pieces of memory that are bigger than the Shared pool is designed to handle.

Prior to the introduction of the Large pool in Oracle 8.0, all memory allocation took place in the Shared pool. This was unfortunate if you were using features that made use of "large" memory allocations such as shared server UGA memory allocations. This issue was further complicated by the fact that processing, which tended to need a lot of memory allocation, would use the memory in a different manner than the way in which the Shared pool managed it. The Shared pool manages memory on a LRU basis, which is perfect for caching and reusing data. Large memory allocations, however, tended to get a chunk of memory, use it, and then were done with it—there was no need to cache this memory.

What Oracle needed was something similar to the Recycle and Keep buffer pools implemented for the block buffer cache. This is exactly what the Large pool and Shared pool are now. The Large pool is a Recycle-style memory space, whereas the Shared pool is more like the Keep buffer pool—if people appear to be using something frequently, then you keep it cached.

Memory allocated in the Large pool is managed in a heap, much in the way C manages memory via malloc() and free(). As soon as you "free" a chunk of memory, it can be used by other processes. In the Shared pool, there really was no concept of freeing a chunk of memory. You would allocate memory, use it, and then stop using it. After a while, if that memory needed to be reused, Oracle would age out your chunk of memory. The problem with using just a Shared pool is that one size doesn't always fit all.

The Large pool is used specifically by

- *Shared server connections*, to allocate the UGA region in the SGA

- *Parallel execution of statements*, to allow for the allocation of interprocess message buffers, which are used to coordinate the parallel query servers

- *Backup* for RMAN disk I/O buffers in some cases

As you can see, none of these memory allocations should be managed in an LRU buffer pool designed to manage small chunks of memory. With shared server connection memory, for example, once a session logs out, this memory is never going to be reused, so it should be immediately returned to the pool. Also, shared server UGA memory allocation tends to be "large." If you review the earlier examples with the SORT_AREA_RETAINED_SIZE or PGA_AGGREGATE_TARGET, the UGA can grow very large and is definitely bigger than 4KB chunks. Putting MTS memory into the Shared pool causes it to fragment into odd-sized pieces of memory and, furthermore, you will find that large pieces of memory that will never be reused will age out memory that could be reused. This forces the database to do more work to rebuild that memory structure later.

The same is true for parallel query message buffers, since they are *not* LRU manageable. They are allocated and cannot be freed until they are done being used. Once they have delivered their message, they are no longer needed and should be released immediately. With backup buffers, this applies to an even greater extent—they are large, and once Oracle is done using them, they should just "disappear."

The Large pool is not mandatory when using shared server connections, but it is highly recommended. If you do not have a Large pool and use a shared server connection, the allocations come out of the Shared pool as they always did in Oracle 7.3 and before. This will definitely lead to degraded performance over some period of time and should be avoided. The Large pool will default to some size if the parameter DBWR_IO_SLAVES or PARALLEL_MAX_SERVERS is set to some positive value. It is recommended that you set the size of the Large pool manually if you are using a feature that uses it. The default mechanism is typically not the appropriate value for your situation.

Java Pool

The *Java pool* was added in version 8.1.5 of Oracle to support running Java in the database. If you code a stored procedure in Java, Oracle will make use of this chunk of memory when processing that code. The parameter JAVA_POOL_SIZE is used to fix the amount of memory allocated to the Java pool for all session-specific Java code and data.

The Java pool is used in different ways, depending on the mode in which the Oracle server is running. In dedicated server mode, the Java pool includes the shared part of each Java class, which is actually used per session. These are basically the read-only parts (execution vectors, methods, etc.) and are about 4KB to 8KB per class.

Thus, in dedicated server mode (which will most likely be the case for applications using purely Java stored procedures), the total memory required for the Java pool is quite modest and can be determined based on the number of Java classes you will be using. It should be noted that none of the per-session state is stored in the SGA in dedicated server mode, as this information is stored in the UGA and, as you will recall, the UGA is included in the PGA in dedicated server mode.

When connecting to Oracle using a shared server connection, the Java pool includes both of the following:

- The shared part of each Java class.

- Some of the UGA used for per-session state of each session, which is allocated from the JAVA_POOL within the SGA. The remainder of the UGA will be located as normal in the Shared pool, or if the Large pool is configured, it will be allocated there instead.

As the total size of the Java pool is fixed in Oracle9*i* and before, application developers will need to estimate the total requirement of their applications and multiply this estimate by the number of concurrent sessions they need to support. This number will dictate the overall size of the Java pool. Each Java UGA will grow or shrink as needed, but bear in mind that the pool must be sized such that all UGAs combined must be able to fit in it at the same time. In Oracle 10*g* and above, this parameter may be modified, and the Java pool may grow and shrink over time without the database being restarted.

Streams Pool

The *Streams pool* is a new SGA structure starting in Oracle 10*g*. Streams itself is a new database feature as of Oracle9*i* Release 2 and above. It was designed as a data sharing/replication tool and is Oracle's stated direction going forward for data replication.

■**Note** The statement that Streams "is Oracle's stated direction going forward for data replication" should not be interpreted as meaning that *Advanced Replication*, Oracle's now legacy replication feature, is going away anytime soon. Rather, Advanced Replication will continue to be supported in future releases. To learn more about Streams itself, see the *Streams Concepts Guide* available on http://otn.oracle.com in the Documentation section.

The Streams pool (or up to 10 percent of the Shared pool if no Streams pool is configured) is used to buffer queue messages used by the Streams process as it is moving/copying data from one database to another. Instead of using permanent disk-based queues, with the attendant overhead associated with them, Streams uses in-memory queues. If these queues fill up, they will spill over to disk eventually. If the Oracle instance with the memory queue fails for some reason, due to an instance failure (software crash), power failure, or whatever, these in-memory queues are rebuilt from the redo logs.

So, the Streams pool will only be important in systems using the Streams database feature. In those environments, it should be set in order to avoid "stealing" 10 percent of the Shared pool for this feature.

Automatic SGA Memory Management

Just as there are two ways to manage PGA memory, there are two ways to manage SGA memory starting in Oracle 10*g*: manually, by setting all of the necessary pool and cache parameters:

and automatically, by setting just a few memory parameters and a single SGA_TARGET parameter. By setting the SGA_TARGET parameter, you are allowing the instance to size and resize various SGA components.

■Note In Oracle9*i* and before, only manual SGA memory management was available—the parameter SGA_TARGET did not exist and the parameter SGA_MAX_SIZE was a limit, not a dynamic target.

In Oracle 10*g*, memory-related parameters are classified into one of two areas:

- *Auto-tuned SGA parameters*: Currently these are DB_CACHE_SIZE, SHARED_POOL_SIZE, LARGE_POOL_SIZE, and JAVA_POOL_SIZE.

- *Manual SGA parameters*: These include LOG_BUFFER, STREAMS_POOL, DB_NK_CACHE_SIZE, DB_KEEP_CACHE_SIZE, and DB_RECYCLE_CACHE_SIZE.

At any time in Oracle 10g, you may query V$SGAINFO to see which components of the SGA are resizable.

■Note To use automatic SGA memory management, the parameter STATISTICS_LEVEL must be set to TYPICAL or ALL. If statistics collection is not enabled, the database will not have the historical information needed to make the necessary sizing decisions.

Under automatic SGA memory management, the primary parameter for sizing the auto-tuned components is SGA_TARGET, which may be dynamically sized while the database is up and running, up to the setting of the SGA_MAX_SIZE parameter (which defaults to be equal to the SGA_TARGET, so if you plan on increasing the SGA_TARGET, you must have set the SGA_MAX_SIZE larger before starting the database instance). The database will use the SGA_TARGET value, minus the size of any of the other manually sized components such as the DB_KEEP_CACHE_SIZE, DB_RECYCLE_CACHE_SIZE, and so on, and use that amount of memory to size the default buffer pool, Shared pool, Large pool, and Java pool. Dynamically at runtime, the instance will allocate and reallocate memory between those four memory areas as needed. Instead of returning an ORA-04031 "Unable to allocate N bytes of shared memory" error to a user when the Shared pool runs out of memory, the instance could instead choose to shrink the buffer cache by some number of megabytes (a granule size) and increase the Shared pool by that amount.

Over time, as the memory needs of the instance are ascertained, the size of the various SGA components would become more or less fixed in size. The database also remembers the sizes of these four components across database startup and shutdown so that it doesn't have to start all over again figuring out the right size for your instance each time. It does this via four double-underscore parameters: __DB_CACHE_SIZE, __JAVA_POOL_SIZE, __LARGE_POOL_SIZE, and __SHARED_POOL_SIZE. During a normal or immediate shutdown, the database will record these values to the stored parameter file and use them upon startup to set the default sizes of each area.

Additionally, if you know you want a certain minimum value to be used for one of the four areas, you may set that parameter in addition to setting the SGA_TARGET. The instance will use your setting as the lower bound, or the smallest size that particular area may be.

Summary

In this chapter, we took a look at the Oracle memory structure. We started at the process and session level, examining the PGA and UGA, and their relationship. We saw how the mode in which we connect to Oracle will dictate how memory is organized. A dedicated server connection implies more memory used in the server process than under a shared server connection, but that use of a shared server connection implies there will be the need for a significantly larger SGA. Then, we discussed the main structures of the SGA itself. We discovered the differences between the Shared pool and the Large pool, and looked at why we might want a Large pool to "save" our Shared pool. We covered the Java pool and how it is used under various conditions, and we looked at the block buffer cache and how that can be subdivided into smaller, more focused pools.

Now we are ready to move on to the physical processes that make up the rest of an Oracle instance.

CHAPTER 5

■■■

Oracle Processes

We've reached the last piece of the architecture puzzle. We've investigated the database and the set of physical files that constitute a database. In covering the memory used by Oracle, we've looked at one half of an instance. The last remaining architectural issue to cover is the set of *processes* that constitute the other half of the instance.

Each process in Oracle will perform a particular task or set of tasks, and each will have internal memory (PGA memory) allocated by it to perform its job. An Oracle instance has three broad classes of processes:

- *Server processes*: These perform work based on a client's request. We have already looked at dedicated and shared servers to some degree. These are the server processes.

- *Background processes*: These are the processes that start up with the database and perform various maintenance tasks, such as writing blocks to disk, maintaining the online redo log, cleaning up aborted processes, and so on.

- *Slave processes*: These are similar to background processes, but they are processes that perform extra work on behalf of either a background or a server process.

Some of these processes, such as the database block writer (DBWn) and the log writer (LGWR), have cropped up already, but here we'll take a closer look at the function of each, and what each does and why.

■**Note** When I use the term "process" in this chapter, consider it to be synonymous with the term "thread" on operating systems where Oracle is implemented with threads (such as Windows). In the context of this chapter, I use the term "process" to cover both processes and threads. If you are using an implementation of Oracle that is multiprocess, such as you see on UNIX, the term "process" is totally appropriate. If you are using a single-process implementation of Oracle, such as you see on Windows, the term "process" will actually mean "thread within the Oracle process." So, for example, when I talk about the DBWn process, the equivalent on Windows is the DBWn thread within the Oracle process.

Server Processes

Server processes are those that perform work on behalf of a client session. They are the processes that ultimately receive and act on the SQL statements our applications send to the database.

In Chapter 2, we briefly touched on two connection types to Oracle, namely the following:

- *Dedicated server*, whereby you get a dedicated process on the server for your connection. There is a one-to-one mapping between a connection to the database and a server process or thread.

- *Shared server*, whereby many sessions share a pool of server processes spawned and managed by the Oracle instance. Your connection is to a database dispatcher, not to a dedicated server process created just for your connection.

■**Note** It is important to understand the difference between a connection and a session in Oracle terminology. A *connection* is just a physical path between a client process and an Oracle instance (e.g., a network connection between you and the instance). A *session*, on the other hand, is a logical entity in the database, where a client process can execute SQL and so on. Many independent sessions can be associated with a single connection, and these sessions can even exist independently of a connection. We will discuss this further shortly.

Both dedicated and shared server processes have the same job: they process all of the SQL you give to them. When you submit a SELECT * FROM EMP query to the database, an Oracle dedicated/shared server process parses the query and places it into the Shared pool (or finds it in the Shared pool already, hopefully). This process comes up with the query plan, if necessary, and executes the query plan, perhaps finding the necessary data in the buffer cache or reading the data from disk into the buffer cache.

These server processes are the workhorse processes. Many times, you will find these processes to be the highest consumers of CPU time on your system, as they are the ones that do your sorting, your summing, your joining—pretty much everything.

Dedicated Server Connections

In dedicated server mode, there will be a one-to-one mapping between a client connection and a server process (or thread, as the case may be). If you have 100 dedicated server connections on a UNIX machine, there will be 100 processes executing on their behalf. Graphically it looks as shown in Figure 5-1.

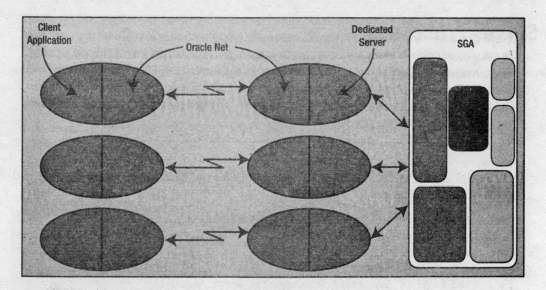

Figure 5-1. *Typical dedicated server connection*

Your client application will have Oracle libraries linked into it. These libraries provide the APIs you need in order to talk to the database. These APIs know how to submit a query to the database and process the cursor that is returned. They know how to bundle your requests into network calls that the dedicated server will know how to unbundle. This piece of software is called *Oracle Net*, although in prior releases you might have known it as *SQL*Net* or *Net8*. This is the networking software/protocol that Oracle employs to allow for client/server processing (even in an n-tier architecture, there is a client/server program lurking). Oracle employs this same architecture even if Oracle Net is not technically involved in the picture. That is, even when the client and server are on the same machine this two-process (also known as *two-task*) architecture is still employed. This architecture provides two benefits:

- *Remote execution*: It is very natural for the client application to be executing on a machine other than the database itself.

- *Address space isolation*: The server process has read-write access to the SGA. An errant pointer in a client process could easily corrupt data structures in the SGA if the client process and server process were physically linked together.

In Chapter 2, we saw how these dedicated servers are "spawned" or created by the Oracle listener process. We won't cover that process again; rather, we'll quickly look at what happens when the listener isn't involved. The mechanism is much the same as it was with the listener, but instead of the listener creating the dedicated server via a fork()/exec() in UNIX or an interprocess communication (IPC) call in Windows, the client process itself creates it.

■Note There are many variants of the fork() and exec() calls, such as vfork(), execve(), and so on. The call used by Oracle may vary by operating system and implementation, but the net effect is the same. fork() creates a new process that is a clone of the parent process, and on UNIX this is the only way to create a new process. exec() loads a new program image over the existing program image in memory, thus starting a new program. So, SQL*Plus can "fork" (copy itself) and then "exec" the Oracle binary, overlaying the copy of itself with this new program.

We can see this parent/child process creation clearly on UNIX when we run the client and server on the same machine:

```
ops$tkyte@ORA10G> select a.spid dedicated_server,
  2              b.process clientpid
  3    from v$process a, v$session b
  4   where a.addr = b.paddr
  5     and b.sid = (select sid from v$mystat where rownum=1)
  6 /


DEDICATED_SE CLIENTPID
------------ ------------
5114         5112

ops$tkyte@ORA10G> !/bin/ps -p 5114 5112
  PID TTY      STAT   TIME COMMAND
 5112 pts/1    R      0:00 sqlplus
 5114 ?        S      0:00 oracleora10g (DESCRIPTION=(LOCAL=YES)..(PROTOCOL=beq)))
```

Here, I used a query to discover the process ID (PID) associated with my dedicated server (the SPID from V$PROCESS is the operating system PID of the process that was being used during the execution of that query).

Shared Server Connections

Let's now take a look at the shared server process in more detail. This type of connection mandates the use of Oracle Net even if the client and server are on the same machine—you cannot use shared server without using the Oracle TNS listener. As described earlier, the client application will connect to the Oracle TNS listener and will be redirected or handed off to a dispatcher. The dispatcher acts as the conduit between the client application and the shared server process. Figure 5-2 is a diagram of the architecture of a shared server connection to the database.

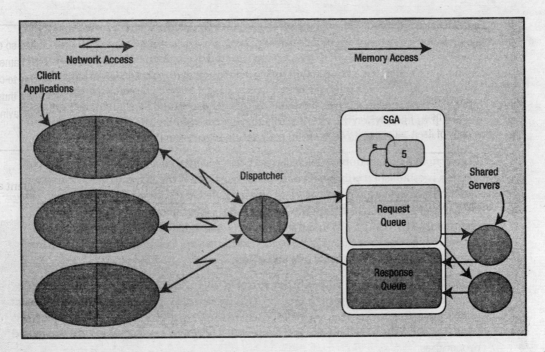

Figure 5-2. *Typical shared server connection*

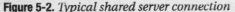

Here, we can see that the client applications, with the Oracle libraries linked in, will be physically connected to a dispatcher process. We may have many dispatchers configured for any given instance, but it is not uncommon to have just one dispatcher for hundreds—even thousands—of users. The dispatcher is simply responsible for receiving inbound requests from the client applications and putting them into a request queue in the SGA. The first available shared server process, which is basically the same as a dedicated server process, will pick up the request from the queue and attach the UGA of the associated session (the boxes labeled "S" in Figure 5-2). The shared server will process that request and place any output from it into the response queue. The dispatcher constantly monitors the response queue for results and transmits them back to the client application. As far as the client is concerned, it cannot really tell if it is connected via a dedicated server or a shared connection—they appear to be the same. Only at the database level is the difference apparent.

Connections vs. Sessions

It surprises many people to discover that a connection is not synonymous with a session. In most people's eyes they are the same, but the reality is they do not have to be. A connection may have zero, one, or more sessions established on it. Each session is separate and independent, even though they all share the same physical connection to the database. A commit in one session does not affect any other session on that connection. In fact, each session using that connection could use different user identities!

In Oracle, a connection is simply a physical circuit between your client process and the database instance—a network connection, most commonly. The connection may be to a dedicated server process or to a dispatcher. As previously stated, a connection may have zero or more sessions, meaning that a connection may exist with no corresponding sessions. Additionally, a session *may or may not* have a connection. Using advanced Oracle Net features such as connection pooling, a physical connection may be dropped by a client, leaving the session intact (but idle). When the client wants to perform some operation in that *session*, it would reestablish the physical *connection*. Let's define these terms in more detail:

- *Connection*: A connection is a physical path from a client to an Oracle instance. A connection is established either over a network or over an IPC mechanism. A connection is typically between a client process and either a dedicated server or a dispatcher. However, using Oracle's Connection Manager (CMAN), a connection may be between a client and CMAN, and CMAN and the database. Coverage of CMAN is beyond the scope of this book, but *Oracle Net Services Administrator's Guide* (freely available from http://otn.oracle.com) covers it in some detail.

- *Session*: A session is a logical entity that exists in the instance. It is your *session state*, or a collection of data structures in memory that represents your unique session. It is what would come first to most people's minds when thinking of a "database connection." It is your session in the server, where you execute SQL, commit transactions, and run stored procedures.

We can use SQL*Plus to see connections and sessions in action, and also to recognize that it could be a very common thing indeed for a connection to have more than one session. We'll simply use the AUTOTRACE command and discover that we have two sessions. Over a single connection, using a single process, we'll establish two sessions. Here is the first:

```
ops$tkyte@ORA10G> select username, sid, serial#, server, paddr, status
  2   from v$session
  3   where username = USER
  4  /

USERNAME   SID  SERIAL# SERVER    PADDR    STATUS
--------- ---- -------- --------- -------- --------
OPS$TKYTE  153     3196 DEDICATED AE4CF614 ACTIVE
```

Now, that shows right now that we have one session: a single dedicated server–connected session. The PADDR column is the address of our sole dedicated server process. Now, we simply turn on AUTOTRACE to see the statistics of statements we execute in SQL*Plus:

```
ops$tkyte@ORA10G> set autotrace on statistics
ops$tkyte@ORA10G> select username, sid, serial#, server, paddr, status
  2   from v$session
  3   where username = USER
  4  /
```

```
USERNAME    SID   SERIAL# SERVER     PADDR     STATUS
---------   ----  ------- ---------  --------  --------
OPS$TKYTE   151      1511 DEDICATED  AE4CF614  INACTIVE
OPS$TKYTE   153      3196 DEDICATED  AE4CF614  ACTIVE


Statistics
----------------------------------------------------------
          0  recursive calls
          0  db block gets
          0  consistent gets
          0  physical reads
          0  redo size
        756  bytes sent via SQL*Net to client
        508  bytes received via SQL*Net from client
          2  SQL*Net roundtrips to/from client
          0  sorts (memory)
          0  sorts (disk)
          2  rows processed
ops$tkyte@ORA10G> set autotrace off
```

In doing so, we now have two sessions, but both are using the same single dedicated server process, as evidenced by them both having the same PADDR value. We can confirm in the operating system that no new processes were created and that we are using a single process—a single connection—for both sessions. Note that one of the sessions (the original session) is ACTIVE. That makes sense: it is running the query to show this information, so of course it is active. But that INACTIVE session—what is that one for? That is the AUTOTRACE session. Its job is to "watch" our real session and report on what it does.

When we enable AUTOTRACE in SQL*Plus, SQL*Plus will perform the following actions when we execute DML operations (INSERT, UPDATE, DELETE, SELECT, and MERGE):

1. It will create a new session using the current connection, if the secondary session does not already exist.

2. It will ask this new session to query the V$SESSTAT view to remember the initial statistics values for the session in which we will run the DML. This is very similar to the function the watch_stat.sql script performed for us in Chapter 4.

3. It will run the DML operation in the original session.

4. Upon completion of that DML statement, SQL*Plus will request the other session to query V$SESSTAT again and produce the report displayed previously showing the difference in the statistics for the session that executed the DML.

If you turn off AUTOTRACE, SQL*Plus will terminate this additional session and you will no longer see it in V$SESSION. A question you might ask is, "Why does SQL*Plus do this trick?" The answer is fairly straightforward. SQL*Plus does it for the same reason that we used a second SQL*Plus session in Chapter 4 to monitor memory and temporary space usage: if we had used a single session to monitor memory usage, we would have been using memory to do the monitoring. By observing the statistics in a single session, we would change those statistics. If SQL*Plus used a single session to report on the number of I/Os performed, how many bytes were transferred over the network, and how many sorts happened, then the queries used to find these details would be adding to the statistics themselves. They could be sorting, performing I/O, transferring data over the network (one would assume they would!), and so on. Hence, we need to use another session to measure correctly.

So far, we've seen a connection with one or two sessions. Now we'd like to use SQL*Plus to see a connection with no session. That one is pretty easy. In the same SQL*Plus window used in the previous example, simply type the "misleading" command, DISCONNECT:

```
ops$tkyte@ORA10G> disconnect
Disconnected from Oracle Database 10g Enterprise Edition Release 10.1.0.3.0 -
Production
With the Partitioning, OLAP and Data Mining options
ops$tkyte@ORA10G>
```

Technically, that command should be called DESTROY_ALL_SESSIONS instead of DISCONNECT, since we haven't really disconnected physically.

■Note The true disconnect in SQL*Plus is "exit," as you would have to exit to completely destroy the connection.

We have, however, closed all of our sessions. If we open another session using some other user account and query (replacing OPS$TKYTE with your account name, of course),

```
sys@ORA10G> select * from v$session where username = 'OPS$TKYTE';
no rows selected
```

we can see that we have no sessions—but we still have a process, a physical connection (using the previous ADDR value):

```
sys@ORA10G> select username, program
  2  from v$process
  3  where addr = hextoraw('AE4CF614');

USERNAME        PROGRAM
--------------- ---------------------------------------------------
tkyte           oracle@localhost.localdomain (TNS V1-V3)
```

So, here we have a "connection" with no sessions associated with it. We can use the also misnamed SQL*Plus CONNECT command to create a new session in this existing process (the CONNECT command might be better named CREATE_SESSION):

```
ops$tkyte@ORA10G> connect /
Connected.

ops$tkyte@ORA10G> select username, sid, serial#, server, paddr, status
  2  from v$session
```

```
3   where username = USER
4   /


USERNAME   SID  SERIAL# SERVER    PADDR     STATUS
--------- ---- -------- --------- --------- --------

OPS$TKYTE  150     233 DEDICATED AE4CF614 ACTIVE
```

So, notice that we have the same PADDR, so we are using the same physical connection, but that we have (potentially) a different SID. I say "potentially" because we could get assigned the same SID—it just depends on whether other people logged in while we were logged out and whether the original SID we had was available.

So far, these tests were performed using a dedicated server connection, so the PADDR was the process address of our dedicated server process. What happens if we use a shared server?

■**Note** To connect via shared server, your database instance would have to have been started with the necessary setup. Coverage of how to configure shared server is beyond the scope of this book, but this topic is explored in detail in *Oracle Net Services Administrator's Guide.*

Well, let's log in using shared server and in that session query:

```
ops$tkyte@ORA10G> select a.username, a.sid, a.serial#, a.server,
  2         a.paddr, a.status, b.program
  3    from v$session a left join v$process b
  4      on (a.paddr = b.addr)
  5   where a.username - 'OPS$TKYTE'
  6   /

USERNAME  SID SERIAL# SERVER  PADDR     STATUS PROGRAM
--------- --- ------- ------- --------- ------ ----------------------

OPS$TKYTE 150    261 SHARED AE4CF118 ACTIVE oracle@localhost(S000)
```

Our shared server connection is associated with a process—the PADDR is there and we can join to V$PROCESS to pick up the name of this process. In this case, we see it is a shared server, as identified by the text S000.

However, if we use another SQL*Plus window to query this same bit of information, while leaving our shared server session idle, we see something like this:

```
sys@ORA10G> select a.username, a.sid, a.serial#, a.server,
  2         a.paddr, a.status, b.program
  3    from v$session a left join v$process b
  4      on (a.paddr = b.addr)
  5   where a.username = 'OPS$TKYTE'
  6   /
```

```
USERNAME  SID SERIAL# SERVER PADDR     STATUS    PROGRAM
--------- --- ------- ------ -------- -------- ------------------------
OPS$TKYTE 150     261 NONE   AE4CEC1C INACTIVE oracle@localhost(D000)
```

Notice that our PADDR is different and the name of the process we are associated with has also changed. Our idle shared server connection is now associated with a dispatcher, D000. Hence we have yet another method for observing multiple sessions pointing to a single process. A dispatcher could have hundreds, or even thousands, of sessions pointing to it.

An interesting attribute of shared server connections is that the shared server process we use can change from call to call. If I were the only one using this system (as I am for these tests), running that query over and over as OPS$TKYTE would tend to produce the same PADDR of AE4CF118 over and over. However, if I were to open up more shared server connections and start to use that shared server in other sessions, then I might notice that the shared server I use varies.

Consider this example. I'll query my current session information, showing the shared server I'm using. Then in another shared server session, I'll perform a long-running operation (i.e., I'll monopolize that shared server). When I ask the database what shared server I'm using again, I'll most likely see a different one (if the original one is off servicing the other session). In the following example, the code in bold represents a second SQL*Plus session that was connected via shared server:

```
ops$tkyte@ORA10G> select a.username, a.sid, a.serial#, a.server,
  2         a.paddr, a.status, b.program
  3    from v$session a left join v$process b
  4      on (a.paddr = b.addr)
  5   where a.username = 'OPS$TKYTE'
  6  /

USERNAME  SID SERIAL# SERVER PADDR     STATUS PROGRAM
--------- --- ------- ------- -------- ------ ----------------------------
OPS$TKYTE 150     261 SHARED AE4CF118 ACTIVE oracle@localhost(S000)

sys@ORA10G> connect system/manager@shared_server.us.oracle.com
Connected.
system@ORA10G> exec dbms_lock.sleep(20)


ops$tkyte@ORA10G> select a.username, a.sid, a.serial#, a.server,
  2         a.paddr, a.status, b.program
  3    from v$session a left join v$process b
  4      on (a.paddr = b.addr)
  5   where a.username = 'OPS$TKYTE'
  6  /

USERNAME  SID SERIAL# SERVER PADDR     STATUS PROGRAM
--------- --- ------- ------ -------- ------ -------
OPS$TKYTE 150 261     SHARED AE4CF614 ACTIVE oracle@localhost(S001)
```

Notice how the first time I queried, I was using S000 as the shared server. Then in another session, I executed a long-running statement that monopolized the shared server, which just happened to be S000 this time. The first nonbusy shared server is the one that gets assigned the work to do, and in this case no one else was asking to use the S000 shared server, so the DBMS_LOCK command took it. Now, when I queried again in the first SQL*Plus session, I got assigned to another shared server process, since the S000 shared server was busy.

It is interesting to note that the parse of a query (returns no rows yet) could be processed by shared server S000, the fetch of the first row by S001, the fetch of the second row by S002, and the closing of the cursor by S003. That is, an individual statement might be processed bit by bit by many shared servers.

So, what we have seen in this section is that a connection—a physical pathway from a client to a database instance—may have zero, one, or more sessions established on it. We have seen one use case of that when using SQL*Plus's AUTOTRACE facility. Many other tools employ this ability as well. For example, Oracle Forms uses multiple sessions on a single connection to implement its debugging facilities. The n-tier proxy authentication feature of Oracle, used to provide end-to-end identification of users from the browser to the database, makes heavy use of the concept of a single connection with multiple sessions, but in each session there would use a potentially different user account. We have seen that sessions can use many processes over time, especially in a shared server environment. Also, if we are using connection pooling with Oracle Net, then our session might not be associated with any process at all; the client would drop the connection after an idle time and reestablish it transparently upon detecting activity.

In short, there is a many-to-many relationship between connections and sessions. However, the most common case, the one most of us see day to day, is a one-to-one relationship between a dedicated server and a single session.

Dedicated Server vs. Shared Server

Before we continue to examine the rest of the processes, let's discuss why there are two connection modes and when one might be more appropriate than the other.

When to Use Dedicated Server

As noted previously, in dedicated server mode there is a one-to-one mapping between client connection and server process. This is by far the most common method of connection to the Oracle database for all SQL-based applications. It is the simplest to set up and provides the easiest way to establish connections. It requires little to no configuration.

Since there is a one-to-one mapping, you do not have to be concerned that a long-running transaction will block other transactions. Those other transactions will simply proceed via their own dedicated processes. Therefore, it is the only mode you should consider using in a non-OLTP environment where you may have long-running transactions. Dedicated server is the recommended configuration for Oracle, and it scales rather nicely. As long as your server has sufficient hardware (CPU and RAM) to service the number of dedicated server processes your system needs, dedicated server may be used for thousands of concurrent connections.

Certain operations must be done in a dedicated server mode, such as database startup and shutdown, so every database will have either both or just a dedicated server setup.

When to Use Shared Server

Shared server setup and configuration, while not difficult, involves an extra step beyond dedicated server setup. The main difference between the two is not, however, in their setup; it is in their mode of operation. With dedicated server, there is a one-to-one mapping between client connections and server processes. With shared server, there is a *many-to-one* relationship: many clients to a shared server.

As its name implies, shared server is a shared resource, whereas a dedicated server is not. When using a shared resource, you must be careful to not monopolize it for long periods of time. As you saw previously, use of a simple DBMS_LOCK.SLEEP(20) in one session would monopolize a shared server process for 20 seconds. Monopolization of these shared server resources can lead to a system that appears to hang.

Figure 5-2 depicts two shared servers. If I have three clients, and all of them attempt to run a 45-second process more or less at the same time, two of them will get their response in 45 seconds and the third will get its response in 90 seconds. This is rule number one for shared server: make sure your transactions are short in duration. They can be frequent, but they should be short (as characterized by OLTP systems). If they are not short, you will get what appears to be a total system slowdown due to shared resources being monopolized by a few processes. In extreme cases, if all of the shared servers are busy, the system will appear to hang for all users except the lucky few who are monopolizing the shared servers.

Another interesting situation that you may observe when using shared server is that of an *artificial deadlock*. With shared server, a number of server processes are being "shared" by a potentially large community of users. Consider a situation where you have five shared servers and one hundred user sessions established. Now, at most, five of those user sessions can be active at any point in time. Suppose one of these user sessions updates a row and does not commit. While that user sits there and ponders his or her modification, five other user sessions try to lock that same row. They will, of course, become blocked and will patiently wait for that row to become available. Now, the user session that holds the lock on this row attempts to commit its transaction (hence releasing the lock on the row). That user session will find that all of the shared servers are being monopolized by the five waiting sessions. We have an artificial deadlock situation here: the holder of the lock will never get a shared server to permit the commit, unless one of the waiting sessions gives up its shared server. But, unless the waiting sessions are waiting for the lock with a timeout, they will never give up their shared server (you could, of course, have an administrator "kill" their session via a dedicated server to release this logjam).

So, for these reasons, shared server is only appropriate for an OLTP system characterized by short, frequent transactions. In an OLTP system, transactions are executed in milliseconds—nothing ever takes more than a fraction of a second. Shared server is highly inappropriate for a data warehouse. Here, you might execute a query that takes one, two, five, or more minutes. Under shared server, this would be deadly. If you have a system that is 90 percent OLTP and 10 percent "not quite OLTP," then you can mix and match dedicated servers and shared server on the same instance. In this fashion, you can reduce the number of server processes on the machine dramatically for the OLTP users, and make it so that the "not quite OLTP" users do not monopolize their shared servers. In addition, the DBA can use the built-in Resource Manager to further control resource utilization.

Of course, a big reason to use shared server is when you have no choice. Many advanced connection features require the use of shared server. If you want to use Oracle Net connection pooling, you must use shared server. If you want to use database link concentration between databases, then you must use shared server for those connections.

■**Note** If you are already using a connection pooling feature in your application (e.g., you are using the J2EE connection pool), and you have sized your connection pool appropriately, using shared server will only be a performance inhibitor. You already sized your connection pool to cater for the number of concurrent connections that you will get at any point in time—you want each of those connections to be a direct dedicated server connection. Otherwise, you just have a connection pooling feature connecting to yet another connection pooling feature.

Potential Benefits of Shared Server

So, what are the benefits of shared server, bearing in mind that you have to be somewhat careful about the transaction types you let use it? Shared server does three things for us mainly: it reduces the number of operating system processes/threads, it artificially limits the degree of concurrency, and it reduces the memory needed on the system. We'll discuss these points in more detail in the sections that follow.

Reduces the Number of Operating System Processes/Threads

On a system with thousands of users, the operating system may quickly become overwhelmed when trying to manage thousands of processes. In a typical system, only a fraction of the thousands of users are concurrently active at any point in time. For example, I've worked on systems recently with 5,000 concurrent users. At any one point in time, at most 50 were active. This system would work effectively with 50 shared server processes, reducing the number of processes the operating system has to manage by two orders of magnitude (100 times). The operating system can now, to a large degree, avoid context switching.

Artificially Limits the Degree of Concurrency

Speaking as a person who has been involved in lots of benchmarks, the benefits of this are obvious to me. When running benchmarks, people frequently ask to run as many users as possible until the system breaks. One of the outputs of these benchmarks is always a chart that shows the number of concurrent users versus the number of transactions (see Figure 5-3).

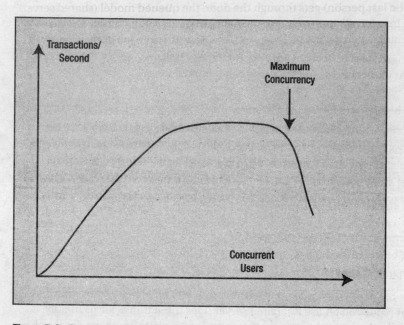

Figure 5-3. *Concurrent users vs. transactions per second*

Initially, as you add concurrent users, the number of transactions increases. At some point, however, adding additional users does not increase the number of transactions you can perform per second—the graph tends to drop off. The throughput has peaked and now response time starts to increase (you are doing the same number of transactions per second, but the end users are observing slower response times). As you continue adding users, you will find that the throughput will actually start to decline. The concurrent user count before this drop-off is the maximum degree of concurrency you want to allow on the system. Beyond this point, the system becomes flooded and queues begin forming to perform work. Much like a backup at a tollbooth, the system can no longer keep up. Not only does response time rise dramatically at this point, but throughput from the system may fall as well as the overhead of simply context switching and sharing resources between too many consumers takes additional resources itself. If we limit the maximum concurrency to the point right before this drop, we can sustain maximum throughput and minimize the increase in response time for most users. Shared server allows us to limit the maximum degree of concurrency on our system to this number.

An analogy for this process could be a simple door. The width of the door and the width of people limit the maximum people per minute throughput. At low "load," there is no problem; however, as more people approach, some forced waiting occurs (CPU time slice). If a lot of people want to get through the door, we get the fallback effect—there are so many saying "after you" and false starts that the throughput falls. Everybody gets delayed getting through. Using a queue means the throughput increases, some people get through the door almost as fast as if there was no queue, while others (the ones put at the end of the queue) experience the greatest delay and might fret that "this was a bad idea." But when you measure how fast everybody (including the last person) gets through the door, the queued model (shared server) performs better than a free-for-all approach (even with polite people; but conjure up the image of the doors opening when a store has a large sale, with everybody pushing very hard to get through).

Reduces the Memory Needed on the System

This is one of the most highly touted reasons for using shared server: it reduces the amount of required memory. It does, but not as significantly as you might think, especially given the new automatic PGA memory management discussed in Chapter 4, where work areas are allocated to a process, used, and released—and their size varies based on the concurrent workload. So, this was a fact that was *truer* in older releases of Oracle but is not as meaningful today. Also, remember that when you use shared server, the UGA is located in the SGA. This means that when switching over to shared server, you must be able to accurately determine your expected UGA memory needs and allocate appropriately in the SGA, via the LARGE_POOL_SIZE parameter. So, the SGA requirements for the shared server configuration are typically very large. This memory must typically be preallocated and, thus, can only be used by the database instance.

■**Note** It is true that with a resizable SGA, you may grow and shrink this memory over time, but for the most part, it will be "owned" by the database instance and will not be usable by other processes.

Contrast this with dedicated server, where anyone can use any memory not allocated to the SGA. So, if the SGA is much larger due to the UGA being located in it, where do the memory savings come from? They comes from having that many fewer PGAs allocated. Each dedicated/shared server has a PGA. This is process information. It is sort areas, hash areas, and other process-related structures. It is this memory need that you are removing from the system by using shared server. If you go from using 5,000 dedicated servers to 100 shared servers, it is the cumulative sizes of the 4,900 PGAs (excluding their UGAs) you no longer need that you are saving with shared server.

Dedicated/Shared Server Wrap-Up

Unless your system is overloaded, or you need to use a shared server for a specific feature, a dedicated server will probably serve you best. A dedicated server is simple to set up (in fact, there is no setup!) and makes tuning easier.

■**Note** With shared server connections, a session's trace information (SQL_TRACE=TRUE output) may be spread across many individual trace files, and reconstructing what that session has done is made more difficult.

If you have a very large user community and *know* that you will be deploying with shared server, I would urge you to *develop and test* with shared server. It will increase your likelihood of failure if you develop under just a dedicated server and never test on shared server. Stress the system, benchmark it, and make sure that your application is well behaved under shared server. That is, make sure it does not monopolize shared servers for too long. If you find that it does so during development, it is much easier to fix than during deployment. You can use features such as the Advanced Queuing (AQ) to turn a long-running process into an apparently short one, but you have to *design* that into your application. These sorts of things are best done when you are developing. Also, there have historically been differences between the feature set available to shared server connections versus dedicated server connections. We already discussed the lack of automatic PGA memory management in Oracle 9*i*, for example, but also in the past things as basic as a hash join between two tables were not available in shared server connections.

Background Processes

The Oracle instance is made up of two things: the SGA and a set of background processes. The background processes perform the mundane maintenance tasks needed to keep the database running. For example, there is a process that maintains the block buffer cache for us, writing blocks out to the data files as needed. Another process is responsible for copying an online redo log file to an archive destination as it fills up. Yet another process is responsible for cleaning up after aborted processes, and so on. Each of these processes is pretty focused on its job, but works in concert with all of the others. For example, when the process responsible for writing to the log files fills one log and goes to the next, it will notify the process responsible for archiving that full log file that there is work to be done.

There is a V$ view you can use to see all of the possible Oracle background processes and determine which ones are currently in use in your system:

```
ops$tkyte@ORA9IR2> select paddr, name, description
  2    from v$bgprocess
  3  order by paddr desc
  4  /

PADDR    NAME DESCRIPTION
-------- ---- -----------------------------------------------------------------
5F162548 ARC1 Archival Process 1
5F162198 ARC0 Archival Process 0
5F161A38 CJQ0 Job Queue Coordinator
5F161688 RECO distributed recovery
5F1612D8 SMON System Monitor Process
5F160F28 CKPT checkpoint
5F160B78 LGWR Redo etc.
5F1607C8 DBW0 db writer process 0
5F160418 PMON process cleanup
00       DIAG diagnosibility process
00       FMON File Mapping Monitor Process
00       LMON global enqueue service monitor
```

```
00        LMD0 global enqueue service daemon 0
...
00        LMS7 global cache service process 7
00        LMS8 global cache service process 8
00        LMS9 global cache service process 9

69 rows selected.
```

Rows in this view with a PADDR other than 00 are processes (threads) configured and running on your system.

There are two classes of background processes: those that have a focused job to do (as just described) and those that do a variety of other jobs (i.e., utility processes). For example, there is a utility background process for the internal job queues accessible via the DBMS_JOB package. This process monitors the job queues and runs whatever is inside them. In many respects, it resembles a dedicated server process, but without a client connection. We will examine each of these background processes now, starting with the ones that have a focused job, and then look into the utility processes.

Focused Background Processes

Figure 5-4 depicts the Oracle background processes that have a focused purpose.

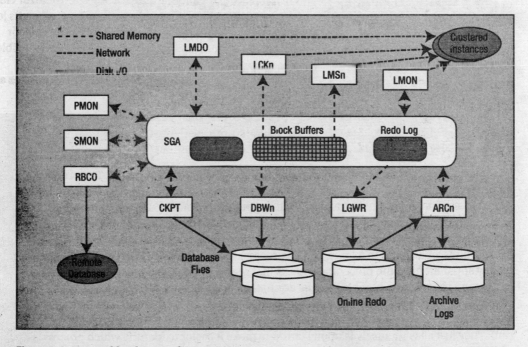

Figure 5-4. *Focused background processes*

You may not see all of these processes when you start your instance, but the majority of them will be present. You will only see ARCn (the archiver) if you are in ARCHIVELOG mode and have enabled automatic archiving. You will only see the LMD0, LCKn, LMON, and LMSn (more details on those processes shortly) processes if you are running Oracle RAC, a configuration of Oracle that allows many instances on different machines in a cluster to mount and open the same physical database.

■Note For the sake of clarity, missing from Figure 5-4 are the shared server dispatcher (Dnnn) and shared server (Snnn) processes.

So, Figure 5-4 depicts roughly what you might "see" if you started an Oracle instance, and mounted and opened a database. For example, on my Linux system, after starting the instance, I have the following processes:

```
$ ps -aef | grep 'ora_.*_ora10g$'
ora10g   5892   1  0 16:17 ?       00:00:00 ora_pmon_ora10g
ora10g   5894   1  0 16:17 ?       00:00:00 ora_mman_ora10g
ora10g   5896   1  0 16:17 ?       00:00:00 ora_dbw0_ora10g
ora10g   5898   1  0 16:17 ?       00:00:00 ora_lgwr_ora10g
ora10g   5900   1  0 16:17 ?       00:00:00 ora_ckpt_ora10g
ora10g   5902   1  0 16:17 ?       00:00:00 ora_smon_ora10g
ora10g   5904   1  0 16:17 ?       00:00:00 ora_reco_ora10g
ora10g   5906   1  0 16:17 ?       00:00:00 ora_cjq0_ora10g
ora10g   5908   1  0 16:17 ?       00:00:00 ora_d000_ora10g
ora10g   5910   1  0 16:17 ?       00:00:00 ora_s000_ora10g
ora10g   5916   1  0 16:17 ?       00:00:00 ora_arc0_ora10g
ora10g   5918   1  0 16:17 ?       00:00:00 ora_arc1_ora10g
ora10g   5920   1  0 16:17 ?       00:00:00 ora_qmnc_ora10g
ora10g   5922   1  0 16:17 ?       00:00:00 ora_mmon_ora10g
ora10g   5924   1  0 16:17 ?       00:00:00 ora_mmnl_ora10g
ora10g   5939   1  0 16:28 ?       00:00:00 ora_q000_ora10g
```

It is interesting to note the naming convention used by these processes. The process name starts with ora_. It is followed by four characters representing the actual name of the process, which are followed by _ora10g. As it happens, my ORACLE_SID (site identifier) is ora10g. On UNIX, this makes it very easy to identify the Oracle background processes and associate them with a particular instance (on Windows, there is no easy way to do this, as the backgrounds are threads in a larger, single process). What is perhaps most interesting, but not readily apparent from the preceding code, is that *they are all really the same exact binary executable program—there is not a separate executable for each "program."* Search as hard as you like, but you will not find the arc0 binary executable on disk anywhere. You will not find LGWR or DBW0. These processes are all really oracle (that's the name of the binary executable that is run). They just alias themselves upon startup to make it easier to identify which process is which. This enables a great deal of object code to be efficiently shared on the UNIX platform. On Windows, this is not nearly as interesting, as they are just threads within the process, so of course they are one big binary.

Let's now take a look at the function performed by each process, starting with the primary Oracle background processes.

PMON: The Process Monitor

This process is responsible for cleaning up after abnormally terminated connections. For example, if your dedicated server "fails" or is killed for some reason, PMON is the process responsible for fixing (recovering or undoing work) and releasing your resources. PMON will initiate the rollback of uncommitted work, release locks, and free SGA resources allocated to the failed process.

In addition to cleaning up after aborted connections, PMON is responsible for monitoring the other Oracle background processes and restarting them if necessary (and if possible). If a shared server or a dispatcher fails (crashes), PMON will step in and restart another one (after cleaning up for the failed process). PMON will watch all of the Oracle processes and either restart them or terminate the instance as appropriate. For example, it is appropriate to fail the instance in the event the database log writer process, LGWR, fails. This is a serious error, and the safest path of action is to terminate the instance immediately and let normal recovery fix the data. (Note that this is a rare occurrence and should be reported to Oracle Support immediately.)

The other thing PMON does for the instance is to register it with the Oracle TNS listener. When an instance starts up, the PMON process polls the well-known port address, unless directed otherwise, to see whether or not a listener is up and running. The well-known/default port used by Oracle is 1521. Now, what happens if the listener is started on some different port? In this case, the mechanism is the same, except that the listener address needs to be explicitly specified by the LOCAL_LISTENER parameter setting. If the listener is running when the database instance is started, PMON communicates with the listener and passes to it relevant parameters, such as the service name and load metrics of the instance. If the listener was not started, PMON will periodically attempt to contact it to register itself.

SMON: The System Monitor

SMON is the process that gets to do all of the "system-level" jobs. Whereas PMON was interested in individual processes, SMON takes a system-level perspective of things and is a sort of "garbage collector" for the database. Some of the jobs it does include the following:

- *Cleans up temporary space*: With the advent of "true" temporary tablespaces, the chore of cleaning up temporary space has lessened, but it has not gone away. For example, when building an index, the extents allocated for the index during the creation are marked as TEMPORARY. If the CREATE INDEX session is aborted for some reason, SMON is responsible for cleaning them up. Other operations create temporary extents that SMON would be responsible for as well.

- *Coalesces free space*: If you are using dictionary-managed tablespaces, SMON is responsible for taking extents that are free in a tablespace and contiguous with respect to each other and coalescing them into one larger free extent. This occurs only on dictionary-managed tablespaces with a default storage clause that has pctincrease set to a nonzero value.

- *Recovers transactions active against unavailable files*: This is similar to its role during database startup. Here, SMON recovers failed transactions that were skipped during instance/crash recovery due to a file(s) not being available to recover. For example, the file may have been on a disk that was unavailable or not mounted. When the file does become available, SMON will recover it.

- *Performs instance recovery of a failed node in RAC*: In an Oracle RAC configuration, when a database instance in the cluster fails (e.g., the machine the instance was executing on fails), some other node in the cluster will open that failed instance's redo log files and perform a recovery of all data for that failed instance.

- *Cleans up* OBJ$: OBJ$ is a low-level data dictionary table that contains an entry for almost every object (table, index, trigger, view, and so on) in the database. Many times, there are entries in here that represent deleted objects, or objects that represent "not there" objects, used in Oracle's dependency mechanism. SMON is the process that removes these rows that are no longer needed.

- *Shrinks rollback segments*: SMON will perform the automatic shrinking of a rollback segment to its optimal size, if it is set.

- *"Offlines" rollback segments*: It is possible for the DBA to *offline*, or make unavailable, a rollback segment that has active transactions. It may be possible that active transactions are using this offlined rollback segment. In this case, the rollback is not really offlined; it is marked as "pending offline." In the background, SMON will periodically try to truly take it offline, until it succeeds.

That should give you a flavor of what SMON does. It does many other things, such as flush the monitoring statistics that show up in the DBA_TAB_MONITORING view, the flush of the SCN to timestamp mapping information found in the SMON_SCN_TIME table, and so on. The SMON process can accumulate quite a lot of CPU over time, and this should be considered normal. SMON periodically wakes up (or is woken up by the other background processes) to perform these housekeeping chores.

RECO: Distributed Database Recovery

RECO has a very focused job: it recovers transactions that are left in a prepared state because of a crash or loss of connection during a *two-phase commit* (*2PC*). A 2PC is a distributed protocol that allows for a modification that affects many disparate databases to be committed atomically. It attempts to close the window for distributed failure as much as possible before committing. In a 2PC between N databases, one of the databases—typically (but not always) the one the client logged into initially—will be the coordinator. This one site will ask the other N-1 sites if they are ready to commit. In effect, this one site will go to the N-1 sites and ask them to be prepared to commit. Each of the N-1 sites reports back its "prepared state" as YES or NO. If any one of the sites votes NO, the entire transaction is rolled back. If all sites vote YES, then the site coordinator broadcasts a message to make the commit permanent on each of the N-1 sites.

If after some site votes YES it is prepared to commit, but before it gets the directive from the coordinator to actually commit the network fails or some other error occurs, the transaction becomes an *in-doubt distributed transaction*. The 2PC tries to limit the window of time in which this can occur, but cannot remove it. If we have a failure right then and there, the transaction will become the responsibility of RECO. RECO will try to contact the coordinator of the transaction to discover its outcome. Until it does that, the transaction will remain in its uncommitted state. When the transaction coordinator can be reached again, RECO will either commit the transaction or roll it back.

It should be noted that if the outage is to persist for an extended period of time, and you have some outstanding transactions, you can commit/roll them back manually yourself. You might want to do this since an in-doubt distributed transaction can cause *writers to block readers*—this is the one time this can happen in Oracle. Your DBA could call the DBA of the other database and ask her to query the status of those in-doubt transactions. Your DBA can then commit or roll them back, relieving RECO of this task.

CKPT: Checkpoint Process

The checkpoint process doesn't, as its name implies, do a checkpoint (checkpoints were discussed in Chapter 3, in the section on redo logs)—that's mostly the job of DBWn. It simply assists with the checkpointing process by updating the file headers of the data files. It used to be that CKPT was an optional process, but starting with version 8.0 of the database, it is always started, so if you do a ps on UNIX, you'll always see it there. The job of updating data files' headers with checkpoint information used to belong to the LGWR; however, as the number of files increased along with the size of a database over time, this additional task for LGWR became too much of a burden. If LGWR had to update dozens, or hundreds, or even thousands of files, there would be a good chance sessions waiting to commit these transactions would have to wait far too long. CKPT removes this responsibility from LGWR.

DBWn: Database Block Writer

The database block writer (DBWn) is the background process responsible for writing dirty blocks to disk. DBWn will write dirty blocks from the buffer cache, usually to make more room in the cache (to free buffers for reads of other data) or to advance a checkpoint (to move forward the position in an online redo log file from which Oracle would have to start reading, to recover the instance in the event of failure). As we discussed in Chapter 3, when Oracle switches log files, a checkpoint is signaled. Oracle needs to advance the checkpoint so that it no longer needs the online redo log file it just filled up. If it hasn't been able to do that by the time we need to reuse that redo log file, we get the "checkpoint not complete" message and we must wait.

■Note Advancing log files is only one of many ways for checkpoint activity to occur. There are incremental checkpoints controlled by parameters such as FAST_START_MTTR_TARGET and other triggers that cause dirty blocks to be flushed to disk.

As you can see, the performance of DBWn can be crucial. If it does not write out blocks fast enough to free buffers (buffers that can be reused to cache some other blocks) for us, we will see both the number and duration of waits on Free Buffer Waits and Write Complete Waits start to grow.

We can configure more than one DBWn; in fact, we can configure up to 20 (DBW0 . . . DBW9, DBWa . . . DBWj). Most systems run with one database block writer, but larger, multi-CPU systems can make use of more than one. This is generally done to distribute the workload of keeping a large block buffer cache in the SGA "clean," flushing the dirtied (modified) blocks to disk.

Optimally, the DBWn uses asynchronous I/O to write blocks to disk. With asynchronous I/O, DBWn gathers up a batch of blocks to be written and gives them to the operating system. DBWn does not wait for the operating system to actually write the blocks out; rather, it goes back and collects the next batch to be written. As the operating system completes the writes, it asynchronously notifies DBWn that it completed the writes. This allows DBWn to work much faster than if it had to do everything serially. We'll see later in the "Slave Processes" section how we can use I/O slaves to simulate asynchronous I/O on platforms or configurations that do not support it.

I would like to make one final point about DBWn. It will, almost by definition, write out blocks scattered all over disk—DBWn does lots of scattered writes. When you do an update, you'll be modifying index blocks that are stored here and there, and data blocks that are also randomly distributed on disk. LGWR, on the other hand, does lots of sequential writes to the redo log. This is an important distinction and one of the reasons that Oracle has a redo log and the LGWR process as well as the DBWn process. Scattered writes are significantly slower than sequential writes. By having the SGA buffer dirty blocks and the LGWR process do large sequential writes that can re-create these dirty buffers, we achieve an increase in performance. The fact that DBWn does its slow job in the background while LGWR does its faster job while the user waits gives us better overall performance. This is true even though Oracle may technically be doing more I/O than it needs to (writes to the log and to the data file)—the writes to the online redo log could *in theory* be skipped if, during a commit, Oracle physically wrote the modified blocks out to disk instead. In practice, it does not happen this way: LGWR writes the redo information to the online redo logs for every transaction, and DBWn flushes the database blocks to disk in the background.

LGWR: Log Writer

The LGWR process is responsible for flushing to disk the contents of the redo log buffer located in the SGA. It does this when one of the following is true:

- Every three seconds

- Whenever a commit is issued by any transaction

- When the redo log buffer is one-third full or contains 1MB of buffered data

For these reasons, having an enormous (hundreds of megabytes) redo log buffer is not practical—Oracle will never be able to use it all. The logs are written to with sequential writes as compared to the scattered I/O DBWn must perform. Doing large batch writes like this is much more efficient than doing many scattered writes to various parts of a file. This is one of the main reasons for having a LGWR and redo logs in the first place. The efficiency in just writing out the changed bytes using sequential I/O outweighs the additional I/O incurred. Oracle could just write database blocks directly to disk when you commit, but that would entail a lot of scattered I/O of full blocks, and this would be significantly slower than letting LGWR write out the changes sequentially.

ARCn: Archive Process

The job of the ARCn process is to copy an online redo log file to another location when LGWR fills it up. These archived redo log files can then be used to perform media recovery. Whereas online redo log is used to "fix" the data files in the event of a power failure (when the instance is terminated), archived redo logs are used to "fix" data files in the event of a hard disk failure. If we lose the disk drive containing the data file, /d01/oradata/ora10g/system.dbf, we can go to our backups from last week, restore that old copy of the file, and ask the database to apply all of the archived and online redo logs generated since that backup took place. This will "catch up" that file with the rest of the data files in our database, and we can continue processing with no loss of data.

ARCn typically copies online redo log files to at least two other locations (redundancy being a key to not losing data!). These other locations may be disks on the local machine or, more appropriately, at least one will be located on another machine altogether, in the event of a catastrophic failure. In many cases, these archived redo log files are copied off by some other process to some tertiary storage device, such as tape. They may also be sent to another machine to be applied to a "standby database," a failover option offered by Oracle. We'll discuss the processes involved in that shortly.

Remaining Focused Processes

Depending on the features of Oracle you are using, other focused processes may be visible. They are listed here with a brief description of their function. The processes described previously are nonnegotiable—you will have them if you have an Oracle instance running. The following processes are optional and will appear only if you make use of the specific feature. The following processes are unique to a database instance using ASM, as discussed in Chapter 3:

- *Automatic Storage Management Background (ASMB) process*: The ASMB process runs in a database instance that is making use of ASM. It is responsible for communicating to the ASM instance that is managing the storage, providing updated statistics to the ASM instance, and providing a "heartbeat" to the ASM instance, letting it know that it is still alive and functioning.

- *Rebalance (RBAL) process*: The RBAL process also runs in a database instance that is making use of ASM. It is responsible for processing a rebalance request (a redistribution request) as disks are added/removed to and from an ASM disk group.

The following processes are found in an Oracle RAC instance. RAC is a configuration of Oracle whereby multiple instances, each running on a separate node (typically a separate physical computer) in a cluster, may mount and open a single database. It gives you the ability to have more than one instance accessing, in a full read-write fashion, a single set of database files. The primary goals of RAC are twofold:

- *High availability*: With Oracle RAC, if one node/computer in the cluster fails due to a software, hardware, or human error, the other nodes may continue to function. The database will be accessible via the other nodes. You might lose some computing power, but you won't lose access to the database.

- *Scalability*: Instead of buying larger and larger machines to handle an increasing workload (known as *vertical scaling*), RAC allows you to add resources in the form of more machines in the cluster (known as *horizontal scaling*). Instead of trading in your 4 CPU machine for one that can grow to 8 or 16 CPUs, RAC gives you the option of adding another relatively inexpensive 4 CPU machine (or more than one).

The following processes are unique to a RAC environment. You will not see them otherwise.

* *Lock monitor (LMON) process*: The LMON process monitors all instances in a cluster to detect the failure of an instance. It then facilitates the recovery of the global locks held by the failed instance. It is also responsible for reconfiguring locks and other resources when instances leave or are added to the cluster (as they fail and come back online, or as new instances are added to the cluster in real time).

* *Lock manager daemon (LMD) process*: The LMD process handles lock manager service requests for the global cache service (keeping the block buffers consistent between instances). It works primarily as a broker sending requests for resources to a queue that is handled by the LMSn processes. The LMD handles global deadlock detection/resolution and monitors for lock timeouts in the global environment.

* *Lock manager server (LMSn) process*: As noted earlier, in a RAC environment, each instance of Oracle is running on a different machine in a cluster, and they all access, in a read-write fashion, the same exact set of database files. To achieve this, the SGA block buffer caches must be kept consistent with respect to each other. This is one of the main goals of the LMSn process. In earlier releases of Oracle Parallel Server (OPS), this was accomplished via a *ping*. That is, if a node in the cluster needed a read-consistent view of a block that was locked in exclusive mode by another node, the exchange of data was done via a disk flush (the block was pinged). This was a very expensive operation just to read data. Now, with the LMSn, this exchange is done via very fast cache-to-cache exchange over the clusters' high-speed connection. You may have up to ten LMSn processes per instance.

* *Lock (LCK0) process*: This process is very similar in functionality to the LMD process described earlier, but it handles requests for all global resources other than database block buffers.

* *Diagnosability daemon (DIAG) process*: The DIAG process is used exclusively in a RAC environment. It is responsible for monitoring the overall "health" of the instance, and it captures information needed in the processing of instance failures.

Utility Background Processes

These background processes are totally optional, based on your need for them. They provide facilities not necessary to run the database day to day, unless you are using them yourself, such as the job queues, or are making use of a feature that uses them, such as the new Oracle 10*g* diagnostic capabilities.

These processes will be visible in UNIX as any other background process would be—if you do a ps, you will see them. In my ps listing from the beginning of the Focused Background Processes section (reproduced in part here), you can see that I have

* Job queues configured. The CJQ0 process is the job queue coordinator.

* Oracle AQ configured, as evidenced by the Q000 (AQ queue process) and QMNC (AQ monitor process).

- Automatic SGA sizing enabled, as evidenced by the memory manager (MMAN) process.

- Oracle 10*g* manageability/diagnostic features enabled, as evidenced by the manageability monitor (MMON) and manageability monitor light (MMNL) processes.

```
ora10g    5894    1   0 16:17 ?        00:00:00 ora_mman_ora10g
ora10g    5906    1   0 16:17 ?        00:00:00 ora_cjq0_ora10g
ora10g    5920    1   0 16:17 ?        00:00:00 ora_qmnc_ora10g
ora10g    5922    1   0 16:17 ?        00:00:00 ora_mmon_ora10g
ora10g    5924    1   0 16:17 ?        00:00:00 ora_mmnl_ora10g
ora10g    5939    1   0 16:28 ?        00:00:00 ora_q000_ora10g
```

Let's take a look at the various processes you might see depending on the features you are using.

CJQ0 and Jnnn Processes: Job Queues

In the first 7.0 release, Oracle provided replication in the form of a database object known as a *snapshot*. Job queues were the internal mechanism by which these snapshots were refreshed, or made current.

A job queue process monitored a job table that told it when it needed to refresh various snapshots in the system. In Oracle 7.1, Oracle Corporation exposed this facility for all to use via a database package called DBMS_JOB. So a process that was solely the domain of the snapshot in 7.0 became the "job queue" in 7.1 and later versions. Over time, the parameters for controlling the behavior of the job queue (how frequently it should be checked and how many queue processes there should be) changed in name from SNAPSHOT_REFRESH_INTERVAL and SNAPSHOT_REFRESH_PROCESSES to JOB_QUEUE_INTERVAL and JOB_QUEUE_PROCESSES, and in current releases only the JOB_QUEUE_PROCESSES parameter is exposed as a user-tunable setting.

You may have up to 1,000 job queue processes. Their names will be J000, J001, . . . , J999. These processes are used heavily in replication as part of the materialized view refresh process. Streams-based replication (new with Oracle9*i* Release 2) uses AQ for replication and therefore does not use the job queue processes. Developers also frequently use the job queues in order to schedule one-off (background) jobs or recurring jobs—for example, to send an e-mail in the background, or process a long-running batch process in the background. By doing some work in the background, you can make a long task seem to take much less time to an impatient end user (he feels like it went faster, even though it might not be done yet). This is similar to what Oracle does with LGWR and DBWn processes—they do much of their work in the background, so you don't have to wait for them to complete all tasks in real time.

The Jnnn processes are very much like a shared server, but with aspects of a dedicated server. They are shared in the sense that they process one job after the other, but they manage memory more like a dedicated server would (their UGA memory is in the PGA, not the SGA). Each job queue process will run exactly one job at a time, one after the other, to completion. That is why we may need multiple processes if we wish to run jobs at the same time. There is no threading or preempting of a job. Once a job is running, it will run to completion (or failure).

You will notice that the Jnnn processes come and go over time—that is, if you configure up to 1,000 of them, you will not see 1,000 of them start up with the database. Rather, a sole process, the job queue coordinator (CJQ0) will start up, and as it sees jobs that need to be run in the job queue table, it will start the Jnnn processes. As the Jnnn processes complete their work and discover no new jobs to process, they will start to exit—to go away. So, if you schedule most of your jobs to run at 2:00 am when no one is around, you might well never actually "see" these Jnnn processes.

QMNC and Qnnn: Advanced Queues

The QMNC process is to the AQ tables what the CJQ0 process is to the job table. It monitors the advanced queues and alerts waiting message "dequeuers" that a message has become available. QMNC and Qnnn are also responsible for queue *propagation*—that is, the ability of a message that was enqueued (added) in one database to be moved to a queue in another database for dequeueing.

The Qnnn processes are to the QMNC process what the Jnnn processes are to the CJQ0 process. They are notified by the QMNC process of work that needs to be performed, and they process the work.

The QMNC and Qnnn processes are optional background processes. The parameter AQ_TM_PROCESSES specifies creation of up to ten of these processes named Q000, . . . , Q009, and a single QMNC process. If AQ_TM_PROCESSES is set to 0, there will be no QMNC or Qnnn processes. Unlike the Jnnn processes used by the job queues, the Qnnn processes are persistent. If you set AQ_TM_PROCESSES to 10, you will see ten Qnnn processes and the QMNC process at database startup and for the entire life of the instance.

EMNn: Event Monitor Processes

The EMNn process is part of the AQ architecture. It is used to notify queue subscribers of messages they would be interested in. This notification is performed asynchronously. There are Oracle Call Interface (OCI) functions available to register a callback for message notification. The callback is a function in the OCI program that will be invoked automatically whenever a message of interest is available in the queue. The EMNn background process is used to notify the subscriber. The EMNn process is started automatically when the first notification is issued for the instance. The application may then issue an explicit message_receive(dequeue) to retrieve the message.

MMAN: Memory Manager

This process is new with Oracle 10g and is used by the automatic SGA sizing feature. The MMAN process coordinates the sizing and resizing of the shared memory components (the default buffer pool, the Shared pool, the Java pool, and the Large pool).

MMON, MMNL, and Mnnn: Manageability Monitors

These processes are used to populate the Automatic Workload Repository (AWR), a new feature in Oracle 10g. The MMNL process flushes statistics from the SGA to database tables on a scheduled basis. The MMON process is used to "auto-detect" database performance issues and implement the new self-tuning features. The Mnnn processes are similar to the Jnnn or Qnnn processes for the job queues; the MMON process will request these slave processes to perform work on its behalf. The Mnnn processes are transient in nature—they will come and go as needed.

CTWR: Change Tracking Processes

This is a new optional process of the Oracle 10*g* database. The CTWR process is responsible for maintaining the new change tracking file, as described in Chapter 3.

RVWR: Recovery Writer

This process, another new optional process of the Oracle 10*g* database, is responsible for maintaining the *before* images of blocks in the Flash Recovery Area (described in Chapter 3) used with the FLASHBACK DATABASE command.

Remaining Utility Background Processes

So, is that the complete list? No, there are others. For example, Oracle Data Guard has a set of processes associated with it to facilitate the shipping of redo information from one database to another and apply it (see the *Data Guard Concepts and Administration Guide* from Oracle for details). There are processes associated with the new Oracle 10*g* Data Pump utility that you will see during certain Data Pump operations. There are Streams apply and capture processes as well. However, the preceding list covers most of the common background processes you will encounter.

Slave Processes

Now we are ready to look at the last class of Oracle processes: the *slave* processes. There are two types of slave processes with Oracle: I/O slaves and parallel query slaves.

I/O Slaves

I/O slaves are used to emulate asynchronous I/O for systems or devices that do not support it. For example, tape devices (which are notoriously slow) do not support asynchronous I/O. By using I/O slaves, we can mimic for tape drives what the operating system normally provides for disk drives. Just as with true asynchronous I/O, the process writing to the device batches a large amount of data and hands it off to be written. When the data is successfully written, the writer (our I/O slave this time, *not* the operating system) signals the original invoker, who removes this batch of data from its list of data that needs to be written. In this fashion, we can achieve a much higher throughput, since the I/O slaves are the ones waiting for the slow device, while their caller is off doing other important work getting the data together for the next write.

I/O slaves are used in a couple of places in Oracle. DBWn and LGWR can make use of them to simulate asynchronous I/O, and RMAN will make use of them when writing to tape.

Two parameters control the use of I/O slaves:

- BACKUP_TAPE_IO_SLAVES: This parameter specifies whether I/O slaves are used by RMAN to back up, copy, or restore data to tape. Since this parameter is designed around *tape* devices, and tape devices may be accessed by only one process at any time, this parameter is a Boolean, and not the number of slaves to use, as you might expect. RMAN will start up as many slaves as necessary for the number of physical devices being used.

When BACKUP_TAPE_IO_SLAVES = TRUE, an I/O slave process is used to write to or read from a tape device. If this parameter is FALSE (the default), then I/O slaves are not used for backups. Instead, the dedicated server process engaged in the backup will access the tape device.

- DBWR_IO_SLAVES: This parameter specifies the number of I/O slaves used by the DBW0 process. The DBW0 process and its slaves always perform the writing to disk of dirty blocks in the buffer cache. By default, the value is 0 and I/O slaves are not used. Note that if you set this parameter to a nonzero value, LGWR and ARCH will use their own I/O slaves as well—up to four I/O slaves for LGWR and ARCH will be permitted.

The DBWR I/O slaves appear with the name I1nn, and the LGWR I/O slaves appear with the name I2nn, where nn is a number.

Parallel Query Slaves

Oracle 7.1.6 introduced the parallel query capability into the database. This is the capability to take a SQL statement such as a SELECT, CREATE TABLE, CREATE INDEX, UPDATE, and so on and create an execution plan that consists of *many* execution plans that can be done simultaneously. The outputs of each of these plans are merged together into one larger result. The goal is to do an operation in a fraction of the time it would take if you did it serially. For example, say you have a really large table spread across ten different files. You have 16 CPUs at your disposal, and you need to execute an ad hoc query on this table. It might be advantageous to break the query plan into 32 little pieces and really make use of that machine, as opposed to just using one process to read and process all of that data serially.

When using parallel query, you will see processes named Pnnn—these are the parallel query slaves themselves. During the processing of a parallel statement, your server process will be known as the *parallel query coordinator*. Its name won't change at the operating system level, but as you read documentation on parallel query, when you see references to the coordinator process, know that it is simply your original server process.

Summary

We've covered the files used by Oracle, from the lowly but important parameter file to data files, redo log files, and so on. We've taken a look inside the memory structures used by Oracle, both in the server processes and the SGA. We've seen how different server configurations, such as shared server versus dedicated server mode for connections, will have a dramatic impact on how memory is used by the system. Lastly, we looked at the processes (or threads, depending on the operating system) that enable Oracle to do what it does. Now we are ready to look at the implementation of some other features of Oracle, such as locking, concurrency controls, and transactions.

CHAPTER 6

■ ■ ■

Locking and Latching

One of the key challenges in developing multiuser, database-driven applications is to maximize concurrent access and, at the same time, ensure that each user is able to read and modify the data in a consistent fashion. The *locking* mechanisms that allow this to happen are key features of any database, and Oracle excels in providing them. However, Oracle's implementation of these features is specific to Oracle—just as SQL Server's implementation is to SQL Server—and it is up to you, the application developer, to ensure that when your application performs data manipulation, it uses these mechanisms correctly. If you fail to do so, your application will behave in an unexpected way, and inevitably the integrity of your data will be compromised (as was demonstrated in Chapter 1).

In this chapter, we'll take a detailed look at how Oracle locks both data (e.g., rows in tables) and shared data structures (such as those found in the SGA). We'll investigate the granularity to which Oracle locks data and what that means to you, the developer. When appropriate, I'll contrast Oracle's locking scheme with other popular implementations, mostly to dispel the myth that row-level locking adds overhead; it adds overhead only if the implementation adds overhead. In the next chapter, we'll continue this discussion and investigate Oracle's multiversioning techniques and how locking strategies interact with them.

What Are Locks?

Locks are mechanisms used to regulate concurrent access to a shared resource. Note how I used the term "shared resource" and not "database row." It is true that Oracle locks table data at the row level, but it also uses locks at many other levels to provide concurrent access to various resources. For example, while a stored procedure is executing, the procedure itself is locked in a mode that allows others to execute it, but it will not permit another user to alter it in any way. Locks are used in the database to permit concurrent access to these shared resources, while at the same time providing data integrity and consistency.

In a single-user database, locks are not necessary. There is, by definition, only one user modifying the information. However, when multiple users are accessing and modifying data or data structures, it is crucial to have a mechanism in place to prevent concurrent modification of the same piece of information. This is what locking is all about.

It is very important to understand that there are as many ways to implement locking in a database as there are databases. Just because you have experience with the locking model of one particular relational database management system (RDBMS) does not mean you know everything about locking. For example, before I got heavily involved with Oracle, I used other databases such as Sybase, Microsoft SQL Server, and Informix. All three of these databases provide locking mechanisms for concurrency control, but there are deep and fundamental differences in the way locking is implemented in each one. To demonstrate this, I'll outline my progression from a SQL Server developer to an Informix user and finally an Oracle developer. This happened many years ago, and the SQL Server fans out there will tell me "But we have row-level locking now!" It is true: SQL Server may now use row-level locking, but the way it is implemented is *totally different* from the way it is done in Oracle. It is a comparison between apples and oranges, and that is the key point.

As a SQL Server programmer, I would hardly ever consider the possibility of multiple users inserting data into a table concurrently. It was something that just didn't often happen in that database. At that time, SQL Server provided only for page-level locking and, since all the data tended to be inserted into the last page of nonclustered tables, concurrent inserts by two users was simply not going to happen.

Note A SQL Server clustered table (a table that has a clustered index) is in some regard similar to, but very different from, an Oracle cluster. SQL Server used to only support page (block) level locking, and if every row inserted was to go to the "end" of the table, you would never have had concurrent inserts, concurrent transactions in that database. The clustered index in SQL Server was used to cause rows to be inserted all over the table, in sorted order by the cluster key, and as such was used to improve concurrency in that database.

Exactly the same issue affected concurrent updates (since an UPDATE was really a DELETE followed by an INSERT). Perhaps this is why SQL Server, by default, commits or rolls back immediately after execution of each and every statement, compromising transactional integrity in an attempt to gain higher concurrency.

So in most cases, with page-level locking, multiple users could not simultaneously modify the same table. Compounding this was the fact that while a table modification was in progress, many queries were also effectively blocked against that table. If I tried to query a table and needed a page that was locked by an update, I waited (and waited and waited). The locking mechanism was so poor that providing support for transactions that took more than a second was deadly—the entire database would appear to "freeze" if you did. I learned a lot of bad habits here. I learned that transactions were "bad" and that you ought to commit rapidly and never hold locks on data. Concurrency came at the expense of consistency. You either wanted to get it right or get it fast. I came to believe that you couldn't have both.

When I moved on to Informix, things were better, but not by much. As long as I remembered to create a table with row-level locking enabled, then I could actually have two people simultaneously insert data into that table. Unfortunately, this concurrency came at a high price. Row-level locks in the Informix implementation were expensive, both in terms of time and memory. It took time to acquire and "unacquire" or release them, and each lock consumed real memory. Also, the total number of locks available to the system had to be computed prior to starting the database. If you exceeded that number, then you were just out of luck. Consequently, most tables were created with page-level locking anyway, and, as with SQL Server, both row and page-level locks would stop a query in its tracks. As a result, I found that once again I would want to commit as fast as I could. The bad habits I picked up using SQL Server were simply reinforced and, furthermore, I learned to treat a lock as a very scarce resource—something to be coveted. I learned that you should manually escalate locks from row level to table level to try to avoid acquiring too many of them and bringing the system down, and bring it down I did—many times.

When I started using Oracle, I didn't really bother reading the manuals to find out how locking worked in this particular database. After all, I had been using databases for quite a while and was considered something of an expert in this field (in addition to Sybase, SQL Server, and Informix, I had used Ingress, DB2, Gupta SQLBase, and a variety of other databases). I had fallen into the trap of believing that I knew how things *should* work, so I thought of course they *would* work in that way. *I was wrong in a big way.*

It was during a benchmark that I discovered just how wrong I was. In the early days of these databases (around 1992/1993), it was common for the vendors to "benchmark" for really large procurements to see who could do the work the fastest, the easiest, with the most features.

The benchmark was between Informix, Sybase, SQL Server, and Oracle. Oracle was first. Their technical people came on-site, read through the benchmark specs, and started setting it up. The first thing I noticed was that the technicians from Oracle were going to use a database table to record their timings, even though we were going to have many dozens of connections doing work, each of which would frequently need to insert and update data in this log table. Not only that, but they were going to *read* the log table during the benchmark as well! Being a nice guy, I pulled one of the Oracle technicians aside to ask him if they were crazy—why would they purposely introduce another point of contention into the system? Wouldn't the benchmark processes all tend to serialize around their operations on this single table? Would they jam the benchmark by trying to read from this table as others were heavily modifying it? Why would they want to introduce all of these extra locks that they would need to manage? I had dozens of "Why would you even consider that?"–type questions. The technical folks from Oracle thought I was a little daft at that point. That is, until I pulled up a window into SQL Server or Informix, and showed them the effects of two people inserting into a table, or someone trying to query a table with others inserting rows (the query returns zero rows per second). The differences between the way Oracle does it and the way almost every other database does it are phenomenal—they are night and day.

Needless to say, neither the Informix nor the SQL Server technicians were too keen on the database log table approach during their attempts. They preferred to record their timings to flat files in the operating system. The Oracle people left with a better understanding of exactly how to compete against SQL Server and Informix: just ask the audience "How many rows per second does your current database return when data is locked?" and take it from there.

The moral to this story is twofold. First, *all databases are fundamentally different.* Second, when designing an application for a new database platform, you must make no assumptions about how that database works. *You must approach each new database as if you had never used a database before.* Things you would do in one database are either not necessary or simply won't work in another database.

In Oracle you will learn that

- Transactions are what databases are all about. They are a "good thing."

- You should defer committing until the correct moment. You should not do it quickly to avoid stressing the system, as it does not stress the system to have long or large transactions. The rule is *commit when you must, and not before.* Your transactions should only be as small or as large as your business logic dictates.

- You should hold locks on data as long as you need to. They are tools for you to use, not things to be avoided. Locks are not a scarce resource. Conversely, you should hold locks on data only as long as you need to. Locks may not be scarce, but they can prevent other sessions from modifying information.

- There is no overhead involved with row-level locking in Oracle—none. Whether you have 1 row lock or 1,000,000 row locks, the number of "resources" dedicated to locking this information will be the same. Sure, you'll do a lot more work modifying 1,000,000 rows rather than 1 row, but the number of resources needed to lock 1,000,000 rows is the same as for 1 row; it is a fixed constant.

- You should never escalate a lock (e.g., use a table lock instead of row locks) because it would be "better for the system." In Oracle, it won't be better for the system—it will save no resources. There are times to use table locks, such as in a batch process, when you know you will update the entire table and you do not want other sessions to lock rows on you. But you are not using a table lock to make it easier for the system by avoiding having to allocate row locks.

- Concurrency and consistency can be achieved simultaneously. You can get the data quickly and accurately, every time. Readers of data are *not* blocked by writers of data. Writers of data are *not* blocked by readers of data. This is one of the fundamental differences between Oracle and most other relational databases.

As we cover the remaining components in this chapter and the next, I'll reinforce these points.

Locking Issues

Before we discuss the various types of locks that Oracle uses, it is useful to look at some locking issues, many of which arise from badly designed applications that do not make correct use (or make no use) of the database's locking mechanisms.

Lost Updates

A *lost update* is a classic database problem. Actually, it is a problem in all multiuser computer environments. Simply put, a lost update happens when the following events occur, in the order presented here:

1. A transaction in Session1 retrieves (queries) a row of data into local memory and displays it to an end user, User1.

2. Another transaction in Session2 retrieves that same row, but displays the data to a different end user, User2.

3. User1, using the application, modifies that row and has the application update the database and commit. Session1's transaction is now complete.

4. User2 modifies that row also, and has the application update the database and commit. Session2's transaction is now complete.

This process is referred to as a "lost update" because all of the changes made in step 3 will be lost. Consider, for example, an employee update screen that allows a user to change an address, work number, and so on. The application itself is very simple: a small search screen to generate a list of employees and then the ability to drill down into the details of each employee. This should be a piece of cake. So, we write the application with no locking on our part, just simple SELECT and UPDATE commands.

Then an end user (User1) navigates to the details screen, changes an address on the screen, clicks Save, and receives confirmation that the update was successful. Fine, except that when User1 checks the record the next day to send out a tax form, the old address is still listed. How could that have happened? Unfortunately, it can happen all too easily. In this case, another end user (User2) queried the same record just after User1 did—after User1 read the data, but before User1 modified it. Then after User2 queried the data, User1 performed her update, received confirmation, and even requeried to see the change for herself. However, User2 then updated the work telephone number field and clicked Save, blissfully unaware of the fact that he just overwrote User1's changes to the address field with the old data! The reason this can happen *in this case* is that the application developer wrote the program such that when one particular field is updated, all fields for that record are "refreshed" (simply because it's easier to update all the columns instead of figuring out exactly which columns changed and only updating those).

Notice that for this to happen, User1 and User2 didn't even need to be working on the record at the exact same time. They simply needed to be working on the record at *about* the same time.

I've seen this database issue crop up time and again when GUI programmers with little or no database training are given the task of writing a database application. They get a working knowledge of SELECT, INSERT, UPDATE, and DELETE and then set about writing the application. When the resulting application behaves in the manner just described, it completely destroys a user's confidence in it, especially since it seems so random, so sporadic, and it is totally irreproducible in a controlled environment (leading the developer to believe it must be a user error).

Many tools, such as Oracle Forms and HTML DB, transparently protect you from this behavior by ensuring the record is unchanged from the time you query it and locked before you make any changes to it, but many others (such as a handwritten Visual Basic or Java program) do not. What the tools that protect you do behind the scenes, or what the developers must do themselves, is use one of two types of locking strategies: pessimistic or optimistic.

Pessimistic Locking

This locking method would be put into action the instant before a user modifies a value on the screen. For example, a row lock would be placed as soon as the user indicates his intention to perform an update on a specific row that he has selected and has visible on the screen (by clicking a button on the screen, say).

Pessimistic locking is useful only in a *stateful* or *connected* environment—that is, one where your application has a continual connection to the database and you are the only one using that connection for at least the life of your transaction. This was the prevalent way of doing things in the early to mid 1990s with client/server applications. Every application would get a direct connection to the database to be used solely by that application instance. This method of connecting, in a stateful fashion, has become less common (though it is not extinct), especially with the advent of application servers in the mid to late 1990s.

Assuming you are using a stateful connection, you might have an application that queries the data without locking anything:

```
scott@ORA10G> select empno, ename, sal from emp where deptno = 10;

    EMPNO ENAME            SAL
---------- ---------- ----------
     7782 CLARK           2450
     7839 KING            5000
     7934 MILLER          1300
```

Eventually, the user picks a row she would like to update. Let's say in this case, she chooses to update the MILLER row. Our application will at that point in time (before the user makes any changes on the screen but after the row has been out of the database for a while) bind the values the user selected so we can query the database and make sure the data hasn't been changed yet. In SQL*Plus, to simulate the bind calls the application would make, we can issue the following:

```
scott@ORA10G> variable empno number
scott@ORA10G> variable ename varchar2(20)
scott@ORA10G> variable sal number
scott@ORA10G> exec :empno := 7934; :ename := 'MILLER'; :sal := 1300;
PL/SQL procedure successfully completed.
```

Now in addition to simply querying the values and verifying that they have not been changed, we are going to lock the row using FOR UPDATE NOWAIT. The application will execute the following query:

```
scott@ORA10G> select empno, ename, sal
  2  from emp
  3  where empno = :empno
  4    and ename = :ename
  5    and sal = :sal
  6    for update nowait
  7  /

    EMPNO ENAME            SAL
---------- ---------- ----------
     7934 MILLER          1300
```

The application supplies values for the bind variables from the data on the screen (in this case 7934, MILLER, and 1300) and requeries this same row from the database, this time locking the row against updates by other sessions; hence, this approach is called *pessimistic* locking. We lock the row before we attempt to update because we doubt—*we are pessimistic*—that the row will remain unchanged otherwise.

Since all tables *should* have a primary key (the preceding SELECT will retrieve at most one record since it includes the primary key, EMPNO) and primary keys should be immutable (we should never update them), we'll get one of three outcomes from this statement:

- If the underlying data has not changed, we will get our MILLER row back, and this row will be locked from updates (but not reads) by others.

- If another user is in the process of modifying that row, we will get an ORA-00054 ➡ resource busy error. We must wait for the other user to finish with it.

- If, in the time between selecting the data and indicating our intention to update, someone has already changed the row, then we will get zero rows back. That implies the data on our screen is stale. To avoid the lost update scenario previously described, the application needs to *requery* and lock the data before allowing the end user to modify it. With pessimistic locking in place, when User2 attempts to update the telephone field the application would now recognize that the address field had been changed and would requery the data. Thus, User2 would not overwrite User1's change with the old data in that field.

Once we have locked the row successfully, the application will bind the new values, and issue the update and commit the changes:

```
scott@ORA10G> update emp
  2   set ename = :ename, sal = :sal
  3   where empno = :empno;
1 row updated.

scott@ORA10G> commit;
Commit complete.
```

We have now very safely changed that row. It is not possible for us to overwrite someone else's changes, as we verified the data did not change between when we initially read it out and when we locked it.

Optimistic Locking

The second method, referred to as *optimistic* locking, defers all locking up to the point right before the update is performed. In other words, we will modify the information on the screen without a lock being acquired. We are optimistic that the data will not be changed by some other user; hence, we wait until the very last moment to find out if we are right.

This locking method works in all environments, but it does increase the probability that a user performing an update will "lose." That is, when that user goes to update her row, she finds that the data has been modified, and she has to start over.

One popular implementation of optimistic locking is to keep the old and new values in the application, and upon updating the data use an update like this:

```
Update table
   Set column1 = :new_column1, column2 = :new_column2, ....
 Where primary_key = :primary_key
   And column1 = :old_column1
   And column2 = :old_column2
   ...
```

Here, we are optimistic that the data doesn't get changed. In this case, if our update updates *one* row, we got lucky; the data didn't change between the time we read it and the time we got around to submitting the update. If we update *zero* rows, we lose; someone else changed the data and now we must figure out what we want to do to continue in the application. Should we make the end user rekey the transaction after querying the new values for the row (potentially causing the user frustration, as there is a chance the row will have changed yet again)? Should we try to merge the values of the two updates by performing update conflict-resolution based on business rules (lots of code)?

The preceding UPDATE will, in fact, avoid a lost update, but it does stand a chance of being blocked—hanging while it waits for an UPDATE of that row by another session to complete. If all of your applications use optimistic locking, then using a straight UPDATE is generally OK since rows are locked for a very short duration as updates are applied and committed. However, if some of your applications use pessimistic locking, which will hold locks on rows for relatively long periods of time, then you will want to consider using a SELECT FOR UPDATE NOWAIT instead, to verify the row was not changed and lock it immediately prior to the UPDATE to avoid getting blocked by another session.

There are many methods of implementing optimistic concurrency control. We've discussed one whereby the application will store all of the before images of the row in the application itself. In the following sections, we'll explore three others, namely

- Using a special column that is maintained by a database trigger or application code to tell us the "version" of the record

- Using a checksum or hash that was computed using the original data

- Using the new Oracle 10*g* feature ORA_ROWSCN

Optimistic Locking Using a Version Column

This is a simple implementation that involves adding a single column to each database table you wish to protect from lost updates. This column is generally either a NUMBER or DATE/TIMESTAMP column. It is typically maintained via a row trigger on the table, which is responsible for incrementing the NUMBER column or updating the DATE/TIMESTAMP column every time a row is modified.

The application you want to implement optimistic concurrency control on would need only to save the value of this additional column, not all of the before images of the other columns. The application would only need to verify that the value of this column in the database at the point when the update is requested matches the value that was initially read out. If these values are the same, then the row has not been updated.

Let's look at an implementation of optimistic locking using a copy of the SCOTT.DEPT table. We could use the following Data Definition Language (DDL) to create the table:

```
ops$tkyte@ORA10G> create table dept
  2  ( deptno    number(2),
  3    dname     varchar2(14),
  4    loc       varchar2(13),
  5    last_mod  timestamp with time zone
  6              default systimestamp
```

```
 7              not null,
 8     constraint dept_pk primary key(deptno)
 9  )
 10 /
Table created.
```

Then we INSERT a copy of the DEPT data into this table:

```
ops$tkyte@ORA10G> insert into dept( deptno, dname, loc )
 2   select deptno, dname, loc
 3     from scott.dept;
4 rows created.

ops$tkyte@ORA10G> commit;
Commit complete.
```

That code re-creates the DEPT table, but with an additional LAST_MOD column that uses the TIMESTAMP WITH TIME ZONE datatype (available in Oracle9*i* and above). We have defined this column to be NOT NULL so that it must be populated, and its default value is the current system time.

This TIMESTAMP datatype has the highest precision in Oracle, typically going down to the microsecond (millionth of a second). For an application that involves user think time, this level of precision on the TIMESTAMP is more than sufficient, as it is highly unlikely that the process of the database retrieving a row and a human looking at it, modifying it, and issuing the update back to the database could take place within a fraction of a second. The odds of two people reading and modifying the same row in the same fraction of a second are very small indeed.

Next, we need way of maintaining this value. We have two choices: either the application can maintain the LAST_MOD column by setting its value to SYSTIMESTAMP when it updates a record or a trigger/stored procedure can maintain it. Having the application maintain LAST_MOD is definitely more performant than a trigger-based approach, since a trigger will add additional processing on part of Oracle to the modification. However, this does mean that you are *relying* on all of the applications to maintain LAST_MOD consistently in all of the places that they modify this table. So, if each application is responsible for maintaining this field, it needs to consistently verify that the LAST_MOD column was not changed and set the LAST_MOD column to the current SYSTIMESTAMP. For example, if an application queries the row where DEPTNO=10

```
ops$tkyte@ORA10G> variable deptno    number
ops$tkyte@ORA10G> variable dname     varchar2(14)
ops$tkyte@ORA10G> variable loc       varchar2(13)
ops$tkyte@ORA10G> variable last_mod varchar2(50)

ops$tkyte@ORA10G> begin
 2       :deptno := 10;
 3       select dname, loc, last_mod
 4         into :dname,:loc,:last_mod
 5         from dept
 6        where deptno = :deptno;
```

```
7  end;
8  /
PL/SQL procedure successfully completed.
```

which we can see is currently

```
ops$tkyte@ORA10G> select :deptno dno, :dname dname, :loc loc, :last_mod lm
  2    from dual;

    DNO DNAME       LOC      LM
---------- ---------- -------- -------------------------------------
     10 ACCOUNTING NEW YORK 25-APR-05 10.54.00.493380 AM -04:00
```

it would use this next update statement to modify the information. The last line does the very important check to make sure the timestamp has not changed and uses the built-in function TO_TIMESTAMP_TZ (TZ is short for TimeZone) to convert the string we saved in from the select back into the proper datatype. Additionally, line 3 of the update updates the LAST_MOD column to be the current time if the row is found to be updated:

```
ops$tkyte@ORA10G> update dept
  2      set dname = initcap(:dname),
  3          last_mod = systimestamp
  4    where deptno = :deptno
  5      and last_mod = to_timestamp_tz(:last_mod);
1 row updated.
```

As you can see, one row was updated—the row of interest. We updated the row by primary key (DEPTNO) and verified that the LAST_MOD column had not been modified by any other session between the time we read it first and the time we did the update. If we were to try to update that same record again, using the same logic, but without retrieving the new LAST_MOD value, we would observe the following:

```
ops$tkyte@ORA10G> update dept
  2      set dname = upper(:dname),
  3          last_mod = systimestamp
  4    where deptno = :deptno
  5      and last_mod = to_timestamp_tz(:last_mod);
0 rows updated.
```

Notice how 0 rows updated is reported this time because the predicate on LAST_MOD was not satisfied. While DEPTNO 10 still exists, the value at the moment we wish to update no longer matches the timestamp value at the moment we queried the row. So, the application knows, based on the fact that no rows were modified, that the data has been changed in the database—and it must now figure out what it wants to do about that.

You would not rely on each application to maintain this field for a number of reasons. For one, it adds code to an application, and it is code that must be repeated and correctly implemented anywhere this table is modified. In a large application, that could be in many places. Furthermore, every application developed in the future must conform to these rules. There are many chances to "miss" a spot in the application code and not have this field properly used.

So, if the application code itself is not to be made responsible for maintaining this LAST_MOD field, then I believe that the application should not be made responsible for checking this LAST_MOD field either (if it can do the check, it can certainly do the update!). So, in this case, I suggest encapsulating the update logic in a stored procedure and not allowing the application to update the table directly at all. If it cannot be trusted to maintain the value in this field, then it cannot be trusted to check it properly either. So, the stored procedure would take as inputs the bind variables we used in the previous updates and do exactly the same update. Upon detecting that zero rows were updated, the stored procedure could raise an exception back to the client to let the client know the update had, in effect, failed.

An alternate implementation uses a trigger to maintain this LAST_MOD field, but for something as simple as this, my recommendation is to avoid the trigger and let the DML take care of it. Triggers introduce a measurable amount of overhead, and in this case they would be unnecessary.

Optimistic Locking Using a Checksum

This is very similar to the previous version column method, but it uses the base data itself to compute a "virtual" version column. I'll quote the Oracle 10g *PL/SQL Supplied Packages Guide* (before showing how to use one of the supplied packages!) to help explain the goal and concepts behind a checksum or hash function:

> *A one-way hash function takes a variable-length input string, the data, and converts it to a fixed-length (generally smaller) output string called a* hash value. *The hash value serves as a unique identifier (like a fingerprint) of the input data. You can use the hash value to verify whether data has been changed or not.*

> *Note that a one-way hash function is a hash function that works in one direction. It is easy to compute a hash value from the input data, but it is hard to generate data that hashes to a particular value.*

The hash value or checksum is not truly unique. It is just designed such that the probability of a collision is sufficiently small—that is, the probability of two random strings having the same checksum or hash is so small as to be negligible.

We can use these hashes or checksums in the same way that we used our version column. We simply compare the hash or checksum value we obtain when we read data out of the database with what we obtain before modifying the data. If someone modified the row's values after we read it out, but before we updated it, then the hash or checksum will almost certainly be different.

There are many ways to compute a hash or checksum. I'll list three of these and demonstrate one in this section. All of these methods are based on supplied database packages:

- OWA_OPT_LOCK.CHECKSUM: This method is available on Oracle8i version 8.1.5 and up. There is a function that given a string returns a 16-bit checksum, and another function that given a ROWID will compute the 16-bit checksum of that row and lock that row at the same time. Possibilities of collision are 1 in 65,536 strings (the highest chance of a false positive).

- DBMS_OBFUSCATION_TOOLKIT.MD5: This method is available in Oracle8*i* version 8.1.7 and up. It computes a 128-bit message digest. The odds of a collision are about 1 in 3.4028E+38 (very small).

- DBMS_CRYPTO.HASH: This method is available in Oracle 10*g* Release 1 and up. It is capable of computing a Secure Hash Algorithm 1 (SHA-1) or MD4/MD5 message digests. It is recommended that you use the SHA-1 algorithm.

■**Note** An array of hash and checksum functions are available in many programming languages, so there may be others at your disposal outside the database.

The following example shows how you might use the DBMS_CRYPTO built-in package in Oracle 10*g* to compute these hashes/checksums. The technique would also be applicable for the other two listed packages; the logic would not be very much different, but the APIs you call would be.

Here we query out the information for department 10 to be displayed in some application. Immediately after querying the information, we compute the hash using the DBMS_CRYPTO package. This is the "version" information that we retain in our application:

```
ops$tkyte@ORA10G> begin
  2      for x in ( select deptno, dname, loc
  3                   from dept
  4                  where deptno = 10 )
  5      loop
  6          dbms_output.put_line( 'Dname:  ' || x.dname );
  7          dbms_output.put_line( 'Loc:    ' || x.loc );
  8          dbms_output.put_line( 'Hash:   ' ||
  9            dbms_crypto.hash
 10            ( utl_raw.cast_to_raw(x.deptno||'/'||x.dname||'/'||x.loc),
 11              dbms_crypto.hash_sh1 ) );
 12      end loop;
 13  end;
 14  /
Dname:  ACCOUNTING
Loc:    NEW YORK
Hash:   C44F7052661CE945D385D5C3F911E70FA99407A6

PL/SQL procedure successfully completed.
```

As you can see, the hash is just a big string of hex digits. The return value from DBMS_CRYPTO is a RAW variable, and when displayed it will be implicitly converted into HEX for us. This is the value we would want to use before updating. To update that row, we would retrieve *and lock* the row in the database as it exists right now, and then compute the hash value of that retrieved row and compare this new hash value with the hash value we computed when we read the data out of the database. The logic for doing so could look like the following (in real life, we would use bind variables for the literal hash values, of course):

```
ops$tkyte@ORA10G> begin
  2      for x in ( select deptno, dname, loc
  3                    from dept
  4                   where deptno = 10
  5                     for update nowait )
  6      loop
  7         if ( hextoraw( 'C44F7052661CE945D385D5C3F911E70FA99407A6' ) <>
  8              dbms_crypto.hash
  9              ( utl_raw.cast_to_raw(x.deptno||'/'||x.dname||'/'||x.loc),
 10                dbms_crypto.hash_sh1 ) )
 11         then
 12              raise_application_error(-20001, 'Row was modified' );
 13         end if;
 14      end loop;
 15      update dept
 16         set dname = lower(dname)
 17       where deptno = 10;
 18      commit;
 19  end;
 20  /

PL/SQL procedure successfully completed.
```

Upon requerying that data and computing the hash again *after the update*, we can see that the hash value is very different. If someone had modified the row before we did, our hash values would not have compared:

```
ops$tkyte@ORA10G> begin
  2      for x in ( select deptno, dname, loc
  3                    from dept
  4                   where deptno = 10 )
  5      loop
  6         dbms_output.put_line( 'Dname: ' || x.dname );
  7         dbms_output.put_line( 'Loc:   ' || x.loc );
  8         dbms_output.put_line( 'Hash:  ' ||
  9           dbms_crypto.hash
 10           ( utl_raw.cast_to_raw(x.deptno||'/'||x.dname||'/'||x.loc),
 11             dbms_crypto.hash_sh1 ) );
 12      end loop;
 13  end;
 14  /
Dname:  accounting
Loc:    NEW YORK
Hash:   F3DE485922D44DF598C2CEBC34C27DD2216FB90F

PL/SQL procedure successfully completed.
```

This example showed how to implement optimistic locking with a hash or checksum. You should bear in mind that computing a hash or checksum is a somewhat CPU-intensive operation—it is computationally expensive. On a system where CPU is a scarce resource, you must take this fact into consideration. However, this approach is much more "network-friendly," as the transmission of a relatively small hash instead of a before and after image of the row (to compare column by column) over the network will consume much less of that resource. Our last example will use a new Oracle 10g function, ORA_ROWSCN, which is small in size like a hash, but not CPU intensive to compute.

Optimistic Locking Using ORA_ROWSCN

Starting with Oracle 10g Release 1, you have the option to use the built-in ORA_ROWSCN function. It works very much like the version column technique described previously, but it can be performed automatically by Oracle—you need no extra column in the table and no extra update/maintenance code to update this value.

ORA_ROWSCN is based on the internal Oracle system clock, the SCN. Every time you commit in Oracle, the SCN advances (other things can advance it as well, but it only advances; it never goes back). The concept is identical to the previous methods in that you retrieve ORA_ROWSCN upon data retrieval, and you verify it has not changed when you go to update. The only reason I give it more than passing mention is that unless you created the table to support the maintenance of ORA_ROWSCN at the row level, it is maintained at the block level. That is, by default many rows on a single block will share the same ORA_ROWSCN value. If you update a row on a block with 50 other rows, then they will all have their ORA_ROWSCN advanced as well. This would almost certainly lead to many false positives, whereby you believe a row was modified that in fact was not. Therefore, you need to be aware of this fact and understand how to change the behavior.

To see the behavior and then change it, we'll use the small DEPT table again:

```
ops$tkyte@ORA10G> create table dept
  2  (deptno, dname, loc, data,
  3   constraint dept_pk primary key(deptno)
  4  )
  5  as
  6  select deptno, dname, loc, rpad('*',3500,'*')
  7    from scott.dept;
Table created.
```

Now we can inspect what block each row is on (it is safe to assume in this case they are in the same file, so a common block number indicates they are on the same block). I was using an 8KB block size with a row width of about 3,550 bytes, so I am expecting there to be two rows per block for this example:

```
ops$tkyte@ORA10G> select deptno, dname,
  2         dbms_rowid.rowid_block_number(rowid) blockno,
  3            ora_rowscn
  4    from dept;
```

```
  DEPTNO DNAME          BLOCKNO ORA_ROWSCN
---------- --------------- ---------- ----------
      10 ACCOUNTING       20972   34676029
      20 RESEARCH         20972   34676029
      30 SALES            20973   34676029
      40 OPERATIONS       20973   34676029
```

And sure enough, that is what we observe in this case. So, let's update the row where
DEPTNO = 10 is on block 20972:

```
ops$tkyte@ORA10G> update dept
  2    set dname = lower(dname)
  3  where deptno = 10;
1 row updated.

ops$tkyte@ORA10G> commit;
Commit complete.
```

What we'll observe next shows the consequences of ORA_ROWSCN being tracked at the block
level. We modified and committed the changes to a single row, but the ORA_ROWSCN values of
both of the rows on block 20972 have been advanced:

```
ops$tkyte@ORA10G> select deptno, dname,
  2         dbms_rowid.rowid_block_number(rowid) blockno,
  3           ora_rowscn
  4    from dept;

  DEPTNO DNAME          BLOCKNO ORA_ROWSCN
---------- --------------- ---------- ----------
      10 accounting       20972   34676046
      20 RESEARCH         20972   34676046
      30 SALES            20973   34676029
      40 OPERATIONS       20973   34676029
```

It would appear to anyone else that had read the DEPTNO=20 row that it had been modified,
even though it was not. The rows on block 20973 are "safe"—we didn't modify them, so they
did not advance. However, if we were to update either of them, both would advance. So the
question becomes how to modify this default behavior. Well, unfortunately, we have to
re-create the segment with ROWDEPENDENCIES enabled.

Row dependency tracking was added to the database with Oracle9*i* in support of
advanced replication to allow for better parallel propagation of changes. Prior to Oracle 10*g*,
its only use was in a replication environment, but starting in Oracle 10*g* we can use it to implement an effective optimistic locking technique with ORA_ROWSCN. It will add 6 bytes of overhead
to each row (so it is not a space saver compared to the do-it-yourself version column) and that
is, in fact, why it requires a table re-create and not just a simple ALTER TABLE: the physical
block structure must be changed to accommodate this feature.

Let's rebuild our table to enable ROWDEPENDENCIES. We could use the online rebuild capabilities in DBMS_REDEFINITION (another supplied package) to do this, but for something so
small, we'll just start over:

```
ops$tkyte@ORA10G> drop table dept;
Table dropped.

ops$tkyte@ORA10G> create table dept
  2  (deptno, dname, loc, data,
  3   constraint dept_pk primary key(deptno)
  4  )
  5  ROWDEPENDENCIES
  6  as
  7  select deptno, dname, loc, rpad('*',3500,'*')
  8    from scott.dept;
Table created.

ops$tkyte@ORA10G> select deptno, dname,
  2         dbms_rowid.rowid_block_number(rowid) blockno,
  3            ora_rowscn
  4    from dept;

   DEPTNO DNAME          BLOCKNO ORA_ROWSCN
---------- -------------- ---------- ----------
       10 ACCOUNTING        21020   34676364
       20 RESEARCH          21020   34676364
       30 SALES             21021   34676364
       40 OPERATIONS        21021   34676364
```

We're back where we were before: four rows on two blocks, all having the same initial ORA_ROWSCN value. Now when we update DEPTNO=10

```
ops$tkyte@ORA10G> update dept
  2     set dname = lower(dname)
  3   where deptno = 10;
1 row updated.

ops$tkyte@ORA10G> commit;
Commit complete.
```

we should observe the following upon querying the DEPT table:

```
ops$tkyte@ORA10G> select deptno, dname,
  2         dbms_rowid.rowid_block_number(rowid) blockno,
  3            ora_rowscn
  4    from dept;

   DEPTNO DNAME          BLOCKNO ORA_ROWSCN
---------- -------------- ---------- ----------
       10 accounting        21020   34676381
       20 RESEARCH          21020   34676364
       30 SALES             21021   34676364
       40 OPERATIONS        21021   34676364
```

The only modified ORA_ROWSCN at this point belongs to DEPTNO = 10, exactly what we wanted. We can now rely on ORA_ROWSCN to detect row-level changes for us.

CONVERTING AN SCN TO WALL CLOCK TIME

There is another benefit of the transparent ORA_ROWSCN column: we can convert an SCN into wall clock time approximately (within about +/−3 seconds) to discover when the row was last modified. So, for example, I can do this:

```
ops$tkyte@ORA10G> select deptno, ora_rowscn, scn_to_timestamp(ora_rowscn) ts
  2  from dept;

    DEPTNO ORA_ROWSCN TS
---------- ---------- ---------------------------------
        10   34676381 25-APR-05 02.37.04.000000000 PM
        20   34676364 25-APR-05 02.34.42.000000000 PM
        30   34676364 25-APR-05 02.34.42.000000000 PM
        40   34676364 25-APR-05 02.34.42.000000000 PM
```

Here you can see that I waited almost three minutes in between the initial creation of the table and the update of DEPTNO = 10. However, this translation of an SCN to a wall clock time has definite limits: about five days of database uptime. For example, if I go to an "old" table and find the oldest ORA_ROWSCN in it (note that I've logged in as SCOTT in this case; I am not using the new table from earlier):

```
scott@ORA10G> select min(ora_rowscn) from dept;

MIN(ORA_ROWSCN)
---------------
         364937
```

If I try to convert that SCN into a timestamp, I might find the following (depending on how old the DEPT table is!):

```
scott@ORA10G> select scn_to_timestamp(min(ora_rowscn)) from dept;
select scn_to_timestamp(min(ora_rowscn)) from dept
       *
ERROR at line 1:
ORA-08181: specified number is not a valid system change number
ORA-06512: at "SYS.SCN_TO_TIMESTAMP", line 1
ORA-06512: at line 1
```

So that conversion cannot be relied on in the long term.

Optimistic or Pessimistic Locking?

So which method is best? In my experience, pessimistic locking works very well in Oracle (but perhaps not in other databases) and has many advantages over optimistic locking. However, it requires a stateful connection to the database, like a client/server connection. This is because locks are not held across connections. This single fact makes pessimistic locking unrealistic in many cases today. In the past, with client/server applications and a couple dozen or hundred users, it would have been my first and only choice. Today, however, optimistic concurrency control is what I would recommend for most applications. Having a connection for the entire duration of a transaction is just too high a price to pay.

Of the methods available, which do I use? I tend to use the version column approach with a timestamp column. It gives me the extra information "when was this row last updated" in a long-term sense. So it adds value in that way. It is less computationally expensive than a hash or checksum, and it doesn't run into the issues potentially encountered with a hash or checksum when processing LONG, LONG RAW, CLOB, BLOB, and other very large columns.

If I had to add optimistic concurrency controls to a table that was still being used with a pessimistic locking scheme (e.g., the table was accessed in both client/server applications and over the Web), I would opt for the ORA_ROWSCN approach. The reason is that the existing legacy application might not appreciate a new column appearing, or even if we took the additional step of hiding the extra column, we might not appreciate the overhead of the necessary trigger to maintain it. The ORA_ROWSCN technique would be nonintrusive and lightweight in that respect (well, after we get over the table re-creation, that is).

The hashing/checksum approach is very database independent, especially if we compute the hashes or checksums outside of the database. However, by performing the computations in the middle tier rather than the database, we will incur higher resource usage penalties, in terms of CPU usage and network transfers.

Blocking

Blocking occurs when one session holds a lock on a resource that another session is requesting. As a result, the requesting session will be blocked—it will "hang" until the holding session gives up the locked resource. In almost every case, blocking is avoidable. In fact, if you do find that your session is blocked in an interactive application, then you have probably been suffering from the lost update bug as well, perhaps without realizing it. That is, your application logic is flawed and that is the cause of the blocking.

The five common DML statements that will block in the database are INSERT, UPDATE, DELETE, MERGE, and SELECT FOR UPDATE. The solution to a blocked SELECT FOR UPDATE is trivial: simply add the NOWAIT clause and it will no longer block. Instead, your application will report back to the end user that the row is already locked. The interesting cases are the remaining four DML statements. We'll look at each of them and see why they should not block and how to correct the situation if they do.

Blocked Inserts

There are few times when an INSERT will block. The most common scenario is when you have a table with a primary key or unique constraint placed on it and two sessions attempt to insert a row with the same value. One of the sessions will block until the other session either commits (in which case the blocked session will receive an error about a duplicate value) or rolls back (in which case the blocked session succeeds). Another case involves tables linked together via referential integrity constraints. An insert into a child table may become blocked if the parent row it depends on is being created or deleted.

Blocked INSERTs typically happen with applications that allow the end user to generate the primary key/unique column value. This situation is most easily avoided by using a sequence to generate the primary key/unique column value. Sequences were designed to be a highly concurrent method of generating unique keys in a multiuser environment. In the event that you cannot use a sequence, you can use the following technique, which avoids the issue by using manual locks implemented via the built-in DBMS_LOCK package.

■**Note** The following example demonstrates how to prevent a session from blocking on an insert due to a primary key or unique constraint. It should be stressed that the "fix" demonstrated here should be considered a short-term solution while the application architecture itself is inspected. This approach adds obvious overhead and should not be implemented lightly. A well-designed application would not encounter this issue. This should be considered a last resort and is definitely not something you want to do to every table in your application "just in case."

With inserts, there's no existing row to select and lock; there's no way to prevent others from inserting a row with the same value, thus blocking our session and causing us to wait indefinitely. Here is where DBMS_LOCK comes into play. To demonstrate this technique, we will create a table with a primary key and a trigger that will prevent two (or more) sessions from inserting the same values simultaneously. The trigger will use DBMS_UTILITY.GET_HASH_VALUE to hash the primary key into some number between 0 and 1,073,741,823 (the range of lock ID numbers permitted for our use by Oracle). In this example, I've chosen a hash table of size 1,024, meaning we will hash our primary keys into one of 1,024 different lock IDs. Then we will use DBMS_LOCK.REQUEST to allocate an exclusive lock based on that ID. Only one session at a time will be able to do that, so if someone else tries to insert a record into our table with the same primary key, then that person's lock request will fail (and the error resource busy will be raised):

■**Note** To successfully compile this trigger, execute permission on DBMS_LOCK must be granted directly to your schema. The privilege to execute DBMS_LOCK may not come from a role.

```
scott@ORA10G> create table demo ( x int primary key );
Table created.

scott@ORA10G> create or replace trigger demo_bifer
  2  before insert on demo
  3  for each row
  4  declare
  5      l_lock_id   number;
```

```
 6        resource_busy    exception;
 7        pragma exception_init( resource_busy, -54 );
 8   begin
 9        l_lock_id :=
10           dbms_utility.get_hash_value( to_char( :new.x ), 0, 1024 );
11        if ( dbms_lock.request
12                  ( id                => l_lock_id,
13                    lockmode          => dbms_lock.x_mode,
14                    timeout           => 0,
15                    release_on_commit => TRUE ) <> 0 )
16        then
17            raise resource_busy;
18        end if;
19   end;
20   /
Trigger created.
```

Now, if in two separate sessions we execute the following:

```
scott@ORA10G> insert into demo values ( 1 );
1 row created.
```

it will succeed in the first session but immediately issue the following in the second session:

```
scott@ORA10G> insert into demo values ( 1 );
insert into demo values ( 1 )
            *
ERROR at line 1:
ORA-00054: resource busy and acquire with NOWAIT specified
ORA-06512: at "SCOTT.DEMO_BIFER", line 14
ORA-04088: error during execution of trigger 'SCOTT.DEMO_BIFER'
```

The concept here is to take the supplied *primary key value* of the table protected by the trigger and put it in a character string. We can then use DBMS_UTILITY.GET_HASH_VALUE to come up with a "mostly unique" hash value for the string. As long as we use a hash table smaller than 1,073,741,823, we can "lock" that value exclusively using DBMS_LOCK.

After hashing, we take that value and use DBMS_LOCK to request that lock ID to be exclusively locked with a timeout of ZERO (this returns immediately if someone else has locked that value). If we timeout or fail for any reason, we raise ORA-54 Resource Busy. Otherwise, we do nothing—it is OK to insert, we won't block.

Of course, if the primary key of your table is an INTEGER and you don't expect the key to go over 1 billion, you can skip the hash and just use the number as the lock ID.

You'll need to play with the size of the hash table (1,024 in this example) to avoid artificial resource busy messages due to different strings hashing to the same number. The size of the hash table will be application (data)-specific, and it will be influenced by the number of concurrent insertions as well. Lastly, bear in mind that although Oracle has unlimited row-level locking, it has a finite number of enqueue locks. If you insert lots of rows this way without committing in your session, then you might find that you create so many enqueue locks that you exhaust the system of enqueue resources (you exceed the maximum value set in the

ENQUEUE_RESOURCES system parameter), as each row will create another *enqueue* (a lock). If this does happen, you'll need to raise the value of the ENQUEUE_RESOURCES parameter. You might also add a flag to the trigger to allow people to turn the check on and off. If I was going to insert hundreds or thousands of records, for example, I might not want this check enabled.

Blocked Merges, Updates, and Deletes

In an interactive application—one where you query some data out of the database, allow an end user to manipulate it, and then "put it back" into the database—a blocked UPDATE or DELETE indicates that *you probably have a lost update problem* in your code (I would call it a bug in your code if you do). You are attempting to UPDATE a row that someone else is already updating (in other words, that someone else already has locked). You can avoid the blocking issue by using the SELECT FOR UPDATE NOWAIT query to

- Verify the data has not changed since you queried it out (preventing lost updates).

- Lock the row (preventing the UPDATE or DELETE from blocking).

As discussed earlier, you can do this regardless of the locking approach you take. Both pessimistic and optimistic locking may employ the SELECT FOR UPDATE NOWAIT query to verify the row has not changed. Pessimistic locking would use that statement the instant the user indicated her intention to modify the data. Optimistic locking would use that statement immediately prior to updating the data in the database. Not only will this resolve the blocking issue in your application, but also it will correct the data integrity issue.

Since a MERGE is simply an INSERT and UPDATE (and in 10*g* with the enhanced MERGE syntax, it's a DELETE as well), you would use both techniques simultaneously.

Deadlocks

Deadlocks occur when you have two sessions, each of which is holding a resource that the other wants. For example, if I have two tables, A and B in my database, and each has a single row in it, I can demonstrate a deadlock easily. All I need to do is open two sessions (e.g., two SQL*Plus sessions). In session A, I update table A. In session B, I update table B. Now, if I attempt to update table A in session B, I will become blocked. Session A has this row locked already. This is not a deadlock; it is just blocking. I have not yet deadlocked because there is a chance that session A will commit or roll back, and session B will simply continue at that point.

If I go back to session A and then try to update table B, I will cause a deadlock. One of the two sessions will be chosen as a "victim" and will have its statement rolled back. For example, the attempt by session B to update table A may be rolled back, with an error such as the following:

```
update a set x = x+1
    *
ERROR at line 1:
ORA-00060: deadlock detected while waiting for resource
```

Session A's attempt to update table B will remain blocked—Oracle will not roll back the entire transaction. Only one of the statements that contributed to the deadlock is rolled back. Session B still has the row in table B locked, and session A is patiently waiting for the row to become available. After receiving the deadlock message, session B must decide whether to commit the outstanding work on table B, roll it back, or continue down an alternate path and commit later. As soon as this session does commit or roll back, the other blocked session will continue on as if nothing happened.

Oracle considers deadlocks to be so rare, so unusual, that it creates a trace file on the server each and every time one does occur. The contents of the trace file will look something like this:

```
*** 2005-04-25 15:53:01.455
*** ACTION NAME:() 2005-04-25 15:53:01.455
*** MODULE NAME:(SQL*Plus) 2005-04-25 15:53:01.455
*** SERVICE NAME:(SYS$USERS) 2005-04-25 15:53:01.455
*** SESSION ID:(145.208) 2005-04-25 15:53:01.455
DEADLOCK DETECTED
Current SQL statement for this session:
update a set x = 1
The following deadlock is not an ORACLE error. It is a
deadlock due to user error in the design of an application
or from issuing incorrect ad-hoc SQL. The following
information may aid in determining the deadlock:...
```

Obviously, Oracle considers these application deadlocks a self-induced error on part of the application and, for the most part, Oracle is correct. Unlike in many other RDBMSs, deadlocks are so rare in Oracle they can be considered almost nonexistent. Typically, you must come up with artificial conditions to get one.

The number one cause of deadlocks in the Oracle database, in my experience, is unindexed foreign keys (the number two cause is bitmap indexes on tables subject to concurrent updates, which we'll cover in Chapter 11). Oracle will place a full table lock on a child table after modification of the parent table in two cases:

- If you update the parent table's primary key (a very rare occurrence if you follow the rule of relational databases stating that primary keys should be immutable), the child table will be locked in the absence of an index on the foreign key.

- If you delete a parent table row, the entire child table will be locked (in the absence of an index on the foreign key) as well.

These full table locks are a short-term occurrence in Oracle9*i* and above, meaning they need to be taken for the duration of the DML operation, not the entire transaction. Even so, they can and do cause large locking issues. As a demonstration of the first point, if we have a pair of tables set up as follows:

```
ops$tkyte@ORA10G> create table p ( x int primary key );
Table created.

ops$tkyte@ORA10G> create table c ( x references p );
Table created.

ops$tkyte@ORA10G> insert into p values ( 1 );
1 row created.
```

```
ops$tkyte@ORA10G> insert into p values ( 2 );
1 row created.

ops$tkyte@ORA10G> commit;
Commit complete.
```

and then we execute the following:

```
ops$tkyte@ORA10G> insert into c values ( 2 );
1 row created.
```

nothing untoward happens yet. But if we go into another session and attempt to delete the first parent record

```
ops$tkyte@ORA10G> delete from p where x = 1;
```

we'll find that session gets immediately blocked. It is attempting to gain a full table lock on table C before it does the delete. Now no other session can initiate a DELETE, INSERT, or UPDATE of any rows in C (the sessions that had already started may continue, but no new sessions may start to modify C).

This blocking would happen with an update of the primary key value as well. Because updating a primary key is a huge no-no in a relational database, this is generally not an issue with updates. Where I have seen this updating of the primary key become a serious issue is when developers use tools that generate SQL for them, and those tools update every single column, regardless of whether the end user actually modified that column or not. For example, say that we use Oracle Forms and create a default layout on any table. Oracle Forms by default will generate an update that modifies every single column in the table we choose to display. If we build a default layout on the DEPT table and include all three fields, Oracle Forms will execute the following command whenever we modify *any* of the columns of the DEPT table:

```
update dept set deptno=:1,dname=:2,loc=:3 where rowid=:4
```

In this case, if the EMP table has a foreign key to DEPT and there is no index on the DEPTNO column in the EMP table, then the entire EMP table will be locked during an update to DEPT. This is something to watch out for carefully if you are using any tools that generate SQL for you. Even though the value of the primary key does not change, the child table EMP will be locked after the execution of the preceding SQL statement. In the case of Oracle Forms, the solution is to set that table's UPDATE CHANGED COLUMNS ONLY property to YES. Oracle Forms will generate an UPDATE statement that includes only the changed columns (not the primary key).

Problems arising from deletion of a row in a parent table are far more common. As I demonstrated, if I delete a row in table P, then the child table, C, will become locked during the DML operation, thus preventing other updates against C from taking place for the duration of the transaction (assuming no one else was modifying C, of course; in which case the delete will wait). This is where the blocking and deadlock issues come in. By locking the entire table C, I have seriously decreased the concurrency in my database to the point where no one will be able to modify anything in C. In addition, I have increased the probability of a deadlock, since I now "own" lots of data until I commit. The probability that some other session will become blocked on C is now much higher; any session that tries to modify C will get blocked. Therefore, I'll start seeing lots of sessions that hold some preexisting locks on other resources getting blocked in the database. If any of these blocked sessions are, in fact, locking a resource that my session also needs, we will have a deadlock. The deadlock in this case is caused by my session preventing access to many more resources (in this case, all of the rows in a single table) than it ever needed. When someone complains of deadlocks in the database, I have them run a script that finds unindexed foreign keys, and 99 percent of the time we locate an offending table. By simply indexing that foreign key, the deadlocks—and lots of other contention issues—go away. The following example demonstrates the use of this script to locate the unindexed foreign key in table C:

```
ops$tkyte@ORA10G> column columns format a30 word_wrapped
ops$tkyte@ORA10G> column tablename format a15 word_wrapped
ops$tkyte@ORA10G> column constraint_name format a15 word_wrapped

ops$tkyte@ORA10G> select table_name, constraint_name,
  2       cname1 || nvl2(cname2,',' ||cname2,null) ||
  3       nvl2(cname3,',' ||cname3,null) || nvl2(cname4,',' ||cname4,null) ||
  4       nvl2(cname5,',' ||cname5,null) || nvl2(cname6,',' ||cname6,null) ||
  5       nvl2(cname7,',' ||cname7,null) || nvl2(cname8,',' ||cname8,null)
  6             columns
  7    from ( select b.table_name,
  8                   b.constraint_name,
  9                   max(decode( position, 1, column_name, null )) cname1,
 10                   max(decode( position, 2, column_name, null )) cname2,
 11                   max(decode( position, 3, column_name, null )) cname3,
 12                   max(decode( position, 4, column_name, null )) cname4,
 13                   max(decode( position, 5, column_name, null )) cname5,
 14                   max(decode( position, 6, column_name, null )) cname6,
 15                   max(decode( position, 7, column_name, null )) cname7,
 16                   max(decode( position, 8, column_name, null )) cname8,
 17                   count(*) col_cnt
 18            from (select substr(table_name,1,30) table_name,
 19                         substr(constraint_name,1,30) constraint_name,
 20                         substr(column_name,1,30) column_name,
 21                         position
 22                  from user_cons_columns ) a,
 23                 user_constraints b
 24          where a.constraint_name = b.constraint_name
 25            and b.constraint_type = 'R'
 26          group by b.table_name, b.constraint_name
 27        ) cons
 28   where col_cnt > ALL
 29          ( select count(*)
 30             from user_ind_columns i
 31            where i.table_name = cons.table_name
 32              and i.column_name in (cname1, cname2, cname3, cname4,
 33                                    cname5, cname6, cname7, cname8 )
```

```
34                and i.column_position <= cons.col_cnt
35             group by i.index_name
36          )
37  /


TABLE_NAME                       CONSTRAINT_NAME COLUMNS
------------------------------   --------------- ---------------------------------
C                                SYS_C009485     X
```

This script works on foreign key constraints that have up to eight columns in them (if you have more than that, you probably want to rethink your design). It starts by building an inline view named CONS in the previous query. This inline view transposes the appropriate column names in the constraint from rows into columns, with the result being a row per constraint and up to eight columns that have the names of the columns in the constraint. Additionally, there is a column, COL_CNT, which contains the number of columns in the foreign key constraint itself. For each row returned from the inline view, we execute a correlated subquery that checks all of the indexes on the table currently being processed. It counts the columns in that index that match columns in the foreign key constraint and then groups them by index name. So, it generates a set of numbers, each of which is a count of matching columns in some index on that table. If the original COL_CNT is greater than *all* of these numbers, then there is no index on that table that supports that constraint. If COL_CNT is less than all of these numbers, then there is at least one index that supports that constraint. Note the use of the NVL2 function, which we used to "glue" the list of column names into a comma-separated list. This function takes three arguments: A, B, and C. If argument A is not null, then it returns argument B; otherwise, it returns argument C. This query assumes that the owner of the constraint is the owner of the table and index as well. If another user indexed the table or the table is in another schema (both rare events), it will not work correctly.

So, this script shows us that table C has a foreign key on the column X, but no index. By indexing X, we can remove this locking issue all together. In addition to this table lock, an unindexed foreign key can also be problematic in the following cases:

- *When you have an ON DELETE CASCADE and have not indexed the child table:* For example, EMP is child of DEPT. DELETE DEPTNO = 10 should CASCADE to EMP. If DEPTNO in EMP is not indexed, you will get a full table scan of EMP for each row deleted from the DEPT table. This full scan is probably undesirable, and if you delete many rows from the parent table, the child table will be scanned once for each parent row deleted.

- *When you query from the parent to the child:* Consider the EMP/DEPT example again. It is very common to query the EMP table in the context of a DEPTNO. If you frequently run the following query (say, to generate a report), you'll find that not having the index in place will slow down the queries:

  - select * from dept, emp

  - where emp.deptno = dept.deptno and dept.deptno = :X;

So, when do you *not* need to index a foreign key? The answer is, in general, when the following conditions are met:

- You do *not* delete from the parent table.

- You do *not* update the parent table's unique/primary key value (watch for unintended updates to the primary key by tools!).

- You do *not* join from the parent to the child (like DEPT to EMP).

If you satisfy all three conditions, feel free to skip the index—it is not needed. If you meet any of the preceding conditions, be aware of the consequences. This is the one rare instance when Oracle tends to "overlock" data.

Lock Escalation

When lock escalation occurs, the system is decreasing the granularity of your locks. An example would be the database system turning your 100 row-level locks against a table into a single table-level lock. You are now using "one lock to lock everything" and, typically, you are also locking a whole lot more data than you were before. Lock escalation is used frequently in databases that consider a lock to be a scarce resource and overhead to be avoided.

Note Oracle will never escalate a lock. *Never*.

Oracle never escalates locks, but it does practice *lock conversion* or *lock promotion*—terms that are often confused with lock escalation.

Note The terms "lock conversion" and "lock promotion" are synonymous. Oracle typically refers to the process as "lock conversion."

Oracle will take a lock at the lowest level possible (i.e., the least restrictive lock possible) and convert that lock to a more restrictive level if necessary. For example, if you select a row from a table with the FOR UPDATE clause, two locks will be created. One lock is placed on the row(s) you selected (and this will be an exclusive lock; no one else can lock that specific row in exclusive mode). The other lock, a ROW SHARE TABLE lock, is placed on the table itself. This will prevent other sessions from placing an exclusive lock on the table and thus prevent them from altering the structure of the table, for example. Another session can modify any other row in this table without conflict. As many commands as possible that could execute successfully given there is a locked row in the table will be permitted.

Lock escalation is not a database "feature." It is not a desired attribute. The fact that a database supports lock escalation implies there is some inherent overhead in its locking mechanism and significant work is performed to manage hundreds of locks. In Oracle, the overhead to have 1 lock or 1 million locks is the same: none.

Lock Types

The three general classes of locks in Oracle are as follows:

- *DML locks*: DML stands for *Data Manipulation Language*. In general this means SELECT, INSERT, UPDATE, MERGE, and DELETE statements. DML locks are the mechanism that allows for concurrent data modifications. DML locks will be, for example, locks on a specific row of data or a lock at the table level that locks every row in the table.

- *DDL locks*: DDL stands for *Data Definition Language* (CREATE and ALTER statements, and so on). DDL locks protect the definition of the structure of objects.

- *Internal locks and latches*: Oracle uses these locks to protect its internal data structures. For example, when Oracle parses a query and generates an optimized query plan, it will "latch" the library cache to put that plan in there for other sessions to use. A *latch* is a lightweight, low-level serialization device employed by Oracle, similar in function to a lock. Do not confuse or be misled by the term "lightweight"—latches are a common cause of contention in the database, as you will see. They are lightweight in their implementation, but not in their effect.

We will now take a more detailed look at the specific types of locks within each of these general classes and the implications of their use. There are more lock types than I can cover here. The ones I cover in the sections that follow are the most common and are held for a long duration. The other types of lock are generally held for very short periods of time.

DML Locks

DML locks are used to ensure that only one person at a time modifies a row and that no one can drop a table upon which you are working. Oracle will place these locks for you, more or less transparently, as you do work.

TX (Transaction) Locks

A *TX lock* is acquired when a transaction initiates its first change, and it is held until the transaction performs a COMMIT or ROLLBACK. It is used as a queuing mechanism so that other sessions can wait for the transaction to complete. Each and every row you modify or SELECT FOR UPDATE in a transaction will "point" to an associated TX lock for that transaction. While this sounds expensive, it is not. To understand why this is, you need a conceptual understanding of where locks "live" and how they are managed. In Oracle, locks are stored as an attribute of the data (see Chapter 10 for an overview of the Oracle block format). Oracle does not have a traditional lock manager that keeps a long list of every row that is locked in the system. Many other databases do it that way because, for them, locks are a scarce resource, the use of which needs to be monitored. The more locks are in use, the more these systems have to manage, so it is a concern in these systems if "too many" locks are being used.

In a database with a traditional memory-based lock manager, the process of locking a row would resemble the following:

1. Find the address of the row you want to lock.

2. Get in line at the lock manager (which must be serialized, as it is a common in-memory structure).

3. Lock the list.

4. Search through the list to see if anyone else has locked this row.

5. Create a new entry in the list to establish the fact that you have locked the row.

6. Unlock the list.

Now that you have the row locked, you can modify it. Later, as you commit your changes you must continue the procedure as follows:

7. Get in line again.

8. Lock the list of locks.

9. Search through the list and release all of your locks.

10. Unlock the list.

As you can see, the more locks acquired, the more time spent on this operation, both before and after modifying the data. Oracle does not do it that way. Oracle's process looks like this:

1. Find the address of the row you want to lock.

2. Go to the row.

3. Lock the row (waiting for the transaction that has it locked to end if it is already locked, unless you are using the NOWAIT option).

That's it. Since the lock is stored as an attribute of the data, Oracle does not need a traditional lock manager. The transaction will simply go to the data and lock it (if it is not locked already). The interesting thing is that the data may appear locked when you get to it, even if it is not. When you lock rows of data in Oracle, the row points to a copy of the transaction ID that is stored with the block containing the data, and when the lock is released that transaction ID is left behind. This transaction ID is unique to your transaction and represents the rollback segment number, slot, and sequence number. You leave that on the block that contains your row to tell other sessions that you "own" this data (not all of the data on the block—just the one row you are modifying). When another session comes along, it sees the lock ID and, using the fact that it represents a transaction, it can quickly see if the transaction holding the lock is still active. If the lock is not active, the session is allowed access to the data. If the lock is still active, that session will ask to be notified as soon as the lock is released. Hence, you have a queuing mechanism: the session requesting the lock will be queued up waiting for that transaction to complete, and then it will get the data.

Here is a small example showing how this happens, using three V$ tables:

- V$TRANSACTION, which contains an entry for every active transaction.

- V$SESSION, which shows us the sessions logged in.

- V$LOCK, which contains an entry for all enqueue locks being held as well as for sessions that are waiting on locks. You will not see a row in this view for each row locked in this table by a session. As stated earlier, that master list of locks at the row level doesn't exist. If a session has one row in the EMP table locked, there will be one row in this view for that session indicating that fact. If a session has millions of rows in the EMP table locked, there will still be just one row in this view. This view shows what enqueue locks individual sessions have.

First, let's start a transaction (if you don't have a copy of the DEPT table, simply make one using a CREATE TABLE AS SELECT):

```
ops$tkyte@ORA10G> update dept set deptno = deptno+10;
4 rows updated.
```

Now, let's look at the state of the system at this point. This example assumes a single-user system; otherwise, you may see many rows in V$TRANSACTION. Even in a single-user system, do not be surprised to see more than one row in V$TRANSACTION, as many of the background Oracle processes may be performing a transaction as well.

```
ops$tkyte@ORA10G> select username,
  2         v$lock.sid,
  3         trunc(id1/power(2,16)) rbs,
  4         bitand(id1,to_number('ffff','xxxx'))+0 slot,
  5         id2 seq,
  6         lmode,
  7         request
  8  from v$lock, v$session
  9  where v$lock.type = 'TX'
 10    and v$lock.sid = v$session.sid
 11    and v$session.username = USER;

USERNAME   SID RBS SLOT    SEQ LMODE REQUEST
---------- ---- --- ---- ------ ----- -------
OPS$TKYTE  145   4  12  16582     6       0

ops$tkyte@ORA10G> select XIDUSN, XIDSLOT, XIDSQN
  2    from v$transaction;

   XIDUSN    XIDSLOT     XIDSQN
---------- ---------- ----------
        4         12      16582
```

The interesting points to note here are as follows:

- The LMODE is 6 in the V$LOCK table and the request is 0. If you refer to the definition of the V$LOCK table in *Oracle Server Reference* manual, you will find that LMODE=6 is an exclusive lock. A value of 0 in the request means you are not making a request; you have the lock.

- There is only one row in this table. This V$LOCK table is more of a queuing table than a lock table. Many people expect there would be four rows in V$LOCK since we have four rows locked. What you must remember, however, is that Oracle does not store a master list of every row locked anywhere. To find out if a row is locked, we must go to that row.

- I took the ID1 and ID2 columns and performed some manipulation on them. Oracle needed to save three 16-bit numbers, but only had two columns in order to do it. So, the first column ID1 holds two of these numbers. By dividing by 2^16 with trunc(id1/power(2,16)) rbs, and by masking out the high bits with bitand(id1,➡ to_number('ffff','xxxx'))+0 slot, I am able to get back the two numbers that are hiding in that one number.

- The RBS, SLOT, and SEQ values match the V$TRANSACTION information. This is my transaction ID.

Now we'll start another session using the same username, update some rows in EMP, and then try to update DEPT:

```
ops$tkyte@ORA10G> update emp set ename = upper(ename);
14 rows updated.

ops$tkyte@ORA10G> update dept set deptno = deptno-10;
```

We're now blocked in this session. If we run the V$ queries again, we see the following:

```
ops$tkyte@ORA10G> select username,
  2          v$lock.sid,
  3          trunc(id1/power(2,16)) rbs,
  4          bitand(id1,to_number('ffff','xxxx'))+0 slot,
  5          id2 seq,
  6          lmode,
  7          request
  8  from v$lock, v$session
  9  where v$lock.type = 'TX'
 10    and v$lock.sid = v$session.sid
 11    and v$session.username = USER;

USERNAME    SID RBS SLOT    SEQ LMODE REQUEST
--------- ---- --- ---- ------ ----- -------
OPS$TKYTE   144   4   12  16582     0       6
OPS$TKYTE   144   5   34   1759     6       0
OPS$TKYTE   145   4   12  16582     6       0
```

```
ops$tkyte@ORA10G> select XIDUSN, XIDSLOT, XIDSQN
  2    from v$transaction;

   XIDUSN    XIDSLOT     XIDSQN
---------- ---------- ----------
        5         34       1759
        4         12      16582
```

What we see here is that a new transaction has begun, with a transaction ID of (5,34,1759). Our new session, SID=144, has two rows in V$LOCK this time. One row represents the locks that it owns (where LMODE=6). It also has a row in there that shows a REQUEST with a value of 6. This is a request for an exclusive lock. The interesting thing to note here is that the RBS/SLOT/SEQ values of this request row are the transaction ID of the *holder* of the lock. The transaction with SID=145 is blocking the transaction with SID=144. We can see this more explicitly simply by doing a self-join of V$LOCK:

```
ops$tkyte@ORA10G> select
  2         (select username from v$session where sid=a.sid) blocker,
  3          a.sid,
  4        ' is blocking '
  5         (select username from v$session where sid=b.sid) blockee,
  6             b.sid
  7    from v$lock a, v$lock b
  8   where a.block = 1
  9     and b.request > 0
 10     and a.id1 = b.id1
 11     and a.id2 = b.id2;

BLOCKER      SID 'ISBLOCKING'  BLOCKEE     SID
---------- ---- -------------- ---------- ----
OPS$TKYTE    145 is blocking   OPS$TKYTE   144
```

Now, if we commit our original transaction, SID=145, and rerun our lock query, we find that the request row has gone:

```
ops$tkyte@ORA10G> select username,
  2         v$lock.sid,
  3         trunc(id1/power(2,16)) rbs,
  4         bitand(id1,to_number('ffff','xxxx'))+0 slot,
  5         id2 seq,
  6         lmode,
  7         request
  8    from v$lock, v$session
  9   where v$lock.type = 'TX'
 10     and v$lock.sid = v$session.sid
 11     and v$session.username = USER;
```

```
USERNAME    SID RBS SLOT    SEQ LMODE REQUEST
--------- ---- --- ---- ------ ----- -------
OPS$TKYTE   144   5   34   1759     6       0

ops$tkyte@ORA10G> select XIDUSN, XIDSLOT, XIDSQN
  2    from v$transaction;

   XIDUSN    XIDSLOT     XIDSQN
---------- ---------- ----------
        5         34       1759
```

The request row disappeared the instant the other session gave up its lock. That request row was the queuing mechanism. The database is able to wake up the blocked sessions the instant the transaction is completed. There are infinitely more "pretty" displays with various GUI tools, but in a pinch, having knowledge of the tables you need to look at is very useful.

However, before we can say that we have a good understanding of how the row locking in Oracle works, we must look at one last topic: how the locking and transaction information is managed with the data itself. It is part of the block overhead. In Chapter 9, we'll get into the details of the block format, but suffice it to say that at the top of a database block is some leading "overhead" space in which to store a transaction table for that block. This transaction table contains an entry for each "real" transaction that has locked some data in that block. The size of this structure is controlled by two physical attribute parameters on the CREATE statement for an object:

- INITRANS: The initial, preallocated size of this structure. This defaults to 2 for indexes and tables (regardless of what *Oracle SQL Reference* says, I have filed the documentation bug regarding that).

- MAXTRANS: The maximum size to which this structure may grow. It defaults to 255 and has a minimum of 2, practically. In Oracle 10g, *this setting has been deprecated*, so it no longer applies. MAXTRANS is 255 regardless in that release.

Each block starts life with, by default, two transaction slots. The number of simultaneous active transactions that a block can ever have is constrained by the value of MAXTRANS and by the availability of space on the block. You may not be able to achieve 255 concurrent transactions on the block if there is not sufficient space to grow this structure.

We can artificially demonstrate how this works by creating a table with a constrained MAXTRANS. We'll need to use Oracle9i or before for this, since in Oracle 10g MAXTRANS is ignored. In Oracle 10g, even if MAXTRANS is set, Oracle will grow the transaction table, as long as there is room on the block to do so. In Oracle9i and before, once the MAXTRANS value is reached for that block, the transaction table will not grow, for example:

```
ops$tkyte@ORA9IR2> create table t ( x int ) maxtrans 2;
Table created.

ops$tkyte@ORA9IR2> insert into t select rownum from all_users;
24 rows created.
```

```
ops$tkyte@ORA9IR2> commit;
Commit complete.

ops$tkyte@ORA9IR2> select distinct dbms_rowid.rowid_block_number(rowid) from t;

DBMS_ROWID.ROWID_BLOCK_NUMBER(ROWID)
------------------------------------
                                  18
```

So, we have 24 rows and we've verified they are all on the same database block. Now, in one session we issue

```
ops$tkyte@ORA9IR2> update t set x = 1 where x = 1;
1 row updated.
```

and in another, we issue

```
ops$tkyte@ORA9IR2> update t set x = 2 where x = 2;
1 row updated.
```

Finally, in a third session, we issue

```
ops$tkyte@ORA9IR2> update t set x = 3 where x = 3;
```

Now, since those three rows are on the same database block, and we set MAXTRANS (the maximum degree of concurrency for that block) to 2, the third session will be blocked.

■**Note** Remember, in Oracle 10*g* this blocking will not happen *in this example*—MAXTRANS is set to 255 regardless. There would have to be insufficient space on the block to grow the transaction table to see this blocking in that release.

This example demonstrates what happens when more than one MAXTRANS transaction attempts to access the same block simultaneously. Similarly, blocking may also occur if the INITRANS is set low and there is not enough space on a block to dynamically expand the transaction. In most cases, the default of 2 for INITRANS is sufficient, as the transaction table will dynamically grow (space permitting), but in some environments you may need to increase this setting to increase concurrency and decrease waits. An example of when you might need to do this would be on a table or, even more frequently, on an index (since index blocks can get many more rows on them than a table can typically hold) that is frequently modified. You may need to increase either PCTFREE (discussed in Chapter 10) or INITRANS to set aside ahead of time sufficient space on the block for the number of expected concurrent transactions. This is especially true if you anticipate the blocks will be nearly full to begin with, meaning there is no room for the dynamic expansion of the transaction structure on the block.

TM (DML Enqueue) Locks

TM locks are used to ensure that the structure of a table is not altered while you are modifying its contents. For example, if you have updated a table, you will acquire a TM lock on that table. This will prevent another user from executing DROP or ALTER commands on that table. If another user attempts to perform DDL on the table while you have a TM lock on it, he'll receive the following error message:

```
drop table dept
          *
ERROR at line 1:
ORA-00054: resource busy and acquire with NOWAIT specified
```

This is a confusing message at first, since there is no method to specify NOWAIT or WAIT on a DROP TABLE at all. It is just the generic message you get when you attempt to perform an operation that would be blocked, but the operation does not permit blocking. As you've seen before, it's the same message you get if you issue a SELECT FOR UPDATE NOWAIT against a locked row.

The following shows how these locks would appear in the V$LOCK table:

```
ops$tkyte@ORA10G> create table t1 ( x int );
Table created.

ops$tkyte@ORA10G> create table t2 ( x int );
Table created.

ops$tkyte@ORA10G> insert into t1 values ( 1 );
1 row created.

ops$tkyte@ORA10G> insert into t2 values ( 1 );
1 row created.

ops$tkyte@ORA10G> select (select username
  2                         from v$session
  3                        where sid = v$lock.sid) username,
  4          sid,
  5          id1,
  6          id2,
  7          lmode,
  8          request, block, v$lock.type
  9     from v$lock
 10    where sid = (select sid
 11                   from v$mystat
 12                  where rownum=1)
 13  /
```

```
USERNAME    SID     ID1    ID2 LMODE REQUEST BLOCK TYPE
---------  ----  -------  ------ ----- ------- ----- ----
OPS$TKYTE  161   262151  16584     6       0     0 TX
OPS$TKYTE  161    62074      0     3       0     0 TM
OPS$TKYTE  161    62073      0     3       0     0 TM

ops$tkyte@ORA10G> select object_name, object_id
  2    from user_objects
  3  where object_name in ('T1','T2')
  4  /


OBJECT_NAME    OBJECT_ID
-----------   ----------
T1                 62073
T2                 62074
```

Whereas we get only one TX lock per transaction, we can get as many TM locks as the objects we modify. Here, the interesting thing is that the ID1 column for the TM lock is the object ID of the DML-locked object, so it easy to find the object on which the lock is being held.

An interesting aside to the TM lock: the total number of TM locks allowed in the system is configurable by you (for details, see the DML_LOCKS parameter definition in the *Oracle Database Reference* manual). It may in fact be set to zero. This does not mean that your database becomes a read-only database (no locks), but rather that *DDL is not permitted*. This is useful in very specialized applications, such as RAC implementations, to reduce the amount of intra-instance coordination that would otherwise take place. You can also remove the ability to gain TM locks on an object-by-object basis using the ALTER TABLE TABLENAME DISABLE TABLE LOCK command. This is a quick way to make it "harder" to accidentally drop a table, as you will have to re-enable the table lock before dropping the table. It can also be used to detect a full table lock as a result of the unindexed foreign key we discussed previously.

DDL Locks

DDL locks are automatically placed against objects during a DDL operation to protect them from changes by other sessions. For example, if I perform the DDL operation ALTER TABLE T, the table T will have an exclusive DDL lock placed against it, preventing other sessions from getting DDL locks and TM locks on this table. DDL locks are held for the duration of the DDL statement and are released immediately afterward. This is done, in effect, by always wrapping DDL statements in implicit commits (or a commit/rollback pair). For this reason, DDL always commits in Oracle. Every CREATE, ALTER, and so on statement is really executed as shown in this pseudo-code:

```
Begin
   Commit;
   DDL-STATEMENT
   Commit;
Exception
   When others then rollback;
End;
```

So, DDL will always commit, even if it is unsuccessful. DDL starts by committing—be aware of this. It commits first so that if it has to roll back, it will not roll back your transaction. If you execute DDL, it will make permanent any outstanding work you have performed, even if the DDL is not successful. If you need to execute DDL, but you do not want it to commit your existing transaction, you may use an autonomous transaction.

There are three types of DDL locks:

- *Exclusive DDL locks*: These prevent other sessions from gaining a DDL lock or TM (DML) lock themselves. This means that you may query a table during a DDL operation, but you may not modify it in any way.

- *Share DDL locks*: These protect the structure of the referenced object against modification by other sessions, but allow modifications to the data.

- *Breakable parse locks*: These allow an object, such as a query plan cached in the Shared pool, to register its reliance on some other object. If you perform DDL against that object, Oracle will review the list of objects that have registered their dependence and invalidate them. Hence, these locks are "breakable"—they do not prevent the DDL from occurring.

Most DDL takes an *exclusive* DDL lock. If you issue a statement such as

```
Alter table t add new_column date;
```

the table T will be unavailable for modifications during the execution of that statement. The table may be queried using SELECT during this time, but most other operations will be prevented, including all DDL statements. In Oracle, some DDL operations may now take place without DDL locks. For example, I can issue the following:

```
create index t_idx on t(x) ONLINE;
```

The ONLINE keyword modifies the method by which the index is actually built. Instead of taking an exclusive DDL lock, preventing modifications of data, Oracle will only attempt to acquire a low-level (mode 2) TM lock on the table. This will effectively prevent other DDL from taking place, but it will allow DML to occur normally. Oracle accomplishes this feat by keeping a record of modifications made to the table during the DDL statement and applying these changes to the new index as it finishes the CREATE. This greatly increases the availability of data.

Other types of DDL take *share* DDL locks. These are taken out against dependent objects when you create stored, compiled objects, such as procedures and views. For example, if you execute

```
Create view MyView
as
select *
  from emp, dept
 where emp.deptno = dept.deptno;
```

share DDL locks will be placed against both EMP and DEPT, while the CREATE VIEW command is being processed. You can modify the contents of these tables, but you cannot modify their structure.

The last type of DDL lock is a *breakable parse* lock. When your session parses a statement, a parse lock is taken against every object referenced by that statement. These locks are taken in order to allow the parsed, cached statement to be invalidated (flushed) in the Shared pool if a referenced object is dropped or altered in some way.

A view that is invaluable for looking at this information is DBA_DDL_LOCKS. There is no V$ view for you to look at. The DBA_DDL_LOCKS view is built on the more mysterious X$ tables and, by default, it will not be installed in your database. You can install this and other locking views by running the catblock.sql script found in the directory [ORACLE_HOME]/rdbms/admin. This script must be executed as the user SYS in order to succeed. Once you have executed this script, you can run a query against the view. For example, in a single-user database I see the following:

```
ops$tkyte@ORA10G> select session_id sid, owner, name, type,
  2      mode_held held, mode_requested request
  3  from dba_ddl_locks;

SID OWNER      NAME                  TYPE                  HELD REQUEST
--- ---------- --------------------- --------------------- ---- ---------
161 SYS        DBMS_UTILITY          Body                  Null None
161 SYS        DBMS_UTILITY          Body                  Null None
161 SYS        DBMS_APPLICATION_INFO Table/Procedure/Type  Null None
161 OPS$TKYTE  OPS$TKYTE             18                    Null None
161 SYS        DBMS_OUTPUT           Body                  Null None
161 SYS        DATABASE              18                    Null None
161 SYS        DBMS_UTILITY          Table/Procedure/Type  Null None
161 SYS        DBMS_UTILITY          Table/Procedure/Type  Null None
161 SYS        PLITBLM               Table/Procedure/Type  Null None
161 SYS        DBMS_APPLICATION_INFO Body                  Null None
161 SYS        DBMS_OUTPUT           Table/Procedure/Type  Null None

11 rows selected.
```

These are all the objects that my session is "locking." I have breakable parse locks on a couple of the DBMS_* packages. These are a side effect of using SQL*Plus; it calls DBMS_APPLICATION_INFO, for example. I may see more than one copy of various objects here—this is normal, and it just means I have more than one thing I'm using in the Shared pool that references these objects. It is interesting to note that in the view, the OWNER column is not the owner of the lock; rather, it is the owner of the object being locked. This is why you see many SYS rows. SYS owns these packages, but they all belong to my session.

To see a breakable parse lock in action, let's first create and run a stored procedure, P:

```
ops$tkyte@ORA10G> create or replace procedure p as begin null; end;
  2  /
Procedure created.

ops$tkyte@ORA10G> exec p
PL/SQL procedure successfully completed.
```

The procedure, P, will now show up in the DBA_DDL_LOCKS view. We have a parse lock on it:

```
ops$tkyte@ORA10G> select session_id sid, owner, name, type,
  2          mode_held held, mode_requested request
  3    from dba_ddl_locks
  4  /

SID OWNER     NAME                  TYPE                  HELD REQUEST
---- --------- --------------------- --------------------- ---- ---------
161 OPS$TKYTE P                     Table/Procedure/Type  Null None
161 SYS       DBMS_UTILITY          Body                  Null None
161 SYS       DBMS_UTILITY          Body                  Null None
...
161 SYS       DBMS_OUTPUT           Table/Procedure/Type  Null None

12 rows selected.
```

We then recompile our procedure and query the view again:

```
ops$tkyte@ORA10G> alter procedure p compile;
Procedure altered.

ops$tkyte@ORA10G> select session_id sid, owner, name, type,
  2          mode_held held, mode_requested request
  3    from dba_ddl_locks
  4  /

SID OWNER     NAME                  TYPE                  HELD REQUEST
---- --------- --------------------- --------------------- ---- ---------
161 SYS       DBMS_UTILITY          Body                  Null None
161 SYS       DBMS_UTILITY          Body                  Null None
...
161 SYS       DBMS_OUTPUT           Table/Procedure/Type  Null None

11 rows selected.
```

We find that P is now missing from the view. Our parse lock has been broken.

This view is useful to you, as a developer, when it is found that some piece of code won't compile in the test or development system—it hangs and eventually times out. This indicates that someone else is using it (actually running it), and you can use this view to see who that might be. The same will happen with GRANTS and other types of DDL against the object. You cannot grant EXECUTE on a procedure that is running, for example. You can use the same method to discover the potential blockers and waiters.

Latches

Latches are lightweight serialization devices used to coordinate multiuser access to shared data structures, objects, and files.

Latches are locks designed to be held for extremely short periods of time—for example, the time it takes to modify an in-memory data structure. They are used to protect certain memory structures, such as the database block buffer cache or the library cache in the Shared pool. Latches are typically requested internally in a "willing to wait" mode. This means that if the latch is not available, the requesting session will sleep for a short period of time and retry the operation later. Other latches may be requested in an "immediate" mode, which is similar in concept to a SELECT FOR UPDATE NOWAIT, meaning that the process will go do something else, such as try to grab an equivalent sibling latch that may be free, rather than sit and wait for this latch to become available. Since many requestors may be waiting for a latch at the same time, you may see some processes waiting longer than others. Latches are assigned rather randomly, based on the luck of the draw, if you will. Whichever session asks for a latch right after it was released will get it. There is no line of latch waiters—just a mob of waiters constantly retrying.

Oracle uses atomic instructions like "test and set" and "compare and swap" for operating on latches. Since the instructions to set and free latches are atomic, the operating system itself guarantees that only one process gets to test and set the latch even though many processes may be going for it simultaneously. Since the instruction is only one instruction, it can be quite fast. Latches are held for short periods of time and provide a mechanism for cleanup in case a latch holder "dies" abnormally while holding it. This cleanup process would be performed by PMON.

Enqueues, which were discussed earlier, are another, more sophisticated serialization device used when updating rows in a database table, for example. They differ from latches in that they allow the requestor to "queue up" and wait for the resource. With a latch request, the requestor session is told right away whether or not it got the latch. With an enqueue lock, the requestor session will be blocked until it can actually attain it.

■**Note** Using SELECT FOR UPDATE NOWAIT or WAIT [n], you can optionally decide not to wait for an enqueue lock if your session would be blocked, but if you do block and wait, you will wait in a queue.

As such, an enqueue is not as fast as a latch can be, but it does provided functionality over and above what a latch can offer. Enqueues may be obtained at various levels, so you can have many shared locks and locks with various degrees of shareability.

Latch "Spinning"

One thing I'd like to drive home with regard to latches is this: latches are a type of lock, locks are serialization devices, and serialization devices inhibit scalability. If your goal is to construct an application that scales well in an Oracle environment, you must look for approaches and solutions that minimize the amount of latching you need to perform.

Even seemingly simple activities, such as parsing a SQL statement, acquire and release hundreds or thousands of latches on the library cache and related structures in the Shared pool. If we have a latch, then someone else might be waiting for it. When we go to get a latch, we may well have to wait for it ourselves.

Waiting for a latch can be an expensive operation. If the latch is not available immediately and we are willing to wait for it, as we likely are most of the time, then on a multi-CPU machine our session will *spin*—trying over and over, in a loop, to get the latch. The reasoning behind this is that *context switching* (i.e., getting "kicked off" the CPU and having to get back on the CPU) is expensive. So, if the process cannot get a latch immediately, we'll stay on the CPU and try again immediately rather than just going to sleep, giving up the CPU, and trying later when we'll have to get scheduled back on the CPU. The hope is that the holder of the latch is busy processing on the other CPU (and since latches are designed to be held for very short periods of time, this is likely) and will give it up soon. If after spinning and constantly trying to get the latch, we still fail to obtain it, only then will our process *sleep*, or take itself off of the CPU, and let some other work take place. The pseudo-code to get a latch get might look like this:

```
Attempt to get Latch
If Latch gotten
Then
   return SUCCESS
Else
   Misses on that Latch = Misses+1;
   Loop
     Sleeps on Latch = Sleeps + 1
       For I in 1 .. 2000
       Loop
         Attempt to get Latch
         If Latch gotten
         Then
            Return SUCCESS
         End if
       End loop
     Go to sleep for short period
   End loop
End if
```

The logic is to try to get the latch and, failing that, to increment the *miss count*—a statistic we can see in a Statspack report or by querying the V$LATCH view directly. Once the process misses, it will loop some number of times (an undocumented parameter controls the number of times and is typically set to 2,000), attempting to get the latch over and over. If one of these get attempts succeeds, then it returns and we continue processing. If they all fail, the process will go to sleep for a short duration of time, after incrementing the *sleep count* for that latch. Upon waking up, the process begins all over again. This implies that the cost of getting a latch is not just the "test and set"-type operation that takes place, but can also be a considerable amount of CPU while we *try* to get the latch. Our system will appear to be very busy (with much CPU being consumed), but not much work is getting done.

Measuring the Cost of Latching a Shared Resource

As an example, we'll study the cost of latching the Shared pool. We'll compare a well-written program (one that uses bind variables) and a program that is not so well written (it uses literal

SQL, or unique SQL for each statement). To do this, we'll use a very small Java program that simply logs into Oracle, turns off auto-commit (as all Java programs should do immediately after connecting to a database), and executes 25,000 unique INSERT statements in a loop. We'll perform two sets of tests: our program will not use bind variables in the first set, and in the second set it will.

To evaluate these programs and their behavior in a multiuser environment, I opted to use Statspack to gather the metrics. as follows:

1. Execute a Statspack snapshot to gather the current state of the system.

2. Run *N* copies of the program, having each program INSERT into its own database table so as to avoid the contention associated with having all programs trying to insert into a single table.

3. Take another snapshot immediately after the last copy of the program finishes.

Then it is a simple matter of printing out the Statspack report and finding out how long it took *N* copies of the program to complete, how much CPU was used, what the major wait events occurred, and so on.

These tests were performed on a dual-CPU machine with hyperthreading enabled (making it appear as if there were four CPUs). Given that there were two physical CPUs, you might expect very linear scaling here—that is, if one user uses 1 unit of CPU to process her inserts, then you might expect that two users would require 2 units of CPU. You'll discover that this premise, while sounding plausible, may well be inaccurate (just how inaccurate depends on your programming technique, as you'll see). It would be correct if the processing we were performing needed no shared resource, but our process will use a shared resource, namely *the Shared pool*. We need to latch the Shared pool to parse SQL statements, and we need to latch the Shared pool because it is a shared data structure, and we cannot modify it while others are reading it and we cannot read it while it is being modified.

Note I've performed these tests using Java, PL/SQL, Pro*C, and other languages. The end results are very much the same every time. This demonstration and discussion applies to all languages and all interfaces to the database. I chose Java for this example as I find Java and Visual Basic applications are most likely to not use bind variables when working with the Oracle database.

Without Bind Variables

In the first instance, our program will not use bind variables, but rather will use string concatenation to insert data:

```
import java.sql.*;
public class instest
{
    static public void main(String args[]) throws Exception
    {
        DriverManager.registerDriver(new oracle.jdbc.driver.OracleDriver());
        Connection
```

```
        conn = DriverManager.getConnection
            ("jdbc:oracle:thin:@dellpe:1521:ora10gr1",
            "scott","tiger");
    conn.setAutoCommit( false );
    Statement stmt = conn.createStatement();
    for( int i = 0; i < 25000; i++ )
    {
      stmt.execute
      ("insert into "+ args[0] +
        " (x) values(" + i + ")" );
    }
    conn.commit();
    conn.close();
  }
}
```

I ran the test in "single user" mode and the Statspack report came back with this information:

```
Elapsed:                 0.52 (mins)

Cache Sizes (end)
~~~~~~~~~~~~~~~~~~

            Buffer Cache:      768M    Std Block Size:      8K
        Shared Pool Size:      244M       Log Buffer:  1,024K

Load Profile
~~~~~~~~~~~~
                              Per Second        Per Transaction
                            ---------------     ---------------
...
                Parses:          810.58            12,564.00
           Hard parses:          807.16            12,511.00
....
Top 5 Timed Events
~~~~~~~~~~~~~~~~~~~
                                                         % Total
Event                              Waits    Time (s) Call Time
------------------------------- ------------ ----------- ---------
CPU time                                          26      55.15
class slave wait                       2          10      21.33
Queue Monitor Task Wait                2          10      21.33
log file parallel write               48           1       1.35
control file parallel write           14           0        .51
```

I included the SGA configuration for reference, but the relevant statistics are as follows:

- Elapsed time of approximately 30 seconds

- 807 hard parses per second

- 26 CPU seconds used

Now, if we were to run two of these programs simultaneously, we might expect the hard parsing to jump to about 1,600 per second (we have two CPUs available, after all) and the CPU time to double to perhaps 52 CPU seconds. Let's take a look:

```
Elapsed:                  0.78 (mins)

Load Profile
~~~~~~~~~~~~~
                                 Per Second        Per Transaction
                                 ----------        ---------------
                     Parses:      1,066.62             16,710.33
                Hard parses:      1,064.28             16,673.67

Top 5 Timed Events
~~~~~~~~~~~~~~~~~~~
                                                              % Total
Event                                  Waits   Time (s) Call Time
--------------------------------------- ------- -------- ---------
CPU time                                             74     97.53
log file parallel write                    53        1      1.27
latch: shared pool                        406        1       .66
control file parallel write                21        0       .45
log file sync                               6        0       .04
```

What we discover is that the hard parsing goes up a little bit, but the CPU time triples rather than doubles! How could that be? The answer lies in Oracle's implementation of latching. On this multi-CPU machine, when we could not immediately get a latch, we "spun." The act of spinning itself consumes CPU. Process 1 attempted many times to get a latch onto the Shared pool only to discover that process 2 held that latch, so process 1 had to spin and wait for it (consuming CPU). The converse would be true for process 2—many times it would find that process 1 was holding the latch to the resource it needed. So, much of our processing time was spent not doing real work, but waiting for a resource to become available. If we page down through the Statspack report to the "Latch Sleep Breakdown" report, we discover the following:

```
Latch Name        Requests     Misses    Sleeps  Sleeps 1->3+
----------------- ----------- ---------- -------- ------------
shared pool       1,126,006    229,537       406  229135/398/4/0
library cache     1,108,039     45,582         7  45575/7/0/0
```

Note how the number 406 appears in the SLEEPS column here? That 406 corresponds to the number of waits reported in the preceding "Top 5 Timed Events" report. This report shows us the number of times we tried to get a latch and failed in the spin loop. That means the "Top 5" report is showing us only the tip of the iceberg with regard to latching issues—the 229,537 misses (which means we spun trying to get the latch) are not revealed in the "Top 5" report for us. After examination of the "Top 5" report, we might not be inclined to think "We have a hard parse problem here," even though we have a very serious one. To perform 2 units of work, we needed to use 3 units of CPU. This was due entirely to the fact that we need that shared resource, the Shared pool—such is the nature of latching. However, it can be very hard to diagnose a latching-related issue, unless we understand the mechanics of how they are implemented. A quick glance at a Statspack report, using the "Top 5" section, might cause us to miss the fact that we have a fairly bad scaling issue on our hands. Only by deeper investigation in the latching section of the Statspack report will we see the problem at hand.

Additionally, it is not normally possible to determine how much of the CPU time used by the system is due to this spinning—all we know in looking at the two-user test is that we used 74 seconds of CPU time and that we missed getting a latch on the Shared pool 229,537 times. We don't know how many times we spun trying to get the latch each time we missed, so we have no real way of gauging how much of the CPU time was spent spinning and how much was spent processing. We need multiple data points to derive that information.

In our tests, because we have the single-user example for comparison, we can conclude that about 22 CPU seconds was spent spinning on the latch, waiting for that resource.

With Bind Variables

Now I'd like to look at the same situation as presented in the previous section, but this time using a program that uses significantly less latches during its processing. We'll take that Java program and code it using bind variables. To accomplish this, we'll change the Statement into a PreparedStatement, parse a single INSERT statement, and then bind and execute that PreparedStatement repeatedly in the loop:

```java
import java.sql.*;
public class instest
{
    static public void main(String args[]) throws Exception
    {
        DriverManager.registerDriver(new oracle.jdbc.driver.OracleDriver());
        Connection
            conn = DriverManager.getConnection
                    ("jdbc:oracle:thin:@dellpe:1521:ora10gr1",
                     "scott","tiger");
        conn.setAutoCommit( false );
        PreparedStatement pstmt =
            conn.prepareStatement
            ("insert into "+ args[0] + " (x) values(?)" );
        for( int i = 0; i < 25000; i++ )
        {
            pstmt.setInt( 1, i );
            pstmt.executeUpdate();
        }
        conn.commit();
        conn.close();
    }
}
```

Let's look at the single and dual user Statspack reports, as we did for the "no bind variable" example. We'll see dramatic differences here. Here is the single-user report:

CHAPTER 6 ■ LOCKING AND LATCHING   228

```
Elapsed:                  0.12 (mins)

Load Profile
~~~~~~~~~~~~~~~
                                  Per Second      Per Transaction
                                  ----------      ---------------
...
                    Parses:          8.43              29.50
               Hard parses:          0.14               0.50


Top 5 Timed Events
~~~~~~~~~~~~~~~~~~~~~~~                                   % Total
Event                             Waits    Time (s) Call Time
-------------------------------- -------- --------- ---------
CPU time                                        4      86.86
log file parallel write             49          0      10.51
control file parallel write          4          0       2.26
log file sync                        4          0        .23
control file sequential read       542          0        .14
```

That is quite dramatic: from 26 CPU seconds in the no bind variables example to 4 CPU seconds here. From 807 hard parses per second to 0.14 per second. Even the elapsed time was dramatically reduced from about 45 seconds down to 8 seconds. When not using bind variables, we spent five-sixths of our CPU time parsing SQL. This was not entirely latch related, as much of the CPU time incurred without bind variables was spent parsing and optimizing the SQL. Parsing SQL is very CPU intensive, but to expend five-sixths of our CPU doing something (parsing) that doesn't really do useful work for us—work we didn't need to perform—is pretty expensive.

When we get to the two-user test, the results continue to look better:

```
Elapsed:                  0.20 (mins)

Load Profile
~~~~~~~~~~~~~~~
                                  Per Second      Per Transaction
                                  ----------      ---------------
                    Parses:          6.58              26.33
               Hard parses:          0.17               0.67


Top 5 Timed Events
~~~~~~~~~~~~~~~~~~~~~~~                                   % Total
Event                             Waits    Time (s) Call Time
-------------------------------- -------- --------- ---------
CPU time                                       11      89.11
log file parallel write             48          1       9.70
control file parallel write          4          0        .88
log file sync                        5          0        .23
log buffer space                     2          0        .05
```

The amount of CPU time is about 2 to 2.5 times the amount reported by the single-user test case.

■Note Due to rounding, the 4 CPU seconds is really anywhere from 3.5 to 4.49, and the 11 is really anywhere from 10.5 to 11.49 seconds.

Further, the amount of CPU used by two users with bind variables is less than half the amount of CPU a single user not using bind variables required! When I went to look at the latch report in this Statspack report, I found it was *missing* in this report—there was so little contention for the Shared pool and library cache that it was not even reported. In fact, digging deeper turned up the fact that the Shared pool latch was requested 50,367 times versus well *over 1,000,000 times in the two-user test just shown.*

Performance/Scalability Comparison

Table 6-1 summarizes the CPU used by each implementation, as well as the latching results as we increase the number of users beyond two. As you can see, the solution using fewer latches will scale much better as the user load goes up.

Table 6-1. *CPU Usage Comparison With and Without Bind Variables*

Users	CPU Seconds/Elapsed Time in Minutes		Shared Pool Latch Requests		Waits for Latches (Number of Waits/Time in Wait in Seconds)	
	No Binds	Binds	No Binds	Binds	No Binds	Binds
1	26/0.52	4/0.10	563,883	25,232	0/0	
2	74/0.78	11/0.20	1,126,006	50,367	406/1	
3	155/1.13	29/0.37	1,712,280	75,541	2,830/4	
4	272/1.50	44/0.45	2,298,179	100,682	9,400/5	
5	370/2.03	64/0.62	2,920,219	125,933	13,800/20	
6	466/2.58	74/0.72	3,526,704	150,957	30,800/80	17/0
7	564/3.15	95/0.92	4,172,492	176,085	40,800/154	
8	664/3.57	106/1.00	4,734,793	201,351	56,300/240	120/1
9	747/4.05	117/1.15	5,360,188	230,516	74,600/374	230/1
10	822/4.42	137/1.30	5,901,981	251,434	60,000/450	354/1

The interesting observation for me is that 10 users using bind variables (and very few latch requests as a result) use the same amount of hardware resources as 2 to 2.5 users that do not use bind variables (i.e., that overuse a latch, or process more than they need to). When you examine the results for 10 users, you see that nonuse of bind variables results in the use of 6 times the CPU and takes 3.4 times the execution time when compared to the bind variable solution. The more users are added over time, the longer each user spends waiting for these latches. We went from an average of 4 seconds/session of wait time for latches with 5 users to an average of 45 seconds/session of wait time with 10 users. However, the implementation that avoided overuse of the latch suffered no ill effects as it scaled up.

Manual Locking and User-Defined Locks

So far we have looked mostly at locks that Oracle places for us transparently. When we update a table, Oracle places a TM lock on it to prevent other sessions from dropping that table (or performing most DDL, in fact). We have TX locks that are left on the various blocks we modify so others can tell what data we "own." The database employs DDL locks to protect objects from change while we ourselves are changing them. It uses latches and locks internally to protect its own structure.

Next, let's take a look at how we can get involved in some of this locking action. Our options are as follows:

- Manually lock data via a SQL statement.

- Create our own locks via the DBMS_LOCK package.

In the following sections, we will briefly discuss why you might want to do each of these.

Manual Locking

We have, in fact, already seen a couple of cases where we might want to use manual locking. The SELECT...FOR UPDATE statement is the predominant method of manually locking data. We used it in previous examples to avoid the lost update issue, whereby one session would over-write another session's changes. We've seen it used as a method to serialize access to detail records to enforce business rules (e.g., the resource scheduler example from Chapter 1).

We can also manually lock data using the LOCK TABLE statement. This statement is actually used rarely, because of the coarseness of the lock. It simply locks the table, not the rows in the table. If you start modifying the rows, they will be "locked" as normal. So, this is not a method to save on resources (as it might be in other RDBMSs). You might use the LOCK TABLE IN EXCLUSIVE MODE statement if you were writing a large batch update that would affect most of the rows in a given table and you wanted to be sure that no one would "block" you. By locking the table in this manner, you can be assured that your update will be able to do all of its work without getting blocked by other transactions. It would be the rare application, however, that has a LOCK TABLE statement in it.

Creating Your Own Locks

Oracle actually exposes to developers the enqueue lock mechanism that it uses internally, via the DBMS_LOCK package. You might be wondering why you would want to create your own locks. The answer is typically application specific. For example, you might use this package to serialize access to some resource external to Oracle. Say you are using the UTL_FILE routine that allows you to write to a file on the server's file system. You might have developed a common message routine that every application calls to record messages. Since the file is external, Oracle won't coordinate the many users trying to modify it simultaneously. In comes the DBMS_LOCK package. Now, before you open, write, and close the file, you will request a lock named after the file in exclusive mode, and after you close the file, you will manually release the lock. In this fashion, only one person at a time will be able to write a message to this file. Everyone else will queue up. The DBMS_LOCK package allows you to manually release a lock when you are done with it, or to give it up automatically when you commit, or even to keep it as long as you are logged in.

Summary

This chapter covered a lot of material that, at times, may have made you scratch your head. While locking is rather straightforward, some of its side effects are not. However, it is vital that you understand these issues. For example, if you were not aware of the table lock Oracle uses to enforce a foreign key relationship when the foreign key is not indexed, then your application would suffer from poor performance. If you did not understand how to review the data dictionary to see who was locking whom, you might never figure that one out. You would just assume that the database "hangs" sometimes. I sometimes wish I had a dollar for every time I was able to solve the insolvable hanging issue by simply running the query to detect unindexed foreign keys and suggesting that we index the one causing the problem—I would be very rich.

CHAPTER 7

■■■

Concurrency and Multi-Versioning

As stated in the last chapter, one of the key challenges in developing multiuser, database-driven applications is to maximize concurrent access but, at the same time, ensure that each user is able to read and modify the data in a consistent fashion. In this chapter, we're going to take a detailed look at how Oracle achieves *multi-version read consistency*, and what that means to you, the developer. I will also introduce a new term, *write consistency*, and use it to describe how Oracle works not only in a read environment with read consistency, but also in a mixed read and write environment.

What Are Concurrency Controls?

Concurrency controls are the collection of functions that the database provides to allow many people to access and modify data simultaneously. As noted in the previous chapter, the *lock* is one of the core mechanisms by which Oracle regulates concurrent access to shared database resources and prevents "interference" between concurrent database transactions. To briefly summarize, Oracle uses a variety of locks, including the following:

- *TX locks*: These locks are acquired for the duration of a data-modifying transaction.

- *TM and DDL locks*: These locks ensure that the structure of an object is not altered while you are modifying its contents (TM lock) or the object itself (DDL lock).

- *Latches*: These are internal locks that Oracle employs to mediate access to its shared data structures.

In each case, there is minimal overhead associated with lock acquisition. TX transaction locks are extremely scalable in terms of both performance and cardinality. TM and DDL locks are applied in the least restrictive mode whenever possible. Latches and enqueues are both very lightweight and fast (enqueues are the slightly heavier of the two, though they're more feature-rich). Problems only arise from poorly designed applications that hold locks for longer than necessary and cause blocking in the database. If you design your code well, Oracle's locking mechanisms will allow for scaleable, highly concurrent applications.

But Oracle's support for concurrency goes beyond efficient locking. It implements a *multi-versioning* architecture (introduced in Chapter 1) that provides controlled, yet highly concurrent access to data. Multi-versioning describes Oracle's ability to simultaneously materialize multiple versions of the data and is the mechanism by which Oracle provides read-consistent views of data (i.e., consistent results with respect to a point in time). A rather pleasant side effect of multi-versioning is that a reader of data will never be blocked by a writer of data. In other words, writes do not block reads. This is one of the fundamental differences between Oracle and other databases. A query that only reads information in Oracle will never be blocked, it will never deadlock with another session, and it will never get an answer that didn't exist in the database.

Note There is a short period of time during the processing of a distributed 2PC where Oracle will prevent read access to information. As this processing is somewhat rare and exceptional (the problem applies only to queries that start between the prepare and the commit phases and try to read the data before the commit arrives), I will not cover it in detail.

Oracle's multi-versioning model for read consistency is applied by default at the *statement level* (for each and every query) and can also be applied at the *transaction level*. This means that each and every SQL statement submitted to the database sees a read-consistent view of the database at least—and if you would like this read-consistent view of the database to be at the level of a transaction (a set of SQL statements), you may do that as well.

The basic purpose of a transaction in the database is to take the database from one consistent state to the next. The ISO SQL standard specifies various *transaction isolation levels*, which define how "sensitive" one transaction is to changes made by another. The greater the level of sensitivity, the greater the degree of isolation the database must provide between transactions executed by your application. In the following section, we'll look at how, via its multi-versioning architecture and with absolutely minimal locking, Oracle can support each of the defined isolation levels.

Transaction Isolation Levels

The ANSI/ISO SQL standard defines four levels of transaction isolation, with different possible outcomes for the same transaction scenario. That is, the same work performed in the same fashion with the same inputs may result in different answers, depending on your isolation level. These isolation levels are defined in terms of three "phenomena" that are either permitted or not at a given isolation level:

- *Dirty read*: The meaning of this term is as bad as it sounds. You are permitted to read uncommitted, or *dirty*, data. You would achieve this effect by just opening an OS file that someone else is writing and reading whatever data happens to be there. Data integrity is compromised, foreign keys are violated, and unique constraints are ignored.

- *Nonrepeatable read*: This simply means that if you read a row at time T1 and attempt to reread that row at time T2, the row may have changed. It may have disappeared, it may have been updated, and so on.

- *Phantom read*: This means that if you execute a query at time T1 and re-execute it at time T2, additional rows may have been added to the database, which will affect your results. This differs from the nonrepeatable read in that with a phantom read, data you already read has not been changed, but rather that *more* data satisfies your query criteria than before.

■**Note** The ANSI/ISO SQL standard defines *transaction*-level characteristics, not just individual statement-by-statement–level characteristics. In the following pages, we'll examine transaction-level isolation, not just statement-level isolation.

The SQL isolation levels are defined based on whether or not they allow each of the preceding phenomena. I find it interesting to note that the SQL standard does not impose a specific locking scheme or mandate particular behaviors, but rather describes these isolation levels in terms of these phenomena, allowing for many different locking/concurrency mechanisms to exist (see Table 7-1).

Table 7-1. *ANSI Isolation Levels*

Isolation Level	Dirty Read	Nonrepeatable Read	Phantom Read
READ UNCOMMITTED	Permitted	Permitted	Permitted
READ COMMITTED		Permitted	Permitted
REPEATABLE READ			Permitted
SERIALIZABLE			

Oracle explicitly supports the READ COMMITTED and SERIALIZABLE isolation levels, as they are defined in the standard. However, this doesn't tell the whole story. The SQL standard was attempting to set up isolation levels that would permit various degrees of consistency for queries performed in each level. REPEATABLE READ is the isolation level that the SQL standard claims will guarantee a read-consistent result from a query. In the SQL standard's definition, READ COMMITTED does not give you consistent results, and READ UNCOMMITTED is the level to use to get non-blocking reads.

However, in Oracle, READ COMMITTED has all of the attributes required to achieve read-consistent queries. In other databases, READ COMMITTED queries can and will return answers that never existed in the database at any point in time. Moreover, Oracle also supports the *spirit* of READ UNCOMMITTED. The goal of providing a dirty read is to supply a non-blocking read, whereby queries are not blocked by, and do not block, updates of the same data. However, Oracle does not need dirty reads to achieve this goal, nor does it support them. Dirty reads are an implementation other databases must use in order to provide non-blocking reads.

In addition to the four defined SQL isolation levels, Oracle provides another level, namely READ ONLY. A READ ONLY transaction is equivalent to a REPEATABLE READ or SERIALIZABLE transaction that cannot perform any modifications in SQL. A transaction using a READ ONLY isolation level only sees those changes that were committed *at the time the transaction began*, but inserts, updates, and deletes are not permitted in this mode (other sessions may update data, but not the READ ONLY transaction). Using this mode, you can achieve REPEATABLE READ and SERIALIZABLE levels of isolation.

Let's now move on to discuss exactly how multi-versioning and read consistency fits into the isolation scheme, and how databases that do not support multi-versioning achieve the same results. This information is instructive for anyone who has used another database and believes he or she understands how the isolation levels must work. It is also interesting to see how a standard that was supposed to remove the differences between the databases, ANSI/ISO SQL, actually allows for them. The standard, while very detailed, can be implemented in very different ways.

READ UNCOMMITTED

The READ UNCOMMITTED isolation level allows dirty reads. Oracle does not make use of dirty reads, nor does it even allow for them. The basic goal of a READ UNCOMMITTED isolation level is to provide a standards-based definition that caters for non-blocking reads. As we have seen, Oracle provides for non-blocking reads by default. You would be hard-pressed to make a SELECT query block in the database (as noted earlier, there is the special case of a distributed transaction). Every single query, be it a SELECT, INSERT, UPDATE, MERGE, or DELETE, executes in a read-consistent fashion. It might seem funny to refer to an UPDATE statement as a query—but it is. UPDATE statements have two components: a read component as defined by the WHERE clause and a write component as defined by the SET clause. UPDATE statements read from and write to the database—as do all DML statements. The special case of a single row INSERT using the VALUES clause is the only exception to this, as such statements have no read component, just the write component.

In Chapter 1, Oracle's method of obtaining read consistency was demonstrated by way of a simple single table query, which retrieved rows that were deleted *after* the cursor was opened. We're now going to explore a real-world example to see what happens in Oracle using multi-versioning, as well as what happens in any number of other databases.

Let's start with the same basic table and query:

```
create table accounts
( account_number number primary key,
  account_balance number not null
);


select sum(account_balance) from accounts;
```

Before the query begins, we have the data shown in Table 7-2.

Table 7-2. ACCOUNTS *Table Before Modifications*

Row	Account Number	Account Balance
1	123	$500.00
2	456	$240.25
...	...	...
342,023	987	$100.00

Now, our select statement starts executing and reads row 1, row 2, and so on. At some point while we are in the middle of the query, a transaction moves $400.00 from account 123 to account 987. This transaction does the two updates, but does not commit. The table now looks as shown in Table 7-3.

Table 7-3. ACCOUNTS *Table During Modifications*

Row	Account Number	Account Balance	Locked?
1	123	($500.00) changed to $100.00	X
2	456	$240.25	
...	...	...	
342,023	987	($100.00) changed to $500.00	X

So, two of those rows are locked. If anyone tried to update them, that user would be blocked. So far, the behavior we are seeing is more or less consistent across all databases. The difference will be in what happens when the query gets to the locked data.

When the query we are executing gets to the block containing the locked row (row 342,023) at the "bottom" of the table, it will notice that the data in the row has changed since the time at which it started execution. To provide a consistent (correct) answer, Oracle will at this point create a copy of the block containing this row *as it existed when the query began.* That is, it will read a value of $100.00, which is the value that existed at the time the query began. Effectively, Oracle takes a detour around the modified data—it reads around it, reconstructing it from the undo (also known as a *rollback*) segment (discussed in detail in Chapter 9). A consistent and correct answer comes back without waiting for the transaction to commit.

Now, a database that allowed a dirty read would simply return the value it saw in account 987 at the time it read it, in this case $500.00. The query would count the transferred $400 twice. Therefore, it not only returns the wrong answer, but also returns a total that never existed in the table at any point in time. In a multiuser database, a dirty read can be a dangerous feature and, personally, I have never seen the usefulness of it. Say that, rather than transferring, the transaction was actually just depositing $400.00 in account 987. The dirty read would count the $400.00 and get the "right" answer, wouldn't it? Well, suppose the uncommitted transaction was rolled back. We have just counted $400.00 that was never actually in the database.

The point here is that dirty read is not a feature; rather, it is a liability. In Oracle, it is just not needed. You get all of the advantages of a dirty read (no blocking) without any of the incorrect results.

READ COMMITTED

The READ COMMITTED isolation level states that a transaction may only read data that has been committed in the database. There are no dirty reads. There may be nonrepeatable reads (i.e., rereads of the same row may return a different answer in the same transaction) and phantom reads (i.e., newly inserted and committed rows become visible to a query that were not visible earlier in the transaction). READ COMMITTED is perhaps the most commonly used isolation level in database applications everywhere, and it is the default mode for Oracle databases. It is rare to see a different isolation level used.

However, achieving READ COMMITTED isolation is not as cut-and-dried as it sounds. If you look at Table 7-1, it appears straightforward. Obviously, given the earlier rules, a query executed in any database using the READ COMMITTED isolation will behave in the same way, will it not? It will not. If you query multiple rows in a single statement then, in almost every other database, READ COMMITTED isolation can be as bad as a dirty read, depending on the implementation.

In Oracle, using multi-versioning and read-consistent queries, the answer we get from the ACCOUNTS query is the same in READ COMMITTED as it was in the READ UNCOMMITTED example. Oracle will reconstruct the modified data as it appeared when the query began, returning the answer that was in the database when the query started.

Let's now take a look at how our previous example might work in READ COMMITTED mode in other databases—you might find the answer surprising. We'll pick up our example at the point described in the previous table:

- We are in the middle of the table. We have read and summed the first N rows.

- The other transaction has moved $400.00 from account 123 to account 987.

- The transaction has not yet committed, so rows containing the information for accounts 123 and 987 are locked.

We know what happens in Oracle when it gets to account 987—it will read around the modified data, find out it should be $100.00, and complete. Table 7-4 shows how another database, running in some default READ COMMITTED mode, might arrive at the answer.

Table 7-4. *Timeline in a Non-Oracle Database Using* READ COMMITTED *Isolation*

Time	Query	Account Transfer Transaction
T1	Reads row 1. Sum = $500.00 so far.	
T2	Reads row 2. Sum = $740.25 so far.	
T3		Updates row 1 and puts an exclusive lock on row 1, preventing other updates and reads. Row 1 now has $100.00.
T4	Reads row N. Sum = . . .	
T5		Updates row 342,023 and puts an exclusive lock on this row. Row 342,023 now has $500.00.
T6	Tries to read row 342,023 and discovers that it is locked. This session will block and wait for this block to become available. *All processing on this query stops.*	
T7		Commits transaction.
T8	Reads row 342,023, sees $500.00, and presents a final answer that includes the $400.00 double-counted.	

The first thing to notice is that this other database, upon getting to account 987, will block our query. This session must wait on that row until the transaction holding the exclusive lock commits. This is one reason why many people have a bad habit of committing every statement, instead of processing well-formed transactions consisting of all of the statements needed to take the database from one consistent state to the next. *Updates interfere with reads in most other databases*. The really bad news in this scenario is that we are making the end user wait for the *wrong* answer. We still receive an answer that never existed in the database at any point in time, as with the dirty read, but this time we made the user wait for the wrong answer. In the next section, we'll look at what these other databases need to do to achieve read-consistent, correct results.

The important lesson here is that various databases executing in the same, apparently safe isolation level can and will return very different answers under the exact same circumstances. It is important to understand that, in Oracle, non-blocking reads are not had at the expense of correct answers. You can have your cake and eat it too, sometimes.

REPEATABLE READ

The goal of REPEATABLE READ is to provide an isolation level that gives consistent, correct answers and prevents lost updates. We'll take a look at examples of both, see what we have to do in Oracle to achieve these goals, and examine what happens in other systems.

Getting a Consistent Answer

If we have a REPEATABLE READ isolation, the results from a given query must be consistent with respect to some point in time. Most databases (not Oracle) achieve repeatable reads via the use of row-level shared read locks. A shared read lock prevents other sessions from modifying data that we have read. This, of course, decreases concurrency. Oracle opted for the more concurrent, multi-versioning model to provide read-consistent answers.

In Oracle, using multi-versioning, we get an answer that is consistent with respect to the point in time the query began execution. In other databases, using shared read locks, we get an answer that is consistent with respect to the point in time the query completes—that is, when we can get the answer at all (more on this in a moment).

In a system that employs a shared read lock to provide repeatable reads, we would observe rows in a table getting locked as the query processed them. So, using the earlier example, as our query reads the ACCOUNTS table, it would leave shared read locks on each row, as shown in Table 7-5.

Table 7-5. *Timeline 1 in Non-Oracle Database Using* READ REPEATABLE *Isolation*

Time	Query	Account Transfer Transaction
T1	Reads row 1. Sum = $500.00 so far. Block 1 has a shared read lock on it.	
T2	Reads row 2. Sum = $740.25 so far. Block 2 has a shared read lock on it.	
T3		Attempts to update row 1 but is blocked. Transaction is suspended until it can obtain an exclusive lock.
T4	Reads row N. Sum = . . .	

Continued

Table 7-5. *Continued*

Time	Query	Account Transfer Transaction
T5	Reads row 342,023, sees $100.00, and presents final answer.	
T6	Commits transaction.	
T7		Updates row 1 and puts an exclusive lock on this block. Row 1 now has $100.00.
T8		Updates row 342,023 and puts an exclusive lock on this block. Row 342,023 now has $500.00. Commits transaction.

Table 7-5 shows that we now get the correct answer, but at the cost of physically blocking one transaction and executing the two transactions sequentially. This is one of the side effects of shared read locks for consistent answers: *readers of data will block writers of data.* This is in addition to the fact that, in these systems, writers of data will block readers of data. Imagine if automatic teller machines (ATMs) worked this way in real life.

So, you can see how shared read locks would inhibit concurrency, but they can also cause spurious errors to occur. In Table 7-6, we start with our original table, but this time with the goal of transferring $50.00 from account 987 to account 123.

Table 7-6. *Timeline 2 in Non-Oracle Database Using* READ REPEATABLE *Isolation*

Time	Query	Account Transfer Transaction
T1	Reads row 1. Sum = $500.00 so far. Block 1 has a shared read lock on it.	
T2	Reads row 2. Sum = $740.25 so far. Block 2 has a shared read lock on it.	
T3		Updates row 342,023 and puts an exclusive lock on block 342,023, preventing other updates and shared read locks. This row now has $50.00.
T4	Reads row N. Sum = . . .	
T5		Attempts to update row 1 but is blocked. Transaction is suspended until it can obtain an exclusive lock.
T6	Attempts to read row 342,023 but cannot as an exclusive lock is already in place.	

We have just reached the classic deadlock condition. Our query holds resources the update needs and vice versa. Our query has just deadlocked with our update transaction. One of them will be chosen as the victim and will be killed. We just spent a lot of time and resources only to fail and get rolled back at the end. This is the second side effect of shared read locks: *readers and writers of data can and frequently will deadlock each other.*

As we have seen in Oracle, we have statement-level read consistency without reads blocking writes or deadlocks. Oracle never uses shared read locks—*ever.* Oracle has chosen the harder-to-implement but infinitely more concurrent multi-versioning scheme.

Lost Updates: Another Portability Issue

A common use of REPEATABLE READ in databases that employ the shared read locks could be for lost update prevention.

■**Note** Lost update detection and solutions to the lost update problem are discussed in Chapter 6.

If we have REPEATABLE READ enabled in a database *that employs shared read locks* (and not multi-versioning), lost update errors cannot happen. The reason lost updates cannot happen in those databases is because the simple act of selecting the data *left a lock on it, once read by our transaction, that data cannot be modified by any other transaction.* Now, if your application assumes that REPEATABLE READ implies "lost updates cannot happen," you are in for a painful surprise when you move your application to a database that does not use shared read locks as an underlying concurrency-control mechanism.

While this sounds good, you must remember that leaving the shared read locks behind on all data as it is read will, of course, severely limit concurrent reads and modifications. So, while this isolation level in those databases provides for lost update prevention, it does so by removing the ability to perform concurrent operations! You cannot always have your cake and eat it too.

SERIALIZABLE

This is generally considered the most restrictive level of transaction isolation, but it provides the highest degree of isolation. A SERIALIZABLE transaction operates in an environment that makes it appear as if there are no other users modifying data in the database. Any row we read is assured to be the same upon a reread, and any query we execute is guaranteed to return the same results for the life of a transaction. For example, if we execute

```
Select * from T;
Begin dbms_lock.sleep( 60*60*24 ); end;
Select * from T;
```

the answers returned from T would be the same, even though we just slept for 24 hours (or we might get an ORA-1555: snapshot too old error, which is discussed in Chapter 8). The isolation level assures us these two queries will always return the same results. Side effects (changes) made by other transactions are not visible to the query regardless of how long it has been running.

In Oracle, a SERIALIZABLE transaction is implemented so that the read consistency we normally get at the statement level is extended to the transaction.

■**Note** As noted earlier, there is also an isolation level in Oracle denoted READ ONLY. It has all of the qualities of the SERIALIZABLE isolation level, but it prohibits modifications. It should be noted that the SYS user (or users connected as SYSDBA) cannot have a READ ONLY or SERIALIZABLE transaction. SYS is special in this regard.

Instead of results being consistent with respect to the start of a statement, they are preordained at the time you begin the transaction. In other words, Oracle uses the rollback segments to reconstruct the data as it existed when our transaction began, instead of just when our statement began.

That's a pretty deep thought there—the database already knows the answer to any question you might ask it, before you ask it.

This degree of isolation comes with a price, and that price is the following possible error:

```
ERROR at line 1:
ORA-08177: can't serialize access for this transaction
```

You will get this message whenever you attempt to update a row that has changed since your transaction began.

■**Note** Oracle attempts to do this purely at the row level, but you may receive an ORA-01877 error even when the row you are interested in modifying has not been modified. The ORA-01877 error may happen due to some other row(s) being modified on the block that contains your row.

Oracle takes an optimistic approach to serialization—it gambles on the fact that the data your transaction wants to update won't be updated by any other transaction. This is typically the way it happens, and usually the gamble pays off, especially in quick-transaction, OLTP-type systems. If no one else updates your data during your transaction, this isolation level, which will generally decrease concurrency in other systems, will provide the same degree of concurrency as it would without SERIALIZABLE transactions. The downside to this is that you may get the ORA-08177 error if the gamble doesn't pay off. If you think about it, however, it's worth the risk. If you're using a SERIALIZABLE transaction, you shouldn't expect to update the same information as other transactions. If you do, you should use the SELECT ... FOR UPDATE as described previously in Chapter 1, and this will serialize the access. So, using an isolation level of SERIALIZABLE will be achievable and effective if you

- Have a high probability of no one else modifying the same data

- Need transaction-level read consistency

- Will be doing short transactions (to help make the first bullet point a reality)

Oracle finds this method scalable enough to run all of their TPC-Cs (an industry standard OLTP benchmark; see www.tpc.org for details). In many other implementations, you will find this being achieved with shared read locks and their corresponding deadlocks, and blocking. Here in Oracle, we do not get any blocking, but we will get the ORA-08177 error if other sessions change the data we want to change as well. However, we will not get the error as frequently as we will get deadlocks and blocks in the other systems.

But—there is always a "but"—you must take care to understand these different isolation levels and their implications. Remember, with isolation set to SERIALIZABLE, you will not see any changes made in the database after the start of your transaction, until you commit. Applications that attempt to enforce their own data integrity constraints, such as the resource scheduler described in Chapter 1, must take extra care in this regard. If you recall, the problem in Chapter 1 was that we could not enforce our integrity constraint in a multiuser system since we could not see changes made by other uncommitted sessions. Using SERIALIZABLE, we would still not see the uncommitted changes, but we would also not see the committed changes made after our transaction began!

As a final point, be aware that SERIALIZABLE *does not* mean that all transactions executed by users will behave as if they were executed one right after another in a serial fashion. It does not imply that there is some serial ordering of the transactions that will result in the same outcome. The phenomena previously described by the SQL standard do not make this happen. This last point is a frequently misunderstood concept, and a small demonstration will clear it up. The following table represents two sessions performing work over time. The database tables A and B start out empty and are created as follows:

```
ops$tkyte@ORA10G> create table a ( x int );
Table created.

ops$tkyte@ORA10G> create table b ( x int );
Table created.
```

Now we have the series of events shown in Table 7-7.

Table 7-7. SERIALIZABLE *Transaction Example*

Time	Session 1 Executes	Session 2 Executes
T1	Alter session set isolation_level= serializable;	
T2		Alter session set isolation_level= serializable;
T3	Insert into a select count(*) from b;	
T4		Insert into b select count(*) from a;
T5	Commit;	
T6		Commit;

Now, when all is said and done, tables A and B will each have a row with the value 0 in it. If there was some "serial" ordering of the transactions, we could not possibly have both tables containing the value 0 in them. If session 1 executed before session 2, then table B would have a row with the value 1 in it. If session 2 executed before session 1, then table A would have a row with the value 1 in it. As executed here, however, both tables will have rows with a value of 0. They just executed as if they were the only transaction in the database at that point in time. No matter how many times session 1 queries table B, the count will be the count that was committed in the database at time T1. Likewise, no matter how many times session 2 queries table A, the count will be the same as it was at time T2.

READ ONLY

READ ONLY transactions are very similar to SERIALIZABLE transactions, the only difference being that they do not allow modifications, so they are not susceptible to the ORA-08177 error. READ ONLY transactions are intended to support reporting needs, where the contents of the report need to be consistent with respect to a single point in time. In other systems, you would use REPEATABLE READ and suffer the associated affects of the shared read lock. In Oracle, you will use the READ ONLY transaction. In this mode, the output you produce in a report that uses 50 SELECT statements to gather the data will be consistent with respect to a single point in time—the time the transaction began. You will be able to do this without locking a single piece of data anywhere.

This aim is achieved by using the same multi-versioning as used for individual statements. The data is reconstructed as needed from the rollback segments and presented to you as it existed when the report began. READ ONLY transactions are not trouble-free, however. Whereas you might see an ORA-08177 error in a SERIALIZABLE transaction, you expect to see an ORA-1555: snapshot too old error with READ ONLY transactions. This will happen on a system where other people are actively modifying the information you are reading. The changes (undo) made to this information are recorded in the rollback segments. But rollback segments are used in a circular fashion in much the same manner as redo logs. The longer the report takes to run, the better the chance that some undo you need to reconstruct your data won't be there anymore. The rollback segment will have wrapped around, and the portion of it you need we be reused by some other transaction. At this point, you will receive the ORA-1555 error and have to start over again.

The only solution to this sticky issue is to have rollback segments that are sized correctly for your system. Time and time again, I see people trying to save a few megabytes of disk space by having the smallest possible rollback segments ("Why 'waste' space on something I don't really need?" is the thought). The problem is that the rollback segments are a key component of the way the database works, and unless they are sized correctly, you will hit this error. In 16 years of using Oracle 6, 7, and 8, I can say I have never hit an ORA-1555 error outside of a testing or development system. In such a case, you know you have not sized the rollback segments correctly and you fix it. We will revisit this issue in Chapter 9.

Implications of Multi-Version Read Consistency

So far, we've seen how multi-versioning provides us with non-blocking reads, and I have stressed that this is a good thing: consistent (correct) answers with a high degree of concurrency. What could be wrong with that? Well, unless you understand that it exists and what it implies, then you are probably doing some of your transactions incorrectly. Recall from Chapter 1 the scheduling resources example whereby we had to employ some manual locking techniques (via SELECT FOR UPDATE to serialize modifications to the SCHEDULES table by resource). But can it affect us in other ways? The answer to that is definitely yes. We'll go into the specifics in the sections that follow.

A Common Data Warehousing Technique That Fails

A common data warehousing technique I've seen people employ goes like this:

1. They use a trigger to maintain a LAST_UPDATED column in the source table, much like the method described in the last chapter, in the "Optimistic Locking" section.

2. To initially populate a data warehouse table, they remember what time it is *right now* by selecting out SYSDATE on the source system. For example, suppose it is exactly 9:00 am right now.

3. They then pull all of the rows from the transactional system—a full SELECT * FROM ➡ TABLE—to get the data warehouse initially populated.

4. To refresh the data warehouse, they remember what time it is *right now* again. For example, suppose an hour has gone by and it is now 10:00 am on the source system. They will remember that fact. They then pull all changed records since 9:00 am—the moment before they started the first pull—and merge them in.

■**Note** This technique may "pull" the same record twice in two consecutive refreshes. This is unavoidable due to the granularity of the clock. A MERGE operation will not be affected by this (i.e., update existing record in the data warehouse or insert a new record).

They believe that they now have all of the records in the data warehouse that were modified since they did the initial pull. They may actually have all of the records, but just as likely they may not. This technique does work on some other databases—ones that employ a locking system whereby reads are blocked by writes and vice versa. But in a system where you have non-blocking reads, the logic is flawed.

To see the flaw in this example, all we need to do is assume that at 9:00 am there was at least one open, uncommitted transaction. At 8:59:30 am, it had updated a row in the table we were to copy. At 9:00 am, when we started pulling the data, reading the data in this table, we would not see the modifications to that row; we would see the last committed version of it. If it was locked when we got to it in our query, we would read around the lock. If it was committed by the time we got to it, we would still read around it since read consistency permits us to read only data that was committed in the database when our statement began. We would *not* read that new version of the row during the 9:00 am initial pull, but nor would we read the modified row during the 10:00 am refresh. The reason? The 10:00 am refresh would only pull records modified since 9:00 am that morning—but this record was modified at 8:59:30 am. We would never pull this changed record.

In many other databases where reads are blocked by writes and a committed but inconsistent read is implemented, this refresh process would work perfectly. If at 9:00 am—when we did the initial pull of data—we hit that row and it was locked, we would have blocked and waited for it, and read the committed version. If it were not locked, we would just read whatever was there, committed.

So, does this mean the preceding logic just cannot be used? No, it means that we need to get the "right now" time a little differently. We need to query V$TRANSACTION and find out which is the earliest of the current time and the time recorded in the START_TIME column of this view. We will need to pull all records changed since the start time of the oldest transaction (or the current SYSDATE value if there are no active transactions):

```
select nvl( min(to_date(start_time,'mm/dd/rr hh24:mi:ss')),sysdate)
  from v$transaction;
```

In this example, that would be 8:59:30 am—when the transaction that modified the row started. When we go to refresh the data at 10:00 am, we pull all of the changes that had occurred since that time, and when we merge these into the data warehouse, we'll have everything we need.

An Explanation for Higher Than Expected I/O on Hot Tables

Another situation where it is vital that you understand read consistency and multi-versioning is when you are faced with a query that in production, under a heavy load, uses many more I/Os than you observe in your test or development systems, and you have no way to account for it. You review the I/O performed by the query and note that it is much higher than you have ever seen—much higher than seems possible. You restore the production instance on test and discover that the I/O is way down. But in production it is still very high (but seems to vary: sometimes it is high, sometimes it is low, and sometimes it is in the middle). The reason, as we'll see, is that in your test system, in isolation, you do not have to undo other transactions' changes. In production, however, when you read a given block, you might have to undo (roll back) the changes of many transactions, and each rollback could involve I/O to retrieve the undo and apply it.

This is probably a query against a table that has many concurrent modifications taking place—you are seeing the reads to the undo segment taking place, the work that Oracle is performing to restore the block back the way it was when your query began. You can see the effects of this easily in a single session, just to understand what is happening. We'll start with a very small table:

```
ops$tkyte@ORA10GR1> create table t ( x int );
Table created.

ops$tkyte@ORA10GR1> insert into t values ( 1 );
1 row created.

ops$tkyte@ORA10GR1> exec dbms_stats.gather_table_stats( user, 'T' );
PL/SQL procedure successfully completed.
ops$tkyte@ORA10GR1> select * from t;

         X
----------
         1
```

Now we'll set our session to use the SERIALIZABLE isolation level, so that no matter how many times we run a query in our session, the results will be "as of" that transaction's start time:

```
ops$tkyte@ORA10GR1> alter session set isolation_level=serializable;
Session altered.
```

Now, we'll query that small table and observe the amount of I/O performed:

```
ops$tkyte@ORA10GR1> set autotrace on statistics
ops$tkyte@ORA10GR1> select * from t;

         X
----------
         1 .
```

```
Statistics
----------------------------------------------------------
          0  recursive calls
          0  db block gets
          3  consistent gets
...
```

So, that query took three I/Os (consistent gets) in order to complete. In *another session*, we'll modify this table repeatedly:

```
ops$tkyte@ORA10GR1> begin
  2          for i in 1 .. 10000
  3          loop
  4              update t set x = x+1;
  5              commit;
  6          end loop;
  7  end;
  8  /

PL/SQL procedure successfully completed.
```

And returning to our SERIALIZABLE session, we'll rerun the same query:

```
ops$tkyte@ORA10GR1> select * from t;

          X
----------
          1


Statistics
----------------------------------------------------------
          0  recursive calls
          0  db block gets
      10004  consistent gets
...
```

It did 10,004 I/Os that time—a marked difference. So, where did all of the I/Os come from? That was Oracle rolling back the changes made to that database block. When we ran the second query, Oracle knew that all of the blocks retrieved and processed by that query had to be "as of" the start time of the transaction. When we got to the buffer cache, we discovered that the block in the cache was simply "too new"—the other session had modified it some 10,000 times. Our query could not see those changes, so it started walking the undo information and undid the last change. It discovered this rolled back block was still too new and did another rollback of the block. It did this repeatedly until finally it found the version of the block that was committed in the database when our transaction began. That was the block we may use—and did use.

■**Note** It is interesting to note that if you were to rerun the SELECT * FROM T, you would likely see the I/O go back down to 3 again; it would not be 10,004. The reason? Oracle has the ability to store multiple versions of the same block in the buffer cache. When you undid the changes to this block, you left that version in the cache, and subsequent executions of your query are able to access it.

So, do we encounter this problem only when using the SERIALIZABLE isolation level? No, not at all. Consider a query that runs for five minutes. During the five minutes the query is running, it is retrieving blocks from the buffer cache. Every time it retrieves a block from the buffer cache, it will perform this check: "Is the block too new? If so, roll it back." And remember, the longer the query runs, the higher the chance that a block it needs has been modified over time.

Now, the database is expecting this check to happen (i.e., to see if a block is "too new" and the subsequent rolling back of the changes), and for just such a reason, the buffer cache may actually contain multiple versions of the same block in memory. In that fashion, chances are that a version you require will be there, ready and waiting to go, instead of having to be materialized using the undo information. A query such as

```
select file#, block#, count(*)
from v$bh
group by file#, block#
having count(*) > 3
order by 3
/
```

may be used to view these blocks. In general, you will find no more than about six versions of a block in the cache at any point in time, but these versions can be used by any query that needs them.

It is generally these small "hot" tables that run into the issue of inflated I/Os due to read consistency. Other queries most often affected by this issue are long-running queries against volatile tables. The longer they run, "the longer they run," because over time they may have to perform more work to retrieve a block from the buffer cache.

Write Consistency

So far, we've looked at read consistency: Oracle's ability to use undo information to provide non-blocking query and consistent (correct) reads. We understand that as Oracle reads blocks for queries out of the buffer cache, it will ensure that the version of the block is "old" enough to be seen by that query.

But that begs the following question: What about writes/modifications? What happens when you run the following UPDATE statement:

```
Update t set x = 2 where y = 5;
```

and while that statement is running, someone updates a row it has yet to read from Y=5 to Y=6 and commits? That is, when your UPDATE began, some row had the value Y=5. As your UPDATE reads the table using consistent reads, it sees that the row was Y=5 when the UPDATE began. But, the current value for Y is now 6—it's not 5 anymore—and before updating the value of X, Oracle will check to see that Y is still 5. Now what happens? How are the updates affected by this?

Obviously, we cannot modify an old version of a block—when we go to modify a row, we must modify the current version of that block. Additionally, Oracle cannot just simply skip this row, as that would be an inconsistent read and unpredictable. What we'll discover is that in such cases, Oracle will restart the write modification from scratch.

Consistent Reads and Current Reads

Oracle does do two types of block gets when processing a modification statement. It performs

- *Consistent reads*: When "finding" the rows to modify

- *Current reads*: When getting the block to actually update the row of interest

We can see this easily using TKPROF. Consider this small one-row example, which reads and updates the single row in table T from earlier:

```
ops$tkyte@ORA10GR1> alter session set sql_trace=true;
Session altered.

ops$tkyte@ORA10GR1> select * from t;

         X
----------
     10001

ops$tkyte@ORA10G> update t t1 set x = x+1;
1 row updated.

ops$tkyte@ORA10G> update t t2 set x = x+1;
1 row updated.
```

When we run TKPROF and view the results, we'll see something like this (note that I removed the ELAPSED, CPU, and DISK columns from this report):

```
select * from t

call      count    query    current    rows
-------  ------   ------   ---------   --------
Parse        1        0          0          0
Execute      1        0          0          0
Fetch        2        3          0          1
-------  ------   ------   ---------   --------
total        4        3          0          1

update t t1 set x = x+1
```

```
call        count   query   current     rows
-------  ------  ------  ----------  ----------
Parse       1       0       0           0
Execute     1       3       3           1
Fetch       0       0       0           0
-------  ------  ------  ----------  ----------
total       2       3       3           1

update t t2 set x = x+1

call        count   query   current     rows
-------  ------  ------  ----------  ----------
Parse       1       0       0           0
Execute     1       3       1           1
Fetch       0       0       0           0
-------  ------  ------  ----------  ----------
total       2       3       1           1
```

So, during just a normal query, we incur three *query (consistent) mode gets*. During the first UPDATE, we incur the same three I/Os (the search component of the update involves finding all of the rows that are in the table when the update began, in this case) and three *current mode gets* as well. The current mode gets are performed in order to retrieve the *table block* as it exists right now, the one with the row on it, to get an *undo segment block* to begin our transaction, and an *undo block*. The second update has exactly one current mode get—since we did not have to do the undo work again, we had only the one current get on the block with the row we want to update. The very presence of the current mode gets tells us that a modification of some sort took place. Before Oracle will modify a block with new information, it must get the most current copy of it.

So, how does read consistency affect a modification? Well, imagine you were executing the following UPDATE statement against some database table:

```
Update t set x = x+1 where y = 5;
```

We understand that the WHERE Y=5 component, the read-consistent phase of the query, will be processed using a consistent read (query mode gets in the TKPROF report). The set of WHERE Y=5 records that was committed in the table at the beginning of the statement's execution are the records it will see (assuming READ COMMITTED isolation—if the isolation is SERIALIZABLE, it would be the set of WHERE Y=5 records that existed when the transaction began). This means if that UPDATE statement were to take five minutes to process from start to finish, and someone added and committed a new record to the table with a value of 5 in the Y column, then that UPDATE would not "see" it because the consistent read would not see it. This is expected, and normal. But, the question is, what happens if two sessions execute the following statements in order?

```
Update t set y = 10 where y = 5;
Update t Set x = x+1 Where y = 5;
```

Table 7-8 demonstrates the timeline.

Table 7-8. *Sequence of Updates*

Time	Session 1	Session 2	Comment
T1	Update t set y = 10 where y = 5;		This updates the one row that matches the criteria.
T2		Update t Set x = x+1 Where y = 5;	Using consistent reads, this will find the record session 1 modified, but it won't be able to update it since session 1 has it blocked. Session 2 will block and wait for this row.
T3	Commit;		This releases session 1; session 1 becomes unblocked. It can finally do the current read on the block containing this row, where Y was equal to 5 when session 1 began its update.

So the record that was Y=5 when you began the UPDATE is no longer Y=5. The consistent read component of the UPDATE says, "You want to update this record because Y was 5 when we began," but the current version of the block makes you think, "Oh, no, I cannot update this row because Y isn't 5 anymore—it would be wrong."

If we just skipped this record at this point and ignored it, then we would have a nondeterministic update. It would be throwing data consistency and integrity out the window. The outcome of the update (how many and which rows were modified) would depend on the order in which rows got hit in the table and what other activity just happened to be going on. You could take the same exact set of rows and in two different databases, each one running the transactions in exactly the same mix, you could observe different results, just because the rows were in different places on the disk.

In this case, Oracle chose to restart the update. When the row that was Y=5 when you started is found to contain the value Y=10, Oracle will silently roll back your update and restart it—assuming you are using READ COMMITTED isolation. If you are using SERIALIZABLE isolation, then at this point you would receive an ORA-08177: can't serialize access error for this transaction. In READ COMMITTED mode, after the transaction rolls back your update, the database will restart the update (i.e., change the point in time at which the update is "as of"), and instead of updating the data again, it will go into SELECT FOR UPDATE mode and attempt to lock all of the rows WHERE Y=5 for your session. Once it does this, it will run the UPDATE against that locked set of data, thus ensuring this time that it can complete without restarting.

But to continue on with the "but what happens . . ." train of thought, what happens if after restarting the update and going into SELECT FOR UPDATE mode (which has the same read-consistent and read current block gets going on as an update does), a row that was Y=5 when you started the SELECT FOR UPDATE is found to be Y=11 when you go to get the current version of it? That SELECT FOR UDPDATE will restart and the cycle begins again.

There are two questions to be addressed here—two questions that interested me, anyway. The first is, Can we observe this? Can we see this actually happen? And the second is, So what? What does this actually mean to us as developers? We'll address these questions in turn now.

Seeing a Restart

It is easier to see a restart than you might at first think. We'll be able to observe one, in fact, using a simple one-row table. This is the table we'll use to test with:

```
ops$tkyte@ORA10G> create table t ( x int, y int );
Table created.

ops$tkyte@ORA10G> insert into t values ( 1, 1 );
1 row created.

ops$tkyte@ORA10G> commit;
Commit complete.
```

To observe the restart, all we need is a trigger to print out some information. We'll use a BEFORE UPDATE FOR EACH ROW trigger to simply print out the before and after image of the row as the result of an update:

```
ops$tkyte@ORA10G> create or replace trigger t_bufer
  2    before update on t for each row
  3    begin
  4            dbms_output.put_line
  5            ( 'old.x = ' || :old.x ||
  6              ', old.y = ' || :old.y );
  7            dbms_output.put_line
  8            ( 'new.x = ' || :new.x ||
  9              ', new.y = ' || :new.y );
 10    end;
 11  /
Trigger created.
```

Now we'll update that row:

```
ops$tkyte@ORA10G> set serveroutput on
ops$tkyte@ORA10G> update t set x = x+1;
old.x = 1, old.y = 1
new.x = 2, new.y = 1
1 row updated.
```

So far, everything is as we expect: the trigger fired once, and we see the old and new values. Note that we have not yet committed, however—the row is still locked. In another session, we'll execute this update:

```
ops$tkyte@ORA10G> set serveroutput on
ops$tkyte@ORA10G> update t set x = x+1 where x > 0;
```

That will immediately block, of course, since the first session has that row locked. If we now go back to the first session and commit, we'll see this output (the update is repeated for clarity) in the second session:

```
ops$tkyte@ORA10G> update t set x = x+1 where x > 0;
old.x = 1, old.y = 1
new.x = 2, new.y = 1
old.x = 2, old.y = 1
new.x = 3, new.y = 1
1 row updated.
```

As you can see, that row trigger saw two versions of that row here. The row trigger was fired two times: once with the original version of the row and what we tried to modify that original version to, and again with the final row that was actually updated. Since this was a BEFORE FOR EACH ROW trigger, Oracle saw the read-consistent version of the record and the modifications we would like to have made to it. However, Oracle retrieved the block in current mode to actually perform the update *after* the BEFORE FOR EACH ROW trigger fired. It waits until after this trigger fires to get the block in current mode, because the trigger can modify the :NEW values. So Oracle cannot modify the block until *after* this trigger executes, and the trigger could take a very long time to execute. Since only one session at a time can hold a block in current mode, Oracle needs to limit the time we have it in that mode.

After this trigger fired, Oracle retrieved the block in current mode and noticed that the column used to find this row, X, had been modified. Since X was used to locate this record and X was modified, the database decided to restart our query. Notice that the update of X from 1 to 2 did not put this row out of scope; we'll still be updating it with this UPDATE statement. Rather, it is the fact that X was used to locate the row, and the consistent read value of X (1 in this case) differs from the current mode read of X (2). Now, upon restart, the trigger sees the value of X=2 (following modification by the other session) as the :OLD value and X=3 as the :NEW value.

So, that shows that these restarts happen. It takes a trigger to see them in action; otherwise, they are generally "undetectable." That does not mean you cannot see other symptoms—such as a large UPDATE statement rolling back work after updating many rows and then discovering a row that causes it to restart—just that it is hard to definitively say, "This symptom is caused by a restart."

An interesting observation is that triggers themselves may cause restarts to occur even when the statement itself doesn't warrant them. Normally, the columns referenced in the WHERE clause of the UPDATE or DELETE statement are used to determine whether or not the modification needs to restart. Oracle will perform a consistent read using these columns and, upon retrieving the block in current mode, it will restart the statement if it detects that any of them have changed. Normally, the other columns in the row are not inspected. For example, let's simply rerun the previous example and use WHERE Y>0 to find the rows:

```
ops$tkyte@ORA10G> update t set x = x+1 where y > 0;
old.x = 1, old.y = 1
new.x = 2, new.y = 1
old.x = 2, old.y = 1
new.x = 3, new.y = 1
1 row updated.
```

You might at first wonder, "Why did Oracle fire the trigger twice when it was looking at the Y value? Does it examine the whole row?" As you can see from the output, the update was in fact restarted and the trigger again fired twice, even though we were searching on Y>0 and did not modify Y at all. But, if we re-create the trigger to simply print out the fact that it fired, rather than reference the :OLD and :NEW values

```
ops$tkyte@ORA10G> create or replace trigger t_bufer
  2  before update on t for each row
  3  begin
  4          dbms_output.put_line( 'fired' );
```

```
 5  end;
 6  /
Trigger created.

ops$tkyte@ORA10G> update t set x = x+1;
fired
1 row updated.
```

and go into that second session again and run the update, we observe it gets blocked (of course). After committing the blocking session, we'll see the following:

```
ops$tkyte@ORA10G> update t set x = x+1 where y > 0;
fired
1 row updated.
```

The trigger fired just once this time, not twice. This shows that the :NEW and :OLD column values, when referenced in the trigger, are also used by Oracle to do the restart checking. When we referenced :NEW.X and :OLD.X in the trigger, X's consistent read and current read values were compared and found to be different. A restart ensued. When we removed the reference to that column from the trigger, there was no restart.

So the rule is that the set of columns used in the WHERE clause to find the rows plus the columns referenced in the row triggers will be compared. The consistent read version of the row will be compared to the current read version of the row, and if any of them are different the modification will restart.

■**Note** You can use this bit of information to further understand why using an AFTER FOR EACH ROW trigger is more efficient than using a BEFORE FOR EACH ROW. The AFTER trigger won't have the same effect.

Which leads us to the "Why do we care?" question.

Why Is a Restart Important to Us?

The first thing that pops out should be "Our trigger fired twice!" We had a one-row table with a BEFORE FOR EACH ROW trigger on it. We updated one row, yet the trigger fired two times.

Think of the potential implications of this. If you have a trigger that does anything non-transactional, this could be a fairly serious issue. For example, consider a trigger that sends an update where the body of the e-mail is "This is what the data used to look like. It has been modified to look like this now." If you sent the e-mail directly from the trigger, using UTL_SMTP in Oracle9*i* or UTL_MAIL in Oracle 10*g* and above, then the user would receive two e-mails, with one of them reporting an update that never actually happened.

Anything you do in a trigger that is nontransactional will be impacted by a restart. Consider the following implications:

- Consider a trigger that maintains some PL/SQL global variables, such as the number of rows processed. When a statement that restarts rolls back, the modifications to PL/SQL variables won't "roll back."

- Virtually any function that starts with UTL_ (UTL_FILE, UTL_HTTP, UTL_SMTP, and so on) should be considered susceptible to a statement restart. When the statement restarts, UTL_FILE won't "un-write" to the file it was writing to.

- Any trigger that is part of an autonomous transaction must be suspect. When the statement restarts and rolls back, the autonomous transaction cannot be rolled back.

All of these consequences must be handled with care in the belief that they may be fired more than once per row or be fired for a row that won't be updated by the statement after all.

The second reason you should care about potential restarts is performance related. We have been using a single-row example, but what happens if you start a large batch update and it is restarted after processing the first 100,000 records? It will roll back the 100,000 row changes, restart in SELECT FOR UPDATE mode, and do the 100,000 row changes again after that.

You might notice, after putting in that simple audit trail trigger (the one that reads the :NEW and :OLD values), that performance is much worse than you can explain, even though nothing else has changed except the new triggers. It could be that you are restarting queries you never used to in the past. Or the addition of a tiny program that updates just a single row here and there makes a batch process that used to run in an hour suddenly run in many hours due to restarts that never used to take place.

This is not a new feature of Oracle—it has been in the database since version 4.0, when read consistency was introduced. I myself was not totally aware of how it worked until the summer of 2003 and, after I discovered what it implied, I was able to answer a lot of "How could that have happened?" questions from my own past. It has made me swear off using autonomous transactions in triggers almost entirely, and it has made me rethink the way some of my applications have been implemented. For example, I'll never send e-mail from a trigger directly; rather, I'll always use DBMS_JOB or the new Oracle 10g scheduler facility to send the e-mail after my transaction commits. This makes the sending of the e-mail "transactional"—that is, if the statement that caused the trigger to fire and send the e-mail is restarted, the rollback it performs will roll back the DBMS_JOB request. Most everything nontransactional that I did in triggers was modified to be done in a job after the fact, making it all transactionally consistent.

Summary

In this chapter, we covered a lot of material that, at times, likely made you scratch your head. However, it is vital that you understand these issues. For example, if you were not aware of the statement-level restart, you might not be able to figure out how a certain set of circumstances could have taken place. That is, you would not be able to explain some of the daily empirical observations you make. In fact, if you were not aware of the restarts, you might wrongly suspect the actual fault to be due to the circumstances or an end user error. It would be one of those unreproducible issues, as it takes many things happening in a specific order to observe.

We took a look at the meaning of the isolation levels set out in the SQL standard and at how Oracle implements them, and at times we contrasted Oracle's implementation with that of other databases. We saw that in other implementations (i.e., ones that employ read locks to provide consistent data), there is a huge trade-off between concurrency and consistency. To get highly concurrent access to data, you would have to decrease your need for consistent answers. To get consistent, correct answers, you would need to live with decreased concurrency. We saw how in Oracle that is not the case, due to its multi-versioning feature.

Table 7-9 sums up what you might expect in a database that employs read locking versus Oracle's multi-versioning.

Table 7-9. *A Comparison of Transaction, Concurrency, and Locking Behavior in Oracle vs. Databases That Employ Read Locking*

Isolation Level	Implementation	Writes Block Reads	Reads Block Writes	Deadlock-Sensitive Reads	Incorrect Query Results	Lost Updates	Lock Escalation or Limits
READ UNCOMMITTED	Not Oracle	No	No	No	Yes	Yes	Yes
READ COMMITTED	Not Oracle	Yes	No	No	Yes	Yes	Yes
READ COMMITTED	Oracle	No	No	No	No	No*	No
REPEATABLE READ	Not Oracle	Yes	Yes	Yes	No	No	Yes
SERIALIZABLE	Not Oracle	Yes	Yes	Yes	No	No	Yes
SERIALIZABLE	Oracle	No	No	No	No	No	No

*With SELECT FOR UPDATE NOWAIT.

Concurrency controls and how the database implements them are definitely things you want to have a good grasp of. I've been singing the praises of multi-versioning and read consistency, but like everything else in the world, they are double-edged swords. If you don't understand that multi-versioning is there and how it works, you will make errors in application design. Consider the resource scheduler example from Chapter 1. In a database without multi-versioning and its associated non-blocking reads, the original logic employed by the program may very well have worked. However, this logic would fall apart when implemented in Oracle—it would allow data integrity to be compromised. Unless you know how it works, you will write programs that corrupt data. It is that simple.

CHAPTER 8

■ ■ ■

Transactions

Transactions are one of the features that set a database apart from a file system. In a file system, if you are in the middle of writing a file and the operating system crashes, this file is likely to be corrupted. It is true there are "journaled" file systems and the like, which may be able to recover your file to some point in time. However, if you need to keep two files synchronized, such as system won't help you there—if you update one file, and the system fails before you finish updating the second, then you will have out-of-sync files.

This is the main purpose of transactions in the database; they take the database from one consistent state to the next. That is their job. When you commit work in the database, you are assured that either all of your changes are saved or none of them is saved. Furthermore, you are assured that the various rules and checks that protect data integrity are implemented.

In the previous chapter, we discussed transactions in terms of concurrency control and how, as a result of Oracle's multi-versioning read-consistent model, Oracle transactions can provide consistent data every time, under highly concurrent data access conditions. Transactions in Oracle exhibit all of the required ACID characteristics. *ACID* is an acronym for

- *Atomicity*: Either all of a transaction happens or none of it happens.

- *Consistency*: A transaction takes the database from one consistent state to the next.

- *Isolation*: The effects of a transaction may not be visible to other transactions until the transaction has committed.

- *Durability*: Once the transaction is committed, it is permanent.

We discussed how Oracle obtains *Consistency* and *Isolation* in the previous chapter. Here we'll focus most of our attention on concept of *Atomicity* and how that is applied in Oracle.

In this chapter, we'll discuss the implications of atomicity and how it affects statements in Oracle. We'll cover transaction control statements such as COMMIT, SAVEPOINT, and ROLLBACK, and we'll discuss how integrity constraints are enforced in a transaction. We'll also look at why you may have some bad transaction habits if you've been developing in other databases. We'll look at distributed transactions and the two-phase commit (2PC). Lastly, we'll examine autonomous transactions, what they are, and the role they play.

Transaction Control Statements

There is no "begin transaction" statement needed in Oracle. A transaction implicitly begins with the first statement that modifies data (the first statement that gets a TX lock). You may explicitly begin a transaction using SET TRANSACTION or the DBMS_TRANSACTION package, but it is not a necessary step, unlike in various other databases. Issuing either a COMMIT or ROLLBACK statement explicitly ends a transaction.

Note A ROLLBACK TO SAVEPOINT command will not end a transaction! Only a full, proper ROLLBACK will.

You should always explicitly terminate your transactions with a COMMIT or ROLLBACK; otherwise, the tool/environment you are using will pick one or the other for you. If you exit your SQL*Plus session normally, without committing or rolling back, SQL*Plus will assume you wish you commit your work and will do so for you. If you just exit from a Pro*C program, on the other hand, an implicit rollback will take place. Never rely on implicit behavior, as it could change in the future. Always explicitly COMMIT or ROLLBACK your transactions.

Transactions are *atomic* in Oracle, meaning that either every statement that comprises the transaction is committed (made permanent) or all of the statements are rolled back. This protection is extended to individual statements as well. Either a statement entirely succeeds or the statement is entirely rolled back. Note that I said the "statement" is rolled back. The failure of one statement does not cause previously executed statements to be automatically rolled back. Their work is preserved and must be either committed or rolled back by you. Before we get into the details of exactly what it means for a statement and transaction to be atomic, let's take a look at the various transaction control statements available to us:

- COMMIT: To use this statement's simplest form, you would just issue COMMIT. You could be more verbose and say COMMIT WORK, but the two are equivalent. A COMMIT ends your transaction and makes any changes permanent (durable). There are extensions to the COMMIT statement used in distributed transactions. These extensions allow you to label a COMMIT (label a transaction) with some meaningful comment and force the commit of an in-doubt distributed transaction.

- ROLLBACK: To use this statement's simplest form, you would just issue ROLLBACK. Again, you could be more verbose and say ROLLBACK WORK, but the two are equivalent. A rollback ends your transaction and undoes any uncommitted changes you have outstanding. It does this by reading information stored in the rollback/undo segments (going forward I'll refer to these exclusively as *undo segments*, the favored terminology for Oracle 10*g*) and restoring the database blocks to the state they were in prior to your transaction beginning.

- SAVEPOINT: A SAVEPOINT allows you to create a "marked point" within a transaction. You may have multiple SAVEPOINTs within a single transaction.

- ROLLBACK TO <SAVEPOINT>: This statement is used with the SAVEPOINT command. You may roll back your transaction to that marked point without rolling back any of the work that preceded it. So, you could issue two UPDATE statements, followed by a SAVEPOINT and then two DELETE statements. If an error or some sort of exceptional condition occurs during execution of the DELETE statements, and you catch that exception and issue the ROLLBACK TO SAVEPOINT command, the transaction will roll back to the named SAVEPOINT, undoing any work performed by the DELETEs, but leaving the work performed by the UPDATE statements intact.

- SET TRANSACTION: This statement allows you to set various transaction attributes, such as the transaction's isolation level and whether it is read-only or read-write. You can also use this statement to instruct the transaction to use a specific undo segment when using manual undo management, but this is not recommended. We'll discuss manual and automatic undo management in more detail in Chapter 9.

That's it—there are no more transaction control statements. The most frequently used control statements are COMMIT and ROLLBACK. The SAVEPOINT statement has a somewhat special purpose. Internally, Oracle uses it frequently, and you may find some use for it in your application as well.

Atomicity

After that brief overview of the transaction control statements, we're ready to see what's meant by statement, procedure, and transaction atomicity.

Statement-Level Atomicity

Consider the following statement:

```
Insert into t values ( 1 );
```

It seems fairly clear that if it were to fail due to a constraint violation, the row would not be inserted. However, consider the following example, where an INSERT or DELETE on table T fires a trigger that adjusts the CNT column in table T2 appropriately:

```
ops$tkyte@ORA10G> create table t2 ( cnt int );
Table created.

ops$tkyte@ORA10G> insert into t2 values ( 0 );
1 row created.

ops$tkyte@ORA10G> commit;
Commit complete.

ops$tkyte@ORA10G> create table t ( x int check ( x>0 ) );
Table created.

ops$tkyte@ORA10G> create trigger t_trigger
  2  before insert or delete on t for each row
```

```
 3  begin
 4      if ( inserting ) then
 5          update t2 set cnt = cnt +1;
 6      else
 7          update t2 set cnt = cnt -1;
 8      end if;
 9      dbms_output.put_line( 'I fired and updated ' ||
10                                   sql%rowcount || ' rows' );
11  end;
12  /
Trigger created.
```

In this situation, it is less clear what should happen. If the error occurs *after* the trigger has fired, should the effects of the trigger be there or not? That is, if the trigger fired and updated T2, but the row was not inserted into T, what should the outcome be? Clearly the answer is that we would not like the CNT column in T2 to be incremented if a row is not actually inserted into T. Fortunately in Oracle, the original statement from the client—INSERT INTO T, in this case—either entirely succeeds or entirely fails. This statement is atomic. We can confirm this, as follows:

```
ops$tkyte@ORA10G> set serveroutput on
ops$tkyte@ORA10G> insert into t values (1);
I fired and updated 1 rows

1 row created.

ops$tkyte@ORA10G> insert into t values(-1);
I fired and updated 1 rows
insert into t values(-1)
*
ERROR at line 1:
ORA-02290: check constraint (OPS$TKYTE.SYS_C009597) violated


ops$tkyte@ORA10G> select * from t2;

       CNT
----------
         1
```

■**Note** When using SQL*Plus from Oracle9*i* Release 2 and before, in order to see that the trigger fired, you will need to add a line of code, exec null, after the second insert. This is because SQL*Plus does not retrieve and display the DBMS_OUTPUT information after a failed DML statement in those releases. In Oracle 10*g* it does.

So, one row was successfully inserted into T and we duly received the message, I fired and updated 1 rows. The next INSERT statement violates the integrity constraint we have on T. The DBMS_OUTPUT message appeared—the trigger on T in fact did fire and we have evidence of that. It performed its updates of T2 successfully. We would maybe expect T2 to have a value of 2 now, but we see it has a value of 1. Oracle made the *original* INSERT atomic—the original INSERT INTO T is the statement, and any side effects of that original INSERT INTO T are considered part of that statement.

Oracle achieves this statement-level atomicity by silently wrapping a SAVEPOINT around each of our calls to the database. The preceding two INSERTs were really treated like this:

```
Savepoint statement1;
    Insert into t values ( 1 );
If error then rollback to statement1;
Savepoint statement2;
    Insert into t values ( -1 );
If error then rollback to statement2;
```

For programmers used to Sybase or SQL Server, this may be confusing at first. In those databases *exactly the opposite is true*. The triggers in those systems execute independently of the firing statement. If they encounter an error, the triggers must explicitly roll back their own work and then raise another error to roll back the triggering statement. Otherwise, the work done by a trigger could persist even if the triggering statement, or some other part of the statement, ultimately fails.

In Oracle, this statement-level atomicity extends as deep as it needs to. If in the preceding example, the INSERT INTO T fires a trigger that updates another table, and that table has a trigger that deletes from another table (and so on, and so on), either *all* of the work succeeds or *none* of it does. You do not need to code anything special to ensure this—it is just the way it works.

Procedure-Level Atomicity

It is interesting to note that Oracle considers PL/SQL anonymous blocks to be statements as well. Consider the following stored procedure:

```
ops$tkyte@ORA10G> create or replace procedure p
  2  as
  3  begin
  4          insert into t values ( 1 );
  5          insert into t values (-1 );
  6  end;
  7  /
Procedure created.

ops$tkyte@ORA10G> select * from t;
no rows selected

ops$tkyte@ORA10G> select * from t2;
```

```
       CNT
----------
         0
```

So, we have a procedure we know will fail. The second INSERT will always fail in this case. Let's see what happens if we run that stored procedure:

```
ops$tkyte@ORA10G> begin
  2          p;
  3  end;
  4  /
I fired and updated 1 rows
I fired and updated 1 rows
begin
*
ERROR at line 1:
ORA-02290: check constraint (OPS$TKYTE.SYS_C009598) violated
ORA-06512: at "OPS$TKYTE.P", line 5
ORA-06512: at line 2


ops$tkyte@ORA10G> select * from t;
no rows selected

ops$tkyte@ORA10G> select * from t2;

       CNT
----------
         0
```

As you can see, Oracle treated the stored procedure call as an atomic statement. The client submitted a block of code, BEGIN P; END;, and Oracle wrapped a SAVEPOINT around it. Since P failed, Oracle restored the database back to the point right before it was called. Now, if we submit a slightly different block, we will get entirely different results:

```
ops$tkyte@ORA10G> begin
  2          p;
  3  exception
  4      when others then null;
  5  end;
  6  /
I fired and updated 1 rows
I fired and updated 1 rows

PL/SQL procedure successfully completed.

ops$tkyte@ORA10G> select * from t;
```

```
        X
----------
        1

ops$tkyte@ORA10G> select * from t2;

      CNT
----------
        1
```

Here, we ran a block of code that ignored any and all errors, and the difference in outcome is huge. Whereas the first call to P effected no changes, here the first INSERT succeeds and the CNT column in T2 is incremented accordingly.

■Note I consider virtually all code that contains a WHEN OTHERS exception handler that does not also include a RAISE to re-raise the exception to be a bug. It silently ignores the error and it changes the transaction semantics. Catching WHEN OTHERS and translating the exception into an old-fashioned return code changes the way the database is supposed to behave.

Oracle considered the "statement" to be the block that the client submitted. This statement succeeded by catching and ignoring the error itself, so the If error then rollback... didn't come into effect and Oracle did not roll back to the SAVEPOINT after execution. Hence, the partial work performed by P was preserved. The reason that this partial work was preserved in the first place is that we have statement-level atomicity within P: each statement in P is atomic. P becomes the client of Oracle when it submits its two INSERT statements. Each INSERT either entirely succeeds or fails. This is evidenced by the fact that we can see that the trigger on T fired twice and updated T2 twice, yet the count in T2 reflects only one UPDATE. The second INSERT executed in P had an implicit SAVEPOINT wrapped around it.

The difference between the two blocks of code is subtle and something you must consider in your applications. Adding an exception handler to a block of PL/SQL code can radically change its behavior. A different way to code this—one that restores the statement-level atomicity to the entire PL/SQL block—is as follows:

```
ops$tkyte@ORA10G> begin
  2        savepoint sp;
  3        p;
  4  exception
  5        when others then
  6            rollback to sp;
  7  end;
  8  /
I fired and updated 1 rows
I fired and updated 1 rows
```

```
PL/SQL procedure successfully completed.

ops$tkyte@ORA10G> select * from t;

no rows selected

ops$tkyte@ORA10G> select * from t2;

       CNT
----------
         0
```

■ **Caution** The preceding code represents an exceedingly bad practice. You should neither catch a WHEN OTHERS in general nor explicitly code what Oracle already provides as far as transaction semantics is concerned.

Here, by mimicking the work Oracle normally does for us with the SAVEPOINT, we are able to restore the original behavior while still catching and "ignoring" the error. I provide this example for illustration only—this would be an exceeding bad coding practice.

Transaction-Level Atomicity

Lastly, there is the concept of transaction-level atomicity. The entire goal of a transaction, a set of SQL statements executed together as a unit of work, is to take the database from one consistent state to another consistent state.

To accomplish this goal, transactions are atomic as well—the entire set of successful work performed by a transaction is either entirely committed and made permanent or rolled back and undone. Just like a statement, the transaction is an atomic unit of work. Upon receipt of "success" from the database after committing a transaction, you know that all of the work performed by the transaction has been made persistent.

Integrity Constraints and Transactions

It is interesting to note exactly when integrity constraints are checked. By default, integrity constraints are checked after the entire SQL statement has been processed. There are also deferrable constraints that permit the validation of integrity constraints to be postponed until either the application requests they be validated by issuing a SET CONSTRAINTS ALL IMMEDIATE command or upon issuing COMMIT.

IMMEDIATE Constraints

For the first part of this discussion, we will assume that constraints are in IMMEDIATE mode, which is the norm. In this case, the integrity constraints are checked immediately after the entire SQL statement has been processed. Note I used the term "SQL statement" and not just "statement." If I have many SQL statements in a PL/SQL stored procedure, then each SQL statement will have its integrity constraints validated immediately after their individual execution, not after the stored procedure completes.

So, why are constraints validated *after* the SQL statement executes? Why not *during*? This is because it is very natural for a single statement to make individual rows in a table momentarily "inconsistent." Taking a look at the partial work by a statement would result in Oracle rejecting the results, even if the end result would be OK. For example, suppose we have a table like this:

```
ops$tkyte@ORA10G> create table t  ( x int unique );
Table created.

ops$tkyte@ORA10G> insert into t values ( 1 );
1 row created.

ops$tkyte@ORA10G> insert into t values ( 2 );
1 row created.
```

And now we want to execute a multiple-row UPDATE:

```
ops$tkyte@ORA10G> update t set x = x+1;
2 rows updated.
```

If Oracle checked the constraint after each row was updated, then on any given day we would stand a 50/50 chance of having the UPDATE fail. The rows in T are accessed in *some* order, and if Oracle updated the X=1 row first, then we would momentarily have a duplicate value for X and it would reject the UPDATE. Since Oracle waits patiently to the end of the statement, the statement succeeds because by the time it is done, there are no duplicates.

DEFERRABLE Constraints and Cascading Updates

Starting with Oracle 8.0, we also have the ability to *defer* constraint checking, which can be quite advantageous for various operations. The one that immediately jumps to mind is the requirement to cascade an UPDATE of a primary key to the child keys. Many people will claim that you should never need to do this—that primary keys are immutable (I am one of those people)—but many others persist in their desire to have a cascading UPDATE. Deferrable constraints make this possible.

■**Note** It is considered an extremely bad practice to perform update cascades to modify a primary key. It violates the intent of the primary key. If you have to do it once to correct bad information, that is one thing, but if you find you are constantly doing it as part of your application, you will want to go back and rethink that process—you have chosen the wrong attributes to be the key!

In prior releases, it was actually possible to do a CASCADE UPDATE, but doing so involved a tremendous amount of work and had certain limitations. With deferrable constraints, it becomes almost trivial. The code could look like this:

```
ops$tkyte@ORA10G> create table p
  2  ( pk  int primary key )
  3  /
Table created.

ops$tkyte@ORA10G> create table c
  2  ( fk  constraint c_fk
  3        references p(pk)
  4        deferrable
  5        initially immediate
  6  )
  7  /
Table created.

ops$tkyte@ORA10G> insert into p values ( 1 );
1 row created.

ops$tkyte@ORA10G> insert into c values ( 1 );
1 row created.
```

We have a parent table, P, and a child table, C. Table C references table P, and the constraint used to enforce that rule is called C_FK (child foreign key). This constraint was created as DEFERRABLE, but it is set to INITIALLY IMMEDIATE. This means we can defer that constraint until COMMIT or to some other time. By default, however, it will be validated at the statement level. This is the most common use of the deferrable constraints. Most existing applications won't check for constraint violations on a COMMIT statement, and it is best not to surprise them with that. As defined, table C behaves in the same fashion that tables always have, but it gives us the ability to explicitly change its behavior. Now let's try some DML on the tables and see what happens:

```
ops$tkyte@ORA10G> update p set pk = 2;
update p set pk = 2
       *
ERROR at line 1:
ORA-02292: integrity constraint (OPS$TKYTE.C_FK) violated - child record found
```

Since the constraint is in IMMEDIATE mode, this UPDATE fails. We'll change the mode and try again:

```
ops$tkyte@ORA10G> set constraint c_fk deferred;
Constraint set.

ops$tkyte@ORA10G> update p set pk = 2;
1 row updated.
```

Now it succeeds. For illustration purposes, I'll show how to check a deferred constraint explicitly before committing, to see if the modifications we made are in agreement with the business rules (in other words, to check that the constraint isn't currently being violated). It's a good idea to do this before committing or releasing control to some other part of the program (which may not be expecting the deferred constraints):

```
ops$tkyte@ORA10G> set constraint c_fk immediate;
set constraint c_fk immediate
*
ERROR at line 1:
ORA-02291: integrity constraint (OPS$TKYTE.C_FK) violated - parent key not found
```

It fails and returns an error immediately as expected, since we knew that the constraint had been violated. The UPDATE to P was not rolled back (that would violate the statement-level atomicity); it is still outstanding. Also note that our transaction is still working with the C_FK constraint deferred because the SET CONSTRAINT command failed. Let's continue on now by cascading the UPDATE to C:

```
ops$tkyte@ORA10G> update c set fk = 2;
1 row updated.

ops$tkyte@ORA10G> set constraint c_fk immediate;
Constraint set.

ops$tkyte@ORA10G> commit;
Commit complete.
```

And that is the way it works. Note that to defer a constraint, you must create them that way—you would have to drop and re-create the constraint to change it from nondeferrable to deferrable.

Bad Transaction Habits

Many developers have some bad habits when it comes to transactions. I see this frequently with developers who have worked with a database that "supports" but does not "promote" the use of transactions. For example, in Informix (by default), Sybase, and SQL Server, you must explicitly BEGIN a transaction; otherwise, each individual statement is a transaction all by itself. In a similar manner to the way in which Oracle wraps a SAVEPOINT around discrete statements, these databases wrap a BEGIN WORK/COMMIT or ROLLBACK around each statement. This is because, in these databases, locks are precious resources, and readers block writers and vice versa. In an attempt to increase concurrency, these databases would like you to make the transaction as short as possible—sometimes at the expense of data integrity.

Oracle takes the opposite approach. Transactions are always implicit, and there is no way to have an "autocommit" unless an application implements it (see the "Using Autocommit" section for more details). In Oracle, every transaction should be committed when it must and never before. Transactions should be as large as they need to be. Issues such as locks, blocking, and so on should not really be considered the driving forces behind transaction size—data integrity is *the driving force* behind the size of your transaction. Locks are not a scarce resource, and there are no contention issues between concurrent readers and writers of data.

This allows you to have robust transactions in the database. These transactions do not have to be short in duration—they should be exactly as long as they need to be (but no longer). Transactions are not for the convenience of the computer and its software; they are to protect your data.

Committing in a Loop

Faced with the task of updating many rows, most programmers will try to figure out some procedural way to do it in a loop, so that they can commit every so many rows. I've heard two main reasons for doing it this way:

- It is faster and more efficient to frequently commit lots of small transactions than it is to process and commit one big transaction.

- We don't have enough undo space.

Both of these conclusions are misguided. Furthermore, committing too frequently leaves you prone to the danger of leaving your database in an "unknown" state should your update fail halfway through. It requires complex logic to write a process that is smoothly restartable in the event of failure. By far the best option is to commit only as frequently as your business processes dictate and to size your undo segments accordingly.

Let's take a look at these issues in more detail.

Performance Implications

It is generally not faster to commit frequently—it is almost always faster to do the work in a single SQL statement. By way of a small example, say we have a table, T, with lots of rows, and we want to update a column value for every row in that table. We'll use two tables, T1 and T2, to demonstrate:

```
ops$tkyte@ORA10G> create table t1 as select * from all_objects;
Table created.

ops$tkyte@ORA10G> exec dbms_stats.gather_table_stats( user, 'T1' );
PL/SQL procedure successfully completed.

ops$tkyte@ORA10G> create table t2 as select * from t1;
Table created.

ops$tkyte@ORA10G> exec dbms_stats.gather_table_stats( user, 'T2' );
PL/SQL procedure successfully completed.
```

Well, when we go to update, we could simply do it in a single UPDATE statement, like this:

```
ops$tkyte@ORA10G> set timing on
ops$tkyte@ORA10G> update t1 set object_name = lower(object_name);
48306 rows updated.

Elapsed: 00:00:00.31
```

Many people—for whatever reason—feel compelled to do it like this:

```
ops$tkyte@ORA10G> begin
  2      for x in ( select rowid rid, object_name, rownum r
  3                   from t2 )
  4      loop
  5          update t2
  6             set object_name = lower(x.object_name)
  7           where rowid = x.rid;
  8           if ( mod(x.r,100) = 0 ) then
  9               commit;
 10           end if;
 11      end loop;
 12      commit;
 13  end;
 14  /
PL/SQL procedure successfully completed.
Elapsed: 00:00:05.38
```

In this simple example, it is many times *slower* to commit frequently in a loop. If you can do it in a *single* SQL statement, do it that way, as it is almost certainly faster. Even if we "optimize" the procedural code, using bulk processing for the updates, as follows:

```
ops$tkyte@ORA10G> declare
  2          type ridArray is table of rowid;
  3          type vcArray is table of t2.object_name%type;
  4
  5          l_rids  ridArray;
  6          l_names vcArray;
  7
  8          cursor c is select rowid, object_name from t2;
  9  begin
 10      open c;
 11      loop
 12          fetch c bulk collect into l_rids, l_names LIMIT 100;
 13          forall i in 1 .. l_rids.count
 14              update t2
 15                 set object_name = lower(l_names(i))
 16               where rowid = l_rids(i);
 17          commit;
 18          exit when c%notfound;
 19      end loop;
 20      close c;
 21  end;
 22  /

PL/SQL procedure successfully completed.
Elapsed: 00:00:02.36
```

it is in fact much faster, but still much slower than it could be. Not only that, but you should notice that the code is getting more and more complex. From the sheer simplicity of a single UPDATE statement, to procedural code, to even more complex procedural code—we are going in the wrong direction!

Now, just to supply a counterpoint to this discussion, recall in Chapter 7 when we discussed the concept of write consistency and how an UPDATE statement, for example, could be made to restart. In the event that the preceding UPDATE statement was to be performed against a subset of the rows (it had a WHERE clause), and other users were modifying the columns this UPDATE was using in the WHERE clause, then there would be a case either for using a series of smaller transactions rather than one large transaction or for locking the table prior to performing the mass update. The goal here would be to reduce the opportunity for restarts to occur. If we were to UPDATE the vast majority of the rows in the table, that would lead us toward using the LOCK TABLE command. In my experience, however, these sorts of large mass updates or mass deletes (the only statement types really that would be subject to the restart) are done in isolation. That large, one-time bulk update or the purge of old data generally is not done during a period of high activity. Indeed, the purge of data should not be affected by this at all, since you would typically use some date field to locate the information to purge, and other applications would not modify this data.

Snapshot Too Old Error

Let's now look at the second reason developers are tempted to commit updates in a procedural loop, which arises from their (misguided) attempts to use a "limited resource" (undo segments) sparingly. This is a configuration issue; you *need* to ensure that you have enough undo space to size your transactions correctly. Committing in a loop, apart from generally being slower, is also the most common cause of the dreaded ORA-01555 error. Let's look at this in more detail.

As you will appreciate after reading Chapters 1 and 7, Oracle's multi-versioning model uses undo segment data to reconstruct blocks as they appeared at the beginning of your statement or transaction (depending on the isolation mode). If the necessary undo information no longer exists, you will receive an ORA-01555: snapshot too old error message, and your query will not complete. So, if you are modifying the table that you are reading (as in the previous example), you are generating undo information required for your query. Your UPDATE generates undo information that your query will probably be making use of to get the read-consistent view of the data it needs to update. If you commit, you are allowing the system to reuse the undo segment space you just filled up. If it does reuse the undo, wiping out old undo data that your query subsequently needs, you are in big trouble. Your SELECT will fail and your UPDATE will stop partway through. You have a part-finished logical transaction and probably no good way to restart it (more about this in a moment).

Let's see this concept in action with a small demonstration. In a small test database, I set up a table:

```
ops$tkyte@ORA10G> create table t as select * from all_objects;
Table created.

ops$tkyte@ORA10G> create index t_idx on t(object_name);
Index created.
```

```
ops$tkyte@ORA10G> exec dbms_stats.gather_table_stats( user, 'T', cascade=>true );
PL/SQL procedure successfully completed.
```

I then created a very small undo tablespace and altered the system to use it. Note that by setting AUTOEXTEND off, I have limited the size of all UNDO to be 2MB or less in this system:

```
ops$tkyte@ORA10G> create undo tablespace undo_small
  2   datafile size 2m
  3   autoextend off
  4  /
Tablespace created.

ops$tkyte@ORA10G> alter system set undo_tablespace = undo_small;
System altered.
```

Now, with only the small undo tablespace in use, I ran this block of code to do the UPDATE:

```
ops$tkyte@ORA10G> begin
  2       for x in ( select /*+ INDEX(t t_idx) */ rowid rid, object_name, rownum r
  3                    from t
  4                   where object_name > ' ' )
  5       loop
  6           update t
  7              set object_name = lower(x.object_name)
  8            where rowid = x.rid;
  9           if ( mod(x.r,100) = 0 ) then
 10               commit;
 11           end if;
 12       end loop;
 13       commit;
 14  end;
 15  /
begin
*
ERROR at line 1:
ORA-01555: snapshot too old: rollback segment number  with name "" too small
ORA-06512: at line 2
```

I get the error. I should point out that I added an index hint to the query and a WHERE clause to make sure I was reading the table randomly (together, they caused the cost-based optimizer to read the table "sorted" by the index key). When we process a table via an index, we will tend to read a block for a single row, and then the next row we want will be on a different block. Ultimately, we will process all of the rows on block 1, just not all at the same time. Block 1 might hold, say, the data for all rows with OBJECT_NAMEs starting with the letters A, M, N, Q, and Z. So we would hit the block many times, since we are reading the data sorted by OBJECT_NAME and presumably many OBJECT_NAMEs start with letters between A and M. Since we are committing frequently and reusing undo space, we eventually revisit a block where we can simply no longer roll back to the point in time our query began, and at that point we get the error.

This was a very artificial example just to show how it happens in a reliable manner. My UPDATE statement was generating undo. I had a very small undo tablespace to play with (2MB in size). I wrapped around in my undo segments many times, since they are used in a circular fashion. Every time I committed, I allowed Oracle to overwrite the undo data I generated. Eventually, I needed some piece of data that I had generated, but it no longer existed and I received the ORA-01555 error.

You would be right to point out that in this case, if I had not committed on line 10 in the preceding example, then I would have received the following error:

```
begin
*
ERROR at line 1:
ORA-30036: unable to extend segment by 8 in undo tablespace 'UNDO_SMALL'
ORA-06512: at line 6
```

The major differences between the two errors are as follows:

- The ORA-01555 example *left my update in a totally unknown state*. Some of the work had been done; some had not.

- There is absolutely *nothing I can do to avoid the* ORA-01555, given that I committed in the cursor FOR loop.

- The ORA-30036 *error can be avoided* by allocating appropriate resources in the system. This error is avoidable by correct sizing; the first error is not. Further, even if I don't avoid this error, at least the update is rolled back and the database is left in a known, consistent state—I'm not left halfway through some large update.

The bottom line here is that you cannot "save" on undo space by committing frequently—you need that undo. I was in a single-user system when I received the ORA-01555 error. It takes only one session to cause that error, and many times even in real life it is a single session causing its own ORA-01555 errors. Developers and DBAs need to work together to size these segments adequately for the jobs that need to be done. There can be no short-changing here. You must discover, through analysis of your system, what your biggest transactions are and size appropriately for them. The dynamic performance view V$UNDOSTAT can be very useful to monitor the amount of undo you are generating and the duration of your longest running queries. Many people consider things like temp, undo, and redo as "overhead"—things to allocate as little storage to as possible. This is reminiscent of a problem the computer industry had on January 1, 2000, which was all caused by trying to save 2 bytes in a date field. These components of the database are not overhead, but rather are key components of the system. They must be sized appropriately (not too big and not too small).

Restartable Processes Require Complex Logic

The most serious problem with the "commit before the logical transaction is over" approach is the fact that it frequently leaves your database in an unknown state if the UPDATE fails halfway through. Unless you planned for this ahead of time, it is very hard to restart the failed process, allowing it to pick up where it left off. For example, say we were not applying the LOWER() function to the column, as in the previous example, but rather some other function of the column such as the following:

```
last_ddl_time = last_ddl_time + 1;
```

If we halted the UPDATE loop partway through, how would we restart it? We could not just rerun it, as we would end up adding 2 to some dates, and 1 to others. If we fail again, we would add 3 to some, 2 to others, 1 to the rest, and so on. We need yet more complex logic—some way to "partition" the data. For example, we could process every OBJECT_NAME that starts with A, and then B, and so on:

```
ops$tkyte@ORA10G> create table to_do
  2  as
  3  select distinct substr( object_name, 1,1 ) first_char
  4    from T
  5  /
Table created.

ops$tkyte@ORA10G> begin
  2          for x in ( select * from to_do )
  3          loop
  4              update t set last_ddl_time = last_ddl_time+1
  5               where object_name like x.first_char || '%';
  6
  7              dbms_output.put_line( sql%rowcount || ' rows updated' );
  8              delete from to_do where first_char = x.first_char;
  9
 10              commit;
 11          end loop;
 12  end;
 13  /
22257 rows updated
1167 rows updated
135 rows updated
1139 rows updated
2993 rows updated
691 rows updated
...
2810 rows updated
6 rows updated
10 rows updated
2849 rows updated
1 rows updated
2 rows updated
7 rows updated

PL/SQL procedure successfully completed.
```

Now, we could restart this process if it fails, since we would not process any object name that had already been processed successfully. The problem with this approach, however, is that unless we have some attribute that evenly partitions the data, we will end up having a very wide distribution of rows. The first UPDATE did more work than all of the others combined. Additionally, if other sessions are accessing this table and modifying the data, they might update the object_name field as well. Suppose that some other session updates the object named Z to be A, *after* we already processed the As—we would miss that record. Furthermore, this is a very inefficient process compared to UPDATE T SET LAST_DDL_TIME = LAST_DDL_TIME+1. We are probably using an index to read every row in the table, or we are full scanning it *n*-times, both of which are undesirable. There are so many bad things to be said about this approach.

The best approach is the one I advocated at the beginning of Chapter 1: do it simply. If it can be done in SQL, do it in SQL. What can't be done in SQL, do in PL/SQL. Do it using the least amount of code you can. Have sufficient resources allocated. Always think about what happens in the event of an error. So many times, I've seen people code update loops that worked great on the test data but then failed halfway through when applied to the real data. Now they are really stuck, as they have no idea where it stopped processing. It is a lot easier to size undo correctly than it is to write a restartable program. If you have truly large tables that need to be updated, then you should be using partitions (more on that in Chapter 10), allowing you to update each partition individually. You can even use parallel DML to perform the update.

Using Autocommit

My final word on bad transaction habits concerns the one that arises from use of the popular programming APIs ODBC and JDBC. These APIs "autocommit" by default. Consider the following statements, which transfer $1,000 from a checking account to a savings account:

```
update accounts set balance = balance - 1000 where account_id = 123;
update accounts set balance = balance + 1000 where account_id = 456;
```

If your program is using JDBC when you submit these statements, JDBC will (silently) inject a commit after *each* UPDATE. Consider the impact of this if the system fails after the first UPDATE and before the second. You've just lost $1,000!

I can sort of understand why ODBC does this. The developers of SQL Server designed ODBC, and this database demands that you use very short transactions due to its concurrency model (writes block reads, reads block writes, and locks are a scarce resource). What I cannot understand is how this got carried over into JDBC, an API that is supposed to be in support of "the enterprise." It is my belief that the very next line of code after opening a connection in JDBC should always be

```
connection conn = DriverManager.getConnection
            ("jdbc:oracle:oci:@database","scott","tiger");

conn.setAutoCommit (false);
```

This will return control over the transaction back to you, the developer, which is where it belongs. You can then safely code your account transfer transaction and commit it after both statements have succeeded. Lack of knowledge of your API can be deadly in this case. I've seen more than one developer unaware of this autocommit "feature" get into big trouble with their application when an error occurred.

Distributed Transactions

One of the really nice features of Oracle is its ability to transparently handle distributed transactions. I can update data in many different databases in the scope of a single transaction. When I commit, either I commit the updates in all of the instances or I commit none of them (they will all be rolled back). I need no extra code to achieve this; I simply "commit."

A key to distributed transactions in Oracle is the *database link*. A database link is a database object that describes how to log into another instance from your instance. However, the purpose of this section is not to cover the syntax of the database link command (it is fully documented), but rather to expose you to its very existence. Once you have a database link set up, accessing remote objects is as easy as this:

```
select * from T@another_database;
```

This would select from table T in the database instance defined by the database link `ANOTHER_DATABASE`. Typically, you would "hide" the fact that T is a remote table by creating a view of it, or a synonym. For example, I can issue the following and then access T as if it were a local table:

```
create synonym T for T@another_database;
```

Now that I have this database link set up and can read some tables, I am also able to modify them (given that I have the appropriate privileges, of course). Performing a distributed transaction is now no different from a local transaction. All I would do is this:

```
update local_table set x = 5;
update remote_table@another_database set y = 10;
commit;
```

That's it. Oracle will commit either in both databases or in neither. It uses a 2PC protocol to do this. 2PC is a distributed protocol that allows for a modification that affects many disparate databases to be committed atomically. It attempts to close the window for distributed failure as much as possible before committing. In a 2PC between many databases, one of the databases—typically the one the client is logged into initially—will be the coordinator for the distributed transaction. This one site will ask the other sites if they are ready to commit. In effect, this one site will go to the other sites and ask them to be prepared to commit. Each of the other sites reports back its "prepared state" as YES or NO. If any one of the sites votes NO, the entire transaction is rolled back. If all sites vote YES, the site coordinator broadcasts a message to make the commit permanent on each of the sites.

This limits the window in which a serious error could occur. Prior to the "voting" on the 2PC, any distributed error would result in all of the sites rolling back. There would be no doubt as to the outcome of the transaction. After the order to commit or roll back, there again is no doubt as to the outcome of the distributed transaction. It is only during the very short window when the coordinator is collecting the votes that the outcome might be in doubt, after a failure.

Assume, for example, we have three sites participating in the transaction with Site 1 being the coordinator. Site 1 has asked Site 2 to prepare to commit, and Site 2 has done so. Site 1 then asks Site 3 to prepare to commit, and it does so. At this point in time, Site 1 is the only site that knows the outcome of the transaction, and it is now responsible for broadcasting the outcome to the other sites. If an error occurs right now—the network fails, Site 1 loses power, whatever—Site 2 and Site 3 will be left "hanging." They will have what is known as an *in-doubt distributed transaction*. The 2PC protocol attempts to close the window of error as much as possible, but it cannot close it entirely. Sites 2 and 3 must keep that transaction open, awaiting notification from Site 1 of the outcome. If you recall from the architecture discussion in Chapter 5, it is the function of the RECO process to resolve this issue. This is also where the COMMIT and ROLLBACK with the FORCE option come into play. If the cause of the problem was a network failure between Sites 1, 2, and 3, then the DBAs at Sites 2 and 3 could actually call the DBA at Site 1, ask him for the outcome, and apply the commit or rollback manually, as appropriate.

There are some, but not many, limitations to what you can do in a distributed transaction, and they are reasonable (to me, they seem reasonable anyway). The big ones are as follows:

- You cannot issue a COMMIT over a database link. That is, you cannot issue a COMMIT@remote_site. You may commit only from the site that initiated the transaction.

- You cannot do DDL over a database link. This is a direct result of the preceding issue. DDL commits. You cannot commit from any other site other then the initiating site, hence you cannot do DDL over a database link.

- You cannot issue a SAVEPOINT over a database link. In short, you cannot issue any transaction control statements over a database link. All transaction control is inherited from the session that opened the database link in the first place; you cannot have different transaction controls in place in the distributed instances in your transaction.

The lack of transaction control over a database link is reasonable, since the initiating site is the only one that has a list of everyone involved in the transaction. If in our three-site configuration, Site 2 attempted to commit, it would have no way of knowing that Site 3 was involved. In Oracle, only Site 1 can issue the commit command. At that point, it is then permissible for Site 1 to delegate responsibility for distributed transaction control to another site.

We can influence which site will be the actual commit site by setting the COMMIT_POINT_STRENGTH (a parameter) of the site. A commit-point strength associates a relative level of importance to a server in a distributed transaction. The more important the server (the more available the data needs to be), the more probable that it will coordinate the distributed transaction. You might want to do this in the event that you need to perform a distributed transaction between your production machine and a test machine. Since the transaction coordinator is *never* in doubt as to the outcome of a transaction, it would be best if the production machine coordinated the distributed transaction. You do not care so much if your test machine has some open transactions and locked resources. You certainly do care if your production machine does.

The inability to do DDL over a database link is actually not so bad at all. First, DDL is "rare." You do it once at installation or during an upgrade. Production systems don't do DDL (well, they *shouldn't* do DDL). Second, there is a method to do DDL over a database link, in a fashion, using the job queue facility, DBMS_JOB or, in Oracle 10*g*, the scheduler package, DBMS_SCHEDULER. Instead of trying to do DDL over the link, you use the link to schedule a remote job to be executed as soon as you commit. In that fashion, the job runs on the remote machine, is not a distributed transaction, and can do the DDL. In fact, this is the method by which the Oracle Replication Services perform distributed DDL to do schema replication.

Autonomous Transactions

Autonomous transactions allow you to create a "transaction within a transaction" that will commit or roll back changes independently of its parent transaction. They allow you to suspend the currently executing transaction, start a new one, do some work, and commit or roll back—all without affecting the currently executing transaction state. Autonomous transactions provide a new method of controlling transactions in PL/SQL and may be used in

- Top-level anonymous blocks

- Local (a procedure in a procedure), stand-alone, or packaged functions and procedures

- Methods of object types

- Database triggers

Before we take a look at how autonomous transactions work, I would like to emphasize that they are a powerful and therefore dangerous tool when used improperly. The true need for an autonomous transaction is very rare indeed. I would be very suspicious of any code that makes use of them—that code would get an extra looking at. It is far too easy to accidentally introduce logical data integrity issues into a system using them. In the sections that follow, we'll discuss when they may safely be used after seeing how they work.

How Autonomous Transactions Work

The best way to demonstrate the actions and consequences of an autonomous transaction is by example. We'll create a simple table to hold a message:

```
ops$tkyte@ORA10G> create table t ( msg varchar2(25) );
Table created.
```

Next, we'll create two procedures, each of which simply INSERTs its name into the message table and commits. However, one of these procedures is a normal procedure and the other is coded as an autonomous transaction. We'll use these objects to show what work persists (is committed) in the database under various circumstances.

First, here's the AUTONOMOUS_INSERT procedure:

```
ops$tkyte@ORA10G> create or replace procedure Autonomous_Insert
  2  as
  3          pragma autonomous_transaction;
  4  begin
  5          insert into t values ( 'Autonomous Insert' );
  6          commit;
  7  end;
  8  /
Procedure created.
```

Note the use of the pragma AUTONOMOUS_TRANSACTION. That directive tells the database that this procedure, when executed, is to be executed as a new autonomous transaction, independent from its parent transaction.

Note A *pragma* is simply a compiler directive, a method to instruct the compiler to perform some compilation option. Other pragmas are available. Refer to the PL/SQL programming manual and you will see a list of them in its index.

And here's the "normal" NONAUTONOMOUS_INSERT procedure:

```
ops$tkyte@ORA10G> create or replace procedure NonAutonomous_Insert
  2  as
  3  begin
  4          insert into t values ( 'NonAutonomous Insert' );
  5          commit;
  6  end;
  7  /
Procedure created.
```

Now let's observe the behavior of the *nonautonomous* transaction in an anonymous block of PL/SQL code:

```
ops$tkyte@ORA10G> begin
  2          insert into t values ( 'Anonymous Block' );
  3          NonAutonomous_Insert;
  4          rollback;
  5  end;
  6  /

PL/SQL procedure successfully completed.

ops$tkyte@ORA10G> select * from t;

MSG
-------------------------
Anonymous Block
NonAutonomous Insert
```

As you can see, the work performed by the anonymous block, its INSERT, was *committed* by the NONAUTONOMOUS_INSERT procedure. Both rows of data were committed, so the ROLLBACK command had nothing to roll back. Compare this to the behavior of the autonomous transaction procedure:

```
ops$tkyte@ORA10G> delete from t;
2 rows deleted.

ops$tkyte@ORA10G> commit;
Commit complete.

ops$tkyte@ORA10G> begin
  2          insert into t values ( 'Anonymous Block' );
```

```
  3              Autonomous_Insert;
  4              rollback;
  5    end;
  6    /
PL/SQL procedure successfully completed.

ops$tkyte@ORA10G> select * from t;

MSG
-------------------------
Autonomous Insert
```

Here, only the work done by and committed in the autonomous transaction persists. The INSERT done in the anonymous block was rolled back by the rollback statement on line 4. The autonomous transaction procedure's COMMIT has no effect on the parent transaction started in the anonymous block. In a nutshell, this captures the essence of autonomous transactions and what they do.

To summarize, if you COMMIT inside a "normal" procedure, it will make durable not only its own work but also any outstanding work performed in that session. However, a COMMIT performed in a procedure with an autonomous transaction will make durable only that procedure's work.

When to Use Autonomous Transactions

The Oracle database has supported autonomous transactions internally for quite a while. We see them all of the time in the form of recursive SQL. For example, a recursive transaction may be performed when selecting from a sequence, in order for you to increment the sequence immediately in the SYS.SEQ$ table. The update of the SYS.SEQ$ table in support of your sequence was immediately committed and visible to other transactions, but your transaction was not committed as yet. Additionally, if you roll back your transaction, the increment to the sequence remained in place; it is not rolled back with your transaction, as it has already been committed. Space management, auditing, and other internal operations are performed in a similar recursive fashion.

This feature has now been exposed for all to use. However, I have found that the legitimate real-world use of autonomous transactions *is very limited*. Time after time, I see them used as a work-around to such problems as a mutating table constraint in a trigger. This almost always leads to data integrity issues, however, since the cause of the mutating table is an attempt to read the table upon which the trigger is firing. Well, by using an autonomous transaction you can query the table, but you are querying the table now without being able to see your changes (which is what the mutating table constraint was trying to do in the first place; the table is in the middle of a modification, so query results would be inconsistent). Any decisions you make based on a query from that trigger would be questionable—you are reading "old" data at that point in time.

A potentially valid use for an autonomous transaction is in custom auditing, but I stress the words "potentially valid." There are more efficient ways to audit information in the database than via a custom written trigger. For example, you can use the DBMS_FGA package or just the AUDIT command itself.

A question that application developers often pose to me is, "How can I audit every attempt to modify secure information and record the values they were trying to modify?" They want to not only *prevent* the attempted modification from taking place, but also create a permanent record of the attempt. Before the advent of autonomous transactions, many developers tried (and failed) to do this using standard triggers without an autonomous transaction. The trigger would detect the UPDATE and, upon discovering a user modifying data she should not, it would create an audit record and fail the UPDATE. Unfortunately, when the trigger failed the UPDATE, it also rolled back the audit record—it was an all-or-nothing failure. With autonomous transactions, it is now possible to securely capture the audit of an attempted operation as well as roll back that operation. In the process, we can inform the end user that she has attempted to modify data that she does not have permission to modify and that a record of the attempt has been made.

It is interesting to note that the native Oracle AUDIT command provided the ability to capture unsuccessful attempts to modify information, using autonomous transactions, for many years. The exposure of this feature to Oracle developers allows us to create our own, more customized auditing.

Here is a small example. Let's place an autonomous transaction trigger on a table that captures an audit trail, detailing *who* tried to update the table and *when* that person tried to do it, along with a descriptive message of which data the person tried to modify. The logic behind this trigger will be that it will prevent any attempt to update the record of an employee who does not (directly or indirectly) report to you.

First, we make a copy of the EMP table from the SCOTT schema to use as our example table:

```
ops$tkyte@ORA10G> create table emp
  2  as
  3  select * from scott.emp;
Table created.

ops$tkyte@ORA10G> grant all on emp to scott;
Grant succeeded.
```

We also create an AUDIT_TAB table in which to store the audit information. Note that we're using the DEFAULT attribute of the columns to have the currently logged in username and the current date/time logged into our audit trail as well:

```
ops$tkyte@ORA10G> create table audit_tab
  2  ( username   varchar2(30) default user,
  3    timestamp  date default sysdate,
  4    msg        varchar2(4000)
  5  )
  6  /
Table created.
```

Next, we create an EMP_AUDIT trigger to audit UPDATE activity on the EMP table:

```
ops$tkyte@ORA10G> create or replace trigger EMP_AUDIT
  2  before update on emp
  3  for each row
  4  declare
```

```
5          pragma autonomous_transaction;
6          l_cnt   number;
7      begin
8
9          select count(*) into l_cnt
10           from dual
11          where EXISTS ( select null
12                           from emp
13                          where empno = :new.empno
14                          start with mgr = ( select empno
15                                               from emp
16                                              where ename = USER )
17                        connect by prior   empno = mgr );
18         if ( l_cnt = 0 )
19         then
20             insert into audit_tab ( msg )
21             values ( 'Attempt to update ' || :new.empno );
22             commit;
23
24             raise_application_error( -20001, 'Access Denied' );
25         end if;
26     end;
27     /
Trigger created.
```

Note the use of the CONNECT BY query. This will resolve the entire hierarchy for us, based on the current user. It will verify that the record we are attempting to update belongs to someone who reports to us at some level.

The main points to note about the action of this trigger are as follows:

- PRAGMA AUTONOMOUS_TRANSACTION is applied to the trigger definition. This entire trigger is an "autonomous transaction" and so it is independent of the parent transaction, the attempted update.

- The trigger actually reads from the table it is protecting, the EMP table, in the query. That in itself would lead to a mutating table error at runtime were it not for the fact that this is an autonomous transaction. The autonomous transaction gets us around this problem—it allows us to read the table, but with the downside being that we're not able to see the changes we ourselves have made to the table. Extreme caution must be exercised in such a case. This logic must be carefully inspected. What if the transaction we were performing was an update to the employee hierarchy itself? We would not see those changes in the trigger, and this must be taken into consideration when evaluating the correctness of this trigger.

- This trigger commits. This has never been possible before—triggers could never commit work. This trigger is not committing the work that actually fired the trigger; rather, it is committing only the work that the trigger has performed (the audit record).

So, we have set up the EMP table that has a nice hierarchical structure (EMPNO, MGR recursive relationship). We also have an AUDIT_TAB table into which we want to record failed attempts to modify information. We have a trigger to enforce our rule that only our manager or our manager's manager (and so on) may modify our record.

Let's see how this works by trying to update a record in the EMP table:

```
ops$tkyte@ORA10G> update emp set sal = sal*10;
update emp set sal = sal*10
       *
ERROR at line 1:
ORA-20001: Access Denied
ORA-06512: at "OPS$TKYTE.EMP_AUDIT", line 21
ORA-04088: error during execution of trigger 'OPS$TKYTE.EMP_AUDIT'

ops$tkyte@ORA10G> select * from audit_tab;

USERNAME   TIMESTAMP  MSG
---------  ---------  ------------------------------------------
OPS$TKYTE  27-APR-05  Attempt to update 7369
```

The trigger caught us and was able to prevent the UPDATE from occurring, while at the same time creating a permanent record of the attempt (notice how it used the DEFAULT keyword on the CREATE TABLE statement for the AUDIT_TAB table to automatically have the USER and SYSDATE values inserted for us). Next, let's log in as a user who can actually do an UPDATE and try some things out:

```
ops$tkyte@ORA10G> connect scott/tiger
Connected.
scott@ORA10G> set echo on
scott@ORA10G> update ops$tkyte.emp set sal = sal*1.05 where ename = 'ADAMS';

1 row updated.

scott@ORA10G> update ops$tkyte.emp set sal = sal*1.05 where ename = 'SCOTT';
update ops$tkyte.emp set sal = sal*1.05 where ename = 'SCOTT'
            *
ERROR at line 1:
ORA-20001: Access Denied
ORA-06512: at "OPS$TKYTE.EMP_AUDIT", line 21
ORA-04088: error during execution of trigger 'OPS$TKYTE.EMP_AUDIT'
```

In the default install of the demonstration table EMP, the employee ADAMS works for SCOTT, so the first UPDATE succeeds. The second UPDATE, where SCOTT tries to give himself a raise, fails since SCOTT does not report to SCOTT. Logging back into the schema that holds the AUDIT_TAB table, we see the following:

```
scott@ORA10G> connect /
Connected.
ops$tkyte@ORA10G> set echo on
ops$tkyte@ORA10G> select * from audit_tab;

USERNAME   TIMESTAMP MSG
---------  --------- ----------------------------------------
OPS$TKYTE  27-APR-05 Attempt to update 7369
SCOTT      27-APR-05 Attempt to update 7788
```

The attempt by SCOTT to perform that UPDATE has been recorded.

Summary

In this chapter, we looked at many aspects of transaction management in Oracle. Transactions are one of the major features that set a database apart from a file system. Understanding how they work and how to use them is necessary to implement applications correctly in any database. Understanding that, in Oracle, all statements are atomic (including their side effects) and that this atomicity is extended to stored procedures is crucial. We saw how the placement of a WHEN OTHERS exception handler in a PL/SQL block could radically affect what changes took place in the database. As database developers, having a good understanding of how transactions work is crucial.

We took a look at the somewhat complex interaction between integrity constraints (unique keys, check constraints, and the like) and transactions in Oracle. We discussed how Oracle typically processes integrity constraints immediately after a statement executes, but that we can defer this constraint validation until the end of the transaction if we wish. This feature is key in implementing complex multitable updates when the tables being modified are all dependent on each other—the cascading update was an example of that.

We moved on to consider some of the bad transaction habits that people tend to pick up from working with databases that "support" rather than "promote" the use of transactions. We looked at the cardinal rule of transactions: they should be as short as they can be but as long as they need to be. *Data integrity drives the transaction size*—that is a key concept to take away from this chapter. The only things that should drive the size of your transactions are the business rules that govern your system. Not undo space, not locks—business rules.

We covered distributed transactions and how they differ from single database transactions. We explored the limitations imposed upon us in a distributed transaction and discussed why they are there. Before you build a distributed system, you need to understand these limitations. What works in a single instance might not work in a distributed database.

The chapter closed with a look at autonomous transactions and covered what they are and, more important, when they should and should not be used. I would like to emphasize once again that the legitimate real-world use of autonomous transactions is exceedingly rare. If you find them to be a feature you are using constantly, you'll want to take a long, hard look at why.

CHAPTER 9

∎∎∎

Redo and Undo

This chapter describes two of the most important pieces of data in an Oracle database: redo and undo. *Redo* is the information Oracle records in online (and archived) redo log files in order to "replay" your transaction in the event of a failure. *Undo* is the information Oracle records in the undo segments in order to reverse, or roll back, your transaction.

In this chapter, we will discuss topics such as how redo and undo (rollback) are generated, and how they fit into transactions, recovery, and so on. We'll start off with a high-level overview of what undo and redo are and how they work together. We'll then drill down into each topic, covering each in more depth and discussing what you, the developer, need to know about them.

The chapter is slanted toward the developer perspective in that we will not cover issues that a DBA should be exclusively in charge of figuring out and tuning. For example, how to find the optimum setting for RECOVERY_PARALLELISM or the FAST_START_MTTR_TARGET parameters are not covered. Nevertheless, redo and undo are topics that bridge the DBA and developer roles. Both need a good, fundamental understanding of the purpose of redo and undo, how they work, and how to avoid potential issues with regard to their use. Knowledge of redo and undo will also help both DBAs and developers better understand how the database operates in general.

In this chapter, I will present the pseudo-code for these mechanisms in Oracle and a conceptual explanation of what actually takes place. Every internal detail of what files get updated with what bytes of data will not be covered. What actually takes place is a little more involved, but having a good understanding of the flow of how it works is valuable and will help you to understand the ramifications of your actions.

What Is Redo?

Redo log files are crucial to the Oracle database. These are the transaction logs for the database. Oracle maintains two types of redo log files: *online* and *archived*. They are used for recovery purposes; their purpose in life is to be used in the event of an instance or media failure.

If the power goes off on your database machine, causing an instance failure, Oracle will use the online redo logs to restore the system to exactly the point it was at immediately prior to the power outage. If your disk drive fails (a media failure), Oracle will use archived redo logs as well as online redo logs to recover a backup of the data that was on that drive to the correct point in time. Additionally, if you "accidentally" truncate a table or remove some critical information and commit the operation, you can restore a backup of the affected data and recover it to the point in time immediately prior to the "accident" using online and archived redo log files.

Archived redo log files are simply copies of old, full online redo log files. As the system fills up log files, the ARCH process will make a copy of the online redo log file in another location, and optionally make several other copies into local and remote locations as well. These archived redo log files are used to perform media recovery when a failure is caused by a disk drive going bad or some other physical fault. Oracle can take these archived redo log files and apply them to backups of the data files to catch them up to the rest of the database. They are the transaction history of the database.

Note With the advent of the Oracle 10*g*, we now have flashback technology. This allows us to perform flashback queries (i.e., query the data as of some point in time in the past), un-drop a database table, put a table back the way it was some time ago, and so on. As a result, the number of occasions where we need to perform a conventional recovery using backups and archived redo logs has decreased. However, performing a recovery is the DBA's most important job. Database recovery is the one thing a DBA is not allowed to get wrong.

Every Oracle database has at least two online redo log groups with at least a single member (redo log file) in each group. These online redo log groups are used in a circular fashion. Oracle will write to the log files in group 1, and when it gets to the end of the files in group 1, it will switch to log file group 2 and begin writing to that one. When it has filled log file group 2, it will switch back to log file group 1 (assuming you have only two redo log file groups; if you have three, Oracle would, of course, proceed to the third group).

Redo logs, or transaction logs, are one of the major features that make a database a database. They are perhaps its most important recovery structure, although without the other pieces such as undo segments, distributed transaction recovery, and so on, nothing works. They are a major component of what sets a database apart from a conventional file system. The online redo logs allow us to effectively recover from a power outage—one that might happen while Oracle is in the middle of a write. The archived redo logs allow us to recover from media failures when, for instance, the hard disk goes bad or human error causes data loss. Without redo logs, the database would not offer any more protection than a file system.

What Is Undo?

Undo is conceptually the opposite of redo. Undo information is generated by the database as you make modifications to data to put it back the way it was before the modifications, in the event the transaction or statement you are executing fails for any reason or if you request it with a ROLLBACK statement. Whereas redo is used to replay a transaction in the event of failure—to recover the transaction—undo is used to reverse the effects of a statement or set of statements. Undo, unlike redo, is stored internally in the database in a special set of segments known as *undo segments*.

■**Note** "Rollback segment" and "undo segment" are considered synonymous terms. Using manual undo management, the DBA will create "rollback segments." Using automatic undo management, the system will automatically create and destroy "undo segments" as necessary. These terms should be considered the same for all intents and purposes in this discussion.

It is a common misconception that undo is used to restore the database *physically* to the way it was before the statement or transaction executed, but this is not so. The database is *logically* restored to the way it was—any changes are logically undone—but the data structures, the database blocks themselves, may well be different after a rollback. The reason for this lies in the fact that, in any multiuser system, there will be tens or hundreds or thousands of concurrent transactions. One of the primary functions of a database is to mediate concurrent access to its data. The blocks that our transaction modifies are, in general, being modified by many other transactions as well. Therefore, we cannot just put a block back exactly the way it was at the start of our transaction—that could undo someone else's work!

For example, suppose our transaction executed an INSERT statement that caused the allocation of a new extent (i.e., it caused the table to grow). Our INSERT would cause us to get a new block, format it for use, and put some data on it. At that point, some other transaction might come along and insert data into this block. If we were to roll back our transaction, obviously we cannot unformat and unallocate this block. Therefore, when Oracle rolls back, it is really doing the logical equivalent of the opposite of what we did in the first place. For every INSERT, Oracle will do a DELETE. For every DELETE, Oracle will do an INSERT. For every UPDATE, Oracle will do an "anti-UPDATE," or an UPDATE that puts the row back the way it was prior to our modification.

■**Note** This undo generation is not true for direct path operations, which have the ability to bypass undo generation on the table. We'll discuss these in more detail shortly.

How can we see this in action? Perhaps the easiest way is to follow these steps:

1. Create an empty table.

2. Full scan the table and observe the amount of I/O performed to read it.

3. Fill the table with many rows (no commit).

4. Roll back that work and undo it.

5. Full scan the table a second time and observe the amount of I/O performed.

First, we'll create an empty table:

```
ops$tkyte@ORA10G> create table t
  2  as
  3  select *
  4    from all_objects
  5   where 1=0;
Table created.
```

And then we'll query it, with AUTOTRACE enabled in SQL*Plus to measure the I/O.

■**Note** In this example, we will full scan the tables twice each time. The goal is to only measure the I/O performed the second time in each case. This avoids counting additional I/Os performed by the optimizer during any parsing and optimization that may occur.

The query initially takes three I/Os to full scan the table:

```
ops$tkyte@ORA10G> select * from t;
no rows selected

ops$tkyte@ORA10G> set autotrace traceonly statistics
ops$tkyte@ORA10G> select * from t;
no rows selected

Statistics
----------------------------------------------------------
          0  recursive calls
          0  db block gets
          3  consistent gets
...
ops$tkyte@ORA10G> set autotrace off
```

Next, we'll add lots of data to the table. We'll make it "grow" but then roll it all back:

```
ops$tkyte@ORA10G> insert into t select * from all_objects;
48350 rows created.

ops$tkyte@ORA10G> rollback;
Rollback complete.
```

Now, if we query the table again, we'll discover that it takes considerably more I/Os to read the table this time:

```
ops$tkyte@ORA10G> select * from t;
no rows selected

ops$tkyte@ORA10G> set autotrace traceonly statistics
```

```
ops$tkyte@ORA10G> select * from t;
no rows selected

Statistics
----------------------------------------------------------
          0  recursive calls
          0  db block gets
        689  consistent gets
...
ops$tkyte@ORA10G> set autotrace off
```

The blocks that our INSERT caused to be added under the table's high-water mark (HWM) are still there—formatted, but empty. Our full scan had to read them to see if they contained any rows. That shows that a rollback is a logical "put the database back the way it was" operation. The database will not be exactly the way it was, just logically the same.

How Redo and Undo Work Together

In this section, we'll take a look at how redo and undo work together in various scenarios. We will discuss, for example, what happens during the processing of an INSERT with regard to redo and undo generation and how Oracle uses this information in the event of failures at various points in time.

An interesting point to note is that undo information, stored in undo tablespaces or undo segments, is protected by redo as well. In other words, undo data is treated just like table data or index data—changes to undo generate some redo, which is logged. Why this is so will become clear in a moment when we discuss what happens when a system crashes. Undo data is added to the undo segment and is cached in the buffer cache just like any other piece of data would be.

Example INSERT-UPDATE-DELETE Scenario

As an example, we will investigate what might happen with a set of statements like this:

```
insert into t (x,y) values  (1,1);
update t set x = x+1 where x = 1;
delete from t where x = 2;
```

We will follow this transaction down different paths and discover the answers to the following questions:

- What happens if the system fails at various points in the processing of these statements?

- What happens if we ROLLBACK at any point?

- What happens if we succeed and COMMIT?

The INSERT

The initial INSERT INTO T statement will generate both redo and undo. The undo generated will be enough information to make the INSERT "go away." The redo generated by the INSERT INTO T will be enough information to make the insert "happen again."

After the insert has occurred, we have the scenario illustrated in Figure 9-1.

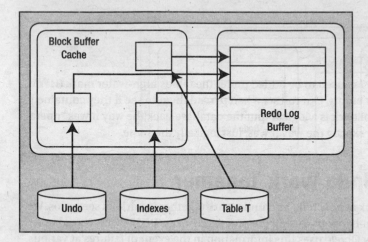

Figure 9-1. *State of the system after an* INSERT

There are some cached, modified undo blocks, index blocks, and table data blocks. Each of these blocks is protected by entries in the redo log buffer.

Hypothetical Scenario: The System Crashes Right Now

Everything is OK. The SGA is wiped out, but we don't need anything that was in the SGA. It will be as if this transaction never happened when we restart. None of the blocks with changes got flushed to disk, and none of the redo got flushed to disk. We have no need of any of this undo or redo to recover from an instance failure.

Hypothetical Scenario: The Buffer Cache Fills Up Right Now

The situation is such that DBWR must make room and our modified blocks are to be flushed from the cache. In this case, DBWR will start by asking LGWR to flush the redo entries that protect these database blocks. Before DBWR can write any of the blocks that are changed to disk, LGWR must flush the redo information related to these blocks. This makes sense: if we were to flush the modified blocks for table T without flushing the redo entries associated with the undo blocks, and the system failed, we would have a modified table T block with no undo information associated with it. We need to flush the redo log buffers before writing these blocks out so that we can redo all of the changes necessary to get the SGA back into the state it is in right now, so that a rollback can take place.

This second scenario shows some of the foresight that has gone into all of this. The set of conditions described by "If we flushed table T blocks *and* did not flush the redo for the undo blocks *and* the system failed" is starting to get complex. It only gets more complex as we add users, and more objects, and concurrent processing, and so on.

At this point, we have the situation depicted in Figure 9-1. We have generated some modified table and index blocks. These have associated undo segment blocks, and all three types of blocks have generated redo to protect them. If you recall from our discussion of the redo log buffer in Chapter 4, it is flushed every three seconds, when it is one-third full or contains 1MB of buffered data, or whenever a commit takes place. It is very possible that at some point during our processing, the redo log buffer will be flushed. In that case, the picture looks like Figure 9-2.

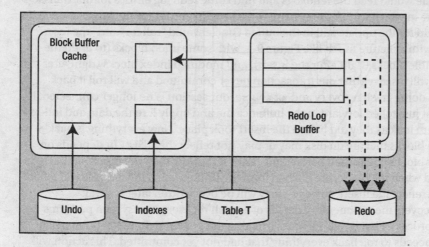

Figure 9-2. *State of the system after a redo log buffer flush*

The UPDATE

The UPDATE will cause much of the same work as the INSERT to take place. This time, the amount of undo will be larger; we have some "before" images to save as a result of the update. Now, we have the picture shown in Figure 9-3.

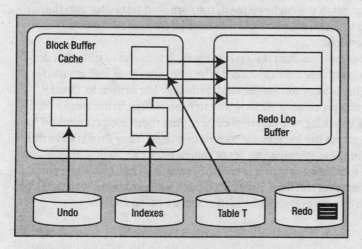

Figure 9-3. *State of the system after the* UPDATE

We have more new undo segment blocks in the block buffer cache. To undo the update, if necessary, we have modified database table and index blocks in the cache. We have also generated more redo log buffer entries. Let's assume that some of our generated redo log from the insert is on disk and some is in cache.

Hypothetical Scenario: The System Crashes Right Now

Upon startup, Oracle would read the redo logs and find some redo log entries for our transaction. Given the state in which we left the system, with the redo entries for the insert in the redo log files and the redo for the update still in the buffer, Oracle would "roll forward" the insert. We would end up with a picture much like Figure 9-1, with some undo blocks (to undo the insert), modified table blocks (right after the insert), and modified index blocks (right after the insert). Oracle will discover that our transaction never committed and will roll it back since the system is doing crash recovery and, of course, our session is no longer connected. It will take the undo it just rolled forward in the buffer cache and apply it to the data and index blocks, making them look as they did before the insert took place. Now everything is back the way it was. The blocks that are on disk may or may not reflect the INSERT (it depends on whether or not our blocks got flushed before the crash). If they do, then the insert has been, in effect, undone, and when the blocks are flushed from the buffer cache, the data file will reflect that. If they do not reflect the insert, so be it—they will be overwritten later anyway.

This scenario covers the rudimentary details of a crash recovery. The system performs this as a two-step process. First it rolls forward, bringing the system right to the point of failure, and then it proceeds to roll back everything that had not yet committed. This action will resynchronize the data files. It replays the work that was in progress and undoes anything that has not yet completed.

Hypothetical Scenario: The Application Rolls Back the Transaction

At this point, Oracle will find the undo information for this transaction either in the cached undo segment blocks (most likely) or on disk if they have been flushed (more likely for very large transactions). It will apply the undo information to the data and index blocks in the buffer cache, or if they are no longer in the cache request, they are read from disk into the cache to have the undo applied to them. These blocks will later be flushed to the data files with their original row values restored.

This scenario is much more common than the system crash. It is useful to note that during the rollback process, the redo logs are never involved. The only time redo logs are read is during recovery and archival. This is a key tuning concept: redo logs are written to. Oracle does not read them during normal processing. As long as you have sufficient devices so that when ARCH is reading a file, LGWR is writing to a different device, then there is no contention for redo logs. Many other databases treat the log files as "transaction logs." They do not have this separation of redo and undo. For those systems, the act of rolling back can be disastrous—the rollback process must read the logs their log writer is trying to write to. They introduce contention into the part of the system that can least stand it. Oracle's goal is to make it so that logs are written sequentially, and no one ever reads them while they are being written.

The DELETE

Again, undo is generated as a result of the DELETE, blocks are modified, and redo is sent over to the redo log buffer. This is not very different from before. In fact, it is so similar to the UPDATE that we are going to move right on to the COMMIT.

The COMMIT

We've looked at various failure scenarios and different paths, and now we've finally made it to the COMMIT. Here, Oracle will flush the redo log buffer to disk, and the picture will look like Figure 9-4.

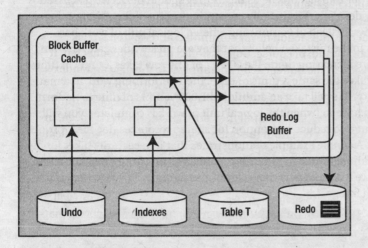

Figure 9-4. *State of the system after a* COMMIT

The modified blocks are in the buffer cache; maybe some of them have been flushed to disk. All of the redo necessary to replay this transaction is safely on disk and the changes are now permanent. If we were to read the data directly from the data files, we probably would see the blocks as they existed *before* the transaction took place, as DBWR most likely has not written them yet. That is OK—the redo log files can be used to bring up to date those blocks in the event of a failure. The undo information will hang around until the undo segment wraps around and reuses those blocks. Oracle will use that undo to provide for consistent reads of the affected objects for any session that needs them.

Commit and Rollback Processing

It is important for us to understand how redo log files might impact us as developers. We will look at how the different ways we can write our code affect redo log utilization. We've already seen the mechanics of redo earlier in the chapter, and now we'll look at some specific issues. Many of these scenarios might be detected by you, but would be fixed by the DBA as they affect the database instance as a whole. We'll start with what happens during a COMMIT, and then get into commonly asked questions and issues surrounding the online redo logs.

What Does a COMMIT Do?

As a developer, you should have a good understanding of exactly what goes on during a COMMIT. In this section, we'll investigate what happens during the processing of the COMMIT statement in Oracle. A COMMIT is generally a very fast operation, regardless of the transaction size. You might think that the bigger a transaction (in other words, the more data it affects), the longer a COMMIT will take. This is not true. The response time of a COMMIT is generally "flat," regardless of the transaction size. This is because a COMMIT does not really have too much work to do, but what it does do is vital.

One of the reasons this is an important fact to understand and embrace is that it will lead you down the path of letting your transactions be as big as they should be. As we discussed in the previous chapter, many developers artificially constrain the size of their transactions, committing every so many rows, instead of committing when a logical unit of work has been performed. They do this in the mistaken belief that they are preserving scarce system resources, when in fact they are increasing them. If a COMMIT of one row takes X units of time, and the COMMIT of 1,000 rows takes the same X units of time, then performing work in a manner that does 1,000 one-row COMMITs will take an additional 1,000*X units of time to perform. By committing only when you have to (when the logical unit of work is complete), you will not only increase performance, but also reduce contention for shared resources (log files, various internal latches, and the like). A simple example demonstrates that it necessarily takes longer. We'll use a Java application, although you should expect similar results from most any client— except, in this case, PL/SQL (we'll discuss why that is after the example). To start, here is the sample table we'll be inserting into:

```
scott@ORA10G> desc test
 Name                    Null?    Type
 ------------------- -------- ------------
 ID                            NUMBER
 CODE                          VARCHAR2(20)
 DESCR                         VARCHAR2(20)
 INSERT_USER                   VARCHAR2(30)
 INSERT_DATE                   DATE
```

Our Java program will accept two inputs: the number of rows to INSERT (iters) and how many rows between commits (commitCnt). It starts by connecting to the database, setting autocommit *off* (which should be done in all Java code), and then calling a doInserts() method a total of three times:

- Once just to warm up the routine (make sure all of the classes are loaded)

- A second time, specifying the number of rows to INSERT along with how many rows to commit at a time (i.e., commit every N rows)

- A final time with the number of rows and number of rows to commit set to the same value (i.e., commit after all rows have been inserted)

It then closes the connection and exits. The main method is as follows:

```
import java.sql.*;
import oracle.jdbc.OracleDriver;
import java.util.Date;
public class perftest
{
  public static void main (String arr[]) throws Exception
  {
    DriverManager.registerDriver(new oracle.jdbc.OracleDriver());
    Connection con = DriverManager.getConnection
            ("jdbc:oracle:thin:@localhost.localdomain:1521:ora10g",
             "scott", "tiger");

    Integer iters = new Integer(arr[0]);
    Integer commitCnt = new Integer(arr[1]);

    con.setAutoCommit(false);
    doInserts( con, 1, 1 );
    doInserts( con, iters.intValue(), commitCnt.intValue() );
    doInserts( con, iters.intValue(), iters.intValue() );
    con.commit();
    con.close();
  }
```

Now, the method doInserts() is fairly straightforward. It starts by preparing (parsing) an INSERT statement so we can repeatedly bind/execute it over and over:

```
static void doInserts(Connection con, int count, int commitCount )
throws Exception
{
  PreparedStatement ps =
    con.prepareStatement
    ("insert into test " +
      "(id, code, descr, insert_user, insert_date)"
    + " values (?,?,?, user, sysdate)");
```

It then loops over the number of rows to insert, binding and executing the INSERT over and over. Additionally, it is checking a row counter to see if it needs to COMMIT or not inside the loop. Note also that before and after the loop we are retrieving the time, so we can monitor elapsed times and report them:

```
  int  rowcnt = 0;
  int  committed = 0;
  long start = new Date().getTime();
  for (int i = 0; i < count; i++ )
  {
    ps.setInt(1,i);
    ps.setString(2,"PS - code" + i);
    ps.setString(3,"PS - desc" + i);
    ps.executeUpdate();
```

```
    rowcnt++;
    if ( rowcnt == commitCount )
    {
      con.commit();
      rowcnt = 0;
      committed++;
    }
  }
  con.commit();
  long end = new Date().getTime();
  System.out.println
  ("pstatement " + count + " times in " +
   (end - start) + " milli seconds committed = "+committed);
 }
}
```

Now we'll run this code repeatedly with different inputs:

```
$ java perftest 10000 1
pstatement 1 times in 4 milli seconds committed = 1
pstatement 10000 times in 11510 milli seconds committed = 10000
pstatement 10000 times in 2708 milli seconds committed = 1

$ java perftest 10000 10
pstatement 1 times in 4 milli seconds committed = 1
pstatement 10000 times in 3876 milli seconds committed = 1000
pstatement 10000 times in 2703 milli seconds committed = 1

$ java perftest 10000 100
pstatement 1 times in 4 milli seconds committed = 1
pstatement 10000 times in 3105 milli seconds committed = 100
pstatement 10000 times in 2694 milli seconds committed = 1
```

As you can see, the more often you commit, the longer it takes (your mileage will vary on this). This is just a single-user scenario—with multiple users doing the same work, all committing too frequently, the numbers will go up rapidly.

We've heard the same story, time and time again, with other similar situations. For example, we've seen how not using bind variables and performing hard parses frequently severely reduces concurrency due to library cache contention and excessive CPU utilization. Even when we switch to using bind variables, soft parsing too frequently, caused by closing cursors even though we are going to reuse them shortly, incurs massive overhead. We must perform operations only when we need to—a COMMIT is just another such operation. It is best to size our transactions based on business need, not based on misguided attempts to lessen resource usage on the database.

There are two contributing factors to the expense of the COMMIT in this example:

- We've obviously increased the round-trips to and from the database. If we commit every record, we are generating that much more traffic back and forth.

- Every time we commit, we must wait for our redo to be written to disk. This will result in a "wait." In this case, the wait is named "log file sync."

We can actually observe the latter easily by slightly modifying the Java application. We'll do two things:

- Add a call to DBMS_MONITOR to enable SQL tracing with wait events. In Oracle9*i*, we would use alter session set events '10046 trace name context forever, level 12' instead, as DBMS_MONITOR is new in Oracle 10*g*.

- Change the con.commit() call to be a call to a SQL statement to perform the commit. If you use the built-in JDBC commit() call, this does not emit a SQL COMMIT statement to the trace file, and TKPROF, the tool used to format a trace file, will not report the time spent doing the COMMIT.

So, we modify the doInserts() method as follows:

```
doInserts( con, 1, 1 );
Statement stmt = con.createStatement ();
stmt.execute
( "begin dbms_monitor.session_trace_enable(waits=>TRUE); end;" );
doInserts( con, iters.intValue(), iters.intValue() );
```

To the main method, we add the following:

```
PreparedStatement commit =
    con.prepareStatement
    ("begin /* commit size = " + commitCount + " */ commit; end;" );

int  rowcnt = 0;
int  committed = 0;
...
   if ( rowcnt == commitCount )
   {
     commit.executeUpdate();
     rowcnt = 0;
     committed++;
```

Upon running that application with 10,000 rows to insert, committing every row, the TKPROF report would show results similar to the following:

```
begin /* commit size = 1 */ commit; end;
....
Elapsed times include waiting on following events:
  Event waited on                             Times    Max. Wait  Total Waited
  ------------------------------------------- Waited  ---------- ------------
  SQL*Net message to client                   10000       0.00         0.01
  SQL*Net message from client                 10000       0.00         0.04
  log file sync                                8288       0.06         2.00
```

If we insert 10,000 rows and only commit when all 10,000 are inserted, we get results similar to the following:

```
begin /* commit size = 10000 */ commit; end;
....
Elapsed times include waiting on following events:
  Event waited on                                Times   Max. Wait  Total Waited
                                                 Waited  ---------- ------------
  log file sync                                    1        0.00       0.00
  SQL*Net message to client                        1        0.00       0.00
  SQL*Net message from client                      1        0.00       0.00
```

When we committed after every INSERT, we waited almost every time—and if you wait a little bit of time but you wait often, then it all adds up. Fully two seconds of our runtime was spent waiting for a COMMIT to complete—in other words, waiting for LGWR to write the redo to disk. In stark contrast, when we committed once, we didn't wait very long (not a measurable amount of time actually). This proves that a COMMIT is a fast operation; we expect the response time to be more or less flat, not a function of the amount of work we've done.

So, why is a COMMIT's response time fairly flat, regardless of the transaction size? Before we even go to COMMIT in the database, we've already done the really hard work. We've already modified the data in the database, so we've already done 99.9 percent of the work. For example, operations such as the following have already taken place:

- Undo blocks have been generated in the SGA.

- Modified data blocks have been generated in the SGA.

- Buffered redo for the preceding two items has been generated in the SGA.

- Depending on the size of the preceding three items, and the amount of time spent, some combination of the previous data may be flushed onto disk already.

- All locks have been acquired.

When we COMMIT, all that is left to happen is the following:

- An SCN is generated for our transaction. In case you are not familiar with it, the SCN is a simple timing mechanism Oracle uses to guarantee the ordering of transactions and to enable recovery from failure. It is also used to guarantee read-consistency and check-pointing in the database. Think of the SCN as a ticker; every time someone COMMITs, the SCN is incremented by one.

- LGWR writes all of our *remaining* buffered redo log entries to disk and records the SCN in the online redo log files as well. This step is actually the COMMIT. If this step occurs, we have committed. Our transaction entry is "removed" from V$TRANSACTION—this shows that we have committed.

- All locks recorded in V$LOCK held by our session are released, and everyone who was enqueued waiting on locks we held will be woken up and allowed to proceed with their work.

- Some of the blocks our transaction modified will be visited and "cleaned out" in a fast mode if they are still in the buffer cache. *Block cleanout* refers to the lock-related information we store in the database block header. Basically, we are cleaning out our transaction information on the block, so the next person who visits the block won't have to. We are doing this in a way that need not generate redo log information, saving considerable work later (this is discussed more fully in the upcoming "Block Cleanout" section).

As you can see, there is very little to do to process a COMMIT. The lengthiest operation is, and always will be, the activity performed by LGWR, as this is physical disk I/O. The amount of time spent by LGWR here will be greatly reduced by the fact that it has already been flushing the contents of the redo log buffer on a recurring basis. LGWR will not buffer all of the work you do for as long as you do it; rather, it will incrementally flush the contents of the redo log buffer in the background as you are going along. This is to avoid having a COMMIT wait for a very long time in order to flush all of your redo at once.

So, even if we have a long-running transaction, much of the buffered redo log it generates would have been flushed to disk, prior to committing. On the flip side of this is the fact that when we COMMIT, we must wait until *all* buffered redo that has not been written yet is safely on disk. That is, our call to LGWR is a *synchronous* one. While LGWR may use asynchronous I/O to write in parallel to our log files, our transaction will wait for LGWR to complete all writes and receive confirmation that the data exists on disk before returning.

Now, earlier I mentioned that we were using a Java program and not PL/SQL for a reason—and that reason is a PL/SQL commit-time optimization. I said that our call to LGWR is a synchronous one, and that we wait for it to complete its write. That is true in Oracle 10*g* Release 1 and before for every programmatic language *except PL/SQL*. The PL/SQL engine, realizing that the client does not know whether or not a COMMIT has happened in the PL/SQL routine until the PL/SQL routine is completed, does an asynchronous commit. It does not wait for LGWR to complete; rather, it returns from the COMMIT call immediately. However, when the PL/SQL routine is completed, when we return from the database to the client, the PL/SQL routine will wait for LGWR to complete any of the outstanding COMMITs. So, if you commit 100 times in PL/SQL and then return to the client, you will likely find you waited for LGWR once—not 100 times—due to this optimization. Does this imply that committing frequently in PL/SQL is a good or OK idea? No, not at all—just that it is not *as bad an idea* as it is in other languages. The guiding rule is to commit when your logical unit of work is complete—not before.

■**Note** This commit-time optimization in PL/SQL may be suspended when you are performing distributed transactions or Data Guard in maximum availability mode. Since there are two participants, PL/SQL must wait for the commit to actually be complete before continuing on.

To demonstrate that a COMMIT is a "flat response time" operation, we'll generate varying amounts of redo and time the INSERTs and COMMITs. To do this, we'll again use AUTOTRACE in SQL*Plus. We'll start with a big table of test data we'll insert into another table and an empty table:

```
ops$tkyte@ORA10G> @big_table 100000
ops$tkyte@ORA10G> create table t as select * from big_table where 1=0;
Table created.
```

And then in SQL*Plus we'll run the following:

```
ops$tkyte@ORA10G> set timing on
ops$tkyte@ORA10G> set autotrace on statistics;
ops$tkyte@ORA10G> insert into t select * from big_table where rownum <= 10;
ops$tkyte@ORA10G> commit;
```

We monitor the *redo size* statistic presented by AUTOTRACE and the timing information presented by set timing on. I performed this test and varied the number of rows inserted from 10 to 100,000 in multiples of 10. Table 9-1 shows my observations.

Table 9-1. *Time to COMMIT by Transaction Size**

Rows Inserted	Time to Insert (Seconds)	Redo Size (Bytes)	Commit Time (Seconds)
10	0.05	116	0.06
100	0.08	3,594	0.04
1,000	0.07	372,924	0.06
10,000	0.25	3,744,620	0.06
100,000	1.94	37,843,108	0.07

* *This test was performed on a single-user machine with an 8MB log buffer and two 512MB online redo log files.*

As you can see, as we generate varying amount of redo, from 116 bytes to 37MB, the difference in time to COMMIT is not measurable using a timer with a one hundredth of a second resolution. As we were processing and generating the redo log, LGWR was constantly flushing our buffered redo information to disk in the background. So, when we generated 37MB of redo log information, LGWR was busy flushing every 1MB or so. When it came to the COMMIT, there wasn't much left to do—not much more than when we created ten rows of data. You should expect to see similar (but not exactly the same) results, regardless of the amount of redo generated.

What Does a ROLLBACK Do?

By changing the COMMIT to ROLLBACK, we can expect a totally different result. The time to roll back will definitely be a function of the amount of data modified. I changed the script developed in the previous section to perform a ROLLBACK instead (simply change the COMMIT to ROLLBACK) and the timings are very different (see Table 9-2).

Table 9-2. *Time to* ROLLBACK *by Transaction Size*

Rows Inserted	Rollback Time (Seconds)	Commit Time (Seconds)
10	0.04	0.06
100	0.05	0.04
1,000	0.06	0.06
10,000	0.22	0.06
100,000	1.46	0.07

This is to be expected, as a ROLLBACK has to physically undo the work we've done. Similar to a COMMIT, a series of operations must be performed. Before we even get to the ROLLBACK, the database has already done a lot of work. To recap, the following would have happened:

- Undo segment records have been generated in the SGA.

- Modified data blocks have been generated in the SGA.

- A buffered redo log for the preceding two items has been generated in the SGA.

- Depending on the size of the preceding three items, and the amount of time spent, some combination of the previous data may be flushed onto disk already.

- All locks have been acquired.

When we ROLLBACK,

- We undo all of the changes made. This is accomplished by reading the data back from the undo segment, and in effect, reversing our operation and then marking the undo entry as applied. If we inserted a row, a ROLLBACK will delete it. If we updated a row, a rollback will reverse the update. If we deleted a row, a rollback will re-insert it again.

- All locks held by our session are released, and everyone who was enqueued waiting on locks we held will be released.

A COMMIT, on the other hand, just flushes any remaining data in the redo log buffers. It does very little work compared to a ROLLBACK. The point here is that you don't want to roll back unless you have to. It is expensive since you spend a lot of time doing the work, and you'll also spend a lot of time undoing the work. Don't do work unless you're sure you are going to want to COMMIT it. This sounds like common sense—of course I wouldn't do all of the work unless I wanted to COMMIT it. Many times, however, I've seen a situation where a developer will use a "real" table as a temporary table, fill it up with data, report on it, and then roll back to get rid of the temporary data. In the next section, we'll talk about true temporary tables and how to avoid this issue.

Investigating Redo

As a developer, it's often important to be able to measure how much redo your operations generate. The more redo you generate, the longer your operations will take, and the slower the entire system will be. You are not just affecting *your* session, but *every* session. Redo management is a point of serialization within the database. There is just one LGWR in any Oracle instance, and eventually all transactions end up at LGWR, asking it to manage their redo and COMMIT their transaction. The more it has to do, the slower the system will be. By seeing how much redo an operation tends to generate, and testing more than one approach to a problem, you can find the best way to do things.

Measuring Redo

It is pretty straightforward to see how much redo is being generated, as shown earlier in the chapter. I used the AUTOTRACE built-in feature of SQL*Plus. But AUTOTRACE works only with simple DML—it cannot, for example, be used to view what a stored procedure call did. For that, we'll need access to two dynamic performance views:

- V$MYSTAT, which has just our session's statistics in it

- V$STATNAME, which tells us what each row in V$MYSTAT represents (the name of the statistic we are looking at)

I do these sorts of measurements so often that I use two scripts I call mystat and mystat2. The mystat.sql script saves the beginning value of the statistic I'm interested in, such as redo size, in a SQL*Plus variable:

```
set verify off
column value new_val V
define S="&1"

set autotrace off
select a.name, b.value
from v$statname a, v$mystat b
where a.statistic# = b.statistic#
and lower(a.name) like '%' || lower('&S')||'%'
/
```

The mystat2.sql script simply prints out the difference between the beginning value and the end value of that statistic:

```
set verify off
select a.name, b.value V, to_char(b.value-&V,'999,999,999,999') diff
from v$statname a, v$mystat b
where a.statistic# = b.statistic#
and lower(a.name) like '%' || lower('&S')||'%'
/
```

Now we're ready to measure how much redo a given transaction would generate. All we need to do is this:

```
@mystat "redo size"
...process...
@mystat2
```

for example:

```
ops$tkyte@ORA10G> @mystat "redo size"

NAME                                VALUE
------------------------------- ----------
redo size                             496

ops$tkyte@ORA10G> insert into t select * from big_table;
100000 rows created.

ops$tkyte@ORA10G> @mystat2

NAME                            V         DIFF
------------------------------- ---------- ----------------
redo size                       37678732       37,678,236
```

As just shown, we generated about 37MB of redo for that INSERT. Perhaps you would like to compare that to the redo generated by a direct path INSERT, as follows:

■**Note** The example in this section was performed on a NOARCHIVELOG mode database. If you are in ARCHIVELOG mode, the table would have to be NOLOGGING to observe this dramatic change. We will investigate the NOLOGGING attribute in more detail shortly in the section "Setting NOLOGGING in SQL." But please make sure to coordinate all nonlogged operations with your DBA on a "real" system.

```
ops$tkyte@ORA10G> @mystat "redo size"

NAME                                VALUE
------------------------------- ----------
redo size                        37678732

ops$tkyte@ORA10G> insert /*+ APPEND */ into t select * from big_table;
100000 rows created.

ops$tkyte@ORA10G> @mystat2
ops$tkyte@ORA10G> set echo off

NAME                                V DIFF
------------------------------- ---------- ----------------
redo size                        37714328           35,596
```

The method I outline using the V$MYSTAT view is useful in general for seeing the side effects of various options. The mystat.sql script is useful for small tests, with one or two operations, but what if we want to perform a big series of tests? This is where a little test harness can come in handy, and in the next section we'll set up and use this test harness alongside a table to log our results, to investigate the redo generated by BEFORE triggers.

Redo Generation and BEFORE/AFTER Triggers

I'm often asked the following question: "Other than the fact that you can modify the values of a row in a BEFORE trigger, are there any other differences between BEFORE and AFTER triggers?" Well, as it turns out, yes there are. A BEFORE trigger tends to add additional redo information, even if it does not modify any of the values in the row. In fact, this is an interesting case study, and using the techniques described in the previous section, we'll discover that

- A BEFORE or AFTER trigger does not affect the redo generated by DELETEs.

- In Oracle9i Release 2 and before, an INSERT generates extra redo in the same amount for either a BEFORE or an AFTER trigger. In Oracle 10g, it generates *no additional redo*.

- In all releases up to (and including) Oracle9i Release 2, the redo generated by an UPDATE is affected only by the existence of a BEFORE trigger. An AFTER trigger adds no additional redo. However, in Oracle 10g, the behavior is once again different. Specifically,

  - Overall, the amount of redo generated during an update on a table without a trigger is less than in Oracle9i and before. This seems to be the crux of what Oracle wanted to achieve: to decrease the amount of redo generated by an update on a table without any triggers.

  - The amount of redo generated during an update on a table with a BEFORE trigger is higher in Oracle 10g than in 9i.

  - The amount of redo generated with the AFTER trigger is the same as in 9i.

To perform this test, we'll use a table T defined as follows:

```
create table t ( x int, y char(N), z date );
```

but we'll create it with varying sizes for N. In this example, we'll use N = 30, 100, 500, 1,000, and 2,000 to achieve rows of varying widths. After we run our test for various sizes of the Y column, we'll analyze the results. I used a simple log table to capture the results of my many runs:

```
create table log ( what varchar2(15),  -- will be no trigger, after or before
                   op varchar2(10),     -- will be insert/update or delete
                   rowsize int,         -- will be the size of Y
                   redo_size int,       -- will be the redo generated
                   rowcnt int )         -- will be the count of rows affected
```

I used the following DO_WORK stored procedure to generate my transactions and record the redo generated. The subprocedure REPORT is a local procedure (only visible in the DO_WORK procedure), and it simply reports what happened on the screen and captures the findings into our LOG table:

```
ops$tkyte@ORA10G> create or replace procedure do_work( p_what in varchar2 )
  2  as
  3    l_redo_size number;
  4    l_cnt       number := 200;
  5
  6    procedure report( l_op in varchar2 )
  7    is
  8    begin
  9      select v$mystat.value-l_redo_size
 10            into l_redo_size
 11            from v$mystat, v$statname
 12           where v$mystat.statistic# = v$statname.statistic#
 13             and v$statname.name = 'redo size';
 14
 15      dbms_output.put_line(l_op || ' redo size = ' || l_redo_size ||
 16                           ' rows = ' || l_cnt || ' ' ||
 17                           to_char(l_redo_size/l_cnt,'99,999.9') ||
 18                           ' bytes/row' );
 19      insert into log
 20      select p_what, l_op, data_length, l_redo_size, l_cnt
 21        from user_tab_columns
 22       where table_name = 'T'
 23         and column_name = 'Y';
 24    end;
```

The local procedure SET_REDO_SIZE queries V$MYSTAT and V$STATNAME to retrieve the current amount of redo our session has generated thus far. It sets the variable L_REDO_SIZE in the procedure to that value:

```
 25    procedure set_redo_size
 26    as
 27    begin
 28      select v$mystat.value
 29        into l_redo_size
 30        from v$mystat, v$statname
 31       where v$mystat.statistic# = v$statname.statistic#
 32             and v$statname.name = 'redo size';
 33    end;
```

And then there is the main routine. It collects the current redo size, runs an INSERT/UPDATE/DELETE, and then saves the redo generated by that operation to the LOG table:

```
 34  begin
 35    set_redo_size;
 36    insert into t
 37    select object_id, object_name, created
 38      from all_objects
 39     where rownum <= l_cnt;
 40    l_cnt := sql%rowcount;
```

```
41      commit;
42      report('insert');
43
44      set_redo_size;
45      update t set y=lower(y);
46      l_cnt := sql%rowcount;
47      commit;
48      report('update');
49
50      set_redo_size;
51      delete from t;
52      l_cnt := sql%rowcount;
53      commit;
54      report('delete');
55   end;
56   /
```

Now, once we have this in place, we set the width of column Y to 2,000. We then run the following script to test the three scenarios, namely no trigger, BEFORE trigger, and AFTER trigger:

```
ops$tkyte@ORA10G> exec do_work('no trigger');
insert redo size = 505960 rows = 200    2,529.8 bytes/row
update redo size = 837744 rows = 200    4,188.7 bytes/row
delete redo size = 474164 rows = 200    2,370.8 bytes/row
PL/SQL procedure successfully completed.

ops$tkyte@ORA10G> create or replace trigger before_insert_update_delete
  2  before insert or update or delete on T for each row
  3  begin
  4          null;
  5  end;
  6  /
Trigger created.

ops$tkyte@ORA10G> truncate table t;
Table truncated.

ops$tkyte@ORA10G> exec do_work('before trigger');
insert redo size = 506096 rows ⇒ 200    2,530.5 bytes/row
update redo size = 897768 rows = 200    4,488.8 bytes/row
delete redo size = 474216 rows = 200    2,371.1 bytes/row
PL/SQL procedure successfully completed.

ops$tkyte@ORA10G> drop trigger before_insert_update_delete;
Trigger dropped.
```

```
ops$tkyte@ORA10G> create or replace trigger after_insert_update_delete
  2  after insert or update or delete on T
  3  for each row
  4  begin
  5          null;
  6  end;
  7  /
Trigger created.

ops$tkyte@ORA10G> truncate table t;
Table truncated.

ops$tkyte@ORA10G> exec do_work( 'after trigger' );
insert redo size = 505972 rows = 200    2,529.9 bytes/row
update redo size = 856636 rows = 200    4,283.2 bytes/row
delete redo size = 474176 rows = 200    2,370.9 bytes/row
PL/SQL procedure successfully completed.
```

The preceding output was from a run where the size of Y was 2,000 bytes. After all of the runs were complete, we are able to query the LOG table and see the following:

```
ops$tkyte@ORA10G> break on op skip 1
ops$tkyte@ORA10G> set numformat 999,999

ops$tkyte@ORA10G> select op, rowsize, no_trig,
                       before_trig-no_trig, after_trig-no_trig
  2  from
  3  ( select op, rowsize,
  4    sum(decode( what, 'no trigger', redo_size/rowcnt,0 ) ) no_trig,
  5    sum(decode( what, 'before trigger', redo_size/rowcnt, 0 ) ) before_trig,
  6 *  sum(decode( what, 'after trigger', redo_size/rowcnt, 0 ) ) after_trig
  7          from log
  8          group by op, rowsize
  9      )
 10   order by op, rowsize
 11  /
```

OP	ROWSIZE	NO_TRIG	BEFORE_TRIG-NO_TRIG	AFTER_TRIG-NO_TRIG
delete	30	291	0	0
	100	364	-1	-0
	500	785	-0	0
	1,000	1,307	-0	-0
	2,000	2,371	0	-0

```
insert         30       296                    0                      -0
              100       367                    0                       0
              500       822                    1                       1
            1,000     1,381                   -0                      -0
            2,000     2,530                    0                       0

update         30       147                  358                     152
              100       288                  363                     157
              500     1,103                  355                     150
            1,000     2,125                  342                     137
            2,000     4,188                  300                      94

15 rows selected.
```

Now, I was curious if the log mode (ARCHIVELOG versus NOARCHIVELOG mode) would affect these results. I discovered that the answer is no, the numbers were identical in both modes. I was curious about why the results were very different from the first edition of *Expert One-on-One Oracle*, upon which this book you are reading is loosely based. That book was released when Oracle8*i* version 8.1.7 was current. The Oracle 10*g* results just shown differed greatly from Oracle8*i*, but the Oracle9*i* results shown in this table resembled the Oracle8*i* results closely:

```
OP         ROWSIZE   NO_TRIG BEFORE_TRIG-NO_TRIG AFTER_TRIG-NO_TRIG
---------- --------- -------- ------------------- -------------------
delete         30       279                   -0                     -0
              100       351                   -0                     -0
              500       768                    1                      0
            1,000     1,288                    0                      0
            2,000     2,356                    0                    -11

insert         30        61                  221                    221
              100       136                  217                    217
              500       599                  199                    198
            1,000     1,160                  181                    181
            2,000     2,311                  147                    147

update         30       302                  197                      0
              100       438                  197                      0
              500     1,246                  195                      0
            1,000     2,262                  185                      0
            2,000     4,325                  195                     -1

15 rows selected.
```

I discovered that the way triggers affect the redo generated by a transaction materially changed between Oracle9*i* Release 2 and Oracle 10*g*. The changes are easy to see here:

- A DELETE was not and is still not affected by the presence of a trigger at all.

- An INSERT was affected in Oracle9*i* Release 2 and before, and at first glance you might say Oracle 10*g* optimized the INSERT so it would not be affected, but if you look at the total redo generated without a trigger in Oracle 10*g*, you'll see it is the same amount that was generated in Oracle9*i* Release 2 and before with a trigger. So, it is not that Oracle 10*g* reduced the amount of redo generated by an INSERT in the presence of a trigger, but rather that the amount of redo generated is constant—and an INSERT in Oracle 10*g* will generate more redo than in Oracle9*i* without a trigger.

- An UPDATE was affected by a BEFORE trigger in 9*i* but not an AFTER trigger. At first glance it would appear that Oracle 10*g* changed that so as both triggers affect it. But upon closer inspection, we can see that what actually happened was that the redo generated by an UPDATE without a trigger was decreased in Oracle 10*g* by the amount that the UPDATE generates with the trigger. So the opposite of what happened with INSERTs between 9*i* and 10*g* happened with UPDATEs—the amount of redo generated without a trigger decreased.

Table 9-3 summarizes the effects of a trigger on the amount of redo generated by a DML operation in both Oracle9*i* and before and Oracle 10*g*.

Table 9-3. *Effect of Triggers on Redo Generation*

DML Operation	AFTER Trigger Pre-10*g*	BEFORE Trigger, Pre-10*g*	AFTER Trigger, 10*g*	BEFORE Trigger, 10*g*
DELETE	No affect	No affect	No affect	No affect
INSERT	Increased redo	Increased redo	Constant redo	Constant redo
UPDATE	Increased redo	No affect	Increased redo	Increased redo

THE IMPORTANCE OF TEST CASES

As I was updating the first edition of this book, it struck me that this example is an excellent example of why having test cases to show something is a really good idea. Had I just written in the first edition "Triggers affect INSERTs, UPDATEs, and DELETEs in this fashion" and not given a method for measuring it, and not supplied the test cases as I did here, it is very likely that I would have continued to say the same thing. Since the test cases when replayed in Oracle9*i* and Oracle 10*g* gave different results, I was able to easily show the change and now know that "something changed" in the database. It has struck me time and time again while going through this update process that without the test cases, I would say many wrong things based on my past knowledge.

So, now you know how to estimate the amount of redo, which every developer should be able to do. You can

- Estimate your "transaction" size (how much data you modify).

- Add 10 to 20 percent overhead of the amount of data you modify, depending on the number of rows you will be modifying. The more rows, the less overhead.

- Double this value for UPDATEs.

In most cases, this will be a good estimate. The doubling on the UPDATEs is a guess—it really depends on how you modify the data. The doubling assumes you take a row of X bytes, and UPDATE it to be a row of X bytes. If you take a small row and make it big, you will not double the value (it will behave more like an INSERT). If you take a big row and make it small, you will not double the value (it will behave like a DELETE). The doubling is a "worst-case" number, as there are various options and features that will impact this—for example, the existence of indexes (or lack thereof, as in my case) will *contribute* to the bottom line. The amount of work that must be done to maintain the index structure may vary from UPDATE to UPDATE, and so on. Side effects from triggers have to be taken into consideration (in addition to the fixed overhead described previously). Implicit operations performed on your behalf, such as an ON DELETE CASCADE setting on a foreign key, must be considered as well. This will allow you to estimate the amount of redo for sizing/performance purposes. Only real-world testing will tell you for sure. Given the preceding script, you can see how to measure this for yourself, for any of your objects and transactions.

Can I Turn Off Redo Log Generation?

This question is often asked. The simple short answer is no, since redo logging is crucial for the database; it is not overhead and it is not a waste. You do need it, regardless of whether you believe you do or not. It is a fact of life, and it is the way the database works. If in fact you "turned off redo," then any temporary failure of disk drives, power, or some software crash would render the entire database unusable and unrecoverable. However, that said, there are some operations that can be done without generating redo log in some cases.

Note As of Oracle9*i* Release 2, a DBA may place the database into FORCE LOGGING mode. In that case, *all* operations are logged. The query SELECT FORCE_LOGGING FROM V$DATABASE may be used to see if logging is going to be forced or not. This feature is in support of Data Guard, a disaster recovery feature of Oracle that relies on redo to maintain a standby database copy.

Setting NOLOGGING in SQL

Some SQL statements and operations support the use of a NOLOGGING clause. This does not mean that all operations against the object will be performed without generating a redo log, just that some very *specific* operations will generate *significantly less* redo than normal. Note that I said "significantly less redo," not "no redo." All operations will generate some redo—all data dictionary operations will be logged regardless of the logging mode. The amount of redo generated can be significantly less. For this example of the NOLOGGING clause, I ran the following in a database running in ARCHIVELOG mode:

```
ops$tkyte@ORA10G> select log_mode from v$database;

LOG_MODE
------------
ARCHIVELOG

ops$tkyte@ORA10G> @mystat "redo size"
ops$tkyte@ORA10G> set echo off

NAME              VALUE
---------- ----------
redo size      5846068

ops$tkyte@ORA10G> create table t
  2  as
  3  select * from all_objects;
Table created.

ops$tkyte@ORA10G> @mystat2
ops$tkyte@ORA10G> set echo off

NAME              V DIFF
---------- ---------- -- -------------
redo size    11454472        5,608,404
```

That CREATE TABLE generated about 5.5MB of redo information. We'll drop and re-create the table, in NOLOGGING mode this time:

```
ops$tkyte@ORA10G> drop table t;
Table dropped.

ops$tkyte@ORA10G> @mystat "redo size"
ops$tkyte@ORA10G> set echo off

NAME              VALUE
---------- ----------
redo size     11459508

ops$tkyte@ORA10G> create table t
  2  NOLOGGING
  3  as
  4  select * from all_objects;
Table created.
```

```
ops$tkyte@ORA10G> @mystat2
ops$tkyte@ORA10G> set echo off

NAME            V   DIFF
----------  ----------  ----------------
redo size    11540676          81,168
```

This time, there is only 80KB of redo generated.

As you can see, this makes a tremendous difference—5.5MB of redo versus 80KB. The 5.5MB is the actual table data itself; it was written directly to disk, with no redo log generated for it.

If you test this on a NOARCHIVELOG mode database, you will not see any differences. The CREATE TABLE will not be logged, with the exception of the data dictionary modifications, in a NOARCHIVELOG mode database. If you would like to see the difference on a NOARCHIVELOG mode database, you can replace the DROP TABLE and CREATE TABLE with DROP INDEX and CREATE INDEX on table T. These operations are logged by default, regardless of the mode in which the database is running. This example also points out a valuable tip: test your system in the mode it will be run in production, as the behavior may be different. Your production system will be running in ARCHIVELOG mode; if you perform lots of operations that generate redo in this mode, but not in NOARCHIVELOG mode, you'll want to discover this during testing, not during rollout to the users!

Of course, it is now obvious that you will do everything you can with NOLOGGING, right? In fact, the answer is a resounding *no*. You must use this mode very carefully, and only after discussing the issues with the person in charge of backup and recovery. Let's say you create this table and it is now part of your application (e.g., you used a CREATE TABLE AS SELECT NOLOGGING as part of an upgrade script). Your users modify this table over the course of the day. That night, the disk that the table is on fails. "No problem," the DBA says. "We are running in ARCHIVELOG mode, and we can perform media recovery." The problem is, however, that the initially created table, since it was not logged, is not recoverable from the archived redo log. This table is unrecoverable and this brings out the most important point about NOLOGGING operations: they must be coordinated with your DBA and the system as a whole. If you use them and others are not aware of that fact, you may compromise the ability of your DBA to recover your database fully after a media failure. They must be used judiciously and carefully.

The important things to note about NOLOGGING operations are as follows:

- Some amount of redo will be generated, as a matter of fact. This redo is to protect the data dictionary. There is no avoiding this at all. It could be of a significantly lesser amount than before, but there will be some.

- NOLOGGING does not prevent redo from being generated by all subsequent operations. In the preceding example, I did not create a table that is never logged. Only the single, individual operation of creating the table was not logged. All subsequent "normal" operations such as INSERTs, UPDATEs, and DELETEs will be logged. Other special operations, such as a direct path load using SQL*Loader, or a direct path insert using the INSERT /*+ APPEND */ syntax, will not be logged (unless and until you ALTER the table and enable full logging again). In general, however, the operations your application performs against this table *will be logged*.

- After performing NOLOGGING operations in an ARCHIVELOG mode database, you must take a new baseline backup of the affected data files as soon as possible, in order to avoid losing subsequent changes to these objects due to media failure. We wouldn't actually lose the subsequent changes, as these are in the redo log; we would lose the data to apply the changes to.

Setting NOLOGGING on an Index

There are two ways to use the NOLOGGING option. You have already seen one method—that of embedding the NOLOGGING keyword in the SQL command. The other method, which involves setting the NOLOGGING attribute on the segment (index or table), allows operations to be performed implicitly in a NOLOGGING mode. For example, I can alter an index or table to be NOLOGGING by default. This means for the index that subsequent rebuilds of this index will not be logged (the index will not generate redo; other indexes and the table itself might, but this index will not):

```
ops$tkyte@ORA10G> create index t_idx on t(object_name);
Index created.

ops$tkyte@ORA10G> @mystat "redo size"
ops$tkyte@ORA10G> set echo off


NAME            VALUE
---------- ----------
redo size    13567908
```

```
ops$tkyte@ORA10G> alter index t_idx rebuild;
Index altered.

ops$tkyte@ORA10G> @mystat2
ops$tkyte@ORA10G> set echo off


NAME            V DIFF
---------- ---------- ----------------
redo size    15603436      2,035,528
```

When the index is in LOGGING mode (the default), a rebuild of it generated 2MB of redo log. However, we can alter the index:

```
ops$tkyte@ORA10G> alter index t_idx nologging;
Index altered.

ops$tkyte@ORA10G> @mystat "redo size"
ops$tkyte@ORA10G> set echo off


NAME            VALUE
---------- ----------
redo size    15605792
```

```
ops$tkyte@ORA10G> alter index t_idx rebuild;
Index altered.

ops$tkyte@ORA10G> @mystat2
ops$tkyte@ORA10G> set echo off

NAME                    V DIFF
----------  ----------  ----------------
redo size    15668084             62,292
```

and now it generates a mere 61KB of redo. But that index is "unprotected" now, if the data files it was located in failed and had to be restored from a backup, we would lose that index data. Understanding that fact is crucial. The index is not recoverable right now—we need a backup to take place. Alternatively, the DBA could just re-create the index as we can re-create the index directly from the table data as well.

NOLOGGING Wrap-Up

The operations that may be performed in a NOLOGGING mode are as follows:

- Index creations and ALTERs (rebuilds).

- Bulk INSERTs into a table using a "direct path insert" such as that available via the /*+ APPEND */ hint or SQL*Loader direct path loads. The table data will not generate redo, but all index modifications will (the indexes on this nonlogged table will generate redo!).

- LOB operations (updates to large objects do not have to be logged).

- Table creations via CREATE TABLE AS SELECT.

- Various ALTER TABLE operations such as MOVE and SPLIT.

Used appropriately on an ARCHIVELOG mode database, NOLOGGING can speed up many operations by dramatically reducing the amount of redo log generated. Suppose you have a table you need to move from one tablespace to another. You can schedule this operation to take place immediately before a backup occurs—you would ALTER the table to be NOLOGGING, move it, rebuild the indexes (without logging as well), and then ALTER the table back to logging mode. Now, an operation that might have taken X hours can happen in X/2 hours perhaps (I'm not promising a 50 percent reduction in runtime!). The appropriate use of this feature includes involvement of the DBA, or whoever is responsible for database backup and recovery or any standby databases. If that person is not aware of the use of this feature, and a media failure occurs, you may lose data, or the integrity of the standby database might be compromised. This is something to seriously consider.

Why Can't I Allocate a New Log?

I get this question all of the time. You are getting warning messages to this effect (this will be found in alert.log on your server):

```
Thread 1 cannot allocate new log, sequence 1466
Checkpoint not complete
  Current log# 3 seq# 1465 mem# 0: /home/ora10g/oradata/ora10g/redo03.log
```

It might say Archival required instead of Checkpoint not complete, but the effect is pretty much the same. This is really something the DBA should be looking out for. This message will be written to alert.log on the server whenever the database attempts to reuse an online redo log file and finds that it cannot. This will happen when DBWR has not yet finished checkpointing the data protected by the redo log or ARCH has not finished copying the redo log file to the archive destination. At this point in time, the database effectively *halts* as far as the end user is concerned. It stops cold. DBWR or ARCH will be given priority to flush the blocks to disk. Upon completion of the checkpoint or archival, everything goes back to normal. The reason the database suspends user activity is that there is simply no place to record the changes the users are making. Oracle is attempting to reuse an online redo log file, but because either the file would be needed to recover the database in the event of a failure (Checkpoint not complete), or the archiver has not yet finished copying it (Archival required), Oracle must wait (and the end users will wait) until the redo log file can safely be reused.

If you see that your sessions spend a lot of time waiting on a "log file switch," "log buffer space," or "log file switch checkpoint or archival incomplete," then you are most likely hitting this. You will notice it during prolonged periods of database modifications if your log files are sized incorrectly, or because DBWR and ARCH need to be tuned by the DBA or system administrator. I frequently see this issue with the "starter" database that has not been customized. The "starter" database typically sizes the redo logs far too small for any sizable amount of work (including the initial database build of the data dictionary itself). As soon as you start loading up the database, you will notice that the first 1,000 rows go fast, and then things start going in spurts: 1,000 go fast, then hang, then go fast, then hang, and so on. These are the indications you are hitting this condition.

There are a couple of things you can do to solve this issue:

- *Make DBWR faster*. Have your DBA tune DBWR by enabling ASYNC I/O, using DBWR I/O slaves, or using multiple DBWR processes. Look at the I/O on the system and see if one disk, or a set of disks, is "hot" so you need to therefore spread out the data. The same general advice applies for ARCH as well. The pros of this are that you get "something for nothing" here—increased performance without really changing any logic/structures/code. There really are no downsides to this approach.

- *Add more redo log files*. This will postpone the Checkpoint not complete in some cases and, after a while, it will postpone the Checkpoint not complete so long that it perhaps doesn't happen (because you gave DBWR enough breathing room to checkpoint). The same applies to the Archival required message. The benefit to this approach is the removal of the "pauses" in your system. The downside is it consumes more disk, but the benefit far outweighs any downside here.

- *Re-create the log files with a larger size.* This will extend the amount of time between the time you fill the online redo log and the time you need to reuse it. The same applies to the Archival required message, if the redo log file usage is "bursty." If you have a period of massive log generation (nightly loads, batch processes) followed by periods of relative calm, then having larger online redo logs can buy enough time for ARCH to catch up during the calm periods. The pros and cons are identical to the preceding approach of adding more files. Additionally, it may postpone a checkpoint from happening until later, since checkpoints happen at each log switch (at least), and the log switches will now be further apart.

- *Cause checkpointing to happen more frequently and more continuously.* Use a smaller block buffer cache (not entirely desirable) or various parameter settings such as FAST_START_MTTR_TARGET, LOG_CHECKPOINT_INTERVAL, and LOG_CHECKPOINT_TIMEOUT. This will force DBWR to flush dirty blocks more frequently. The benefit to this approach is that recovery time from a failure is reduced. There will always be less work in the online redo logs to be applied. The downside is that blocks may be written to disk more frequently if they are modified often. The buffer cache will not be as effective as it could be, and it can defeat the block cleanout mechanism discussed in the next section.

The approach you take will depend on your circumstances. This is something that must be fixed at the database level, taking the entire instance into consideration.

Block Cleanout

In this section, we'll discuss *block cleanouts*, or the removal of "locking"-related information on the database blocks we've modified. This concept is important to understand when we talk about the infamous ORA-01555: snapshot too old error in a subsequent section.

If you recall in Chapter 6, we talked about data locks and how they are managed. I described how they are actually attributes of the data, stored on the block header. A side effect of this is that the next time that block is accessed, we may have to "clean it out"—in other words, remove the transaction information. This action generates redo and causes the block to become *dirty* if it wasn't already, meaning that a simple SELECT *may generate redo* and may cause lots of blocks to be written to disk with the next checkpoint. Under most normal circumstances, however, this will not happen. If you have mostly small- to medium-sized transactions (OLTP), or you have a data warehouse that performs direct path loads or uses DBMS_STATS to analyze tables after load operations, then you'll find the blocks are generally "cleaned" for you. If you recall from the earlier section titled "What Does a COMMIT Do?" one of the steps of COMMIT-time processing is to revisit our blocks if they are still in the SGA, if they are accessible (no one else is modifying them), and then clean them out. This activity is known as a *commit cleanout* and is the activity that cleans out the transaction information on our modified block. Optimally, our COMMIT can clean out the blocks so that a subsequent SELECT (read) will not have to clean it out. Only an UPDATE of this block would truly clean out our residual transaction information, and since the UPDATE is already generating redo, the cleanout is not noticeable.

We can force a cleanout to *not* happen, and therefore observe its side effects, by understanding how the commit cleanout works. In a commit list associated with our transaction, Oracle will record lists of blocks we have modified. Each of these lists is 20 blocks long, and Oracle will allocate as many of these lists as it needs—up to a point. If the sum of the blocks we modify exceeds 10 percent of the block buffer cache size, Oracle will stop allocating new lists for us. For example, if our buffer cache is set to cache 3,000 blocks, Oracle will maintain a list of up to 300 blocks (10 percent of 3,000) for us. Upon COMMIT, Oracle will process each of these lists of 20 block pointers, and if the block is still available, it will perform a fast cleanout. So, as long as the number of blocks we modify does not exceed 10 percent of the number of blocks in the cache *and* our blocks are still in the cache and available to us, Oracle will clean them out upon COMMIT. Otherwise, it just skips them (i.e., does not clean them out).

Given this understanding, we can set up artificial conditions to see how the cleanout works. I set my DB_CACHE_SIZE to a low value of 4MB, which is sufficient to hold 512 8KB blocks (my blocksize is 8KB). Then, I created a table such that a row fits on exactly one block—I'll never have two rows per block. Then, I fill this table up with 500 rows and COMMIT. I'll measure the amount of redo I have generated so far, run a SELECT that will visit each block, and then measure the amount of redo that SELECT generated.

Surprising to many people, the SELECT will have generated redo. Not only that, but it will also have "dirtied" these modified blocks, causing DBWR to write them again. This is due to the block cleanout. Next, I'll run the SELECT once again and see that no redo is generated. This is expected, as the blocks are all "clean" at this point.

```
ops$tkyte@ORA10G> create table t
  2  ( x char(2000),
  3    y char(2000),
  4    z char(2000)
  5  )
  6  /
Table created.
ops$tkyte@ORA10G> set autotrace traceonly statistics
ops$tkyte@ORA10G> insert into t
  2  select 'x', 'y', 'z'
  3    from all_objects
  4   where rownum <= 500;
500 rows created.
Statistics
----------------------------------------------------------
...
   3297580  redo size
...
       500  rows processed
ops$tkyte@ORA10G> commit;
Commit complete.
```

So, this is my table with one row per block (in my 8KB blocksize database). Now I will measure the amount of redo generated during the read of the data:

```
ops$tkyte@ORA10G> select *
  2    from t;
500 rows selected.

Statistics
----------------------------------------------------------
```

```
...
      36484  redo size
...
       500  rows processed
```

So, this SELECT generated about 35KB of redo during its processing. This represents the block headers it modified during the full scan of T. DBWR will be writing these modified blocks back out to disk at some point in the future. Now, if I run the query again

```
ops$tkyte@ORA10G> select *
  2    from t;
500 rows selected.

Statistics
---------------------------------------------------------
...
         0  redo size
...
       500  rows processed

ops$tkyte@ORA10G> set autotrace off
```

I see that no redo is generated—the blocks are all clean.

If we were to rerun the preceding example with the buffer cache set to hold at least 5,000 blocks, we'll find that we generate little to no redo on any of the SELECTs—we will not have to clean dirty blocks during either of our SELECT statements. This is because the 500 blocks we modified fit comfortably into 10 percent of our buffer cache, and we are the only users. There is no one else mucking around with the data, and no one else is causing our data to be flushed to disk or accessing those blocks. In a live system, it will be normal for at least some of the blocks to not be cleaned out sometimes.

This behavior will most affect you after a large INSERT (as just demonstrated), UPDATE, or DELETE—one that affects many blocks in the database (anything more than 10 percent of the size of the cache will definitely do it). You will notice that the first query to touch the block after this will generate a little redo and dirty the block, possibly causing it to be rewritten if DBWR had already flushed it or the instance had been shut down, clearing out the buffer cache altogether. There is not too much you can do about it. It is normal and to be expected. If Oracle did not do this deferred cleanout of a block, a COMMIT could take as long to process as the transaction itself. The COMMIT would have to revisit each and every block, possibly reading them in from disk again (they could have been flushed).

If you are not aware of block cleanouts and how they work, it will be one of those mysterious things that just seems to happen for no reason. For example, say you UPDATE a lot of data and COMMIT. Now you run a query against that data to verify the results. The query appears to generate tons of write I/O and redo. It seems impossible if you are unaware of block cleanouts; it was to me the first time I saw it. You go and get someone to observe this behavior with you, but it is not reproducible, as the blocks are now "clean" on the second query. You simply write it off as one of those database mysteries.

In an OLTP system, you will probably never see this happening, since those systems are characterized by small, short transactions that affect a few blocks. By design, all or most of the transactions are short and sweet. Modify a couple of blocks and they all get cleaned out. In a warehouse where you make massive UPDATEs to the data after a load, block cleanouts may be a factor in your design. Some operations will create data on "clean" blocks. For example, CREATE TABLE AS SELECT, direct path loaded data, and direct path inserted data will all create "clean" blocks. An UPDATE, normal INSERT, or DELETE may create blocks that need to be cleaned with the first read. This could really affect you if your processing consists of

- Bulk loading lots of new data into the data warehouse

- Running UPDATEs on all of the data you just loaded (producing blocks that need to be cleaned out)

- Letting people query the data

You will have to realize that the first query to touch the data will incur some additional processing if the block needs to be cleaned. Realizing this, you yourself should "touch" the data after the UPDATE. You just loaded or modified a ton of data; you need to analyze it at the very least. Perhaps you need to run some reports yourself to validate the load. This will clean the block out and make it so the next query doesn't have to do this. Better yet, since you just bulk loaded the data, you now need to refresh the statistics anyway. Running the DBMS_STATS utility to gather statistics may well clean out all of the blocks, as it just uses SQL to query the information and would naturally clean out the blocks as it goes along.

Log Contention

This, like the cannot allocate new log message, is something the DBA must fix, typically in conjunction with the system administrator. However, it is something a developer might detect as well if the DBA isn't watching closely enough.

If you are faced with the log contention, what you might observe is a large wait time on the "log file sync" event and long write times evidenced in the "log file parallel write" event in a Statspack report. If you observe this, you may be experiencing contention on the redo logs; they are not being written fast enough. This can happen for many reasons. One application reason (one the DBA cannot fix, but the developer must fix) is that you are committing too frequently—committing inside of a loop doing INSERTs, for example. As demonstrated in the "What Does a Commit Do?" section, committing too frequently, aside from being a bad programming practice, is a surefire way to introduce lots of log file sync waits. Assuming all of your transactions are correctly sized (you are not committing more frequently than your business rules dictate), the most common causes for log file waits that I've seen are as follows:

- *Putting redo on a slow device*: The disks are just performing poorly. It is time to buy faster disks.

- *Putting redo on the same device as other files that are accessed frequently*: Redo is designed to be written with sequential writes and to be on dedicated devices. If other components of your system—even other Oracle components—are attempting to read and write to this device at the same time as LGWR, you will experience some degree of contention. Here, you want to ensure LGWR has exclusive access to these devices if at all possible.

- *Mounting the log devices in a buffered manner*: Here, you are using a "cooked" file system (not RAW disks). The operating system is buffering the data, and the database is also buffering the data (redo log buffer). Double buffering slows things down. If possible, mount the devices in a "direct" fashion. How to do this varies by operating system and device, but it is usually possible.

- *Putting redo on a slow technology, such as RAID-5*: RAID-5 is great for reads, but it is terrible for writes. As we saw earlier regarding what happens during a COMMIT, we must wait for LGWR to ensure the data is on disk. Using any technology that slows this down is not a good idea.

If at all possible, you really want at least five dedicated devices for logging and optimally six to mirror your archives as well. In these days of 9GB, 20GB, 36GB, 200GB, 300GB, and larger disks, this is getting harder, but if you can set aside four of the smallest, fastest disks you can find and one or two big ones, you can affect LGWR and ARCH in a positive fashion. To lay out the disks, you would break them into three groups (see Figure 9-5):

- *Redo log group 1*: Disks 1 and 3

- *Redo log group 2*: Disks 2 and 4

- *Archive*: Disk 5 and optionally disk 6 (the big disks)

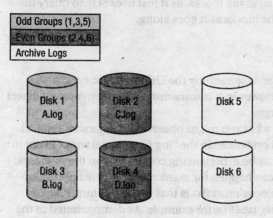

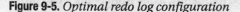

Figure 9-5. *Optimal redo log configuration*

You would place redo log group 1 with members A and B onto disk 1. You would place redo log group 2 with members C and D onto disk 2. If you have groups 3, 4, and so on, they'll go onto the odd and respectively even groups of disks. The effect of this is that LGWR, when the database is currently using group 1, will write to disks 1 and 3 simultaneously. When this group fills up, LGWR will move to disks 2 and 4. When they fill up, LGWR will go back to disks 1 and 3. Meanwhile, ARCH will be processing the full online redo logs and writing them to disks 5 and 6, the big disks. The net effect is neither ARCH nor LGWR is ever reading a disk being written to, or writing to a disk being read from, so there is no contention (see Figure 9-6).

So, when LGWR is writing group 1, ARCH is reading group 2 and writing to the archive disks. When LGWR is writing group 2, ARCH is reading group 1 and writing to the archive disks. In this fashion, LGWR and ARCH each have their own dedicated devices and will not be contending with anyone, not even each other.

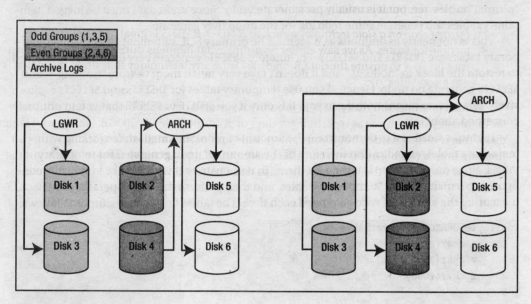

Figure 9-6. *Redo log flow*

Online redo log files are the one set of Oracle files that benefit the most from the use of RAW disks. If there is one type of file you might consider for RAW, log files would be it. There is much back and forth discussion on the pros and cons of using RAW versus cooked file systems. As this is not a book on DBA/SA tasks, I won't get into them. I'll just mention that if you are going to use RAW devices anywhere, online redo log files would be the best candidates. You never back up online redo log files, so the fact that they are on RAW partitions versus a cooked file system won't impact any backup scripts you might have. ARCH can always turn the RAW logs into cooked file system files (you cannot use a RAW device to archive to), hence the "mystique" of RAW devices is very much minimized in this case.

Temporary Tables and Redo/Undo

Temporary tables are still considered a relatively new feature of Oracle, having been introduced only in Oracle8*i* version 8.1.5. As such, there is some confusion surrounding them, in particular in the area of logging. In Chapter 10, we will cover how and why you might use temporary tables. In this section, we will explore only the question "How do temporary tables work with respect to logging of changes?"

Temporary tables generate no redo for their blocks. Therefore, an operation on a temporary table is not "recoverable." When you modify a block in a temporary table, no record of this change will be made in the redo log files. However, temporary tables do generate undo, and the undo is logged. Hence, temporary tables will generate some redo. At first glance, it doesn't seem to make total sense: why would they need to generate undo? This is because you can roll back to a SAVEPOINT within a transaction. You might erase the last 50 INSERTs into a temporary table, leaving the first 50. Temporary tables can have constraints and everything else a normal table can have. They might fail a statement on the five-hundredth row of a 500-row INSERT, necessitating a rollback of that statement. Since temporary tables behave in general just like "normal" tables, temporary tables must generate undo. Since undo data must be logged, temporary tables will generate some redo log for the undo they generate.

This is not nearly as ominous as it seems. The primary SQL statements used against temporary tables are INSERTs and SELECTs. Fortunately, INSERTs generate very little undo (you need to restore the block to "nothing," and it doesn't take very much room to store "nothing"), and SELECTs generate no undo. Hence, if you use temporary tables for INSERTs and SELECTs exclusively, this section means nothing to you. It is only if you UPDATE or DELETE that you might be concerned about this.

I set up a small test to demonstrate the amount of redo generated while working with temporary tables, an indication therefore of the amount of undo generated for temporary tables, since only the undo is logged for them. To demonstrate this, I will take identically configured "permanent" and "temporary" tables, and then perform the same operations on each, measuring the amount of redo generated each time. The tables I used were simply as follows:

```
ops$tkyte@ORA10G> create table perm
  2  ( x char(2000) ,
  3    y char(2000) ,
  4    z char(2000)  )
  5  /
Table created.

ops$tkyte@ORA10G> create global temporary table temp
  2  ( x char(2000) ,
  3    y char(2000) ,
  4    z char(2000)  )
  5  on commit preserve rows
  6  /
Table created.
```

I set up a small stored procedure to allow me to perform arbitrary SQL and report the amount of redo generated by that SQL. I will use this routine to perform INSERTs, UPDATEs, and DELETEs against both the temporary and permanent tables:

```
ops$tkyte@ORA10G> create or replace procedure do_sql( p_sql in varchar2 )
  2  as
  3      l_start_redo    number;
  4      l_redo          number;
  5  begin
  6      select v$mystat.value
  7        into l_start_redo
  8        from v$mystat, v$statname
  9       where v$mystat.statistic# = v$statname.statistic#
 10         and v$statname.name = 'redo size';
 11
 12      execute immediate p_sql;
```

```
13        commit;
14
15        select v$mystat.value-l_start_redo
16          into l_redo
17          from v$mystat, v$statname
18         where v$mystat.statistic# = v$statname.statistic#
19           and v$statname.name = 'redo size';
20
21        dbms_output.put_line
22        ( to_char(l_redo,'9,999,999') ||' bytes of redo generated for "' ||
23           substr( replace( p_sql, chr(10), ' '), 1, 25 ) || '"...' );
24   end;
25   /
Procedure created.
```

Then, I ran equivalent INSERTs, UPDATEs, and DELETEs against the PERM and TEMP tables:

```
ops$tkyte@ORA10G> set serveroutput on format wrapped
ops$tkyte@ORA10G> begin
  2        do_sql( 'insert into perm
  3                select 1,1,1
  4                  from all_objects
  5                 where rownum <= 500' );
  6
  7        do_sql( 'insert into temp
  8                select 1,1,1
  9                  from all_objects
 10                 where rownum <= 500' );
 11          dbms_output.new_line;
 12
 13      do_sql( 'update perm set x = 2' );
 14      do_sql( 'update temp set x = 2' );
 15          dbms_output.new_line;
 16
 17      do_sql( 'delete from perm' );
 18      do_sql( 'delete from temp' );
 19   end;
 20   /
3,297,752 bytes of redo generated for "insert into perm        "...
   66,488 bytes of redo generated for "insert into temp        "...

2,182,200 bytes of redo generated for "update perm set x = 2"...
1,100,252 bytes of redo generated for "update temp set x = 2"...

3,218,804 bytes of redo generated for "delete from perm"...
3,212,084 bytes of redo generated for "delete from temp"...

PL/SQL procedure successfully completed.
```

As you can see,

- The INSERT into the "real" table generated a lot of redo. Almost no redo was generated for the temporary table. This makes sense—there is very little undo data generated for INSERTs and only undo data is logged for temporary tables.

- The UPDATE of the real table generated about twice the amount of redo as the temporary table. Again, this makes sense. About half of that UPDATE, the "before image," had to be saved. The "after image" (redo) for the temporary table did not have to be saved.

- The DELETEs took about the same amount of redo space. This makes sense, as the undo for a DELETE is big, but the redo for the modified blocks is very small. Hence, a DELETE against a temporary table takes place very much in the same fashion as a DELETE against a permanent table.

■**Note** If you see the temporary table generating more redo than the permanent table with the INSERT statement, you are observing a product issue in the database that is fixed in at least Oracle 9.2.0.6 and 10.1.0.4 patch releases (the current shipping releases as of this writing).

Therefore, the following generalizations may be made regarding DML activity on temporary tables:

- An INSERT will generate little to no undo/redo activity.

- A DELETE will generate the same amount of redo as a normal table.

- An UPDATE of a temporary table will generate about half the redo of an UPDATE of a normal table.

There are notable exceptions to the last statement. For example, if I UPDATE a column that is entirely NULL with 2,000 bytes of data, there will be very little undo data generated. This UPDATE will behave like the INSERT. On the other hand, if I UPDATE a column with 2,000 bytes of data to be NULL, it will behave like the DELETE as far as redo generation is concerned. On average, you can expect an UPDATE against a temporary table to produce about 50 percent of the undo/redo you would experience with a real table.

In general, common sense prevails on the amount of redo created. If the operation you perform causes undo data to be created, then determine how easy or hard it will be to reverse (undo) the effect of your operation. If you INSERT 2,000 bytes, the reverse of this is easy. You simply go back to no bytes. If you DELETE 2,000 bytes, the reverse is INSERTing 2,000 bytes. In this case, the redo is substantial.

Armed with this knowledge, you will avoid deleting from temporary tables. You can use TRUNCATE (bearing in mind, of course, that TRUNCATE is DDL that will commit your transaction and, in Oracle9*i* and before, invalidate your cursors) or just let the temporary tables empty themselves automatically after a COMMIT or when your session terminated. All of these methods generate no undo and, therefore, no redo. You will try to avoid updating a temporary table unless you really have to for some reason. You will use temporary tables mostly as something to be INSERTed into and SELECTed from. In this fashion, you'll make optimum use of their unique ability to not generate redo.

Investigating Undo

We've already discussed a lot of undo segment topics. We've seen how they are used during recovery, how they interact with the redo logs, and how they are used for consistent, non-blocking reads of data. In this section, we'll look at the most frequently raised issues with undo segments.

The bulk of our time will be spent on the infamous ORA-01555: snapshot too old error, as this single issue causes more confusion than any other topic in the entire set of database topics. Before we do this, however, we'll investigate one other undo-related issue in the next section: the question of what type of DML operation generates the most and least undo (you might already be able to answer that yourself, given the preceding examples with temporary tables).

What Generates the Most and Least Undo?

This is a frequently asked but easily answered question. The presence of indexes (or the fact that a table is an index-organized table) may affect the amount of undo generated dramatically, as indexes are complex data structures and may generate copious amounts of undo information.

That said, an INSERT will, in general, generate the least amount of undo, since all Oracle needs to record for this is a rowid to "delete." An UPDATE is typically second in the race (in most cases). All that needs to be recorded are the changed bytes. It is most common that you UPDATE some small fraction of the entire row's data. Therefore, a small fraction of the row must be remembered in the undo. Many of the previous examples run counter to this rule of thumb, but that is because they update large, fixed-sized rows, and they update the entire row. It is much more common to UPDATE a row and change a small percentage of the total row. A DELETE will, in general, generate the most undo. For a DELETE, Oracle must record the entire row's before image into the undo segment. The previous temporary table example, with regard to redo generation, demonstrated that fact: the DELETE generated the most redo, and since the only logged element of the DML operation on a temporary table is the undo, we in fact observed that the DELETE generated the most undo. The INSERT generated very little undo that needed to be logged. The UPDATE generated an amount equal to the before image of the data that was changed, and the DELETE generated the entire set of data written into the undo segment.

As previously mentioned, you must also take into consideration the work performed on an index. You will find that an update of an unindexed column not only executes much faster, but will tend to generate significantly less undo than an update of an indexed column. For example, we'll create a table with two columns both containing the same information and index one of them:

```
ops$tkyte@ORA10G> create table t
  2  as
  3  select object_name unindexed,
  4         object_name indexed
  5    from all_objects
  6  /
Table created.
```

```
ops$tkyte@ORA10G> create index t_idx on t(indexed);
Index created.

ops$tkyte@ORA10G> exec dbms_stats.gather_table_stats(user,'T');
PL/SQL procedure successfully completed.
```

Now we'll update the table, first updating the unindexed column and then the indexed column. We'll need a new V$ query to measure the amount of undo we've generated in each case. The following query accomplishes this for us. It works by getting our session ID (SID) from V$MYSTAT, using that to find our record in the V$SESSION view, and retrieving the transaction address (TADDR). It uses the TADDR to pull up our V$TRANSACTION record (if any) and selects the USED_UBLK column—the number of used undo blocks. Since we currently are not in a transaction, the query is expected to return 0 rows right now:

```
ops$tkyte@ORA10G> select used_ublk
  2    from v$transaction
  3   where addr = (select taddr
  4                   from v$session
  5                  where sid = (select sid
  6                                 from v$mystat
  7                                where rownum = 1
  8                              )
  9                )
 10  /
no rows selected
```

This is the query I'll use after each UPDATE, but I won't repeat it in the text—I'll just show the results.

Now we are ready to perform the updates and measure the number of undo blocks used by each:

```
ops$tkyte@ORA10G> update t set unindexed = lower(unindexed);
48771 rows updated.

ops$tkyte@ORA10G> select used_ublk
...
 10  /

USED_UBLK
----------
       401

ops$tkyte@ORA10G> commit;
Commit complete.
```

That UPDATE used 401 blocks to store its undo. The commit would "free" that up, or release it, so if we rerun the query against V$TRANSACTION it would once again show us no rows selected. When we update the same data—only indexed this time—we'll observe the following:

```
ops$tkyte@ORA10G> update t set indexed = lower(indexed);
48771 rows updated. .

ops$tkyte@ORA10G> select used_ublk
...
 10  /

USED_UBLK
----------
      1938
```

As you can see, updating that indexed column in this example generated almost five times the undo. This is due to the inherit complexity of the index structure itself and the fact that we updated every single row in the table—moving every single index key value in this structure.

ORA-01555: snapshot too old Error

In the last chapter, we briefly investigated the ORA-01555 error and looked at one cause of it: committing too frequently. Here we are going to take a much more detailed look at the causes and solutions for the ORA-01555 error. ORA-01555 is one of those errors that confound people. It is the foundation for many myths, inaccuracies, and suppositions.

■**Note** ORA-01555 is not related to data corruption or data loss at all. It is a "safe" error in that regard; the only outcome is that the query that received this error is unable to continue processing.

The error is actually straightforward and has only two real causes, but since there is a special case of one of them that happens so frequently, I'll say that there are three:

- The undo segments are too small for the work you perform on your system.

- Your programs fetch across COMMITs (actually a variation on the preceding point). We covered this in the last chapter.

- Block cleanout.

The first two points are directly related to Oracle's read consistency model. As you recall from Chapter 7, the results of your query are *pre-ordained*, meaning they are well defined before Oracle goes to retrieve even the first row. Oracle provides this consistent point in time "snapshot" of the database by using the undo segments to roll back blocks that have changed since your query began. Every statement you execute, such as the following:

```
update t set x = 5 where x = 2;
insert into t select * from t where x = 2;
delete from t where x = 2;
select * from t where x = 2;
```

will see a read-consistent view of T and the set of rows where X=2, regardless of any other concurrent activity in the database.

■Note The four statements presented here are just examples of the types of statements that would see a read-consistent view of T. They were not meant to be run as a single transaction in the database, as the first update would cause the following three statements to see no records. They are purely illustrative.

All statements that "read" the table take advantage of this read consistency. In the example just shown, the UPDATE reads the table to find rows where x=2 (and then UPDATEs them). The INSERT reads the table to find where X=2, and then INSERTs them, and so on. It is this dual use of the undo segments, both to roll back failed transactions and to provide for read consistency, that results in the ORA-01555 error.

The third item in the previous list is a more insidious cause of ORA-01555, in that it can happen in a database where there is a single session, and this session is not modifying the tables that are being queried when the ORA-01555 error is raised! This doesn't seem possible—why would we need undo data for a table we can guarantee is not being modified? We'll find out shortly.

Before we take a look at all three cases with illustrations, I'd like to share with you the solutions to the ORA-1555 error, in general:

- Set the parameter UNDO_RETENTION properly (larger than the amount of time it takes to execute your longest running transaction). V$UNDOSTAT can be used to determine the duration of your long-running queries. Also, ensure sufficient space on disk has been set aside so the undo segments are allowed to grow to the size they need to be based on the requested UNDO_RETENTION.

- Increase or add more rollback segments when using manual undo management. This decreases the likelihood of undo data being overwritten during the course of your long-running query. This method goes toward solving all three of the previous points.

- Reduce the runtime of your query (tune it). This is always a good thing if possible, so it might be the first thing you try. This will reduce the need for larger undo segments. This method goes toward solving all three of the previous points.

- Gather statistics on related objects. This will help avoid the third point listed earlier. Since the block cleanout is the result of a very large mass UPDATE or INSERT, this needs to be done anyway after a mass UPDATE or large load.

We'll come back to these solutions, as they are important facts to know. It seemed appropriate to display them prominently before we begin.

Undo Segments Are in Fact Too Small

The scenario is this: you have a system where the transactions are small. As a result of this, you need very little undo segment space allocated. Say, for example, the following is true:

- Each transaction generates 8KB of undo on average.

- You do five of these transactions per second on average (40KB of undo per second, 2,400KB per minute).

- You have a transaction that generates 1MB of undo that occurs once per minute on average. In total, you generate about 3.5MB of undo per minute.

- You have 15MB of undo configured for the system.

That is more than sufficient undo for this database when processing transactions. The undo segments will wrap around and reuse space about every three to four minutes or so, on average. If you were to size undo segments based on your transactions that do modifications, you did all right.

In this same environment, however, you have some reporting needs. Some of these queries take a really long time to run—five minutes, perhaps. Here is where the problem comes in. If these queries take five minutes to execute *and* they need a view of the data as it existed when the query began, you have a very good probability of the ORA-01555 error occurring. Since your undo segments will wrap during this query execution, you know that some undo information generated since your query began is gone—it has been overwritten. If you hit a block that was modified near the time you started your query, the undo information for this block will be missing, and you will receive the ORA-01555 error.

Here is a small example. Let's say we have a table with blocks 1, 2, 3, . . . 1,000,000 in it. Table 9-4 shows a sequence of events that could occur.

Table 9-4. *Long-Running Query Timeline*

Time (Minutes:Seconds)	Action
0:00	Our query begins.
0:01	Another session UPDATEs block 1,000,000. Undo information for this is recorded into some undo segment.
0:01	This UPDATE session COMMITs. The undo data it generated is still there, but is now subject to being overwritten if we need the space.
1:00	Our query is still chugging along. It is at block 200,000.
1:01	Lots of activity going on. We have generated a little over 14MB of undo by now.
3:00	Our query is still going strong. We are at block 600,000 or so by now.
4:00	Our undo segments start to wrap around and reuse the space that was active when our query began at time 0:00. Specifically, we have just reused the undo segment space that the UPDATE to block 1,000,000 used back at time 0:01.
5:00	Our query finally gets to block 1,000,000. It finds it has been modified since the query began. It goes to the undo segment and attempts to find the undo for that block to get a consistent read on it. At this point, it discovers the information it needs no longer exists. ORA-01555 is raised and the query fails.

This is all it takes. If your undo segments are sized such that they have a good chance of being reused during the execution of your queries, and your queries access data that will probably be modified, you stand a very good chance of hitting the ORA-01555 error on a recurring basis. It is at this point you must set your UNDO_RETENTION parameter higher and let Oracle take care of figuring out how much undo to retain (that is the suggested approach; it is much easier than trying to figure out the perfect undo size yourself) or resize your undo segments and make them larger (or have more of them). You need enough undo configured to last as long as your long-running queries. The system was sized for the transactions that modify data—and you forgot to size for the other components of the system.

With Oracle9i and above, there are two methods to manage undo in the system:

- *Automatic undo management*: Here, Oracle is told how long to retain undo for, via the UNDO_RETENTION parameter. Oracle will determine how many undo segments to create based on concurrent workload and how big each should be. The database can even reallocate extents between individual undo segments at runtime to meet the UNDO_RETENTION goal set by the DBA. This is the recommended approach for undo management.

- *Manual undo management*: Here, the DBA does the work. The DBA determines how many undo segments to manually create, based on the estimated or observed workload. The DBA determines how big the segments should be based on transaction volume (how much undo is generated) and the length of the long-running queries.

Under manual undo management, where a DBA figures out how many undo segments to have and how big each should be, is where one of the points of confusion comes into play. People will say, "Well, we have XMB of undo configured, but they can grow. We have MAXEXTENTS set at 500 and each extent is 1MB, so the undo can get quite large." The problem is that the manually managed undo segments will never grow due to a query; they will grow only due to INSERTs, UPDATEs, and DELETEs. The fact that a long-running query is executing does not cause Oracle to grow a manual rollback segment to retain the data in case it might need it. Only a long-running UPDATE transaction would do this. In the preceding example, even if the manual rollback segments had the potential to grow, they will not. What you need to do for this system is have manual rollback segments that are already big. You need to permanently allocate space to the rollback segments, not give them the opportunity to grow on their own.

The only solutions to this problem are to either make it so that the manual rollback segments are sized so they do not wrap but every six to ten minutes, or make it so your queries never take more than two to three minutes to execute. The first suggestion is based on the fact that you have queries that take five minutes to execute. In this case, the DBA needs to make the amount of permanently allocated undo two to three times larger. The second (perfectly valid) suggestion is equally appropriate. Any time you can make the queries go faster, you should. If the undo generated since the time your query began is never overwritten, you will avoid ORA-01555.

Under automatic undo management, things are much easier from the ORA-01555 perspective. Rather than having to figure out how big the undo space needs to be and pre-allocating it, the DBA tells the database how long the longest-running query is and sets that value in the UNDO_RETENTION parameter. Oracle will attempt to preserve undo for at least that duration of time. If sufficient space to grow has been allocated, Oracle will extend an undo segment and not wrap around—in trying to obey the UNDO_RETENTION period. This is in direct contrast to manually managed undo, which will wrap around and reuse undo space as soon as it can. It is primarily for this reason, the support of the UNDO_RETENTION parameter, that I highly recommend *automatic undo management* whenever possible. That single parameter reduces the possibility of an ORA-01555 error greatly (when it is set appropriately!).

When using manual undo management, it is also important to remember that the probability of an ORA-01555 error is dictated by the *smallest* rollback segment in your system, not the largest and not the average. Adding one "big" rollback segment will not make this problem go away. It only takes the smallest rollback segment to wrap around while a query is processing, and this query stands a chance of an ORA-01555 error. This is why I was a big fan of equi-sized rollback segments when using the legacy rollback segments. In this fashion, each rollback segment is both the smallest and the largest. This is also why I avoid using "optimally" sized rollback segments. If you shrink a rollback segment that was forced to grow, you are throwing away a lot of undo that may be needed right after that. It discards the oldest rollback data when it does this, minimizing the risk, but still the risk is there. I prefer to manually shrink rollback segments during off-peak times if at all.

I am getting a little too deep into the DBA role at this point, so we'll be moving on to the next case. It's just important that you understand that the ORA-01555 error in this case is due to the system not being sized correctly for your workload. The only solution is to size correctly for your workload. It is not your fault, but it is your problem since you hit it. It is the same as if you run out of temporary space during a query. You either configure sufficient temporary space for the system, or you rewrite the queries so they use a plan that does not require temporary space.

To demonstrate this effect, we can set up a small, but somewhat artificial test. We'll create a very small undo tablespace with one session that will generate many small transactions, virtually assuring us that it will wrap around and reuse its allocated space many times—regardless of the UNDO_RETENTION setting, since we are not permitting the undo tablespace to grow. The session that uses this undo segment will be modifying a table, T. It will use a full scan of T and read it from "top" to "bottom." In another session, we will execute a query that will read the table T via an index. In this fashion, it will read the table somewhat randomly: it will read row 1, then row 1,000, then row 500, then row 20,001, and so on. In this way, we will tend to visit blocks very randomly and perhaps many times during the processing of our query. The odds of getting an ORA-01555 error in this case are virtually 100 percent. So, in one session we start with the following:

```
ops$tkyte@ORA10G> create undo tablespace undo_small
  2  datafile size 2m
  3  autoextend off
  4  /
Tablespace created.

ops$tkyte@ORA10G> alter system set undo_tablespace = undo_small;
System altered.
```

Now, we'll set up the table T used to query and modify. Note that we are ordering the data randomly in this table. The CREATE TABLE AS SELECT tends to put the rows in the blocks in the order it fetches them from the query. We'll just scramble the rows up so they are not artificially sorted in any order, randomizing their distribution:

```
ops$tkyte@ORA10G> create table t
  2  as
  3  select *
  4    from all_objects
  5   order by dbms_random.random;
Table created.

ops$tkyte@ORA10G> alter table t add constraint t_pk primary key(object_id)
  2  /
Table altered.

ops$tkyte@ORA10G> exec dbms_stats.gather_table_stats( user, 'T', cascade=> true );
PL/SQL procedure successfully completed.
```

And now we are ready to do our modifications:

```
ops$tkyte@ORA10G> begin
  2      for x in ( select rowid rid from t )
  3      loop
  4          update t set object_name = lower(object_name) where rowid = x.rid;
  5          commit;
  6      end loop;
  7  end;
  8  /
```

Now, while that is running, we run a query in another session. This query was reading this table T and processing each record. I spent about 1/100 of a second processing each record before fetching the next (simulated using DBMS_LOCK.SLEEP(0.01)). I used the FIRST_ROWS hint in the query to have it use the index we created to read the rows out of the table via the index sorted by OBJECT_ID. Since the data was randomly inserted into the table, we would tend to query blocks in the table rather randomly. This block ran for only a couple of seconds before failing:

```
ops$tkyte@ORA10G> declare
  2      cursor c is
  3      select /*+ first_rows */ object_name
  4        from t
  5       order by object_id;
  6
  7      l_object_name t.object_name%type;
  8      l_rowcnt      number := 0;
  9  begin
 10      open c;
 11      loop
 12          fetch c into l_object_name;
 13          exit when c%notfound;
 14          dbms_lock.sleep( 0.01 );
 15          l_rowcnt := l_rowcnt+1;
 16      end loop;
```

```
17       close c;
18   exception
19       when others then
20           dbms_output.put_line( 'rows fetched = ' || l_rowcnt );
21           raise;
22   end;
23   /
rows fetched = 253
declare
*
ERROR at line 1:
ORA-01555: snapshot too old: rollback segment number 23 with name "_SYSSMU23$"
too small
ORA-06512: at line 21
```

As you can see, it got to process only 253 records before failing with the ORA-01555: snapshot too old error. To correct this, we want to make sure two things are done:

- UNDO_RETENTION is set in the database to be at least long enough for this read process to complete. That will allow the database to grow the undo tablespace to hold sufficient undo for us to complete.

- The undo tablespace is allowed to grow or you manually allocate more disk space to it.

For this example, I have determined my long-running process takes about 600 seconds to complete. My UNDO_RETENTION is set to 900 (this is in seconds, so the undo retention is about 15 minutes). I altered the undo tablespace's data file to permit it to grow by 1MB at a time, up to 2GB in size:

```
ops$tkyte@ORA10G> column file_name new_val F
ops$tkyte@ORA10G> select file_name
  2  from dba_data_files
  3  where tablespace_name = 'UNDO_SMALL';

FILE_NAME
------------------------------
/home/ora10g/oradata/ora10g/OR
A10G/datafile/o1_mf_undo_sma_1
729wn1h_.dbf

ops$tkyte@ORA10G> alter database
  2  datafile '&F'
  3  autoextend on
  4  next 1m
  5  maxsize 2048m;
old   2: datafile '&F'
new   2: datafile '/home/ora10g/.../o1_mf_undo_sma_1729wn1h_.dbf'
Database altered.
```

When I ran the processes concurrently again, both ran to completion. The undo table-space's data file grew this time, because it was allowed to and the undo retention I set up said to:

```
ops$tkyte@ORA10G> select bytes/1024/1024
  2  from dba_data_files
  3  where tablespace_name = 'UNDO_SMALL';

BYTES/1024/1024
---------------
             11
```

So, instead of receiving an error, we completed successfully, and the undo grew to be large enough to accommodate our needs. It is true that in this example, getting the error was purely due to the fact that we read the table T via the index and performed random reads all over the table. If we had full scanned the table instead, there is a good chance we would not get the ORA-01555 *in this particular case*. This is because both the SELECT and UPDATE would have been full scanning T, and the SELECT could most likely race ahead of the UPDATE during its scan (the SELECT just has to read, but the UPDATE must read and update and therefore could go slower). By doing the random reads, we increase the probability that the SELECT will need to read a block, which the UPDATE modified and committed many rows ago. This just demonstrates the somewhat insidious nature of ORA-01555. Its occurrence depends on how concurrent sessions access and manipulate the underlying tables.

Delayed Block Cleanout

This cause of the ORA-01555 error is hard to eliminate entirely, but it is rare anyway, as the circumstances under which it occurs do not happen frequently (at least not in Oracle8*i* and above anymore). We have already discussed the block cleanout mechanism, but to summarize, it is the process whereby the next session to access a block after it has been modified may have to check to see if the transaction that last modified the block is still active. Once the process determines that the transaction is not active, it cleans out the block so that the next session to access it does not have to go through the same process again. To clean out the block, Oracle determines the undo segment used for the previous transaction (from the blocks header) and then determines if the undo header indicates whether it has been committed or not. This confirmation is accomplished in one of two ways. One way is that Oracle can determine that the transaction committed a long time ago, even though its transaction slot has been overwritten in the undo segment transaction table. The other way is that the COMMIT SCN is still in the transaction table of the undo segment, meaning the transaction committed a short time ago, and its transaction slot hasn't been overwritten.

To receive the ORA-01555 error from a delayed block cleanout, all of the following conditions must be met:

- A modification is made and COMMITed, and the blocks are not cleaned out automatically (e.g., it modified more blocks than can fit in 10 percent of the SGA block buffer cache).

- These blocks are not touched by another session and will not be touched until our unfortunate query (displayed shortly) hits it.

- A long-running query begins. This query will ultimately read some of those blocks from earlier. This query starts at SCN t1, the read consistent SCN it must roll back data to in order to achieve read consistency. The transaction entry for the modification transaction is still in the undo segment transaction table when we began.

- During the query, many commits are made in the system. These transactions do not touch the blocks in question (if they did, then we wouldn't have the impending problem).

- The transaction tables in the undo segments roll around and reuse slots due to the high degree of COMMITs. Most important, the transaction entry for the original modification transaction is cycled over and reused. In addition, the system has reused undo segment extents, so as to prevent a consistent read on the undo segment header block itself.

- Additionally, the lowest SCN recorded in the undo segment now exceeds t1 (it is higher than the read-consistent SCN of the query), due to the large number of commits.

When our query gets to the block that was modified and committed before it began, it is in trouble. Normally, it would go to the undo segment pointed to by the block and find the status of the transaction that modified it (in other words, it would find the COMMIT SCN of that transaction). If the COMMIT SCN is less than t1, our query can use this block. If the COMMIT SCN is greater than t1, our query must roll back that block. The problem is, however, that our query is unable to determine in this particular case if the COMMIT SCN of the block is greater than or less than t1. It is unsure as to whether it can use that block image or not. The ORA-01555 error then results.

To see this, we will create many blocks in a table that need to be cleaned out. We will then open a cursor on that table and allow many small transactions to take place against some other table—not the table we just updated and opened the cursor on. Finally, we will attempt to fetch the data for the cursor. Now, we *know* that the data required by the cursor will be "OK"—we should be able to see all of it since the modifications to the table would have taken place and been committed *before* we open the cursor. When we get an ORA-01555 error this time, it will be because of the previously described problem. To set up for this example, we'll use

- The 2MB UNDO_SMALL undo tablespace (again).

- A 4MB buffer cache, which is enough to hold about 500 blocks. This is so we can get some dirty blocks flushed to disk to observe this phenomenon.

Before we start, we'll create the big table we'll be querying:

```
ops$tkyte@ORA10G> create table big
  2  as
  3  select a.*, rpad('*',1000,'*') data
  4    from all_objects a;
Table created.

ops$tkyte@ORA10G> exec dbms_stats.gather_table_stats( user, 'BIG' );
PL/SQL procedure successfully completed.
```

That table will have lots of blocks as we get about six or seven rows per block using that big data field. Next, we'll create the small table that the many little transactions will modify:

```
ops$tkyte@ORA10G> create table small ( x int, y char(500) );
Table created.

ops$tkyte@ORA10G> insert into small select rownum, 'x' from all_users;
38 rows created.
ops$tkyte@ORA10G> commit;
Commit complete.

ops$tkyte@ORA10G> exec dbms_stats.gather_table_stats( user, 'SMALL' );
PL/SQL procedure successfully completed.
```

Now, we'll dirty up that big table. We have a very small undo tablespace, so we'll want to update as many blocks of this big table as possible, all while generating the least amount of undo possible. We'll be using a fancy UPDATE statement to do that. Basically, the following subquery is finding the "first" rowid of a row on every block. That subquery will return a rowid for each and every database block identifying a single row on it. We'll update that row, setting a VARCHAR2(1) field. This will let us update all of the blocks in the table (some 8,000 plus in the example), flooding the buffer cache with dirty blocks that will have to be written out (we have room for only 500 right now). We'll make sure we are using that small undo tablespace as well. To accomplish this and not exceed the capacity of our undo tablespace, we'll craft an UPDATE statement that will update just the "first row" on each block. The ROW_NUMBER() built-in analytic function is instrumental in this operation; it assigns the number 1 to the "first row" by database block in the table, which would be the single row on the block we would update:

```
ops$tkyte@ORA10G> alter system set undo_tablespace = undo_small;
System altered.

ops$tkyte@ORA10G> update big
  2      set temporary = temporary
  3    where rowid in
  4    (
  5    select r
  6      from (
  7    select rowid r, row_number() over
             (partition by dbms_rowid.rowid_block_number(rowid) order by rowid) rn
  8       from big
  9          )
 10     where rn = 1
 11    )
 12   /
8045 rows updated.

ops$tkyte@ORA10G> commit;
Commit complete.
```

OK, so now we know that we have lots of dirty blocks on disk. We definitely wrote some of them out, but we just did not have the room to hold them all. Next, we opened a cursor, but did not yet fetch a single row. Remember, when we open the cursor, the result set is preordained, so even though Oracle did not actually process a row of data, the act of opening that result set fixed the point in time the results must be "as of." Now since we will be fetching the data we just updated and committed, and we know no one else is modifying the data, we should be able to retrieve the rows without needing any undo at all. But that is where the delayed block cleanout rears its head. The transaction that modified these blocks is so new that Oracle will be obliged to verify that it committed before we begin, and if we overwrite that information (also stored in the undo tablespace), the query will fail. So, here is the opening of the cursor:

```
ops$tkyte@ORA10G> variable x refcursor
ops$tkyte@ORA10G> exec open :x for select * from big;
PL/SQL procedure successfully completed.

ops$tkyte@ORA10G> !./run.sh
```

run.sh is a shell script. It simply fired off nine SQL*Plus sessions using a command:

```
$ORACLE_HOME/bin/sqlplus / @test2 1 &
```

where each SQL*Plus session was passed a different number (that was number 1; there was a 2, 3, and so on). The script test2.sql they each ran is as follows:

```
begin
    for i in 1 .. 1000
    loop
        update small set y = i where x= &1;
        commit;
    end loop;
end;
/
exit
```

So, we had nine sessions inside of a tight loop initiate many transactions. The run.sh script waited for the nine SQL*Plus sessions to complete their work, and then we returned to our session, the one with the open cursor. Upon attempting to print it out, we observe the following:

```
ops$tkyte@ORA10G> print x
ERROR:
ORA-01555: snapshot too old: rollback segment number 23 with name "_SYSSMU23$"
too small
no rows selected
```

As I said, the preceding is a rare case. It took a lot of conditions, all of which must exist simultaneously to occur. We needed blocks that were in need of a cleanout to exist, and these blocks are rare in Oracle8i and above. A DBMS_STATS call to collect statistics gets rid of them so the most common causes—large mass updates and bulk loads—should not be a concern, since the tables need to be analyzed after such operations anyway. Most transactions tend to touch less then 10 percent of the block buffer cache; hence, they do not generate blocks that need to be cleaned out. In the event that you believe you've encountered this issue, in which a SELECT against a table that has no other DML applied to it is raising ORA-01555, try the following solutions:

- Ensure you are using "right-sized" transactions in the first place. Make sure you are not committing more frequently than you should.

- Use DBMS_STATS to scan the related objects, cleaning them out after the load. Since the block cleanout is the result of a very large mass UPDATE or INSERT, this needs to be done anyway.

- Allow the undo tablespace to grow by giving it the room to extend and increasing the undo retention. This decreases the likelihood of an undo segment transaction table slot being overwritten during the course of your long-running query. This is the same as the solution for the other cause of an ORA-01555 error (the two are very much related; you are experiencing undo segment reuse during the processing of your query). In fact, I reran the preceding example with the undo tablespace set to autoextend 1MB at a time, with an undo retention of 900 seconds. The query against the table BIG completed successfully.

- Reduce the runtime of your query (tune it). This is always a good thing if possible, so it might be the first thing you try.

Summary

In this chapter, we took a look at redo and undo, and what they mean to the developer. I've mostly presented here things for you to be on the lookout for, since it is actually the DBAs or SAs who must correct these issues. The most important things to take away from this chapter are the significance of redo and undo, and the fact that they are not overhead—they are integral components of the database, and are necessary and mandatory. Once you have a good understanding of how they work and what they do, you'll be able to make better use of them. Understanding that you are not "saving" anything by committing more frequently than you should (you are actually wasting resources, as it takes more CPU, more disk, and more programming) is probably the most important point. Understand what the database needs to do, and then let the database do it.

CHAPTER 10

■ ■ ■

Database Tables

In this chapter, we will discuss the various types of database tables and cover when you might want to use each type (i.e., when one type of table is more appropriate than another). We will concentrate on the physical storage characteristics of the tables: how the data is organized and stored.

Once upon a time, there was only one type of table, really: a "normal" table. It was managed in the same way a "heap of stuff" is managed (the definition of which appears in the next section). Over time, Oracle added more sophisticated types of tables. Now, in addition to the heap organized table, there are clustered tables (three types of those), index organized tables, nested tables, temporary tables, and object tables. Each table type has different characteristics that make it suitable for use in different application areas.

Types of Tables

We will define each type of table before getting into the details. There are nine major table types in Oracle:

- *Heap organized tables*: These are "normal," standard database tables. Data is managed in a heap-like fashion. As data is added, the first free space found in the segment that can fit the data will be used. As data is removed from the table, it allows space to become available for reuse by subsequent INSERTs and UPDATEs. This is the origin of the name "heap" as it refers to this type of table. A *heap* is a bunch of space, and it is used in a somewhat random fashion.

- *Index organized tables*: These tables are stored in an index structure. This imposes physical order on the rows themselves. Whereas in a heap the data is stuffed wherever it might fit, in index organized tables (IOTs) the data is stored in sorted order, according to the primary key.

- *Index clustered tables*: *Clusters* are groups of one or more tables, physically stored on the same database blocks, with all rows that share a common cluster key value being stored physically "near" each other. Two goals are achieved in this structure. First, many tables may be stored physically joined together. Normally, you would expect data from only one table to be found on a database block, but with clustered tables, data from many tables may be stored on the same block. Second, all data that contains the same cluster key value, such as DEPTNO=10, will be physically stored together. The data is "clustered" around the cluster key value. A cluster key is built using a B*Tree index.

- *Hash clustered tables*: These tables are similar to clustered tables, but instead of using a B*Tree index to locate the data by cluster key, the hash cluster hashes the key to the cluster to arrive at the database block the data should be on. In a hash cluster, the data is the index (metaphorically speaking). These tables are appropriate for data that is read frequently via an equality comparison on the key.

- *Sorted hash clustered tables*: This table type is new in Oracle 10*g* and combines some aspects of a hash clustered table with those of an IOT. The concept is as follows: you have some key value that rows will be hashed by (say, CUSTOMER_ID), and then a series of records related to that key that arrive in sorted order (timestamp-based records) and are processed in that sorted order. For example, a customer places orders in your order entry system, and these orders are retrieved and processed in a first in, first out (FIFO) manner. In such as system, a sorted hash cluster may be the right data structure for you.

- *Nested tables*: These are part of the object-relational extensions to Oracle. They are simply system-generated and -maintained child tables in a parent/child relationship. They work in much the same way as EMP and DEPT in the SCOTT schema. EMP is considered to be a child of the DEPT table, since the EMP table has a foreign key, DEPTNO, that points to DEPT. The main difference is that they are not "stand-alone" tables like EMP.

- *Temporary tables*: These tables store scratch data for the life of a transaction or the life of a session. These tables allocate temporary extents, as needed, from the current user's temporary tablespace. Each session will see only the extents that session allocates; it will never see any of the data created in any other session.

- *Object tables*: These tables are created based on an object type. They have special attributes not associated with non-object tables, such as a system-generated REF (object identifier) for each row. Object tables are really special cases of heap, index organized, and temporary tables, and they may include nested tables as part of their structure as well.

- *External tables*: These tables are not stored in the database itself; rather, they reside outside of the database in ordinary operating system files. External tables in Oracle9*i* and above give you the ability to query a file residing outside the database as if it were a normal table inside the database. They are most useful as a means of getting data into the database (they are a very powerful data-loading tool). Furthermore, in Oracle 10*g*, which introduces an external table unload capability, they provide an easy way to move data between Oracle databases without using database links. We will look at external tables in some detail in Chapter 15.

Here is some general information about tables, regardless of their type:

- A table can have up to 1,000 columns, although I recommend against a design that does contain the maximum number of columns, unless there is some pressing need. Tables are most efficient with far fewer than 1,000 columns. Oracle will internally store a row with more than 254 columns in separate row pieces that point to each other and must be reassembled to produce the entire row image.

- A table can have a virtually unlimited number of rows, although you will hit other limits that prevent this from happening. For example, typically a tablespace can have at most 1,022 files (although there are new BIGFILE tablespaces in Oracle 10*g* that will get you beyond these file size limits, too). Say you have 32GB files—that is to say, 32,704GB per tablespace. This would be 2,143,289,344 blocks, each of which is 16KB in size. You might be able to fit 160 rows of between 80 to 100 bytes per block. This would give you 342,926,295,040 rows. If you partition the table, though, you can easily multiply this number many times. For example, consider a table with 1,024 hash partitions—that would be 1024 × 342,926,295,040 rows. There are limits, but you'll hit other practical limitations before even coming close to these figures.

- A table can have as many indexes as there are permutations of columns (and permutations of functions on those columns). With the advent of function-based indexes, the true number of indexes you could create theoretically becomes infinite! Once again, however, practical restrictions will limit the actual number of indexes you will create and maintain.

- There is no limit to the number of tables you may have, even within a single database. Yet again, practical limits will keep this number within reasonable bounds. You will not have millions of tables (this many is impracticable to create and manage), but you may have thousands of tables.

In the next section, we'll look at some of the parameters and terminology relevant to tables. After that, we'll jump into a discussion of the basic heap-organized table, and then move on to examine the other types.

Terminology

In this section, we will cover the various storage parameters and terminology associated with tables. Not all parameters are used for every table type. For example, the PCTUSED parameter is not meaningful in the context of an IOT. We'll cover the relevant parameters as part of the discussion of each individual table type. The goal is to introduce the terms and define them. As appropriate, more information on using specific parameters is covered in subsequent sections.

Segment

A *segment* in Oracle is an object that consumes storage on disk. While there are many segment types, the most popular are as follows:

- *Cluster*: This segment type is capable of storing tables. There are two types of clusters: B*Tree and hash. Clusters are commonly used to store related data from multiple tables "prejoined" on the same database block and to store related information from a single table together. The term "cluster" refers to this segment's ability to cluster related information physically together.

- *Table*: A table segment holds data for a database table and is perhaps the most common segment type used in conjunction with an index segment.

- *Table partition or subpartition*: This segment type is used in partitioning and is very similar to a table segment. A table partition or subpartition segment holds just a slice of the data from a table. A partitioned table is made up of one or more table partition segments, and a composite partitioned table is made up of one or more table subpartition segments.

- *Index*: This segment type holds an index structure.

- *Index partition*: Similar to a table partition, this segment type contains some slice of an index. A partitioned index consists of one or more index partition segments.

- *Lob partition, lob subpartition, lobindex, and lobsegment*: The lobindex and lobsegment segments hold the structure of a *large object*, or *LOB*. When a table containing a LOB is partitioned, the lobsegment will be partitioned as well—the lob partition segment is used for that. It is interesting to note that there is not a lobindex partition segment type—for whatever reason, Oracle marks the partitioned lobindex as an index partition (one wonders why a lobindex is given a special name!).

- *Nested table*: This is the segment type assigned to nested tables, a special kind of "child" table in a master/detail relationship that we'll discuss later.

- *Rollback and Type2 undo*: This is where undo data is stored. Rollback segments are those manually created by the DBA. Type2 undo segments are automatically created and managed by Oracle.

So, for example, a table may be a segment. An index *may be* a segment. I stress the words "*may be*" because we can partition an index into separate segments. So, the index object itself would just be a definition, not a physical segment—and the index would be made up of many index partitions, and each *index partition* would be a segment. A table may be a segment or not. For the same reason, we might have many table segments due to partitioning, or we might create a table in a segment called a cluster. Here the table will reside, perhaps with other tables in the same cluster segment.

The most common case, however, is that a table will be a segment and an index will be a segment. That is the easiest way to think of it for now. When you create a table, you are normally creating a new table segment and, as discussed in Chapter 3, that segment consists of extents, and extents consist of blocks. That is the normal storage hierarchy. But it is important to note that only the "common" case has this one-to-one relationship. For example, consider this simple CREATE TABLE statement:

```
Create table t ( x int primary key, y clob, z blob );
```

This statement creates six segments. If you issue this CREATE TABLE statement in a schema that owns nothing, you'll observe the following:

```
ops$tkyte@ORA10G> select segment_name, segment_type
  2    from user_segments;
no rows selected

ops$tkyte@ORA10G> create table t ( x int primary key, y clob, z blob );
Table created.
```

```
ops$tkyte@ORA10G> select segment_name, segment_type
  2    from user_segments;

SEGMENT_NAME                      SEGMENT_TYPE
--------------------------------  --------------------
SYS_IL0000063631C00002$$          LOBINDEX
SYS_LOB0000063631C00003$$         LOBSEGMENT
SYS_C009783                       INDEX
SYS_IL0000063631C00003$$          LOBINDEX
SYS_LOB0000063631C00002$$         LOBSEGMENT
T                                 TABLE

6 rows selected.
```

The table itself created a segment in this example: the last row in the output. The primary key constraint created an index segment in this case in order to enforce uniqueness.

■**Note** A unique or primary key constraint may or may not create a new index. If there is an existing index on the constrained columns, and these columns are on the leading edge of the index, the constraint can and will use them.

Additionally, each of the LOB columns created two segments: one segment to store the actual chunks of data pointed to by the character large object (CLOB) or binary large object (BLOB) pointer, and one segment to "organize" them. LOBs provide support for very large chunks of information, up to many gigabytes in size. They are stored in chunks in the lobsegment, and the lobindex is used to keep track of where the LOB chunks are and the order in which they should be accessed.

Segment Space Management

Starting in Oracle9*i*, there are two methods for managing space in segments:

- *Manual Segment Space Management*: You set various parameters such as FREELISTS, FREELIST GROUPS, PCTUSED, and others to control how space is allocated, used, and reused in a segment over time. I will refer to this space management method in this chapter as *MSSM*, but bear in mind that that is a made-up abbreviation that you will not find in the Oracle documentation.

- *Automatic Segment Space Management (ASSM)*: You control one parameter relating to how space is used: PCTFREE. The others are accepted when the segment is created, but they are ignored.

MSSM is the legacy implementation in Oracle. It has been around for many years, over many versions. ASSM was first introduced in Oracle9*i* Release 1 and its design intention was to eliminate the need to fine-tune the myriad parameters used to control space allocation and provide high concurrency. For example, by having the FREELISTS parameter set to the default of 1, you might find that your insert/update-intensive segments may be suffering from contention on free space allocation. When Oracle goes to insert a row into a table, or update an index key entry, or update a row causing the row to migrate (more on that in a moment as well), it may need to get a block from the list of free blocks associated with the segment. If there is only one list, only one transaction at a time may review and modify this list—they would have to wait for each other. Multiple FREELISTS and FREELIST GROUPS serve the purpose of increasing concurrency in such a case, as the transactions may each be looking at different lists and not contending with each other.

When I discuss the storage settings shortly, I will mention which are for manual and which are for automatic segment space management, but in the area of storage/segment characteristics, the only storage settings that apply to ASSM segments are as follows:

- BUFFER_POOL

- PCTFREE

- INITRANS

- MAXTRANS (only in 9i; in 10g this is ignored for all segments)

The remaining storage and physical attribute parameters do not apply to ASSM segments.

Segment space management is an attribute inherited from the tablespace in which a segment is contained (and segments never span tablespaces). For a segment to use ASSM, it would have to reside in a tablespace that supported that method of space management.

High-Water Mark

This is a term used with table segments stored in the database. If you envision a table, for example, as a "flat" structure or as a series of blocks laid one after the other in a line from left to right, the *high-water mark* (*HWM*) would be the rightmost block that ever contained data, as illustrated in Figure 10-1.

Figure 10-1 shows that the HWM starts at the first block of a newly created table. As data is placed into the table over time and more blocks get used, the HWM rises. If we delete some (or even *all*) of the rows in the table, we might have many blocks that no longer contain data, but they are still *under* the HWM, and they will remain under the HWM until the object is rebuilt, truncated, or shrunk (shrinking of a segment is a new Oracle 10g feature that is supported only if the segment is in an ASSM tablespace).

The HWM is relevant since Oracle will scan all blocks under the HWM, even when they contain *no* data, during a full scan. This will impact the performance of a full scan—especially if most of the blocks under the HWM are empty. To see this, just create a table with 1,000,000 rows (or create any table with a large number of rows), and then execute a SELECT COUNT(*) from this table. Now, DELETE every row in it and you will find that the SELECT COUNT(*) takes just as long (or longer, if you need to clean out the block; refer to the "Block Cleanout" section of Chapter 9) to count *0* rows as it did to count 1,000,000. This is because Oracle is busy reading all of the blocks below the HWM to see if they contain data. You should compare this to what happens if you used TRUNCATE on the table instead of deleting each individual row. TRUNCATE will reset the HWM of a table back to "zero" and will truncate the associated indexes on the table as well. If you plan on deleting every row in a table, TRUNCATE—if it can be used— would be the method of choice for this reason.

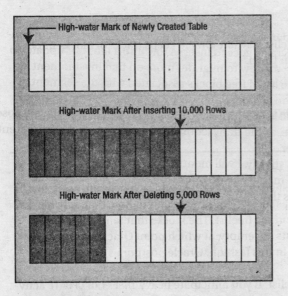

Figure 10-1. *HWM depiction*

In an MSSM tablespace, segments have a definite HWM. In an ASSM tablespace, however, there is an HWM *and* a low HWM (see Figure 10-2). In MSSM, when the HWM is advanced (e.g., as rows are inserted), all of the blocks are formatted and valid, and Oracle can read them safely. With ASSM, however, when the HWM is advanced, Oracle doesn't format *all of* the blocks immediately—they are only formatted and made safe to read upon their first use. So, when full scanning a segment, we have to know if the blocks to be read are "safe" or unformatted (meaning they contain nothing of interest and we do not process them). To make it so that not every block in the table need go through this safe/not safe check, Oracle maintains a low HWM and an HWM. Oracle will full scan the table up to the HWM—and for all of the blocks below the low HWM, it will just read and process them. For blocks between the low HWM and the HWM, it must be more careful and refer to the ASSM bitmap information used to manage these blocks to see which of them it should read and which it should just ignore.

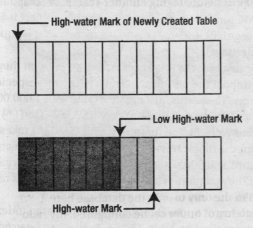

Figure 10-2. *Low HWM depiction*

FREELISTS

When you use an MSSM tablespace, the freelist is where Oracle keeps tracks of blocks under the HWM for objects that have free space on them.

Note Freelists and freelist groups do not pertain to ASSM tablespaces at all; only MSSM tablespaces use this technique.

Each object will have at least one freelist associated with it, and as blocks are used, they will be placed on or taken off of the freelist as needed. It is important to note that only blocks under the HWM of an object will be found on the freelist. The blocks that remain above the HWM will be used only when the freelists are empty, at which point Oracle advances the HWM and adds these blocks to the freelist. In this fashion, Oracle postpones increasing the HWM for an object until it has to.

An object may have more than one freelist. If you anticipate heavy INSERT or UPDATE activity on an object by many concurrent users, then configuring more than one freelist can have a major positive impact on performance (at the cost of possible additional storage). Having sufficient freelists for your needs is crucial.

FREELISTS can be a huge positive performance influence (or inhibitor) in an environment with many concurrent inserts and updates. An extremely simple test can show the benefits of setting FREELISTS correctly. Consider this relatively simple table:

```
ops$tkyte@ORA10GR1> create table t ( x int, y char(50) ) tablespace MSSM;
Table created.
```

Using five concurrent sessions, we start inserting into this table like wild. If we measure the systemwide wait events for block-related waits both before and after inserting, we will find large waits, especially on data blocks (trying to insert data). This is frequently caused by insufficient freelists on tables (and on indexes, but we'll cover that in detail in the next chapter). I used Statspack for this—I took a statspack.snap, executed a script that started the five concurrent SQL*Plus sessions, and waited for them to exit before taking another statspack.snap. The script these sessions ran was simply as follows:

```
begin
    for i in 1 .. 100000
    loop
        insert into t values ( i, 'x' );
    end loop;
    commit;
end;
/
exit;
```

Now, this is a very simple block of code, and I'm the only user in the database here. I should get the best possible performance. I have plenty of buffer cache configured, my redo logs are sized appropriately, indexes won't be slowing things down, and I'm running on a machine with two hyperthreaded Xeon CPUs—this should run fast. What I discovered afterward, however, is the following:

```
               Snap Id    Snap Time        Sessions Curs/Sess Comment
             ---------  ------------------  -------- --------- -------------------
Begin Snap:      793 29-Apr-05 13:45:36       15       3.9
  End Snap:      794 29-Apr-05 13:46:34       15       5.7
  Elapsed:               0.97 (mins)

Top 5 Timed Events
~~~~~~~~~~~~~~~~~~~
                                                             % Total
Event                                     Waits    Time (s) Call Time
-------------------------------------- ----------- --------- ---------
CPU time                                               165     53.19
buffer busy waits                         368,698        119     38.43
log file parallel write                     1,323         21      6.86
latch: cache buffers chains                   355          2       .67
enq: HW - contention                        2,828          1       .24
```

I collectively waited 119 seconds, or about 24 seconds per session, on buffer busy waits. These waits are caused entirely by the fact that there are not enough freelists configured on my table for the type of concurrent activity that is taking place. I can eliminate most of that wait time easily, just by creating the table with multiple freelists:

```
ops$tkyte@ORA10GR1> create table t ( x int, y char(50) )
  2  storage( freelists 5 ) tablespace MSSM;
Table created.
```

or by altering the object:

```
ops$tkyteORA10GR1> alter table t storage ( FREELISTS 5 );
Table altered.
```

You will find that the buffer busy waits goes way down, and the amount of CPU needed (since you are doing less work here; competing for a latched data structure can really burn CPU) also goes down along with the elapsed time:

```
               Snap Id    Snap Time        Sessions Curs/Sess Comment
             ---------  ------------------  -------- --------- -------------------
Begin Snap:      809 29-Apr-05 14:04:07       15       4.0
  End Snap:      810 29-Apr-05 14:04:41       14       6.0
  Elapsed:               0.57 (mins)

Top 5 Timed Events
~~~~~~~~~~~~~~~~~~~
                                                             % Total
Event                                     Waits    Time (s) Call Time
-------------------------------------- ----------- --------- ---------
CPU time                                               122     74.66
```

buffer busy waits	76,538	24	14.94
log file parallel write	722	14	8.45
latch: cache buffers chains	144	1	.63
enq: HW - contention	678	1	.46

What you want to do for a table is try to determine the maximum number of concurrent (truly concurrent) inserts or updates that will require more space. What I mean by "truly concurrent" is how often you expect two people at exactly the same instant to request a free block for that table. This is not a measure of overlapping transactions; it is a measure of how many sessions are doing inserts at the same time, regardless of transaction boundaries. You want to have about as many freelists as concurrent inserts into the table to increase concurrency.

You should just set freelists really high and then not worry about it, right? Wrong—of course, that would be too easy. When you use multiple freelists, there is a master freelist and process freelists. If a segment has a single freelist, then the master and process freelists are one and the same thing. If you have two freelists, you'll really have one master freelist and two process freelists. A given session will be assigned to a single process freelist based on a hash of its session ID. Now, each process freelist will have very few blocks on it—the remaining free blocks are on the master freelist. As a process freelist is used, it will pull a few blocks from the master freelist as needed. If the master freelist cannot satisfy the space requirement, then Oracle will advance the HWM and add empty blocks to the master freelist. So, over time, the master freelist will fan out its storage over the many process freelists (again, each of which has only a few blocks on it). So, each process will use a single process freelist. It will not go from process freelist to process freelist to find space. This means that if you have ten process freelists on a table, and the one your process is using exhausts the free buffers on its list, it will not go to another process freelist for space—even if the other nine process freelists have five blocks each (45 blocks in total), it will go to the master freelist. Assuming the master freelist cannot satisfy the request for a free block, it would cause the table to advance the HWM or, if the table's HWM cannot be advanced (all the space is used), to extend (to get another extent). It will then continue to use the space on its freelist only (which is no longer empty). There is a tradeoff to be made with multiple freelists. On one hand, use of multiple freelists is a huge performance booster. On the other hand, it will probably cause the table to use slightly more disk space than absolutely necessary. You will have to decide which is less bothersome in your environment.

Do not underestimate the usefulness of the FREELISTS parameter, especially since you can alter it up and down at will with Oracle 8.1.6 and later. What you might do is alter it to a large number to perform some load of data in parallel with the conventional path mode of SQL*Loader. You will achieve a high degree of concurrency for the load with minimum waits. After the load, you can reduce the value to some more reasonable, day-to-day number. The blocks on the many existing freelists will be merged into the one master freelist when you alter the space down.

Another way to solve the previously mentioned issue of buffer busy waits is to use an ASSM managed tablespace. If you take the preceding example and create the table T in an ASSM managed tablespace as follows:

```
ops$tkyte@ORA10GR1> create tablespace assm
  2  datafile size 1m autoextend on next 1m
  3  segment space management auto;
Tablespace created.

ops$tkyte@ORA10GR1> create table t ( x int, y char(50) ) tablespace ASSM;
Table created.
```

you'll find the buffer busy waits, CPU time, and elapsed time to have decreased for this case as well—without having to figure out the optimum number of required freelists:

	Snap Id	Snap Time	Sessions	Curs/Sess	Comment
Begin Snap:	812	29-Apr-05 14:12:37	15	3.9	
End Snap:	813	29-Apr-05 14:13:07	15	5.6	
Elapsed:		0.50 (mins)			

Top 5 Timed Events
~~~~~~~~~~~~~~~~~~~~

Event	Waits	Time (s)	% Total Call Time
CPU time		107	78.54
log file parallel write	705	12	9.13
buffer busy waits	12,485	12	8.52
latch: library cache	68	1	.70
LGWR wait for redo copy	3,794	1	.47

This is one of ASSM's main purposes: to remove the need to manually determine the correct settings for many key storage parameters.

PCTFREE and PCTUSED

In general, the PCTFREE parameter tells Oracle how much space should be reserved on a block for future updates. By default, this is 10 percent. If there is a higher percentage of free space than the value specified in PCTFREE, then the block is considered to be "free." PCTUSED tells Oracle the percentage of free space that needs to be present on a block that is not currently "free" in order for it to become free again. The default value is 40 percent.

As noted earlier, when used with a table (but not an IOT, as we'll see), PCTFREE tells Oracle how much space should be reserved on a block for future updates. This means if we use an 8KB blocksize, as soon as the addition of a new row onto a block causes the free space on the block to drop below about 800 bytes, Oracle will use another block from the FREELIST instead of the existing block. This 10 percent of the data space on the block is set aside for updates to the rows on that block.

> **■Note** PCTFREE and PCTUSED are implemented differently for different table types. Some table types employ both, whereas others only use PCTFREE, and even then only when the object is created. IOTs use PCTFREE upon creation to set aside space in the table for future updates, but do not use PCTFREE to decide when to stop inserting rows into a given block, for example.

The exact effect of these two parameters varies depending on whether you are using ASSM or MSSM tablespaces. When you are using MSSM, these parameter settings control when the block will be put on and taken off the freelist. If you are using the default values for PCTFREE (10) and PCTUSED (40), then a block will remain on the freelist until it is 90 percent full (10 percent free space). Once it hits 90 percent, it will be taken off the freelist and remain off the freelist until the free space on the block exceeds 60 percent of the block.

When you are using ASSM, PCTFREE still limits if a new row may be inserted into a block, but it does not control whether a block is on a freelist or not, as ASSM does not use freelists at all. In ASSM, PCTUSED is simply ignored.

There are three settings for PCTFREE: too high, too low, and just about right. If you set PCTFREE for blocks too high, you will waste space. If you set PCTFREE to 50 percent and you never update the data, you have just wasted 50 percent of every block. On another table, however, 50 percent may be very reasonable. If the rows start out small and tend to double in size, setting PCTFREE too small will cause row migration as you update the rows.

Row Migration

What exactly is row migration? *Row migration* is when a row is forced to leave the block it was created on because it grew too large to fit on that block with the rest of the rows. I'll illustrate a row migration in this section. We'll start with a block that looks like Figure 10-3.

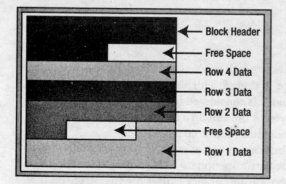

Figure 10-3. *Data block before update*

Approximately one-seventh of the block is free space. However, we would like to more than double the amount of space used by row 4 via an UPDATE (it currently consumes one-seventh of the block). In this case, even if Oracle coalesced the space on the block as shown in Figure 10-4, there is still insufficient room double the size of row 4 because the size of the free space is less than the current size of row 4.

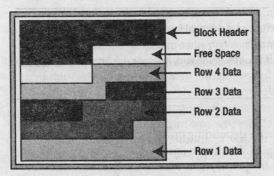

Figure 10-4. *Data block as it would appear after coalescing free space*

If the row fit into the coalesced space, then this would have happened. This time, however, Oracle will not perform this coalescing and the block will remain as it is. Since row 4 would have to span more than one block if it stayed on this block, Oracle will move, or migrate, the row. However, Oracle cannot just move the row—it must leave behind a "forwarding address." There may be indexes that physically point to this address for row 4. A simple update will not modify the indexes as well. (Note that there is a special case with partitioned tables that a rowid, the address of a row, will change. We will look at this case in Chapter 13.) Therefore, when Oracle migrates the row, it will leave behind a pointer to where the row really is. After the update, the blocks might look as shown in Figure 10-5.

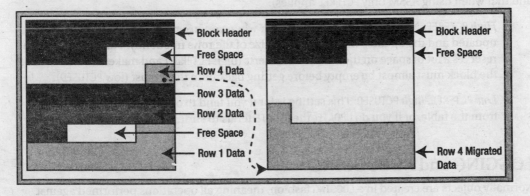

Figure 10-5. *Migrated row depiction*

So, a *migrated row* is a row that had to move from the block it was inserted into, onto some other block. Why is this an issue? Your application will never know; the SQL you use is no different. It only matters for performance reasons. If you go to read this row via an index, the index will point to the original block. That block will point to the new block. Instead of doing the two or so I/Os to read the index plus one I/O to read the table, you'll need to do yet one more I/O to get to the actual row data. In isolation, this is no big deal—you won't even notice it. However, when you have a sizable percentage of your rows in this state, with lots of users accessing them, you'll begin to notice this side effect. Access to this data will start to slow down (additional I/Os and the associated latching that goes with the I/O add to the access time), your buffer cache efficiency goes down (you need to buffer two blocks instead of just the one you would if the rows were not migrated), and your table grows in size and complexity. For these reasons, you do not want migrated rows.

It is interesting to note what Oracle will do if the row that was migrated from the block on the left to the block on the right, in Figure 10-5, has to migrate *again* at some future point in time. This would be due to other rows being added to the block it was migrated to and then updating this row to make it even larger. Oracle will actually migrate the row *back* to the original block and, if there is sufficient space, leave it there (the row might become "unmigrated"). If there isn't sufficient space, Oracle will migrate the row to another block altogether and change the forwarding address on the *original* block. As such, row migrations will always involve one level of indirection.

So, now we are back to PCTFREE and what it is used for: it is the setting that will help you to minimize row chaining when set properly.

Setting PCTFREE and PCTUSED Values

Setting PCTFREE and PCTUSED is an important—and greatly overlooked—topic. In summary, PCTUSED and PCTFREE are both *crucial* when using MSSM; with ASSM, only PCTFREE is. On one hand, you need to use them to avoid too many rows from migrating. On the other hand, you use them to avoid wasting too much space. You need to look at your objects and describe how they will be used, and then you can come up with a logical plan for setting these values. Rules of thumb may very well fail you on these settings; they really need to be set based on usage. You might consider the following (keeping in mind that "high" and "low" are *relative* terms, and that when using ASSM only PCTFREE applies):

- *High* PCTFREE, *low* PCTUSED: This setting is for when you insert lots of data that will be updated and the updates will increase the size of the rows frequently. This setting reserves a lot of space on the block after inserts (high PCTFREE) and makes it so that the block must almost be empty before getting back onto the freelist (low PCTUSED).

- *Low* PCTFREE, *high* PCTUSED: This setting is for if you tend to only ever INSERT or DELETE from the table, or if you do UPDATE, the UPDATE tends to shrink the row in size.

LOGGING and NOLOGGING

Normally objects are created in a LOGGING fashion, meaning all operations performed against them that can generate redo will generate it. NOLOGGING allows certain operations to be performed against that object without the generation of redo; we covered this in the last chapter in some detail. NOLOGGING affects only a few specific operations, such as the initial creation of the object, or direct path loads using SQL*Loader, or rebuilds (see the *Oracle SQL Reference* manual for the database object you are working with to see which operations apply).

This option does not disable redo log generation for the object in general—only for very specific operations. For example, if I create a table as SELECT NOLOGGING and then INSERT INTO THAT_TABLE VALUES (1), the INSERT will be logged, but the table creation might not have been (the DBA can force logging at the database or tablespace level).

INITRANS and MAXTRANS

Each block in a segment has a block header. Part of this block header is a transaction table. Entries will be made in the transaction table to describe which transactions have what rows/elements on the block locked. The initial size of this transaction table is specified by the INITRANS setting for the object. For tables, this defaults to 2 (indexes default to 2). This transaction table will grow dynamically as needed up to MAXTRANS entries in size (given sufficient free space on the block, that is). Each allocated transaction entry consumes 23 to 24 bytes of storage in the block header. Note that as of Oracle 10g, MAXTRANS is ignored—all segments have a MAXTRANS of 255.

Heap Organized Tables

A heap organized table is probably used 99 percent (or more) of the time in applications, although that might change over time with the advent of IOTs, since they can themselves be indexed. A heap organized table is the type of table you get by default when you issue the CREATE TABLE statement. If you want any other type of table structure, you need to specify that in the CREATE statement itself.

A *heap* is a classic data structure studied in computer science. It is basically a big area of space, disk, or memory (disk in the case of a database table, of course), which is managed in an apparently random fashion. Data will be placed where it fits best, rather than in any specific sort of order. Many people expect data to come back out of a table in the same order it was put into it, but with a heap, this is definitely not assured. In fact, rather the opposite is guaranteed: the rows will come out in a wholly unpredictable order. This is quite easy to demonstrate.

In this example, I will set up a table such that in my database I can fit one full row per block (I am using an 8KB blocksize). You do not need to have the case where you only have one row per block—I am just taking advantage of that to demonstrate a predictable sequence of events. The following sort of behavior (that rows have no order) will be observed on tables of all sizes, in databases with any blocksize:

```
ops$tkyte@ORA10GR1> create table t
  2  ( a int,
  3    b varchar2(4000) default rpad('*',4000,'*'),
  4    c varchar2(3000) default rpad('*',3000,'*')
  5  )
  6  /
Table created.

ops$tkyte@ORA10GR1> insert into t (a) values ( 1);
1 row created.

ops$tkyte@ORA10GR1> insert into t (a) values ( 2);
1 row created.

ops$tkyte@ORA10GR1> insert into t (a) values ( 3);
1 row created.
```

```
ops$tkyte@ORA10GR1> delete from t where a = 2 ;
1 row deleted.

ops$tkyte@ORA10GR1> insert into t (a) values ( 4);
1 row created.

ops$tkyte@ORA10GR1> select a from t;

         A
----------
         1
         4
         3
```

Adjust columns B and C to be appropriate for your blocksize if you would like to reproduce this. For example, if you have a 2KB blocksize, you do not need column C, and column B should be a VARCHAR2(1500) with a default of 1,500 asterisks. Since data is managed in a heap in a table like this, as space becomes available, it will be reused.

■**Note** When using ASSM or MSSM, you'll find rows end up in "different places." The underlying space management routines are very different, and the same operations executed against a table in ASSM and MSSM may well result in different physical order. The data will logically be the same, but it will be stored in different ways.

A full scan of the table will retrieve the data as it hits it, never in the order of insertion. This is a key concept to understand about database tables: in general, they are inherently unordered collections of data. You should also note that I do not need to use a DELETE in order to observe this effect; I could achieve the same results using *only* INSERTs. If I insert a small row, followed by a very large row that will not fit on the block with the small row, and then a small row again, I may very well observe that the rows come out by default in the order "small row, small row, large row." They will not be retrieved in the order of insertion. Oracle will place the data where it fits, not in any order by date or transaction.

If your query needs to retrieve data in order of insertion, you must add a column to the table that you can use to order the data when retrieving it. That column could be a number column, for example, maintained with an increasing sequence (using the Oracle SEQUENCE object). You could then approximate the insertion order using a SELECT that did an ORDER BY on this column. It will be an approximation because the row with sequence number 55 may very well have committed before the row with sequence 54, therefore it was officially "first" in the database.

You should think of a heap organized table as a big unordered collection of rows. These rows will come out in a seemingly random order, and depending on other options being used (parallel query, different optimizer modes, and so on), they may come out in a different order with the same query. Do not ever count on the order of rows from a query unless you have an ORDER BY statement on your query!

That aside, what is important to know about heap tables? Well, the CREATE TABLE syntax spans some 72 pages in the *Oracle SQL Reference* manual, so there are lots of options that go along with them. There are so many options that getting a hold on all of them is pretty difficult. The "wire diagrams" (or "train track" diagrams) alone take 18 pages to cover. One trick I use to see most of the options available to me in the CREATE TABLE statement for a given table is to create the table as simply as possible, for example:

```
ops$tkyte@ORA10GR1> create table t
  2  ( x int primary key,
  3    y date,
  4    z clob
  5  )
  6  /
Table created.
```

Then, using the standard supplied package DBMS_METADATA, I query the definition of it and see the verbose syntax:

```
ops$tkyte@ORA10GR1> select dbms_metadata.get_ddl( 'TABLE', 'T' ) from dual;

DBMS_METADATA.GET_DDL('TABLE','T')
--------------------------------------------------------------------------------

  CREATE TABLE "OPS$TKYTE"."T"
   (    "X" NUMBER(*,0),
        "Y" DATE,
        "Z" CLOB,
         PRIMARY KEY ("X")
  USING INDEX PCTFREE 10 INITRANS 2 MAXTRANS 255
  STORAGE(INITIAL 65536 NEXT 1048576 MINEXTENTS 1 MAXEXTENTS 2147483645
  PCTINCREASE 0 FREELISTS 1 FREELIST GROUPS 1 BUFFER_POOL DEFAULT)
  TABLESPACE "USERS"  ENABLE
   ) PCTFREE 10 PCTUSED 40 INITRANS 1 MAXTRANS 255 NOCOMPRESS LOGGING
  STORAGE(INITIAL 65536 NEXT 1048576 MINEXTENTS 1 MAXEXTENTS 2147483645
  PCTINCREASE 0 FREELISTS 1 FREELIST GROUPS 1 BUFFER_POOL DEFAULT)
  TABLESPACE "USERS"
 LOB ("Z") STORE AS (
  TABLESPACE "USERS" ENABLE STORAGE IN ROW CHUNK 8192 PCTVERSION 10
  NOCACHE
  STORAGE(INITIAL 65536 NEXT 1048576 MINEXTENTS 1 MAXEXTENTS 2147483645
  PCTINCREASE 0 FREELISTS 1 FREELIST GROUPS 1 BUFFER_POOL DEFAULT))
```

The nice thing about this trick is that it shows many of the options for my CREATE TABLE statement. I just have to pick data types and such, and Oracle will produce the verbose version for me. I can now customize this verbose version, perhaps changing the ENABLE STORAGE IN ROW to DISABLE STORAGE IN ROW, which would disable the storage of the LOB data in the row with the structured data, causing it to be stored in another segment. I use this trick all of the time to save the couple minutes of confusion I would otherwise have if I were trying to figure this all out from the huge wire diagrams. I can also use this technique to learn what options are available to me on the CREATE TABLE statement under different circumstances.

Now that you know how to see most of the options available to you on a given CREATE TABLE statement, which are the important ones you need to be aware of for *heap* tables? In my opinion, there are two with ASSM and four with MSSM:

- FREELISTS: MSSM only. Every table manages the blocks it has allocated in the heap on a freelist. A table may have more than one freelist. If you anticipate heavy insertion into a table by many concurrent users, configuring more than one freelist can have a major positive impact on performance (at the cost of possible additional storage). Refer to the previous discussion and example in the section "FREELISTS" for the sort of impact this setting can have on performance.

- PCTFREE: Both ASSM and MSSM. A measure of how full a block can be is made during the INSERT process. As shown earlier, this is used to control whether a row may be added to a block or not based on how full the block currently is. This option is also used to control row migrations caused by subsequent updates and needs to be set based on how you use the table.

- PCTUSED: MSSM only. A measure of how empty a block must become before it can be a candidate for insertion again. A block that has less than PCTUSED space used is a candidate for insertion of new rows. Again, like PCTFREE, you must consider how you will be using your table to set this option appropriately.

- INITRANS: Both ASSM and MSSM. The number of transaction slots initially allocated to a block. If set too low (it defaults to and has a minimum of 2), this option can cause concurrency issues in a block that is accessed by many users. If a database block is nearly full and the transaction list cannot be dynamically expanded, sessions will queue up waiting for this block, as each concurrent transaction needs a transaction slot. If you believe you will have many concurrent updates to the same blocks, you should consider increasing this value

---

■**Note** LOB data that is stored out of line in the LOB segment does not make use of the PCTFREE/PCTUSED parameters set for the table. These LOB blocks are managed differently: they are always filled to capacity and returned to the freelist only when completely empty.

These are the parameters you want to pay particularly close attention to. With the introduction of locally managed tablespaces, which are highly recommended, I find that the rest of the storage parameters (such as PCTINCREASE, NEXT, and so on) are simply not relevant anymore.

Index Organized Tables

Index organized tables (IOTs) are, quite simply, tables stored in an index structure. Whereas a table stored in a heap is unorganized (i.e., data goes wherever there is available space), data in an IOT is stored and sorted by primary key. IOTs behave just like "regular" tables do as far as your application is concerned; you use SQL to access them as normal. They are especially useful for information retrieval, spatial, and OLAP applications.

What is the point of an IOT? You might ask the converse, actually: what is the point of a heap organized table? Since all tables in a relational database are supposed to have a primary key anyway, isn't a heap organized table just a waste of space? We have to make room for both the table and the index on the primary key of the table when using a heap organized table. With an IOT, the space overhead of the primary key index is removed, as the index is the data and the data is the index. The fact is that an index is a complex data structure that requires a lot of work to manage and maintain, and the maintenance requirements increase as the width of the row to store increases. A heap, on the other hand, is trivial to manage by comparison. There are efficiencies in a heap organized table over an IOT. That said, IOTs have some definite advantages over their heap counterparts. For example, I remember once building an inverted list index on some textual data (this predated the introduction of interMedia and related technologies). I had a table full of documents, and I would parse the documents and find words within them. I had a table that then looked like this:

```
create table keywords
( word varchar2(50),
  position  int,
  doc_id int,
  primary key(word,position,doc_id)
);
```

Here I had a table that consisted solely of columns of the primary key. I had *over* 100 percent overhead; the size of my table and primary key index were comparable (actually, the primary key index was larger since it physically stored the rowid of the row it pointed to, whereas a rowid is not stored in the table—it is inferred). I only used this table with a WHERE clause on the WORD or WORD and POSITION columns. That is, I never used the table—I used only the index on the table. The table itself was no more than overhead. I wanted to find all documents containing a given word (or "near" another word, and so on). The heap table was useless, and it just slowed down the application during maintenance of the KEYWORDS table and doubled the storage requirements. This is a perfect application for an IOT.

Another implementation that begs for an IOT is a code lookup table. Here you might have ZIP_CODE to STATE lookup, for example. You can now do away with the heap table and just use an IOT itself. Anytime you have a table that you access via its primary key exclusively, it is a candidate for an IOT.

When you want to enforce co-location of data or you want data to be physically stored in a specific order, the IOT is the structure for you. For users of Sybase and SQL Server, this is where you would have used a clustered index, but IOTs go one better. A clustered index in those databases may have up to a 110 percent overhead (similar to the previous KEYWORDS table example). Here, we have a 0 percent overhead since the data is stored only once. A classic example of when you might want this physically co-located data would be in a parent/child relationship. Let's say the EMP table had a child table containing addresses. You might have a home address entered into the system when the employee is initially sent an offer letter for a job, and later he adds his work address. Over time, he moves and changes the home address to a previous address and adds a new home address. Then he has a school address he added when he went back for a degree, and so on. That is, the employee has three or four (or more) detail records, but these details arrive randomly over time. In a normal heap-based table, they just go "anywhere." The odds that two or more of the address records would be on the same database block in the heap table are very near zero. However, when you query an employee's information, you always pull the address detail records as well. The rows that arrive over time are always retrieved together. To make the retrieval more efficient, you can use an IOT for the child table to put all of the records for a given employee "near" each other upon insertion, so when you retrieve them over and over again, you do less work.

An example will easily show the effects of using an IOT to physically co-locate the child table information. Let's create and populate an EMP table:

```
ops$tkyte@ORA10GR1> create table emp
  2  as
  3  select object_id    empno,
  4         object_name  ename,
  5         created      hiredate,
  6         owner        job
  7    from all_objects
  8  /
Table created.

ops$tkyte@ORA10GR1> alter table emp add constraint emp_pk primary key(empno)
  2  /
Table altered.

ops$tkyte@ORA10GR1> begin
  2      dbms_stats.gather_table_stats( user, 'EMP', cascade=>true );
  3  end;
  4  /
PL/SQL procedure successfully completed.
```

Next, we'll implement the child table two times: once as a conventional heap table and again as an IOT:

```
ops$tkyte@ORA10GR1> create table heap_addresses
  2  ( empno     references emp(empno) on delete cascade,
  3    addr_type varchar2(10),
  4    street    varchar2(20),
  5    city      varchar2(20),
  6    state     varchar2(2),
  7    zip       number,
  8    primary key (empno,addr_type)
  9  )
 10  /
Table created.

ops$tkyte@ORA10GR1> create table iot_addresses
  2  ( empno     references emp(empno) on delete cascade,
  3    addr_type varchar2(10),
  4    street    varchar2(20),
  5    city      varchar2(20),
  6    state     varchar2(2),
```

```
 7    zip        number,
 8    primary key (empno,addr_type)
 9  )
10  ORGANIZATION INDEX
11  /
Table created.
```

I populated these tables by inserting into them a work address for each employee, then a home address, then a previous address, and finally a school address. A heap table would tend to place the data at "the end" of the table; as the data arrives, the heap table would simply add it to the end, due to the fact that the data is just arriving and no data is being deleted. Over time, if addresses are deleted the inserts would become more random throughout the table. But suffice it to say that the odds an employee's work address would be on the same block as his home address in the heap table is near zero. For the IOT, however, since the key is on EMPNO,ADDR_TYPE, we'll be pretty sure that all of the addresses for a given EMPNO are located on one or maybe two index blocks together. The inserts used to populate this data were

```
ops$tkyte@ORA10GR1> insert into heap_addresses
  2  select empno, 'WORK', '123 main street', 'Washington', 'DC', 20123
  3    from emp;
48250 rows created.

ops$tkyte@ORA10GR1> insert into iot_addresses
  2  select empno, 'WORK', '123 main street', 'Washington', 'DC', 20123
  3    from emp;
48250 rows created.
```

I did that three more times, changing WORK to HOME, PREV, and SCHOOL in turn. Then I gathered statistics:

```
ops$tkyte@ORA10GR1> exec dbms_stats.gather_table_stats( user, 'HEAP_ADDRESSES' );
PL/SQL procedure successfully completed.

ops$tkyte@ORA10GR1> exec dbms_stats.gather_table_stats( user, 'IOT_ADDRESSES' );
PL/SQL procedure successfully completed.
```

Now we are ready to see what measurable difference we could expect to see. Using AUTOTRACE, we'll get a feeling for the change:

```
ops$tkyte@ORA10GR1> set autotrace traceonly
ops$tkyte@ORA10GR1> select *
  2    from emp, heap_addresses
  3   where emp.empno = heap_addresses.empno
  4     and emp.empno = 42;


Execution Plan
----------------------------------------------------------
  0      SELECT STATEMENT Optimizer=ALL_ROWS (Cost=8 Card=4 Bytes=336)
  1    0   NESTED LOOPS (Cost=8 Card=4 Bytes=336)
```

```
2    1      TABLE ACCESS (BY INDEX ROWID) OF 'EMP' (TABLE) (Cost=2 Card=1...
3    2        INDEX (UNIQUE SCAN) OF 'EMP_PK' (INDEX (UNIQUE)) (Cost=1 Card=1)
4    1      TABLE ACCESS (BY INDEX ROWID) OF 'HEAP_ADDRESSES' (TABLE) (Cost=6...
5    4        INDEX (RANGE SCAN) OF 'SYS_C008078' (INDEX (UNIQUE)) (Cost=2 Card=4)

Statistics
----------------------------------------------------------
...
      11  consistent gets
...
       4  rows processed
```

That is a pretty common plan: go to the EMP table by primary key; get the row; then using that EMPNO, go to the address table; and using the index, pick up the child records. We did 11 I/Os to retrieve this data. Now running the same query, but using the IOT for the addresses

```
ops$tkyte@ORA10GR1> select *
  2     from emp, iot_addresses
  3   where emp.empno = iot_addresses.empno
  4      and emp.empno = 42;

Execution Plan
----------------------------------------------------------
   0      SELECT STATEMENT Optimizer=ALL_ROWS (Cost=4 Card=4 Bytes=336)
   1    0   NESTED LOOPS (Cost=4 Card=4 Bytes=336)
   2    1      TABLE ACCESS (BY INDEX ROWID) OF 'EMP' (TABLE) (Cost=2 Card=1...
   3    2        INDEX (UNIQUE SCAN) OF 'EMP_PK' (INDEX (UNIQUE)) (Cost=1 Card=1)
   4    1      INDEX (RANGE SCAN) OF 'SYS_IOT_TOP_59615' (INDEX (UNIQUE)) (Cost=2...

Statistics
----------------------------------------------------------
...
       7  consistent gets
...
       4  rows processed

ops$tkyte@ORA10GR1> set autotrace off
```

we did four fewer I/Os (the four should have been guessable); we skipped four TABLE ACCESS ➥ (BY INDEX ROWID) steps. The more child records we have, the more I/Os we would anticipate skipping.

So, what is four I/Os? Well, in this case it was over one-third of the I/O performed for the query, and if we execute this query repeatedly, that would add up. Each I/O and each consistent get requires an access to the buffer cache, and while it is true that reading data out of the buffer cache is faster than disk, it is also true that the buffer cache gets are *not free and not totally cheap*. Each will require many latches of the buffer cache, and latches are serialization devices that will inhibit our ability to scale. We can measure both the I/O reduction as well as latching reduction by running a PL/SQL block such as this:

```
ops$tkyte@ORA10GR1> begin
  2      for x in ( select empno from emp )
  3      loop
  4          for y in ( select emp.ename, a.street, a.city, a.state, a.zip
  5                       from emp, heap_addresses a
  6                      where emp.empno = a.empno
  7                        and emp.empno = x.empno )
  8          loop
  9              null;
 10          end loop;
 11      end loop;
 12  end;
 13  /
PL/SQL procedure successfully completed.
```

Here, we are just emulating a busy period and running the query some 45,000 times, once for each EMPNO. If we run that for the HEAP_ADRESSES and IOT_ADDRESSES tables, TKPROF shows us the following:

```
SELECT EMP.ENAME, A.STREET, A.CITY, A.STATE, A.ZIP
  FROM EMP, HEAP_ADDRESSES A
 WHERE EMP.EMPNO = A.EMPNO AND EMP.EMPNO = :B1
```

call	count	cpu	elapsed	disk	query	current	rows
Parse	1	0.00	0.00	0	0	0	0
Execute	48244	7.66	7.42	0	0	0	0
Fetch	48244	6.29	6.56	0	483393	0	192976
total	96489	13.95	13.98	0	483393	0	192976

```
Rows     Row Source Operation
-------  ---------------------------------------------------
 192976  NESTED LOOPS  (cr=483393 pr=0 pw=0 time=5730335 us)
  48244    TABLE ACCESS BY INDEX ROWID EMP (cr=144732 pr=0 pw=0 time=1594981 us)
  48244     INDEX UNIQUE SCAN EMP_PK (cr=96488 pr=0 pw=0 time=926147 us)...
 192976    TABLE ACCESS BY INDEX ROWID HEAP_ADDRESSES (cr=338661 pr=0 pw=0 time=...
 192976     INDEX RANGE SCAN SYS_C008073 (cr=145685 pr=0 pw=0 time=1105135 us)...
********************************************************************************
SELECT EMP.ENAME, A.STREET, A.CITY, A.STATE, A.ZIP
  FROM EMP, IOT_ADDRESSES A
 WHERE EMP.EMPNO = A.EMPNO AND EMP.EMPNO = :B1
```

call	count	cpu	elapsed	disk	query	current	rows
Parse	1	0.00	0.00	0	0	0	0
Execute	48244	8.17	8.81	0	0	0	0
Fetch	48244	4.31	4.12	0	292918	0	192976

```
-------  ------  --------  ----------  ----------  ----------  ----------  ----------
total    96489    12.48      12.93            0      292918            0      192976

Rows      Row Source Operation
-------   -----------------------------------------------
 192976   NESTED LOOPS  (cr=292918 pr=0 pw=0 time=3429753 us)
  48244    TABLE ACCESS BY INDEX ROWID EMP (cr=144732 pr=0 pw=0 time=1615024 us)
  48244     INDEX UNIQUE SCAN EMP_PK (cr=96488 pr=0 pw=0 time=930931 us)...
 192976     INDEX RANGE SCAN SYS_IOT_TOP_59607 (cr=148186 pr=0 pw=0 time=1417238 us)...
```

Both queries fetched exactly the same number of rows, but the HEAP table performed considerably more logical I/O. As the degree of concurrency on the system goes up, we would likewise expect the CPU used by the HEAP table to go up more rapidly as well, while the query possibly waits for latches into the buffer cache. Using runstats (a utility of my own design), we can measure the difference in latching. On my system, I observed the following:

```
STAT...consistent gets            484,065     293,566    -190,499
STAT...no work - consistent re    194,546       4,047    -190,499
STAT...consistent gets from ca    484,065     293,566    -190,499
STAT...session logical reads      484,787     294,275    -190,512
STAT...table fetch by rowid       241,260      48,260    -193,000
STAT...buffer is not pinned co    337,770      96,520    -241,250
LATCH.cache buffers chains        732,960     349,380    -383,580

Run1 latches total versus runs -- difference and pct
Run1         Run2        Diff       Pct
990,344      598,750     -391,594   165.40%
```

where Run1 was the HEAP_ADDRESSES table and Run2 was the IOT_ADDRESSES table. As you can see, there was a dramatic and repeatable decrease in the latching taking place, mostly due to the cache buffers chains latch (the one that protects the buffer cache). The IOT in this case would provide the following benefits:

- Increased buffer cache efficiency, as any given query needs to have fewer blocks in the cache

- Decreased buffer cache access, which increases scalability

- Less overall work to retrieve our data, as it is faster

- Less physical I/O per query possibly, as fewer distinct blocks are needed for any given query and a single physical I/O of the addresses most likely retrieves all of them (not just one of them, as the heap table implementation does)

The same would be true if you frequently use BETWEEN queries on a primary or unique key. Having the data stored physically sorted will increase the performance of those queries as well. For example, I maintain a table of stock quotes in my database. Every day, for hundreds of stocks, I gather together the stock ticker, date, closing price, days high, days low, volume, and other related information. The table looks like this:

```
ops$tkyte@ORA10GR1> create table stocks
  2  ( ticker       varchar2(10),
  3    day          date,
  4    value        number,
  5    change       number,
  6    high         number,
  7    low          number,
  8    vol          number,
  9    primary key(ticker,day)
 10  )
 11  organization index
 12  /
Table created.
```

I frequently look at one stock at a time for some range of days (e.g., computing a moving average). If I were to use a heap organized table, the probability of two rows for the stock ticker ORCL existing on the same database block are almost zero. This is because every night, I insert the records for the day for all of the stocks. That fills up at least one database block (actually, many of them). Therefore, every day I add a new ORCL record, but it is on a block different from every other ORCL record already in the table. If I query as follows:

```
Select * from stocks
 where ticker = 'ORCL'
   and day between sysdate-100 and sysdate;
```

Oracle would read the index and then perform table access by rowid to get the rest of the row data. Each of the 100 rows I retrieve would be on a different database block due to the way I load the table—each would probably be a physical I/O. Now consider that I have this same data in an IOT. That same query only needs to read the relevant index blocks, and it already has all of the data. Not only is the table access removed, but all of the rows for ORCL in a given range of dates are physically stored "near" each other as well. Less logical I/O and less physical I/O is incurred.

Now you understand when you might want to use IOTs and how to use them. What you need to understand next is what the options are with these tables. What are the caveats? The options are very similar to the options for a heap organized table. Once again, we'll use DBMS_METADATA to show us the details. Let's start with the three basic variations of the IOT:

```
ops$tkyte@ORA10GR1> create table t1
  2  ( x int primary key,
  3    y varchar2(25),
  4    z date
  5  )
  6  organization index;
Table created.

ops$tkyte@ORA10GR1> create table t2
  2  ( x int primary key,
  3    y varchar2(25),
  4    z date
```

```
  5  )
  6  organization index
  7  OVERFLOW;
Table created.

ops$tkyte@ORA10GR1> create table t3
  2  (  x int primary key,
  3     y varchar2(25),
  4     z date
  5  )
  6  organization index
  7  overflow INCLUDING y;
Table created.
```

We'll get into what OVERFLOW and INCLUDING do for us, but first let's look at the detailed SQL required for the first table:

```
ops$tkyte@ORA10GR1> select dbms_metadata.get_ddl( 'TABLE', 'T1' ) from dual;

DBMS_METADATA.GET_DDL('TABLE','T1')
-------------------------------------------------------------------------------

  CREATE TABLE "OPS$TKYTE"."T1"
   (    "X" NUMBER(*,0),
        "Y" VARCHAR2(25),
        "Z" DATE,
         PRIMARY KEY ("X") ENABLE
   )
ORGANIZATION INDEX
NOCOMPRESS
PCTFREE 10 INITRANS 2 MAXTRANS 255 LOGGING
STORAGE(INITIAL 65536 NEXT 1048576 MINEXTENTS 1 MAXEXTENTS 2147483645
        PCTINCREASE 0 FREELISTS 1 FREELIST GROUPS 1 BUFFER_POOL DEFAULT)
TABLESPACE "USERS"
PCTTHRESHOLD 50
```

This table introduces two new options, NOCOMPRESS and PCTTHRESHOLD, which we'll look at in a moment. You might have noticed that something is missing from the preceding CREATE ➥ TABLE syntax: there is no PCTUSED clause, but there is a PCTFREE. This is because an index is a complex data structure that isn't randomly organized like a heap, so data must go where it "belongs." Unlike in a heap, where blocks are sometimes available for inserts, blocks are always available for new entries in an index. If the data belongs on a given block because of its values, it will go there regardless of how full or empty the block is. Additionally, PCTFREE is used only when the object is created and populated with data in an index structure. It is not used like it is in the heap organized table. PCTFREE will reserve space on a newly created index, but not for subsequent operations on it, for much the same reason as PCTUSED is not used at all. The same considerations for freelists we had on heap organized tables apply in whole to IOTs.

Now, on to the newly discovered option NOCOMPRESS. This option is available to indexes in general. It tells Oracle to store each and every value in an index entry (i.e., do not compress). If the primary key of the object were on columns A, B, and C, every occurrence of A, B, and C would physically be stored. The converse to NOCOMPRESS is COMPRESS N, where N is an integer that represents the number of columns to compress. This removes repeating values and factors them out at the block level, so that the values of A and perhaps B that repeat over and over are no longer physically stored. Consider, for example, a table created like this:

```
ops$tkyte@ORA10GR1> create table iot
  2  ( owner, object_type, object_name,
  3    primary key(owner,object_type,object_name)
  4  )
  5  organization index
  6  NOCOMPRESS
  7  as
  8  select owner, object_type, object_name from all_objects
  9  /
Table created.
```

It you think about it, the value of OWNER is repeated many hundreds of times. Each schema (OWNER) tends to own lots of objects. Even the value pair of OWNER,OBJECT_TYPE repeats many times—a given schema will have dozens of tables, dozens of packages, and so on. Only all three columns together do not repeat. We can have Oracle suppress these repeating values. Instead of having an index block with the values shown in Table 10-1, we could use COMPRESS 2 (factor out the leading two columns) and have a block with the values shown in Table 10-2.

Table 10-1. *Index Leaf Block,* NOCOMPRESS

Sys,table,t1	Sys,table,t2	Sys,table,t3	Sys,table,t4
Sys,table,t5	Sys,table,t6	Sys,table,t7	Sys,table,t8
...	...	...	...
Sys,table,t100	Sys,table,t101	Sys,table,t102	Sys,table,t103

Table 10-2. *Index Leaf Block,* COMPRESS 2

Sys,table	t1	t2	t3
t4	t5	...	...
...	t103	t104	...
t300	t301	t302	t303

That is, the values SYS and TABLE appear once, and then the third column is stored. In this fashion, we can get many more entries per index block than we could otherwise. This does not decrease concurrency—we are still operating at the row level in all cases—or functionality at all. It *may* use slightly more CPU horsepower, as Oracle has to do more work to put together the keys again. On the other hand, it may significantly reduce I/O and allow more data to be cached in the buffer cache, since we get more data per block. That is a pretty good tradeoff.

Let's demonstrate the savings by doing a quick test of the preceding CREATE TABLE as SELECT with NOCOMPRESS, COMPRESS 1, and COMPRESS 2. We'll start by creating our IOT without compression:

```
ops$tkyte@ORA10GR1> create table iot
  2  ( owner, object_type, object_name,
  3    constraint iot_pk primary key(owner,object_type,object_name)
  4  )
  5  organization index
  6  NOCOMPRESS
  7  as
  8  select distinct owner, object_type, object_name
  9    from all_objects
 10  /
Table created.
```

Now we can measure the space used. We'll use the ANALYZE INDEX VALIDATE STRUCTURE command for this. This command populates a dynamic performance view named INDEX_STATS, which will contain only one row at most with the information from the last execution of that ANALYZE command:

```
ops$tkyte@ORA10GR1> analyze index iot_pk validate structure;
Index analyzed.

ops$tkyte@ORA10GR1> select lf_blks, br_blks, used_space,
  2         opt_cmpr_count, opt_cmpr_pctsave
  3    from index_stats;

   LF_BLKS    BR_BLKS USED_SPACE OPT_CMPR_COUNT OPT_CMPR_PCTSAVE
---------- ---------- ---------- -------------- ----------------
       284          3    2037248              2               33
```

So, that shows our index is currently using 284 leaf blocks (where our data is) and 3 branch blocks (blocks Oracle uses to navigate the index structure) to find the leaf blocks. The space used is about 2MB (2,038,248 bytes). The other two oddly named columns are trying to tell us something. The OPT_CMPR_COUNT (optimum compression count) column is trying to say, "If you made this index COMPRESS 2, you would achieve the best compression." The OPT_CMPR_PCTSAVE (optimum compression percentage saved) is telling us if we did the COMPRESS 2, we would save about one-third of the storage and the index would consume just two-thirds the disk space it is now.

■**Note** The next chapter covers the index structure in more detail.

To test that theory, we'll rebuild the IOT with COMPRESS 1 first:

```
ops$tkyte@ORA10GR1> alter table iot move compress 1;
Table altered.

ops$tkyte@ORA10GR1> analyze index iot_pk validate structure;
Index analyzed.

ops$tkyte@ORA10GR1> select lf_blks, br_blks, used_space,
  2          opt_cmpr_count, opt_cmpr_pctsave
  3     from index_stats;

   LF_BLKS    BR_BLKS USED_SPACE OPT_CMPR_COUNT OPT_CMPR_PCTSAVE
---------- ---------- ---------- -------------- ----------------
       247          1    1772767              2               23
```

As you can see, the index is in fact smaller: about 1.7MB, with fewer leaf blocks and many fewer branch blocks. But now it is saying, "You still can get another 23 percent off," as we didn't chop off that much yet. Let's rebuild with COMPRESS 2:

```
ops$tkyte@ORA10GR1> alter table iot move compress 2;
Table altered.

ops$tkyte@ORA10GR1> analyze index iot_pk validate structure;
Index analyzed.

ops$tkyte@ORA10GR1> select lf_blks, br_blks, used_space,
  2          opt_cmpr_count, opt_cmpr_pctsave
  3     from index_stats;

   LF_BLKS    BR_BLKS USED_SPACE OPT_CMPR_COUNT OPT_CMPR_PCTSAVE
---------- ---------- ---------- -------------- ----------------
       190          1    1359357              2                0
```

Now we are significantly reduced in size, both by the number of leaf blocks as well as overall used space, about 1.3MB. If we go back to the original numbers,

```
ops$tkyte@ORA10GR1> select (2/3) * 2037497 from dual;

(2/3)*2037497
-------------
   1358331.33
```

then we can see the OPT_CMPR_PCTSAVE was dead-on accurate. The preceding example points out an interesting fact with IOTs. They are tables, but only in name. Their segment is truly an index segment.

I am going to defer discussion of the PCTTHRESHOLD option at this point, as it is related to the next two options for IOTs: OVERFLOW and INCLUDING. If we look at the full SQL for the next two sets of tables, T2 and T3, we see the following (I've used a DBMS_METADATA routine to suppress the storage clauses, as they are not relevant to the example):

```
ops$tkyte@ORA10GR1> begin
  2     dbms_metadata.set_transform_param
  3     ( DBMS_METADATA.SESSION_TRANSFORM, 'STORAGE', false );
  4   end;
/

ops$tkyte@ORA10GR1> select dbms_metadata.get_ddl( 'TABLE', 'T2' ) from dual;

DBMS_METADATA.GET_DDL('TABLE','T2')
-------------------------------------------------------------------------------
  CREATE TABLE "OPS$TKYTE"."T2"
   (    "X" NUMBER(*,0),
        "Y" VARCHAR2(25),
        "Z" DATE,
         PRIMARY KEY ("X") ENABLE
   ) ORGANIZATION INDEX NOCOMPRESS PCTFREE 10 INITRANS 2 MAXTRANS 255 LOGGING
  TABLESPACE "USERS"
 PCTTHRESHOLD 50 OVERFLOW
 PCTFREE 10 PCTUSED 40 INITRANS 1 MAXTRANS 255 LOGGING
  TABLESPACE "USERS"

ops$tkyte@ORA10GR1> select dbms_metadata.get_ddl( 'TABLE', 'T3' ) from dual;

DBMS_METADATA.GET_DDL('TABLE','T3')
-------------------------------------------------------------------------------
  CREATE TABLE "OPS$TKYTE"."T3"
   (    "X" NUMBER(*,0),
        "Y" VARCHAR2(25),
        "Z" DATE,
         PRIMARY KEY ("X") ENABLE
   ) ORGANIZATION INDEX NOCOMPRESS PCTFREE 10 INITRANS 2 MAXTRANS 255 LOGGING
  TABLESPACE "USERS"
 PCTTHRESHOLD 50 INCLUDING "Y" OVERFLOW
 PCTFREE 10 PCTUSED 40 INITRANS 1 MAXTRANS 255 LOGGING
  TABLESPACE "USERS"
```

So, now we have PCTTHRESHOLD, OVERFLOW, and INCLUDING left to discuss. These three items are intertwined, and their goal is to make the index leaf blocks (the blocks that hold the actual index data) able to efficiently store data. An index typically is on a subset of columns. You will generally find many more times the number of row entries on an index block than you would on a heap table block. An index counts on being able to get many rows per block. Oracle would spend large amounts of time maintaining an index otherwise, as each INSERT or UPDATE would probably cause an index block to split in order to accommodate the new data.

The OVERFLOW clause allows you to set up another segment (making an IOT a multiseg-ment object, much like having a CLOB column does) where the row data for the IOT can overflow onto when it gets too large.

Note The columns making up the primary key cannot overflow—they must be placed on the leaf blocks directly.

Notice that an OVERFLOW reintroduces the PCTUSED clause to an IOT when using MSSM. PCTFREE and PCTUSED have the same meanings for an OVERFLOW segment as they did for a heap table. The conditions for using an overflow segment can be specified in one of two ways:

- PCTTHRESHOLD: When the amount of data in the row exceeds that percentage of the block, the trailing columns of that row will be stored in the overflow. So, if PCTTHRESHOLD was 10 percent and your blocksize was 8KB, any row that was greater than about 800 bytes in length would have part of it stored elsewhere, off the index block.

- INCLUDING: All of the columns in the row up to and including the one specified in the INCLUDING clause are stored on the index block, and the remaining columns are stored in the overflow.

Given the following table with a 2KB blocksize:

```
ops$tkyte@ORA10GR1> create table iot
  2  ( x    int,
  3    y    date,
  4    z    varchar2(2000),
  5    constraint iot_pk primary key (x)
  6  )
  7  organization index
  8  pctthreshold 10
  9  overflow
 10  /
Table created.
```

Graphically, it could look as shown in Figure 10-6.

The gray boxes are the index entries, part of a larger index structure (in Chapter 11, you'll see a larger picture of what an index looks like). Briefly, the index structure is a tree, and the leaf blocks (where the data is stored) are in effect a doubly linked list to make it easier to tra-verse the nodes in order once we've found where we want to start in the index. The white box represents an OVERFLOW segment. This is where data that exceeds our PCTTHRESHOLD setting will be stored. Oracle will work backward from the last column up to but not including the last col-umn of the primary key to find out what columns need to be stored in the overflow segment. In this example, the number column X and the date column Y will always fit in the index block. The last column, Z, is of varying length. When it is less than about 190 bytes or so (10 percent of a 2KB block is about 200 bytes; subtract 7 bytes for the date and 3 to 5 for the number), it will be stored on the index block. When it exceeds 190 bytes, Oracle will store the data for Z in the overflow segment and set up a pointer (a rowid, in fact) to it.

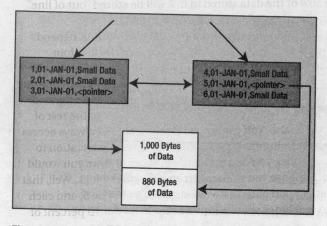

Figure 10-6. *IOT with overflow segment,* PCTTHRESHOLD *clause*

The other option is to use the INCLUDING clause. Here we are stating explicitly what columns we want stored on the index block and which should be stored in the overflow. Given a CREATE TABLE like this:

```
ops$tkyte@ORA10GR1> create table iot
  2  ( x     int,
  3    y     date,
  4    z     varchar2(2000),
  5    constraint iot_pk primary key (x)
  6  )
  7  organization index
  8  including y
  9  overflow
 10  /
Table created.
```

what we can expect to find is illustrated in Figure 10-7.

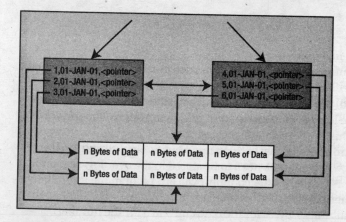

Figure 10-7. *IOT with* OVERFLOW *segment,* INCLUDING *clause*

In this situation, regardless of the size of the data stored in it, Z will be stored "out of line" in the overflow segment.

Which is better, then: PCTTHRESHOLD, INCLUDING, or some combination of both? It depends on your needs. If you have an application that always, or almost always, uses the first four columns of a table and rarely accesses the last five columns, using INCLUDING would be appropriate. You would include up to the fourth column and let the other five be stored out of line. At runtime, if you need them, the columns will be retrieved in much the same way as a migrated or chained row would be. Oracle will read the "head" of the row, find the pointer to the rest of the row, and then read that. If, on the other hand, you cannot say that you almost always access these columns and hardly ever access those columns, you should give some consideration to PCTTHRESHOLD. Setting PCTTHRESHOLD is easy once you determine the number of rows you would like to store per index block on average. Suppose you wanted 20 rows per index block. Well, that means each row should be one-twentieth (5 percent). Your PCTTHRESHOLD would be 5, and each chunk of the row that stays on the index leaf block should consume no more than 5 percent of the block.

The last thing to consider with IOTs is indexing. You can have an index on an IOT itself—sort of like having an index *on* an index. These are called *secondary indexes*. Normally, an index contains the physical address of the row it points to, the rowid. An IOT secondary index cannot do this; it must use some other way to address the row. This is because a row in an IOT can move around a lot, and it does not "migrate" in the way a row in a heap organized table would. A row in an IOT is expected to be at some position in the index structure, based on its primary key value; it will only be moving because the size and shape of the index itself is changing. (We'll cover more about how index structures are maintained in the next chapter.) To accommodate this, Oracle introduced a *logical rowid*. These logical rowids are based on the IOT's primary key. They may also contain a "guess" as to the current location of the row, although this guess is almost always wrong because after a short while, data in an IOT tends to move. The guess is the physical address of the row in the IOT when it was first placed into the secondary index structure. If the row in the IOT has to move to another block, the guess in the secondary index becomes "stale." Therefore, an index on an IOT is slightly less efficient than an index on a regular table. On a regular table, an index access typically requires the I/O to scan the index structure and then a single read to read the table data. With an IOT, typically two scans are performed: one on the secondary structure and the other on the IOT itself. That aside, indexes on IOTs provide fast and efficient access to the data in the IOT using columns other than the primary key.

Index Organized Tables Wrap-Up

Getting the right mix of data on the index block versus data in the overflow segment is the most critical part of the IOT setup. Benchmark various scenarios with different overflow conditions, and see how they will affect your INSERTs, UPDATEs, DELETEs, and SELECTs. If you have a structure that is built once and read frequently, stuff as much of the data onto the index block as you can. If you frequently modify the structure, you will have to achieve some balance between having all of the data on the index block (great for retrieval) versus reorganizing data in the index frequently (bad for modifications). The freelist consideration you had for heap tables applies to IOTs as well. PCTFREE and PCTUSED play two roles in an IOT. PCTFREE is not nearly as important for an IOT as for a heap table, and PCTUSED doesn't come into play normally.

When considering an OVERFLOW segment, however, PCTFREE and PCTUSED have the same interpretation as they do for a heap table; set them for an overflow segment using the same logic as you would for a heap table.

Index Clustered Tables

I generally find people's understanding of what a cluster is in Oracle to be inaccurate. Many people tend to confuse a cluster with a SQL Server or Sybase "clustered index." They are not the same. A cluster is a way to store a group of tables that share some common column(s) in the same database blocks and to store related data together on the same block. A clustered index in SQL Server forces the rows to be stored in sorted order according to the index key, similar to an IOT as just described. With a cluster, a single block of data may contain data from many tables. Conceptually, you are storing the data "prejoined." It can also be used with single tables, where you are storing data together grouped by some column. For example, all of the employees in department 10 will be stored on the same block (or as few blocks as possible, if they all don't fit). It is not storing the data sorted—that is the role of the IOT. It is storing the data clustered by some key, but in a heap. So, department 100 might be right next to department 1, and very far away (physically on disk) from departments 101 and 99.

Graphically, you might think of it as shown in Figure 10-8. On the left side of the image, we are using conventional tables. EMP will be stored in its segment. DEPT will be stored on its own. They may be in different files and different tablespaces, and they are definitely in separate extents. On the right side of the image, we see what would happen if we clustered these two tables together. The square boxes represent database blocks. We now have the value 10 factored out and stored once. Then, all of the data from all of the tables in the cluster for department 10 is stored in that block. If all of the data for department 10 does not fit on the block, then additional blocks will be chained to the original block to contain the overflow, in the same fashion as the overflow blocks for an IOT.

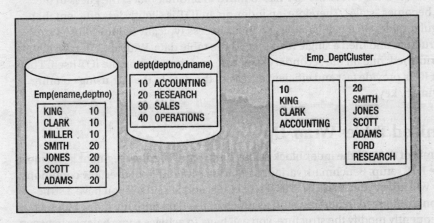

Figure 10-8. *Index clustered data*

So, let's look at how we might go about creating a clustered object. Creating a cluster of tables in the object is straightforward. The definition of the storage of the object (PCTFREE, PCTUSED, INITIAL, and so on) is associated with the CLUSTER, not the tables. This makes sense since there will be many tables in the cluster, and they will be on the same block. Having different PCTFREEs would not make sense. Therefore, a CREATE CLUSTER looks a lot like a CREATE TABLE with a small number of columns (just the cluster key columns):

```
ops$tkyte@ORA10GR1> create cluster emp_dept_cluster
  2  ( deptno number(2) )
  3  size 1024
  4  /
Cluster created.
```

Here, we have created an *index cluster* (the other type being a *hash cluster*, which we'll look at in the next section). The clustering column for this cluster will be the DEPTNO column. The columns in the tables do not have to be called DEPTNO, but they *must* be NUMBER(2), to match this definition. We have, on the cluster definition, a SIZE 1024 option. This is used to tell Oracle that we expect about 1,024 bytes of data to be associated with each cluster key value. Oracle will use that to compute the *maximum* number of cluster keys that could fit per block. Given that we have an 8KB blocksize, Oracle will fit up to seven cluster keys (but maybe fewer if the data is larger than expected) per database block. This is, the data for departments 10, 20, 30, 40, 50, 60, and 70 would tend to go onto one block, and as soon as we insert department 80, a new block will be used. That does not mean that the data is stored in a sorted manner; it just means that if we inserted the departments in that order, they would naturally tend to be put together. If we inserted the departments in the order 10, 80, 20, 30, 40, 50, 60, and then 70, the final department, 70, would tend to be on the newly added block. As we'll see shortly, both the size of the data and the order in which the data is inserted will affect the number of keys we can store per block.

The SIZE parameter therefore controls the maximum number of cluster keys per block. It is the single largest influence on the space utilization of our cluster. Set the size too high, and we'll get very few keys per block and we'll use more space than we need. Set the size too low, and we'll get excessive chaining of data, which offsets the purpose of the cluster to store all of the data together on a single block. It is the most important parameter for a cluster.

Now for the cluster index on our cluster. We need to index the cluster before we can put data in it. We could create tables in the cluster right now, but we're going to create and populate the tables simultaneously, and we need a cluster index *before* we can have any data. The cluster index's job is to take a cluster key value and return the block address of the block that contains that key. It is a primary key in effect, where each cluster key value points to a single block in the cluster itself. So, when we ask for the data in department 10, Oracle will read the cluster key, determine the block address for that, and then read the data. The cluster key index is created as follows:

```
ops$tkyte@ORA10GR1> create index emp_dept_cluster_idx
  2  on cluster emp_dept_cluster
  3  /
Index created.
```

It can have all of the normal storage parameters of an index and can be stored in another tablespace. It is just a regular index, so it can be on multiple columns; it just happens to index into a cluster and can also include an entry for a completely null value (see Chapter 11 for the reason why this is interesting to note). Note that we do *not* specify a list of columns in this CREATE INDEX statement—that is derived from the CLUSTER definition itself. Now we are ready to create our tables in the cluster:

```
ops$tkyte@ORA10GR1> create table dept
  2  ( deptno number(2) primary key,
  3    dname  varchar2(14),
  4    loc    varchar2(13)
  5  )
  6  cluster emp_dept_cluster(deptno)
  7  /
Table created.

ops$tkyte@ORA10GR1> create table emp
  2  ( empno   number primary key,
  3    ename   varchar2(10),
  4    job     varchar2(9),
  5    mgr     number,
  6    hiredate date,
  7    sal     number,
  8    comm    number,
  9    deptno number(2) references dept(deptno)
 10  )
 11  cluster emp_dept_cluster(deptno)
 12  /
Table created.
```

Here, the only difference from a "normal" table is that we used the CLUSTER keyword and told Oracle which column of the base table will map to the cluster key in the cluster itself. Remember, the cluster is the segment here, therefore this table will never have segment attributes such as TABLESPACE, PCTFREE, and so on—they are attributes of the cluster segment, not the table we just created. We can now load them up with the initial set of data:

```
ops$tkyte@ORA10GR1> begin
  2      for x in ( select * from scott.dept )
  3      loop
  4          insert into dept
  5          values ( x.deptno, x.dname, x.loc );
  6          insert into emp
  7          select *
  8            from scott.emp
  9           where deptno = x.deptno;
 10      end loop;
 11  end;
 12  /
PL/SQL procedure successfully completed.
```

You might be wondering, "Why didn't we just insert all of the DEPT data and then all of the EMP data, or vice versa? Why did we load the data DEPTNO by DEPTNO like that?" The reason is in the design of the cluster. We are simulating a large, initial bulk load of a cluster. If we had loaded all of the DEPT rows first, we definitely would have gotten our seven keys per block (based on the SIZE 1024 setting we made), since the DEPT rows are very small (just a couple of bytes). When it came time to load up the EMP rows, we might have found that some of the departments had many more than 1,024 bytes of data. This would cause excessive chaining on those cluster key blocks. Oracle would chain, or link together, a list of blocks to contain this information. By loading all of the data for a given cluster key at the same time, we pack the blocks as tightly as possible and start a new block when we run out of room. Instead of Oracle putting up to seven cluster key values per block, it will put as many as can fit.

A quick example will show the difference between these two approaches. We'll add a large column to the EMP table: a CHAR(1000). This column will be used to make the EMP rows much larger than they are now. We'll load the cluster tables in two ways: we'll load DEPT and then EMP. The second time, we'll load by department number: a DEPT row, then all the EMP rows that go with it, and then the next DEPT. We'll look at the blocks each row ends up on, in the given case, to see which one best achieves the goal of co-locating the data by DEPTNO. Our EMP table looks like this:

```
ops$tkyte@ORA10GR1> create table emp
  2  ( empno     number primary key,
  3    ename     varchar2(10),
  4    job       varchar2(9),
  5    mgr       number,
  6    hiredate  date,
  7    sal       number,
  8    comm      number,
  9    deptno    number(2) references dept(deptno),
 10    data      char(1000)
 11  )
 12  cluster emp_dept_cluster(deptno)
 13  /
Table created.
```

When we load the data into the DEPT and the EMP tables, we see that many of the EMP rows are not on the same block as the DEPT row anymore (DBMS_ROWID is a supplied package useful for peeking at the contents of a row ID):

```
ops$tkyte@ORA10GR1> insert into dept
  2  select * from scott.dept;
4 rows created.

ops$tkyte@ORA10GR1> insert into emp
  2  select emp.*, '*' from scott.emp;
14 rows created.

ops$tkyte@ORA10GR1> select dept_blk, emp_blk,
  2         case when dept_blk <> emp_blk then '*' end flag,
  3              deptno
  4     from (
  5   select dbms_rowid.rowid_block_number(dept.rowid) dept_blk,
  6          dbms_rowid.rowid_block_number(emp.rowid) emp_blk,
  7          dept.deptno
```

```
 8     from emp, dept
 9    where emp.deptno = dept.deptno
10         )
11    order by deptno
12  /

  DEPT_BLK    EMP_BLK F    DEPTNO
---------- ---------- - ----------
      4792       4788 *        10
      4792       4788 *        10
      4792       4791 *        10
      4792       4788 *        20
      4792       4788 *        20
      4792       4792          20
      4792       4792          20
      4792       4791 *        20
      4792       4788 *        30
      4792       4792          30
      4792       4792          30
      4792       4792          30
      4792       4792          30
      4792       4788 *        30

14 rows selected.
```

More than half of the EMP rows are not on the block with the DEPT row. Loading the data using the cluster key instead of the table key, we get the following:

```
ops$tkyte@ORA10GR1> begin
 2      for x in ( select * from scott.dept )
 3      loop
 4          insert into dept
 5          values ( x.deptno, x.dname, x.loc );
 6          insert into emp
 7          select emp.*, 'x'
 8            from scott.emp
 9           where deptno = x.deptno;
10      end loop;
11  end;
12  /
PL/SQL procedure successfully completed.

ops$tkyte@ORA10GR1> select dept_blk, emp_blk,
 2          case when dept_blk <> emp_blk then '*' end flag,
 3              deptno
 4    from (
 5  select dbms_rowid.rowid_block_number(dept.rowid) dept_blk,
 6          dbms_rowid.rowid_block_number(emp.rowid) emp_blk,
```

```
  7          dept.deptno
  8     from emp, dept
  9   where emp.deptno = dept.deptno
 10         )
 11   order by deptno
 12   /
```

```
 DEPT_BLK    EMP_BLK F      DEPTNO
---------- ---------- - ----------
        12         12             10
        12         12             10
        12         12             10
        11         11             20
        11         11             20
        11         11             20
        11         12 *           20
        11         11             20
        10         10             30
        10         10             30
        10         10             30
        10         10             30
        10         10             30
        10         11 *           30

14 rows selected.
```

■Note Your mileage may vary here, as the order in which the rows are fetched from the SCOTT.DEPT table can and will change the results, and the use of ASSM versus MSSM may as well. The concept should be clear, however: if you put the row for DEPTNO=*n* on a given block, and then the employee rows for DEPTNO=*n*, you should achieve the best clustering possible.

Most of the EMP rows are on the same block as the DEPT rows. This example is somewhat contrived in that I woefully undersized the SIZE parameter on the cluster to make a point, but the approach suggested is correct for an initial load of a cluster. It will ensure that if for some of the cluster keys, you exceed the estimated SIZE, you will still end up with most of the data clustered on the same block. If you load a table at a time, you will not.

This technique applies only to the initial load of a cluster—after that, you would use it as your transactions deem necessary. You will not adapt your application to work specifically with a cluster.

Here is a bit of puzzle to amaze and astound your friends with. Many people mistakenly believe a rowid uniquely identifies a row in a database, and that given a rowid you can tell what table the row came from. In fact, *you cannot*. You can and will get duplicate rowids from a cluster. For example, after executing the preceding code you should find

```
ops$tkyte@ORA10GR1> select rowid from emp
  2  intersect
  3  select rowid from dept;

ROWID
------------------
AAAOniAAJAAAAAKAAA
AAAOniAAJAAAAAKAAB
AAAOniAAJAAAAALAAA
AAAOniAAJAAAAAMAAA
```

Every rowid assigned to the rows in DEPT has been assigned to the rows in EMP as well. That is because it takes a table *and* row ID to uniquely identify a row. The rowid pseudo-column is unique only within a table.

I also find that many people believe the cluster object to be an esoteric object that no one really uses—everyone just uses normal tables. The fact is, you use clusters every time you use Oracle. Much of the data dictionary is stored in various clusters, for example:

```
sys@ORA10GR1> break on cluster_name
sys@ORA10GR1> select cluster_name, table_name
  2  from user_tables
  3  where cluster_name is not null
  4  order by 1;

CLUSTER_NAME                     TABLE_NAME
-------------------------------- --------------------------------
C_COBJ#                          CCOL$
                                 CDEF$
C_FILE#_BLOCK#                   UET$
                                 SEG$
C_MLOG#                          MLOG$
                                 SLOG$
C_OBJ#                           ICOL$
                                 CLU$
                                 COL$
                                 TYPE_MISC$
                                 VIEWTRCOL$
                                 ATTRCOL$
                                 SUBCOLTYPE$
                                 COLTYPE$
                                 LOB$
                                 TAB$
                                 IND$
                                 ICOLDEP$
                                 OPQTYPE$
                                 REFCON$
```

```
                                   LIBRARY$
                                   NTAB$
C_OBJ#_INTCOL#                     HISTGRM$
C_RG#                              RGROUP$
                                   RGCHILD$
C_TOID_VERSION#                    TYPE$
                                   COLLECTION$
                                   METHOD$
                                   RESULT$
                                   PARAMETER$
                                   ATTRIBUTE$
C_TS#                    ·         TS$
                                   FET$
C_USER#                            USER$
                                   TSQ$
SMON_SCN_TO_TIME                   SMON_SCN_TIME

36 rows selected.
```

As you can see, most of the object-related data is stored in a single cluster (the C_OBJ# cluster): 16 tables sharing the same block. It is mostly column-related information stored there, so all of the information about the set of columns of a table or index is stored physically on the same block. This makes sense, as when Oracle parses a query, it wants to have access to the data for all of the columns in the referenced table. If this data were spread all over the place, it would take a while to get it together. Here, it is on a single block typically and readily available.

When would you use a cluster? It is easier perhaps to describe when not to use one:

- *If you anticipate the tables in the cluster will be modified heavily*: You must be aware that an index cluster will have certain negative side effects on DML performance (INSERT statements in particular). It takes more work to manage the data in a cluster.

- *If you need to perform full scans of tables in clusters*: Instead of just having to full scan the data in your table, you have to full scan the data for (possibly) many tables. There is more data to scan through, so full scans will take longer.

- *If you believe you will frequently need to* TRUNCATE *and load the table*: Tables in clusters cannot be truncated. That is obvious—since the cluster stores more than one table on a block, you must delete the rows in a cluster table.

So, if you have data that is mostly read (that does *not* mean "never written"; it is perfectly OK to modify cluster tables) and read via indexes, either the cluster key index or other indexes you put on the tables in the cluster, and join this information together frequently, a cluster would be appropriate. Look for tables that are logically related and always used together, like the people who designed the Oracle data dictionary when they clustered all column-related information together.

Index Clustered Tables Wrap-Up

Clustered tables give you the ability to physically "prejoin" data together. You use clusters to store related data from many tables on the same database block. Clusters can help read-intensive operations that always join data together or access related sets of data (e.g., everyone in department 10).

Clustered tables reduce the number of blocks that Oracle must cache. Instead of keeping ten blocks for ten employees in the same department, Oracle will put them in one block and therefore increase the efficiency of your buffer cache. On the downside, unless you can calculate your SIZE parameter setting correctly, clusters may be inefficient with their space utilization and can tend to slow down DML-heavy operations.

Hash Clustered Tables

Hash clustered tables are very similar in concept to the index clustered tables just described with one main exception: the cluster key index is replaced with a hash function. The data in the table is the index; there is no physical index. Oracle will take the key value for a row, hash it using either an internal function or one you supply, and use that to figure out where the data should be on disk. One side effect of using a hashing algorithm to locate data, however, is that you cannot range scan a table in a hash cluster without adding a conventional index to the table. In an index cluster, the query

```
select * from emp where deptno between 10 and 20
```

would be able to make use of the cluster key index to find these rows. In a hash cluster, this query would result in a full table scan unless you had an index on the DEPTNO column. Only exact equality searches (including in lists and subqueries) may be made on the hash key without using an index that supports range scans.

In a perfect world, with nicely distributed hash key values and a hash function that distributes them evenly over all of the blocks allocated to the hash cluster, we can go straight from a query to the data with one I/O. In the real world, we will end up with more hash key values hashing to the same database block address than fit on that block. This will result in Oracle having to chain blocks together in a linked list to hold all of the rows that hash to this block. Now, when we need to retrieve the rows that match our hash key, we might have to visit more than one block.

Like a hash table in a programming language, hash tables in the database have a fixed "size." When you create the table, you must determine the number of hash keys your table will have, forever. That does not limit the amount of rows you can put in there.

Figure 10-9 shows a graphical representation of a hash cluster with table EMP created in it. When the client issues a query that uses the hash cluster key in the predicate, Oracle will apply the hash function to determine which block the data should be in. It will then read that one block to find the data. If there have been many collisions, or the SIZE parameter to the CREATE CLUSTER was underestimated, Oracle will have allocated overflow blocks that are chained off the original block.

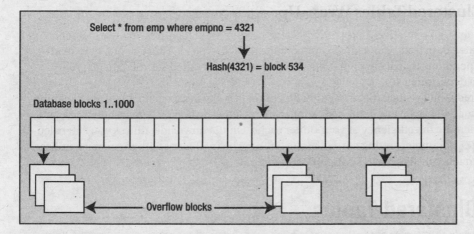

Figure 10-9. *Hash cluster depiction*

When you create a hash cluster, you'll use the same CREATE CLUSTER statement you used to create the index cluster with different options. You'll just be adding a HASHKEYS option to it to specify the size of the hash table. Oracle will take your HASHKEYS value and round it up to the nearest prime number (the number of hash keys will always be a prime). Oracle will then compute a value based on the SIZE parameter multiplied by the modified HASHKEYS value. It will allocate at least that much space in bytes for the cluster. This is a big difference from the preceding index cluster, which dynamically allocates space as it needs it. A hash cluster pre-allocates enough space to hold (HASHKEYS/trunc(blocksize/SIZE)) bytes of data. For example, if you set your SIZE to 1,500 bytes and you have a 4KB blocksize, Oracle will expect to store two keys per block. If you plan on having 1,000 HASHKEYs, Oracle will allocate 500 blocks.

It is interesting to note that unlike a conventional hash table in a computer language, it is OK to have hash collisions—in fact, it is desirable in many cases. If you take the same DEPT/EMP example from earlier, you could set up a hash cluster based on the DEPTNO column. Obviously, many rows will hash to the same value, and you expect them to (they have the same DEPTNO). This is what the cluster is about in some respects: clustering like data together. This is why Oracle asks you to specify the HASHKEYs (how many department numbers you anticipate over time) and SIZE (what the size of the data is that will be associated with each department number). It allocates a hash table to hold HASHKEY number of departments of SIZE bytes each. What you do want to avoid is unintended hash collisions. It is obvious that if you set the size of the hash table to 1,000 (really 1,009, since the hash table size is always a prime number and Oracle rounds up for you), and you put 1,010 departments in the table, there will be at least one collision (two different departments hashing to the same value). Unintended hash collisions are to be avoided, as they add overhead and increase the probability of block chaining occurring.

To see what sort of space hash clusters take, we'll use a small utility stored procedure, SHOW_SPACE (for details on this procedure, see the "Setup" section at the beginning of the book), that we'll use in this chapter and in the next chapter. This routine just uses the DBMS_SPACE-supplied package to get details about the storage used by segments in the database.

Now if we issue a CREATE CLUSTER statement such as the following, we can see the storage it allocated:

```
ops$tkyte@ORA10GR1> create cluster hash_cluster
  2  ( hash_key number )
  3  hashkeys 1000
  4  size 8192
  5  tablespace mssm
  6  /
Cluster created.

ops$tkyte@ORA10GR1> exec show_space( 'HASH_CLUSTER', user, 'CLUSTER' )
Free Blocks.............................           0
Total Blocks............................       1,024
Total Bytes.............................   8,388,608
Total MBytes............................           8
Unused Blocks...........................          14
Unused Bytes............................     114,688
Last Used Ext FileId....................           9
Last Used Ext BlockId...................       1,033
Last Used Block.........................         114

PL/SQL procedure successfully completed.
```

We can see that the total number of blocks allocated to the table is 1,024. Fourteen of these blocks are unused (free). One block goes to table overhead, to manage the extents. Therefore, 1,009 blocks are under the HWM of this object, and these are used by the cluster. The prime 1,009 just happens to be the next largest prime over 1,000, and since the blocksize is 8KB, we can see that Oracle did in fact allocate (8192 × 1009) blocks. The figure is a little higher than this, due to the way extents are rounded and/or by using locally managed table-spaces with uniformly sized extents.

This example points out one of the issues with hash clusters you need to be aware of. Normally, if you create an empty table, the number of blocks under the HWM for that table is 0. If you full scan it, it reaches the HWM and stops. With a hash cluster, the tables will start out big and will take longer to create, as Oracle must initialize each block, an action that normally takes place as data is added to the table. They have the potential to have data in their first block and their last block, with nothing in between. Full scanning a virtually empty hash cluster will take as long as full scanning a full hash cluster. This is not necessarily a bad thing; you built the hash cluster to have very fast access to the data by a hash key lookup. You did not build it to full scan it frequently.

Now we can start placing tables into the hash cluster in the same fashion we did with index clusters:

```
Ops$tkyte@ORA10GR1> create table hashed_table
  2  ( x number, data1 varchar2(4000), data2 varchar2(4000) )
  3  cluster hash_cluster(x);
Table created.
```

To see the difference a hash cluster can make, I set up a small test. I created a hash cluster, loaded some data in it, copied this data to a "regular" table with a conventional index on it, and then did random reads on each table (the same "random" reads on each). Using runstats, SQL_TRACE, and TKPROF, I was able to determine the characteristics of each. The following is the setup I performed, followed by the analysis:

```
ops$tkyte@ORA10GR1> create cluster hash_cluster
  2  ( hash_key number )
  3  hashkeys 75000
  4  size 150
  5  /
Cluster created.

ops$tkyte@ORA10GR1> create table t_hashed
  2  cluster hash_cluster(object_id)
  3  as
  4  select *
  5    from all_objects
  6  /
Table created.

ops$tkyte@ORA10GR1> alter table t_hashed add constraint
  2  t_hashed_pk primary key(object_id)
  2  /
Table altered.

ops$tkyte@ORA10GR1> begin
  2     dbms_stats.gather_table_stats( user, 'T_HASHED', cascade=>true );
  3  end;
  4  /
PL/SQL procedure successfully completed.
```

I created the hash cluster with a SIZE of 150 bytes. This is because I determined the average row size for a row in my table would be about 100 bytes, but would vary up and down based on the data. I then created and populated a table in that cluster as a copy of ALL_OBJECTS.

Next, I created the "conventional clone" of the table:

```
ops$tkyte@ORA10GR1> create table t_heap
  2  as
  3  select *
  4    from t_hashed
  5  /
Table created.

ops$tkyte@ORA10GR1> alter table t_heap add constraint
  2  t_heap_pk primary key(object_id)
  3  /
Table altered.
```

```
ops$tkyte@ORA10GR1> begin
  2      dbms_stats.gather_table_stats( user, 'T_HEAP', cascade=>true );
  3  end;
  4  /
PL/SQL procedure successfully completed.
```

Now, all I needed was some "random" data to pick rows from each of the tables with. To achieve that, I simply selected all of the OBJECT_IDs into an array and had them sorted randomly, to hit the table all over in a scattered fashion. I used a PL/SQL package to define and declare the array and a bit of PL/SQL code to "prime" the array, to fill it up:

```
ops$tkyte@ORA10GR1> create or replace package state_pkg
  2  as
  3      type array is table of t_hashed.object_id%type;
  4      g_data array;
  5  end;
  6  /
Package created.

ops$tkyte@ORA10GR1> begin
  2      select object_id bulk collect into state_pkg.g_data
  3        from t_hashed
  4        order by dbms_random.random;
  5  end;
  6  /
PL/SQL procedure successfully completed.
```

To see the work performed by each, I used the following block of code (if you replace occurrences of the word HASHED with HEAP, you have the other block of code you need to test against):

```
ops$tkyte@ORA10GR1> declare
  2      l_rec t_hashed%rowtype;
  3  begin
  4      for i in 1 .. state_pkg.g_data.count
  5      loop
  6          select * into l_rec from t_hashed
  7          where object_id = state_pkg.g_data(i);
  8      end loop;
  9  end;
 10  /
PL/SQL procedure successfully completed.
```

Next, I ran the preceding block of code three times (and the copy of that block of code where HASHED is replaced with HEAP as well). The first run was to "warm up" the system, to get any hard parses out of the way. The second time I ran the blocks of code, I used runstats to see the material differences between the two: running first the hashed implementation and then the heap. The third time I ran the blocks of code, I did so with SQL_TRACE enabled so I could see a TKPROF report. The runstats run reported the following:

```
ops$tkyte@ORA10GR1> exec runstats_pkg.rs_stop(10000);
Run1 ran in 263 hsecs
Run2 ran in 268 hsecs
run 1 ran in 98.13% of the time

Name                           Run1       Run2       Diff
LATCH.cache buffers chains   99,891    148,031     48,140
STAT...Cached Commit SCN refer 48,144        0    -48,144
STAT...no work - consistent re 48,176        0    -48,176
STAT...cluster key scans       48,176        0    -48,176
STAT...cluster key scan block  48,176        0    -48,176
STAT...table fetch by rowid         0   48,176     48,176
STAT...rows fetched via callba      0   48,176     48,176
STAT...buffer is not pinned co 48,176   96,352     48,176
STAT...index fetch by key           0   48,176     48,176
STAT...session logical reads   48,901  145,239     96,338
STAT...consistent gets         48,178  144,530     96,352
STAT...consistent gets from ca 48,178  144,530     96,352
STAT...consistent gets - exami      1  144,529    144,528


Run1 latches total versus runs -- difference and pct
Run1        Run2       Diff       Pct
347,515     401,961      54,446    86.45%
```

Now, these two simulations ran in about the same amount of time by the wall clock. As I had a buffer cache larger than large enough to cache these results, I was expecting that. The material difference to note, however, is the large reduction in cache buffers chains latches. The first implementation (hashed) used significantly fewer, meaning the hashed implementation should scale better in a read-intensive environment, since it needs fewer resources that require some level of serialization. This was due entirely to the fact that the I/O needed by the hashed implementation was significantly reduced over the HEAP table—you can see the statistic consistent gets in that report bears this out. The TKPROF shows it even more clearly:

```
SELECT * FROM T_HASHED WHERE OBJECT_ID = :B1

call     count       cpu    elapsed      disk      query    current       rows
-------  ------  --------  ---------- ---------- ---------- ---------- ----------
Parse        1      0.00       0.00          0          0          0          0
Execute  48174      4.77       4.83          0          2          0          0
Fetch    48174      1.50       1.46          0      48174          0      48174
-------  ------  --------  ---------- ---------- ---------- ---------- ----------
total    96349      6.27       6.30          0      48176          0      48174

Rows     Row Source Operation
-------  ---------------------------------------------------
  48174  TABLE ACCESS HASH T_HASHED (cr=48174 pr=0 pw=0 time=899962 us)
*****************************************************************************
SELECT * FROM T_HEAP WHERE OBJECT_ID = :B1
```

call	count	cpu	elapsed	disk	query	current	rows
Parse	1	0.00	0.00	0	0	0	0
Execute	48174	5.37	5.02	0	0	0	0
Fetch	48174	1.36	1.32	0	144522	0	48174
total	96349	6.73	6.34	0	144522	0	48174

```
Rows     Row Source Operation
-------  -----------------------------------------------------
  48174  TABLE ACCESS BY INDEX ROWID T_HEAP (cr=144522 pr=0 pw=0 time=1266695 us)
  48174   INDEX UNIQUE SCAN T_HEAP_PK (cr=96348 pr=0 pw=0 time=700017 us)(object ...
```

The HASHED implementation simply converted the OBJECT_ID passed into the query into a FILE/BLOCK to be read and read it—no index. The HEAP table, however, had to do two I/Os on the index for each row. The cr=96348 in the TKPROF Row Source Operation line shows us exactly how many consistent reads were done against the index. Each time I looked up OBJECT_ID = :B1, Oracle had to get the root block of the index and then find the leaf block containing the location of that row. Then, I had to take the leaf block information, which included the ROWID of that row, and access that row in the table for a third I/O. The HEAP table did three times the I/O of the HASHED implementation.

The points of interest here are as follows:

- The hash cluster did significantly less I/O (query column). This is what we anticipated. The query simply took the random OBJECT_IDs, performed the hash on them, and went to the block. The hash cluster has to do at least one I/O to get the data. The conventional table with an index had to perform index scans followed by a table access by rowid to get the same answer. The indexed table has to do at least three I/Os in this case to get the data.

- The hash cluster query took the same amount of CPU for all intents and purposes, even though it went to the buffer cache one-third as many times. This, too, could be anticipated. The act of performing a hash is very CPU intensive. The act of performing an index lookup is I/O intensive. It was a tradeoff here. However, as we scale up users, we would expect the hash cluster query to scale better, as it has to get in line to access the buffer cache less frequently.

This last point is the important one. When working with computers, it is all about resources and their utilization. If we are I/O bound and perform queries that do lots of keyed reads like I just did, a hash cluster may improve performance. If we are already CPU bound, a hash cluster may possibly decrease performance since it needs more CPU horsepower to hash, but if the extra CPU we are burning is due to spinning on cache buffers chains latches, the hash cluster could significantly reduce the CPU needed. This is one of the main reasons why rules of thumb do not work on real-world systems: what works for you might not work for others in similar but different conditions.

There is a special case of a hash cluster called a *single table hash cluster*. This is an optimized version of the general hash cluster we've already looked at. It supports only one table in the cluster at a time (you have to DROP the existing table in a single table hash cluster before you can create another). Additionally, if there is a one-to-one mapping between hash keys and data rows, the access to the rows is somewhat faster as well. These hash clusters are designed for those occasions when you want to access a table by primary key and do not care to cluster other tables with it. If you need fast access to an employee record by EMPNO, a single table hash cluster might be called for. I did the preceding test on a single table hash cluster as well and found the performance to be even better than just a hash cluster. You could even go a step further with this example, however, and take advantage of the fact that Oracle will allow you to write your own specialized hash function (instead of using the default one provided by Oracle). You are limited to using only the columns available in the table, and you may use only the Oracle built-in functions (e.g., no PL/SQL code) when writing these hash functions. By taking advantage of the fact that OBJECT_ID is a number between 1 and 75,000 in the preceding example, I made my "hash function" simply be the OBJECT_ID column itself. In this fashion, I am guaranteed to never have a hash collision. Putting it all together, I'll create a single table hash cluster with my own hash function via

```
ops$tkyte@ORA10GR1> create cluster hash_cluster
  2  ( hash_key number(10) )
  3  hashkeys 75000
  4  size 150
  5  single table
  6  hash is HASH_KEY
  7  /
Cluster created.
```

I've simply added the key words SINGLE TABLE to make it a single table hash cluster. My HASH IS function is simply the HASH_KEY cluster key in this case. This is a SQL function, so I could have used trunc(mod(hash_key/324+278,555)/abs(hash_key+1)) if I wanted (not that this is a good hash function—it just demonstrates that we can use a complex function there if we wish). I used a NUMBER(10) instead of just a number. Since the hash value must be an integer, it cannot have any fractional components. Then, I create the table in that cluster

```
ops$tkyte@ORA10GR1> create table t_hashed
  2  cluster hash_cluster(object_id)
  3  as
  4  select OWNER, OBJECT_NAME, SUBOBJECT_NAME,
  5         cast( OBJECT_ID as number(10) ) object_id,
  6         DATA_OBJECT_ID, OBJECT_TYPE, CREATED,
  7         LAST_DDL_TIME, TIMESTAMP, STATUS, TEMPORARY,
  8         GENERATED, SECONDARY
  9   from all_objects
 10  /
Table created.
```

to build the hashed table. Note the use of the CAST built-in function to make the datatype of OBJECT_ID be what it must be. I ran the test as before (three runs of each block), and this time the runstats output was consistently even more positive:

```
Run1 ran in 224 hsecs
Run2 ran in 269 hsecs
run 1 ran in 83.27% of the time

Name                                    Run1        Run2        Diff
STAT...index fetch by key                  0      48,178      48,178
STAT...buffer is not pinned co        48,178      96,356      48,178
STAT...table fetch by rowid                0      48,178      48,178
STAT...cluster key scans              48,178           0     -48,178
STAT...session logical reads          48,889     145,245      96,356
STAT...consistent gets                48,184     144,540      96,356
STAT...consistent gets from ca        48,184     144,540      96,356
STAT...consistent gets - exami        48,184     144,540      96,356
LATCH.cache buffers chains            51,663     148,019      96,356

Run1 latches total versus runs -- difference and pct
Run1        Run2        Diff        Pct
298,987     402,085     103,098     74.36%

PL/SQL procedure successfully completed.
```

This single table hash cluster required even less latching into the buffer cache to process (it can stop looking for data sooner, and it has more information). As a result, the TKPROF report shows a measurable decrease in CPU utilization this time around:

```
SELECT * FROM T_HASHED WHERE OBJECT_ID = :B1

call     count      cpu   elapsed      disk     query   current      rows
------- ------ -------- ---------- ---------- ---------- ---------- ----------
Parse        1     0.00      0.00         0         0         0         0
Execute  48178     4.45      4.52         0         2         0         0
Fetch    48178     0.67      0.82         0     48178         0     48178
------- ------ -------- ---------- ---------- ---------- ---------- ----------
total    96357     5.12      5.35         0     48180         0     48178

Rows     Row Source Operation
------- ---------------------------------------------------
  48178   TABLE ACCESS HASH T_HASHED (cr=48178 pr=0 pw=0 time=551123 us)
********************************************************************************
SELECT * FROM T_HEAP WHERE OBJECT_ID = :B1

call     count      cpu   elapsed      disk     query   current      rows
------- ------ -------- ---------- ---------- ---------- ---------- ----------
Parse        1     0.00      0.00         0         0         0         0
Execute  48178     5.38      4.99         0         0         0         0
Fetch    48178     1.25      1.65         0    144534         0     48178
------- ------ -------- ---------- ---------- ---------- ---------- ----------
total    96357     6.63      6.65         0    144534         0     48178
```

```
Rows     Row Source Operation
-------  --------------------------------------------------------
 48178   TABLE ACCESS BY INDEX ROWID T_HEAP (cr=144534 pr=0 pw=0 time=1331049 us)
 48178    INDEX UNIQUE SCAN T_HEAP_PK (cr=96356 pr=0 pw=0 time=710295 us)(object...
```

Hash Clustered Tables Wrap-Up

That is the nuts and bolts of a hash cluster. Hash clusters are similar in concept to index clusters, except a cluster index is not used. *The data is the index* in this case. The cluster key is hashed into a block address and the data is expected to be there. The important things to understand about hash clusters are as follows:

- The hash cluster is allocated right from the beginning. Oracle will take your HASHKEYS/trunc(blocksize/SIZE) and allocate and format that space right away. As soon as the first table is put in that cluster, any full scan will hit every allocated block. This is different from every other table in this respect.

- The number of HASHKEYs in a hash cluster is a fixed size. You cannot change the size of the hash table without a rebuild of the cluster. This does not in any way limit the amount of data you can store in this cluster; it simply limits the number of unique hash keys that can be generated for this cluster. That may affect performance due to unintended hash collisions if the value was set too low.

- Range scanning on the cluster key is not available. Predicates such as WHERE cluster_key BETWEEN 50 AND 60 cannot use the hashing algorithm. There are an infinite number of possible values between 50 and 60, and the server would have to generate them all to hash each one and see if there was any data there. This is not possible. The cluster will be full scanned if you use a range on a cluster key and have not indexed it using a conventional index.

Hash clusters are suitable in the following situations:

- You know with a good degree of accuracy how many rows the table will have over its life, or you have some reasonable upper bound. Getting the size of the HASHKEYs and SIZE parameters right is crucial to avoid a rebuild.

- DML, especially inserts, is light with respect to retrieval. This means you have to balance optimizing data retrieval with new data creation. Light inserts might be 100,000 per unit of time for one person and 100 per unit of time for another—all depending on their data retrieval patterns. Updates do not introduce significant overhead, unless you update the HASHKEY, which would not be a good idea, as it would cause the row to migrate.

- You access the data by the HASHKEY value constantly. For example, say you have a table of parts, and these parts are accessed by part number. Lookup tables are especially appropriate for hash clusters.

Sorted Hash Clustered Tables

Sorted hash clusters are new in Oracle 10*g*. They combine the qualities of the hash cluster just described with those of an IOT. They are most appropriate when you constantly retrieve data using a query similar to this:

```
Select *
  From t
 Where KEY=:x
 Order by SORTED_COLUMN
```

That is, you retrieve the data by some key and need that data ordered by some other column. Using a sorted hash cluster, Oracle can return the data without performing a sort at all. It accomplishes this by storing the data upon insert in sorted order physically—by key. Suppose you have a customer order table:

```
ops$tkyte@ORA10G> select cust_id, order_dt, order_number
  2    from cust_orders
  3    order by cust_id, order_dt;

CUST_ID ORDER_DT                        ORDER_NUMBER
------- ------------------------------- ------------
      1 31-MAR-05 09.13.57.000000 PM           21453
        11-APR-05 08.30.45.000000 AM           21454
        28-APR-05 06.21.09.000000 AM           21455
      2 08-APR-05 03.42.45.000000 AM           21456
        19-APR-05 08.59.33.000000 AM           21457
        27-APR-05 06.35.34.000000 AM           21458
        30-APR-05 01.47.34.000000 AM           21459

7 rows selected.
```

The table is stored in a sorted hash cluster, whereby the HASH key is CUST_ID and the field to sort on is ORDER_DT. Graphically, it might look like Figure 10-10, where 1, 2, 3, 4, . . . represent the records stored sorted on each block.

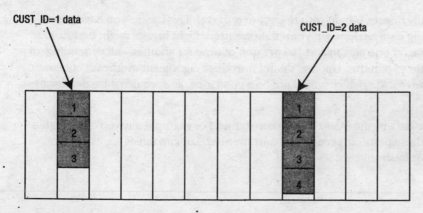

Figure 10-10. *Sorted hash cluster depiction*

Creating a sorted hash cluster is much the same as the other clusters. To set up a sorted hash cluster capable of storing the above data, we could use the following:

```
ops$tkyte@ORA10G> CREATE CLUSTER shc
  2  (
  3     cust_id      NUMBER,
  4     order_dt     timestamp SORT
  5  )
  6  HASHKEYS 10000
  7  HASH IS cust_id
  8  SIZE  8192
  9  /
Cluster created.
```

We've introduced a new keyword here: SORT. When we created the cluster, we identified the HASH IS CUST_ID and we added an ORDER_DT of type timestamp with the keyword SORT. This means the data will be located by CUST_ID (where CUST_ID=:X) and physically retrieved and sorted by ORDER_DT. Technically, it really means we'll store some data that will be retrieved via a NUMBER column and sorted by the TIMESTAMP. The column names here are not relevant, as they were not in the B*Tree or HASH clusters, but convention would have us name them after what they represent.

The CREATE TABLE for our CUST_ORDERS would look like this:

```
ops$tkyte@ORA10G> CREATE TABLE cust_orders
  2  ( cust_id        number,
  3    order_dt       timestamp SORT,
  4    order_number   number,
  5    username       varchar2(30),
  6    ship_addr      number,
  7    bill_addr      number,
  8    invoice_num    number
  9  )
 10  CLUSTER shc ( cust_id, order_dt )
 11  /
Table created.
```

We've mapped the CUST_ID column of this table to the hash key for the sorted hash cluster and the ORDER_DT column to the SORT column. We can observe using AUTOTRACE in SQL*Plus that the normal sort operations we expect are missing when accessing the sorted hash cluster:

```
ops$tkyte@ORA10G> set autotrace traceonly explain
ops$tkyte@ORA10G> variable x number
ops$tkyte@ORA10G> select cust_id, order_dt, order_number
  2    from cust_orders
  3   where cust_id = :x
  4   order by order_dt;
```

```
Execution Plan
----------------------------------------------------------
   0      SELECT STATEMENT Optimizer=ALL_ROWS (Cost=0 Card=4 Bytes=76)
   1    0   TABLE ACCESS (HASH) OF 'CUST_ORDERS' (CLUSTER (HASH))

ops$tkyte@ORA10G> select job, hiredate, empno
   2    from scott.emp
   3  where job = 'CLERK'
   4  order by hiredate;

Execution Plan
----------------------------------------------------------
   0      SELECT STATEMENT Optimizer=ALL_ROWS (Cost=3 Card=3 Bytes=60)
   1    0   SORT (ORDER BY) (Cost=3 Card=3 Bytes=60)
   2    1     TABLE ACCESS (BY INDEX ROWID) OF 'EMP' (TABLE) (Cost=2 Card=3 ...
   3    2       INDEX (RANGE SCAN) OF 'JOB_IDX' (INDEX) (Cost=1 Card=3)

ops$tkyte@ORA10G> set autotrace off
```

I added the query against the normal SCOTT.EMP table (after indexing the JOB column for this demonstration) to compare what we normally expect to see: the SCOTT.EMP query plan versus what the sorted hash cluster can do for us when we want to access the data in a FIFO mode (like a queue). As you can see, the sorted hash cluster has one step: it takes the CUST_ID=:X, hashes the input, finds the first row, and just starts reading the rows, as they are in order already. The regular table is much different: it finds all the JOB='CLERK' rows (which could be anywhere in that heap table), sorts them, and then returns the first one.

So, the sorted hash cluster has all the retrieval aspects of the hash cluster, in that it can get to the data without having to traverse an index, and many of the features of the IOT, in that the data will be sorted within that key by some field of your choice. This data structure works well when the input data arrives "in order" by the sort field, by key. That is, over time the data arrives in increasing sort order for any given key value. Stock information fits this requirement as an example. Every night you get a new file full of stock symbols, the date (the date would be the sort key and the stock symbol would be the hash key), and related information. You receive and load this data in sort key order. The stock data for stock symbol ORCL for yesterday does not arrive after today—you would load yesterday's value, and then today's value, and later tomorrow's value. If the information arrives randomly (not in sort order), this data structure quickly breaks down during the insert process, as much data has to be moved to put the rows physically in order on disk. A sorted hash cluster is not recommended in that case (an IOT, on the other hand, could well be useful for that data).

When considering using this structure, you should employ the same considerations from the hash cluster section, in addition to the constraint that the data should arrive sorted for each key value over time.

Nested Tables

Nested tables are part of the object-relational extensions to Oracle. A nested table, one of the two collection types in Oracle, is very similar to a child table in a traditional parent/child table pair in the relational model. It is an unordered set of data elements, all of the same data type, which could be either a built-in data type or an object data type. It goes one step further, however, since it is designed to give the illusion that each row in the parent table has its *own* child table. If there are 100 rows in the parent table, then there are *virtually* 100 nested tables. Physically, there is only the single parent and the single child table. There are large syntactic and semantic differences between nested tables and parent/child tables as well, and we'll look at those in this section.

There are two ways to use nested tables. One is in your PL/SQL code as a way to extend the PL/SQL language. The other is as a physical storage mechanism for persistent storage of collections. I personally use them in PL/SQL all of the time, but have never used them as a permanent storage mechanism.

In this section, I'll briefly introduce the syntax to create, query, and modify nested tables. Then we'll look at some of the implementation details and what is important to know about how Oracle really stores nested tables.

Nested Tables Syntax

The creation of a table with a nested table is fairly straightforward—it is the syntax for manipulating it that gets a little complex. Let's use the simple EMP and DEPT tables to demonstrate. We're familiar with that little data model that is implemented relationally as follows:

```
ops$tkyte@ORA10GR1> create table dept
  2  (deptno  number(2) primary key,
  3   dname        varchar2(14),
  4   loc          varchar2(13)
  5  );
Table created.

ops$tkyte@ORA10GR1> create table emp
  2  (empno       number(4) primary key,
  3   ename       varchar2(10),
  4   job         varchar2(9),
  5   mgr         number(4) references emp,
  6   hiredate    date,
  7   sal         number(7, 2),
  8   comm        number(7, 2),
  9   deptno      number(2) references dept
 10  );
Table created.
```

with primary and foreign keys. We'll do the equivalent implementation using a nested table for the EMP table:

```
ops$tkyte@ORA10GR1> create or replace type emp_type
  2  as object
  3  (empno       number(4),
  4   ename       varchar2(10),
  5   job         varchar2(9),
  6   mgr         number(4),
```

```
  7    hiredate      date,
  8    sal           number(7, 2),
  9    comm          number(7, 2)
 10  );
 11  /
Type created.

ops$tkyte@ORA10GR1> create or replace type emp_tab_type
  2  as table of emp_type
  3  /
Type created.
```

To create a table with a nested table, we need a nested table type. The preceding code creates a complex object type, EMP_TYPE, and a nested table type of that, EMP_TAB_TYPE. In PL/SQL, this will be treated much like an array would. In SQL, it will cause a physical nested table to be created. Here is the simple CREATE TABLE statement that uses it:

```
ops$tkyte@ORA10G> create table dept_and_emp
  2  (deptno number(2) primary key,
  3   dname      varchar2(14),
  4   loc        varchar2(13),
  5   emps       emp_tab_type
  6  )
  7  nested table emps store as emps_nt;
Table created.

ops$tkyte@ORA10G> alter table emps_nt add constraint
  2  emps_empno_unique unique(empno)
  3  /
Table altered.
```

The important part of this CREATE TABLE is the inclusion of the column EMPS of EMP_TAB_TYPE and the corresponding NESTED TABLE EMPS STORE AS EMPS_NT. This created a real physical table, EMPS_NT, separate from and in addition to the table DEPT_AND_EMP. We add a constraint on the EMPNO column directly on the nested table to make the EMPNO unique as it was in our original relational model. We cannot implement our full data model; however, there is the self-referencing constraint:

```
ops$tkyte@ORA10G> alter table emps_nt add constraint mgr_fk
  2  foreign key(mgr) references emps_nt(empno);
alter table emps_nt add constraint mgr_fk
*
ERROR at line 1:
ORA-30730: referential constraint not allowed on nested table column
```

This will simply not work. Nested tables do not support referential integrity constraints, as they cannot reference any other table—even themselves. So, we'll just skip that for now. Next, we'll populate this table with the existing EMP and DEPT data:

CHAPTER 10 ■ DATABASE TABLES   392

```
ops$tkyte@ORA10G> insert into dept_and_emp
  2  select dept.*,
  3     CAST( multiset( select empno, ename, job, mgr, hiredate, sal, comm
  4                       from SCOTT.EMP
  5                      where emp.deptno = dept.deptno ) AS emp_tab_type )
  6    from SCOTT.DEPT
  7  /
4 rows created.
```

There are two things to notice here:

- Only "four" rows were created. There are really only four rows in the DEPT_AND_EMP table. The 14 EMP rows don't exist independently.

- The syntax is getting pretty exotic. CAST and MULTISET is syntax most people have never used. You will find lots of exotic syntax when dealing with object-relational components in the database. The MULTISET keyword is used to tell Oracle the subquery is expected to return more than one row (subqueries in a SELECT list have previously been limited to returning one row). CAST is used to instruct Oracle to treat the returned set as a collection type—in this case, we CAST the MULTISET to be an EMP_TAB_TYPE. CAST is a general-purpose routine not limited to use in collections. For example, if we wanted to fetch the EMPNO column from EMP as a VARCHAR2(20) instead of a NUMBER(4) type, we may use the query SELECT CAST(EMPNO AS VARCHAR2(20)) E FROM EMP.

We're now ready to query the data. Let's see what one row might look like:

```
ops$tkyte@ORA10G> select deptno, dname, loc, d.emps AS employees
  2  from dept_and_emp d
  3  where deptno = 10
  4  /

   DEPTNO DNAME          LOC            EMPLOYEES(EMPNO, ENAME, JOB,
---------- -------------- -------------- ----------------------------
       10 ACCOUNTING     NEW YORK       EMP_TAB_TYPE(EMP_TYPE(7782,
                                        'CLARK', 'MANAGER', 7839, '0
                                        9-JUN-81', 2450, NULL), EMP_
                                        TYPE(7839, 'KING', 'PRESIDEN
                                        T', NULL, '17-NOV-81', 5000,
                                         NULL), EMP_TYPE(7934, 'MILL
                                        ER', 'CLERK', 7782, '23-JAN-
                                        82', 1300, NULL))
```

All of the data is there, in a single column. Most applications, unless they are specifically written for the object-relational features, will not be able to deal with this particular column. For example, ODBC doesn't have a way to deal with a nested table (JDBC, OCI, Pro*C, PL/SQL, and most other APIs and languages do). For those cases, Oracle provides a way to un-nest a collection and treat it much like a relational table:

```
ops$tkyte@ORA10G> select d.deptno, d.dname, emp.*
  2  from dept_and_emp D, table(d.emps) emp
  3  /
```

DEPTNO	DNAME	EMPNO	ENAME	JOB	MGR	HIREDATE	SAL	COMM
10	ACCOUNTING	7782	CLARK	MANAGER	7839	09-JUN-81	2450	
10	ACCOUNTING	7839	KING	PRESIDENT		17-NOV-81	5000	
10	ACCOUNTING	7934	MILLER	CLERK	7782	23-JAN-82	1300	
20	RESEARCH	7369	SMITH	CLERK	7902	17-DEC-80	800	
20	RESEARCH	7566	JONES	MANAGER	7839	02-APR-81	2975	
20	RESEARCH	7788	SCOTT	ANALYST	7566	09-DEC-82	3000	
20	RESEARCH	7876	ADAMS	CLERK	7788	12-JAN-83	1100	
20	RESEARCH	7902	FORD	ANALYST	7566	03-DEC-81	3000	
30	SALES	7499	ALLEN	SALESMAN	7698	20-FEB-81	1600	300
30	SALES	7521	WARD	SALESMAN	7698	22-FEB-81	1250	500
30	SALES	7654	MARTIN	SALESMAN	7698	28-SEP-81	1250	1400
30	SALES	7698	BLAKE	MANAGER	7839	01-MAY-81	2850	
30	SALES	7844	TURNER	SALESMAN	7698	08-SEP-81	1500	0
30	SALES	7900	JAMES	CLERK	7698	03-DEC-81	950	

```
14 rows selected.
```

We are able to cast the EMPS column as a table and it naturally did the join for us—no join conditions were needed. In fact, since our EMP type doesn't have the DEPTNO column, there is nothing for us apparently to join on. Oracle takes care of that nuance for us.

So, how can we update the data? Let's say we want to give department 10 a $100 bonus. We would code the following:

```
ops$tkyte@ORA10G> update
  2     table( select emps
  3              from dept_and_emp
  4                where deptno = 10
  5          )
  6  set comm = 100
  7  /
3 rows updated.
```

Here is where the "virtually a table for every row" comes into play. In the SELECT predicate shown earlier, it may not have been obvious that there was a table per row; especially since the joins and such aren't there, it looks a little like "magic." The UPDATE statement, however, shows that there is a table per row. We selected a discrete table to UPDATE—this table has no name, only a query to identify it. If we use a query that does not SELECT *exactly* one table, we will receive the following:

```
ops$tkyte@ORA10G> update
  2     table( select emps
  3              from dept_and_emp
  4                where deptno = 1
```

```
  5       )
  6   set comm = 100
  7   /
update
*
ERROR at line 1:
ORA-22908: reference to NULL table value

ops$tkyte@ORA10G> update
  2     table( select emps
  3             from dept_and_emp
  4               where deptno > 1
  5         )
  6   set comm = 100
  7   /
  table( select emps
         *
ERROR at line 2:
ORA-01427: single-row subquery returns more than one row
```

If we return fewer than one row (one nested table instance), the update fails. Normally an update of zero rows is OK, but not in this case—it returns an error the same as if we left the table name off the update. If we return more than one row (more than one nested table instance), the update fails. Normally an update of many rows is perfectly OK. This shows that Oracle considers each row in the DEPT_AND_EMP table to point to another table, not just another set of rows as the relational model does.

This is the semantic difference between a nested table and a parent/child relational table. In the nested table model, there is one table per parent row. In the relational model, there is one set of rows per parent row. This difference can make nested tables somewhat cumbersome to use at times. Consider this model we are using, which provides a very nice view of the data from the perspective of single department. It is a terrible model if we want to ask questions like "What department does KING work for?", "How many accountants do we have working for us?", and so on. These questions are best asked of the EMP relational table, but in this nested table model we can only access the EMP data via the DEPT data. We must always join; we cannot query the EMP data alone. Well, we can't do it in a supported, documented method, but we can use a trick (more on this trick later). If we needed to update every row in the EMPS_NT, we would have to do four updates: one each for the rows in DEPT_AND_EMP to update the virtual table associated with each row.

Another thing to consider is that when we updated the employee data for department 10, we were semantically updating the EMPS column in the DEPT_AND_EMP table. We understand that physically there are two tables involved, but semantically there is only one. Even though we updated no data in the department table, the row that contains the nested table we did modify is locked from update by other sessions. In a traditional parent/child table relationship, this would not be the case.

These are the reasons why I tend to stay away from nested tables as a persistent storage mechanism. It is the *rare* child table that is not queried stand-alone. In the preceding example, the EMP table should be a strong entity. It stands alone, so it needs to be queried alone. I find this to be the case almost all of the time. I tend to use nested tables via views on relational tables.

So, now that we have seen how to update a nested table instance, inserting and deleting are pretty straightforward. Let's add a row to the nested table instance department 10 and remove a row from department 20:

```
ops$tkyte@ORA10G> insert into table
  2  ( select emps from dept_and_emp where deptno = 10 )
  3  values
  4  ( 1234, 'NewEmp', 'CLERK', 7782, sysdate, 1200, null );
1 row created.

ops$tkyte@ORA10G> delete from table
  2  ( select emps from dept_and_emp where deptno = 20 )
  3  where ename = 'SCOTT';
1 row deleted.

ops$tkyte@ORA10G> select d.dname, e.empno, ename
  2  from dept_and_emp d, table(d.emps) e
  3  where d.deptno in ( 10, 20 );

DNAME              EMPNO ENAME
-------------- ---------- ----------
ACCOUNTING          7782 CLARK
ACCOUNTING          7839 KING
ACCOUNTING          7934 MILLER
RESEARCH            7369 SMITH
RESEARCH            7566 JONES
RESEARCH            7876 ADAMS
RESEARCH            7902 FORD
ACCOUNTING          1234 NewEmp

8 rows selected.
```

That is the basic syntax of how to query and modify nested tables. You will find many times that you must un-nest these tables as we just did, especially in queries, to make use of them. Once you conceptually visualize the "virtual table per row" concept, working with nested tables becomes much easier.

Previously I stated, "We must always join; we cannot query the EMP data alone," but then I followed that up with a caveat: "You can if you really need to." It is undocumented and not supported, so use it *only* as a last ditch method. Where it will come in most handy is if you ever need to mass update the nested table (remember, you would have to do that through the DEPT table with a join). There is an underdocumented hint (it is mentioned briefly and not fully documented), NESTED_TABLE_GET_REFS, which is used by various tools such as EXP and IMP to deal with nested tables. It is also a way to see a little more about the physical structure of the nested tables. If you use this hint, you can query to get some "magic" results. The following query is what EXP (a data unload utility) uses to extract the data from this nested table:

```
ops$tkyte@ORA10G> SELECT /*+NESTED_TABLE_GET_REFS*/
  2          NESTED_TABLE_ID,SYS_NC_ROWINFO$
  3    FROM "OPS$TKYTE"."EMPS_NT"
  4  /


NESTED_TABLE_ID                    SYS_NC_ROWINFO$(EMPNO, EN
---------------------------------- -------------------------
F60DEEE0FF7D7BC1E030007F01001321 EMP_TYPE(7782, 'CLARK', '
                                   MANAGER', 7839, '09-JUN-8
                                   1', 2450, 100)


F60DEEE0FF7D7BC1E030007F01001321 EMP_TYPE(7839, 'KING', 'P
                                   RESIDENT', NULL, '17-NOV-
                                   81', 5000, 100) ...
```

Well, this is somewhat surprising if you describe this table:

```
ops$tkyte@ORA10G> desc emps_nt
 Name                          Null?    Type
 ----------------------------- -------- --------------------
 EMPNO                                  NUMBER(4)
 ENAME                                  VARCHAR2(10)
 JOB                                    VARCHAR2(9)
 MGR                                    NUMBER(4)
 HIREDATE                               DATE
 SAL                                    NUMBER(7,2)
 COMM                                   NUMBER(7,2)
```

These two columns don't even show up. They are part of the hidden implementation of nested tables. The NESTED_TABLE_ID is really a foreign key to the parent table DEPT_AND_EMP. DEPT_AND_EMP actually has a hidden column in it that is used to join to EMPS_NT. The SYS_NC_ROWINF$ "column" is a magic column; it is more of a function than a column. The nested table here is really an object table (it is made of an object type), and SYS_NC_INFO$ is the internal way Oracle references the row as an object, instead of referencing each of the scalar columns. Under the covers, all Oracle has done for us is implement a parent/child table with system-generated primary and foreign keys. If we dig a little deeper, we can query the "real" data dictionary to see all of the columns in the DEPT_AND_EMP table:

```
sys@ORA10G> select name
  2    from sys.col$
  3   where obj# = ( select object_id
  4                    from dba_objects
  5                   where object_name = 'DEPT_AND_EMP'
  6                     and owner = 'OPS$TKYTE' )
  7  /

NAME
------------------------------------
DEPTNO
```

```
DNAME
EMPS
LOC
SYS_NC0000400005$
```

Selecting this column out from the nested table, we'll see something like this:

```
ops$tkyte@ORA10G> select SYS_NC0000400005$ from dept_and_emp;

SYS_NC0000400005$
--------------------------------
F60DEEE0FF887BC1E030007F01001321
F60DEEE0FF897BC1E030007F01001321
F60DEEE0FF8A7BC1E030007F01001321
F60DEEE0FF8B7BC1E030007F01001321
```

The weird-looking column name, SYS_NC0000400005$, is the system-generated key placed into the DEPT_AND_EMP table. If we dig even deeper, we will find that Oracle has placed a unique index on this column. Unfortunately, however, it neglected to index the NESTED_TABLE_ID in EMPS_NT. This column really needs to be indexed, as we are always joining *from* DEPT_AND_EMP *to* EMPS_NT. This is an important thing to remember about nested tables if you use them with all of the defaults as just done: *always index* the NESTED_TABLE_ID in the nested tables!

I've gotten off track, though, at this point—I was talking about how to treat the nested table as if it were a real table. The NESTED_TABLE_GET_REFS hint does that for us. We can use the hint like this:

```
ops$tkyte@ORA10G> select /*+ nested_table_get_refs */ empno, ename
  2      from emps_nt where ename like '%A%';

    EMPNO ENAME
---------- ----------
     7782 CLARK
     7876 ADAMS
     7499 ALLEN
     7521 WARD
     7654 MARTIN
     7698 BLAKE
     7900 JAMES
7 rows selected.

ops$tkyte@ORA10G> update /*+ nested_table_get_refs */ emps_nt
  2      set ename = initcap(ename);
14 rows updated.

ops$tkyte@ORA10G> select /*+ nested_table_get_refs */ empno, ename
  2      from emps_nt where ename like '%a%';
```

```
     EMPNO ENAME
---------- ----------
      7782 Clark
      7876 Adams
      7521 Ward
      7654 Martin
      7698 Blake
      7900 James
6 rows selected.
```

Again, this is not a thoroughly documented and supported feature. It has a specific functionality for EXP and IMP to work. This is the only environment it is assured to work in. Use it at your own risk, and resist putting it into production code. In fact, if you find you *need to use it*, then by definition you didn't mean to use a nested table at all! It is the wrong construct for you. Use it for one-off fixes of data or to see what is in the nested table out of curiosity. The supported way to report on the data is to un-nest it like this:

```
ops$tkyte@ORA10G> select d.deptno, d.dname, emp.*
  2  from dept_and_emp D, table(d.emps) emp
  3  /
```

This is what you should use in queries and production code.

Nested Table Storage

We have already seen some of the storage of the nested table structure. In this section, we'll take an in-depth look at the structure created by Oracle by default and what sort of control over that we have. Working with the same CREATE statement as before

```
ops$tkyte@ORA10G> create table dept_and_emp
  2  (deptno number(2) primary key,
  3   dname      varchar2(14),
  4   loc        varchar2(13),
  5   emps       emp_tab_type
  6  )
  7  nested table emps store as emps_nt;
Table created.

ops$tkyte@ORA10G> alter table emps_nt add constraint emps_empno_unique
  2             unique(empno)
  3  /
Table altered.
```

we know that Oracle really creates a structure like the one shown in Figure 10-11.

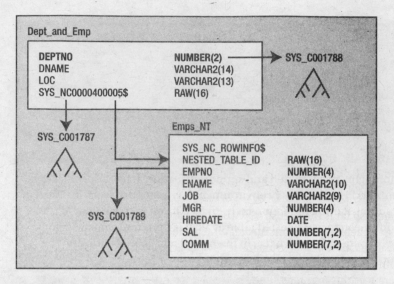

Figure 10-11. *Nested table physical implementation*

The code created two real tables. The table we asked to have is there, but it has an extra hidden column (we'll have one extra hidden column by default for *each* nested table column in a table). It also created a *unique* constraint on this hidden column. Oracle created the nested table, EMPS_NT, for us. This table has two hidden columns, one of which, SYS_NC_ ROWINFO$, is not really a column but a virtual column that returns all of the scalar elements as an object. The other is the foreign key called NESTED_TABLE_ID, which can be joined back to the parent table. Notice the *lack* of an index on this column. Finally, Oracle added an index on the DEPTNO column in the DEPT_AND_EMP table to enforce the primary key. So, we asked for a table and got a lot more than we bargained for. If you look at it, it is a lot like what you might create for a parent/child relationship, but you would have used the existing primary key on DEPTNO as the foreign key in EMPS_NT instead of generating a surrogate RAW(16) key.

If we look at the DBMS_METADATA.GET_DDL dump of our nested table example, we see the following:

```
ops$tkyte@ORA10G> begin
  2      dbms_metadata.set_transform_param
  3      ( DBMS_METADATA.SESSION_TRANSFORM, 'STORAGE', false );
  4  end;
  5  /
PL/SQL procedure successfully completed.

ops$tkyte@ORA10G> select dbms_metadata.get_ddl( 'TABLE', 'DEPT_AND_EMP' ) from dual;

DBMS_METADATA.GET_DDL('TABLE','DEPT_AND_EMP')
--------------------------------------------------------------------------------

  CREATE TABLE "OPS$TKYTE"."DEPT_AND_EMP"
   (    "DEPTNO" NUMBER(2,0),
```

```
        "DNAME" VARCHAR2(14),
        "LOC" VARCHAR2(13),
        "EMPS" "OPS$TKYTE"."EMP_TAB_TYPE" ,
         PRIMARY KEY ("DEPTNO")
 USING INDEX PCTFREE 10 INITRANS 2 MAXTRANS 255
 TABLESPACE "USERS"  ENABLE
  ) PCTFREE 10 PCTUSED 40 INITRANS 1 MAXTRANS 255 NOCOMPRESS LOGGING
 TABLESPACE "USERS"
NESTED TABLE "EMPS" STORE AS "EMPS_NT"
(PCTFREE 10 PCTUSED 40 INITRANS 1 MAXTRANS 255 LOGGING
 TABLESPACE "USERS" ) RETURN AS VALUE
```

The only new thing here so far is the RETURN AS VALUE. It is used to describe how the nested table is returned to a client application. By default, Oracle will return the nested table by value to the client; the actual data will be transmitted with each row. This can also be set to RETURN AS LOCATOR, meaning the client will get a pointer to the data, not the data itself. If—and only if—the client dereferences this pointer will the data be transmitted to it. So, if you believe the client will typically not look at the rows of a nested table for each parent row, you can return a locator instead of the values, saving on the network round-trips. For example, if you have a client application that displays the lists of departments and when the user double-clicks a department it shows the employee information, you may consider using the locator. This is because the details are usually not looked at—that is the exception, not the rule.

So, what else can we do with the nested table? First, the NESTED_TABLE_ID column must be indexed. Since we always access the nested table *from* the parent *to* the child, we really need that index. We can index that column using CREATE INDEX, but a better solution is to use an IOT to store the nested table. The nested table is another perfect example of what an IOT is excellent for. It will physically store the child rows co-located by NESTED_TABLE_ID (so retrieving the table is done with less physical I/O). It will remove the need for the redundant index on the RAW(16) column. Going one step further, since the NESTED_TABLE_ID will be the leading column in the IOT's primary key, we should also incorporate index key compression to suppress the redundant NESTED_TABLE_IDs that would be there otherwise. In addition, we can incorporate our UNIQUE and NOT NULL constraint on the EMPNO column into the CREATE TABLE command. Therefore, if we take the preceding CREATE TABLE and modify it slightly, as follows:

```
ops$tkyte@ORA10G> CREATE TABLE "OPS$TKYTE"."DEPT_AND_EMP"
  2  ("DEPTNO" NUMBER(2, 0),
  3   "DNAME"  VARCHAR2(14),
  4   "LOC"    VARCHAR2(13),
  5  "EMPS" "EMP_TAB_TYPE")
  6  PCTFREE 10 PCTUSED 40 INITRANS 1 MAXTRANS 255 LOGGING
  7  STORAGE(INITIAL 131072 NEXT 131072
  8          MINEXTENTS 1 MAXEXTENTS 4096
  9          PCTINCREASE 0 FREELISTS 1 FREELIST GROUPS 1
 10          BUFFER_POOL DEFAULT)
 11  TABLESPACE "USERS"
 12  NESTED TABLE "EMPS"
 13    STORE AS "EMPS_NT"
 14    ( (empno NOT NULL, unique (empno), primary key(nested_table_id,empno))
```

```
15        organization index compress 1 )
16     RETURN AS VALUE
17   /
Table created.
```

we now get the following set of objects. Instead of having a conventional table EMP_NT, we have an IOT EMPS_NT as signified by the index structure overlaid on the table in Figure 10-12.

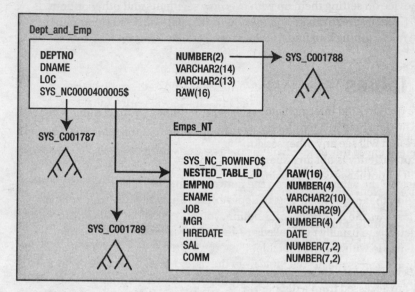

Figure 10-12. *Nested table implemented as an IOT*

Where the EMPS_NT is an IOT using compression, it should take less storage than the original default nested table *and* it has the index we badly need.

Nested Tables Wrap-Up

I do not use nested tables as a permanent storage mechanism myself, for the following reasons:

- The unnecessary storage overhead of the RAW(16) columns that are added. Both the parent and child table will have this extra column. The parent table will have an extra 16-byte RAW for each nested table column it has. Since the parent table typically already has a primary key (DEPTNO in my examples), it makes sense to use this key in the child tables, not a system-generated key.

- The unnecessary overhead of the additional unique constraint on the parent table, when it typically already has a unique constraint.

- The nested table is not easily used by itself, without using unsupported constructs (NESTED_TABLE_GET_REFS). It can be un-nested for queries, but not mass updates. I have yet to find a table in real life that isn't queried "by itself."

I do use nested tables heavily as a programming construct and in views. This is where I believe they are in their element. As a storage mechanism, I much prefer creating the parent/ child tables myself. After creating the parent/child tables, we can, in fact, create a view that makes it appear as if we had a real nested table. That is, we can achieve all of the advantages of the nested table construct without incurring the overhead.

If you do use a nested table as a storage mechanism, be sure to make it an IOT to avoid the overhead of an index on the NESTED_TABLE_ID and the nested table itself. See the previous section on IOTs for advice on setting them up with overflow segments and other options. If you do not use an IOT, make sure to create an index on the NESTED_TABLE_ID column in the nested table to avoid full scanning it to find the child rows.

Temporary Tables

Temporary tables are used to hold intermediate resultsets, for the duration of either a transaction or a session. The data held in a temporary table is only ever visible to the current session—no other session will see any other session's data, even if the current session COMMITs the data. Multiuser concurrency is not an issue with regard to temporary tables either, as one session can never block another session by using a temporary table. Even if we "lock" the temporary table, it will not prevent other sessions using their temporary table. As we observed in Chapter 9, temporary tables generate significantly less redo than regular tables. However, since they must generate undo information for the data they contain, they will generate some amount of redo. UPDATEs and DELETEs will generate the largest amount; INSERTs and SELECTs the least amount.

Temporary tables will allocate storage from the currently logged-in user's temporary tablespace, or if they are accessed from a definer rights procedure, the temporary tablespace of the owner of that procedure will be used. A global temporary table is really just a template for the table itself. The act of creating a temporary table involves no storage allocation; no INITIAL extent is allocated, as it would be for a regular table. Rather, at runtime when a session first puts data into the temporary table, a temporary segment for that session will be created. Since each session gets its own temporary segment (not just an extent of an existing segment), every user might be allocating space for her temporary table in different tablespaces. USER1 might have his temporary tablespace set to TEMP1, so his temporary tables will be allocated from this space. USER2 might have TEMP2 as her temporary tablespace, and her temporary tables will be allocated there.

Oracle's temporary tables are similar to temporary tables in other relational databases, with the main exception being that they are "statically" defined. You create them once per database, not once per stored procedure in the database. They always exist—they will be in the data dictionary as objects, but they will always appear empty until your session puts data into them. The fact that they are statically defined allows you to create views that reference temporary tables, to create stored procedures that use static SQL to reference them, and so on.

Temporary tables may be *session* based (data survives in the table across commits but not a disconnect/reconnect). They may also be *transaction* based (data disappears after a commit). Here is an example showing the behavior of both. I used the SCOTT.EMP table as a template:

```
ops$tkyte@ORA10G> create global temporary table temp_table_session
  2  on commit preserve rows
  3  as
  4  select * from scott.emp where 1=0
  5  /
Table created.
```

The ON COMMIT PRESERVE ROWS clause makes this a session-based temporary table. Rows will stay in this table until my session disconnects or I physically remove them via a DELETE or TRUNCATE. Only my session can see these rows; no other session will ever see "my" rows, even after I COMMIT.

```
ops$tkyte@ORA10G> create global temporary table temp_table_transaction
  2  on commit delete rows
  3  as
  4  select * from scott.emp where 1=0
  5  /
Table created.
```

The ON COMMIT DELETE ROWS makes this a transaction-based temporary table. When my session commits, the rows disappear. The rows will disappear by simply giving back the temporary extents allocated to my table—there is no overhead involved in the automatic clearing of temporary tables.

Now, let's look at the differences between the two types:

```
ops$tkyte@ORA10G> insert into temp_table_session select * from scott.emp;
14 rows created.

ops$tkyte@ORA10G> insert into temp_table_transaction select * from scott.emp;
14 rows created.
```

We've just put 14 rows into each TEMP table, and this shows we can "see" them:

```
ops$tkyte@ORA10G> select session_cnt, transaction_cnt
  2     from ( select count(*) session_cnt from temp_table_session ),
  3          ( select count(*) transaction_cnt from temp_table_transaction );

SESSION_CNT TRANSACTION_CNT
----------- ---------------
         14              14

ops$tkyte@ORA10G> commit;
```

Since we've committed, we'll see the session-based rows but not the transaction-based rows:

```
ops$tkyte@ORA10G> select session_cnt, transaction_cnt
  2     from ( select count(*) session_cnt from temp_table_session ),
  3          ( select count(*) transaction_cnt from temp_table_transaction );
```

```
SESSION_CNT TRANSACTION_CNT
----------- ---------------
         14               0

ops$tkyte@ORA10G>
ops$tkyte@ORA10G> disconnect
Disconnected from Oracle Database 10g Enterprise Edition Release 10.1.0.3.0
With the Partitioning, OLAP and Data Mining options
ops$tkyte@ORA10G> connect /
Connected.
```

Since we've started a new session, we'll see no rows in either table:

```
ops$tkyte@ORA10G> select session_cnt, transaction_cnt
  2     from ( select count(*) session_cnt from temp_table_session ),
  3          ( select count(*) transaction_cnt from temp_table_transaction );

SESSION_CNT TRANSACTION_CNT
----------- ---------------
          0               0
```

If you have experience with temporary tables in SQL Server and/or Sybase, the major consideration for you is that instead of executing SELECT X, Y, Z INTO #TEMP FROM SOME_TABLE to dynamically create and populate a temporary table, you will

- Create all your global temporary tables once, as part of the application installation, just as you create permanent tables.

- In your procedures, simply INSERT INTO TEMP (X,Y,Z) SELECT X,Y,Z FROM SOME_TABLE.

Just to drive home the point, the goal here is to not create tables in your stored procedures at runtime. That is not the proper way to use temporary tables in Oracle. DDL is an expensive operation; you want to avoid doing that at runtime. The temporary tables for an application should be created during the application installation—*never* at runtime.

Temporary tables can have many of the attributes of a permanent table. They may have triggers, check constraints, indexes, and so on. Features of permanent tables that they do not support include the following:

- They cannot have referential integrity constraints. Neither can they be the *target* of a foreign key, nor can they have a foreign key defined on them.

- They cannot have NESTED TABLE type columns. In Oracle9*i* and earlier, they cannot have VARRAY type columns either; this restriction was lifted in Oracle 10*g*.

- They cannot be IOTs.

- They cannot be in a cluster of any type.

- They cannot be partitioned.

- They cannot have statistics generated via the ANALYZE table command.

One of the drawbacks of a temporary table in any database is the fact that the optimizer has no real statistics on it normally. When using the *cost-based optimizer* (*CBO*), valid statistics are vital to the optimizer's success (or failure). In the absence of statistics, the optimizer will make guesses as to the distribution of data, the amount of data, and the selectivity of an index. When these guesses are wrong, the query plans generated for queries that make heavy use of temporary tables could be less than optimal. In many cases, the correct solution is to not use a temporary table at all, but rather to use an INLINE VIEW (for an example of an INLINE VIEW, refer to the SELECT just run—it has two of them) in its place. In this fashion, Oracle will have access to all of the relevant statistics for a table and can come up with an optimal plan.

I find many times people use temporary tables because they learned in other databases that joining too many tables in a single query is a "bad thing." This is a practice that must be unlearned for Oracle development. Rather than trying to outsmart the optimizer and breaking what should be a single query into three or four queries that store their subresults into temporary tables, and then combining the temporary tables, you should just code a single query that answers the original question. Referencing many tables in a single query is OK; the temporary table crutch is not needed in Oracle for this purpose.

In other cases, however, the use of a temporary table in a process is the correct approach. For example, I once wrote a Palm sync application to synchronize the date book on a Palm Pilot with calendar information stored in Oracle. The Palm gives me a list of all records that have been modified since the last hot synchronization. I must take these records and compare them against the live data in the database, update the database records, and then generate a list of changes to be applied to the Palm. This is a perfect example of when a temporary table is very useful. I used a temporary table to store the changes from the Palm in the database. I then ran a stored procedure that bumps the Palm-generated changes against the live (and very large) permanent tables to discover what changes need to be made to the Oracle data, and then to find the changes that need to come from Oracle back down to the Palm. I have to make a couple of passes on this data. First, I find all records that were modified only on the Palm and make the corresponding changes in Oracle. Next, I find all records that were modified on both the Palm and my database since the last synchronization and rectify them. Then I find all records that were modified only on the database and place their changes into the temporary table. Lastly, the Palm sync application pulls the changes from the temporary table and applies them to the Palm device itself. Upon disconnection, the temporary data goes away.

The issue I encountered, however, is that because the permanent tables were analyzed, the CBO was being used. The temporary table had no statistics on it (you can analyze the temporary table, but no statistics are gathered), and the CBO would "guess" many things about it. I, as the developer, knew the average number of rows I might expect, the distribution of the data, the selectivity of the indexes, and so on. I needed a way to inform the optimizer of these *better* guesses. There are three ways to give the optimizer statistics on the global temporary tables. One is via dynamic sampling (new in Oracle9*i* Release 2 and above) and the other is the DBMS_STATS package, which has two ways to accomplish this. First, let's look at dynamic sampling.

Dynamic sampling is the optimizer's ability, when hard parsing a query, to scan segments in the database (sample them) to collect statistics useful in optimizing that particular query. It is akin to doing a "miniature gather statistics" command during a hard parse. In Oracle 10*g*, dynamic sampling will work out of the box, because the default setting has been increased from 1 to 2, and at level 2, the optimizer will dynamically sample any unanalyzed object referenced in a query processed by the optimizer prior to evaluating the query plan. In 9*i* Release 2,

the setting of 1 would cause dynamic sampling to be used much less often. We can use an
ALTER SESSION|SYSTEM command in Oracle9*i* Release 2 to make it behave the way Oracle 10*g*
does by default, or we can use the dynamic sampling hint as follows:

```
ops$tkyte@ORA9IR2> create global temporary table gtt
  2 as
  3 select * from scott.emp where 1=0;
Table created.

ops$tkyte@ORA9IR2> insert into gtt select * from scott.emp;
14 rows created.

ops$tkyte@ORA9IR2> set autotrace traceonly explain
ops$tkyte@ORA9IR2> select /*+ first_rows */ * from gtt;

Execution Plan
----------------------------------------------------------
   0      SELECT STATEMENT Optimizer=HINT: FIRST_ROWS (Cost=17 Card=8168 Bytes...
   1    0    TABLE ACCESS (FULL) OF 'GTT' (Cost=17 Card=8168 Bytes=710616)

ops$tkyte@ORA9IR2> select /*+ first_rows dynamic_sampling(gtt 2) */ * from gtt;

Execution Plan
----------------------------------------------------------
   0      SELECT STATEMENT Optimizer=HINT: FIRST_ROWS (Cost=17 Card=14 Bytes=1218)
   1    0    TABLE ACCESS (FULL) OF 'GTT' (Cost=17 Card=14 Bytes=1218)

ops$tkyte@ORA9IR2> set autotrace off
```

Here, we set the dynamic sampling to level 2 for the table GTT in this query. Left to itself,
the optimizer guessed 8,168 rows would be returned from the table GTT. Using dynamic sampling, the estimated cardinality will be much closer to reality (which leads to better query
plans overall). Using the level 2 setting, the optimizer quickly scans the table to come up with
more-realistic estimates of the true size of this table. In Oracle 10*g*, we should find this to be
less of a problem, because the defaults will cause dynamic sampling to take place:

```
ops$tkyte@ORA10G> create global temporary table gtt
  2 as
  3 select * from scott.emp where 1=0;
Table created.

ops$tkyte@ORA10G> insert into gtt select * from scott.emp;
14 rows created.

ops$tkyte@ORA10G> set autotrace traceonly explain
ops$tkyte@ORA10G> select * from gtt;
```

```
Execution Plan
-----------------------------------------------------------
   0      SELECT STATEMENT Optimizer=ALL_ROWS (Cost=2 Card=14 Bytes=1218)
   1    0    TABLE ACCESS (FULL) OF 'GTT' (TABLE (TEMP)) (Cost=2 Card=14 Bytes=1218)

ops$tkyte@ORA10G> set autotrace off
```

We get the right cardinality without having to ask for it. Dynamic sampling does not come free, however—there is a cost associated with having to perform it at query parse time. If we gathered appropriate representative statistics ahead of time, we could avoid this at hard parse time. That leads us in to DBMS_STATS.

There are three methods to use DBMS_STATS to gather representative statistics. The first way is to use DBMS_STATS with the GATHER_SCHEMA_STATS or GATHER_DATABASE_STATS call. These procedures allow you to pass in a parameter, GATHER_TEMP, which is a Boolean and defaults to FALSE. When set to TRUE, any ON COMMIT PRESERVE ROWS global temporary table will have statistics gathered and stored (this technique will *not* work on ON COMMIT DELETE ROWS tables). Consider the following (note that this was done in an empty schema; the only objects are those you see created):

```
ops$tkyte@ORA10G> create table emp as select * from scott.emp;
Table created.

ops$tkyte@ORA10G> create global temporary table gtt1 ( x number )
  2  on commit preserve rows;
Table created.

ops$tkyte@ORA10G> create global temporary table gtt2 ( x number )
  2  on commit delete rows;
Table created.

ops$tkyte@ORA10G> insert into gtt1 select user_id from all_users;
38 rows created.

ops$tkyte@ORA10G> insert into gtt2 select user_id from all_users;
38 rows created.

ops$tkyte@ORA10G> exec dbms_stats.gather_schema_stats( user );
PL/SQL procedure successfully completed.

ops$tkyte@ORA10G> select table_name, last_analyzed, num_rows from user_tables;

TABLE_NAME                        LAST_ANAL   NUM_ROWS
-------------------------------   ---------   ----------
EMP                               01-MAY-05          14
GTT1
GTT2
```

As we can see, only the EMP table was analyzed in this case; the two global temporary tables were ignored. We can change that behavior by calling GATHER_SCHEMA_STATS with GATHER_TEMP => TRUE:

```
ops$tkyte@ORA10G> insert into gtt2 select user_id from all_users;
38 rows created.

ops$tkyte@ORA10G> exec dbms_stats.gather_schema_stats( user, gather_temp=>TRUE );
PL/SQL procedure successfully completed.

ops$tkyte@ORA10G> select table_name, last_analyzed, num_rows from user_tables;

TABLE_NAME                            LAST_ANAL   NUM_ROWS
------------------------------------- ---------   ----------
EMP                                   01-MAY-05         14
GTT1                                  01-MAY-05         38
GTT2                                  01-MAY-05          0
```

Notice that the ON COMMIT PRESERVE rows table has accurate statistics, but the ON COMMIT DELETE ROWS does not. DBMS_STATS commits, and that wipes out any information in that table. Do note, however, that GTT2 does now have statistics, which in itself is *a bad thing*, because the statistics are very much incorrect! It is doubtful the table will have 0 rows in it at runtime. So, if you use this approach, be aware of two things:

- Make sure to populate your global temporary tables with representative data *in the session that gathers the statistics*. If not, they will appear empty to DBMS_STATS.

- If you have ON COMMIT DELETE ROWS global temporary tables, this approach should not be used, as you will definitely gather inappropriate values.

The second technique that works with ON COMMIT PRESERVE ROWS global temporary tables is to use GATHER_TABLE_STATS directly on the table. You would populate the global temporary table as we just did, and then execute GATHER_TABLE_STATS on that global temporary table. Note that just as before, this *does not work* for ON COMMIT DELETE ROWS global temporary tables, as the same issues as just described would come into play.

The last technique using DBMS_STATS uses a manual process to populate the data dictionary with representative statistics for our temporary tables. For example, if on average the number of rows in the temporary table will be 500, the average row size will be 100 bytes, and the number of blocks will be 7, we could simply use the following:

```
ops$tkyte@ORA10G> create global temporary table t ( x int, y varchar2(100) );
Table created.

ops$tkyte@ORA10G> begin
  2      dbms_stats.set_table_stats( ownname => USER,
  3                                  tabname => 'T',
  4                                  numrows => 500,
  5                                  numblks => 7,
  6                                  avgrlen => 100 );
  7  end;
```

```
  8  /
PL/SQL procedure successfully completed.

ops$tkyte@ORA10G> select table_name, num_rows, blocks, avg_row_len
  2               from user_tables
  3               where table_name = 'T';

TABLE_NAME                       NUM_ROWS     BLOCKS AVG_ROW_LEN
------------------------------ ---------- ---------- -----------
T                                     500          7         100
```

Now, the optimizer won't use its best guess—it will use *our* best guess for this information.

Temporary Tables Wrap-Up

Temporary tables can be useful in an application where you need to temporarily store a set of rows to be processed against other tables, for either a session or a transaction. They are not meant to be used as a means to take a single larger query and "break it up" into smaller result sets that would be combined back together (which seems to be the most popular use of temporary tables in other databases). In fact, you will find in almost all cases that a single query broken up into smaller temporary table queries performs more slowly in Oracle than the single query would have. I've seen this behavior time and time again, when given the opportunity to rewrite the series of INSERTs into temporary tables as SELECTs in the form of one large query, the resulting single query executes much faster than the original multistep process.

Temporary tables generate a minimum amount of redo, but they still generate some redo, and there is no way to disable that. The redo is generated for the rollback data, and in most typical uses it will be negligible. If you only INSERT and SELECT from temporary tables, the amount of redo generated will not be noticeable. Only if you DELETE or UPDATE a temporary table heavily will you see large amounts of redo generated.

Statistics used by the CBO can be generated on a temporary table with care; however, a better guess set of statistics may be set on a temporary table using the DBMS_STATS package or dynamically collected by the optimizer at hard parse time using dynamic sampling.

Object Tables

We have already seen a partial example of an object table with nested tables. An *object table* is a table that is created based on a TYPE, not as a collection of columns. Normally, a CREATE TABLE would look like this:

```
create table t ( x int, y date, z varchar2(25) );
```

An object table creation statement looks more like this:

```
create table t of Some_Type;
```

The attributes (columns) of T are derived from the definition of SOME_TYPE. Let's quickly look at an example involving a couple of types, and then we'll review the resulting data structures:

```
ops$tkyte@ORA10G> create or replace type address_type
  2  as object
  3  ( city    varchar2(30),
  4    street  varchar2(30),
  5    state   varchar2(2),
  6    zip     number
  7  )
  8  /
Type created.

ops$tkyte@ORA10G> create or replace type person_type
  2  as object
  3  ( name          varchar2(30),
  4    dob           date,
  5    home_address  address_type,
  6    work_address  address_type
  7  )
  8  /
Type created.

ops$tkyte@ORA10G> create table people of person_type
  2  /
Table created.

ops$tkyte@ORA10G> desc people
 Name                                      Null?    Type
 ---------------------------------------- -------- -----------------------------
 NAME                                               VARCHAR2(30)
 DOB                                                DATE
 HOME_ADDRESS                                       ADDRESS_TYPE
 WORK_ADDRESS                                       ADDRESS_TYPE
```

That's all there is to it. We create some type definitions, and then we can create tables of that type. The table appears to have four columns representing the four attributes of the PERSON_TYPE we created. We are at the point where we can now perform DML on the object table to create and query data:

```
ops$tkyte@ORA10G> insert into people values ( 'Tom', '15-mar-1965',
  2  address_type( 'Reston', '123 Main Street', 'Va', '45678' ),
  3  address_type( 'Redwood', '1 Oracle Way', 'Ca', '23456' ) );
1 row created.

ops$tkyte@ORA10G> select * from people;

NAME  DOB       HOME_ADDRESS(CITY, S WORK_ADDRESS(CITY, S
----- --------- -------------------- --------------------
Tom   15-MAR-65 ADDRESS_TYPE('Reston ADDRESS_TYPE('Redwoo
```

```
                        ', '123 Main Street' d', '1 Oracle Way',
                        , 'Va', 45678)        'Ca', 23456)

ops$tkyte@ORA10G> select name, p.home_address.city from people p;

NAME  HOME_ADDRESS.CITY
----- ------------------------------
Tom   Reston
```

We're starting to see some of the object syntax necessary to deal with object types. For example, in the INSERT statement we had to wrap the HOME_ADDRESS and WORK_ADDRESS with a CAST. We cast the scalar values to be of an ADDRESS_TYPE. Another way of saying this is that we create an ADDRESS_TYPE instance for that row by using the default constructor for the ADDRESS_TYPE object.

Now, as far as the external face of the table is concerned, there are four columns in our table. By now, after seeing the hidden magic that took place for the nested tables, we can probably guess that there is something else going on. Oracle stores all object-relational data in plain old relational tables—at the end of the day it is all in rows and columns. If we dig into the "real" data dictionary, we can see what this table really looks like:

```
ops$tkyte@ORA10G> select name, segcollength
  2    from sys.col$
  3   where obj# = ( select object_id
  4                    from user_objects
  5                   where object_name = 'PEOPLE' )
  6  /

NAME                         SEGCOLLENGTH
---------------------------- ------------
SYS_NC_OID$                            16
SYS_NC_ROWINFO$                         1
NAME                                   30
DOB                                     7
HOME_ADDRESS                            1
SYS_NC00006$                           30
SYS_NC00007$                           30
SYS_NC00008$                            2
SYS_NC00009$                           22
WORK_ADDRESS                            1
SYS_NC00011$                           30
SYS_NC00012$                           30
SYS_NC00013$                            2
SYS_NC00014$                           22
 14 rows selected.
```

This looks quite different from what DESCRIBE tells us. Apparently, there are 14 columns in this table, not 4. In this case, they are

- **SYS_NC_OID$**: This is the system-generated object ID of the table. It is a unique RAW(16) column. It has a unique constraint on it, and there is a corresponding unique index created on it as well.

- **SYS_NC_ROWINFO**: This is the same "magic" function we observed with the nested table. If we select that from the table, it returns the entire row as a single column:

```
ops$tkyte@ORA10G> select sys_nc_rowinfo$ from people;

SYS_NC_ROWINFO$(NAME, DOB, HOME_ADDRESS(CITY,STREET,STATE,ZIP), WORK_ADDRESS
---------------------------------------------------------------------------
PERSON_TYPE('Tom', '15-MAR-65', ADDRESS_TYPE('Reston', '123 Main Street',
'Va', 45678), ADDRESS_TYPE('Redwood', '1 Oracle Way', 'Ca', 2346))
```

- **NAME, DOB**: These are the scalar attributes of our object table. They are stored much as we would expect, as regular columns.

- **HOME_ADDRESS, WORK_ADDRESS**: These are "magic" functions as well. They return the collection of columns they represent as a single object. These consume no real space except to signify NULL or NOT NULL for the entity.

- **SYS_NCnnnnn$**: These are the scalar implementations of our embedded object types. Since the PERSON_TYPE had the ADDRESS_TYPE embedded in it, Oracle needed to make room to store them in the appropriate type of columns. The system-generated names are necessary since a column name must be unique, and there is nothing stopping us from using the same object type more than once as we did here. If the names were not generated, we would have ended up with the ZIP column twice.

So, just like with the nested table, there is a lot going on here. A pseudo primary key of 16 bytes was added, there are virtual columns, and an index was created for us. We can change the default behavior with regard to the value of the object identifier assigned to an object, as we'll see in a moment. First, let's look at the full verbose SQL that would generate our table for us. Again, this was generated using EXP/IMP since I wanted to easily see the dependent objects, including all of the SQL needed to re-create this object. This was achieved via the following:

```
[tkyte@localhost tkyte]$ exp userid=/ tables=people rows=n
Export: Release 10.1.0.3.0 - Production on Sun May 1 14:04:16 2005
Copyright (c) 1982, 2004, Oracle.  All rights reserved.

Connected to: Oracle Database 10g Enterprise Edition Release 10.1.0.3.0 - Production
With the Partitioning, OLAP and Data Mining options
Export done in WE8ISO8859P1 character set and AL16UTF16 NCHAR character set
Note: table data (rows) will not be exported

About to export specified tables via Conventional Path ...
. . exporting table                      PEOPLE
Export terminated successfully without warnings.
```

```
[tkyte@localhost tkyte]$ imp userid=/ indexfile=people.sql full=y
Import: Release 10.1.0.3.0 - Production on Sun May 1 14:04:33 2005
Copyright (c) 1982, 2004, Oracle.  All rights reserved.

Connected to: Oracle Database 10g Enterprise Edition Release 10.1.0.3.0 - Production
With the Partitioning, OLAP and Data Mining options

Export file created by EXPORT:V10.01.00 via conventional path
import done in WE8ISO8859P1 character set and AL16UTF16 NCHAR character set
Import terminated successfully without warnings.
```

Review of the people.sql file that results would show this:

```
CREATE TABLE "OPS$TKYTE"."PEOPLE"
OF "PERSON_TYPE" OID 'F610318AC3D8981FE030007F01001464'
OIDINDEX (PCTFREE 10 INITRANS 2 MAXTRANS 255
          STORAGE(INITIAL 131072 NEXT 131072
                MINEXTENTS 1 MAXEXTENTS 4096
                PCTINCREASE 0 FREELISTS 1 FREELIST GROUPS 1
                BUFFER_POOL DEFAULT)
TABLESPACE "USERS")
PCTFREE 10 PCTUSED 40
INITRANS 1 MAXTRANS 255
LOGGING STORAGE(INITIAL 131072 NEXT 131072
                MINEXTENTS 1 MAXEXTENTS 4096
                PCTINCREASE 0 FREELISTS 1 FREELIST GROUPS 1
                BUFFER_POOL DEFAULT) TABLESPACE "USERS" NOCOMPRESS
/

ALTER TABLE "OPS$TKYTE"."PEOPLE" MODIFY
("SYS_NC_OID$" DEFAULT SYS_OP_GUID())
/
```

This gives us a little more insight into what is actually taking place here. We see the OIDINDEX clause clearly now, and we see a reference to the SYS_NC_OID$ column. This is the hidden primary key of the table. The function SYS_OP_GUID is the same as the function SYS_GUID. They both return a globally unique identifier that is a 16-byte RAW field.

The OID '<big hex number>' syntax is not documented in the Oracle documentation. All this is doing is ensuring that during an EXP and subsequent IMP, the underlying type PERSON_TYPE is in fact the *same* type. This will prevent an error that would occur if we performed the following steps:

1. Create the PEOPLE table.

2. Export the table.

3. Drop the table and the underlying PERSON_TYPE.

4. Create a new PERSON_TYPE with different attributes.

5. Import the old PEOPLE data.

Obviously, this export cannot be imported into the new structure—it will not fit. This check prevents that from occurring.

If you remember, I mentioned that we can change the behavior of the object identifier assigned to an object instance. Instead of having the system generate a pseudo primary key for us, we can use the natural key of an object. At first, this might appear self-defeating—the SYS_NC_OID$ will still appear in the table definition in SYS.COL$ and, in fact, it will appear to consume massive amounts of storage as compared to the system-generated column. Once again, however, there is "magic" at work here. The SYS_NC_OID$ column for an object table that is based on a *primary key* and not *system* generated is a virtual column and consumes no real storage on disk.

Here is an example that shows what happens in the data dictionary and demonstrates that there is no physical storage consumed for the SYS_NC_OID$. We'll start with an analysis of the system-generated OID table:

```
ops$tkyte@ORA10G> create table people of person_type
  2  /
Table created.

ops$tkyte@ORA10G> select name, type#, segcollength
  2     from sys.col$
  3   where obj# = ( select object_id
  4                    from user_objects
  5                   where object_name = 'PEOPLE' )
  6     and name like 'SYS\_NC\_%' escape '\'
  7  /

NAME                         TYPE# SEGCOLLENGTH
---------------------------- ----------- ------------
SYS_NC_OID$                     23            16
SYS_NC_ROWINFO$                121             1

ops$tkyte@ORA10G> insert into people(name)
  2  select rownum from all_objects;
48217 rows created.

ops$tkyte@ORA10G> exec dbms_stats.gather_table_stats( user, 'PEOPLE' );
PL/SQL procedure successfully completed.

ops$tkyte@ORA10G> select table_name, avg_row_len from user_object_tables;

TABLE_NAME                      AVG_ROW_LEN
------------------------------- ------------
PEOPLE                              23
```

We see here that the average row length is 23 bytes: 16 bytes for the SYS_NC_OID$ and 7 bytes for the NAME. Now, let's do the same thing, but use a primary key on the NAME column as the object identifier:

```
ops$tkyte@ORA10G> CREATE TABLE "PEOPLE"
  2  OF "PERSON_TYPE"
  3  ( constraint people_pk primary key(name) )
  4  object identifier is PRIMARY KEY
  5  /
Table created.

ops$tkyte@ORA10G> select name, type#, segcollength
  2    from sys.col$
  3   where obj# = ( select object_id
  4                    from user_objects
  5                   where object_name = 'PEOPLE' )
  6     and name like 'SYS\_NC\_%' escape '\'
  7  /

NAME                                TYPE# SEGCOLLENGTH
----------------------------------- ----- ------------
SYS_NC_OID$                            23           81
SYS_NC_ROWINFO$                       121            1
```

According to this, instead of a small 16-byte column, we have a large 81-byte column! In reality, there is no data stored in there. It will be null. The system will generate a unique ID based on the object table, its underlying type, and the value in the row itself. We can see this in the following:

```
ops$tkyte@ORA10G> insert into people (name)
  2  values ( 'Hello World!' );
1 row created.

ops$tkyte@ORA10G> select sys_nc_oid$ from people p;

SYS_NC_OID$
--------------------------------------------------------------------------------
F610733A48F865F9E030007F0100149A00000017260100010001002900000000000C07001E01000
02A00078401FE000000140C48656C6C6F20576F726C6421000000000000000000000000000000000
0000

ops$tkyte@ORA10G> select utl_raw.cast_to_raw( 'Hello World!' ) data
  2  from dual;

DATA
--------------------------------------------------------------------------------
48656C6C6F20576F726C6421

ops$tkyte@ORA10G> select utl_raw.cast_to_varchar2(sys_nc_oid$) data
  2  from people;
```

```
DATA
--------------------------------------------------------------------------------
<garbage bits and bytes..>Hello World!
```

If we select out the SYS_NC_OID$ column and inspect the HEX dump of the string we inserted, we see that the row data itself is embedded in the object ID. Converting the object ID into a VARCHAR2, we can confirm that visually. Does that mean our data is stored twice with a lot of overhead with it? No, it is not—it is just factored into that magic thing that is the SYS_NC_OID$ column upon retrieval. Oracle synthesizes the data upon selecting from the table.

Now for an opinion. The object-relational components (nested tables and object tables) are primarily what I call "syntactic sugar." They are always translated into good old relational rows and columns. I prefer not to use them as physical storage mechanisms personally. There are too many bits of "magic" happening—side effects that are not clear. You get hidden columns, extra indexes, surprise pseudo columns, and so on. *This does not mean that the object-relational components are a waste of time*—on the contrary, I use them in PL/SQL constantly. I use them with object views. I can achieve the benefits of a nested table construct (less data returned over the network for a master/detail relationship, conceptually easier to work with, and so on) without any of the physical storage concerns. That is because I can use object views to synthesize my objects from my relational data. This solves most of my concerns with object tables/nested tables in that the physical storage is dictated by me, the join conditions are set up by me, and the tables are available as relational tables (which is what many third-party tools and applications will demand) naturally. The people who require an object view of relational data can have it, and the people who need the relational view can have it. Since object tables are really relational tables in disguise, we are doing the same thing Oracle does for us behind the scenes, only we can do it more efficiently, since we don't have to do it generically as they do. For example, using the types defined earlier, I could just as easily use the following:

```
ops$tkyte@ORA10G> create table people_tab
  2  ( name          varchar2(30) primary key,
  3    dob           date,
  4    home_city     varchar2(30),
  5    home_street   varchar2(30),
  6    home_state    varchar2(2),
  7    home_zip      number,
  8    work_city     varchar2(30),
  9    work_street   varchar2(30),
 10    work_state    varchar2(2),
 11    work_zip      number
 12  )
 13  /
Table created.

ops$tkyte@ORA10G> create view people of person_type
  2  with object identifier (name)
  3  as
  4  select name, dob,
  5    address_type(home_city,home_street,home_state,home_zip) home_adress,
```

```
    6        address_type(work_city,work_street,work_state,work_zip) work_adress
    7        from people_tab
    8    /
View created.


ops$tkyte@ORA10G> insert into people values ( 'Tom', '15-mar-1965',
   2    address_type( 'Reston', '123 Main Street', 'Va', '45678' ),
   3    address_type( 'Redwood', '1 Oracle Way', 'Ca', '23456' ) );
1 row created.
```

However I achieve very much the same effect, I know exactly what is stored, how it is stored, and where it is stored. For more complex objects, we may have to code INSTEAD OF triggers on the object views to allow for modifications through the view.

Object Tables Wrap-Up

Object tables are used to implement an object relational model in Oracle. A single object table will create many physical database objects typically, and add additional columns to your schema to manage everything. There is some amount of "magic" associated with object tables. Object views allow you to take advantage of the syntax and semantics of "objects," while at the same time retaining complete control over the physical storage of the data and allowing for relational access to the underlying data. In that fashion, you can achieve the best of both the relational and object-relational worlds.

Summary

Hopefully after reading this chapter, you have come to the conclusion that not all tables are created equal. Oracle provides a rich variety of table types that you can exploit. In this chapter, we have covered many of the salient aspects of tables in general and explored the many different table types Oracle provides for us to use.

We began by looking at some terminology and storage parameters associated with tables. We looked at the usefulness of freelists in a multiuser environment where a table is frequently inserted/updated by many people simultaneously, and how the use of ASSM tablespaces could make it so we don't even have to think about that. We investigated the meaning of PCTFREE and PCTUSED, and developed some guidelines for setting them correctly.

Then we got into the different types of tables, starting with the common heap. The heap organized table is by far the most commonly used table in most Oracle applications, and it is the default table type. We moved on to examine index organized tables (IOTs), which provide us with the ability store our table data in an index structure instead of a heap table. We saw how these are applicable for various uses, such as lookup tables and inverted lists, where a heap table would just be a redundant copy of the data. Later, we saw how IOTs can really be useful when mixed with other table types, specifically the nested table type.

We looked at cluster objects, of which Oracle has three kinds: index, hash, and sorted hash. The goals of the cluster are twofold:

- To give us the ability to store data from many tables together on the same database block(s).

- To give us the ability to force like data to be stored physically "together" based on some cluster key. In this fashion all of the data for department 10 (from many tables) may be stored together.

These features allow us to access related data very quickly, with minimal physical I/O. We observed the main differences between index clusters and hash clusters, and discussed when each would (and would not) be appropriate.

Next, we moved on to cover nested tables. We reviewed the syntax, semantics, and usage of nested tables. We saw how they are in a fact a system-generated and -maintained parent/child pair of tables, and we discovered how Oracle physically does this for us. We looked at using different table types for nested tables, which by default use a heap-based table. We found that there will probably never be a reason not to use an IOT instead of a heap table for nested tables.

Then we looked into the ins and outs of temporary tables, including how to create them, where they get their storage from, and the fact that they introduce no concurrency-related issues at runtime. We explored the differences between session-level and transaction-level temporary tables, and we discussed the appropriate method for using temporary tables in an Oracle database.

This chapter finished with a look at the inner workings of object tables. As with nested tables, we discovered there is a lot going on under the covers with object tables in Oracle. We discussed how object views on top of relational tables can give us the functionality of an object table, while at the same time offering easy access to the underlying relational data.

CHAPTER 11

■ ■ ■

Indexes

Indexing is a crucial aspect of your application design and development. Too many indexes and the performance of DML will suffer. Too few indexes and the performance of queries (including inserts, updates, and deletes) will suffer. Finding the right mix is critical to your application's performance.

Frequently, I find that indexes are an afterthought in application development. I believe that this is the wrong approach. From the very beginning, if you understand how the data will be used, you should be able to come up with the representative set of indexes you will use in your application. Too many times the approach seems to be to throw the application out there and then see where indexes are needed. This implies you have not taken the time to understand how the data will be used and how many rows you will ultimately be dealing with. You'll be adding indexes to this system forever as the volume of data grows over time (i.e., you'll perform reactive tuning). You'll have indexes that are redundant and never used, and this wastes not only space but also computing resources. A few hours at the start spent properly considering when and how to index your data will save you many hours of "tuning" further down the road (note that I said doing so "will," not "might," save you many hours).

The basic aim of this chapter is to give an overview of the indexes available for use in Oracle and discuss when and where you might use them. This chapter differs from others in this book in terms of its style and format. Indexing is a huge topic—you could write an entire book on the subject—in part because indexing bridges the developer and DBA roles. The developer must be aware of indexes, how indexes apply to their applications, when to use indexes (and when not to use them), and so on. The DBA is concerned with the growth of an index, the use of storage within an index, and other physical properties. We will be tackling indexes mainly from the standpoint of their practical use in applications. The first half of this chapter represents the basic knowledge I believe you need to make intelligent choices about when to index and what type of index to use. The second half of the chapter answers some of the most frequently asked questions about indexes.

The various examples in this chapter require different feature releases of Oracle. When a specific example requires features found in Oracle Enterprise or Personal Edition but not Standard Edition, I'll specify that.

An Overview of Oracle Indexes

Oracle provides many different types of indexes for us to use. Briefly, they are as follows:

- *B*Tree indexes*: These are what I refer to as "conventional" indexes. They are by far the most common indexes in use in Oracle and most other databases. Similar in construct to a binary tree, B*Tree indexes provide fast access, by key, to an individual row or range of rows, normally requiring few reads to find the correct row. It is important to note, however, that the "B" in "B*Tree" does not stand for *binary* but rather for *balanced*. A B*Tree index is not a binary tree at all, as we'll see when we look at how one is physically stored on disk. The B*Tree index has several subtypes:

  - *Index organized tables*: These are tables stored in a B*Tree structure. Whereas rows of data in a heap table are stored in an unorganized fashion (data goes wherever there is available space), data in an IOT is stored and sorted by primary key. IOTs behave just like "regular" tables as far as your application is concerned; you use SQL to access them as normal. IOTs are especially useful for information retrieval, spatial, and OLAP applications. We discussed IOTs in some detail in the previous chapter.

  - *B*Tree cluster indexes*: These are a slight variation of conventional B*Tree indexes. They are used to index the cluster keys (see the section "Index Clustered Tables" in Chapter 10) and will not be discussed again in this chapter. Rather than having a key that points to a row, as for a conventional B*Tree, a B*Tree cluster has a cluster key that points to the block that contains the rows related to that cluster key.

  - *Descending indexes*: Descending indexes allow for data to be sorted from "big to small" (descending) instead of "small to big" (ascending) in the index structure. We'll take a look at why that might be important and how they work.

  - *Reverse key indexes*: These are B*Tree indexes whereby the bytes in the key are "reversed." Reverse key indexes can be used to obtain a more even distribution of index entries throughout an index that is populated with increasing values. For example, if I am using a sequence to generate a primary key, the sequence will generate values like 987500, 987501, 987502, and so on. These values are sequential, so if I were using a conventional B*Tree index, they would all tend to go the same right-hand-side block, thus increasing contention for that block. With a reverse key index, Oracle will logically index 205789, 105789, 005789, and so on instead. Oracle will reverse the bytes of the data to be stored before placing them in the index, so values that would have been next to each other in the index before the byte reversal will instead be far apart. This reversing of the bytes spreads out the inserts into the index over many blocks.

- *Bitmap indexes*: Normally in a B*Tree, there is a one-to-one relationship between an index entry and a row: an index entry points to a row. With bitmap indexes, a single index entry uses a bitmap to point to many rows simultaneously. They are appropriate for highly repetitive data (data with few distinct values *relative to the total number of rows in the table*) that is mostly read-only. Consider a column that takes on three possible values—Y, N, and NULL—in a table of 1 million rows. This might be a good candidate for a bitmap index if, for example, you need to frequently count how many rows have a value of Y. That is not to say that a bitmap index on a column with 1,000 distinct values in that same table would not be valid—it certainly can be. Bitmap indexes should never be considered in an OLTP database for concurrency-related issues (which we'll discuss in due course). Note that bitmap indexes require the Enterprise or Personal Edition of Oracle.

- *Bitmap join indexes*: These provide a means of denormalizing data in an index structure, instead of in a table. For example, consider the simple EMP and DEPT tables. Someone might ask the question, "How many people work in departments located in the city of Boston?" EMP has a foreign key to DEPT, and in order to count the employees in departments with a LOC value of Boston, we would normally have to join the tables to get the LOC column joined to the EMP records to answer this question. Using a bitmap join index, we can instead index the LOC column against the EMP table.

- *Function-based indexes*: These are B*Tree or bitmap indexes that store the computed result of a function on a row's column(s), not the column data itself. You can consider them an index on a virtual (or derived) column—in other words, a column that is not physically stored in the table. These may be used to speed up queries of the form SELECT * FROM T WHERE FUNCTION(DATABASE_COLUMN) = SOME_VALUE, since the value FUNCTION(DATABASE_COLUMN) has already been computed and stored in the index.

- *Application domain indexes*: These are indexes you build and store yourself, either in Oracle or perhaps even outside of Oracle. You tell the optimizer how selective your index is and how costly it is to execute, and the optimizer will decide whether or not to use your index based on that information. The Oracle text index is an example of an application domain index; it is built using the same tools you may use to build your own index. It should be noted that the "index" created here need not use a traditional index structure. The Oracle text index, for example, uses a set of tables to implement its concept of an index.

As you can see, there are many index types to choose from. In the following sections, I'll present some technical details on how each one works and when it should be used. I would like to stress again that we will not cover certain DBA-related topics. For example, we will not discuss the mechanics of an online rebuild; rather, we will concentrate on practical application-related details.

B*Tree Indexes

B*Tree—or what I call "conventional"—indexes are the most commonly used type of indexing structure in the database. They are similar in implementation to a binary search tree. Their goal is to minimize the amount of time Oracle spends searching for data. Loosely speaking, if you have an index on a number column, then the structure might conceptually look like Figure 11-1.

■**Note** There are block-level optimizations and compression of data that take place that make the real block structure look different from Figure 11-1.

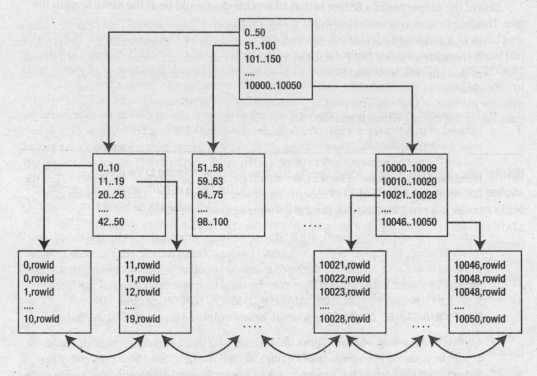

Figure 11-1. *Typical B*Tree index layout*

The lowest level blocks in the tree, called *leaf nodes* or *leaf blocks*, contain every indexed key and a rowid that points to the row it is indexing. The interior blocks, above the leaf nodes, are known as *branch blocks*. They are used to navigate through the structure. For example, if we wanted to find the value 42 in the index, we would start at the top of the tree and go to the left. We would inspect that block and discover we needed to go to the block in the range "42..50". This block would be the leaf block and point us to the rows that contained the number 42. It is interesting to note that the leaf nodes of the index are actually a doubly linked list. Once we find out where to "start" in the leaf nodes (i.e., once we have found that first value), doing an ordered scan of values (also known as an *index range scan*) is very easy. We don't have to navigate the structure any more; we just go forward or backward through the leaf nodes as needed. That makes satisfying a predicate, such as the following, pretty simple:

```
where x between 20 and 30
```

Oracle finds the first index leaf block that contains the lowest key value that is 20 or greater, and then it just walks horizontally through the linked list of leaf nodes until it finally hits a value that is greater than 30.

There really is no such thing as a nonunique entry in a B*Tree index. In a nonunique index, Oracle simply stores the rowid by appending it to the key as an extra column with a length byte to make the key unique. For example, an index such as CREATE INDEX I ON T(X,Y) is conceptually CREATE **UNIQUE** INDEX I ON T(X,Y,**ROWID**). In a unique index, as defined by you, Oracle does not add the rowid to the index key. In a nonunique index, you will find that the data is sorted first by index key values (in the order of the index key) and then by rowid ascending. In a unique index, the data is sorted only by the index key values.

One of the properties of a B*Tree is that all leaf blocks should be at the same level in the tree. This level is also known as the *height* of the index, meaning that any traversal from the root block of the index to a leaf block will visit the same number of blocks. That is, to get to the leaf block to retrieve the first row for a query of the form "SELECT INDEXED_COL FROM T WHERE ➥ INDEXED_COL = :X" will take the same number of I/Os regardless of the value of :X that is used. In other words, the index is *height balanced*. Most B*Tree indexes will have a height of 2 or 3, even for millions of records. This means that it will take, in general, two or three I/Os to find your key in the index—which is not too bad.

■**Note** Oracle uses two terms with slightly different meanings when referring to the number of blocks involved in traversing from an index root block to a leaf block. The first is HEIGHT, which is the number of blocks required to go from the root block to the leaf block. The HEIGHT value can be found from the INDEX_STATS view after the index has been analyzed using the ANALYZE INDEX <name> VALIDATE STRUCTURE command. The other is BLEVEL, which is the number of branch levels and differs from HEIGHT by one (it does not count the leaf blocks). The value of BLEVEL is found in the normal dictionary tables such as USER_INDEXES after statistics have been gathered.

For example, say we have a 10,000,000-row table with a primary key index on a number column:

```
big_table@ORA9IR2> select index_name, blevel, num_rows
  2  from user_indexes
  3  where table_name = 'BIG_TABLE';


INDEX_NAME                              BLEVEL   NUM_ROWS
--------------------------------------  -------  ----------
BIG_TABLE_PK                                  2    10441513
```

The BLEVEL is 2, meaning the HEIGHT is 3, and it will take two I/Os to find a leaf (resulting in a third I/O). So we would expect three I/Os to retrieve any given key value from this index:

```
big_table@ORA9IR2> select id from big_table where id = 42;

Execution Plan
----------------------------------------------------------
   0      SELECT STATEMENT Optimizer=CHOOSE (Cost=2 Card=1 Bytes=6)
   1    0   INDEX (UNIQUE SCAN) OF 'BIG_TABLE_PK' (UNIQUE) (Cost=2 Card=1 Bytes=6)

Statistics
----------------------------------------------------------
...
       3 consistent gets
...
       1 rows processed
```

```
big_table@ORA9IR2> select id from big_table where id = 12345;

Statistics
----------------------------------------------------------
...          3  consistent gets
...          1  rows processed

big_table@ORA9IR2> select id from big_table where id = 1234567;

Statistics
----------------------------------------------------------
...
    3 consistent gets
...
    1 rows processed
```

The B*Tree is an excellent general-purpose indexing mechanism that works well for large and small tables, and experiences little, if any, degradation in retrieval performance as the size of the underlying table grows.

Index Key Compression

One of the interesting things you can do with a B*Tree index is "compress" it. This is not compression in the same manner that ZIP files are compressed; rather, this is compression that removes redundancies from concatenated (multicolumn) indexes.

We covered compressed key indexes in some detail in the section "Index Organized Tables" in Chapter 10, and we will take a brief look at them again here. The basic concept behind a compressed key index is that every entry is broken into two pieces: a "prefix" and "suffix" component. The prefix is built on the leading columns of the concatenated index and will have many repeating values. The suffix is built on the trailing columns in the index key and is the unique component of the index entry within the prefix.

By way of example, we'll create a table and a concatenated index and measure its space without compression using ANALYZE INDEX. We'll then re-create the index with index key compression, compressing a different number of key entries, and see the difference. Let's start with this table and index:

```
ops$tkyte@ORA10G> create table t
  2  as
  3  select * from all_objects;
Table created.

ops$tkyte@ORA10G> create index t_idx on
  2  t(owner,object_type,object_name);
Index created.

ops$tkyte@ORA10G> analyze index t_idx validate structure;
Index analyzed.
```

We then create an IDX_STATS table in which to save INDEX_STATS information, and we label the rows in the table as "noncompressed":

```
ops$tkyte@ORA10G> create table idx_stats
  2  as
  3  select 'noncompressed' what, a.*
  4    from index_stats a;
Table created.
```

Now, we could realize that the OWNER component is repeated many times, meaning that a single index block in this index will have dozens of entries, as shown in Figure 11-2.

```
Sys.Package.Dbms_Alert
Sys.Package.Dbms_Application_Info
Sys.Package.Dbms_Aq
Sys.Package.Dbms_Aqadm
Sys.Package.Dbms_Aqadm_Sys
Sys.Package.Dbms_Aqadm_Syscalls
Sys.Package.Dbms_Aqin
Sys.Package.Dbms_Aqjms
...
```

Figure 11-2. *Index block with* OWNER *column repeated*

We could factor the repeated OWNER column out of this, resulting in a block that looks more like Figure 11-3.

```
Sys
Package.Dbms_Alert
Package.Dbms_Application_Info
Package.Dbms_Aq
Package.Dbms_Aqadm
Package.Dbms_Aqadm_Sys
Package.Dbms_Aqadm_Syscalls
Package.Dbms_Aqin
Package.Dbms_Aqjms
...
```

Figure 11-3. *Index block with* OWNER *column factored out*

In Figure 11-3, the owner name appears once on the leaf block—not once per repeated entry. We run the following script, passing in the number 1, to re-create the scenario whereby the index is using compression on just the leading column:

```
drop index t_idx;
create index t_idx on
t(owner,object_type,object_name)
compress &1;
```

```
analyze index t_idx validate structure;
insert into idx_stats
select 'compress &1', a.*
 from index_stats a;
```

For comparison reasons, we run this script not only with one column, but also two and three compressed columns, to see what happens. At the end, we query IDX_STATS and should observe this:

```
ops$tkyte@ORA10G> select what, height, lf_blks, br_blks,
  2          btree_space, opt_cmpr_count, opt_cmpr_pctsave
  3     from idx_stats
  4  /
```

WHAT	HEIGHT	LF_BLKS	BR_BLKS	BTREE_SPACE	OPT_CMPR_COUNT	OPT_CMPR_PCTSAVE
noncompressed	3	337	3	2718736	2	28
compress 1	3	300	3	2421684	2	19
compress 2	2	240	1	1926108	2	0
compress 3	3	375	3	3021084	2	35

We see that the COMPRESS 1 index is about 89 percent the size of the noncompressed index (comparing BTREE_SPACE). The number of leaf blocks has decreased measurably. Further, when we use COMPRESS 2, the savings are even more impressive. The resulting index is about 70 percent the size of the original, and so much data is able to be placed on individual blocks that the height of the index actually decreased from 3 to 2. In fact, using the column OPT_CMPR_PCTSAVE, which stands for *optimum compression percent saved* or the expected savings from compression, we could have guessed the size of the COMPRESS 2 index:

```
ops$tkyte@ORA10G> select 2718736*(1-0.28) from dual;

2718736*(1-0.28)
----------------
      1957489.92
```

■**Note**   The ANALYZE command against the noncompressed index populated the OPT_CMPR_PCTSAVE/OPT_CMPR_COUNT columns and estimated a 28 percent savings with COMPRESS 2, and we achieved just about exactly that.

But notice what happens with COMPRESS 3. The resulting index is actually larger: 110 percent the size of the original index. This is due to the fact that each repeated prefix we remove saves the space of N copies, but adds 4 bytes of overhead on the leaf block as part of the compression scheme. By adding in the OBJECT_NAME column to the compressed key, we made that key unique—in this case, meaning there were no duplicate copies to factor out. Therefore, we ended up *adding* 4 bytes to every single index key entry and factoring out no repeating data. The OPT_CMPR_COUNT column in IDX_STATS is dead accurate at providing the best compression count to be used, and OPT_CMPR_PCTSAVE will tell you exactly how much savings to expect.

Now, you do not get this compression for free. The compressed index structure is now more complex than it used to be. Oracle will spend more time processing the data in this structure, both while maintaining the index during modifications and when you search the index during a query. What we are doing here is trading off increased CPU time for reduced I/O time. With compression, our block buffer cache will be able to hold more index entries than before, our cache-hit ratio might go up, and our physical I/Os should go down, but it will take a little more CPU horsepower to process the index, and it will also increase the chance of block contention. Just as in our discussion of the hash cluster, where it might take more CPU to retrieve a million random rows but half the I/O, we must be aware of the tradeoff. If you are currently CPU bound, adding compressed key indexes may slow down your processing. On the other hand, if you are I/O bound, using them may speed up things.

Reverse Key Indexes

Another feature of a B*Tree index is the ability to "reverse" its keys. At first you might ask yourself, "Why would I want to do that?" B*Tree indexes were designed for a specific environment and for a specific issue. They were implemented to reduce contention for index leaf blocks in "right-hand-side" indexes, such as indexes on columns populated by a sequence value or a timestamp, in an Oracle RAC environment.

■**Note** We discussed RAC in Chapter 2.

RAC is a configuration of Oracle in which multiple instances can mount and open the same database. If two instances need to modify the same block of data simultaneously, they will share the block by passing it back and forth over a hardware *interconnect*, a private network connection between the two (or more) machines. If you have a primary key index on a column populated from a sequence (a very popular implementation), everyone will be trying to modify the one block that is currently the left block on the right-hand side of the index structure as they insert new values (see Figure 11-1, which shows that higher values in the index go to the right, and lower values go to the left). Modifications to indexes on columns populated by sequences are focused on a small set of leaf blocks. Reversing the keys of the index allows insertions to be distributed across all the leaf keys in the index, though it could tend to make the index much less efficiently packed.

■**Note** You may also find reverse key indexes useful as a method to reduce contention, even in a single instance of Oracle. Again, you will mainly use them to alleviate buffer busy waits on the right-hand side of a busy index, as described in this section.

Before we look at how to measure the impact of a reverse key index, let's discuss what a reverse key index physically does. A reverse key index simply reverses the bytes of each column in an index key. If we consider the numbers 90101, 90102, and 90103, and look at their internal representation using the Oracle DUMP function, we will find they are represented as follows:

```
ops$tkyte@ORA10GR1> select 90101, dump(90101,16) from dual
  2  union all
  3  select 90102, dump(90102,16) from dual
  4  union all
  5  select 90103, dump(90103,16) from dual
  6  /

     90101 DUMP(90101,16)
---------- ---------------------
     90101 Typ=2 Len=4: c3,a,2,2
     90102 Typ=2 Len=4: c3,a,2,3
     90103 Typ=2 Len=4: c3,a,2,4
```

Each one is 4 bytes in length and only the last byte is different. These numbers would end up right next to each other in an index structure. If we reverse their bytes, however, Oracle will insert the following:

```
ops$tkyte@ORA10GR1> select 90101, dump(reverse(90101),16) from dual
  2  union all
  3  select 90102, dump(reverse(90102),16) from dual
  4  union all
  5  select 90103, dump(reverse(90103),16) from dual
  6  /

     90101 DUMP(REVERSE(90101),1
---------- ---------------------
     90101 Typ=2 Len=4: 2,2,a,c3
     90102 Typ=2 Len=4: 3,2,a,c3
     90103 Typ=2 Len=4: 4,2,a,c3
```

■**Note** REVERSE is an undocumented function and, as such, should be used carefully. I do not recommend using REVERSE in "real" code, as its undocumented nature implies that it is not supported.

The numbers will end up "far away" from each other. This reduces the number of RAC instances going after the same block (the rightmost block) and reduces the number of block transfers between RAC instances. One of the drawbacks to a reverse key index is that you cannot use it in all cases where a regular index can be applied. For example, in answering the following predicate, a reverse key index on X would not be useful:

```
where x > 5
```

The data in the index is not sorted by X before it is stored, but rather by REVERSE(X), hence the range scan for X > 5 will not be able to use the index. On the other hand, some range scans can be done on a reverse key index. If I have a concatenated index on (X, Y), the following predicate will be able to make use of the reverse key index and will "range scan" it:

```
where x = 5
```

This is because the bytes for X are reversed, and then the bytes for Y are reversed. Oracle does not reverse the bytes of (X || Y), but rather stores (REVERSE(X) || REVERSE(Y)). This means all of the values for X = 5 will be stored together, so Oracle can range scan that index to find them all.

Now, assuming you have a surrogate primary key on a table populated via a sequence, and you do not need to use range scanning on this index—that is, you don't need to query for MAX(primary_key), MIN(primary_key), WHERE primary_key < 100, and so on—then you could consider a reverse key index in high insert scenarios even in a single instance of Oracle. I set up two different tests, one in a pure PL/SQL environment and one using Pro*C to demonstrate the differences between inserting into a table with a reverse key index on the primary key and one with a conventional index. In both cases, the table used was created with the following DDL (we will avoid contention on table blocks by using ASSM so we can isolate the contention on the index blocks):

```
create table t tablespace assm
as
select 0 id, a.*
  from all_objects a
 where 1=0;

alter table t
add constraint t_pk
primary key (id)
using index (create index t_pk on t(id) &indexType tablespace assm);

create sequence s cache 1000;
```

whereby &indexType was replaced with either the keyword REVERSE, creating a reverse key index, or with nothing, thus using a "regular" index. The PL/SQL that would be run by 1, 2, 5, 10, or 15 users concurrently was

```
create or replace procedure do_sql
as
begin
    for x in ( select rownum r, all_objects.* from all_objects )
    loop
        insert into t
        ( id, OWNER, OBJECT_NAME, SUBOBJECT_NAME,
          OBJECT_ID, DATA_OBJECT_ID, OBJECT_TYPE, CREATED,
          LAST_DDL_TIME, TIMESTAMP, STATUS, TEMPORARY,
          GENERATED, SECONDARY )
        values
```

```
        ( s.nextval, x.OWNER, x.OBJECT_NAME, x.SUBOBJECT_NAME,
          x.OBJECT_ID, x.DATA_OBJECT_ID, x.OBJECT_TYPE, x.CREATED,
          x.LAST_DDL_TIME, x.TIMESTAMP, x.STATUS, x.TEMPORARY,
          x.GENERATED, x.SECONDARY );
        if ( mod(x.r,100) = 0 )
        then
            commit;
        end if;
    end loop;
    commit;
end;
/
```

Now, since we discussed the PL/SQL commit time optimization in Chapter 9, I wanted to run a test that was using a different environment as well, so as to not be misled by this commit time optimization. I used Pro*C to emulate a data warehouse extract, transform, load (ETL) routine that processed rows in batches of 100 at a time between commits:

```
exec sql declare c cursor for select * from all_objects;
exec sql open c;
exec sql whenever notfound do break;
for(;;)
{
    exec sql
    fetch c into :owner:owner_i,
    :object_name:object_name_i, :subobject_name:subobject_name_i,
    :object_id:object_id_i, :data_object_id:data_object_id_i,
    :object_type:object_type_i, :created:created_i,
    :last_ddl_time:last_ddl_time_i, :timestamp:timestamp_i,
    :status:status_i, :temporary:temporary_i,
    :generated:generated_i, :secondary:secondary_i;

    exec sql
    insert into t
    ( id, OWNER, OBJECT_NAME, SUBOBJECT_NAME,
      OBJECT_ID, DATA_OBJECT_ID, OBJECT_TYPE, CREATED,
      LAST_DDL_TIME, TIMESTAMP, STATUS, TEMPORARY,
      GENERATED, SECONDARY )
    values
    ( s.nextval, :owner:owner_i, :object_name:object_name_i,
      :subobject_name:subobject_name_i, :object_id:object_id_i,
      :data_object_id:data_object_id_i, :object_type:object_type_i,
      :created:created_i, :last_ddl_time:last_ddl_time_i,
      :timestamp:timestamp_i, :status:status_i,
      :temporary:temporary_i, :generated:generated_i,
      :secondary:secondary_i );
```

```
    if ( (++cnt%100) == 0 )
    {
        exec sql commit;
    }
}
exec sql whenever notfound continue;
exec sql commit;
exec sql close c;
```

The Pro*C was precompiled with a PREFETCH of 100, making this C code analogous to the PL/SQL code in Oracle 10g.

Note In Oracle 10g Release 1 and above, a simple FOR X IN (SELECT * FROM T) in PL/SQL will silently array fetch 100 rows at a time, whereas in Oracle9i and before, it fetches just a single row at a time. Therefore, if you want to reproduce this example on Oracle9i and before, you will need to modify the PL/SQL code to also array fetch with the BULK COLLECT syntax.

Both would fetch 100 rows at a time and then single row insert the data into another table. The following tables summarize the differences between the various runs, starting with the single user test in Table 11-1.

Table 11-1. *Performance Test for Use of Reverse Key Indexes with PL/SQL and Pro*C: Single User*

	Reverse PL/SQL	No Reverse PL/SQL	Reverse Pro*C	No Reverse Pro*C
Transaction/second	38.24	43.45	17.35	19.08
CPU time (seconds)	25	22	33	31
Buffer busy waits number/time	0/0	0/0	0/0	0/0
Elapsed time (minutes)	0.42	0.37	0.92	0.83
Log file sync number/time		6/0	1,940/7	1,940/7

From the first single-user test, we can see that PL/SQL was measurably more efficient than Pro*C in performing this operation, a trend we'll continue to see as we scale up the user load. Part of the reason Pro*C won't scale as well as PL/SQL will be the log file sync waits that Pro*C must wait for, but which PL/SQL has an optimization to avoid.

It would appear from this single-user test that reverse key indexes consume more CPU. This makes sense because the database must perform extra work as it carefully reverses the bytes in the key. But, we'll see that this logic won't hold true as we scale up the users. As we introduce contention, the overhead of the reverse key index will completely disappear. In fact, even by the time we get the two-user test, the overhead is mostly offset by the contention on the right-hand side of the index, as shown in Table 11-2.

Table 11-2. *Performance Test for Use of Reverse Key Indexes with PL/SQL and Pro*C: Two Users*

	Reverse PL/SQL	No Reverse PL/SQL	Reverse Pro*C	No Reverse Pro*C
Transaction/second	46.59	49.03	20.07	20.29
CPU time (seconds)	77	73	104	101
Buffer busy waits number/time	4,267/2	133,644/2	3,286/0	23,688/1
Elapsed time (minutes)	0.68	0.65	1.58	1.57
Log file sync number/time	19/0	18/0	3,273/29	2,132/29

As you can see from this two-user test, PL/SQL still outperforms Pro*C, but the use of the reverse key index is showing some positive benefits on the PL/SQL side and not so much on the Pro*C side. That too is a trend that will continue. The reverse key index is solving the buffer busy wait problem we have due to the contention for the rightmost block in the index structure; however, it does nothing for the log file sync waits that affect the Pro*C program. This was the main reason for performing both a PL/SQL and a Pro*C test: to see the differences between these two environments. This begs the question, why would a reverse key index apparently benefit PL/SQL but not Pro*C in this case? It comes down to the log file sync wait event. PL/SQL was able to continuously insert and rarely had to wait for the log file sync wait event upon commit, whereas Pro*C was waiting every 100 rows. Therefore, PL/SQL in this case was impacted more heavily by buffer busy waits than Pro*C was. Alleviating the buffer busy waits in the PL/SQL case allowed it to process more transactions, and so the reverse key index positively benefited PL/SQL. But in the Pro*C case, the buffer busy waits were not the issue—they were not the major performance bottleneck, so removing the waits had no impact on overall performance.

Let's move on to the five-user test, shown in Table 11-3.

Table 11-3. *Performance Test for Use of Reverse Key Indexes with PL/SQL and Pro*C: Five Users*

	Reverse PL/SQL	No Reverse PL/SQL	Reverse Pro*C	No Reverse Pro*C
Transaction/second	43.84	39.78	19.22	18.15
CPU time (seconds)	389	395	561	588
Buffer busy waits number/time	19,259/45	221,353/153	19,118/9	157,967/56
Elapsed time (minutes)	1.82	2.00	4.13	4.38
Log file sync number/time		691/14	6,655/73	5,391/82

We see more of the same. PL/SQL, running full steam ahead with few log file sync waits, was very much impacted by the buffer busy waits. With a conventional index and all five users attempting to insert into the right-hand side of the index structure, PL/SQL suffered the most from the buffer busy waits and, therefore, benefited the most when they were reduced.

Now, taking a look at the ten-user test in Table 11-4, we can see the trend continues.

Table 11-4. *Performance Test for Use of Reverse Key Indexes with PL/SQL and Pro*C: Ten Users*

	Reverse PL/SQL	No Reverse PL/SQL	Reverse Pro*C	No Reverse Pro*C
Transaction/second	45.90	35.38	17.88	16.05
CPU time (seconds)	781	789	1,256	1,384
Buffer busy waits number/time	26,846/279	456,231/1,382	25,871/134	364,556/1,702
Elapsed time (minutes)	3.47	4.50	8.90	9.92
Log file sync number/time		2,602/72	11,032/196	12,653/141

PL/SQL, in the absence of the log file sync wait, is very much helped by removing the buffer busy wait events. Pro*C is experiencing more buffer busy wait contention now but, due to the fact it is waiting on log file sync events frequently, is not benefiting. One way to improve the performance of the PL/SQL implementation with a regular index would be to introduce a small wait. That would reduce the contention on the right-hand side of the index and increase overall performance. For space reasons, I will not include the 15- and 20-user tests here, but I will confirm that the trend observed in this section continued.

We can take away two things from this demonstration. A reverse key index can help allevi-ate a buffer busy wait situation, but depending on other factors you will get varying returns on investment. In looking at Table 11-4 for the ten-user test, the removal of buffer busy waits (the most waited for wait event in that case) affected transaction throughput marginally, but it did show increased scalability with higher concurrency levels. Doing the same thing for PL/SQL had a markedly different impact on performance: we achieved a measurable increase in throughput by removing that bottleneck.

Descending Indexes

Descending indexes were introduced in Oracle8*i* to extend the functionality of a B*Tree index. They allow for a column to be stored sorted in descending order (from big to small) in the index instead of ascending order (from small to big). Prior releases of Oracle, pre-Oracle8*i*, always supported the DESC (descending) keyword *syntactically*, but basically ignored it—it had no effect on how the data was stored or used in the index. In Oracle8*i* and above, however, the DESC keyword changes the way the index is created and used.

Oracle has had the ability to read an index backward for quite a while, so you may be wondering why this feature is relevant. For example, if we use the table T from earlier and query it as follows:

```
ops$tkyte@ORA10G> set autotrace traceonly explain
ops$tkyte@ORA10G> select owner, object_type
  2    from t
  3   where owner between 'T' and 'Z'
  4     and object_type is not null
  5   order by owner DESC, object_type DESC;

Execution Plan
----------------------------------------------------------
   0      SELECT STATEMENT Optimizer=ALL_ROWS (Cost=82 Card=11395 Bytes=170925)
   1    0    INDEX (RANGE SCAN DESCENDING) OF 'T_IDX' (INDEX) (Cost=82 Card=11395...
```

Oracle will just read the index backward. There is no final sort step in this plan; the data is sorted. Where this descending index feature comes into play, however, is when you have a mixture of columns, and some are sorted ASC (ascending) and some DESC (descending), for example:

```
ops$tkyte@ORA10G> select owner, object_type
  2    from t
  3   where owner between 'T' and 'Z'
  4     and object_type is not null
  5   order by owner DESC, object_type ASC;

Execution Plan
-----------------------------------------------------------
   0      SELECT STATEMENT Optimizer=ALL_ROWS (Cost=85 Card=11395 Bytes=170925)
   1    0   SORT (ORDER BY) (Cost=85 Card=11395 Bytes=170925)
   2    1     INDEX (RANGE SCAN) OF 'T_IDX' (INDEX) (Cost=82 Card=11395 ...
```

Oracle isn't able to use the index we have in place on (OWNER, OBJECT_TYPE, OBJECT_NAME) anymore to *sort* the data. It could have read it backward to get the data sorted by OWNER DESC, but it needs to read it "forward" to get OBJECT_TYPE sorted ASC. Instead, it collected together all of the rows and then sorted. Enter the DESC index:

```
ops$tkyte@ORA10G> create index desc_t_idx on t(owner desc,object_type asc);
Index created.

ops$tkyte@ORA10G> exec dbms_stats.gather_index_stats( user, 'DESC_T_IDX' );
PL/SQL procedure successfully completed.

ops$tkyte@ORA10G> select owner, object_type
  2    from t
  3   where owner between 'T' and 'Z'
  4     and object_type is not null
  5   order by owner DESC, object_type ASC;

Execution Plan
-----------------------------------------------------------
   0      SELECT STATEMENT Optimizer=ALL_ROWS (Cost=2 Card=11395 Bytes=170925)
   1    0   INDEX (RANGE SCAN) OF 'DESC_T_IDX' (INDEX) (Cost=2 Card=11395 ...
```

Now, once more, we are able to read the data sorted, and there is no extra sort step at the end of the plan. It should be noted that unless your *compatible* init.ora parameter is set to 8.1.0 or higher, the DESC option on the CREATE INDEX will be silently ignored—no warning or error will be produced, as this was the default behavior in prior releases.

■**Note** Do not be tempted to ever leave an ORDER BY off a query. Just because your query plan includes an index does not mean the data will be returned in "some order." The *only way* to retrieve data from the database in some sorted order is to include an ORDER BY on your query. There is no substitute for ORDER BY.

When Should You Use a B*Tree Index?

Not being a big believer in "rules of thumb" (there are exceptions to every rule), I don't have any rules of thumb for when to use (or not to use) a B*Tree index. To demonstrate why I don't have any rules of thumb for this case, I'll present two equally valid ones:

- Only use B*Tree to index columns if you are going to access a very small percentage of the rows in the table via the index.

- Use a B*Tree index if you are going to process many rows of a table and the index can be used *instead of* the table.

These rules seem to offer conflicting advice, but in reality, they do not—they just cover two extremely different cases. There are two ways to use an index given the preceding advice:

- *As the means to access rows in a table*: You will read the index to get to a row in the table. Here you want to access a very small percentage of the rows in the table.

- *As the means to answer a query*: The index contains enough information to answer the entire query—we will not have to go to the table at all. The index will be used as a "thinner" version of the table.

There are other ways as well—for example, we could be using an index to retrieve *all* of the rows in a table, including columns that are not in the index itself. That seemingly goes counter to both rules of thumb just presented. The case that would be true would be an interactive application where you are getting some of the rows and displaying them, then some more, and so on. You want to have the query optimized for initial response time, not overall throughput.

The first case (i.e., use the index if you are going to access a small percentage of the table) says if you have a table T (using the same table T from earlier) and you have a query plan that looks like this:

```
ops$tkyte@ORA10G> set autotrace traceonly explain
ops$tkyte@ORA10G> select owner, status
  2  from t
  3  where owner = USER;

Execution Plan
----------------------------------------------------------
   0      SELECT STATEMENT Optimizer=ALL_ROWS (Cost=3 Card=1947 Bytes=25311)
   1    0   TABLE ACCESS (BY INDEX ROWID) OF 'T' (TABLE) (Cost=3 Card=1947 ....
   2    1     INDEX (RANGE SCAN) OF 'DESC_T_IDX' (INDEX) (Cost=2 Card=8)
```

then you should be accessing a very small percentage of this table. The issue to look at here is the INDEX (RANGE SCAN) followed by the TABLE ACCESS BY INDEX ROWID. This means that Oracle will read the index and then, for the index entries, it will perform a database block read (logical or physical I/O) to get the row data. This is not the most efficient method if you are going to have to access a large percentage of the rows in T via the index (shortly we will define what a large percentage might be).

In the second case (i.e., when the index can be used *instead* of the table), you can process 100 percent (or any percentage, in fact) of the rows via the index. You might use an index just to create a "thinner" version of a table. The following query demonstrates this concept:

```
ops$tkyte@ORA10G> select count(*)
  2  from t
  3  where owner = user;

Execution Plan
----------------------------------------------------------
   0      SELECT STATEMENT Optimizer=ALL_ROWS (Cost=16 Card=1 Bytes=6)
   1    0   SORT (AGGREGATE)
   2    1     INDEX (RANGE SCAN) OF 'T_IDX' (INDEX) (Cost=16 Card=1947
```

Here, only the index was used to answer the query—it would not matter now what percentage of rows we were accessing, as we would use the index only. We can see from the plan that the underlying table was never accessed; we simply scanned the index structure itself.

It is important to understand the difference between the two concepts. When we have to do a TABLE ACCESS BY INDEX ROWID, we must ensure we are accessing only a small percentage of the total blocks in the table, which typically equates to a small percentage of the rows, or that we *need* the first rows to be retrieved as fast as possible (the end user is waiting for them impatiently). If we access too high a percentage of the rows (larger than somewhere between 1 and 20 percent of the rows), then it will generally take longer to access them via a B*Tree than by just full scanning the table.

With the second type of query, where the answer is found entirely in the index, we have a different story. We read an index block and pick up many "rows" to process, then we go on to the next index block, and so on—we never go to the table. There is also a *fast full scan* we can perform on indexes to make this even faster in certain cases. A fast full scan is when the database reads the index blocks in no particular order; it just starts reading them. It is no longer using the index as an index, but even more like a table at that point. Rows do not come out ordered by index entries from a fast full scan.

In general, a B*Tree index would be placed on columns that we use frequently in the predicate of a query, and we would expect some small fraction of the data from the table to be returned or else the end user demands immediate feedback. On a *thin* table (i.e., a table with few or small columns), this fraction may be very small. A query that uses this index should expect to retrieve 2 to 3 percent or less of the rows to be accessed in the table. On a *fat* table (i.e., a table with many columns or very wide columns), this fraction *might* go all the way up to 20 to 25 percent of the table. This advice doesn't always seem to make sense to everyone immediately; it is not intuitive, but it is accurate. An index is stored sorted by index key. The index will be accessed in sorted order by key. The blocks that are pointed to are stored randomly in a heap. Therefore, as we read through an index to access the table, we will perform lots of *scattered*, random I/O. By "scattered," I mean that the index will tell us to read block 1, block 1,000, block 205, block 321, block 1, block 1,032, block 1, and so on—it won't ask us to read block 1, then block 2, and then block 3 in a consecutive manner. We will tend to read and reread blocks in a very haphazard fashion. This single block I/O can be very slow.

As a simplistic example of this, let's say we are reading that thin table via an index, and we are going to read 20 percent of the rows. Assume we have 100,000 rows in the table. Twenty percent of that is 20,000 rows. If the rows are about 80 bytes apiece in size, on a database with an 8KB blocksize, we will find about 100 rows per block. That means the table has approximately 1,000 blocks. From here, the math is very easy. We are going to read 20,000 rows via the index; this will mean, quite likely 20,000 TABLE ACCESS BY ROWID operations. We will process 20,000 table blocks to execute this query. There are only about 1,000 blocks in the entire table, however! We would end up reading and processing each block in the table on average 20 times. Even if we increased the size of the row by an order of magnitude to 800 bytes per row, and 10 rows per block, we now have 10,000 blocks in the table. Index accesses for 20,000 rows would cause us to still read each block on average two times. In this case, a full table scan will be much more efficient than using an index, as it has to touch each block only once. Any query that used this index to access the data would not be very efficient until it accesses on average less than 5 percent of the data for the 800-byte column (then we access about 5,000 blocks) and even less for the 80-byte column (about 0.5 percent or less).

Physical Organization

How the data is organized physically on disk deeply impacts these calculations, as it materially affects how expensive (or inexpensive) index access will be. Suppose you have a table where the rows have a primary key populated by a sequence. As data is added to the table, rows with sequential sequence numbers might be in general "next" to each other.

■Note The use of features such as ASSM or multiple freelist/freelist groups will affect how the data is organized on disk. Those features tend to spread the data out, and this natural clustering by primary key may not be observed.

The table is naturally clustered in order by the primary key (since the data is added in more or less that order). It will not be strictly clustered in order by the key, of course (we would have to use an IOT to achieve that), but in general rows with primary keys that are close in value will be "close" together in physical proximity. Now when you issue the query

```
select * from T where primary_key between :x and :y
```

the rows you want are typically located on the same blocks. In this case, an index range scan may be useful even if it accesses a large percentage of rows, simply because the database blocks that we need to read and reread will most likely be cached, since the data is co-located. On the other hand, if the rows are not co-located, using that same index may be disastrous for performance. A small demonstration will drive this fact home. We'll start with a table that is pretty much ordered by its primary key:

```
ops$tkyte@ORA10G> create table colocated ( x int, y varchar2(80) );
Table created.

ops$tkyte@ORA10G> begin
  2        for i in 1 .. 100000
  3        loop
  4            insert into colocated(x,y)
  5            values (i, rpad(dbms_random.random,75,'*') );
```

```
 6      end loop;
 7  end;
 8  /
PL/SQL procedure successfully completed.

ops$tkyte@ORA10G> alter table colocated
 2  add constraint colocated_pk
 3  primary key(x);
Table altered.

ops$tkyte@ORA10G> begin
 2  dbms_stats.gather_table_stats( user, 'COLOCATED', cascade=>true );
 3  end;
 4  /
PL/SQL procedure successfully completed.
```

This table fits the description we laid out earlier with about 100 rows/block in an 8KB database. In this table, there is a very good chance that the rows with X = 1, 2, 3 are on the same block. Now, we'll take this table and purposely "disorganize" it. In the COLOCATED table, we created the Y column with a leading random number, and we'll use that fact to "disorganize" the data so that it will definitely not be ordered by primary key anymore:

```
ops$tkyte@ORA10G> create table disorganized
 2  as
 3  select x,y
 4    from colocated
 5   order by y;
Table created.

ops$tkyte@ORA10G> alter table disorganized
 2  add constraint disorganized_pk
 3  primary key (x);
Table altered.

ops$tkyte@ORA10G> begin
 2  dbms_stats.gather_table_stats( user, 'DISORGANIZED', cascade=>true );
 3  end;
 4  /
PL/SQL procedure successfully completed.
```

Arguably, these are the same tables—it is a relational database, so physical organization has no bearing on the answers returned (at least that's what they teach in theoretical database courses). In fact, the performance characteristics of these two tables are as different as night and day, while the answers returned are identical. Given the same exact question, using the same exact query plans, and reviewing the TKPROF (SQL trace) output, we see the following:

```
select * from colocated where x between 20000 and 40000

call     count       cpu    elapsed      disk      query    current        rows
------- ------  -------- ---------- ---------- ---------- ---------- ----------
Parse        5      0.00       0.00          0          0          0          0
Execute      5      0.00       0.00          0          0          0          0
Fetch     6675      0.59       0.60          0      14495          0     100005
------- ------  -------- ---------- ---------- ---------- ---------- ----------
total     6685      0.59       0.60          0      14495          0     100005

Rows    Row Source Operation
------- -------------------------------------------------------
  20001  TABLE ACCESS BY INDEX ROWID COLOCATED (cr=2899 pr=0 pw=0 time=120134 us)
  20001   INDEX RANGE SCAN COLOCATED_PK (cr=1374 pr=0 pw=0 time=40081 us)(object id...
**************************************************************************
select /*+ index( disorganized disorganized_pk ) */* from disorganized
    where x between 20000 and 40000

call     count       cpu    elapsed      disk      query    current        rows
------- ------  -------- ---------- ---------- ---------- ---------- ----------
Parse        5      0.00       0.00          0          0          0          0
Execute      5      0.00       0.00          0          0          0          0
Fetch     6675      0.85       0.87          0     106815          0     100005
------- ------  -------- ---------- ---------- ---------- ---------- ----------
total     6685      0.85       0.87          0     106815          0     100005

Rows    Row Source Operation
------- -------------------------------------------------------
  20001  TABLE ACCESS BY INDEX ROWID DISORGANIZED (cr=21363 pr=0 pw=0 time=220144 ...
  20001   INDEX RANGE SCAN DISORGANIZED_PK (cr=1374 pr=0 pw=0 time=40311 us)(...
```

■**Note** I ran each query five times in order to get a good "average" runtime for each.

I think this is pretty incredible. What a difference physical data layout can make! Table 11-5 summarizes the results.

Table 11-5. *Investigating the Effect of Physical Data Layout on the Cost of Index Access*

Table	CPU Time	Logical I/O
Co-located	0.59 seconds	14,495
Disorganized	0.85 seconds	106,815
Co-located %	70%	13%

In my database using an 8KB blocksize, these tables had the following number of total blocks apiece:

```
ops$tkyte@ORA10G> select table_name, blocks
  2  from user_tables
  3  where table_name in ( 'COLOCATED', 'DISORGANIZED' );

TABLE_NAME                       BLOCKS
------------------------------ ----------
COLOCATED                          1252
DISORGANIZED                       1219
```

The query against the disorganized table bears out the simple math we did earlier: we did 20,000+ logical I/Os (100,000 total blocks queried and five runs of the query). We processed each and every block 20 times! On the other hand, the physically COLOCATED data took the logical I/Os way down. Here is the perfect illustration of why rules of thumb are so hard to provide—in one case, using the index works great, and in the other case it doesn't. Consider this the next time you dump data from your production system and load it into development, as it may very well provide at least part of the answer to the question, "Why is it running differently on this machine—aren't they identical?" They are not identical.

■**Note** Recall from Chapter 6 that increased logical I/O is the tip of the iceberg here. Each logical I/O involves one or more latches into the buffer cache. In a multiuser/CPU situation, the CPU used by the second query would have undoubtedly gone up many times faster than the first as we spin and wait for latches. The second example query not only performs more work, but also will not scale as well as the first.

THE EFFECT OF ARRAYSIZE ON LOGICAL I/O

It is interesting to note the effect of the ARRAYSIZE on logical I/O performed. ARRAYSIZE is the number of rows Oracle returns to a client when they ask for the next row. The client will then buffer these rows and use them before asking the database for the next set of rows. The ARRAYSIZE may have a very material affect on the logical I/O performed by a query, resulting from the fact that if you have to access the same block over and over again across calls (across fetch calls specifically in this case) to the database, Oracle must retrieve that block again from the buffer cache. Therefore, if you ask for 100 rows from the database in a single call, Oracle might be able to fully process a database block and not need to retrieve that block again. If you ask for 15 rows at a time, Oracle might well have to get the same block over and over again to retrieve the same set of rows.

In the example earlier in this section, we were using SQL*Plus's default array fetch size of 15 rows (if you divide the total rows fetched by the number of fetch calls, the result is very close to 15). If we were to compare the execution of the previous queries using 15 rows per fetch versus 100 rows per fetch, we would observe the following for the COLOCATED table:

```
select * from colocated a15 where x between 20000 and 40000

Rows     Row Source Operation
-------  -----------------------------------------------------
  20001  TABLE ACCESS BY INDEX ROWID COLOCATED (cr=2899 pr=0 pw=0 time=120125...
  20001   INDEX RANGE SCAN COLOCATED_PK (cr=1374 pr=0 pw=0 time=40072 us)(...

select * from colocated a100 where x between 20000 and 40000

Rows   Row Source Operation
-------  -----------------------------------------------------
  20001  TABLE ACCESS BY INDEX ROWID COLOCATED (cr=684 pr=0 pw=0 ...)
  20001  INDEX RANGE SCAN COLOCATED_PK (cr=245 pr=0 pw=0 ...
```

The first query was executed with the ARRAYSIZE of 15, and the (cr=nnnn) values in the Row ➡ Source Operation shows we performed 1,374 logical I/Os against the index and then 1,625 logical I/Os against the table (2,899–1,374; the numbers are cumulative in the Row Source Operation steps). When we increased the ARRAYSIZE to 100 from 15, the amount of logical I/O against the index dropped to 245, which was the direct result of not having to reread the index leaf blocks from the buffer cache every 15 rows, but only every 100 rows. To understand this, assume that we were able to store 200 rows per leaf block. As we are scanning through the index reading 15 rows at a time, we would have to retrieve the first leaf block 14 times to get all 200 entries off it. On the other hand, when we array fetch 100 rows at a time, we need to retrieve this same leaf block only two times from the buffer cache to exhaust all of its entries.

The same thing happened in this case with the table blocks. Since the table was sorted in the same order as the index keys, we would tend to retrieve each table block less often, as we would get more of the rows from it with each fetch call.

So, if this was good for the COLOCATED table, it must have been just as good for the DISORGANIZED table, right? Not so. The results from the DISORGANIZED table would look like this:

```
select /*+ index( a15 disorganized_pk ) */ *
from disorganized a15 where x between 20000 and 40000

Rows     Row Source Operation
-------  -----------------------------------------------------
  20001  TABLE ACCESS BY INDEX ROWID DISORGANIZED (cr=21357 pr=0 pw=0 ...
  20001   INDEX RANGE SCAN DISORGANIZED_PK (cr=1374 pr=0 pw=0 ...

select /*+ index( a100 disorganized_pk ) */ *
from disorganized a100 where x between 20000 and 40000

Rows     Row Source Operation
-------  -----------------------------------------------------
  20001  TABLE ACCESS BY INDEX ROWID OBJ#(75652) (cr=20228 pr=0 pw=0 ...
  20001   INDEX RANGE SCAN OBJ#(75653) (cr=245 pr=0 pw=0 time=20281 us)(...
```

The results against the index here were identical, which makes sense, as the data is stored in the index is just the same regardless of how the *table* is organized. The logical I/O went from 1,374 for a single execution of this query to 245, just as before. But overall the amount of logical I/O performed by this query did not differ significantly: 21,357 versus 20,281. The reason? The amount of logical I/O performed against the table did not differ at all—if you subtract the logical I/O against the index from the total logical I/O performed by each query, you'll find that both queries did 19,983 logical I/Os against the table. This is because every time we wanted N rows from the database—the odds that any two of those rows would be on the same block was very small—there was no opportunity to get multiple rows from a table block in a single call.

Every professional programming language I have seen that can interact with Oracle implements this concept of array fetching. In PL/SQL, you may use BULK COLLECT or rely on the implicit array fetch of 100 that is performed for implicit cursor for loops. In Java/JDBC, there is a prefetch method on a connect or statement object. Oracle Call Interface (OCI; a C API) allows you to programmatically set the prefetch size, as does Pro*C. As you can see, this can have a material and measurable affect on the amount of logical I/O performed by your query, and it deserves your attention.

Just to wrap up this example, let's look at what happens when we full scan the DISORGANIZED table:

```
select * from disorganized where x between 20000 and 40000

call     count      cpu    elapsed       disk      query    current        rows
-------  ------  -------- ----------  ---------- ---------- ----------  ----------
Parse        5     0.00       0.00          0          0          0           0
Execute      5     0.00       0.00          0          0          0           0
Fetch     6675     0.53       0.54          0      12565          0      100005
-------  ------  -------- ----------  ---------- ---------- ----------  ----------
total     6685     0.53       0.54          0      12565          0      100005

Rows     Row Source Operation
-------  -------------------------------------------------------------
  20001  TABLE ACCESS FULL DISORGANIZED (cr=2513 pr=0 pw=0 time=60115 us)
```

That shows that in this particular case, the full scan is very appropriate due to the way the data is physically stored on disk. This begs the question, "Why didn't the optimizer full scan in the first place for this query?" Well, it would have if left to its own design, but in the first example query against DISORGANIZED I purposely hinted the query and told the optimizer to construct a plan that used the index. In the second case, I let the optimizer pick the best overall plan.

The Clustering Factor

Next, let's look at some of the information Oracle will use. We are specifically going to look at the CLUSTERING_FACTOR column found in the USER_INDEXES view. The *Oracle Reference* manual tells us this column has the following meaning:

Indicates the amount of order of the rows in the table based on the values of the index:

- *If the value is near the number of blocks, then the table is very well ordered. In this case, the index entries in a single leaf block tend to point to rows in the same data blocks.*

- *If the value is near the number of rows, then the table is very randomly ordered. In this case, it is unlikely that index entries in the same leaf block point to rows in the same data blocks.*

We could also view the clustering factor as a number that represents the number of logi-cal I/Os against the table that would be performed to read the entire table via the index. That is, the CLUSTERING_FACTOR is an indication of how ordered the table is with respect to the index itself, and when we look at these indexes we find the following:

```
ops$tkyte@ORA10G> select a.index_name,
  2            b.num_rows,
  3            b.blocks,
  4            a.clustering_factor
  5    from user_indexes a, user_tables b
  6   where index_name in ('COLOCATED_PK', 'DISORGANIZED_PK' )
  7     and a.table_name = b.table_name
  8  /

INDEX_NAME          NUM_ROWS      BLOCKS CLUSTERING_FACTOR
---------------   ----------   ---------- ------------------
COLOCATED_PK         100000         1252              1190
DISORGANIZED_PK      100000         1219             99932
```

■**Note** I used an ASSM-managed tablespace for this section's example, which explains why the clustering factor for the COLOCATED table is less than the number of blocks in the table. There are unformatted blocks in the COLOCATED table below the HWM that do not contain data, as well as blocks used by ASSM itself to manage space, and we will not read these blocks ever in an index range scan. Chapter 10 explains HWMs and ASSM in more detail.

So the database is saying, "If we were to read every row in COLOCATED via the index COLOCATED_PK from start to finish, we would perform 1,190 I/Os. However, if we did the same to DISORGANIZED, we would perform 99,932 I/Os against the table." The reason for the large difference is that as Oracle range scans through the index structure, if it discovers the next row in the index is on the same database block as the prior row, it does not perform another I/O to get the table block from the buffer cache. It already has a handle to one and just uses it. However, if the next row is *not* on the same block, then it will release that block and perform another I/O into the buffer cache to retrieve the next block to be processed. Hence the COLOCATED_PK index, as we range scan through it, will discover that the next row is almost always on the same block as the prior row. The DISORGANIZED_PK index will discover the oppo-site is true. In fact, we can actually see this measurement is very accurate. Using hints to have the optimizer use an index full scan to read the entire table and just count the number of non-null Y values—we can see exactly how many I/Os it will take to read the entire table via the index:

```
select count(Y)
from
 (select /*+ INDEX(COLOCATED COLOCATED_PK) */ * from colocated)

call     count      cpu    elapsed     disk      query    current       rows
-------  ------  --------  ----------  --------  --------  ----------  ----------
Parse        1     0.00      0.00         0          0          0           0
Execute      1     0.00      0.00         0          0          0           0
Fetch        2     0.10      0.16         0       1399          0           1
-------  ------  --------  ----------  --------  --------  ----------  ----------
total        4     0.10      0.16         0       1399          0           1

Rows     Row Source Operation
-------  --------------------------------------------------
      1  SORT AGGREGATE (cr=1399 pr=0 pw=0 time=160325 us)
 100000   TABLE ACCESS BY INDEX ROWID COLOCATED (cr=1399 pr=0 pw=0 time=500059 us)
 100000    INDEX FULL SCAN COLOCATED_PK (cr=209 pr=0 pw=0 time=101057 us)(object ...
********************************************************************************
select count(Y)
from
 (select /*+ INDEX(DISORGANIZED DISORGANIZED_PK) */ * from disorganized)

call     count      cpu    elapsed     disk      query    current       rows
-------  ------  --------  ----------  --------  --------  ----------  ----------
Parse        1     0.00      0.00         0          0          0           0
Execute      1     0.00      0.00         0          0          0           0
Fetch        2     0.34      0.40         0     100141          0           1
-------  ------  --------  ----------  --------  --------  ----------  ----------
total        4     0.34      0.40         0     100141          0           1

Rows     Row Source Operation
-------  --------------------------------------------------
      1  SORT AGGREGATE (cr=100141 pr=0 pw=0 time=401109 us)
 100000   TABLE ACCESS BY INDEX ROWID OBJ#(66615) (cr=100141 pr=0 pw=0 time=800058...
 100000    INDEX FULL SCAN OBJ#(66616) (cr=209 pr=0 pw=0 time=101129 us)(object...
```

In both cases, the index needed to perform 209 logical I/Os (cr=209 in the Row Source ➡ Operation lines). If you subtract 209 from the total consistent reads and measure just the number of I/Os against the table, then you'll find that they are identical to the clustering factor for each respective index. The COLOCATED_PK is a classic "the table is well ordered" example, whereas the DISORGANIZE_PK is a classic "the table is very randomly ordered" example. It is interesting to see how this affects the optimizer now. If we attempt to retrieve 25,000 rows, Oracle will now choose a full table scan for both queries (retrieving 25 percent of the rows via an index is not the optimal plan, even for the very ordered table). However, if we select only 10 percent of the table data, we observe the following:

```
ops$tkyte@ORA10G> select * from colocated where x between 20000 and 30000;

Execution Plan
----------------------------------------------------------
   0      SELECT STATEMENT Optimizer=ALL_ROWS (Cost=143 Card=10002 Bytes=800160)
   1    0   TABLE ACCESS (BY INDEX ROWID) OF 'COLOCATED' (TABLE) (Cost=143 ...
   2    1    INDEX (RANGE SCAN) OF 'COLOCATED_PK' (INDEX (UNIQUE)) (Cost=22 ...


ops$tkyte@ORA10G> select * from disorganized where x between 20000 and 30000;

Execution Plan
----------------------------------------------------------
   0      SELECT STATEMENT Optimizer=ALL_ROWS (Cost=337 Card=10002 Bytes=800160)
   1    0   TABLE ACCESS (FULL) OF 'DISORGANIZED' (TABLE) (Cost=337 Card=10002 ...
```

Here we have the same table structures and the same indexes, but different clustering factors. The optimizer, in this case, chose an index access plan for the COLOCATED table and a full scan access plan for the DISORGANIZED table. Bear in mind that 10 percent is not a threshold value—it is just a number that is less than 25 percent and that caused an index range scan to happen in this case (for the COLOCATED table).

The key point to this discussion is that indexes are not always the appropriate access method. The optimizer may very well be correct in choosing to not use an index, as the preceding example demonstrates. Many factors influence the use of an index by the optimizer, *including* physical data layout. You might be tempted, therefore, to run out and try to rebuild all of your tables now to make all indexes have a good clustering factor, but that would *be a waste of time* in most cases. It will affect cases where you do index range scans of a large percentage of a table. Additionally, you must keep in mind that in general the table will have only *one* index with a good clustering factor! The rows in a table may be sorted in only one way. In the example just shown, if I had another index on the column Y, it would be very poorly clustered in the COLOCATED table, but very nicely clustered in the DISORGANIZED table. If having the data physically clustered is important to you, consider the use of an IOT, a B*Tree cluster, or a hash cluster over continuous table rebuilds.

B*Trees Wrap-Up

B*Tree indexes are by far the most common and well-understood indexing structures in the Oracle database. They are an excellent general-purpose indexing mechanism. They provide very scalable access times, returning data from a 1,000-row index in about the same amount of time as a 100,000-row index structure.

When to index and what columns to index are things you need to pay attention to in your design. An index does not always mean faster access; in fact, you will find that indexes will decrease performance in many cases if Oracle uses them. It is purely a function of how large of a percentage of the table you will need to access via the index and how the data happens to be laid out. If you can use the index to "answer the question," then accessing a large percentage of the rows makes sense, since you are avoiding the extra scattered I/O to read the table. If you use the index to access the table, then you will need to ensure that you are processing a small percentage of the total table.

You should consider the design and implementation of indexes *during* the design of your application, not as an afterthought (as I so often see). With careful planning and due consideration of how you are going to access the data, the indexes you need will be apparent in most all cases.

Bitmap Indexes

Bitmap indexes were added to Oracle in version 7.3 of the database. They are currently available with the Oracle Enterprise and Personal Editions, but not the Standard Edition. Bitmap indexes are designed for data warehousing/ad hoc query environments where the full set of queries that may be asked of the data is not totally known at system implementation time. They are specifically *not* designed for OLTP systems or systems where data is frequently updated by many concurrent sessions.

Bitmap indexes are structures that store pointers to many rows with a single index key entry, as compared to a B*Tree structure where there is parity between the index keys and the rows in a table. In a bitmap index, there will be a very small number of index entries, each of which points to many rows. In a conventional B*Tree, one index entry points to a single row.

Let's say we are creating a bitmap index on the JOB column in the EMP table as follows:

```
Ops$tkyte@ORA10G> create BITMAP index job_idx on emp(job);
Index created.
```

Oracle will store something like what is shown in Table 11-6 in the index.

Table 11-6. *Representation of How Oracle Would Store the* JOB-IDX *Bitmap Index*

Value/Row	1	2	3	4	5	6	7	8	9	10	11	12	13	14
ANALYST	0	0	0	0	0	0	0	1	0	1	0	0	1	0
CLERK	1	0	0	0	0	0	0	0	0	0	1	1	0	1
MANAGER	0	0	0	1	0	1	1	0	0	0	0	0	0	0
PRESIDENT	0	0	0	0	0	0	0	0	1	0	0	0	0	0
SALESMAN	0	1	1	0	1	0	0	0	0	0	0	0	0	0

Table 11-6 shows that rows 8, 10, and 13 have the value ANALYST, whereas rows 4, 6, and 7 have the value MANAGER. It also shows us that no rows are null (bitmap indexes store null entries; the lack of a null entry in the index implies there are no null rows). If we wanted to count the rows that have the value MANAGER, the bitmap index would do this very rapidly. If we wanted to find all the rows such that the JOB was CLERK or MANAGER, we could simply combine their bitmaps from the index, as shown in Table 11-7.

Table 11-7. *Representation of a Bitwise* OR

Value/Row	1	2	3	4	5	6	7	8	9	10	11	12	13	14
CLERK	1	0	0	0	0	0	0	0	0	0	1	1	0	1
MANAGER	0	0	0	1	0	1	1	0	0	0	0	0	0	0
CLERK or MANAGER	1	0	0	1	0	1	1	0	0	0	1	1	0	1

Table 11-7 rapidly shows us that rows 1, 4, 6, 7, 11, 12, and 14 satisfy our criteria. The bitmap Oracle stores with each key value is set up so that each position represents a rowid in the underlying table, if we need to actually retrieve the row for further processing. Queries such as the following:

```
select count(*) from emp where job = 'CLERK' or job = 'MANAGER'
```

will be answered directly from the bitmap index. A query such as this:

```
select * from emp where job = 'CLERK' or job = 'MANAGER'
```

on the other hand, will need to get to the table. Here, Oracle will apply a function to turn the fact that the i'th bit is on in a bitmap, into a rowid that can be used to access the table.

When Should You Use a Bitmap Index?

Bitmap indexes are most appropriate on *low distinct cardinality* data (i.e., data with relatively few discrete values when compared to the cardinality of the entire set). It is not really possible to put a value on this—in other words, it is difficult to define what low distinct cardinality truly is. In a set of a couple thousand records, 2 would be low distinct cardinality, but 2 would not be low distinct cardinality in a two-row table. In a table of tens or hundreds of millions records, 100,000 could be low distinct cardinality. So, low distinct cardinality is relative to the size of the resultset. This is data where the number of distinct items in the set of rows divided by the number of rows is a small number (near zero). For example, a GENDER column might take on the values M, F, and NULL. If you have a table with 20,000 employee records in it, then you would find that 3/20000 = 0.00015. Likewise, 100,000 unique values out of 10,000,000 results in a ratio of 0.01—again, very small. These columns would be candidates for bitmap indexes. They probably would *not* be candidates for a having B*Tree indexes, as each of the values would tend to retrieve an extremely large percentage of the table. B*Tree indexes should be selective in general, as outlined earlier. Bitmap indexes should not be selective—on the contrary, they should be very "unselective" in general.

Bitmap indexes are extremely useful in environments where you have lots of ad hoc queries, especially queries that reference many columns in an ad hoc fashion or produce aggregations such as COUNT. For example, suppose you have a large table with three columns: GENDER, LOCATION, and AGE_GROUP. In this table, GENDER has a value of M or F, LOCATION can take on the values 1 through 50, and AGE_GROUP is a code representing 18 and under, 19-25, 26-30, 31-40, and 41 and over. You have to support a large number of ad hoc queries that take the following form:

```
Select count(*)
  from T
 where gender = 'M'
   and location in ( 1, 10, 30 )
   and age_group = '41 and over';

select *
  from t
 where (   ( gender = 'M' and location = 20 )
       or ( gender = 'F' and location = 22 ))
   and age_group = '18 and under';

select count(*) from t where location in (11,20,30);

select count(*) from t where age_group = '41 and over' and gender = 'F';
```

You would find that a conventional B*Tree indexing scheme would fail you. If you wanted to use an index to get the answer, you would need at least three and up to six combinations of possible B*Tree indexes to access the data via the index. Since any of the three columns or any subset of the three columns may appear, you would need large concatenated B*Tree indexes on

- GENDER, LOCATION, AGE_GROUP: For queries that used all three, or GENDER with LOCATION, or GENDER alone

- LOCATION, AGE_GROUP: For queries that used LOCATION and AGE_GROUP or LOCATION alone

- AGE_GROUP, GENDER: For queries that used AGE_GROUP with GENDER or AGE_GROUP alone

To reduce the amount of data being searched, other permutations might be reasonable as well, to decrease the size of the index structure being scanned. This is ignoring the fact that a B*Tree index on such low cardinality data is not a good idea.

Here the bitmap index comes into play. With three small bitmap indexes, one on each of the individual columns, you will be able to satisfy all of the previous predicates efficiently. Oracle will simply use the functions AND, OR, and NOT, with the bitmaps of the three indexes together, to find the solution set for any predicate that references any set of these three columns. It will take the resulting merged bitmap, convert the 1s into rowids if necessary, and access the data (if you are just counting rows that match the criteria, Oracle will just count the 1 bits). Let's take a look at an example. First, we'll generate test data that matches our specified distinct cardinalities—index it and gather statistics. We'll make use of the DBMS_RANDOM package to generate random data fitting our distribution:

```
ops$tkyte@ORA10G> create table t
  2  ( gender   not null,
  3    location not null,
  4    age_group not null,
  5    data
  6  )
  7  as
  8  select decode( ceil(dbms_random.value(1,2)),
```

```
  9                      1, 'M',
 10                      2, 'F' ) gender,
 11          ceil(dbms_random.value(1,50)) location,
 12          decode( ceil(dbms_random.value(1,5)),
 13                   1,'18 and under',
 14                   2,'19-25',
 15                   3,'26-30',
 16                   4,'31-40',
 17                   5,'41 and over'),
 18          rpad( '*', 20, '*')
 19     from big_table.big_table
 20    where rownum <= 100000;
Table created.

ops$tkyte@ORA10G> create bitmap index gender_idx on t(gender);
Index created.

ops$tkyte@ORA10G> create bitmap index location_idx on t(location);
Index created.

ops$tkyte@ORA10G> create bitmap index age_group_idx on t(age_group);
Index created.

ops$tkyte@ORA10G> exec dbms_stats.gather_table_stats( user, 'T', cascade=>true );
PL/SQL procedure successfully completed.
```

Now we'll take a look at the plans for our various ad hoc queries from earlier:

```
ops$tkyte@ORA10G> Select count(*)
  2      from T
  3    where gender = 'M'
  4      and location in ( 1, 10, 30 )
  5      and age_group = '41 and over';

Execution Plan
-----------------------------------------------------------
  0        SELECT STATEMENT Optimizer=ALL_ROWS (Cost=5 Card=1 Bytes=13)
  1    0     SORT (AGGREGATE)
  2    1       BITMAP CONVERSION (COUNT) (Cost=5 Card=1 Bytes=13)
  3    2         BITMAP AND
  4    3           BITMAP INDEX (SINGLE VALUE) OF 'GENDER_IDX' (INDEX (BITMAP))
  5    3           BITMAP OR
  6    5             BITMAP INDEX (SINGLE VALUE) OF 'LOCATION_IDX' (INDEX (BITMAP))
  7    5             BITMAP INDEX (SINGLE VALUE) OF 'LOCATION_IDX' (INDEX (BITMAP))
  8    5             BITMAP INDEX (SINGLE VALUE) OF 'LOCATION_IDX' (INDEX (BITMAP))
  9    3           BITMAP INDEX (SINGLE VALUE) OF 'AGE_GROUP_IDX' (INDEX (BITMAP))
```

This example shows the power of the bitmap indexes. Oracle is able to see the location in (1,10,30) and knows to read the index on location for these three values and logically OR together the "bits" in the bitmap. It then takes that resulting bitmap and logically ANDs that with the bitmaps for AGE_GROUP='41 AND OVER' and GENDER='M'. Then a simple count of 1s and the answer is ready.

```
ops$tkyte@ORA10G> select *
  2     from t
  3    where (   ( gender = 'M' and location = 20 )
  4           or ( gender = 'F' and location = 22 ))
  5      and age_group = '18 and under';

Execution Plan
--------------------------------------------------------------
   0          SELECT STATEMENT Optimizer=ALL_ROWS (Cost=77 Card=507 Bytes=16731)
   1     0    TABLE ACCESS (BY INDEX ROWID) OF 'T' (TABLE) (Cost=77 Card=507 ...
   2     1      BITMAP CONVERSION (TO ROWIDS)
   3     2        BITMAP AND
   4     3          BITMAP INDEX (SINGLE VALUE) OF 'AGE_GROUP_IDX' (INDEX (BITMAP))
   5     3          BITMAP OR
   6     5            BITMAP AND
   7     6              BITMAP INDEX (SINGLE VALUE) OF 'LOCATION_IDX' (INDEX (BITMAP))
   8     6              BITMAP INDEX (SINGLE VALUE) OF 'GENDER_IDX' (INDEX (BITMAP))
   9     5            BITMAP AND
  10     9              BITMAP INDEX (SINGLE VALUE) OF 'GENDER_IDX' (INDEX (BITMAP))
  11     9              BITMAP INDEX (SINGLE VALUE) OF 'LOCATION_IDX' (INDEX (BITMAP))
```

This shows similar logic: the plan shows the OR'd conditions are each evaluated by AND-ing together the appropriate bitmaps and then OR-ing together those results. Throw in another AND to satisfy the AGE_GROUP='18 AND UNDER' and we have it all. Since we asked for the actual rows this time, Oracle will convert each bitmap 1 and 0 into rowids to retrieve the source data.

In a data warehouse or a large reporting system supporting many ad hoc SQL queries, this ability to use as many indexes as make sense simultaneously comes in very handy indeed. Using conventional B*Tree indexes here would not be nearly as usual or usable, and as the number of columns that are to be searched by the ad hoc queries increases, the number of combinations of B*Tree indexes you would need increases as well.

However, there are times when bitmaps are *not* appropriate. They work well in a read-intensive environment, but they are extremely ill suited for a write-intensive environment. The reason is that a single bitmap index key entry points to *many* rows. If a session modifies the indexed data, then all of the rows that index entry points to are effectively locked in most cases. Oracle cannot lock an individual bit in a bitmap index entry; it locks the entire bitmap index entry. Any other modifications that need to update *that same bitmap index entry* will be locked out. This will seriously inhibit concurrency, as each update will appear to lock potentially hundreds of rows preventing their bitmap columns from being concurrently updated. It will not lock *every* row as you might think—just many of them. Bitmaps are stored in chunks, so using the earlier EMP example we might find that the index key ANALYST appears in the index many times, each time pointing to hundreds of rows. An update to a row that modifies the JOB column will need to get exclusive access to two of these index key entries: the index key entry for the *old* value and the index key entry for the *new* value. The hundreds of rows these two entries point to will be unavailable for modification by other sessions until that UPDATE commits.

Bitmap Join Indexes

Oracle9*i* introduced a new index type: the bitmap join index. Normally an index is created on a single table, using only columns from that table. A bitmap join index breaks that rule and allows you to index a given table using columns from some other table. In effect, this allows you to denormalize data in an index structure instead of in the tables themselves.

Consider the simple EMP and DEPT tables. EMP has a foreign key to DEPT (the DEPTNO column). The DEPT table has the DNAME attribute (the name of the department). The end users will frequently ask questions such as "How many people work in sales?", "Who works in sales?", "Can you show me the top N performing people in sales?" Note that they do not ask, "How many people work in DEPTNO 30?" They don't use those key values; rather, they use the human-readable department name. Therefore, they end up running queries such as the following:

```
select count(*)
from emp, dept
where emp.deptno = dept.deptno
and dept.dname = 'SALES'
/
select emp.*
from emp, dept
where emp.deptno = dept.deptno
and dept.dname = 'SALES'
/
```

Those queries almost necessarily have to access the DEPT table and the EMP table using conventional indexes. We might use an index on DEPT.DNAME to find the SALES row(s) and retrieve the DEPTNO value for SALES, and then using an INDEX on EMP.DEPTNO find the matching rows, but by using a bitmap join index we can avoid all of that. The bitmap join index allows us to index the DEPT.DNAME column, but have that index point not at the DEPT table, but at the EMP table. This is a pretty radical concept—to be able to index attributes from other tables—and it might change the way to implement your data model in a reporting system. You can, in effect, have your cake and eat it, too. You can keep your normalized data structures intact, yet get the benefits of denormalization at the same time.

Here's the index we would create for this example:

```
ops$tkyte@ORA10G> create bitmap index emp_bm_idx
  2  on emp( d.dname )
  3  from emp e, dept d
  4  where e.deptno = d.deptno
  5  /
Index created.
```

Note how the beginning of the CREATE INDEX looks "normal" and creates the index INDEX_NAME on the table. But from there on, it deviates from "normal." We see a reference to a column in the DEPT table: D.DNAME. We see a FROM clause, making this CREATE INDEX statement resemble a query. We have a join condition between multiple tables. This CREATE INDEX statement indexes the DEPT.DNAME column, but in the context of the EMP table. If we ask those questions mentioned earlier, we would find the database never accesses the DEPT at all, and it need not do so because the DNAME column now exists in the index pointing to rows in the EMP table. For purposes of illustration, we will make the EMP and DEPT tables appear "large" (to avoid having the CBO think they are small and full scanning them instead of using indexes):

```
ops$tkyte@ORA10G> begin
  2 dbms_stats.set_table_stats( user, 'EMP',
  3                                numrows => 1000000, numblks => 300000 );
  4 dbms_stats.set_table_stats( user, 'DEPT',
  5                                numrows => 100000, numblks => 30000 );
  6 end;
  7 /
PL/SQL procedure successfully completed.
```

and then we'll perform our queries:

```
ops$tkyte@ORA10G> set autotrace traceonly explain
ops$tkyte@ORA10G> select count(*)
  2 from emp, dept
  3 where emp.deptno = dept.deptno
  4 and dept.dname = 'SALES'
  5 /
Execution Plan
----------------------------------------------------------
  0      SELECT STATEMENT Optimizer=ALL_ROWS (Cost=1 Card=1 Bytes=13)
  1   0    SORT (AGGREGATE)
  2   1      BITMAP CONVERSION (COUNT) (Cost=1 Card=10000 Bytes=130000)
  3   2        BITMAP INDEX (SINGLE VALUE) OF 'EMP_BM_IDX' (INDEX (BITMAP))
```

As you can see, to answer this particular question, we did not have to actually access either the EMP or DEPT table—the entire answer came from the index itself. All the information needed to answer the question was available in the index structure.

Further, we were able to skip accessing the DEPT table and, using the index on EMP that incorporated the data we needed from DEPT, gain direct access to the required rows:

```
ops$tkyte@ORA10G> select emp.*
  2 from emp, dept
  3 where emp.deptno = dept.deptno
  4 and dept.dname = 'SALES'
  5 /
Execution Plan
----------------------------------------------------------
  0      SELECT STATEMENT Optimizer=ALL_ROWS (Cost=6145 Card=10000 Bytes=870000)
  1   0    TABLE ACCESS (BY INDEX ROWID) OF 'EMP' (TABLE) (Cost=6145 Card=10000 ...
  2   1      BITMAP CONVERSION (TO ROWIDS)
  3   2        BITMAP INDEX (SINGLE VALUE) OF 'EMP_BM_IDX' (INDEX (BITMAP))
```

Bitmap join indexes do have a prerequisite. The join condition must join to a primary or unique key in the other table. In the preceding example, `DEPT.DEPTNO` is the primary key of the `DEPT` table, and the primary key must be in place, otherwise an error will occur:

```
ops$tkyte@ORA10G> create bitmap index emp_bm_idx
  2  on emp( d.dname )
  3  from emp e, dept d
  4  where e.deptno = d.deptno
  5  /
from emp e, dept d
        *
ERROR at line 3:
ORA-25954: missing primary key or unique constraint on dimension
```

Bitmap Indexes Wrap-Up

When in doubt, try it out. It is trivial to add a bitmap index to a table (or a bunch of them) and see what it does for you. Also, you can usually create bitmap indexes much faster than B*Tree indexes. Experimentation is the best way to see if they are suited for your environment. I am frequently asked, "What defines low cardinality?" There is no cut-and-dried answer for this. Sometimes it is 3 values out of 100,000. Sometimes it is 10,000 values out of 1,000,000. Low cardinality doesn't imply single-digit counts of distinct values. Experimentation is the way to discover if a bitmap is a good idea for your application. In general, if you have a large, mostly read-only environment with lots of ad hoc queries, a set of bitmap indexes may be exactly what you need.

Function-Based Indexes

Function-based indexes were added to Oracle 8.1.5. They are now a feature of Standard Edition, whereas in releases prior to Oracle9i Release 2 they were a feature of Enterprise Edition.

Function-based indexes give us the ability to index computed columns and use these indexes in a query. In a nutshell, this capability allows you to have case-insensitive searches or sorts, search on complex equations, and extend the SQL language efficiently by implementing your own functions and operators and then searching on them.

There are many reasons why you would want to use a function-based index, with the following chief among them:

- They are easy to implement and provide immediate value.

- They can be used to speed up existing applications without changing any of their logic or queries.

Important Implementation Details

Unlike B*Tree and bitmap indexes, in Oracle9i Release 1 function-based indexes require some initial setup before we can create and then use them.

> **■Note** The following information applies only to Oracle9*i* Release 1 and before. In Oracle9*i* Release 2 and above, function-based indexes are usable without any setup. The *Oracle SQL Reference* manual for Oracle9*i* Release 2 is not correct in this regard—it says you need these privileges, when in fact you do not.

There are some system parameter or session settings you must use and, to be able to create them, a privilege you must have:

- You must have the system privilege QUERY REWRITE to create function-based indexes on tables in your own schema.

- You must have the system privilege GLOBAL QUERY REWRITE to create function-based indexes on tables in other schemas.

- For the optimizer to use function-based indexes, the following session or system variables must be set: QUERY_REWRITE_ENABLED=TRUE and QUERY_REWRITE_INTEGRITY=TRUSTED. You may enable these either at the session level with ALTER SESSION, or at the system level via ALTER SYSTEM, or by setting them in the init.ora parameter file. QUERY_REWRITE_ENABLED allows the optimizer to rewrite the query to use the function-based index. QUERY_REWRITE_INTEGRITY tells the optimizer to "trust" that the code marked deterministic by the programmer is in fact deterministic (the following section contains examples of deterministic code and its meaning). If the code is in fact not deterministic (i.e., it returns different output given the same inputs), the resulting rows retrieved via the index may be incorrect. You must take care to ensure that a function defined as deterministic is in fact deterministic.

In all releases, the following points apply:

- *Use the cost-based optimizer (CBO)*. The virtual columns (columns with functions applied to them) in the function-based indexes are only visible to the CBO and will not be used by the rule-based optimizer (RBO) ever. The RBO can make use of the leading-edge columns in a function-based index that have no functions applied to them.

- *Use SUBSTR to constrain return values from user-written functions that return VARCHAR2 or RAW types.* Optionally hide the SUBSTR in a view (recommended). Again, the following section contains examples of this.

Once the preceding criteria have been satisfied, function-based indexes are as easy to use as the CREATE INDEX command. The optimizer will find and use your indexes at runtime for you.

A Simple Function-Based Index Example

Consider the following example. We want to perform a case-insensitive search on the ENAME column of the EMP table. Prior to function-based indexes, we would have approached this in a very different manner. We would have added an extra column to the EMP table called UPPER_ENAME, for example. This column would have been maintained by a database trigger on

INSERT and UPDATE; that trigger would simply have set NEW.UPPER_NAME := UPPER(:NEW.ENAME). This extra column would have been indexed. Now with function-based indexes, we remove the need for the extra column.

We begin by creating a copy of the demo EMP table in the SCOTT schema and adding some data to it:

```
ops$tkyte@ORA10G> create table emp
  2  as
  3  select *
  4    from scott.emp
  5   where 1=0;
Table created.

ops$tkyte@ORA10G> insert into emp
  2  (empno,ename,job,mgr,hiredate,sal,comm,deptno)
  3  select rownum empno,
  4         initcap(substr(object_name,1,10)) ename,
  5            substr(object_type,1,9) JOB,
  6         rownum MGR,
  7         created hiredate,
  8         rownum SAL,
  9         rownum COMM,
 10         (mod(rownum,4)+1)*10 DEPTNO
 11    from all_objects
 12   where rownum < 10000;
9999 rows created.
```

Next, we will create an index on the UPPER value of the ENAME column, effectively creating a case-insensitive index:

```
ops$tkyte@ORA10G> create index emp_upper_idx on emp(upper(ename));
Index created.
```

Finally, we'll analyze the table since, as noted previously, we need to make use of the CBO to use function-based indexes. In Oracle 10g, this step is technically unnecessary, as the CBO is used by default and dynamic sampling would gather the needed information, but gathering statistics is a more correct approach.

```
ops$tkyte@ORA10G> begin
  2      dbms_stats.gather_table_stats
  3      (user,'EMP',cascade=>true);
  4  end;
  5  /
PL/SQL procedure successfully completed.
```

We now have an index on the UPPER value of a column. Any application that already issues "case-insensitive" queries like this:

```
ops$tkyte@ORA10G> set autotrace traceonly explain
ops$tkyte@ORA10G> select *
  2    from emp
  3    where upper(ename) = 'KING';

Execution Plan
----------------------------------------------------------
  0        SELECT STATEMENT Optimizer=ALL_ROWS (Cost=2 Card=2 Bytes=92)
  1    0     TABLE ACCESS (BY INDEX ROWID) OF 'EMP' (TABLE) (Cost=2 Card=2 Bytes=92)
  2    1        INDEX (RANGE SCAN) OF 'EMP_UPPER_IDX' (INDEX) (Cost=1 Card=2)
```

will make use of this index, gaining the performance boost an index can deliver. Before this feature was available, every row in the EMP table would have been scanned, uppercased, and compared. In contrast, with the index on UPPER(ENAME), the query takes the constant KING to the index, range scans a little data, and accesses the table by rowid to get the data. This is very fast.

This performance boost is most visible when indexing user-written functions on columns. Oracle 7.1 added the ability to use user-written functions in SQL, so we could do something like this:

```
SQL> select my_function(ename)
  2    from emp
  3    where some_other_function(empno) > 10
  4    /
```

This was great because we could now effectively extend the SQL language to include application-specific functions. Unfortunately, however, the performance of the preceding query was a bit disappointing at times. Say the EMP table had 1,000 rows in it. The function SOME_OTHER_FUNCTION would be executed 1,000 times during the query, once per row. In addition, assuming the function took one-hundredth of a second to execute, this relatively simple query now takes at least ten seconds.

Let's look at a real example, where we'll implement a modified SOUNDEX routine in PL/SQL. Additionally, we'll use a package global variable as a counter in our procedure, which will allow us to execute queries that make use of the MY_SOUNDEX function and see exactly how many times it was called:

```
ops$tkyte@ORA10G> create or replace package stats
  2    as
  3          cnt number default 0;
  4    end;
  5    /
Package created.

ops$tkyte@ORA10G> create or replace
  2    function my_soundex( p_string in varchar2 ) return varchar2
  3    deterministic
  4    as
  5        l_return_string varchar2(6) default substr( p_string, 1, 1 );
  6        l_char        varchar2(1);
```

```
7       l_last_digit    number default 0;
8
9       type vcArray is table of varchar2(10) index by binary_integer;
10      l_code_table    vcArray;
11
12  begin
13      stats.cnt := stats.cnt+1;
14
15      l_code_table(1) := 'BPFV';
16      l_code_table(2) := 'CSKGJQXZ';
17      l_code_table(3) := 'DT';
18      l_code_table(4) := 'L';
19      l_code_table(5) := 'MN';
20      l_code_table(6) := 'R';
21
22
23      for i in 1 .. length(p_string)
24      loop
25          exit when (length(l_return_string) = 6);
26          l_char := upper(substr( p_string, i, 1 ) );
27
28          for j in 1 .. l_code_table.count
29          loop
30          if (instr(l_code_table(j), l_char ) > 0 AND j <> l_last_digit)
31          then
32              l_return_string := l_return_string || to_char(j,'fm9');
33              l_last_digit := j;
34          end if;
35          end loop;
36      end loop;
37
38      return rpad( l_return_string, 6, '0' );
39  end;
40  /
```

Function created.

Notice in this function, we are using a new keyword, DETERMINISTIC. This declares that the preceding function, when given the same inputs, will always return the exact same output. This is needed to create an index on a user-written function. We must tell Oracle that the function is DETERMINISTIC and will return a consistent result given the same inputs. We are telling Oracle that this function should be trusted to return the same value, call after call, given the same inputs. If this were not the case, we would receive different answers when accessing the data via the index versus a full table scan. This deterministic setting implies, for example, that we cannot create an index on the function DBMS_RANDOM.RANDOM, the random number generator. Its results are not deterministic; given the same inputs, we'll get random output. The built-in SQL function UPPER used in the first example, on the other hand, is deterministic, so we can create an index on the UPPER value of a column.

Now that we have the function MY_SOUNDEX, let's see how it performs without an index. This uses the EMP table we created earlier with about 10,000 rows in it:

```
ops$tkyte@ORA10G> set timing on
ops$tkyte@ORA10G> set autotrace on explain
ops$tkyte@ORA10G> select ename, hiredate
  2      from emp
  3    where my_soundex(ename) = my_soundex('Kings')
  4  /

ENAME      HIREDATE
---------- ---------
Ku$_Chunk_ 10-AUG-04
Ku$_Chunk_ 10-AUG-04
Elapsed: 00:00:01.07

Execution Plan
----------------------------------------------------------
   0      SELECT STATEMENT Optimizer=ALL_ROWS (Cost=32 Card=100 Bytes=1900)
   1    0    TABLE ACCESS (FULL) OF 'EMP' (TABLE) (Cost=32 Card=100 Bytes=1900)

ops$tkyte@ORA10G> set autotrace off
ops$tkyte@ORA10G> set timing off
ops$tkyte@ORA10G> set serveroutput on
ops$tkyte@ORA10G> exec dbms_output.put_line( stats.cnt );
19998
PL/SQL procedure successfully completed.
```

We can see this query took over one second to execute and had to do a full scan on the table. The function MY_SOUNDEX was invoked almost 20,000 times (according to our counter), twice for each row.

Let's see how indexing the function can speed up things. The first thing we'll do is create the index as follows:

```
ops$tkyte@ORA10G> create index emp_soundex_idx on
  2  emp( substr(my_soundex(ename),1,6) )
  3  /
Index created.
```

The interesting thing to note in this CREATE INDEX command is the use of the SUBSTR function. This is because we are indexing a function that returns a string. If we were indexing a function that returned a number or date, this SUBSTR would not be necessary. The reason we must SUBSTR the user-written function that returns a string is that such functions return VARCHAR2(4000) types. That may well be too big to be indexed—index entries must fit within about three quarters the size of a block. If we tried, we would receive (in a tablespace with a 4KB blocksize) the following:

```
ops$tkyte@ORA10G> create index emp_soundex_idx on
  2  emp( my_soundex(ename) ) tablespace ts4k;
emp( my_soundex(ename) ) tablespace ts4k
                *
ERROR at line 2:
ORA-01450: maximum key length (3118) exceeded
```

It is not that the index actually contains any keys that large, but that *it could* as far as the database is concerned. But the database understands SUBSTR. It sees the inputs to SUBSTR of 1 and 6, and knows the biggest return value from this is six characters; hence, it permits the index to be created. This size issue can get you, especially with concatenated indexes. Here is an example on an 8KB blocksize tablespace:

```
ops$tkyte@ORA10G> create index emp_soundex_idx on
  2  emp( my_soundex(ename), my_soundex(job) );
emp( my_soundex(ename), my_soundex(job) )
                    *
ERROR at line 2:
ORA-01450: maximum key length (6398) exceeded
```

Here, the database thinks the maximum key size is 8,000 bytes and fails the CREATE once again. So, to index a user-written function that returns a string, we should constrain the return type in the CREATE INDEX statement. In the example, knowing that MY_SOUNDEX returns at most six characters, we are substringing the first six characters.

We are now ready to test the performance of the table with the index on it. We would like to monitor the effect of the index on INSERTs as well as the speedup for SELECTs to see the effect on each. In the unindexed test case, our queries take over one second, and if we were to run SQL_TRACE and TKPROF during the inserts, we could observe that without the index, the insert of 9,999 records took about .5 seconds:

```
insert into emp NO_INDEX
(empno,ename,job,mgr,hiredate,sal,comm,deptno)
select rownum empno,
       initcap(substr(object_name,1,10)) ename,
           substr(object_type,1,9) JOB,
       rownum MGR,
       created hiredate,
       rownum SAL,
       rownum COMM,
       (mod(rownum,4)+1)*10 DEPTNO
  from all_objects
 where rownum < 10000
```

call	count	cpu	elapsed	disk	query	current	rows
Parse	1	0.03	0.06	0	0	0	0
Execute	1	0.46	0.43	0	15439	948	9999

call	count	cpu	elapsed	disk	query	current	rows
Fetch	0	0.00	0.00	0	0	0	0
total	2	0.49	0.50	0	15439	948	9999

But with the index, it takes about 1.2 seconds:

call	count	cpu	elapsed	disk	query	current	rows
Parse	1	0.03	0.04	0	0	0	0
Execute	1	1.14	1.12	2	15650	7432	9999
Fetch	0	0.00	0.00	0	0	0	0
total	2	1.17	1.16	2	15650	7432	9999

This was the overhead introduced in the management of the new index on the MY_SOUNDEX function—both in the performance overhead of simply having an index (any type of index will affect insert performance) and the fact that this index had to call a stored procedure 9,999 times.

Now, to test the query, we'll just rerun the query:

```
ops$tkyte@ORA10G> REM reset our counter
ops$tkyte@ORA10G> exec stats.cnt := 0
PL/SQL procedure successfully completed.

ops$tkyte@ORA10G> set timing on
ops$tkyte@ORA10G> set autotrace on explain
ops$tkyte@ORA10G> select ename, hiredate
  2  from emp
  3  where substr(my_soundex(ename),1,6) = my_soundex('Kings')
  4  /

ENAME       HIREDATE
----------  ---------
Ku$_Chunk_  10-AUG-04
Ku$_Chunk_  10-AUG-04
Elapsed: 00:00:00.02

Execution Plan
----------------------------------------------------------
   0      SELECT STATEMENT Optimizer=ALL_ROWS (Cost=2 Card=1 Bytes=16)
   1    0   TABLE ACCESS (BY INDEX ROWID) OF 'EMP' (TABLE) (Cost=2 Card=1 Bytes=16)
   2    1     INDEX (RANGE SCAN) OF 'EMP_SOUNDEX_IDX' (INDEX) (Cost=1 Card=35)

ops$tkyte@ORA10G> set autotrace off
ops$tkyte@ORA10G> set timing off
ops$tkyte@ORA10G> set serveroutput on
ops$tkyte@ORA10G> exec dbms_output.put_line( stats.cnt );
2

PL/SQL procedure successfully completed.
```

If we compare the two examples (unindexed versus indexed), we find that the insert was affected by a little more than doubling the runtime. However, the select went from over a second to effectively "instantly." The important things to note here are the following:

- The insertion of 9,999 records took approximately two times longer. Indexing a user-written function will necessarily affect the performance of inserts and some updates. You should realize that any index will impact performance, of course. For example, I did a simple test without the MY_SOUNDEX function, just indexing the ENAME column itself. That caused the INSERT to take about one second to execute—the PL/SQL function is not responsible for the entire overhead. Since most applications insert and update singleton entries, and each row took less than 1/10,000 of a second to insert, you probably won't even notice this in a typical application. Since we insert a row only once, we pay the price of executing the function on the column once, not the thousands of times we query the data.

- While the insert ran two times slower, the query ran many times faster. It evaluated the MY_SOUNDEX function a few times instead of almost 20,000 times. The difference in performance of our query here is measurable and quite large. Also, as the size of our table grows, the full scan query will take longer and longer to execute. The index-based query will always execute with nearly the same performance characteristics as the table gets larger.

- We had to use SUBSTR in our query. This is not as nice as just coding WHERE MY_SOUNDEX(ename)=MY_SOUNDEX('King'), but we can easily get around that, as we will see shortly.

So, the insert was affected, but the query ran incredibly fast. The payoff for a small reduction in insert/update performance is huge. Additionally, if you never update the columns involved in the MY_SOUNDEX function call, the updates are not penalized at all (MY_SOUNDEX is invoked only if the ENAME column is *modified* and its value changed).

Now let's see how to make it so the query does not have use the SUBSTR function call. The use of the SUBSTR call could be error-prone—our end users have to know to SUBSTR from 1 for six characters. If they use a different size, the index will not be used. Also, we want to control in the server the number of bytes to index. This will allow us to reimplement the MY_SOUNDEX function later with 7 bytes instead of 6 if we want to. We can hide the SUBSTR with a view quite easily as follows:

```
ops$tkyte@ORA10G> create or replace view emp_v
  2  as
  3  select ename, substr(my_soundex(ename),1,6) ename_soundex, hiredate
  4    from emp
  5  /
View created.

ops$tkyte@ORA10G> exec stats.cnt := 0;
PL/SQL procedure successfully completed.

ops$tkyte@ORA10G> set timing on
ops$tkyte@ORA10G> select ename, hiredate
```

```
 2      from emp_v
 3    where ename_soundex = my_soundex('Kings')
 4  /
ENAME        HIREDATE
---------- ---------
Ku$_Chunk_ 10-AUG-04
Ku$_Chunk_ 10-AUG-04

Elapsed: 00:00:00.03
ops$tkyte@ORA10G> set timing off
ops$tkyte@ORA10G> exec dbms_output.put_line( stats.cnt )
2
PL/SQL procedure successfully completed.
```

We see the same sort of query plan we did with the base table. All we have done here is hidden the SUBSTR(F(X), 1, 6) in the view itself. The optimizer still recognizes that this virtual column is, in fact, the indexed column and does the "right thing." We see the same performance improvement and the same query plan. Using this view is as good as using the base table—better even because it hides the complexity and allows us to change the size of the SUBSTR later.

Indexing Only Some of the Rows

In addition to transparently helping out queries that use built-in functions like UPPER, LOWER, and so on, function-based indexes can be used to selectively index only some of the rows in a table. As we'll discuss a little later, B*Tree indexes do not contain entries for entirely NULL keys. That is, if you have an index I on a table T:

```
Create index I on t(a,b);
```

and you have a row where A and B are both NULL, there will be no entry in the index structure. This comes in handy when you are indexing just some of the rows in a table.

Consider a large table with a NOT NULL column called PROCESSED_FLAG that may take one of two values, Y or N, with a default value of N. New rows are added with a value of N to signify not processed, and as they are processed, they are updated to Y to signify processed. We would like to index this column to be able to retrieve the N records rapidly, but there are millions of rows and almost all of them are going to have a value of Y. The resulting B*Tree index will be large, and the cost of maintaining it as we update from N to Y will be high. This table sounds like a candidate for a bitmap index (this is low cardinality, after all!), but this is a transactional system and lots of people will be inserting records at the same time with the processed column set to N and, as we discussed earlier, bitmaps are not good for concurrent modifications. When we factor in the constant updating of N to Y in this table as well, then bitmaps would be out of the question, as this process would serialize entirely.

So, what we would really like is to index only the records of interest (the N records). We'll see how to do this with function-based indexes, but before we do, let's see what happens if we just use a regular index. Using the standard BIG_TABLE script described in the setup, we'll update the TEMPORARY column, flipping the Ys to Ns and the Ns to Ys:

```
ops$tkyte@ORA10G> update big_table set temporary = decode(temporary,'N','Y','N');
1000000 rows updated.
```

And we'll check out the ratio of Ys to Ns:

```
ops$tkyte@ORA10G> select temporary, cnt,
  2          round( (ratio_to_report(cnt) over ()) * 100, 2 ) rtr
  3    from (
  4  select temporary, count(*) cnt
  5    from big_table
  6   group by temporary
  7          )
  8  /


T        CNT        RTR
- ---------- ----------
N       1779        .18
Y     998221      99.82
```

As we can see, of the 1,000,000 records in the table, only about one-fifth of 1 percent of the data should be indexed. If we use a conventional index on the TEMPORARY column (which is playing the role of the PROCESSED_FLAG column in this example), we would discover that the index has 1,000,000 entries, consumes over 14MB of space, and has a height of 3:

```
ops$tkyte@ORA10G> create index processed_flag_idx
  2  on big_table(temporary);
Index created.

ops$tkyte@ORA10G> analyze index processed_flag_idx
  2  validate structure;
Index analyzed.

ops$tkyte@ORA10G> select name, btree_space, lf_rows, height
  2    from index_stats;

NAME                             BTREE_SPACE   LF_ROWS    HEIGHT
-------------------------------- ----------- ---------- ----------
PROCESSED_FLAG_IDX                 14528892   1000000         3
```

Any retrieval via this index would incur three I/Os to get to the leaf blocks. This index is not only "wide," but also "tall." To get the first unprocessed record, we will have to perform at least four I/Os (three against the index and one against the table).

How can we change all of this? We need to make it so the index is much smaller and easier to maintain (with less runtime overhead during the updates). Enter the function-based index, which allows us to simply write a function that returns NULL when we don't want to index a given row and returns a non-NULL value when we do. For example, since we are interested just in the N records, let's index just those:

```
ops$tkyte@ORA10G> drop index processed_flag_idx;
Index dropped.

ops$tkyte@ORA10G> create index processed_flag_idx
  2  on big_table( case temporary when 'N' then 'N' end );
Index created.

ops$tkyte@ORA10G> analyze index processed_flag_idx
  2  validate structure;
Index analyzed.

ops$tkyte@ORA10G> select name, btree_space, lf_rows, height
  2      from index_stats;

NAME                             BTREE_SPACE    LF_ROWS     HEIGHT
-------------------------------- -----------  ---------- ----------
PROCESSED_FLAG_IDX                     40012        1779          2
```

That is quite a difference—the index is some 40KB, not 14.5MB. The height has decreased as well. If we use this index, we'll perform one less I/O than we would using the previous taller index.

Implementing Selective Uniqueness

Another useful technique with function-based indexes is to use them to enforce certain types of complex constraints. For example, suppose you have a table with versioned information, such as a projects table. Projects have one of two statuses: either ACTIVE or INACTIVE. You need to enforce a rule such that "Active projects must have a unique name; inactive projects do not." That is, there can only be one active "project X," but you could have as many inactive project Xs as you like.

The first response from a developer when they hear this requirement is typically, "We'll just run a query to see if there are any active project Xs, and if not, we'll create ours." If you read Chapter 7 (which covers concurrency control and multi-versioning), you understand that such a simple implementation cannot work in a multiuser environment. If two people attempt to create a new active project X at the same time, they'll both succeed. We need to serialize the creation of project X, but the only way to do that is to lock the entire projects table (not very concurrent) or use a function-based index and let the database do it for us.

Building on the fact that we can create indexes on functions, that entire null entries are not made in B*Tree indexes, and that we can create a UNIQUE index, we can easily do the following:

```
Create unique index active_projects_must_be_unique
On projects ( case when status = 'ACTIVE' then name end );
```

That would do it. When the status column is ACTIVE, the NAME column will be uniquely indexed. Any attempt to create active projects with the same name will be detected, and concurrent access to this table is not compromised at all.

Caveat on CASE

There is a bug in certain Oracle releases whereby a function referenced in a function-based index is rewritten in a manner that prevents the index from apparently being used. For example, the previous CASE statement

```
Case when temporary = 'N' then 'N' end
```

will silently be rewritten into the more efficient

```
CASE "TEMPORARY" WHEN 'N' THEN 'N' END
```

But this function doesn't match the one we created anymore, so queries will not be able to use it. This simple test case, performed in 10.1.0.3 and then again in 10.1.0.4 (where it is corrected), demonstrates this (in 10.1.0.3):

```
ops$tkyte@ORA10GR1> create table t ( x int );
Table created.

ops$tkyte@ORA10GR1> create index t_idx on
  2  t( case when x = 42 then 1 end );
Index created.

ops$tkyte@ORA10GR1> set autotrace traceonly explain
ops$tkyte@ORA10GR1> select /*+ index( t t_idx ) */ *
  2    from t
  3   where (case when x = 42 then 1 end ) = 1;

Execution Plan
----------------------------------------------------------
   0      SELECT STATEMENT Optimizer=ALL_ROWS (Cost=2 Card=1 Bytes=13)
   1    0   TABLE ACCESS (FULL) OF 'T' (TABLE) (Cost=2 Card=1 Bytes=13)
```

It would appear that the function-based index just won't work and isn't available. But in fact, the FBI is available, because the underlying function was rewritten, and we can verify this by peeking at the view USER_IND_EXPRESSIONS to see what Oracle has rewritten it to

```
ops$tkyte@ORA10GR1> select column_expression
  2    from user_ind_expressions
  3   where index_name = 'T_IDX';

COLUMN_EXPRESSION
----------------------------------------------------------------------------
CASE "X" WHEN 42 THEN 1 END
```

In Oracle 10.1.0.4, the rewrite still takes place in the function-based index, but the index use takes place:

```
ops$tkyte@ORA10G> set autotrace traceonly explain
ops$tkyte@ORA10G> select /*+ index( t t_idx ) */ *
  2    from t
  3   where (case when x = 42 then 1 end ) = 1;
```

```
Execution Plan
------------------------------------------------------------
   0        SELECT STATEMENT Optimizer=ALL_ROWS (Cost=1 Card=1 Bytes=13)
   1    0     TABLE ACCESS (BY INDEX ROWID) OF 'T' (TABLE) (Cost=1 Card=1 Bytes=13)
   2    1       INDEX (RANGE SCAN) OF 'T_IDX' (INDEX) (Cost=1 Card=1)
```

This is because the database is now not only rewriting the function in the CREATE INDEX, but also in the query itself, so they match.

The workaround in prior releases is to do one of the following:

- Use DECODE instead of CASE, as DECODE is not rewritten and what you see is what you get.

- Use the searched CASE syntax in the first place (anticipate the optimization that will take place).

But in any situation where your function-based index is not getting used and you cannot see any good reason why it should not be, check out USER_IND_EXPRESSIONS to verify that you are using the correct function.

Caveat Regarding ORA-01743

One quirk I have noticed with function-based indexes is that if you create one on the built-in function TO_DATE, it will not succeed in some cases, for example:

```
ops$tkyte@ORA10GR1> create table t ( year varchar2(4) );
Table created.

ops$tkyte@ORA10GR1> create index t_idx on t( to_date(year,'YYYY') );
create index t_idx on t( to_date(year,'YYYY') )
                                      *
ERROR at line 1:
ORA-01743: only pure functions can be indexed
```

This seems strange, since we can *sometimes* create a function using TO_DATE, for example:

```
ops$tkyte@ORA10GR1> create index t_idx on t( to_date('01'||year,'MMYYYY') );
Index created.
```

The error message that accompanies this isn't too illuminating either:

```
ops$tkyte@ORA10GR1> !oerr ora 1743
01743, 00000, "only pure functions can be indexed"
// *Cause: The indexed function uses SYSDATE or the user environment.
// *Action: PL/SQL functions must be pure (RNDS, RNPS, WNDS, WNPS).  SQL
//          expressions must not use SYSDATE, USER, USERENV(), or anything
//          else dependent on the session state.  NLS-dependent functions
//          are OK.
```

We are not using SYSDATE. We are not using the "user environment" (or are we?). No PL/SQL functions are used, and nothing about the session state is involved. The trick lies in the format we used: YYYY. That format, given the same exact inputs, will return different answers depending on what month you call it in. For example, anytime in the month of May

```
ops$tkyte@ORA10GR1> select to_char( to_date('2005','YYYY'),
  2                                  'DD-Mon-YYYY HH24:MI:SS' )
  3      from dual;

TO_CHAR(TO_DATE('200
--------------------
01-May-2005 00:00:00
```

the YYYY format will return May 1, in June it will return June 1, and so on. It turns out that TO_DATE, when used with YYYY, is not deterministic! That is why the index cannot be created; it would only work correctly in the month you created it in (or insert/updated a row in). So, it is due to the user environment, which includes the current date itself.

To use TO_DATE in a function-based index, you *must* use a date format that is unambiguous and deterministic—regardless of what day it is currently.

Function-Based Indexes Wrap-Up

Function-based indexes are easy to use and implement, and they provide immediate value. They can be used to speed up existing applications without changing any of their logic or queries. Many orders of magnitude improvement may be observed. You can use them to precompute complex values without using a trigger. Additionally, the optimizer can estimate selectivity more accurately if the expressions are materialized in a function-based index. You can use function-based indexes to selectively index only rows of interest as demonstrated earlier with the PROCESSED_FLAG example. You can, in effect, index a WHERE clause using that technique. Lastly, we explored how to use function-based indexes to implement a certain kind of integrity constraint: selective uniqueness (e.g., "The fields X,Y, and Z must be unique when some condition is true").

Function-based indexes will affect the performance of inserts and updates. Whether or not that warning is relevant to you is something you must decide. If you insert and very infrequently query the data, this might not be an appropriate feature for you. On the other hand, keep in mind that you typically insert a row once and you query it thousands of times. The performance hit on the insert (which your individual end user will probably never notice) may be offset many thousands of times by speeding up the queries. In general, the pros heavily outweigh any of the cons in this case.

Application Domain Indexes

Application domain indexes are what Oracle calls *extensible indexing*. They allow you to create your own index structures that work just like indexes supplied by Oracle. When someone issues a CREATE INDEX statement using your index type, Oracle will run your code to generate the index. If someone analyzes the index to compute statistics on it, Oracle will execute your code to generate statistics in whatever format you care to store them in. When Oracle parses a query and develops a query plan that may make use of your index, Oracle will ask you how costly this function is to perform as it is evaluating the different plans. In short, application domain indexes give you the ability to implement a new index type that does not exist in the database as of yet. For example, if you develop software that analyzes images stored in the database, and you produce information about the images, such as the colors found in them, you could create your own *image* index. As images are added to the database, your code is invoked to extract the colors from the images and store them somewhere (wherever you want to store them). At query time, when the user asks for all "blue images," Oracle will ask you to provide the answer from your index when appropriate.

The best example of this is Oracle's own *text index*. This index is used to provide keyword searching on large text items. You may create a simple text index like this:

```
ops$tkyte@ORA10G> create index myindex on mytable(docs)
  2  indextype is ctxsys.context
  3  /
Index created.
```

and then use the text operators the creators of that index introduced into the SQL language:

```
select * from mytable where contains( docs, 'some words' ) > 0;
```

It will even respond to commands such as the following:

```
ops$tkyte@ORA10GR1> begin
  2    dbms_stats.gather_index_stats( user, 'MYINDEX' );
  3  end;
  4  /
PL/SQL procedure successfully completed.
```

It will participate with the optimizer at runtime to determine the relative cost of using a text index over some other index or a full scan. The interesting thing about all of this is that you or I could have developed this index. The implementation of the text index was done without "inside kernel knowledge." It was done using the dedicated, documented, and exposed API. The Oracle database kernel is not aware of how the text index is stored (the APIs store it in many physical database tables per index created). Oracle is not aware of the processing that takes place when a new row is inserted. Oracle text is really an application built on top of the database, but in a wholly integrated fashion. To you and me, it looks just like any other Oracle database kernel function, but it is not.

I personally have not found the need to go and build a new exotic type of index structure. I see this particular feature as being of use mostly to third-party solution providers that have innovative indexing techniques.

I think the most interesting thing about application domain indexes is that they allow others to supply new indexing technology I can use in my applications. Most people will never make use of this particular API to build a new index type, but most of us will use the end results. Virtually every application I work on seems to have some *text* associated with it, *XML* to be dealt with, or *images* to be stored and categorized. The interMedia set of functionality, implemented using the Application Domain Indexing feature, provides these capabilities. As time passes, the set of available index types grows. We'll take a more in-depth look at the text index in a subsequent chapter.

Frequently Asked Questions and Myths About Indexes

As I said in the introduction to this book, I field lots of questions about Oracle. I am the Tom behind "Ask Tom" column in *Oracle Magazine* and at http://asktom.oracle.com, where I answer people's questions about the Oracle database and tools. In my experience, the topic of indexes attracts the most questions of all. In this section, I answer some of the most frequently asked questions. Some of the answers may seem like common sense, while other answers might surprise you. Suffice it to say, there are lots of myths and misunderstandings surrounding indexes.

Do Indexes Work on Views?

A related question is, "How can I index a view?" Well, the fact is that a view is nothing more than a stored query. Oracle will replace the text of the query that accesses the view with the view definition itself. Views are for the convenience of the end user or programmer—the optimizer works with the query against the base tables. Any and all indexes that could have been used if the query had been written against the base tables will be considered when you use the view. To "index a view," you simply index the base tables.

Do Nulls and Indexes Work Together?

B*Tree indexes, except in the special case of cluster B*Tree indexes, do not store completely null entries, but bitmap and cluster indexes do. This side effect can be a point of confusion, but it can actually be used to your advantage when you understand what not storing entirely null keys implies.

To see the effect of the fact that null values are *not* stored, consider this example:

```
ops$tkyte@ORA10GR1> create table t ( x int, y int );
Table created.

ops$tkyte@ORA10GR1> create unique index t_idx on t(x,y);
Index created.

ops$tkyte@ORA10GR1> insert into t values ( 1, 1 );
1 row created.

ops$tkyte@ORA10GR1> insert into t values ( 1, NULL );
1 row created.

ops$tkyte@ORA10GR1> insert into t values ( NULL, 1 );
1 row created.

ops$tkyte@ORA10GR1> insert into t values ( NULL, NULL );
1 row created.
```

```
ops$tkyte@ORA10GR1> analyze index t_idx validate structure;
Index analyzed.

ops$tkyte@ORA10GR1> select name, lf_rows from index_stats;

NAME                             LF_ROWS
-------------------------------- ----------
T_IDX                                  3
```

The table has four rows, whereas the index only has three. The first three rows, where at least *one* of the index key elements was *not* null, are in the index. The last row with (NULL, NULL) is not in the index. One of the areas of confusion is when the index is a unique index, as just shown. Consider the effect of the following three INSERT statements:

```
ops$tkyte@ORA10GR1> insert into t values ( NULL, NULL );
1 row created.

ops$tkyte@ORA10GR1> insert into t values ( NULL, 1 );
insert into t values ( NULL, 1 )
*
ERROR at line 1:
ORA-00001: unique constraint (OPS$TKYTE.T_IDX) violated

ops$tkyte@ORA10GR1> insert into t values ( 1, NULL );
insert into t values ( 1, NULL )
*
ERROR at line 1:
ORA-00001: unique constraint (OPS$TKYTE.T_IDX) violated
```

The new (NULL, NULL) row is not considered to be the same as the old row with (NULL, NULL):

```
ops$tkyte@ORA10GR1> select x, y, count(*)
  2  from t
  3  group by x,y
  4  having count(*) > 1;

         X          Y   COUNT(*)
---------- ---------- ----------
                               2
```

This seems impossible; our unique key isn't unique if we consider all null entries. The fact is that, in Oracle, (NULL, NULL) is not the same as (NULL, NULL) when considering uniqueness—the SQL standard mandates this. (NULL,NULL) and (NULL,NULL) are considered the same with regard to aggregation, however. The two are unique for comparisons but are the same as far as the GROUP BY clause is concerned. That is something to consider: each *unique* constraint should have at least one NOT NULL column to be truly unique.

The question that comes up with regard to indexes and null values is, "Why isn't my query using the index?" The query in question is something like the following:

```
select * from T where x is null;
```

This query cannot use the index we just created—the row (NULL, NULL) simply is not in the index, hence the use of the index would in fact return the wrong answer. Only if at least *one* of the columns is defined as NOT NULL can the query use an index. For example, the following shows Oracle will use an index for an X IS NULL predicate if there is an index with X on the leading edge and at least one other column in the index is NOT NULL:

```
ops$tkyte@ORA10GR1> create table t ( x int, y int NOT NULL );
Table created.

ops$tkyte@ORA10GR1> create unique index t_idx on t(x,y);
Index created.

ops$tkyte@ORA10GR1> insert into t values ( 1, 1 );
1 row created.

ops$tkyte@ORA10GR1> insert into t values ( NULL, 1 );
1 row created.

ops$tkyte@ORA10GR1> begin
  2     dbms_stats.gather_table_stats(user,'T');
  3  end;
  4  /
PL/SQL procedure successfully completed.
```

When we go to query that table this time, we'll discover this:

```
ops$tkyte@ORA10GR1> set autotrace on
ops$tkyte@ORA10GR1> select * from t where x is null;

         X          Y
---------- ----------
                    1

Execution Plan
----------------------------------------------------------
   0       SELECT STATEMENT Optimizer=ALL_ROWS (Cost=1 Card=1 Bytes=5)
   1    0    INDEX (RANGE SCAN) OF 'T_IDX' (INDEX (UNIQUE)) (Cost=1 Card=1 Bytes=5)
```

Previously, I said that you can use to your advantage the fact that totally null entries are not stored in a B*Tree index—here is how. Say you have a table with a column that takes exactly two values. The values are very skewed; say, 90 percent or more of the rows take on one value and 10 percent or less take on the other value. You can index this column efficiently to gain quick access to the minority rows. This comes in handy when you would like to use an index to get to the minority rows, but you want to full scan to get to the majority rows, and you want to conserve space. The solution is to use a null for majority rows and whatever value you want for minority rows or, as demonstrated earlier, use a function-based index to index only the non-null return values from a function.

Now that you know how a B*Tree will treat null values, you can use that to your advantage and take precautions with unique constraints on sets of columns that all allow nulls (be prepared to have more than one row that is all null as a possibility in this case).

Should Foreign Keys Be Indexed?

The question of whether or not foreign keys should be indexed comes up frequently. We touched on this subject in Chapter 6 when discussing deadlocks. There, I pointed out that unindexed foreign keys are the biggest single cause of deadlocks that I encounter, due to the fact that an update to a parent table's primary key or the removal of a parent record will place a table lock on the child table (no modifications to the child table will be allowed until the statement completes). This locks many more rows than it should and decreases concurrency. I see it frequently when people are using a tool that generates the SQL to modify a table. The tool generates an updates that updates every column in the table, regardless of whether or not the value was UPDATE statement modified. This in effect updates the primary key (even though they never changed the value). For example, Oracle Forms will do this by default, unless you tell it to just send modified columns over to the database. In addition to the table lock issue that might hit you, an unindexed foreign key is bad in the following cases as well:

- When you have an ON DELETE CASCADE and have not indexed the child table. For example, EMP is child of DEPT. DELETE FROM DEPT WHERE DEPTNO = 10 should cascade to EMP. If DEPTNO in EMP is not indexed, you will get a full table scan of EMP. This full scan is probably undesirable, and if you delete many rows from the parent table, the child table will be scanned once for each parent row deleted.

- When you query from the parent to the child. Consider the EMP/DEPT example again. It is very common to query the EMP table in the context of a DEPTNO. If you frequently query

```
select *
  from dept, emp
 where emp.deptno = dept.deptno
   and dept.dname = :X;
```

to generate a report or something, you'll find not having the index in place will slow down the queries. This is the same argument I gave for indexing the NESTED_COLUMN_ID of a nested table in Chapter 10. The hidden NESTED_COLUMN_ID of a nested table is nothing more than a foreign key.

So, when do you *not* need to index a foreign key? In general, when the following conditions are met:

- You do *not* delete from the parent table.

- You do *not* update the parent table's unique/primary key value, either purposely or by accident (via a tool).

- You do *not* join from the parent table to the child table, or more generally the foreign key columns do not support an important access path to the child table and you do not use them in predicates to select data from this table (such as DEPT to EMP).

If you satisfy all three criteria, feel free to skip the index—it is not needed and will slow down DML on the child table. If you do any of the three, be aware of the consequences.

As a side note, if you believe that a child table is getting locked via an unindexed foreign key and you would like to prove it (or just prevent it in general), you can issue the following:

```
ALTER TABLE <child table name> DISABLE TABLE LOCK;
```

Now, any UPDATE or DELETE to the parent table that would cause the table lock will receive

```
ERROR at line 1:
ORA-00069: cannot acquire lock -- table locks disabled for <child table name>
```

This is useful in tracking down the piece of code that is doing what you believe should not be done (no UPDATEs or DELETEs of the parent primary key), as the end users will immediately report this error back to you.

Why Isn't My Index Getting Used?

There are many possible causes of this. In this section, we'll take a look at some of the most common.

Case 1

We're using a B*Tree index, and our predicate does not use the leading edge of an index. In this case, we might have a table T with an index on T(x,y). We query SELECT * FROM T WHERE Y = 5. The optimizer will tend not to use the index since our predicate did not involve the column X—it might have to inspect each and every index entry in this case (we'll discuss an index skip scan shortly where this is not true). It will typically opt for a full table scan of T instead. That does not preclude the index from being used. If the query was SELECT X,Y FROM T WHERE Y = 5, the optimizer would notice that it did not have to go to the table to get either X or Y (they are in the index) and may very well opt for a fast full scan of the index itself, as the index is typically much smaller than the underlying table. Note also that this access path is only available with the CBO.

There is another case whereby the index on T(x,y) could be used with the CBO is during an index skip scan. The skip scan works well if and only if the leading edge of the index (X in the previous example) has very few distinct values and the optimizer understands that. For example, consider an index on (GENDER, EMPNO) where GENDER has the values M and F, and EMPNO is unique. A query such as

```
select * from t where empno = 5;
```

might consider using that index on T to satisfy the query in a *skip scan* method, meaning the query will be processed conceptually like this:

```
select * from t where GENDER='M' and empno = 5
UNION ALL
select * from t where GENDER='F' and empno = 5;
```

It will skip throughout the index, pretending it is two indexes: one for Ms and one for Fs. We can see this in a query plan easily. We'll set up a table with a bivalued column and index it:

```
ops$tkyte@ORA10GR1> create table t
  2  as
  3  select decode(mod(rownum,2), 0, 'M', 'F' ) gender, all_objects.*
  4    from all_objects
  5  /
Table created.

ops$tkyte@ORA10GR1> create index t_idx on t(gender,object_id)
  2  /
Index created.

ops$tkyte@ORA10GR1> begin
  2          dbms_stats.gather_table_stats
  3          ( user, 'T', cascade=>true );
  4  end;
  5  /
PL/SQL procedure successfully completed.
```

Now, when we query this, we should see the following:

```
ops$tkyte@ORA10GR1> set autotrace traceonly explain
ops$tkyte@ORA10GR1> select * from t t1 where object_id = 42;

Execution Plan
----------------------------------------------------------------
   0      SELECT STATEMENT Optimizer=ALL_ROWS (Cost=4 Card=1 Bytes=95)
   1    0   TABLE ACCESS (BY INDEX ROWID) OF 'T' (TABLE) (Cost=4 Card=1 Bytes=95)
   2    1     INDEX (SKIP SCAN) OF 'T_IDX' (INDEX) (Cost=3 Card=1)
```

The INDEX SKIP SCAN step tells us that Oracle is going to skip throughout the index, looking for points where GENDER changes values and read down the tree from there, looking for OBJECT_ID=42 in each virtual index being considered. If we increase the number of distinct values for GENDER measurably, as follows:

```
ops$tkyte@ORA10GR1> update t
  2      set gender = chr(mod(rownum,256));
48215 rows updated.

ops$tkyte@ORA10GR1> begin
  2          dbms_stats.gather_table_stats
  3          ( user, 'T', cascade=>true );
  4  end;
  5  /
PL/SQL procedure successfully completed.
```

we'll see that Oracle stops seeing the skip scan as being a sensible plan. It would have 256 mini indexes to inspect, and it opts for a full table scan to find our row:

```
ops$tkyte@ORA10GR1> set autotrace traceonly explain
ops$tkyte@ORA10GR1> select * from t t1 where object_id = 42;

Execution Plan
------------------------------------------------------------
   0      SELECT STATEMENT Optimizer=ALL_ROWS (Cost=158 Card=1 Bytes=95)
   1    0   TABLE ACCESS (FULL) OF 'T' (TABLE) (Cost=158 Card=1 Bytes=95)
```

Case 2

We're using a SELECT COUNT(*) FROM T query (or something similar) and we have a B*Tree index on table T. However, the optimizer is full scanning the table, rather than counting the (much smaller) index entries. In this case, the index is probably on a set of columns that can contain nulls. Since a totally null index entry would never be made, the count of rows in the index will not be the count of rows in the table. Here the optimizer is doing the right thing—it would get the wrong answer if it used the index to count rows.

Case 3

For an indexed column, we query using the following:

```
select * from t where f(indexed_column) = value
```

and find that the index on INDEX_COLUMN is not used. This is due to the use of the function on the column. We indexed the values of INDEX_COLUMN, not the value of F(INDEXED_COLUMN). The ability to use the index is curtailed here. We can index the function if we choose to do it.

Case 4

We have indexed a character column. This column contains only numeric data. We query using the following syntax:

```
select * from t where indexed_column = 5
```

Note that the number 5 in the query is the constant *number* 5 (not a character string). The index on INDEXED_COLUMN is not used. This is because the preceding query is the same as the following:

```
select * from t where to_number(indexed_column) = 5
```

We have implicitly applied a function to the column and, as noted in case 3, this will preclude the use of the index. This is very easy to see with a small example. In this example, we're going to use the built-in package DBMS_XPLAN. This package is available only with Oracle9*i* Release 2 and above (in Oracle9*i* Release 1, we will use AUTOTRACE instead to see the plan easily, but we will not see the predicate information—that is only available in Oracle9*i* Release 2 and above):

```
ops$tkyte@ORA10GR1> create table t ( x char(1) constraint t_pk primary key,
  2  y date );
Table created.

ops$tkyte@ORA10GR1> insert into t values ( '5', sysdate );
1 row created.

ops$tkyte@ORA10GR1> delete from plan_table;
3 rows deleted.

ops$tkyte@ORA10GR1> explain plan for select * from t where x = 5;
Explained.

ops$tkyte@ORA10GR1> select * from table(dbms_xplan.display);

PLAN_TABLE_OUTPUT
-----------------------------------------------
Plan hash value: 749696591

-------------------------------------------------------------------------------
| Id  | Operation          | Name  | Rows  | Bytes | Cost (%CPU)| Time     |
-------------------------------------------------------------------------------
|   0 | SELECT STATEMENT   |       |     1 |    12 |     2   (0)| 00:00:01 |
|*  1 |   TABLE ACCESS FULL| T     |     1 |    12 |     2   (0)| 00:00:01 |
-------------------------------------------------------------------------------

Predicate Information (identified by operation id):
-----------------------------------------------------

   1 - filter(TO_NUMBER("X")=5)
```

As you can see, it full scanned the table, and even if we were to hint the query

```
ops$tkyte@ORA10GR1> explain plan for select /*+ INDEX(t t_pk) */ * from t
  2  where x = 5;
Explained.

ops$tkyte@ORA10GR1> select * from table(dbms_xplan.display);

PLAN_TABLE_OUTPUT
-----------------------------------------
Plan hash value: 3473040572

-------------------------------------------------------------------------------------
| Id  | Operation                    | Name  | Rows  | Bytes | Cost (%CPU)| Time     |
-------------------------------------------------------------------------------------
|   0 | SELECT STATEMENT             |       |     1 |    12 |    34   (0)| 00:00:01 |
|   1 |  TABLE ACCESS BY INDEX ROWID | T     |     1 |    12 |    34   (0)| 00:00:01 |
|*  2 |   INDEX FULL SCAN            | T_PK  |     1 |       |    26   (0)| 00:00:01 |
-------------------------------------------------------------------------------------
```

```
Predicate Information (identified by operation id):
---------------------------------------------------

  2 - filter(TO_NUMBER("X")=5)
```

it uses the index, but not for a UNIQUE SCAN as we might expect—it is FULL SCANNING this index. The reason lies in the last line of output there: filter(TO_NUMBER("X")=5). There is an implicit function being applied to the database column. The character string stored in X must be converted to a number prior to comparing to the value 5. We cannot convert 5 to a string, since our NLS settings control what 5 might look like in a string (it is not deterministic), so we convert the string into a number, and that precludes the use of the index to rapidly find this row. If we simply compare strings to strings

```
ops$tkyte@ORA10GR1> delete from plan_table;
2 rows deleted.

ops$tkyte@ORA10GR1> explain plan for select * from t where x = '5';
Explained.

ops$tkyte@ORA10GR1> select * from table(dbms_xplan.display);

PLAN_TABLE_OUTPUT
-----------------------------------------------------------------
Plan hash value: 1301177541

-----------------------------------------------------------------------------------
| Id  | Operation                    | Name | Rows | Bytes | Cost (%CPU)| Time     |
-----------------------------------------------------------------------------------
|   0 | SELECT STATEMENT             |      |    1 |   12  |    1   (0)| 00:00:01 |
|   1 |  TABLE ACCESS BY INDEX ROWID | T    |    1 |   12  |    1   (0)| 00:00:01 |
|*  2 |   INDEX UNIQUE SCAN          | T_PK |    1 |       |    1   (0)| 00:00:01 |
-----------------------------------------------------------------------------------

Predicate Information (identified by operation id):
---------------------------------------------------

  2 - access("X"='5')
```

we get the expected INDEX UNIQUE SCAN, and we can see the function is not being applied. You should *always* avoid implicit conversions anyway. Always compare apples to apples and oranges to oranges. Another case where this comes up frequently is with dates. We try to query:

```
-- find all records for today
select * from t where trunc(date_col) = trunc(sysdate);
```

and discover that the index on DATE_COL will not be used. We can either index the TRUNC(DATE_COL) or, perhaps more easily, query using range comparison operators. The following demonstrates the use of greater than and less than on a date. Once we realize that the condition

```
TRUNC(DATE_COL) = TRUNC(SYSDATE)
```

is the same as the condition

```
select *
  from t
 where date_col >= trunc(sysdate)
   and date_col < trunc(sysdate+1)
```

this moves all of the functions to the right-hand side of the equation, allowing us to use the index on DATE_COL (and it has the same exact effect as WHERE TRUNC(DATE_COL) = ➡ TRUNC(SYSDATE)).

　　If possible, you should always remove the functions from database columns when they are in the predicate. Not only will doing so allow for more indexes to be considered for use, but also it will reduce the amount of processing the database needs to do. In the preceding case, when we used

```
where date_col >= trunc(sysdate)
   and date_col < trunc(sysdate+1)
```

the TRUNC values are computed once for the query, and then an index could be used to find just the qualifying values. When we used TRUNC(DATE_COL) = TRUNC(SYSDATE), the TRUNC(DATE_COL) had to be evaluated once *per row* for every row in the entire table (no indexes).

Case 5

The index, if used, would actually be slower. I see this a lot—people assume that, of course, an index will always make a query go faster. So, they set up a small table, analyze it, and find that the optimizer doesn't use the index. The optimizer is doing exactly the right thing in this case. Oracle (under the CBO) will use an index only when it makes sense to do so. Consider this example:

```
ops$tkyte@ORA10GR1> create table t
  2  ( x, y , primary key (x) )
  3  as
  4  select rownum x, object_name
  5    from all_objects
  6  /
Table created.

ops$tkyte@ORA10GR1> begin
  2      dbms_stats.gather_table_stats
  3      ( user, 'T', cascade=>true );
  4  end;
  5  /
PL/SQL procedure successfully completed.
```

If we run a query that needs a relatively small percentage of the table, as follows:

```
ops$tkyte@ORA10GR1> set autotrace on explain
ops$tkyte@ORA10GR1> select count(y) from t where x < 50;

  COUNT(Y)
----------
        49

Execution Plan
----------------------------------------------------------
0    SELECT STATEMENT Optimizer=ALL_ROWS (Cost=3 Card=1 Bytes=28)
1  0   SORT (AGGREGATE)
2  1    TABLE ACCESS (BY INDEX ROWID) OF 'T' (TABLE) (Cost=3 Card=41 Bytes=1148)
3  2     INDEX (RANGE SCAN) OF 'SYS_C009167' (INDEX (UNIQUE)) (Cost=2 Card=41)
```

it will happily use the index; however, we'll find that when the estimated number of rows to be retrieved via the index crosses a threshold (which varies depending on various optimizer settings, physical statistics, and so on), we'll start to observe a full table scan:

```
ops$tkyte@ORA10GR1> select count(y) from t where x < 15000;

  COUNT(Y)
----------
     14999

Execution Plan
----------------------------------------------------------
  0      SELECT STATEMENT Optimizer=ALL_ROWS (Cost=57 Card=1 Bytes=28)
  1  0    SORT (AGGREGATE)
  2  1     TABLE ACCESS (FULL) OF 'T' (TABLE) (Cost=57 Card=14994 Bytes=419832)
```

This example shows the optimizer won't *always* use an index and, in fact, it makes the right choice in skipping indexes. While tuning your queries, if you discover that an index isn't used when you think it "ought to be," don't just force it to be used—test and prove first that the index is indeed faster (via elapsed and I/O counts) before overruling the CBO. Reason it out.

Case 6

We haven't analyzed our tables in a while. They used to be small, but now when we look at them, they have grown quite large. An index will now make sense, whereas it didn't originally. If we analyze the table, it will use the index.

Without correct statistics, the CBO *cannot* make the correct decisions.

Index Case Summary

In my experience, these six cases are the *main* reasons I find that indexes are not being used. It usually boils down to a case of "They cannot be used—using them would return incorrect results" or "They should not be used—if they were used, performance would be terrible."

Myth: Space Is Never Reused in an Index

This is a myth that I would like to dispel once and for all: space *is* reused in an index. The myth goes like this: you have a table, T, in which there is a column, X. At some point, you put the value X = 5 in the table. Later you delete it. The myth is that the space used by X = 5 will not be reused unless you put X = 5 back into the index later. The myth states that once an index slot is used, it will be there forever and can be reused only by the same value. A corollary to this is the myth that free space is never returned to the index structure, and a block will never be reused. Again, this is simply not true.

The first part of the myth is trivial to disprove. All we need to do is to create a table like this:

```
ops$tkyte@ORA10GR1> create table t ( x int, constraint t_pk primary key(x) );
Table created.

ops$tkyte@ORA10GR1> insert into t values (1);
1 row created.

ops$tkyte@ORA10GR1> insert into t values (2);
1 row created.

ops$tkyte@ORA10GR1> insert into t values (9999999999);
1 row created.

ops$tkyte@ORA10GR1> analyze index t_pk validate structure;
Index analyzed.

ops$tkyte@ORA10GR1> select lf_blks, br_blks, btree_space
  2    from index_stats;

  LF_BLKS    BR_BLKS BTREE_SPACE
---------- ---------- -----------
        1          0        7996
```

So, according to the myth, if I delete from T where X = 2, that space will never be reused unless I reinsert the number 2. Currently, this index is using one leaf block of space. If the index key entries are never reused upon deletion, and I keep inserting and deleting and never reuse a value, this index should grow like crazy. Let's see:

```
ops$tkyte@ORA10GR1> begin
  2          for i in 2 .. 999999
  3          loop
  4                  delete from t where x = i;
  5                  commit;
  6                  insert into t values (i+1);
  7                  commit;
  8          end loop;
  9  end;
 10  /
PL/SQL procedure successfully completed.
```

```
ops$tkyte@ORA10GR1> analyze index t_pk validate structure;
Index analyzed.

ops$tkyte@ORA10GR1> select lf_blks, br_blks, btree_space
  2    from index_stats;

  LF_BLKS    BR_BLKS BTREE_SPACE
---------- ---------- -----------
        1          0        7996
```

This shows the space in the index was reused. As with most myths, however, there is a nugget of truth in there. The truth is that the space used by that initial number 2 (in between 1 and 9,999,999,999) would remain on that index block forever. The index will not "coalesce" itself. This means if I load a table with values 1 to 500,000 and then delete every other row (all of the even numbers), there will be 250,000 "holes" in the index on that column. Only if I reinsert data that will fit onto a block where there is a hole will the space be reused. Oracle will make no attempt to "shrink" or compact the index. This can be done via an ALTER INDEX REBUILD or COALESCE command. On the other hand, if I load a table with values 1 to 500,000 and then delete from the table every row where the value was 250,000 or less, I would find the blocks that were cleaned out of the index were put back onto the freelist for the index. This space can be totally reused.

If you recall, this was the second myth: index space is never "reclaimed." It states that once an index block is used, it will be stuck in that place in the index structure forever and will only be reused if you insert data that would go into that place in the index anyway. We can show that this is false as well. First, we need to build a table with about 500,000 rows in it. For that, we'll use the big_table script. After we have that table with its corresponding primary key index, we'll measure how many leaf blocks are in the index and how many blocks are on the freelist for the index. Remember, with an index, a block will only be on the freelist if the block is entirely empty, unlike a table. So any blocks we see on the freelist are completely empty and available for reuse:

```
ops$tkyte@ORA10GR1> select count(*) from big_table;

  COUNT(*)
----------
    500000

ops$tkyte@ORA10GR1> declare
  2      l_freelist_blocks number;
  3  begin
  4      dbms_space.free_blocks
  5      ( segment_owner => user,
  6        segment_name => 'BIG_TABLE_PK',
  7        segment_type => 'INDEX',
  8        freelist_group_id => 0,
  9        free_blks => l_freelist_blocks );
 10      dbms_output.put_line( 'blocks on freelist = ' || l_freelist_blocks );
 11  end;
```

```
 12  /
blocks on freelist = 0
PL/SQL procedure successfully completed.

ops$tkyte@ORA10GR1> select leaf_blocks from user_indexes
  2  where index_name = 'BIG_TABLE_PK';

LEAF_BLOCKS
-----------
       1043
```

Before we perform this mass deletion, we have no blocks on the freelist and there are 1,043 blocks in the "leafs" of the index, holding data. Now, we'll perform the delete and measure the space utilization again:

```
ops$tkyte@ORA10GR1> delete from big_table where id <= 250000;
250000 rows deleted.

ops$tkyte@ORA10GR1> commit;
Commit complete.

ops$tkyte@ORA10GR1> declare
  2      l_freelist_blocks number;
  3  begin
  4      dbms_space.free_blocks
  5      ( segment_owner => user,
  6        segment_name => 'BIG_TABLE_PK',
  7        segment_type => 'INDEX',
  8        freelist_group_id => 0,
  9        free_blks => l_freelist_blocks );
 10      dbms_output.put_line( 'blocks on freelist = ' || l_freelist_blocks );
 11          dbms_stats.gather_index_stats
 12          ( user, 'BIG_TABLE_PK' );
 13  end;
 14  /
blocks on freelist = 520
PL/SQL procedure successfully completed.

ops$tkyte@ORA10GR1> select leaf_blocks from user_indexes
  2  where index_name = 'BIG_TABLE_PK';

LEAF_BLOCKS
-----------
        523
```

As we can see, over half of the index is on the freelist now (520 blocks) and there are only 523 leaf blocks. If we add 523 and 520, we get the original 1043. This means the blocks are totally empty and ready to be reused (blocks on the freelist for an index must be empty, unlike blocks on the freelist for a heap organized table).

This demonstration highlights two points:

- Space is reused on index blocks as soon as a row comes along that can reuse it.

- When an index block is emptied, it can be taken out of the index structure and may be reused later. This is probably the genesis of this myth in the first place: blocks are not visible as having "free space" on them in an index structure as they are in a table. In a table, you can see blocks on the freelists, even if they have data on them. In an index, you will only see completely empty blocks on the freelists; blocks that have at least one index entry (and remaining free space) will not be as clearly visible.

Myth: Most Discriminating Elements Should Be First

This seems like common sense. If you are going to create an index on the columns C1 and C2 in a table with 100,000 rows, and you find C1 has 100,000 distinct values and C2 has 25,000 distinct values, you would want to create the index on T(C1,C2). This means that C1 should be first, which is the "commonsense" approach. The fact is, when comparing vectors of data (consider C1, C2 to be a vector), it doesn't matter which you put first. Consider the following example. We will create a table based on ALL_OBJECTS and an index on the OWNER, OBJECT_TYPE, and OBJECT_NAME columns (least discriminating to most discriminating) and also on OBJECT_NAME, OBJECT_TYPE, and OWNER:

```
ops$tkyte@ORA10GR1> create table t
  2  as
  3  select * from all_objects;
Table created.

ops$tkyte@ORA10GR1> create index t_idx_1 on t(owner,object_type,object_name);
Index created.

ops$tkyte@ORA10GR1> create index t_idx_2 on t(object_name,object_type,owner);
Index created.

ops$tkyte@ORA10GR1> select count(distinct owner), count(distinct object_type),
  2     count(distinct object_name ), count(*)
  3  from t;

DISTINCTOWNER DISTINCTOBJECT_TYPE DISTINCTOBJECT_NAME  COUNT(*)
------------- ------------------- ------------------- --------
           28                  36               28537    48243
```

Now, to show that neither is more efficient space-wise, we'll measure their space utilization:

```
ops$tkyte@ORA10GR1> analyze index t_idx_1 validate structure;
Index analyzed.

ops$tkyte@ORA10GR1> select btree_space, pct_used, opt_cmpr_count, opt_cmpr_pctsave
  2  from index_stats;
```

```
BTREE_SPACE    PCT  OPT_CMPR_COUNT OPT_CMPR_PCTSAVE
-----------  ------ -------------- ----------------
    2702744   89.0               2               28

ops$tkyte@ORA10GR1> analyze index t_idx_2 validate structure;
Index analyzed.

ops$tkyte@ORA10GR1> select btree_space, pct_used, opt_cmpr_count, opt_cmpr_pctsave
  2 from index_stats;

BTREE_SPACE    PCT  OPT_CMPR_COUNT OPT_CMPR_PCTSAVE
-----------  ------ -------------- ----------------
    2702744   89.0               1               13
```

They use exactly the same amount of space, down to the byte—there are no differences there. However, the first index is a lot more *compressible* if we use index key compression, as evidenced by the OPT_CMP_PCTSAVE value. There is an argument for arranging the columns in the index in order from the least discriminating to the most discriminating. Now let's see how they perform, to determine if either index is generally more efficient than the other. To test this, we'll use a PL/SQL block with hinted queries (so as to use one index or the other):

```
ops$tkyte@ORA10GR1> alter session set sql_trace=true;
Session altered.

ops$tkyte@ORA10GR1> declare
  2        cnt int;
  3  begin
  4    for x in ( select /*+FULL(t)*/ owner, object_type, object_name from t )
  5    loop
  6        select /*+ INDEX( t t_idx_1 ) */ count(*) into cnt
  7          from t
  8        where object_name = x.object_name
  9          and object_type = x.object_type
 10          and owner = x.owner;
 11
 12        select /*+ INDEX( t t_idx_2 ) */ count(*) into cnt
 13          from t
 14        where object_name = x.object_name
 15          and object_type = x.object_type
 16          and owner = x.owner;
 17    end loop;
 18  end;
 19  /
PL/SQL procedure successfully completed.
```

These queries read every single row in the table by means of the index. The TKPROF report shows us the following:

```
SELECT /*+ INDEX( t t_idx_1 ) */ COUNT(*) FROM T
WHERE OBJECT_NAME = :B3 AND OBJECT_TYPE = :B2 AND OWNER = :B1
```

call	count	cpu	elapsed	disk	query	current	rows
Parse	1	0.00	0.00	0	0	0	0
Execute	48243	10.63	10.78	0	0	0	0
Fetch	48243	1.90	1.77	0	145133	0	48243
total	96487	12.53	12.55	0	145133	0	48243

```
Rows     Row Source Operation
-------  ---------------------------------------------------
 48243   SORT AGGREGATE (cr=145133 pr=0 pw=0 time=2334197 us)
 57879    INDEX RANGE SCAN T_IDX_1 (cr=145133 pr=0 pw=0 time=1440672 us)(object...
```

```
*******************************************************************************
```

```
SELECT /*+ INDEX( t t_idx_2 ) */ COUNT(*) FROM T
WHERE OBJECT_NAME = :B3 AND OBJECT_TYPE = :B2 AND OWNER = :B1
```

call	count	cpu	elapsed	disk	query	current	rows
Parse	1	0.00	0.00	0	0	0	0
Execute	48243	11.00	10.78	0	0	0	0
Fetch	48243	1.87	2.10	0	145168	0	48243
total	96487	12.87	12.88	0	145168	0	48243

```
Rows     Row Source Operation
-------  ---------------------------------------------------
 48243   SORT AGGREGATE (cr=145168 pr=0 pw=0 time=2251857 us)
 57879    INDEX RANGE SCAN T_IDX_2 (cr=145168 pr=0 pw=0 time=1382547 us)(object...
```

They processed the same exact number of rows and very similar numbers of blocks (minor variations coming from accidental ordering of rows in the table and consequential optimizations made by Oracle), used equivalent amounts of CPU time, and ran in about the same elapsed time (run this same test again and the CPU and ELAPSED numbers will be a little different, but on average they will be the same). There are no inherent efficiencies to be gained by placing the columns in order of how discriminating they are, and as stated previously, with index key compression there is an argument for putting the least selective first. If you run the preceding example with COMPRESS 2 on the indexes, you'll find that the first index will perform about two-thirds the I/O of the second, given the nature of the query in this case.

However, the fact is that the decision to put column C1 before C2 *must* be driven by how the index is used. If you have lots of queries like the following:

```
select * from t where c1 = :x and c2 = :y;
select * from t where c2 = :y;
```

it makes more sense to place the index on T(C2,C1). This single index could be used by either of the queries. Additionally, using index key compression (which we looked at with regard to IOTs and will examine further later), we can build a smaller index if C2 is first. This is because each value of C2 repeats itself on average four times in the index. If C1 and C2 are both, on average, 10 bytes in length, the index entries for this index would nominally be 2,000,000 bytes (100,000 × 20). Using index key compression on (C2, C1), we could shrink this index to 1,250,000 (100,000 × 12.5), since three out of four repetitions of C2 could be suppressed.

In Oracle 5 (yes, version 5!), there was an argument for placing the most selective columns first in an index. It had to do with the way version 5 implemented index compression (not the same as index key compression). This feature was removed in version 6 with the addition of row-level locking. Since then, it is not true that putting the most discriminating entries first in the index will make the index smaller or more efficient. It seems like it will, but it will not. With index key compression, there is a compelling argument to go the other way since it can make the index smaller. However, it should be driven by *how* you use the index, as previously stated.

Summary

In this chapter, we covered the different types of indexes Oracle has to offer. We started with the basic B*Tree index and looked at various subtypes of this index, such as the reverse key index (designed for Oracle RAC) and descending indexes for retrieving data sorted in a mix of descending and ascending order. We spent some time looking at when you should use an index and why an index may not be useful in various circumstances.

We then looked at bitmap indexes, an excellent method for indexing low to medium cardinality data in a data warehouse (read-intensive, non-OLTP) environment. We covered the times it would be appropriate to use a bitmapped index and why you would never consider one for use in an OLTP environment—or any environment where multiple users must concurrently update the same column.

We moved on to cover function-based indexes, which are actually special cases of B*Tree and bitmapped indexes. A function-based index allows us to create an index on a function of a column (or columns), which means that we can precompute and store the results of complex calculations and user-written functions for blazing-fast index retrieval later. We looked at some important implementation details surrounding function-based indexes, such as the necessary system- and session-level settings that must be in place for them to be used. We followed that with examples of function-based indexes both on built-in Oracle functions and user-written ones. Lastly, we looked at a few caveats with regard to function-based indexes.

We then examined a very specialized index type called the application domain index. Rather than go into how to build one of those from scratch (which involves a long, complex sequence of events), we looked at an example that had already been implemented: the text index.

We closed with some of the most frequently asked questions on indexes that I receive as well as some myths about indexes. This section covered topics ranging from the simple question "Do indexes work with views?" to the more complex and sublime myth "Space is never reused in an index." We answered these questions and debunked the myths mostly through example, demonstrating the concepts as we went along.

CHAPTER 12

Datatypes

Choosing the right datatype seems so easy and straightforward, but many times I see it done incorrectly. The most basic decision—what type you use to store your data in—will have repercussions on your applications and data for years to come. Choosing the appropriate datatype is paramount and hard to change after the fact—that is, once you implement it you might be stuck with it for quite a while.

In this chapter, we'll take a look at all of the Oracle basic datatypes available and discuss how they are implemented and when each might be appropriate to use. We won't examine user-defined datatypes, as they're simply compound objects derived from the built-in Oracle datatypes. We'll investigate what happens when you use the wrong datatype for the job, or even just the wrong parameters to the datatype (length, precision, scale, and so on). By the end of this chapter, you'll have an understanding of the types available to you, how they're implemented, when to use each type and, as important, why using the right type for the job is key.

An Overview of Oracle Datatypes

Oracle provides 22 different SQL data types for us to use. Briefly, they are as follows:

- CHAR: A fixed-length character string that will be blank padded with spaces to its maximum length. A non-null CHAR(10) will always contain 10 *bytes* of information using the default National Language Support (NLS) settings. We will cover NLS implications in more detail shortly. A CHAR field may store up to 2,000 *bytes* of information.

- NCHAR: A fixed-length character string that contains UNICODE formatted data. Unicode is a character-encoding standard developed by the Unicode Consortium with the aim of providing a universal way of encoding characters of any language, regardless of the computer system or platform being used. The NCHAR type allows a database to contain data in two different character sets: the CHAR type and NCHAR type use the database's character set and the national character set, respectively. A non-null NCHAR(10) will always contain 10 *characters* of information (note that it differs from the CHAR type in this respect). An NCHAR field may store up to 2,000 *bytes* of information.

- VARCHAR2: Also currently synonymous with VARCHAR. This is a variable-length character string that differs from the CHAR type in that it is not blank padded to its maximum length. A VARCHAR2(10) may contain between 0 and 10 *bytes* of information using the default NLS settings. A VARCHAR2 may store up to 4,000 *bytes* of information.

- NVARCHAR2: A variable-length character string that contains UNICODE formatted data. An NVARCHAR2(10) may contain between 0 and 10 *characters* of information. An NVARCHAR2 may store up to 4,000 *bytes* of information.

- RAW: A variable-length binary datatype, meaning that no character set conversion will take place on data stored in this datatype. It is considered a string of binary bytes of information that will simply be stored by the database. It may store up to 2,000 bytes of information.

- NUMBER: This datatype is capable of storing numbers with up to 38 digits of precision. These numbers may vary between $1.0 \times 10(-130)$ and up to but not including $1.0 \times 10(126)$. Each number is stored in a *variable-length* field that varies between 0 bytes (for NULL) and 22 bytes. Oracle NUMBER types are very precise—much more so than normal FLOAT and DOUBLE types found in many programming languages.

- BINARY_FLOAT: This is a new type available only in Oracle 10*g* Release 1 and later. This is a 32-bit single-precision floating-point number. It can support at least 6 digits of precision and will consume 5 bytes of storage on disk.

- BINARY_DOUBLE: This is a new type available only in Oracle 10*g* Release 1 and later. This is a 64-bit double-precision floating-point number. It can support at least 15 digits of precision and will consume 9 bytes of storage on disk.

- LONG: This type is capable of storing up to 2GB of character data (2 *gigabytes*, not characters, as each character may take multiple bytes in a multibyte character set). As LONG types have many restrictions that we'll discuss later and are provided for backward compatibility, it is strongly recommended you do not use them in new applications and, when possible, convert them from LONG to CLOB types in existing applications.

- LONG RAW: The LONG RAW type is capable of storing up to 2GB of binary information. For the same reasons as noted for LONGs, it is recommended you use the BLOB type in all future development and, when possible, in existing applications as well.

- DATE: This is a fixed-width 7-byte date/time datatype. It will always contain the seven attributes of the century, the year within the century, the month, the day of the month, the hour, the minute, and the second.

- TIMESTAMP: This is a fixed-width 7- or 11-byte date/time datatype. It differs from the DATE datatype in that it may contain fractional seconds; up to 9 digits to the right of the decimal point may be preserved for TIMESTAMPs with fractional seconds.

- TIMESTAMP WITH TIME ZONE: This is a fixed-width 13-byte TIMESTAMP as the preceding entry, but it also provides for TIME ZONE support. Additional information regarding the time zone is stored with the TIMESTAMP in the data, so the TIME ZONE originally inserted is preserved with the data.

- TIMESTAMP WITH LOCAL TIME ZONE: This is a fixed-width 7- or 11-byte date/time datatype just as the TIMESTAMP is; however, it is time zone sensitive. Upon modification in the database, the TIME ZONE supplied with the data is consulted, and the date/time component is normalized to the database time zone. So, if you were to insert a date/time using the time zone U.S./Pacific and the database time zone was U.S./Eastern, the final date/time information would be converted to the Eastern time zone and stored as a TIMESTAMP would be. Upon retrieval, the TIMESTAMP stored in the database would be converted to the time in the session's time zone.

- INTERVAL YEAR TO MONTH: This is a fixed-width 5-byte datatype that stores a duration of time, in this case as a number of years and months. You may use intervals in date arithmetic to add or subtract a period of time from a DATE or the TIMESTAMP types.

- INTERVAL DAY TO SECOND: This is a fixed-width 11-byte datatype that stores a duration of time, in this case as a number of days and hours, minutes, and seconds, optionally with up to 9 digits of fractional seconds.

- BFILE: This datatype permits you to store an Oracle directory object (a pointer to an operating system directory) and a file name in a database column and to read this file. This effectively allows you to access operating system files available on the database server in a read-only fashion, as if they were stored in the database table itself.

- BLOB: This datatype permits for the storage of up to 4GB of data in Oracle9*i* and earlier or (4GB)×(database blocksize) bytes of data in Oracle 10*g* and later. BLOBs contain "binary" information that is not subject to character set conversion. This would be an appropriate type to store a spreadsheet, a word processing document, image files, and the like.

- CLOB: This datatype permits for the storage of up to 4GB of data in Oracle9*i* and earlier or (4GB)×(database blocksize) bytes of data in Oracle 10*g* and later. CLOBs contain information that is subject to character set conversion. This would be an appropriate type to store plain-text information in.

- NCLOB: This datatype permits for the storage of up to 4GB of data in Oracle9*i* and earlier or (4GB)×(database blocksize) bytes of data in Oracle 10*g* and later. NCLOBs store information encoded in the national character set of the database and are subject to character set conversions just as CLOBs are.

- ROWID: A ROWID is effectively a 10-byte address of a row in a database. Sufficient information is encoded in the ROWID to locate the row on disk, as well as identify the object the ROWID points to (the table and so on).

- UROWID: A UROWID is a universal ROWID and is used for tables, such as IOTs and tables accessed via gateways to heterogeneous databases, that do not have fixed ROWIDs. The UROWID is a representation of the primary key value of the row and, hence, will vary in size depending on the object it points to.

Many types are apparently missing from the preceding list, such as INT, INTEGER, SMALLINT, FLOAT, REAL, and others. These types are actually implemented on top of one of the base types in the preceding list—that is, they are synonyms for the native Oracle type. Additionally, datatypes such as XMLType, SYS.ANYTYPE, and SDO_GEOMETRY are not listed either, as we will not cover them in this book. They are complex object types comprising a collection of attributes along with the methods (functions) that operate on those attributes. They are made up of the basic datatypes listed previously and are not truly datatypes in the conventional sense, but rather an implementation, a set of functionality, that you may make use of in your applications.

Now, let's take a closer look at these basic datatypes.

Character and Binary String Types

Character datatypes in Oracle, namely CHAR, VARCHAR2, and their "N" variants, NCHAR and NVARCHAR2, are capable of storing either 2,000 bytes or 4,000 bytes of text. This text is converted between various character sets as needed by the database. A *character set* is a binary representation of individual characters in bits and bytes. Many different character sets are available, and each is capable of representing different characters, for example:

- The US7ASCII character set is the ASCII standard representation of 128 characters. It uses the low 7 bits of a byte to represent these 128 characters.

- The WE8ISO8859P1 character set is a Western European character set capable of representing the 128 ASCII characters as well as 128 extended characters, using all 8 bits of a byte.

Before we get into the details of CHAR, VARCHAR2, and their "N" variants, it would benefit us to get a cursory understanding of what these different character sets mean to us.

NLS Overview

As stated earlier, *NLS* stands for *National Language Support*. NLS is a very powerful feature of the database, but one that is often not as well understood as it should be. NLS controls many aspects of our data. For example, it controls how data is sorted, and whether we see commas and a single period in a number (e.g., 1,000,000.01) or many periods and a single comma (e.g., 1.000.000,01). But most important, it controls the following:

- Encoding of the textual data as stored persistently on disk

- Transparent conversion of data from character set to character set

It is this transparent part that confuses people the most—it is so transparent, you cannot even really see it happening. Let's look at a small example.

Suppose you are storing 8-bit data in a WE8ISO8859P1 character set in your database, but you have some clients that connect using a 7-bit character set such as US7ASCII. These clients are not expecting 8-bit data and need to have the data from the database converted into something they can use. While this sounds wonderful, if you are not aware of it taking place, then you might well find that your data "loses" characters over time as the characters that are not available in US7ASCII are translated into some character that is. This is due to the character set translation taking place. In short, if you retrieve data from the database in character set 1, convert it to character set 2, and then insert it back (reversing the process), there is a very good chance that you have materially modified the data. Character set conversion is typically a process that will change the data, and you are usually mapping a large set of characters (in this example, the set of 8-bit characters) into a smaller set (that of the 7-bit characters). This is a *lossy conversion*—the characters get modified because it is quite simply not possible to represent every character. But this conversion must take place. If the database is storing data in a single-byte character set but the client (say, a Java application, since the Java language uses Unicode) expects it in a multibyte representation, then it must be converted simply so the client application can work with it.

You can see character set conversion very easily. For example, I have a database whose character set is set to WE8ISO8859P1, a typical Western European character set:

```
ops$tkyte@ORA10G> select *
  2  from nls_database_parameters
  3  where parameter = 'NLS_CHARACTERSET';

PARAMETER                      VALUE
------------------------------ --------------------------------------------
NLS_CHARACTERSET               WE8ISO8859P1
```

Now, if I ensure my NLS_LANG is set the same as my database character set (Windows users would change/verify this setting in their registry) as follows:

```
ops$tkyte@ORA10G> host echo $NLS_LANG
AMERICAN_AMERICA.WE8ISO8859P1
```

then I can create a table and put in some "8-bit" data. This data that will not be usable by a 7-bit client that is expecting only 7-bit ASCII data:

```
ops$tkyte@ORA10G> create table t ( data varchar2(1) );
Table created.
ops$tkyte@ORA10G> insert into t values ( chr(224) );
1 row created.

ops$tkyte@ORA10G> insert into t values ( chr(225) );
1 row created.

ops$tkyte@ORA10G> insert into t values ( chr(226) );
1 row created.

ops$tkyte@ORA10G> select data, dump(data) dump
  2     from t;
D DUMP
- --------------------
à Typ=1 Len=1: 224
á Typ=1 Len=1: 225
â Typ=1 Len=1: 226
ops$tkyte@ORA10G> commit;
```

Now, if I go to another window and specify "a 7-bit ASCII" client, I'll see quite different results:

```
[tkyte@desktop tkyte]$ export NLS_LANG=AMERICAN_AMERICA.US7ASCII
[tkyte@desktop tkyte]$ sqlplus /
SQL*Plus: Release 10.1.0.4.0 - Production on Mon May 30 15:58:46 2005
Copyright © 1982, 2005, Oracle.  All rights reserved.
Connected to:
Oracle Database 10g Enterprise Edition Release 10.1.0.4.0 - Production
With the Partitioning, OLAP and Data Mining options
ops$tkyte@ORA10G> select data, dump(data) dump
  2   from t;
D DUMP
- --------------------
a Typ=1 Len=1: 224
a Typ=1 Len=1: 225
a Typ=1 Len=1: 226
```

Notice how in the 7-bit session I received the letter "a" three times, with no diacritical marks. However, the DUMP function is showing me that in the database there are in fact three separate distinct characters, not just the letter "a." The data in the database hasn't changed—just the values this client received. And in fact, if this client were to retrieve that data into host variables as follows:

```
ops$tkyte@ORA10G> variable d varchar2(1)
ops$tkyte@ORA10G> variable r varchar2(20)
ops$tkyte@ORA10G> begin
  2   select data, rowid into :d, :r from t where rownum = 1;
  3   end;
  4   /
PL/SQL procedure successfully completed.
```

and do nothing whatsoever with it, just send it back to the database:

```
ops$tkyte@ORA10G> update t set data = :d where rowid = chartorowid(:r);
1 row updated.
ops$tkyte@ORA10G> commit;
Commit complete.
```

then I would observe in the original 8-bit session that I have lost one of the original characters. It has been replaced with the lowly 7-bit a, not the fancy à I had previously:

```
ops$tkyte@ORA10G> select data, dump(data) dump
  2   from t;

D DUMP
- --------------------
a Typ=1 Len=1: 97
á Typ=1 Len=1: 225
â Typ=1 Len=1: 226
```

That demonstrates the immediate impact of an environment with a heterogeneous character set, whereby the clients and database use different NLS settings. It is something to be aware of because it comes into play in many circumstances. For example, if the DBA uses the EXP tool to extract information, he may observe the following warning:

```
[tkyte@desktop tkyte]$ exp userid=/ tables=t
Export: Release 10.1.0.4.0 - Production on Mon May 30 16:19:09 2005
Copyright © 1982, 2004, Oracle.  All rights reserved.

Connected to: Oracle Database 10g Enterprise Edition Release 10.1.0.4.0 - Production
With the Partitioning, OLAP and Data Mining options
Export done in US7ASCII character set and AL16UTF16 NCHAR character set
server uses WE8ISO8859P1 character set (possible charset conversion)
...
```

Such warnings should be treated very seriously. If you were exporting this table with the goal of dropping the table and then using IMP to re-create it, you would find that *all* of your data in that table was now lowly 7-bit data! Beware the unintentional character set conversion.

But also be aware that, in general, character set conversions are necessary. If clients are expecting data in a specific character set, then it would be disastrous to send them the information in a different character set.

■**Note** I highly encourage everyone to read through the *Oracle Globalization Support Guide* document. It covers NLS-related issues to a depth we will not cover here. Anyone creating applications that will be used around the globe (or even across international boundaries), and who isn't today, needs to master the information contained in that document.

Now that we have a cursory understanding of character sets and the impact they will have on us, let's take a look at the character string types provided by Oracle.

Character Strings

There are four basic character string types in Oracle, namely CHAR, VARCHAR2, NCHAR, and NVARCHAR2. All of the strings are stored in the same format in Oracle. On the database block, they will have a leading length field of 1 to 3 bytes followed by the data, or when they are NULL they will be represented as a single byte value of 0xFF.

■**Note** Trailing NULL columns consume 0 bytes of storage in Oracle. This means that if the "last column" in a table is NULL, Oracle stores nothing for it. If the last two columns are both NULL, there will be nothing stored for either of them. But if any column after a NULL column in position is *not null*, then Oracle will use the null flag described in this section to indicate the missing value.

If the length of the string is less than or equal to 250 (0x01 to 0xFA), Oracle will use 1 byte for the length. All strings exceeding 250 bytes in length will have a flag byte of 0xFE followed by 2 bytes that represent the length. So, a VARCHAR2(80) holding the words Hello World might look like Figure 12-1 on a block.

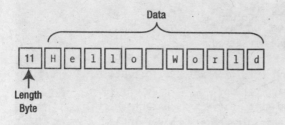

Figure 12-1. Hello World *stored in a* VARCHAR2(80)

A CHAR(80) holding the same data, on the other hand, would look like Figure 12-2.

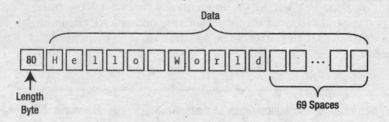

Figure 12-2. Hello World *stored in a* CHAR(80)

The fact that a CHAR/NCHAR is really nothing more than a VARCHAR2/NVARCHAR2 in disguise makes me of the opinion that there are really only two character string types to ever consider, namely VARCHAR2 and NVARCHAR2. I have never found a use for the CHAR type in any application. Since a CHAR type *always* blank pads the resulting string out to a fixed width, we discover rapidly that it consumes maximum storage both in the table segment and any index segments. That would be bad enough, but there is another important reason to avoid CHAR/NCHAR types: they create confusion in applications that need to retrieve this information (many cannot "find" their data after storing it). The reason for this relates to the rules of character string comparison and the strictness with which they are performed. Let's use the 'Hello World' string in a simple table to demonstrate:

```
ops$tkyte@ORA10G> create table t
  2  ( char_column      char(20),
  3    varchar2_column  varchar2(20)
  4  )
  5  /
Table created.

ops$tkyte@ORA10G> insert into t values ( 'Hello World', 'Hello World' );
1 row created.
```

```
ops$tkyte@ORA10G> select * from t;
CHAR_COLUMN          VARCHAR2_COLUMN
-------------------- --------------------
Hello World          Hello World
ops$tkyte@ORA10G> select * from t where char_column = 'Hello World';
CHAR_COLUMN          VARCHAR2_COLUMN
-------------------- --------------------
Hello World          Hello World

ops$tkyte@ORA10G> select * from t where varchar2_column = 'Hello World';
CHAR_COLUMN          VARCHAR2_COLUMN
-------------------- --------------------
Hello World          Hello World
```

So far, the columns look identical but, in fact, some implicit conversion has taken place and the CHAR(11) literal has been promoted to a CHAR(20) and blank padded when compared to the CHAR column. This must have happened since Hello World......... is *not the same* as Hello World without the trailing spaces. We can confirm that these two strings are materially different:

```
ops$tkyte@ORA10G> select * from t where char_column = varchar2_column;
no rows selected
```

They are not equal to each other. We would have to either blank pad out the VARCHAR2_COLUMN to be 20 bytes in length or trim the trailing blanks from the CHAR_COLUMN, as follows:

```
ops$tkyte@ORA10G> select * from t where trim(char_column) = varchar2_column;
CHAR_COLUMN          VARCHAR2_COLUMN
-------------------- --------------------
Hello World          Hello World
ops$tkyte@ORA10G> select * from t where char_column = rpad( varchar2_column, 20 );
CHAR_COLUMN          VARCHAR2_COLUMN
-------------------- --------------------
Hello World          Hello World
```

■**Note** There are many ways to blank pad the VARCHAR2_COLUMN, such as using the CAST() function.

The problem arises with applications that use variable-length strings when they bind inputs, with the resulting "no data found" that is sure to follow:

```
ops$tkyte@ORA10G> variable varchar2_bv varchar2(20)
ops$tkyte@ORA10G> exec :varchar2_bv := 'Hello World';
PL/SQL procedure successfully completed.

ops$tkyte@ORA10G> select * from t where char_column = :varchar2_bv;
no rows selected
```

```
ops$tkyte@ORA10G> select * from t where varchar2_column = :varchar2_bv;
CHAR_COLUMN          VARCHAR2_COLUMN
-------------------- --------------------
Hello World          Hello World
```

Here, the search for the VARCHAR2 string worked, but the CHAR column did not. The VARCHAR2 bind variable will not be promoted to a CHAR(20) in the same way as a character string literal. At this point, many programmers form the opinion that "bind variables don't work; we have to use literals." That would be a very bad decision indeed. The solution is to bind using a CHAR type:

```
ops$tkyte@ORA10G> variable char_bv char(20)
ops$tkyte@ORA10G> exec :char_bv := 'Hello World';

PL/SQL procedure successfully completed.
ops$tkyte@ORA10G>
ops$tkyte@ORA10G> select * from t where char_column = :char_bv;
CHAR_COLUMN          VARCHAR2_COLUMN
-------------------- --------------------
Hello World          Hello World
ops$tkyte@ORA10G> select * from t where varchar2_column = :char_bv;
no rows selected
```

However, if you mix and match VARCHAR2 and CHAR, you'll be running into this issue constantly. Not only that, but the developer is now having to consider the field width in her applications. If the developer opts for the RPAD() trick to convert the bind variable into something that will be comparable to the CHAR field (it is preferable, of course, to pad out the bind variable, rather than TRIM the database column, as applying the function TRIM to the column could easily make it impossible to use existing indexes on that column), she would have to be concerned with column length changes over time. If the size of the field changes, then the application is impacted, as it must change its field width.

It is for these reasons—the fixed-width storage, which tends to make the tables and related indexes much larger than normal, coupled with the bind variable issue—that I avoid the CHAR type in all circumstances. I cannot even make an argument for it in the case of the one-character field, because in that case it is really of no material difference. The VARCHAR2(1) and CHAR(1) are identical in all aspects. There is no compelling reason to use the CHAR type in that case, and to avoid any confusion, I "just say no," even for the CHAR(1) field.

Character String Syntax

The syntax for the four basic string types is straightforward, as described in Table 12-1.

Table 12-1. *Four Basic String Types*

String Type	Description
VARCHAR2(<SIZE> <BYTE|CHAR>)	<SIZE> is a number between 1 and 4,000 for up to 4,000 bytes of storage. In the following section, we'll examine in detail the differences and nuances of the BYTE versus CHAR modifier in that clause.
CHAR(<SIZE> <BYTE|CHAR>)	<SIZE> is a number between 1 and 2,000 for up to 2,000 bytes of storage.
NVARCHAR2(<SIZE>)	<SIZE> is a number greater than 0 whose upper bound is dictated by your national character set.
NCHAR(<SIZE>)	<SIZE> is a number greater than 0 whose upper bound is dictated by your national character set.

Bytes or Characters

The VARCHAR2 and CHAR types support two methods of specifying lengths:

- *In bytes*: VARCHAR2(10 byte). This will support up to 10 bytes of data, which could be as few as two characters in a multibyte character set.

- *In characters*: VARCHAR2(10 char). This will support to up 10 *characters* of data, which could be as much as 40 bytes of information.

When using a multibyte character set such as UTF8, you would be well advised to use the CHAR modifier in the VARCHAR2/CHAR definition—that is, use VARCHAR2(80 CHAR), not VARCHAR2(80), since your intention is likely to define a column that can in fact store 80 characters of data. You may also use the session or system parameter NLS_LENGTH_SEMANTICS to change the default behavior from BYTE to CHAR. I do not recommend changing this setting at the system level; rather, use it as part of an ALTER SESSION setting in your database schema installation scripts. Any application that requires a database to have a specific set of NLS settings makes for an "unfriendly" application. Such applications, generally, cannot be installed into a database with other applications that do not desire these settings, but rely on the defaults to be in place.

One other important thing to remember is that the upper bound of the number of bytes stored in a VARCHAR2 is 4,000. However, even if you specify VARCHAR2(4000 CHAR), you may not be able to fit 4,000 characters into that field. In fact, you may be able to fit as few as 1,000 characters in that field if all of the characters take 4 bytes to be represented in your chosen character set!

The following small example demonstrates the differences between BYTE and CHAR, and how the upper bounds come into play. We'll create a table with three columns, the first two of which will be 1 byte and 1 character, respectively, with the last column being 4,000 characters. Notice that we're performing this test on a multibyte character set database using the character set AL32UTF8, which supports the latest version of the Unicode standard and encodes characters in a variable-length fashion using from 1 to 4 bytes for each character:

```
ops$tkyte@010GUTF> select *
  2    from nls_database_parameters
  3    where parameter = 'NLS_CHARACTERSET';

PARAMETER                         VALUE
------------------------------    --------------------
NLS_CHARACTERSET                  AL32UTF8
ops$tkyte@010GUTF> create table t
  2  ( a varchar2(1),
  3    b varchar2(1 char),
  4    c varchar2(4000 char)
  5  )
  6  /
Table created.
```

Now, if we try to insert into our table a single character that is 2 bytes long in UTF, we observe the following:

```
ops$tkyte@010GUTF> insert into t (a) values (unistr('\00d6'));
insert into t (a) values (unistr('\00d6'))
                         *
ERROR at line 1:
ORA-12899: value too large for column "OPS$TKYTE"."T"."A"
(actual: 2, maximum: 1)
```

This example demonstrates two things:

- VARCHAR2(1) is in bytes, not characters. We have single Unicode character, but it won't fit into a single byte.

- As you migrate an application from a single-byte, fixed-width character set to a multi-byte character set, you might find that the text that used to fit into your fields no longer does.

The reason for the second point is that a 20-character string in a single-byte character set is 20 bytes long and will absolutely fit in a VARCHAR2(20). However a 20-character field could be as long as 80 bytes in a multibyte character set, and 20 Unicode characters may well not fit in 20 bytes. You might consider modifying your DDL to be VARCHAR2(20 CHAR) or using the NLS_LENGTH_SEMANTICS session parameter mentioned previously when running your DDL to create your tables.

If we insert that single character into a field set up to hold a single character, we will observe the following:

```
ops$tkyte@010GUTF> insert into t (b) values (unistr('\00d6'));
1 row created.
ops$tkyte@010GUTF> select length(b), lengthb(b), dump(b) dump from t;
LENGTH(B) LENGTHB(B) DUMP
---------- ---------- --------------------
         1          2 Typ=1 Len=2: 195,150
```

The INSERT succeeded, and we can see that the LENGTH of the inserted data is one character—all of the character string functions work "character-wise." So the length of the field is
one character, but the LENGTHB (length in bytes) function shows it takes 2 bytes of storage,
and the DUMP function shows us exactly what those bytes are. That example demonstrates one
very common issue people encounter when using multibyte character sets, namely that a
VARCHAR2(N) doesn't necessarily hold N *characters*, but rather N *bytes*.

The next issue people confront frequently is that the maximum length in bytes of a
VARCHAR2 is 4,000, and in a CHAR it is 2,000:

```
ops$tkyte@010GUTF> declare
  2           l_data varchar2(4000 char);
  3           l_ch   varchar2(1 char) := unistr( '\00d6' );
  4   begin
  5           l_data := rpad( l_ch, 4000, l_ch );
  6           insert into t ( c ) values ( l_data );
  7   end;
  8   /
declare
*
ERROR at line 1:
ORA-01461: can bind a LONG value only for insert into a LONG column
ORA-06512: at line 6
```

That shows that a 4,000-character string that is really 8,000 bytes long cannot be stored
permanently in a VARCHAR2(4000 CHAR) field. It fits in the PL/SQL variable because in PL/SQL
a VARCHAR2 is allowed to be up to 32KB in size. However, when it is stored in a table, the hard
limit is 4,000 bytes. We can store 2,000 of these characters successfully:

```
ops$tkyte@010GUTF> declare
  2           l_data varchar2(4000 char);
  3           l_ch   varchar2(1 char) := unistr( '\00d6' );
  4   begin
  5           l_data := rpad( l_ch, 2000, l_ch );
  6           insert into t ( c ) values ( l_data );
  7   end;
  8   /

PL/SQL procedure successfully completed.
ops$tkyte@010GUTF> select length( c ), lengthb( c )
  2     from t
  3   where c is not null;

LENGTH(C)  LENGTHB(C)
---------- ----------
     2000        4000
```

And as you can see, they consume 4,000 bytes of storage.

The "N" Variant

So, of what use are the NVARCHAR2 and NCHAR (for completeness)? They are used in systems where the need to manage and store multiple character sets arises. This typically happens in a database where the predominant character set is a single-byte, fixed-width one (such as WE8ISO8859P1), but the need arises to maintain and store some multibyte data. There are many systems that have legacy data but need to support multibyte data for some new applications, or systems that want the efficiency of a single-byte character set for most operations (string operations on a fixed-width string are more efficient than on a string where each character may store a different number of bytes) but need the flexibility of multibyte data at some points.

The NVARCHAR2 and NCHAR datatypes support this need. They are generally the same as their VARCHAR2 and CHAR counterparts, with the following exceptions:

- Their text is stored and managed in the database's national character set, not the default character set.

- Their lengths are always provided in characters, whereas a CHAR/VARCHAR2 may specify either bytes or characters.

In Oracle9*i* and later, the database's national character set may take one of two values: UTF8 or AL16UTF16 (UTF16 in 9*i*; AL16UTF16 in 10*g*). This makes the NCHAR and NVARCHAR types suitable for storing only multibyte data, which is a change from earlier releases of the database (Oracle8*i* and earlier allowed you to choose any character set for the national character set).

Binary Strings: RAW Types

Oracle supports the storage of binary data as well as text. Binary data is not subject to the character set conversions we discussed earlier with regard to the CHAR and VARCHAR2 types. Therefore, binary datatypes are not suitable for storing user-supplied text, but are suitable for storing encrypted information—encrypted data is not "text," but a binary representation of the original text, word processing documents containing binary markup information, and so on. Anything that should not be considered by the database to be "text" and that should not have character set conversion applied to it should be stored in a binary datatype.

Oracle supports three datatypes for storing binary data:

- The RAW type, which we focus on in this section and is suitable for storing RAW data up to 2,000 bytes in size.

- The BLOB type, which supports binary data of much larger sizes, coverage of which we'll defer to the "LOB Types" section later in the chapter.

- The LONG RAW type, which is supported for backward compatibility and should not be considered for new applications.

The syntax for the binary RAW type is straightforward:

```
RAW( <size> )
```

For example, the following code creates a table capable of storing 16 bytes of binary information per row:

```
ops$tkyte@ORA10GR1> create table t ( raw_data raw(16) );
Table created.
```

The RAW type is much like the VARCHAR2 type in terms of storage on disk. The RAW type is a variable-length binary string, meaning that the table T just created, for example, may store anywhere from 0 to 16 bytes of binary data. It is not padded out like the CHAR type.

When dealing with RAW data, you will likely find it being implicitly converted to a VARCHAR2 type—that is, many tools such as SQL*Plus will not display the RAW data directly, but will convert it to a hexadecimal format for display. In the following example, we create some binary data in our table using SYS_GUID(), a built-in function that returns a 16-byte RAW string that is globally unique (*GUID* stands for *globally unique identifier*):

```
ops$tkyte@ORA10GR1> insert into t values ( sys_guid() );
1 row created.
ops$tkyte@ORA10GR1> select * from t;

RAW_DATA
--------------------------------
FD1EB03D3718077BE030007F01002FF5
```

You can immediately note two things here. First, the RAW data looks like a character string. That is just how SQL*Plus retrieved and printed it, and that is not how it is stored on disk. SQL*Plus cannot print arbitrary binary data on your screen, as that could have serious side effects on the display. Remember that binary data may include control characters such as a carriage return or linefeed, or maybe a Ctrl+G character that would cause your terminal to "beep."

Second, the RAW data looks much larger than 16 bytes—in fact, in this example, you can see 32 characters. This is due to the fact that every binary byte takes two hexadecimal characters to display. The stored RAW data is really 16 bytes in length, and you can see this using the Oracle DUMP function. Here, I am "dumping" the value of the binary string and using the optional parameter to specify the base that should be used when displaying the value of each byte. I am using base 16, so we can compare the results of dump with the previous string:

```
ops$tkyte@ORA10GR1> select dump(raw_data,16) from t;

DUMP(RAW_DATA,16)
---------------------------------------------------------------------------
Typ=23 Len=16: fd,1e,b0,3d,37,18,7,7b,e0,30,0,7f,1,0,2f,f5
```

So, DUMP shows us this binary string is in fact 16 bytes long (LEN=16) and displays the binary data byte by byte. As we can see, this dump display matches up with the implicit conversion performed when SQL*Plus fetched the RAW data into a string. This implicit conversion goes the other direction as well:

```
ops$tkyte@ORA10GR1> insert into t values ( 'abcdef' );
1 row created.
```

That did not insert the string abcdef, but rather a 3-byte RAW with the bytes AB, CD, EF, or in decimal with the bytes 171, 205, 239. If you attempt to use a string that does not consist of valid hex characters, you will receive an error message:

```
ops$tkyte@ORA10GR1> insert into t values ( 'abcdefgh' );
insert into t values ( 'abcdefgh' )
                            *
ERROR at line 1:
ORA-01465: invalid hex number
```

The RAW type may be indexed and used in predicates—it is as functional as any other datatype. However, you must take care to avoid unwanted implicit conversions, and you must be aware that they will occur.

I prefer and recommend using *explicit* conversions in all cases, which can be performed using the following built-in functions:

- HEXTORAW: To convert strings of hexadecimal characters to the RAW type

- RAWTOHEX: To convert RAW strings to hexadecimal strings

The RAWTOHEX function is invoked implicitly by SQL*Plus when it fetches a RAW type into a string, and the HEXTORAW function is invoked implicitly when inserting the string. It is a good practice to avoid implicit conversions and to always be explicit when coding. So the previous examples could have been written as follows:

```
ops$tkyte@ORA10GR1> select rawtohex(raw_data) from t;

RAWTOHEX(RAW_DATA)
---------------------------------
FD1EB03D3718077BE030007F01002FF5

ops$tkyte@ORA10GR1> insert into t values ( hextoraw('abcdef') );
1 row created.
```

Number Types

Oracle 10*g* supports three native datatypes suitable for storing numbers. Oracle9*i* Release 2 and earlier support exactly one native datatype suitable for storing numeric data. In this list, the NUMBER type is supported by all releases, and the subsequent two types are new datatypes supported only in Oracle 10*g* and later:

- NUMBER: The Oracle NUMBER type is capable of storing numbers with an extremely large degree of precision—38 digits of precision, in fact. The underlying data format is similar to a "packed decimal" representation. The Oracle NUMBER type is a variable-length format from 0 to 22 bytes in length. It is appropriate for storing any number as small as $10e^{-130}$ and numbers up to but not including $10e^{126}$. This is by far the most common NUMBER type in use today.

- BINARY_FLOAT: This is an IEEE native single-precision floating-point number. On disk it will consume 5 bytes of storage: 4 fixed bytes for the floating-point number and 1 length byte. It is capable of storing numbers in the range of ~ $\pm 10^{38.53}$ with 6 digits of precision.

- BINARY_DOUBLE: This is an IEEE native double-precision floating-point number. On disk it will consume 9 bytes of storage: 8 fixed bytes for the floating-point number and 1 length byte. It is capable of storing numbers in the range of ~ ± $10^{308.25}$ with 13 digits of precision.

As you can see from this quick overview, the Oracle NUMBER type has significantly larger precision than the BINARY_FLOAT and the BINARY_DOUBLE types, but a much smaller range than the BINARY_DOUBLE. That is, you can store numbers very precisely with many significant digits in a NUMBER type, but you can store much smaller and larger numbers in the BINARY_FLOAT and BINARY_DOUBLE types. As a quick example, we can create a table with the various datatypes in them and see what is stored given the same inputs:

```
ops$tkyte@ORA10GR1> create table t
  2  ( num_col   number,
  3    float_col binary_float,
  4    dbl_col   binary_double
  5  )
  6  /
Table created.

ops$tkyte@ORA10GR1> insert into t ( num_col, float_col, dbl_col )
  2  values ( 1234567890.0987654321,
  3           1234567890.0987654321,
  4           1234567890.0987654321 );
1 row created.

ops$tkyte@ORA10GR1> set numformat 99999999999.99999999999
ops$tkyte@ORA10GR1> select * from t;

              NUM_COL                 FLOAT_COL                  DBL_COL
-------------------------- -------------------------- --------------------------
 1234567890.09876543210     1234567940.00000000000    1234567890.09876540000
```

Note that the NUM_COL returns the exact number we provided as input. There are fewer than 38 significant digits in the input number (I supplied a number with 20 significant digits), so the exact number is preserved. The FLOAT_COL, however, using the new BINARY_FLOAT type, was not able to accurately represent this number. In fact, it preserved only 7 digits accurately. The DBL_COL faired much better, accurately representing the number in this case out to 17 digits. Overall, though, this should be a good indication that the BINARY_FLOAT and BINARY_DOUBLE types will not be appropriate for financial applications! If you play around with different values, you'll see different results:

```
ops$tkyte@ORA10GR1> delete from t;
1 row deleted.

ops$tkyte@ORA10GR1> insert into t ( num_col, float_col, dbl_col )
  2  values ( 9999999999.9999999999,
  3           9999999999.9999999999,
```

```
   4              9999999999.9999999999 );
1 row created.

ops$tkyte@ORA10GR1> select * from t;
```

NUM_COL	FLOAT_COL	DBL_COL
9999999999.99999999990	10000000000.00000000000	10000000000.00000000000

Once again, the NUM_COL accurately represented the number, but the FLOAT_COL and DBL_COL cannot. This does not mean that the NUMBER type is able to store things with "infinite" accuracy/precision—just that it has a much larger precision associated with it. It is easy to observe similar results from the NUMBER type:

```
ops$tkyte@ORA10GR1> delete from t;
1 row deleted.

ops$tkyte@ORA10GR1> insert into t ( num_col )
  2  values ( 123 * 1e20 + 123*1e-20 ) ;
1 row created.

ops$tkyte@ORA10GR1> set numformat 99999999999999999999999.99999999999999999999999999
ops$tkyte@ORA10GR1> select num_col, 123*1e20, 123*1e-20 from t;
```

NUM_COL
123*1E20
123*1E-20
1230000000000000000000000.0000000000000000000000000
1230000000000000000000000.0000000000000000000000000
.00000000000000001230000

As you can see, when we put together a very large number (123*1e20) and a very small number (123*1e-20), we lost precision because this arithmetic requires more than 38 digits of precision. The large number by itself can be faithfully represented, as can the small number, but the result of the larger minus the smaller cannot. We can verify this is not just a display/formatting issue as follows:

```
ops$tkyte@ORA10GR1> select num_col from t where num_col = 123*1e20;
```

NUM_COL
1230000000000000000000000.0000000000000000000000000

The value in NUM_COL is equal to 123*1e20, and not the value we attempted to insert.

NUMBER Type Syntax and Usage

The syntax for the NUMBER type is straightforward:

```
NUMBER( p,s )
```

where P and S are optional and are used to specify the following:

- *Precision*, or the total number of digits. By default, the precision is 38 and has valid values in the range of 1 to 38. The character * may be used to represent 38 as well.

- *Scale*, or the number of digits to the right of the decimal point. Valid values for the scale are –84 to 127, and its default value depends on whether or not the precision is specified. If no precision is specified, then scale defaults to the maximum range. If a precision is specified, then scale defaults to 0 (no digits to the right of the decimal point). So, for example, a column defined as NUMBER stores floating-point numbers (with decimal places), whereas a NUMBER(38) stores only integer data (no decimals), since the scale defaults to 0 in the second case.

You should consider the precision and scale to be *edits* for your data—data integrity tools in a way. The precision and scale *do not affect* at all how the data is stored on disk, only what values are permitted and how numbers are to be rounded. For example, if a value exceeds the precision permitted, Oracle returns an error:

```
ops$tkyte@ORA10GR1> create table t ( num_col number(5,0) );
Table created.

ops$tkyte@ORA10GR1> insert into t (num_col) values ( 12345 );
1 row created.

ops$tkyte@ORA10GR1> insert into t (num_col) values ( 123456 );
insert into t (num_col) values ( 123456 )
                                 *
ERROR at line 1:
ORA-01438: value larger than specified precision allows for this column
```

So, you can use the precision to enforce some data integrity constraints. In this case, NUM_COL is a column that is not allowed to have more than five digits.

The scale, on the other hand, is used to control "rounding" of the number, for example:

```
ops$tkyte@ORA10GR1> create table t ( msg varchar2(10), num_col number(5,2) );
Table created.

ops$tkyte@ORA10GR1> insert into t (msg,num_col) values ( '123.45',  123.45 );
1 row created.

ops$tkyte@ORA10GR1> insert into t (msg,num_col) values ( '123.456', 123.456 );
1 row created.

ops$tkyte@ORA10GR1> select * from t;
```

```
MSG          NUM_COL
----------   ----------
123.45          123.45
123.456         123.46
```

Notice how the number 123.456, with more than five digits, succeeded this time. That is because the scale we used in this example was used to round 123.456 to two digits, resulting in 123.46, *and then* 123.46 was validated against the precision, found to fit, and inserted. However, if we attempt the following insert, it fails:

```
ops$tkyte@ORA10GR1> insert into t (msg,num_col) values ( '1234', 1234 );
insert into t (msg,num_col) values ( '1234', 1234 )
                                              *
ERROR at line 1:
ORA-01438: value larger than specified precision allows for this column
```

because the number 1234.00 has more than five digits in total. When you specify the scale of 2, at most three digits may be to the left of the decimal place and two to the right. Hence, that number does not fit. The NUMBER(5,2) column can hold all values between 999.99 and –999.99.

It may seem strange to allow the scale to vary from –84 to 127. What purpose could a negative scale fulfill? It allows you to round values to the left of the decimal place. Just as the NUMBER(5,2) rounded values to the nearest .01, so a NUMBER(5,-2) would round to the nearest 100, for example:

```
ops$tkyte@ORA10GR1> create table t ( msg varchar2(10), num_col number(5,-2) );
Table created.

ops$tkyte@ORA10GR1> insert into t (msg,num_col) values ( '123.45',  123.45 );
1 row created.

ops$tkyte@ORA10GR1> insert into t (msg,num_col) values ( '123.456', 123.456 );
1 row created.

ops$tkyte@ORA10GR1> select * from t;

MSG          NUM_COL
----------   ----------
123.45          100
123.456         100
```

The numbers were rounded up to the nearest 100. We still have five digits of precision, but there are now seven digits (including the trailing two 0s) permitted to the left of the decimal point:

```
ops$tkyte@ORA10GR1> insert into t (msg,num_col) values ( '1234567', 1234567 );
1 row created.

ops$tkyte@ORA10GR1> select * from t;
```

```
MSG            NUM_COL
----------     ----------
123.45                100
123.456               100
1234567           1234600

ops$tkyte@ORA10GR1> insert into t (msg,num_col) values ( '12345678', 12345678 );
insert into t (msg,num_col) values ( '12345678', 12345678 )
                                                  *

ERROR at line 1:
ORA-01438: value larger than specified precision allows for this column
```

So, the precision dictates how many digits are permitted in the number after rounding, using the scale to determine how to round. The precision is an integrity constraint, whereas the scale is an "edit."

It is interesting and useful to note that the NUMBER type is, in fact, a variable-length datatype on disk and will consume between 0 and 22 bytes of storage. Many times, programmers consider a numeric datatype to be a fixed-length type, as that is what they typically see when programming with 2- or 4-byte integers and 4- or 8-byte floats. The Oracle NUMBER type is similar to a variable-length character string. We can see what happens with numbers that contain differing amounts of significant digits. We'll create a table with two NUMBER columns and populate the first column with many numbers that have 2, 4, 6, . . . 28 significant digits. Then, we'll simply add 1 to each of them:

```
ops$tkyte@ORA10GR1> create table t ( x number, y number );
Table created.

ops$tkyte@ORA10GR1> insert into t ( x )
  2  select to_number(rpad('9',rownum*2,'9'))
  3    from all_objects
  4   where rownum <= 14;
14 rows created.

ops$tkyte@ORA10GR1> update t set y = x+1;
14 rows updated.
```

Now, if we use the built-in VSIZE function that shows how much storage the column takes, we can review the size differences between the two numbers in each row:

```
ops$tkyte@ORA10GR1> set numformat 9999999999999999999999999999
ops$tkyte@ORA10GR1> column v1 format 99
ops$tkyte@ORA10GR1> column v2 format 99
ops$tkyte@ORA10GR1> select x, y, vsize(x) v1, vsize(y) v2
  2    from t order by x;

                              X                                Y  V1  V2
------------------------------ ------------------------------ --- ---
                            99                              100   2   2
                          9999                            10000   3   2
```

999999	1000000	4	2
99999999	100000000	5	2
9999999999	10000000000	6	2
999999999999	1000000000000	7	2
99999999999999	100000000000000	8	2
9999999999999999	1000000000000000000	9	2
999999999999999999	100000000000000000000	10	2
99999999999999999999	1000000000000000000000	11	2
9999999999999999999999	10000000000000000000000	12	2
999999999999999999999999	1000000000000000000000000	13	2
99999999999999999999999999	100000000000000000000000000	14	2
9999999999999999999999999999	10000000000000000000000000000	15	2

14 rows selected.

We can see that as we added significant digits to X, the amount of storage required took increasingly more room. Every two significant digits added another byte of storage. But a number just one larger consistently took 2 bytes. When Oracle stores a number, it does so by storing as little as it can to represent that number. It does this by storing the significant digits, an exponent used to place the decimal place, and information regarding the sign of the number (positive or negative). So, the more *significant* digits a number contains, the more storage it consumes.

That last fact explains why it is useful to know that numbers are stored in varying width fields. When attempting to size a table (e.g., to figure out how much storage 1,000,000 rows would need in a table), you have to consider the NUMBER fields carefully. Will your numbers take 2 bytes or 20 bytes? What is the average size? This makes accurately sizing a table without representative test data very hard. You can get the worst-case size and the best-case size, but the real size will likely be some value in between.

BINARY_FLOAT/BINARY_DOUBLE Type Syntax and Usage

Oracle 10*g* introduced two new numeric types for storing data; they are not available in any release of Oracle prior to version 10g. These are the IEEE standard floating-points many programmers are used to working with. For a full description of what these number types look like and how they are implemented, I suggest reading http://en.wikipedia.org/wiki/ Floating-point. It is interesting to note the following in the basic definition of a floating-point number in that reference (emphasis mine):

> *A floating-point number is a digital representation for a number in a certain subset of the rational numbers, and is often used **to approximate an** arbitrary real number on a computer. In particular, it represents an integer or fixed-point number (the significand or, informally, the mantissa) multiplied by a base (usually 2 in computers) to some integer power (the exponent). When the base is 2, it is the binary analogue of scientific notation (in base 10).*

They are used to *approximate* numbers; they are not nearly as precise as the built-in Oracle NUMBER type described previously. Floating-point numbers are commonly used in scientific applications and are useful in many types of applications due to the fact that they allow arithmetic to be done in hardware (on the CPU, the chip) rather than in Oracle subroutines. Therefore, the arithmetic is much faster if you are doing real number-crunching in a scientific application, but you would not want to use floating-points to store financial information.

The syntax for declaring columns of this type in a table is very straightforward:

```
BINARY_FLOAT
BINARY_DOUBLE
```

That is it. There are no options to these types whatsoever.

Non-Native Number Types

In addition to the NUMBER, BINARY_FLOAT, and BINARY_DOUBLE types, Oracle syntactically supports the following numeric datatypes:

■**Note** When I say "syntactically supports," I mean that a CREATE statement may use these datatypes, but under the covers they are all really the NUMBER type. There are precisely three native numeric formats in Oracle 10*g* Release 1 and later and only one native numeric format in Oracle9*i* Release 2 and earlier. The use of any other numeric datatype was always mapped to the native Oracle NUMBER type.

- NUMERIC(p,s): Maps exactly to a NUMBER(p,s). If p is not specified, it defaults to 38.

- DECIMAL(p,s) *or* DEC(p,s): Maps exactly to a NUMBER(p,s). If p is not specified, it defaults to 38.

- INTEGER *or* INT: Maps exactly to the NUMBER(38) type.

- SMALLINT: Maps exactly to the NUMBER(38) type.

- FLOAT(b): Maps to the NUMBER type.

- DOUBLE PRECISION: Maps to the NUMBER type.

- REAL: Maps to the NUMBER type.

Performance Considerations

In general, the Oracle NUMBER type is the best overall choice for most applications. However, there are performance implications associated with that type. The Oracle NUMBER type is a *software datatype*—it is implemented in the Oracle software itself. We cannot use native hardware operations to add two NUMBER types together, as it is emulated in the software. The floating-point types, however, do not have this implementation. When we add two floating-point numbers together, Oracle will use the hardware to perform the operation.

This is fairly easy to see. If we create a table that contains about 50,000 rows and place the same data in there using the NUMBER and BINARY_FLOAT/BINARY_DOUBLE types as follows:

```
ops$tkyte@ORA10G> create table t
  2  ( num_type      number,
  3    float_type    binary_float,
  4    double_type   binary_double
  5  )
  6  /
Table created.

ops$tkyte@ORA10G> insert /*+ APPEND */  into t
  2  select rownum, rownum, rownum
  3    from all_objects
  4  /
48970 rows created.

ops$tkyte@ORA10G> commit;
Commit complete.
```

We then execute the same query against each type of column, using a complex mathematical function such as LN (natural log). We observe radically different CPU utilization:

```
select sum(ln(num_type)) from t

call      count       cpu    elapsed
-------  ------   --------  ----------
total         4      2.73        2.73

select sum(ln(float_type)) from t

call      count       cpu    elapsed
-------  ------   --------  ----------
total         4      0.06        0.12

select sum(ln(double_type)) from t

call      count       cpu    elapsed
-------  ------   --------  ----------
total         4      0.05        0.11
```

The Oracle NUMBER type used some 50 times the CPU of the floating-point types. But, you have to remember that we did not receive precisely the same answer from all three queries! The floating-point numbers were an approximation of the number, with between 6 and 13 digits of precision. The answer from the NUMBER type is much more "precise" than from the floats. But when you are performing data mining or complex numerical analysis of scientific data, this loss of precision is typically acceptable and the performance gain to be had can be dramatic.

■Note If you are interested in the gory details of floating-point arithmetic and the subsequent loss of precision, see http://docs.sun.com/source/806-3568/ncg_goldberg.html.

It should be noted that we can sort of have our cake and eat it too, here. Using the built-in CAST function, we can perform an on-the-fly conversion of the Oracle NUMBER type to a floating-point type, prior to performing the complex math on it. This results in a CPU usage that is much nearer to that of the native floating-point types:

```
select sum(ln(cast( num_type as binary_double ) )) from t

call     count       cpu    elapsed
-------  ------   --------  ----------
total        4      0.12       0.17
```

This implies that we may store our data very precisely, and when the need for raw speed arises, and the floating-point types significantly outperform the Oracle NUMBER type, we can use the CAST function to accomplish that goal.

LONG Types

LONG types come in two flavors in Oracle:

- A LONG text type capable of storing 2GB of text. The text stored in the LONG type is subject to character set conversion, much like a VARCHAR2 or CHAR type.

- A LONG RAW type capable of storing 2GB of raw binary data (data that is not subject to character set conversion).

The LONG types date back to version 6 of Oracle, when they were limited to 64KB of data. In version 7, they were enhanced to support up to 2GB of storage, but by the time version 8 was released, they were superseded by the LOB types, which we will discuss shortly.

Rather than explain how to use the LONG type, I will explain why you do not want to use the LONG (or LONG RAW) type in your applications. First and foremost, the Oracle documentation is very clear in its treatment of the LONG types. The *Oracle SQL Reference* manual states the following:

> *Do not create tables with* LONG *columns. Use LOB columns* (CLOB, NCLOB, BLOB) *instead.* LONG *columns are supported only for backward compatibility.*

Restrictions on LONG and LONG RAW Types

The LONG and LONG RAW types are subject to the restrictions outlined in Table 12-2. Even though it might be considered jumping ahead, I've added a column to say whether the corresponding LOB type, which is the replacement for the LONG/LONG RAW types, is subject to the same restriction.

Table 12-2. LONG *Types Compared to LOBs*

LONG/LONG RAW Type	CLOB/BLOB Type
You may have only one LONG or LONG RAW column per table.	You may have up to 1,000 columns of CLOB or BLOB type per table.
User-defined types may not be defined with attributes of type LONG/LONG RAW.	User-defined types may fully use CLOB and BLOB types.
LONG types may not be referenced in the WHERE clause.	LOBs may be referenced in the WHERE clause, and a host of functions is supplied in the DBMS_LOB package to manipulate them.
LONG types may not be referenced in integrity constraints, with the exception of NOT NULL.	LOB types may be referenced in integrity constraints.
LONG types do not support distributed transactions.	LOBs do support distributed transactions.
LONG types cannot be replicated using basic or advanced replication.	LOBs fully support replication.
LONG columns cannot be in a GROUP BY, ORDER BY, or CONNECT BY, or in a query that uses DISTINCT, UNIQUE, INTERSECT, MINUS, or UNION.	LOBs may appear in these clauses provided a function is applied to the LOB that converts it into a scalar SQL type such as a VARCHAR2, NUMBER, or DATE.
PL/SQL functions/procedures cannot accept an input of type LONG.	PL/SQL works fully with LOB types.
SQL built-in functions cannot be used against LONG columns (e.g., SUBSTR).	SQL functions may be used against LOB types.
You cannot use a LONG type in a CREATE TABLE AS SELECT statement.	LOBs support CREATE TABLE AS SELECT.
You cannot use ALTER TABLE MOVE on a table containing LONG types.	You may move tables containing LOBs.

As you can see, Table 12-2 presents quite a long list; there are many things you just cannot do when you have a LONG column in the table. For all new applications, do not even consider using the LONG type. Instead, use the appropriate LOB type. For existing applications, you should seriously consider converting the LONG type to the corresponding LOB type if you are hitting any of the restrictions in Table 12-2. Care has been taken to provide backward compatibility so that an application written for LONG types will work against the LOB type transparently.

■**Note** It almost goes without saying that you should perform a full functionality test against your application(s) before modifying your production system from LONG to LOB types.

Coping with Legacy LONG Types

A question that arises frequently is, "What about the data dictionary in Oracle?" It is littered with LONG columns, and this makes using the dictionary columns problematic. For example, it is not possible using SQL to search the ALL_VIEWS dictionary view to find all views that contain the text HELLO:

```
ops$tkyte@ORA10G> select *
  2  from all_views
  3  where text like '%HELLO%';
where text like '%HELLO%'
      *
ERROR at line 3:
ORA-00932: inconsistent datatypes: expected NUMBER got LONG
```

This issue is not limited to the ALL_VIEWS view—many views are affected:

```
ops$tkyte@ORA10G> select table_name, column_name
  2  from dba_tab_columns
  3  where data_type in ( 'LONG', 'LONG RAW' )
  4  and owner = 'SYS'
  5  and table_name like 'DBA%';
```

TABLE_NAME	COLUMN_NAME
DBA_VIEWS	TEXT
DBA_TRIGGERS	TRIGGER_BODY
DBA_TAB_SUBPARTITIONS	HIGH_VALUE
DBA_TAB_PARTITIONS	HIGH_VALUE
DBA_TAB_COLUMNS	DATA_DEFAULT
DBA_TAB_COLS	DATA_DEFAULT
DBA_SUMMARY_AGGREGATES	MEASURE
DBA_SUMMARIES	QUERY
DBA_SUBPARTITION_TEMPLATES	HIGH_BOUND
DBA_SQLTUNE_PLANS	OTHER
DBA_SNAPSHOTS	QUERY
DBA_REGISTERED_SNAPSHOTS	QUERY_TXT
DBA_REGISTERED_MVIEWS	QUERY_TXT
DBA_OUTLINES	SQL_TEXT
DBA_NESTED_TABLE_COLS	DATA_DEFAULT
DBA_MVIEW_ANALYSIS	QUERY
DBA_MVIEW_AGGREGATES	MEASURE
DBA_MVIEWS	QUERY
DBA_IND_SUBPARTITIONS	HIGH_VALUE
DBA_IND_PARTITIONS	HIGH_VALUE
DBA_IND_EXPRESSIONS	COLUMN_EXPRESSION
DBA_CONSTRAINTS	SEARCH_CONDITION
DBA_CLUSTER_HASH_EXPRESSIONS	HASH_EXPRESSION

```
23 rows selected.
```

So, what is the solution? If you want to make use of these columns in SQL, then you'll need to convert them to a SQL-friendly type. You can use a user-defined function for doing so. The following example demonstrates how to accomplish this using a LONG SUBSTR function that will allow you to effectively convert any 4,000 bytes of a LONG type into a VARCHAR2, for use with SQL. When you are done, you'll be able to query:

```
ops$tkyte@ORA10G> select *
  2    from (
  3  select owner, view_name,
  4         long_help.substr_of( 'select text
  5                                 from dba_views
  6                                where owner = :owner
  7                                  and view_name = :view_name',
  8                              1, 4000,
  9                              'owner', owner,
 10                              'view_name', view_name ) substr_of_view_text
 11    from dba_views
 12   where owner = user
 13         )
 14   where upper(substr_of_view_text) like '%INNER%'
 15  /
```

You've converted the first 4,000 bytes of the VIEW_TEXT column from LONG to VARCHAR2 and can now use a predicate on it. Using the same technique, you could implement your own INSTR, LIKE, and so forth for LONG types as well. In this book, I'll only demonstrate how to get the substring of a LONG type.

The package we will implement has the following specification:

```
ops$tkyte@ORA10G> create or replace package long_help
  2  authid current_user
  3  as
  4      function substr_of
  5  ( p_query in varchar2,
  6      p_from  in number,
  7      p_for   in number,
  8      p_name1 in varchar2 default NULL,
  9      p_bind1 in varchar2 default NULL,
 10      p_name2 in varchar2 default NULL,
 11      p_bind2 in varchar2 default NULL,
 12      p_name3 in varchar2 default NULL,
 13      p_bind3 in varchar2 default NULL,
 14      p_name4 in varchar2 default NULL,
 15      p_bind4 in varchar2 default NULL )
 16      return varchar2;
 17  end;
 18  /
Package created.
```

Note that on line 2, we specify AUTHID CURRENT_USER. This makes the package run as the invoker, with all roles and grants in place. This is important for two reasons. First, we'd like the database security to not be subverted—this package will only return substrings of columns we (the invoker) are allowed to see. Second, we'd like to install this package once in the database and have its functionality available for all to use; using invoker rights allows us to do that. If we used the default security model of PL/SQL—definer rights—the package would run with the privileges of the owner of the package, meaning it would only be able to see data the owner of the package could see, which may not include the set of data the invoker is allowed to see.

The concept behind the function SUBSTR_OF is to take a query that selects at most one row and one column: the LONG value we are interested in. SUBSTR_OF will parse that query if needed, bind any inputs to it, and fetch the results programmatically, returning the necessary piece of the LONG value.

The package body, the implementation, begins with two global variables. The G_CURSOR variable holds a persistent cursor open for the duration of our session. This is to avoid having to repeatedly open and close the cursor and to avoid parsing SQL more than we need to. The second global variable, G_QUERY, is used to remember the text of the last SQL query we've parsed in this package. As long as the query remains constant, we'll just parse it once. So, even if we query 5,000 rows in a query, as long as the SQL query we pass to this function doesn't change, we'll have only one parse call:

```
ops$tkyte@ORA10G> create or replace package body long_help
  2  as
  3
  4      g_cursor number := dbms_sql.open_cursor;
  5      g_query  varchar2(32765);
  6
```

Next in this package is a private procedure, BIND_VARIABLE, that we'll use to bind inputs passed to us by the caller. We implemented this as a separate private procedure only to make life easier; we want to bind only when the input name is NOT NULL. Rather than perform that check four times in the code for each input parameter, we do it once in this procedure:

```
  7  procedure bind_variable( p_name in varchar2, p_value in varchar2 )
  8  is
  9  begin
 10      if ( p_name is not null )
 11      then
 12          dbms_sql.bind_variable( g_cursor, p_name, p_value );
 13      end if;
 14  end;
 15
```

Next is the actual implementation of SUBSTR_OF in the package body. This routine begins with a function declaration from the package specification and the declaration for some local variables. L_BUFFER will be used to return the value, and L_BUFFER_LEN will be used to hold the length returned by an Oracle-supplied function:

```
16
17   function substr_of
18   ( p_query in varchar2,
19     p_from  in number,
20     p_for   in number,
21     p_name1 in varchar2 default NULL,
22     p_bind1 in varchar2 default NULL,
23     p_name2 in varchar2 default NULL,
24     p_bind2 in varchar2 default NULL,
25     p_name3 in varchar2 default NULL,
26     p_bind3 in varchar2 default NULL,
27     p_name4 in varchar2 default NULL,
28     p_bind4 in varchar2 default NULL )
29   return varchar2
30   as
31       l_buffer        varchar2(4000);
32       l_buffer_len    number;
33   begin
```

Now, the first thing our code does is a sanity check on the P_FROM and P_FOR inputs. P_FROM must be a number greater than or equal to 1, and P_FOR must be between 1 and 4,000—just like the built-in function SUBSTR:

```
34       if ( nvl(p_from,0) <= 0 )
35       then
36           raise_application_error
37           (-20002, 'From must be >= 1 (positive numbers)' );
38       end if;
39       if ( nvl(p_for,0) not between 1 and 4000 )
40       then
41           raise_application_error
42           (-20003, 'For must be between 1 and 4000' );
43       end if;
44
```

Next, we'll check to see if we are getting a new query that needs to be parsed. If the last query we parsed is the same as the current query, we can skip this step. It is very important to note that on line 47 we are verifying that the P_QUERY passed to us is just a SELECT—we will use this package *only* to execute SQL SELECT statements. This check validates that for us:

```
45       if ( p_query <> g_query or g_query is NULL )
46       then
47           if ( upper(trim(nvl(p_query,'x'))) not like 'SELECT%')
48           then
49               raise_application_error
50               (-20001, 'This must be a select only' );
51           end if;
52           dbms_sql.parse( g_cursor, p_query, dbms_sql.native );
53           g_query := p_query;
54       end if;
```

We are ready to bind the inputs to this query. Any non-NULL names that were passed to us will be "bound" to the query, so when we execute it, it finds the right row:

```
55        bind_variable( p_name1, p_bind1 );
56        bind_variable( p_name2, p_bind2 );
57        bind_variable( p_name3, p_bind3 );
58        bind_variable( p_name4, p_bind4 );
59
```

And now we can execute the query and fetch the row. Then using DBMS_SQL.COLUMN_VALUE_LONG, we extract the necessary substring of the LONG and return it:

```
60        dbms_sql.define_column_long(g_cursor, 1);
61        if (dbms_sql.execute_and_fetch(g_cursor)>0)
62        then
63            dbms_sql.column_value_long
64            (g_cursor, 1, p_for, p_from-1,
65             l_buffer, l_buffer_len );
66        end if;
67        return l_buffer;
68    end substr_of;
69
70    end;
71    /
Package body created.
```

That's it—you should be able to use that package against *any* legacy LONG column in your database, allowing you to perform many WHERE clause operations that were not possible before. For example, you can now find all partitions in your schema such that the HIGH_VALUE has the year 2003 in it:

```
ops$tkyte@ORA10G> select *
  2     from (
  3   select table_owner, table_name, partition_name,
  4          long_help.substr_of
  5          ( 'select high_value
  6              from all_tab_partitions
  7             where table_owner = :o
  8               and table_name = :n
  9               and partition_name = :p',
 10           1, 4000,
 11           'o', table_owner,
 12           'n', table_name,
 13           'p', partition_name ) high_value
 14     from all_tab_partitions
 15    where table_name = 'T'
 16      and table_owner = user
 17          )
 18    where high_value like '%2003%'
 19   /
```

```
TABLE_OWN TABLE PARTIT HIGH_VALUE
--------- ----- ------ -------------------------------
OPS$TKYTE T     PART1  TO_DATE(' 2003-03-13 00:00:00'
                       , 'SYYYY-MM-DD HH24:MI:SS', 'N
                       LS_CALENDAR=GREGORIAN')

OPS$TKYTE T     PART2  TO_DATE(' 2003-03-14 00:00:00'
                       , 'SYYYY-MM-DD HH24:MI:SS', 'N
                       LS_CALENDAR=GREGORIAN')
```

Using this same technique—that of processing the result of a query that returns a single row with a single LONG column in a function—you can implement your own INSTR, LIKE, and so on as needed.

This implementation works well on the LONG type, but it will not work on LONG RAW types. LONG RAWs are not piecewise accessible (there is no COLUMN_VALUE_LONG_RAW function in DBMS_SQL). Fortunately, this is not too serious of a restriction since LONG RAWs are not used in the dictionary and the need to "substring" so you can search on it is rare. If you do have a need to do so, however, you will not use PL/SQL unless the LONG RAW is 32KB or less, as there is simply no method for dealing with LONG RAWs over 32KB in PL/SQL itself. Java, C, C++, Visual Basic, or some other language would have to be used.

Another approach is to temporarily convert the LONG or LONG RAW into a CLOB or BLOB using the TO_LOB built-in function and a global temporary table. Your PL/SQL procedure could be as follows:

```
Insert into global_temp_table ( blob_column )
select to_lob(long_raw_column) from t where...
```

This would work well in an application that occasionally needs to work with a single LONG RAW value. You would not want to continuously do that, however, due to the amount of work involved. If you find yourself needing to resort to this technique frequently, you should definitely convert the LONG RAW to a BLOB once and be done with it.

DATE, TIMESTAMP, and INTERVAL Types

The native Oracle datatypes of DATE, TIMESTAMP, and INTERVAL are closely related. The DATE and TIMESTAMP types store fixed date/times with varying degrees of precision. The INTERVAL type is used to store an amount of time, such as "8 hours" or "30 days," easily. The result of subtracting two dates might be an interval; for example, the result of adding an interval of 8 hours to a TIMESTAMP results in a new TIMESTAMP that is 8 hours later.

The DATE datatype has been part of Oracle for many releases—as far back as my experience with Oracle goes, which means at least back to version 5 and probably before. The TIMESTAMP and INTERVAL types are relative newcomers to the scene by comparison, as they were introduced with Oracle9i Release 1. For this simple reason, you will find the DATE datatype to be the most prevalent type for storing date/time information. But many new applications are using the TIMESTAMP type for two reasons: it has support for fractions of seconds, while the DATE type does not; and it has support for time zones, something the DATE type also does not have.

We'll take a look at each type after discussing DATE/TIMESTAMP formats and their uses.

Formats

I am not going to attempt to cover all of the DATE, TIMESTAMP, and INTERVAL formats here. That is well covered in the *Oracle SQL Reference* manual, which is freely available to all. A wealth of formats is available to you, and a good understanding of what they are is vital. It is strongly recommended that you investigate them.

I'd like to discuss what the formats do here, as there are a great many misconceptions surrounding this topic. The formats are used for two things:

- To format the data on the way out of the database in a style that pleases you

- To tell the database how to convert an input string into a DATE, TIMESTAMP, or INTERVAL

And that is all. The common misconception I've observed over the years is that the format used somehow affects what is stored on disk and how the data is actually saved. *The format has no effect at all on how the data is stored. The format is only used to convert the single binary format used to store a* DATE *into a string or to convert a string into the single binary format that is used to store a* DATE. The same is true for TIMESTAMPs and INTERVALs.

My advice on formats is simply this: use them. Use them when you send a string to the database that represents a DATE, TIMESTAMP, or INTERVAL. Do *not* rely on default date formats—defaults can and probably will at some point in the future be changed by someone. If you rely on a default date format and it changes, your application may be negatively affected. It might raise an error back to the end user if the date cannot be converted or, worse still, it might silently insert *the wrong data*. Consider the follow INSERT statement, which relies on a default date mask:

```
Insert into t ( date_column ) values ( '01/02/03' );
```

Suppose the application was relying on a default date mask of DD/MM/YY to be in place. That would be February 1, 2003 (assuming that code was executed after the year 2000, but we'll visit the implications of that in a moment). Now, say someone decides the correct and proper date format is MM/DD/YY. All of a sudden, that previous date changes to January 2, 2003. Or someone decides YY/MM/DD is right, and now you have February 3, 2001. In short, without a date format to accompany that date string, there are many ways to interpret it. That INSERT statement should be

```
Insert into t ( date_column ) values ( to_date( '01/02/03', 'DD/MM/YY' ) );
```

And if you want my opinion, it has to be

```
Insert into t ( date_column ) values ( to_date( '01/02/2003', 'DD/MM/YYYY' ) );
```

That is, it must use a four-character year. Not too long ago, our industry learned the hard way how much time and effort was spent remedying software that attempted to "save" 2 bytes—we seem to have lost that lesson over time. There is no excuse in the year 2005 and beyond *not* to use a four-character year!

This same discussion applies to data leaving the database. If you execute SELECT DATE_COLUMN FROM T and fetch that column into a string in your application, then you should apply an explicit date format to it. Whatever format your application is expecting should be explicitly applied there. Otherwise, at some point in the future when someone changes the default date format, your application may break or behave incorrectly.

Next, let's look at the datatypes themselves in more detail.

DATE Type

The DATE type is a fixed-width 7-byte date/time datatype. It will always contain the seven attributes of the century, the year within the century, the month, the day of the month, the hour, the minute, and the second. Oracle uses an internal format to represent that information, so it is not really storing 20, 05, 06, 25, 12, 01, 00 for June 25, 2005, at 12:01:00. Using the built-in DUMP function, we can see what Oracle really stores:

```
ops$tkyte@ORA10G> create table t ( x date );
Table created.

ops$tkyte@ORA10G> insert into t (x) values
  2  ( to_date( '25-jun-2005 12:01:00',
  3            'dd-mon-yyyy hh24:mi:ss' ) );
1 row created.

ops$tkyte@ORA10G> select x, dump(x,10) d from t;

X         D
--------- ----------------------------------
25-JUN-05 Typ=12 Len=7: 120,105,6,25,13,2,1
```

The century and year bytes (the 120,105 in the DUMP output) are stored in an excess-100 notation. You would have to subtract 100 from them to determine the correct century and year. The reason for the excess-100 notation is support of BC and AD dates. If you subtract 100 from the century byte and get a negative number, it is a BC date, for example:

```
ops$tkyte@ORA10G> insert into t (x) values
  2  ( to_date( '01-jan-4712bc',
  3            'dd-mon-yyyybc hh24:mi:ss' ) );
1 row created.

ops$tkyte@ORA10G> select x, dump(x,10) d from t;

X         D
--------- ----------------------------------
25-JUN-05 Typ=12 Len=7: 120,105,6,25,13,2,1
01-JAN-12 Typ=12 Len=7: 53,88,1,1,1,1,1
```

So, when we insert 01-JAN-4712BC, the century byte is 53 and 53 − 100 = −47, the century we inserted. Because it is negative, we know that it is a BC date. This storage format also allows the dates to be naturally sortable in a binary sense. Since 4712 BC is "less than" 4710 BC, we'd like a binary representation that supports that. By dumping those two dates, we can see that 01-JAN-4710BC is "larger" than the same day in 4712 BC, so they will sort and compare nicely:

```
ops$tkyte@ORA10G> insert into t (x) values
  2  ( to_date( '01-jan-4710bc',
  3            'dd-mon-yyyybc hh24:mi:ss' ) );
1 row created.
```

```
ops$tkyte@ORA10G> select x, dump(x,10) d from t;

X         D
--------- -----------------------------------
25-JUN-05 Typ=12 Len=7: 120,105,6,25,13,2,1
01-JAN-12 Typ=12 Len=7: 53,88,1,1,1,1,1
01-JAN-10 Typ=12 Len=7: 53,90,1,1,1,1,1
```

The month and day bytes, the next two fields, are stored naturally, without any modification. So, June 25 used a month byte of 6 and a day byte of 25. The hour, minute, and second fields are stored in excess-1 notation, meaning we must subtract 1 from each component to see what time it really was. Hence midnight is represented as 1,1,1 in the date field.

This 7-byte format is naturally sortable, as you have seen—it is a 7-byte field that can be sorted in a binary fashion from small to larger (or vice versa) very efficiently. Additionally, its structure allows for easy truncation, without converting the date into some other format. For example, truncating the date we just stored, 25-JUN-2005 12:01:00, to the day (remove the hours, minutes, seconds) is very straightforward. Just set the trailing three bytes to 1,1,1 and the time component is as good as erased. Consider a fresh table, T, with the following inserts:

```
ops$tkyte@ORA10G> create table t ( what varchar2(10), x date );
Table created.

ops$tkyte@ORA10G> insert into t (what, x) values
  2  ( 'orig',
  3    to_date( '25-jun-2005 12:01:00',
  4             'dd-mon-yyyy hh24:mi:ss' ) );
1 row created.

ops$tkyte@ORA10G> insert into t (what, x)
  2  select 'minute', trunc(x,'mi') from t
  3  union all
  4  select 'day', trunc(x,'dd') from t
  5  union all
  6  select 'month', trunc(x,'mm') from t
  7  union all
  8  select 'year', trunc(x,'y') from t
  9  /
4 rows created.

ops$tkyte@ORA10G> select what, x, dump(x,10) d from t;

WHAT     X         D
-------- --------- -----------------------------------
orig     25-JUN-05 Typ=12 Len=7: 120,105,6,25,13,2,1
minute   25-JUN-05 Typ=12 Len=7: 120,105,6,25,13,2,1
day      25-JUN-05 Typ=12 Len=7: 120,105,6,25,1,1,1
month    01-JUN-05 Typ=12 Len=7: 120,105,6,1,1,1,1
year     01-JAN-05 Typ=12 Len=7: 120,105,1,1,1,1,1
```

To truncate that date down to the year, all the database had to do was put 1s in the last 5 bytes—a very fast operation. We now have a sortable, comparable DATE field that is truncated to the year level, and we got it as efficiently as possible. What many people do instead of using TRUNC, however, is use a date format in the TO_CHAR function. For example, they will use

```
Where to_char(date_column,'yyyy') = '2005'
```

instead of

```
Where trunc(date_column,'y') = to_date('01-jan-2005','dd-mon-yyyy')
```

The latter is a far more performant and less resource-intensive approach. If we make a copy of ALL_OBJECTS and save out just the CREATED column

```
ops$tkyte@ORA10G> create table t
  2  as
  3  select created from all_objects;
Table created.

ops$tkyte@ORA10G> exec dbms_stats.gather_table_stats( user, 'T' );
PL/SQL procedure successfully completed.
```

and then, with SQL_TRACE enabled, we repeatedly query this table using both techniques, we see the following results:

```
select count(*)
from
 t where to_char(created,'yyyy') = '2005'
```

call	count	cpu	elapsed	disk	query	current	rows
Parse	4	0.01	0.05	0	0	0	0
Execute	4	0.00	0.00	0	0	0	0
Fetch	8	0.41	0.59	0	372	0	4
total	16	0.42	0.64	0	372	0	4

```
select count(*)
from
 t where trunc(created,'y') = to_date('01-jan-2005','dd-mon-yyyy')
```

call	count	cpu	elapsed	disk	query	current	rows
Parse	4	0.00	0.00	0	0	0	0
Execute	4	0.00	0.00	0	0	0	0
Fetch	8	0.04	0.16	0	372	0	4
total	16	0.04	0.16	0	372	0	4

You can see the obvious difference. Using TO_CHAR consumed an order of magnitude more CPU than using TRUNC. That is because TO_CHAR must convert the date to a string, using a much larger code path, taking all of the NLS we have in place to do so. Then we had to compare a string to a string. The TRUNC, on the other hand, just had to set the last 5 bytes to 1. Then it compared 7 binary bytes to 7 binary bytes, and it was done. So, you should never use TO_CHAR on a DATE column simply to truncate it.

Additionally, avoid applying a function at all to the DATE column when possible. Taking the preceding example one step further, we can see that the goal was to retrieve all data in the year 2005. Well, what if CREATED had an index on it and a very small fraction of the values in that table were in the year 2005? We would like to be able to use that index by avoiding a function on the database and column using a simple predicate:

```
select count(*) from t
where created >= to_date('01-jan-2005','dd-mon-yyyy')
  and created <  to_date('01-jan-2006','dd-mon-yyyy');
```

We would achieve two things:

- An index on CREATED could be considered.

- The TRUNC function would not have to be invoked at all, and that overhead would go away entirely.

This technique of using a range comparison instead of TRUNC or TO_CHAR applies equally to the TIMESTAMP type discussed shortly. When you can avoid applying a function to a database column in a query, you should. In general, avoiding the function will be more performant and allow the optimizer to choose from a wider variety of access paths.

Adding Time to or Subtracting Time from a DATE

A question I am frequently asked is, "How do I add time to or subtract time from a DATE type?" For example, how do you add one day to a DATE, or eight hours, or one year, or one month, and so on? There are three techniques you'll commonly use:

- Simply add a NUMBER to the DATE. Adding 1 to a DATE is a method to add 1 day. Adding 1/24 to a DATE therefore adds 1 hour, and so on.

- You may use the INTERVAL type, as described shortly, to add units of time. INTERVAL types support two levels of granularity, years and months, or days/hours/minutes/seconds. That is, you may have an interval of so many years and months *or* an interval of so many days, hours, minutes, and seconds.

- Add months using the built-in ADD_MONTHS function. Since adding a month is generally not as simple as adding 28 to 31 days, a special-purpose function was implemented to facilitate this.

Table 12-3 demonstrates the techniques you would use to add N units of time to a date (or subtract N units of time from a date, of course).

Table 12-3. *Adding Time to a Date*

Unit of Time	Operation	Description
N seconds	DATE + n/24/60/60 DATE + n/86400 DATE + NUMTODSINTERVAL(n,'second')	There are 86,400 seconds in a day. Since adding 1 adds one day, adding 1/86400 adds one second to a date. I prefer the n/24/60/60 technique over the 1/86400 technique. They are equivalent. An even more readable method is to use the NUMTODSINTERVAL (number to day/second interval) to add N seconds.
N minutes	DATE + n/24/60 DATE + n/1440 DATE + NUMTODSINTERVAL(n,'minute')	There are 1,440 minutes in a date. Adding 1/1440 therefore adds one minute to a DATE. An even more readable method is to use the NUMTODSINTERVAL function.
N hours	DATE + n/24 DATE + NUMTODSINTERVAL(n,'hour')	There are 24 hours in a day. Adding 1/24 therefore adds one hour to a DATE. An even more readable method is to use the NUMTODSINTERVAL function.
N days	DATE + n	Simply add N to the DATE to add or subtract N days.
N weeks	DATE + 7*n	A week is seven days, so just multiply 7 by the number of weeks to add or subtract.
N months	ADD_MONTHS(DATE,n) DATE + NUMTOYMINTERVAL(n,'month')	You may use the ADD_MONTHS built-in function or add an interval of N months to the DATE. Please see the important caveat noted shortly regarding using month intervals with DATEs.
N years	ADD_MONTHS(DATE,12*n) DATE + NUMTOYMINTERVAL(n,'year')	You may use the ADD_MONTHS built-in function with 12*n to add or subtract N years. Similar goals may be achieved with a year interval, but please see the important caveat noted shortly regarding using year intervals with dates.

In general, when using the Oracle DATE type I recommend the following:

- Use the NUMTODSINTERVAL built-in function to add hours, minutes, and seconds.

- Add a simple number to add days.

- Use the ADD_MONTHS built-in function to add months and years.

I do not recommend using the NUMTOYMINTERVAL function. The reason has to do with how the functions behave at the months' end.

The ADD_MONTHS function treats the end of month days specially. It will in effect "round" the dates for us; for example, if we add one month to a month that has 31 days and the next month has fewer than 31 days, ADD_MONTHS will return the last day of the next month. Additionally, adding one month to the last day of a month results in the last day of the next month. We see this when adding one month to a month with 30 or fewer days:

```
ops$tkyte@ORA10G> alter session set nls_date_format = 'dd-mon-yyyy hh24:mi:ss';
Session altered.

ops$tkyte@ORA10G> select dt, add_months(dt,1)
  2     from (select to_date('29-feb-2000','dd-mon-yyyy') dt from dual )
  3  /
DT                   ADD_MONTHS(DT,1)
-------------------- --------------------
29-feb-2000 00:00:00 31-mar-2000 00:00:00

ops$tkyte@ORA10G> select dt, add_months(dt,1)
  2     from (select to_date('28-feb-2001','dd-mon-yyyy') dt from dual )
  3  /
DT                   ADD_MONTHS(DT,1)
-------------------- --------------------
28-feb-2001 00:00:00 31-mar-2001 00:00:00

ops$tkyte@ORA10G> select dt, add_months(dt,1)
  2     from (select to_date('30-jan-2001','dd-mon-yyyy') dt from dual )
  3  /
DT                   ADD_MONTHS(DT,1)
-------------------- --------------------
30-jan-2001 00:00:00 28-feb-2001 00:00:00

ops$tkyte@ORA10G> select dt, add_months(dt,1)
  2     from (select to_date('30-jan-2000','dd-mon-yyyy') dt from dual )
  3  /
DT                   ADD_MONTHS(DT,1)
-------------------- --------------------
30-jan-2000 00:00:00 29-feb-2000 00:00:00
```

See how the result of adding one month to February 29, 2000, results in March 31, 2000? February 29 was the last day of that month, so ADD_MONTHS returned the last day of the next month. Additionally, notice how adding one month to January 30, 2000 and 2001 results in the last day of February 2000 and 2001, respectively.

If we compare this to how adding an interval would work, we see very different results:

```
ops$tkyte@ORA10G> select dt, dt+numtoyminterval(1,'month')
  2     from (select to_date('29-feb-2000','dd-mon-yyyy') dt from dual )
  3  /
DT                   DT+NUMTOYMINTERVAL(1
-------------------- --------------------
29-feb-2000 00:00:00 29-mar-2000 00:00:00
```

```
ops$tkyte@ORA10G> select dt, dt+numtoyminterval(1,'month')
  2      from (select to_date('28-feb-2001','dd-mon-yyyy') dt from dual )
  3  /
DT                    DT+NUMTOYMINTERVAL(1
-------------------- --------------------
28-feb-2001 00:00:00 28-mar-2001 00:00:00
```

Notice how the resulting date is not the last day of the next month, but rather the *same* day of the next month. It is arguable that this behavior is acceptable, but consider what happens when the resulting month doesn't have that many days:

```
ops$tkyte@ORA10G> select dt, dt+numtoyminterval(1,'month')
  2      from (select to_date('30-jan-2001','dd-mon-yyyy') dt from dual )
  3  /
select dt, dt+numtoyminterval(1,'month')
           *
ERROR at line 1:
ORA-01839: date not valid for month specified

ops$tkyte@ORA10G> select dt, dt+numtoyminterval(1,'month')
  2      from (select to_date('30-jan-2000','dd-mon-yyyy') dt from dual )
  3  /
select dt, dt+numtoyminterval(1,'month')
               *
ERROR at line 1:
ORA-01839: date not valid for month specified
```

In my experience, that makes using a month interval in date arithmetic impossible in general. A similar issue arises with a year interval: adding one year to February 29, 2000, results in a runtime error as well, because there is no February 29, 2001.

Getting the Difference Between Two DATEs

Another frequently asked question is, "How do I retrieve the difference between two dates?" The answer is deceptively simple: you just subtract them. This will return a number representing the number of days between the two dates. Additionally, you have the built-in function MONTHS_BETWEEN that will return a number representing the number of months—including fractional months—between two dates. Lastly, with the INTERVAL types, you have yet another method to see the elapsed time between two dates. The following SQL query demonstrates the outcome of subtracting two dates (showing the number of days between them), using the MONTHS_BETWEEN function and then the two functions used with INTERVAL types:

```
ops$tkyte@ORA10G> select dt2-dt1 ,
  2          months_between(dt2,dt1) months_btwn,
  3          numtodsinterval(dt2-dt1,'day') days,
  4          numtoyminterval(months_between(dt2,dt1),'month') months
  5     from (select to_date('29-feb-2000 01:02:03','dd-mon-yyyy hh24:mi:ss') dt1,
  6                  to_date('15-mar-2001 11:22:33','dd-mon-yyyy hh24:mi:ss') dt2
  7              from dual )
  8  /
```

```
  DT2-DT1 MONTHS_BTWN DAYS                          MONTHS
---------- ----------- ------------------------------ -------------
380.430903  12.5622872 +000000380 10:20:30.000000000  +000000001-00
```

Those are all "correct" values, but not of great use to us yet. Most applications would like to display the years, months, days, hours, minutes, and seconds between the dates. Using a combination of the preceding functions, we can achieve that goal. We'll select out two intervals: one for the years and months, and the other for just the day, hours, and so on. We'll use the MONTHS_BETWEEN built-in function to determine the decimal number of months between the two dates, and then we'll use the NUMTOYMINTERVAL built-in function to convert that number into the years and months. Additionally, we'll use MONTHS_BETWEEN to subtract the integer number of months between the two dates from the larger of the two dates to get down to the days and hours between them:

```
ops$tkyte@ORA10G> select numtoyminterval
  2          (months_between(dt2,dt1),'month')
  3               years_months,
  4          numtodsinterval
  5            (dt2-add_months( dt1, trunc(months_between(dt2,dt1)) ),
  6             'day' )
  7             days_hours
  8    from (select to_date('29-feb-2000 01:02:03','dd-mon-yyyy hh24:mi:ss') dt1,
  9                 to_date('15-mar-2001 11:22:33','dd-mon-yyyy hh24:mi:ss') dt2
 10           from dual )
 11  /

YEARS_MONTHS       DAYS_HOURS
---------------    ------------------------------
+000000001-00      +000000015 10:20:30.000000000
```

Now it is clear that there is 1 year, 15 days, 10 hours, 20 minutes, and 30 seconds between the two DATEs.

TIMESTAMP Type

The TIMESTAMP type is very much like the DATE, with the addition of support for fractional seconds and time zones. We'll look at the TIMESTAMP type in the following three sections: one with regard to just the fractional second support but no time zone support, and the other two with regard to the two methods of storing the TIMESTAMP with time zone support.

TIMESTAMP

The syntax of the basic TIMESTAMP datatype is straightforward:

```
TIMESTAMP(n)
```

where N is optional and is used to specify the scale of the seconds component in the TIMESTAMP and may take on values between 0 and 9. If you specify 0, then a TIMESTAMP is functionally equivalent to a DATE and in fact stores the same values in the same manner:

```
ops$tkyte@ORA10G> create table t
  2  ( dt    date,
  3    ts    timestamp(0)
  4  )
  5  /
Table created.

ops$tkyte@ORA10G> insert into t values ( sysdate, systimestamp );
1 row created.

ops$tkyte@ORA10G> select dump(dt,10) dump, dump(ts,10) dump
  2    from t;

DUMP                                      DUMP
----------------------------------------- -------------------------------------
Typ=12 Len=7: 120,105,6,28,11,35,41  Typ=180 Len=7: 120,105,6,28,11,35,41
```

The datatypes are different (the TYP=FIELD indicates that), but the manner in which they store data is identical. The TIMESTAMP datatype will differ in length from the DATE type when you specify some number of fractional seconds to preserve, for example:

```
ops$tkyte@ORA10G> create table t
  2  ( dt    date,
  3    ts    timestamp(9)
  4  )
  5  /
Table created.

ops$tkyte@ORA10G> insert into t values ( sysdate, systimestamp );
1 row created.

ops$tkyte@ORA10G> select dump(dt,10) dump, dump(ts,10) dump
  2    from t;

DUMP                                    DUMP
-------------------------------------- --------------------------------------
Typ=12 Len=7: 120,105,6,28,11,46,21  Typ=180 Len=11: 120,105,6,28,11,46,21
                                       ,44,101,192,208
```

Now the TIMESTAMP consumes 11 bytes of storage, and the extra 4 bytes at the end contain the fractional seconds, which we can see by looking at the time that was stored:

```
ops$tkyte@ORA10G> alter session set nls_date_format = 'dd-mon-yyyy hh24:mi:ss';
Session altered.

ops$tkyte@ORA10G> select * from t;
```

```
DT                       TS
-------------------- --------------------------------
28-jun-2005 10:45:20 28-JUN-05 10.45.20.744866000 AM

ops$tkyte@ORA10G> select dump(ts,16) dump from t;

DUMP
----------------------------------------------------
Typ=180 Len=11: 78,69,6,1c,b,2e,15,2c,65,c0,d0

ops$tkyte@ORA10G> select to_number('2c65c0d0','xxxxxxxx') from dual;

TO_NUMBER('2C65C0D0','XXXXXXXX')
--------------------------------
                       744866000
```

We can see the fractional seconds that were stored are there in the last 4 bytes. We used the DUMP function to inspect the data in HEX this time (base 16) so we could easily convert the 4 bytes into the decimal representation.

Adding Time to or Subtracting Time from a TIMESTAMP

The same techniques we applied to DATE for date arithmetic work with a TIMESTAMP, but *the TIMESTAMP will be converted into a DATE in many cases using the preceding techniques*, for example:

```
ops$tkyte@ORA10G> alter session set nls_date_format = 'dd-mon-yyyy hh24:mi:ss';
Session altered.

ops$tkyte@ORA10G> select systimestamp ts, systimestamp+1 dt
  2  from dual;

TS                                      DT
------------------------------------    --------------------
28-JUN-05 11.04.49.833097 AM -04:00     29-jun-2005 11:04:49
```

Note that adding 1 did, in fact, advance the SYSTIMESTAMP by a day, but the fractional seconds are gone, as would be the time zone information. This is where using INTERVALs will be more important:

```
ops$tkyte@ORA10G> select systimestamp ts, systimestamp +numtodsinterval(1,'day') dt
  2  from dual;

TS                                      DT
------------------------------------    -----------------------------------------
28-JUN-05 11.08.03.958866 AM -04:00     29-JUN-05 11.08.03.958866000 AM -04:00
```

Using the function that returns an INTERVAL type preserved the fidelity of the TIMESTAMP. You will need to exercise caution when using TIMESTAMPs, to avoid the implicit conversions.

But bear in mind the caveat about adding intervals of months or years to a TIMESTAMP. If the resulting day isn't a valid date, the operation fails (adding one month to the last day in January will always fail if the month is added via an INTERVAL).

Getting the Difference Between Two TIMESTAMPs

This is where the DATE and TIMESTAMP types diverge significantly. Whereas the results of subtracting a DATE from a DATE was a NUMBER, the result of doing the same to a TIMESTAMP is an INTERVAL:

```
ops$tkyte@ORA10G> select dt2-dt1
  2    from (select to_timestamp('29-feb-2000 01:02:03.122000',
  3                              'dd-mon-yyyy hh24:mi:ss.ff') dt1,
  4               to_timestamp('15-mar-2001 11:22:33.000000',
  5                              'dd-mon-yyyy hh24:mi:ss.ff') dt2
  6          from dual )
  7  /

DT2-DT1
---------------------------------------------------------------------------
+000000380 10:20:29.878000000
```

The difference between two TIMESTAMP values is an INTERVAL, and this shows us the number of days and hours/minutes/seconds between the two. If we desire to have the years, months, and so forth, we are back to using a query similar to the one we used with dates:

```
ops$tkyte@ORA10G> select numtoyminterval
  2          (months_between(dt2,dt1),'month')
  3             years_months,
  4          dt2-add_months(dt1,trunc(months_between(dt2,dt1)))
  5             days_hours
  6    from (select to_timestamp('29-feb-2000 01:02:03.122000',
  7                              'dd-mon-yyyy hh24:mi:ss.ff') dt1,
  8               to_timestamp('15-mar-2001 11:22:33.000000',
  9                              'dd-mon-yyyy hh24:mi:ss.ff') dt2
 10          from dual )
 11  /

YEARS_MONTHS   DAYS_HOURS
-------------  ------------------------------
+000000001-00  +000000015 10:20:30.000000000
```

Note in this case, since we used ADD_MONTHS, DT1 was converted implicitly into a DATE type and we lost the fractional seconds. We would have to add yet more code to preserve them. We could use NUMTOYMINTERVAL to add the months and preserve the TIMESTAMP; however, we would be subject to runtime errors:

```
ops$tkyte@ORA10G> select numtoyminterval
  2          (months_between(dt2,dt1),'month')
  3             years_months,
  4          dt2-(dt1 + numtoyminterval( trunc(months_between(dt2,dt1)),'month' ))
  5               days_hours
  6    from (select to_timestamp('29-feb-2000 01:02:03.122000',
  7                              'dd-mon-yyyy hh24:mi:ss.ff') dt1,
  8                  to_timestamp('15-mar-2001 11:22:33.000000',
  9                              'dd-mon-yyyy hh24:mi:ss.ff') dt2
 10            from dual )
 11  /
        dt2-(dt1 + numtoyminterval( trunc(months_between(dt2,dt1)),'month' ))
              *
ERROR at line 4:
ORA-01839: date not valid for month specified
```

I personally find this unacceptable. The fact is, though, that by the time you are displaying information with years and months, the fidelity of the TIMESTAMP is destroyed already. A year is not fixed in duration (it may be 365 or 366 days in length) and neither is a month. If you are displaying information with years and months, the loss of microseconds is not relevant; having the information displayed down to the second is more than sufficient at that point.

TIMESTAMP WITH TIME ZONE Type

The TIMESTAMP WITH TIME ZONE type inherits all of the qualities of the TIMESTAMP type and adds time zone support. The TIMESTAMP WITH TIME ZONE type consumes 13 bytes of storage, with the extra 2 bytes being used to preserve the time zone information. It differs from a TIMESTAMP structurally only by the addition of these 2 bytes:

```
ops$tkyte@ORA10G> create table t
  2  (
  3    ts     timestamp,
  4    ts_tz timestamp with time zone
  5  )
  6  /
Table created.

ops$tkyte@ORA10G> insert into t ( ts, ts_tz )
  2  values ( systimestamp, systimestamp );
1 row created.

ops$tkyte@ORA10G> select * from t;

TS                          TS_TZ
--------------------------- -----------------------------------
28-JUN-05 01.45.08.087627 PM 28-JUN-05 01.45.08.087627 PM -04:00

ops$tkyte@ORA10G> select dump(ts), dump(ts_tz) from t;
```

```
DUMP(TS)
--------------------------------------------------------------------------------
DUMP(TS_TZ)
--------------------------------------------------------------------------------
Typ=180 Len=11: 120,105,6,28,14,46,9,5,57,20,248
Typ=181 Len=13: 120,105,6,28,18,46,9,5,57,20,248,16,60
```

As you can see, upon retrieval the default TIMESTAMP format included the time zone information (I was on East Coast US time during daylight saving time when this was executed).

TIMESTAMP WITH TIME ZONEs store the data in whatever time zone was specified when the data was stored. The time zone becomes part of the data itself. Note how the TIMESTAMP WITH TIME ZONE field stored ...18,46,9... for the hour, minutes, and seconds (in excess-1 notation, so that is 17:45:08), whereas the TIMESTAMP field stored simply ...14,46,9..., which is 13:45:09—the exact time in the string we inserted. The TIMESTAMP WITH TIME ZONE had four hours added to it, in order to store in GMT (also known as UTC) time. The trailing 2 bytes are used upon retrieval to properly adjust the TIMESTAMP value.

It is not my intention to cover all of the nuances of time zones here in this book; that is a topic well covered elsewhere. To that end, I'll just point out that time zone support is more relevant in applications today than ever before. A decade ago, applications were not nearly as global as they are now. In the days before widespread Internet use, applications were many times distributed and decentralized, and the time zone was implicitly based on where the server was located. Today, with large centralized systems being used by people worldwide, the need to track and use time zones is very relevant.

Before time zone support was built into a datatype, you had to store the DATE in one column and the time zone information in another, and then it was the application's job to apply functions to convert DATEs from one time zone to another. Now that is the job of the database, and it is able to store data in multiple time zones:

```
ops$tkyte@ORA10G> create table t
  2  ( ts1  timestamp with time zone,
  3    ts2  timestamp with time zone
  4  )
  5  /
Table created.

ops$tkyte@ORA10G> insert into t (ts1, ts2)
  2  values ( timestamp'2005-06-05 17:02:32.212 US/Eastern',
  3           timestamp'2005-06-05 17:02:32.212 US/Pacific' );

1 row created.
```

and perform correct TIMESTAMP arithmetic on them:

```
ops$tkyte@ORA10G> select ts1-ts2 from t;

TS1-TS2
--------------------------------------------------------------------------------
-000000000 03:00:00.000000
```

Since there is a three-hour time difference between those two time zones, even though they show the "same time" of 17:02:32.212, the interval reported is a three-hour difference. When performing TIMESTAMP arithmetic on TIMESTAMPS WITH TIME ZONE types, Oracle automatically converts both types to UTC time first and then performs the operation.

TIMESTAMP WITH LOCAL TIME ZONE Type

This type works much like the TIMESTAMP type. It is a 7- or 11-byte field (depending on the precision of the TIMESTAMP), but it is normalized to be stored in database's time zone. To see this, we'll use the DUMP command once again. First, we create a table with three columns—a DATE, a TIMESTAMP WITH TIME ZONE, and a TIMESTAMP WITH LOCAL TIME ZONE—and then we insert the same value into all three columns:

```
ops$tkyte@ORA10G> create table t
  2  ( dt    date,
  3    ts1   timestamp with time zone,
  4    ts2   timestamp with local time zone
  5  )
  6  /
Table created.

ops$tkyte@ORA10G> insert into t (dt, ts1, ts2)
  2  values ( timestamp'2005-06-05 17:02:32.212 US/Pacific',
  3           timestamp'2005-06-05 17:02:32.212 US/Pacific',
  4           timestamp'2005-06-05 17:02:32.212 US/Pacific' );
1 row created.

ops$tkyte@ORA10G> select dbtimezone from dual;

DBTIMEZONE
----------
US/Eastern
```

Now, when we dump those values as follows:

```
ops$tkyte@ORA10G> select dump(dt), dump(ts1), dump(ts2) from t;

DUMP(DT)
-------------------------------------
DUMP(TS1)
-------------------------------------
DUMP(TS2)
-------------------------------------
Typ=12 Len=7:   120,105,6,5,18,3,33
Typ=181 Len=13: 120,105,6,6,1,3,33,12,162,221,0,137,156
Typ=231 Len=11: 120,105,6,5,21,3,33,12,162,221,0
```

We can see that in this case, three totally different date/time representations were stored:

- DT: This column stored the date/time 5-JUN-2005 17:02:32. The time zone and fractional seconds are lost because we used the DATE type. No time zone conversions were performed at all. We stored the exact date/time inserted, but lost the time zone.

- TS1: This column preserved the TIME ZONE information and was normalized to be in UTC with respect to that TIME ZONE. The inserted TIMESTAMP value was in the US/Pacific time zone, which at the time of this writing was seven hours off UTC. Therefore, the stored date/time was 6-JUN-2005 00:02:32.212. It advanced our input time by seven hours to make it UTC time, and it saved the time zone US/Pacific as the last 2 bytes so this data can be properly interpreted later.

- TS2: This column *is assumed to be in the database's time zone, which is US/Eastern.* Now, 17:02:32 US/Pacific is 20:02:32 US/Eastern, so that is what was stored in the bytes ...21,3,33... (excess-1 notation; remember to subtract 1).

Since the TS1 column preserved the original time zone in the last 2 bytes, we'll see the following upon retrieval:

```
ops$tkyte@ORA10G> select ts1, ts2 from t;

TS1
----------------------------------------
TS2
----------------------------------------
05-JUN-05 05.02.32.212000 PM US/PACIFIC
05-JUN-05 08.02.32.212000 PM
```

The database would be able to show that information, but the TS2 column with the LOCAL TIME ZONE (the time zone of the database) shows the time in the database's time zone, which is the assumed time zone for that column (and, in fact, all columns in this database with the LOCAL TIME ZONE). My database was in the US/Eastern time zone, so 17:02:32 US/Pacific on the way in is now displayed as 8:00 pm East Coast time on the way out.

The TIMESTAMP WITH LOCAL TIME ZONE provides sufficient support for most applications, if you need not remember the source time zone, but only need a datatype that provides consistent worldwide handling of date/time types. Additionally, the TIMESTAMP(0) WITH LOCAL ⇒ TIMEZONE provides you the equivalent of a DATE type with time zone support; it consumes 7 bytes of storage and allows you to store dates "normalized" in UTC form.

One caveat with regard to the TIMESTAMP WITH LOCAL TIME ZONE type is that once you create tables with this column, you will find your database's time zone is "frozen," and you will not be able to change it:

```
ops$tkyte@ORA10G> alter database set time_zone = 'PST';
alter database set time_zone = 'PST'
*
ERROR at line 1:
ORA-30079: cannot alter database timezone when database has
           TIMESTAMP WITH LOCAL TIME ZONE columns
```

```
ops$tkyte@ORA10G> !oerr ora 30079
30079, 00000, "cannot alter database timezone when database has
              TIMESTAMP WITH LOCAL TIME ZONE columns"
// *Cause:  An attempt was made to alter database timezone with
//          TIMESTAMP WITH LOCAL TIME ZONE column in the database.
// *Action: Either do not alter database timezone or first drop all the
//          TIMESTAMP WITH LOCAL TIME ZONE columns.
```

The reason is that if you were able to change the database's time zone, you would have to rewrite every single table with a TIMESTAMP WITH LOCAL TIME ZONE—their current values would be wrong given the new time zone!

INTERVAL Type

We briefly saw INTERVAL type used in the previous section. It is a way to represent a duration of time or an interval of time. We'll discuss two INTERVAL types in this section: the YEAR TO MONTH type, which is capable of storing a duration of time specified in years and months, and the DATE TO SECOND type, which is capable of storing a duration of time in days, hours, minutes, and seconds (including fractional seconds).

Before we get into the specifics of the two INTERVAL types, I'd like to look at the EXTRACT built-in function, which can be very useful when working with this type. The EXTRACT built-in function works on TIMESTAMPs and INTERVALs, and returns various bits of information from them, such as the time zone from a TIMESTAMP or the hours/days/minutes from an INTERVAL. Using the previous example, where we got the INTERVAL of 380 days, 10 hours, 20 minutes, and 29.878 seconds

```
ops$tkyte@ORA10G> select dt2-dt1
  2     from (select to_timestamp('29-feb-2000 01:02:03.122000',
  3                               'dd-mon-yyyy hh24:mi:ss.ff') dt1,
  4                to_timestamp('15-mar-2001 11:22:33.000000',
  5                               'dd-mon-yyyy hh24:mi:ss.ff') dt2
  6           from dual )
  7  /

DT2-DT1
---------------------------------------------------------------------------
+000000380 10:20:29.878000000
```

we can use EXTRACT to see how easy it is to pull out each bit of information:

```
ops$tkyte@ORA10G> select extract( day    from dt2-dt1 ) day,
  2            extract( hour   from dt2-dt1 ) hour,
  3            extract( minute from dt2-dt1 ) minute,
  4            extract( second from dt2-dt1 ) second
  5     from (select to_timestamp('29-feb-2000 01:02:03.122000',
  6                               'dd-mon-yyyy hh24:mi:ss.ff') dt1,
  7                to_timestamp('15-mar-2001 11:22:33.000000',
  8                               'dd-mon-yyyy hh24:mi:ss.ff') dt2
```

```
 9          from dual )
10   /


        DAY       HOUR      MINUTE     SECOND
---------- ---------- ---------- ----------
        380        10         20      29.878
```

Additionally, we've already seen the NUMTOYMINTERVAL and the NUMTODSINTERVAL for creating YEAR TO MONTH and DAY TO SECOND intervals. I find these functions to be the easiest way to create instances of INTERVAL types—over and above the string conversion functions. Rather than concatenate a bunch of numbers representing the days, hours, minutes, and seconds representing some interval together, I'd rather add up four calls to NUMTODSINTERVAL to do the same.

The INTERVAL type can be used to store not just durations, but "times" as well in a way. For example, if you want to store a specific date and time, you have the DATE or TIMESTAMP types. But what if you want to store just the time 8:00 am? The INTERVAL type would be handy for that (the INTERVAL DAY TO SECOND type in particular).

INTERVAL YEAR TO MONTH

The syntax for INTERVAL YEAR TO MONTH is straightforward:

```
INTERVAL YEAR(n) TO MONTH
```

where N is an optional number of digits to support for the number of years and varies from 0 to 9, with a default of 2 (to store a number of years from 0 to 99). It allows you to store any number of years (up to nine digits' worth, anyway) and months. The function I prefer to use to create INTERVAL instances of this type is NUMTOYMINTERVAL. For example, to create an interval of five years and two months, we can use the following:

```
ops$tkyte@ORA10G> select numtoyminterval(5,'year')+numtoyminterval(2,'month')
  2  from dual;

NUMTOYMINTERVAL(5,'YEAR')+NUMTOYMINTERVAL(2,'MONTH')
-------------------------------------------------------------------------
+000000005-02
```

Or, using a single call and the fact that a year has 12 months, we can use the following:

```
ops$tkyte@ORA10G> select numtoyminterval(5*12+2,'month')
  2  from dual;

NUMTOYMINTERVAL(5*12+2,'MONTH')
-------------------------------------------------------------------------
+000000005-02
```

Either approach works well. Another function, TO_YMINTERVAL, can be used to convert a string into a year/month INTERVAL type:

```
ops$tkyte@ORA10G> select to_yminterval( '5-2' ) from dual;

TO_YMINTERVAL('5-2')
-----------------------------------------------------------------------
+000000005-02
```

But since the vast majority of the time I have the year and months in two NUMBER fields in my application, I find the NUMTOYMINTERVAL function to be more useful, as opposed to building a formatted string from the numbers.

Lastly, you can just use the INTERVAL type right in SQL, bypassing the functions altogether:

```
ops$tkyte@ORA10G> select interval '5-2' year to month from dual;

INTERVAL'5-2'YEARTOMONTH
-----------------------------------------------------------------------
+05-02
```

INTERVAL DAY TO SECOND

The syntax for the INTERVAL DAY TO SECOND type is straightforward:

```
INTERVAL DAY(n) TO SECOND(m)
```

where N is an optional number of digits to support for the day component and varies from 0 to 9, with a default of 2. M is the number of digits to preserve in the fractional part of the seconds field and varies from 0 to 9, with a default of 6. Once again, the function I prefer to use to create instances of this INTERVAL type is NUMTODSINTERVAL:

```
ops$tkyte@ORA10G> select numtodsinterval( 10, 'day' )+
  2  numtodsinterval( 2, 'hour' )+
  3  numtodsinterval( 3, 'minute' )+
  4  numtodsinterval( 2.3312, 'second' )
  5  from dual;

NUMTODSINTERVAL(10,'DAY')+NUMTODSINTERVAL(2,'HOUR')+NUMTODSINTERVAL(3,'MINU
-----------------------------------------------------------------------
+000000010 02:03:02.331200000
```

or simply

```
ops$tkyte@ORA10G> select numtodsinterval( 10*86400+2*3600+3*60+2.3312, 'second' )
  2  from dual;

NUMTODSINTERVAL(10*86400+2*3600+3*60+2.3312,'SECOND')
-----------------------------------------------------------------------
+000000010 02:03:02.331200000
```

using the fact that there are 86,400 seconds in a day, 3,600 seconds in an hour, and so on. Alternatively, as before, we can use the TO_DSINTERVAL function to convert a string into a DAY TO SECOND interval:

```
ops$tkyte@ORA10G> select to_dsinterval( '10 02:03:02.3312' )
  2  from dual;

TO_DSINTERVAL('1002:03:02.3312')
---------------------------------------------------------------------------
+000000010 02:03:02.331200000
```

or just use an INTERVAL literal in SQL itself:

```
ops$tkyte@ORA10G> select interval '10 02:03:02.3312' day to second
  2  from dual;

INTERVAL'1002:03:02.3312'DAYTOSECOND
---------------------------------------------------------------------------
+10 02:03:02.331200
```

LOB Types

LOBs, or *large objects*, are the source of much confusion, in my experience. They are a misunderstood datatype, both in terms of how they are implemented and how best to use them. This section provides an overview of how LOBs are stored physically and the considerations you must take into account when using a LOB type. They have many optional settings, and getting the right mix for your application is crucial.

There are four types of LOBs supported in Oracle:

- CLOB: A character LOB. This type is used to store large amounts of textual information, such as XML or just plain text. This datatype is subject to character set translation—that is, the characters in this field will be converted from the database's character set to the client's character set upon retrieval, and from the client's character set to the database's character set upon modification.

- NCLOB: Another type of character LOB. The character set of the data stored in this column is the national character set of the database, not the default character set of the database.

- BLOB: A binary LOB. This type is used to stored large amounts of binary information, such as word documents, images, and anything else you can imagine. It is not subject to character set translation. Whatever bits and bytes the application writes into a BLOB are what are returned by the BLOB.

- BFILE: A binary file LOB. This is more of a pointer than a database-stored entity. The only thing stored in the database with a BFILE is a pointer to a file in the operating system. The file is maintained outside of the database and is not really part of the database at all. A BFILE provides read-only access to the contents of the file.

When discussing LOBs, I'll break the preceding list into two pieces: LOBs stored in the database, or internal LOBs, which include CLOB, BLOB, and NCLOB; and LOBs stored outside of the database, or the BFILE type. I will not discuss CLOB, BLOB, or NCLOB independently, since from a storage and option perspective they are the same. It is just that a CLOB and NCLOB support textual information and a BLOB does not. But the options we specify for them—the CHUNKSIZE, PCTVERSION, and so on—and the considerations are the same, regardless of the base type. Since BFILEs are significantly different, we'll discuss them separately.

Internal LOBs

The syntax for a LOB is, on the face of it, very simple—deceptively simple. You may create tables with column datatypes of CLOB, BLOB, or NCLOB, and that is it. They are as simple to use as the NUMBER, DATE, or VARCHAR2 type:

```
ops$tkyte@ORA10G> create table t
  2  ( id int primary key,
  3    txt clob
  4  )
  5  /
Table created.
```

Or are they? That small example shows the tip of the iceberg—the bare minimum you can specify about a LOB. Using DBMS_METADATA, we can get the entire picture:

```
ops$tkyte@ORA10G> select dbms_metadata.get_ddl( 'TABLE', 'T' )
  2      from dual;

DBMS_METADATA.GET_DDL('TABLE','T')
--------------------------------------------------------------------------------

  CREATE TABLE "OPS$TKYTE"."T"
   (    "ID" NUMBER(*,0),
        "TXT" CLOB,
         PRIMARY KEY ("ID")
  USING INDEX PCTFREE 10 INITRANS 2 MAXTRANS 255
  STORAGE(INITIAL 65536 NEXT 1048576 MINEXTENTS 1 MAXEXTENTS 2147483645
  PCTINCREASE 0 FREELISTS 1 FREELIST GROUPS 1 BUFFER_POOL DEFAULT)
  TABLESPACE "USERS"  ENABLE
   ) PCTFREE 10 PCTUSED 40 INITRANS 1 MAXTRANS 255 NOCOMPRESS LOGGING
  STORAGE(INITIAL 65536 NEXT 1048576 MINEXTENTS 1 MAXEXTENTS 2147483645
  PCTINCREASE 0 FREELISTS 1 FREELIST GROUPS 1 BUFFER_POOL DEFAULT)
  TABLESPACE "USERS"
  LOB ("TXT") STORE AS (
  TABLESPACE "USERS" ENABLE STORAGE IN ROW CHUNK 8192 PCTVERSION 10
  NOCACHE
  STORAGE(INITIAL 65536 NEXT 1048576 MINEXTENTS 1 MAXEXTENTS 2147483645
  PCTINCREASE 0 FREELISTS 1 FREELIST GROUPS 1 BUFFER_POOL DEFAULT))
```

The LOB apparently has the following attributes:

- A tablespace (USERS in this example)

- ENABLE STORAGE IN ROW as a default attribute

- CHUNK 8192

- PCTVERSION 10

- NOCACHE

- A full storage clause

This implies there is a lot going on in the background with LOBs, and in fact there is. A LOB column always results in what I call a *multisegment object*, meaning the table will use multiple physical segments. If we had created that table in an empty schema, we would discover the following:

```
ops$tkyte@ORA10G> select segment_name, segment_type
  2  from user_segments;

SEGMENT_NAME                        SEGMENT_TYPE
----------------------------------  ------------------
SYS_C0011927                        INDEX
SYS_IL0000071432C00002$$            LOBINDEX
SYS_LOB0000071432C00002$$           LOBSEGMENT
T                                   TABLE
```

An index was created in support of the primary key constraint—that is normal—but what about the other two segments, the lobindex and the lobsegment? Those were created in support of our LOB column. The lobsegment is where our actual data will be stored (well, it might be stored in the table T also, but we'll cover that in more detail when we get to the ENABLE ⇒ STORAGE IN ROW clause). The lobindex is used to navigate our LOB, to find the pieces of it. When we create a LOB column, in general what is stored in the row is a *pointer*, or *LOB locator*. This LOB locator is what our application retrieves. When we ask for "bytes 1,000 through 2,000" of the LOB, the LOB locator is used against the lobindex to find where those bytes are stored, and then the lobsegment is accessed. The lobindex is used to find the pieces of the LOB easily. You can think of a LOB then as a master/detail sort of relation. A LOB is stored in "chunks" or pieces, and any piece is accessible to us. If we were to implement a LOB using just tables, for example, we might do so as follows:

```
Create table parent
( id int primary key,
  other-data...
);

Create table lob
( id references parent on delete cascade,
  chunk_number int,
  data <datatype>(n),
  primary key (id,chunk_number)
);
```

Conceptually, the LOB is stored very much like that—in creating those two tables, we would have a primary key on the LOB table on the ID, CHUNK_NUMBER (analogous to the lobindex created by Oracle), and we would have a table LOB storing the chunks of data (analogous to the lobsegment). The LOB column implements this master/detail structure for us transparently. Figure 12-3 might make this idea clearer.

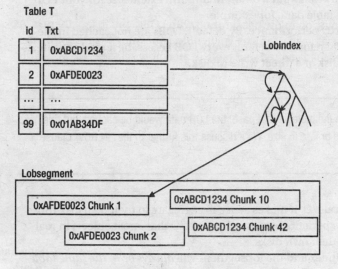

Figure 12-3. *Table to lobindex to lobsegment*

The LOB in the table really just points to the lobindex, and the lobindex in turn points to all of the pieces of the LOB itself. To get bytes N through M of the LOB, you would dereference the pointer in the table (the LOB locator), walk the lobindex structure to find the needed chunks, and then access them in order. This makes random access to any piece of the LOB equally fast—you can get the front, the middle, or the end of a LOB equally fast, as you don't always just start at the beginning and walk the LOB.

Now that you understand conceptually how a LOB is stored, I'd like to walk through each of the optional settings listed previously, and explain what they are used for and what exactly they imply.

LOB Tablespace

The CREATE TABLE statement returned from DBMS_METADATA included the following:

```
LOB ("TXT") STORE AS ( TABLESPACE "USERS" ...
```

The TABLESPACE specified here is the tablespace where the lobsegment and lobindex will be stored, and this may be different from the tablespace where the table itself resides. That is, the tablespace that holds the LOB data may be separate and distinct from the tablespace that holds the actual table data.

The main reasons you might consider using a different tablespace for the LOB data versus the table data relate mainly to administration and performance. From the administrative angle, a LOB datatype represents a sizable amount of information. If the table had millions of rows, and each row had a sizeable LOB associated with it, the LOB data would be huge. It would make sense to segregate the table from the LOB data just to facilitate backup and recovery and space management. You may well want a different uniform extent size for your LOB data than you have for your regular table data, for example.

The other reason could be for I/O performance. By default, LOBs are not cached in the buffer cache (more on that later). Therefore, by default every LOB access, be it read or write, is a physical I/O—a direct read from disk or a direct write to disk.

Note LOBs may be *inline*, or stored in the table. In that case, the LOB data would be cached, but this applies only to LOBs that are 4,000 bytes or less in size. We'll discuss this further in the "IN ROW Clause" section.

Because each access is a physical I/O, it makes sense to segregate to their own disk those objects you know for a fact will be experiencing more physical I/O than most objects in real time (as the user accesses them) to their own disks.

It should be noted that the lobindex and the lobsegment will *always be in the same tablespace*. You cannot have the lobindex and lobsegment in separate tablespaces. Much earlier releases of Oracle allowed you to separate them, but versions 8*i* Release 3 and later do not allow you to specify separate tablespaces for the lobindex and lobsegment. In fact, all storage characteristics of the lobindex are inherited from the lobsegment, as we'll see shortly.

IN ROW Clause

The CREATE TABLE statement returned from DBMS_METADATA earlier included the following:

```
LOB ("TXT") STORE AS (... ENABLE STORAGE IN ROW ...
```

This controls whether the LOB data is always stored separately from the table, in the lobsegment, or if it can sometimes be stored right in the table itself without being placed into the lobsegment. If ENABLE STORAGE IN ROW is set, as opposed to DISABLE STORAGE IN ROW, small LOBs of up to 4,000 bytes will be stored in the table itself, much like a VARCHAR2 would be. Only when LOBs exceed 4,000 bytes will they be moved "out of line" into the lobsegment.

Enabling storage in the row is the default and, in general, should be the way to go if you know the LOBs will generally fit in the table itself. For example, you might have an application with a DESCRIPTION field of some sort in it. The DESCRIPTION might store between 0 and 32KB of data (or maybe even more, but mostly 32KB or less). Many of the descriptions are known to be very short, consisting of a couple hundred characters. Rather than suffering the overhead of storing these out of line and accessing them via the index every time you retrieve them, you can store them inline, in the table itself. Further, if the LOB is using the default of NOCACHE (the lobsegment data is not cached in the buffer cache), then a LOB stored in the table will avoid the physical I/O required to retrieve the LOB.

We can see the effect of this with a rather simple example. We'll create a table with a LOB that can store data in row and one that cannot:

```
ops$tkyte@ORA10G> create table t
  2  ( id int     primary key,
  3    in_row   clob,
  4    out_row  clob
  5  )
  6  lob (in_row)  store as ( enable  storage in row )
  7  lob (out_row) store as ( disable storage in row )
  8  /
Table created.
```

Into this table we'll insert some string data, all of which is less than 4,000 bytes in length:

```
ops$tkyte@ORA10G> insert into t
  2  select rownum,
  3         owner || ' ' || object_name || ' ' || object_type || ' ' || status,
  4         owner || ' ' || object_name || ' ' || object_type || ' ' || status
  5    from all_objects
  6  /
48592 rows created.

ops$tkyte@ORA10G> commit;
Commit complete.
```

Now, if we try to read out each row and, using the DBMS_MONITOR package, do this with SQL_TRACE enabled, we'll be able to see the performance upon data retrieval of each:

```
ops$tkyte@ORA10G> declare
  2          l_cnt    number;
  3          l_data   varchar2(32765);
  4  begin
  5          select count(*)
  6            into l_cnt
  7            from t;
  8
  9          dbms_monitor.session_trace_enable;
 10          for i in 1 .. l_cnt
 11          loop
 12                  select in_row  into l_data from t where id = i;
 13                  select out_row into l_data from t where id = i;
 14          end loop;
 15  end;
 16  /
PL/SQL procedure successfully completed.
```

When we review the TKPROF report for this small simulation, the results are rather obvious:

```
SELECT IN_ROW FROM T WHERE ID = :B1

call      count       cpu     elapsed       disk       query     current         rows
-------  ------  --------  ----------  ---------- ----------- -----------  -----------
Parse         1      0.00        0.00           0           0           0            0
Execute   48592      2.99        2.78           0           0           0            0
Fetch     48592      1.84        1.80           0      145776           0        48592
-------  ------  --------  ----------  ---------- ----------- -----------  -----------
total     97185      4.83        4.59           0      145776           0        48592

Rows      Row Source Operation
-------   ----------------------------------------------------
  48592   TABLE ACCESS BY INDEX ROWID T (cr=145776 pr=0 pw=0 time=1770453 us)
  48592    INDEX UNIQUE SCAN SYS_C0011949 (cr=97184 pr=0 pw=0 time=960814 us)
********************************************************************************
SELECT OUT_ROW FROM T WHERE ID = :B1

call      count       cpu     elapsed       disk       query     current         rows
-------  ------  --------  ----------  ---------- ----------- -----------  -----------
Parse         1      0.00        0.00           0           0           0            0
Execute   48592      2.21        2.13           0           0           0            0
Fetch     48592      7.33        8.49       48592      291554           0        48592
-------  ------  --------  ----------  ---------- ----------- -----------  -----------
total     97185      9.54       10.62       48592      291554           0        48592

Rows      Row Source Operation
-------   ----------------------------------------------------
  48592   TABLE ACCESS BY INDEX ROWID T (cr=145776 pr=0 pw=0 time=1421463 us)
  48592    INDEX UNIQUE SCAN SYS_C0011949 (cr=97184 pr=0 pw=0 time=737992 us)


Elapsed times include waiting on following events:
  Event waited on                              Times   Max. Wait  Total Waited
  ---------------------------------------      Waited  ---------- ------------
  direct path read                             48592        0.00          0.25
```

The retrieval of the IN_ROW column was significantly faster and consumed far fewer resources. We can see that it used 145,776 logical I/Os (query mode gets), whereas the OUT_ROW column used some two times as many logical I/Os. At first it is not clear where these extra logical I/Os are coming from, but if you remember how LOBs are stored, it will become obvious. These are the I/Os against the lobindex segment in order to find the pieces of the LOB. Those extra logical I/Os are all against this lobindex.

Additionally, you can see that, for the OUT_ROW column, the retrieval of 48,592 rows incurred 48,592 physical I/Os and resulted in the same number of I/O waits for "direct path read." These were the reads of the noncached LOB data. We could reduce them in this case by enabling caching on the LOB data, but then we'd have to ensure we had sufficient additional buffer cache to be used for this. Also, if there were some really large LOBs in there, we might not really want this data to be cached.

This in-row/out-of-row storage will affect modifications as well as reads. If we were to update the first 100 rows with short strings and insert 100 new rows with short strings, and use the same techniques to monitor performance, we would observe the following:

```
ops$tkyte@ORA10G> create sequence s start with 100000;
Sequence created.

ops$tkyte@ORA10G> declare
  2          l_cnt    number;
  3          l_data   varchar2(32765);
  4  begin
  5          dbms_monitor.session_trace_enable;
  6          for i in 1 .. 100
  7          loop
  8                  update t set in_row =
                     to_char(sysdate,'dd-mon-yyyy hh24:mi:ss') where id = i;
  9                  update t set out_row =
                     to_char(sysdate,'dd-mon-yyyy hh24:mi:ss') where id = i;
 10                  insert into t (id, in_row) values ( s.nextval, 'Hello World' );
 11                  insert into t (id,out_row) values ( s.nextval, 'Hello World' );
 12          end loop;
 13  end;
 14  /
PL/SQL procedure successfully completed.
```

We would discover findings similar to this in the resulting TKPROF report:

```
UPDATE T SET IN_ROW = TO_CHAR(SYSDATE,'dd-mon-yyyy hh24:mi:ss')
WHERE ID = :B1

call     count      cpu    elapsed       disk      query    current        rows
------- ------  -------- ----------  ---------- ---------- ----------  ----------
Parse        1     0.00       0.00          0          0          0           0
Execute    100     0.05       0.02          0        200        202         100
Fetch        0     0.00       0.00          0          0          0           0
------- ------  -------- ----------  ---------- ---------- ----------  ----------
total      101     0.05       0.02          0        200        202         100

Rows     Row Source Operation
-------  ---------------------------------------------------
    100   UPDATE  (cr=200 pr=0 pw=0 time=15338 us)
    100    INDEX UNIQUE SCAN SYS_C0011949 (cr=200 pr=0 pw=0 time=2437 us)
********************************************************************************
UPDATE T SET OUT_ROW = TO_CHAR(SYSDATE,'dd-mon-yyyy hh24:mi:ss')
WHERE ID = :B1
```

```
call      count     cpu    elapsed        disk      query    current       rows
-------  ------  --------  ----------  ----------  ----------  ----------  ----------
Parse        1     0.00      0.00           0          0          0.          0
Execute    100     0.07      0.14           0       1100        2421        100
Fetch        0     0.00      0.00           0          0          0           0
-------  ------  --------  ----------  ----------  ----------  ----------  ----------
total      101      .0.07     0.14           0       1100        2421        100

Rows       Row Source Operation
-------    -----------------------------------------------------------
   100     UPDATE  (cr=1100 pr=0 pw=100 time=134959 us)
   100      INDEX UNIQUE SCAN SYS_C0011949 (cr=200 pr=0 pw=0 time=2180 us)

Elapsed times include waiting on following events:
  Event waited on                                   Times    Max. Wait  Total Waited
  -------------------------------------------      Waited    ----------  ------------
  direct path write                                  200        0.00         0.00
```

As you can see, the update of the out-of-line LOB consumed measurably more resources. It spent some amount of time doing direct path writes (physical I/O) and performed many more current mode gets as well as query mode gets. These were in response to the fact that the lobindex and lobsegment had to be maintained in addition to the table itself. The INSERT activity shows the same disparity:

```
INSERT INTO T (ID, IN_ROW) VALUES ( S.NEXTVAL, 'Hello World' )

call      count     cpu    elapsed        disk      query    current       rows
-------  ------  --------  ----------  ----------  ----------  ----------  ----------
Parse        1     0.00      0.00           0          0          0           0
Execute    100     0.03      0.02           0          2        316        100
Fetch        0     0.00      0.00           0          0          0           0
-------  ------  --------  ----------  ----------  ----------  ----------  ----------
total      101     0.03      0.02           0          2        316        100
******************************************************************************
INSERT INTO T (ID,OUT_ROW) VALUES ( S.NEXTVAL, 'Hello World' )

call      count     cpu    elapsed        disk      query    current       rows
-------  ------  --------  ----------  ----------  ----------  ----------  ----------
Parse        1     0.00      0.00           0          0          0           0
Execute    100     0.08      0.13           0        605       1839        100
Fetch        0     0.00      0.00           0          0          0          .0
-------  ------  --------  ----------  ----------  ----------  ----------  ----------
total      101     0.08      0.13           0        605       1839        100

Elapsed times include waiting on following events:
  Event waited on                                   Times    Max. Wait  Total Waited
  -------------------------------------------      Waited    ----------  ------------
  direct path write                                  200        0.00         0.00
```

Note the increased I/O usage, both on the read and writes. All in all, this shows that if you use a CLOB, and many of the strings are expected to fit "in the row" (i.e., will be less than 4,000 bytes), then using the default of ENABLE STORAGE IN ROW is a good idea.

CHUNK Clause

The CREATE TABLE statement returned from DBMS_METADATA previously included the following:

```
LOB ("TXT") STORE AS ( ... CHUNK 8192 ... )
```

LOBs are stored in chunks; the index that points to the LOB data points to individual chunks of data. *Chunks* are logically contiguous sets of blocks and are the smallest unit of allocation for LOBs, whereas normally a block is the smallest unit of allocation. The CHUNK size must be an integer multiple of your Oracle blocksize—this is the only valid value.

You must take care to choose a CHUNK size from two perspectives. First, each LOB instance (each LOB value stored out of line) will consume at least one CHUNK. A single CHUNK is used by a single LOB value. If a table has 100 rows and each row has a LOB with 7KB of data in it, you can be sure that there will be 100 chunks allocated. If you set the CHUNK size to 32KB, you will have 100 32KB chunks allocated. If you set the CHUNK size to 8KB, you will have (probably) 100 8KB chunks allocated. The point is, a chunk is used by only one LOB entry (two LOBs will not use the same CHUNK). If you pick a CHUNK size that does not meet your expected LOB sizes, you could end up wasting an excessive amount of space. For example, if you have that table with 7KB LOBs on average, and you use a CHUNK size of 32k, you will be "wasting" approximately 25k of space per LOB instance. On the other hand, if you use an 8KB CHUNK, you will minimize any sort of waste.

You also need to be careful when you want to minimize the number of CHUNKs you have per LOB instance. As you have seen, there is a lobindex used to point to the individual chunks, and the more chunks you have, the larger this index is. If you have a 4MB LOB and use an 8KB CHUNK, you will need at least 512 CHUNKs to store that information. That means you need at least as many lobindex entries to point to these chunks. That might not sound like a lot, but you have to remember that this is per LOB instance, so if you have thousands of 4MB LOBs, you now have many thousands of entries. This will also affect your retrieval performance, as it takes longer to read and manage many small chunks than it does to read fewer, but larger, chunks. The ultimate goal is to use a CHUNK size that minimizes your "waste," but also efficiently stores your data.

PCTVERSION Clause

The CREATE TABLE statement returned from DBMS_METADATA previously included the following:

```
LOB ("TXT") STORE AS ( ... PCTVERSION 10 ... )
```

This is used to control the read consistency of the LOB. In previous chapters, we've discussed read consistency, multi-versioning, and the role that undo plays in them. Well, when it comes to LOBs, the way read consistency is implemented changes. The lobsegment does not use undo to record its changes; rather, it versions the information directly in the lobsegment itself. The lobindex generates undo just as any other segment would, but the lobsegment does not. Instead, when you modify a LOB, Oracle allocates a new CHUNK and leaves the old CHUNK in place. If you roll back your transaction, the changes to the LOB index are rolled back and the

index will point to the old CHUNK again. So the undo maintenance is performed right in the
LOB segment itself. As you modify the data, the old data is left in place and new data is created.

This is also relevant when reading the LOB data. LOBs are read consistent, just as all other
segments are. If you retrieve a LOB locator at 9:00 am, the LOB data you retrieve from it will be
"as of 9:00 am." Just like if you open a cursor (a resultset) at 9:00 am, the rows it produces will
be as of that point in time. Even if someone else comes along and modifies the LOB data and
commits (or not), your LOB locator will be "as of 9:00 am," just like your resultset would be.
Here, Oracle uses the lobsegment along with the read-consistent view of the lobindex to undo
the changes to the LOB, to present you with the LOB data as it existed when you retrieved the
LOB locator. It does not use the undo information for the lobsegment, since none was generated for the lobsegment itself.

We can easily demonstrate that LOBs are read consistent. Consider this small table with
an out-of-line LOB (it is stored in the lobsegment):

```
ops$tkyte@ORA10G> create table t
  2  ( id int    primary key,
  3    txt       clob
  4  )
  5  lob( txt) store as ( disable storage in row )
  6  /
Table created.

ops$tkyte@ORA10G> insert into t values ( 1, 'hello world' );
1 row created.

ops$tkyte@ORA10G> commit;
Commit complete.
```

If we fetch out the LOB locator and open a cursor on this table as follows:

```
ops$tkyte@ORA10G> declare
  2          l_clob  clob;
  3
  4          cursor c is select id from t;
  5          l_id    number;
  6  begin
  7          select txt into l_clob from t;
  8          open c;
```

and then we modify that row and commit:

```
  9
 10          update t set id = 2, txt = 'Goodbye';
 11          commit;
 12
```

we'll see, upon working with the LOB locator and opened cursor, that the data is presented "as
of the point in time we retrieved or opened them":

```
13              dbms_output.put_line( dbms_lob.substr( l_clob, 100, 1 ) );
14              fetch c into l_id;
15              dbms_output.put_line( 'id = ' || l_id );
16              close c;
17   end;
18   /
hello world
id = 1

PL/SQL procedure successfully completed.
```

But the data is most certainly updated/modified in the database:

```
ops$tkyte@ORA10G> select * from t;

        ID TXT
---------- ----------------
         2 Goodbye
```

The read-consistent images for the cursor C came from the undo segments, whereas the read-consistent images for the LOB came from the LOB segment itself.

So, that gives us a reason to be concerned: if the undo segments are not used to store rollback for LOBs *and* LOBs support read consistency, how can we prevent the dreaded ORA-1555: snapshot too old error from occurring? And, as important, how do we control the amount of space used by these old versions? That is where PCTVERSION comes into play.

PCTVERSION controls the percentage of allocated (used by LOBs at some point and blocks under the lobsegment's HWM) LOB space that should be used for versioning of LOB data. The default of 10 percent is adequate for many uses, since many times you only ever INSERT and retrieve LOBs (updating of LOBs is typically not done; LOBs tend to be inserted once and retrieved many times). Therefore, not much space, if any, needs to be set aside for LOB versioning.

However, if you have an application that does modify the LOBs often, the default of 10 percent may be too small if you frequently read LOBs at the same time some other session is modifying them. If you hit an ORA-22924 error while processing a LOB, the solution is not to increase the size of your undo tablespace, or increase the undo retention, or add more RBS space if you are using manual undo management. Rather, you should use the following:

```
ALTER TABLE tabname MODIFY LOB (lobname) ( PCTVERSION n );
```

and increase the amount of space to be used in that lobsegment for versioning of data.

RETENTION Clause

This is a mutually exclusive alternative to the PCTVERSION clause, and it is valid when you are using automatic undo management in the database. Rather than reserving some percentage of space in the lobsegment to version LOBs, the RETENTION clause uses the same time-based mechanism to retain data. The database would have the parameter UNDO_RETENTION set to specify how long to retain undo information for consistent reads. This parameter would also apply to LOB data in this case.

It should be noted that you cannot specify the retention time using this clause; rather, it is inherited from the database setting of UNDO_RETENTION itself.

CACHE Clause

The CREATE TABLE statement returned from DBMS_METADATA previously included the following:

```
LOB ("TXT") STORE AS (...   NOCACHE ... )
```

The alternative to NOCACHE is CACHE or CACHE READS. This clause controls whether or not the lobsegment data is stored in the buffer cache. The default NOCACHE implies that every access will be a direct read from disk and every write/modification will likewise be a direct read from disk. CACHE READS allows LOB data that is read from disk to be buffered, but writes of LOB data will be done directly to disk. CACHE permits the caching of LOB data during both reads and writes.

In many cases, the default might not be what you want. If you have small- to medium-sized LOBs (e.g., you are using them to store descriptive fields of just a couple of kilobytes), caching them makes perfect sense. If they are not cached, when the user updates the description field, that user must also wait for the I/O to write the data to disk (an I/O the size of a CHUNK will be performed, and the user will wait for this I/O to complete). If you are performing a large load of many LOBs, you will have to wait for the I/O to complete on each row as they are loaded. It makes sense to enable caching on these LOBs. You may turn caching on and off easily to see the effect this may have on you:

```
ALTER TABLE tabname MODIFY LOB (lobname) ( CACHE );
ALTER TABLE tabname MODIFY LOB (lobname) ( NOCACHE );
```

For a large initial load, it would make sense to enable caching of the LOBs and allow DBWR to write the LOB data out to disk in the background while your client application keeps loading more. For small- to medium-sized LOBs that are frequently accessed or modified, caching makes sense so as to not have the end users wait for physical I/O to complete in real time. For a LOB that is 50MB in size, however, it probably does not make sense to have that in the cache.

Bear in mind that you can make excellent use of the Keep or Recycle pool here. Instead of caching the lobsegment data in the default cache with all of the "regular" data, you can use the Keep or Recycle pool to separate it out. In that fashion, you can achieve the goal of caching LOB data without affecting the caching of existing data in your system.

LOB STORAGE Clause

And lastly, the CREATE TABLE statement returned from DBMS_METADATA previously included the following:

```
LOB ("TXT") STORE AS ( ... STORAGE(INITIAL 65536 NEXT 1048576
MINEXTENTS 1 MAXEXTENTS 2147483645 PCTINCREASE 0 FREELISTS 1
FREELIST GROUPS 1 BUFFER_POOL DEFAULT ) ... )
```

That is, it had a full storage clause that you can use to control the physical storage characteristics. It should be noted that this storage clause applies to the lobsegment *and* the lobindex equally—a setting for one is used for the other. Assuming a locally-managed tablespace, the relevant settings for a LOB would be FREELISTS, FREELIST GROUPS, and BUFFER_POOL. We discussed the relevance of FREELISTS and FREELIST GROUPS in Chapter 10 in relation to table segments. The same rules apply to the lobindex segment, as the lobindex is managed as any other index segment would be. If you have highly concurrent modifications of LOBs, multiple FREELISTS on the index segment might be recommended.

As mentioned in the previous section, using the Keep or Recycle pool for LOB segments can be a useful technique to allow you to cache LOB data, without "damaging" your existing default buffer cache. Rather than having the LOBs age out block buffers from normal tables, you can set aside a dedicated piece of memory in the SGA just for these objects. The BUFFER_POOL clause could be used to achieve that.

BFILEs

The last of the LOB types to talk about is the BFILE type. A BFILE type is simply a pointer to a file in the operating system. It is used to provide *read-only* access to these operating system files.

■**Note** The built-in package UTL_FILE provides read and write access to operating system files as well. It does not use the BFILE type, however.

When you use BFILEs, you will also be using an Oracle DIRECTORY object. The DIRECTORY object simply maps an operating system directory to a "string" or a name in the database (providing for portability; you refer to a string in your BFILEs, not an operating system–specific file-naming convention). As a quick example, let's create a table with a BFILE column, create a DIRECTORY object, and insert a row referencing a file in the file system:

```
ops$tkyte@ORA10G> create table t
  2  ( id       int primary key,
  3    os_file  bfile
  4  )
  5  /
Table created.

ops$tkyte@ORA10G> create or replace directory my_dir as '/tmp/'
  2  /
Directory created.

ops$tkyte@ORA10G> insert into t values ( 1, bfilename( 'MY_DIR', 'test.dbf' ) );
1 row created.
```

Now the BFILE can be treated as if it were a LOB—because it is. So, for example, we can do the following:

```
ops$tkyte@ORA10G> select dbms_lob.getlength(os_file) from t;

DBMS_LOB.GETLENGTH(OS_FILE)
---------------------------
                    1056768
```

We can see the file pointed to is 1MB in size. Note that the use of MY_DIR in the INSERT statement was intentional. If we use mixed case or lowercase, we would get the following:

```
ops$tkyte@ORA10G> update t set os_file = bfilename( 'my_dir', 'test.dbf' );
1 row updated.

ops$tkyte@ORA10G> select dbms_lob.getlength(os_file) from t;
select dbms_lob.getlength(os_file) from t
       *
ERROR at line 1:
ORA-22285: non-existent directory or file for GETLENGTH operation
ORA-06512: at "SYS.DBMS_LOB", line 566
```

That example just points out that DIRECTORY objects in Oracle are identifiers, and identifiers are stored in uppercase by default. The BFILENAME built-in function accepts a string, and this string's case must match the case of the DIRECTORY object exactly as stored in the data dictionary. So, we must either use uppercase in the BFILENAME function or use quoted identifiers when creating the DIRECTORY object:

```
ops$tkyte@ORA10G> create or replace directory "my_dir" as '/tmp/'
  2  /

Directory created.

ops$tkyte@ORA10G> select dbms_lob.getlength(os_file) from t;

DBMS_LOB.GETLENGTH(OS_FILE)
---------------------------
                    1056768
```

I recommend against using quoted identifiers; rather, use the uppercase name in the BFILENAME call. Quoted identifiers are not "usual" and tend to create confusion downstream.

A BFILE consumes a varying amount of space on disk depending on the length of the DIRECTORY object name and the file name. In the preceding example, the resulting BFILE was about 35 bytes in length. In general, you'll find the BFILE consumes approximately 20 bytes of overhead *plus* the length of the DIRECTORY object name *plus* the length of the file name itself.

BFILE data is not "read consistent" as other LOB data is. Since the BFILE is managed outside of the database, whatever happens to be in the file when you dereference the BFILE is what you will get. So, repeated reads from the same BFILE may produce different results—unlike a LOB locator used against a CLOB, BLOB, or NCLOB.

ROWID/UROWID Types

The last datatypes to discuss are the ROWID and UROWID types. A ROWID is the address of a row in a database. Sufficient information is encoded in the ROWID to locate the row on disk, as well as identify the object the ROWID points to (the table and so on). ROWID's close relative, UROWID, is a universal ROWID and is used for tables, such as IOTs, and tables accessed via gateways to heterogeneous databases that do not have fixed ROWIDs. The UROWID is a representation of the primary key value of the row and, hence, will vary in size depending on the object it points to.

Every row in every table has either a ROWID or a UROWID associated with it. They are considered *pseudo columns* when retrieved from a table, meaning they are not actually stored with the row, but rather are a derived attribute of the row. A ROWID is generated based on the physical location of the row; it is not stored with it. A UROWID is generated based on the row's primary key, so in a sense it is stored with the row, but not really, as the UROWID does not exist as a discrete column, but rather as a function of the existing columns.

It used to be that for rows with ROWIDs (the most common "type" of rows in Oracle; with the exception of rows in IOTs, all rows have ROWIDs), the ROWIDs were immutable. When a row was inserted, it would be associated with a ROWID, an address, and that ROWID would be associated with that row until it was deleted—until it was physically removed from the database. Over time, this is becoming less true, as there are now operations that may cause a row's ROWID to change, for example:

- Updating the partition key of a row in a partitioned table such that the row must move from one partition to another

- Using the FLASHBACK table command to restore a database table to a prior point in time

- Performing MOVE operations and many partition operations such as splitting or merge partitions

- Using the ALTER TABLE SHRINK SPACE command to perform a segment shrink

Now, since ROWIDs can change over time (since they are no longer immutable), it is not recommended to physically store them as columns in database tables. That is, using a ROWID as a datatype of a database column is considered a bad practice and should be avoided. The primary key of the row (which should be immutable) should be used instead, and referential integrity can be in place to ensure data integrity is preserved. You cannot do this with the ROWID types—you cannot create a foreign key from a child table to a parent table by ROWID, and you cannot enforce integrity across tables like that. You must use the primary key constraint.

Of what use is the ROWID type, then? It is still useful in applications that allow the end user to interact with the data—the ROWID, being a physical address of a row, is the fastest way to access a single row in any table. An application that reads data out of the database and presents it to the end user can use the ROWID upon attempting to update that row. The application must use the ROWID in combination with other fields or checksums (refer to Chapter 7 for further information on application locking). In this fashion, you can update the row in question with the least amount of work (e.g., no index lookup to find the row again) and ensure the row is the same row you read out in the first place by verifying the column values have not changed. So, a ROWID is useful in applications that employ optimistic locking.

Summary

In this chapter, we examined the 22 basic datatypes provided by Oracle and saw how they are physically stored and what options are available with each. We started with character strings, the most basic of types, and looked into considerations surrounding multibyte characters and raw binary data. Next, we studied the numeric types, including the very precise Oracle NUMBER type and the new floating-point types provided with Oracle 10g and later.

We also gave consideration to the legacy LONG and LONG RAW types, concentrating on how we might work around their existence, as the functionality provided by these types falls far short of that provided by the LOB types. Next, we looked at the datatypes capable of storing dates and times. We covered the basics of date arithmetic, a perplexing issue until you've seen it demonstrated. Lastly, in the section on DATEs and TIMESTAMPs, we looked at the INTERVAL type and how best to use it.

The most detailed part of the chapter from a physical storage perspective was the LOB section. The LOB type is frequently misunderstood by developers and DBAs alike, so the bulk of the section was spent looking at how they are physically implemented as well as certain performance considerations.

The last datatype we looked at was the ROWID/UROWID type. For what now should be obvious reasons, you should not use this datatype as a database column, since ROWIDs are not immutable and no integrity constraints could enforce the parent/child relationship. Rather, you want to store primary keys if you need to "point" to another row.

Partitioning

Partitioning, first introduced in Oracle 8.0, is the process of physically breaking a table or index into many smaller, more manageable pieces. As far as the application accessing the database is concerned, there is logically only one table or one index, but physically that table or index may comprise many dozens of physical partitions. Each partition is an independent object that may be manipulated either by itself or as part of the larger object.

■Note Partitioning is an extra cost option to the Enterprise Edition of the Oracle database. It is not available in the Standard Edition.

In this chapter, we will investigate why you might consider using partitioning. The reasons range from increased availability of data to reduced administrative (DBA) burdens and, in certain situations, increased performance. Once you have a good understanding of the reasons for using partitioning, we'll look at how you may partition tables and their corresponding indexes. The goal of this discussion is not to teach you the details of administering partitions, but rather to present a practical guide to implementing your applications with partitions.

We will also discuss the important fact that partitioning of tables and indexes is not a guaranteed "fast = true" setting for the database. It has been my experience that many developers and DBAs believe that increased performance is an automatic side effect of partitioning an object. Partitioning is just a tool, and one of three things will happen when you partition an index or table: the application using these partitioned tables might run slower, might run faster, or might be not be affected one way or the other. I put forth that if you just apply partitioning without understanding how it works and how your application can make use of it, then the odds are you will negatively impact performance by just turning it on.

Lastly, we'll investigate a very common use of partitions in today's world: supporting a large online audit trail in an OLTP and other operational systems. We'll discuss how to incorporate partitioning and segment space compression to efficiently store online a large audit trail and provide the ability to archive old records out of this audit trail with minimal work.

Partitioning Overview

Partitioning facilitates the management of very large tables and indexes using "divide and conquer" logic. Partitioning introduces the concept of a *partition key* that is used to segregate data based on a certain range value, a list of specific values, or the value of a hash function. If I were to put the benefits of partitioning in some sort of order, it would be

1. *Increases availability of data*: This attribute is applicable to all system types, be they OLTP or warehouse systems by nature.

2. *Eases administration of large segments by removing them from the database*: Performing administrative operations on a 100GB table, such as a reorganization to remove migrated rows or to reclaim "whitespace" left in the table after a purge of old information, would be much more onerous than performing the same operation ten times on individual 10GB table partitions. Additionally, using partitions, we might be able to conduct a purge routine without leaving whitespace behind at all, removing the need for a reorganization entirely!

3. *Improves the performance of certain queries*: This is mainly beneficial in a large warehouse environment where we can use partitioning to eliminate large ranges of data from consideration, avoiding accessing this data at all. This will not be as applicable in a transactional system, since we are accessing small volumes of data in that system already.

4. *May reduce contention on high-volume OLTP systems by spreading out modifications across many separate partitions*: If you have a segment experiencing high contention, turning it into many segments could have the side effect of reducing that contention proportionally.

Let's take a look at each of these potential benefits of using partitioning.

Increased Availability

Increased availability derives from the independence of each partition. The availability (or lack thereof) of a single partition in an object does not mean the object itself is unavailable. The optimizer is aware of the partitioning scheme that is in place and will remove unreferenced partitions from the query plan accordingly. If a single partition is unavailable in a large object, and your query can eliminate this partition from consideration, then Oracle will successfully process the query.

To demonstrate this increased availability, we'll set up a hash partitioned table with two partitions, each in a separate tablespace. We'll create an EMP table that specifies a partition key on the EMPNO column; EMPNO will be our partition key. In this case, this structure means that for each row inserted into this table, the value of the EMPNO column is hashed to determine the partition (and hence the tablespace) into which the row will be placed:

```
ops$tkyte@ORA10G> CREATE TABLE emp
  2  ( empno    int,
  3    ename    varchar2(20)
  4  )
  5  PARTITION BY HASH (empno)
```

```
 6  ( partition part_1 tablespace p1,
 7    partition part_2 tablespace p2
 8  )
 9  /
Table created.
```

Next, we insert some data into the EMP table and then, using the partition-extended table name, inspect the contents of each partition:

```
ops$tkyte@ORA10G> insert into emp select empno, ename from scott.emp
  2  /
14 rows created.

ops$tkyte@ORA10G> select * from emp partition(part_1);

     EMPNO ENAME
---------- --------------------
      7369 SMITH
      7499 ALLEN
      7654 MARTIN
      7698 BLAKE
      7782 CLARK
      7839 KING
      7876 ADAMS
      7934 MILLER
8 rows selected.

ops$tkyte@ORA10G> select * from emp partition(part_2);

     EMPNO ENAME
---------- --------------------
      7521 WARD
      7566 JONES
      7788 SCOTT
      7844 TURNER
      7900 JAMES
      7902 FORD
6 rows selected.
```

You should note that the data is somewhat randomly assigned. That is by design here. Using hash partitioning, we are asking Oracle to randomly—but hopefully evenly—distribute our data across many partitions. We cannot control the partition into which data goes; Oracle decides that based on the hash key values that it generates. Later, when we look at range and list partitioning, we'll see how we can control what partitions receive which data.

Now, we take one of the tablespaces offline (simulating, for example, a disk failure), thus making the data unavailable in that partition:

```
ops$tkyte@ORA10G> alter tablespace p1 offline;
Tablespace altered.
```

Next, we run a query that hits every partition, and we see that this query fails:

```
ops$tkyte@ORA10G> select * from emp;
select * from emp
              *
ERROR at line 1:
ORA-00376: file 12 cannot be read at this time
ORA-01110: data file 12:
'/home/ora10g/oradata/ora10g/ORA10G/datafile/p1.dbf'
```

However, a query that does not access the offline tablespace will function as normal; Oracle will eliminate the offline partition from consideration. I use a bind variable in this particular example just to demonstrate that even though Oracle does not know at query optimization time which partition will be accessed, it is nonetheless able to perform this elimination at runtime:

```
ops$tkyte@ORA10G> variable n number
ops$tkyte@ORA10G> exec :n := 7844;
PL/SQL procedure successfully completed.

ops$tkyte@ORA10G> select * from emp where empno = :n;

    EMPNO ENAME
---------- --------------------
     7844 TURNER
```

In summary, when the optimizer can eliminate partitions from the plan, it will. This fact increases availability for those applications that use the partition key in their queries.

Partitions also increase availability by reducing downtime. If you have a 100GB table, for example, and it is partitioned into 50 2GB partitions, then you can recover from errors that much faster. If one of the 2GB partitions is damaged, the time to recover is now the time it takes to restore and recover a 2GB partition, not a 100GB table. So availability is increased in two ways:

- Partition elimination by the optimizer means that many users may never even notice that some of the data was unavailable.

- Downtime is reduced in the event of an error because of the significantly reduced amount of work that is required to recover.

Reduced Administrative Burden

The administrative burden relief is derived from the fact that performing operations on small objects is inherently easier, faster, and less resource intensive than performing the same operation on a large object.

For example, say you have a 10GB index in your database. If you need to rebuild this index and it is not partitioned, then you will have to rebuild the entire 10GB index as a single unit of work. While it is true that you could rebuild the index online, it requires a huge number of resources to completely rebuild an entire 10GB index. You'll need at least 10GB of free storage elsewhere to hold a copy of both indexes, you'll need a temporary transaction log table to record the changes made against the base table during the time you spend rebuilding the index, and so on. On the other hand, if the index itself had been partitioned into ten 1GB partitions, then you could rebuild each index partition individually, one by one. Now you need 10 percent of the free space you needed previously. Likewise, the individual index rebuilds will each be much faster (ten times faster, perhaps), so far fewer transactional changes occurring during an online index rebuild need to be merged into the new index, and so on.

Also, consider what happens in the event of a system or software failure just before completing the rebuilding of a 10GB index. The entire effort is lost. By breaking the problem down and partitioning the index into 1GB partitions, at most you would lose 10 percent of the total work required to rebuild the index.

Alternatively, it may be that you need to rebuild only 10 percent of the total aggregate index—for example, only the "newest" data (the active data) is subject to this reorganization, and all of the "older" data (which is relatively static) remains unaffected.

Finally, consider the situation whereby you discover 50 percent of the rows in your table are "migrated" rows (see Chapter 10 for details on chained/migrated rows), and you would like to fix this. Having a partitioned table will facilitate the operation. To "fix" migrated rows, you must typically rebuild the object—in this case, a table. If you have one 100GB table, you will need to perform this operation in one very large "chunk," serially, using ALTER TABLE MOVE. On the other hand, if you have 25 partitions, each 4GB in size, then you can rebuild each partition one by one. Alternatively, if you are doing this during off-hours and have ample resources, you can even do the ALTER TABLE MOVE statements in parallel, in separate sessions, potentially reducing the amount of time the whole operation will take. Virtually everything you can do to a nonpartitioned object, you can do to an individual partition of a partitioned object. You might even discover that your migrated rows are concentrated in a very small subset of your partitions, hence you could rebuild one or two partitions instead of the entire table.

Here is a quick example demonstrating the rebuild of a table with many migrated rows. Both BIG_TABLE1 and BIG_TABLE2 were created from a 10,000,000-row instance of BIG_TABLE (see the "Setup" section for the BIG_TABLE creation script). BIG_TABLE1 is a regular, nonpartitioned table, whereas BIG_TABLE2 is a hash partitioned table in eight partitions (we'll cover hash partitioning in a subsequent section; suffice it to say, it distributed the data rather evenly into eight partitions):

```
ops$tkyte@ORA10GR1> create table big_table1
  2  ( ID, OWNER, OBJECT_NAME, SUBOBJECT_NAME,
  3    OBJECT_ID, DATA_OBJECT_ID,
  4    OBJECT_TYPE, CREATED, LAST_DDL_TIME,
  5    TIMESTAMP, STATUS, TEMPORARY,
  6    GENERATED, SECONDARY )
  7  tablespace big1
  8  as
  9  select ID, OWNER, OBJECT_NAME, SUBOBJECT_NAME,
 10         OBJECT_ID, DATA_OBJECT_ID,
 11         OBJECT_TYPE, CREATED, LAST_DDL_TIME,
 12         TIMESTAMP, STATUS, TEMPORARY,
 13         GENERATED, SECONDARY
 14    from big_table.big_table;
Table created.
```

```
ops$tkyte@ORA10GR1> create table big_table2
  2  ( ID, OWNER, OBJECT_NAME, SUBOBJECT_NAME,
  3    OBJECT_ID, DATA_OBJECT_ID,
  4    OBJECT_TYPE, CREATED, LAST_DDL_TIME,
  5    TIMESTAMP, STATUS, TEMPORARY,
  6    GENERATED, SECONDARY )
  7  partition by hash(id)
  8  (partition part_1 tablespace big2,
  9   partition part_2 tablespace big2,
 10   partition part_3 tablespace big2,
 11   partition part_4 tablespace big2,
 12   partition part_5 tablespace big2,
 13   partition part_6 tablespace big2,
 14   partition part_7 tablespace big2,
 15   partition part_8 tablespace big2
 16  )
 17  as
 18  select ID, OWNER, OBJECT_NAME, SUBOBJECT_NAME,
 19         OBJECT_ID, DATA_OBJECT_ID,
 20         OBJECT_TYPE, CREATED, LAST_DDL_TIME,
 21         TIMESTAMP, STATUS, TEMPORARY,
 22         GENERATED, SECONDARY
 23    from big_table.big_table;
Table created.
```

Now, each of those tables is in its own tablespace, so we can easily query the data dictionary to see the allocated and free space in each tablespace:

```
ops$tkyte@ORA10GR1> select b.tablespace_name,
  2         mbytes_alloc,
  3         mbytes_free
  4    from ( select round(sum(bytes)/1024/1024) mbytes_free,
  5                  tablespace_name
  6             from dba_free_space
  7            group by tablespace_name ) a,
  8         ( select round(sum(bytes)/1024/1024) mbytes_alloc,
  9                  tablespace_name
 10             from dba_data_files
 11            group by tablespace_name ) b
 12   where a.tablespace_name (+) = b.tablespace_name
 13     and b.tablespace_name in ('BIG1','BIG2')
 14  /

TABLESPACE MBYTES_ALLOC MBYTES_FREE
---------- ------------ -----------
BIG1               1496         344
BIG2               1496         344
```

BIG1 and BIG2 are both about 1.5GB in size and each have 344MB free. We'll try to rebuild the first table, BIG_TABLE1:

```
ops$tkyte@ORA10GR1> alter table big_table1 move;
alter table big_table1 move
            *
ERROR at line 1:
ORA-01652: unable to extend temp segment by 1024 in tablespace BIG1
```

That fails—we needed sufficient free space in tablespace BIG1 to hold an entire copy of BIG_TABLE1 at the same time as the old copy was there—in short, we would need about two times the storage for a short period (maybe more, maybe less—it depends on the resulting size of the rebuilt table). We now attempt the same operation on BIG_TABLE2:

```
ops$tkyte@ORA10GR1> alter table big_table2 move;
alter table big_table2 move
            *
ERROR at line 1:
ORA-14511: cannot perform operation on a partitioned object
```

That is Oracle telling us we cannot do the MOVE operation on the "table"; we must perform the operation on each partition of the table instead. We can move (hence rebuild and reorganize) each partition one by one:

```
ops$tkyte@ORA10GR1> alter table big_table2 move partition part_1;
Table altered.
ops$tkyte@ORA10GR1> alter table big_table2 move partition part_2;
Table altered.
ops$tkyte@ORA10GR1> alter table big_table2 move partition part_3;
Table altered.
ops$tkyte@ORA10GR1> alter table big_table2 move partition part_4;
Table altered.
ops$tkyte@ORA10GR1> alter table big_table2 move partition part_5;
Table altered.
ops$tkyte@ORA10GR1> alter table big_table2 move partition part_6;
Table altered.
ops$tkyte@ORA10GR1> alter table big_table2 move partition part_7;
Table altered.
ops$tkyte@ORA10GR1> alter table big_table2 move partition part_8;
Table altered.
```

Each individual move only needed sufficient free space to hold a copy of one-eighth of the data! Therefore, these commands succeeded given the same amount of free space as we had before. We needed significantly less temporary resources and, further, if the system failed (e.g., due to a power outage) after we moved PART_4 but before PART_5 finished "moving," we would not have lost all of the work performed as we would have with a single MOVE statement. The first four partitions would still be "moved" when the system recovered, and we may resume processing at partition PART_5.

Some may look at that and say, "Wow, eight statements—that is a lot of typing," and it's true that this sort of thing would be unreasonable if you had hundreds of partitions (or more). Fortunately, it is very easy to script a solution, and the previous would become simply

```
ops$tkyte@ORA10GR1> begin
  2      for x in ( select partition_name
  3                   from user_tab_partitions
  4                  where table_name = 'BIG_TABLE2' )
  5      loop
  6          execute immediate
  7          'alter table big_table2 move partition ' ||
  8           x.partition_name;
  9      end loop;
 10  end;
 11  /
PL/SQL procedure successfully completed.
```

All of the information you need is there in the Oracle data dictionary, and most sites that have implemented partitioning also have a series of stored procedures they use to make managing large numbers of partitions easy. Additionally, many GUI tools such as Enterprise Manager have the built-in capability to perform these operations as well, without your needing to type in the individual commands.

Another factor to consider with regard to partitions and administration is the use of "sliding windows" of data in data warehousing and archiving. In many cases, you need to keep data online that spans the last N units of time. For example, say you need to keep the last 12 months or the last 5 years online. Without partitions, this is generally a massive INSERT followed by a massive DELETE. Lots of DML, and lots of redo and undo generated. Now with partitions, you can simply do the following:

1. Load a separate table with the new months' (or years', or whatever) data.

2. Index the table fully. (These steps could even be done in another instance and transported to this database.)

3. Attach this newly loaded and indexed table onto the *end* of the partitioned table using a fast DDL command: ALTER TABLE EXCHANGE PARTITION.

4. Detach the oldest partition off the other end of the partitioned table.

So, you can now very easily support extremely large objects containing time-sensitive information. The old data can easily be removed from the partitioned table and simply *dropped* if you do not need it, or it can be archived off elsewhere. New data can be loaded into a separate table, so as to not affect the partitioned table until the loading, indexing, and so on is complete. We will take a look at a complete example of a sliding window later in this chapter.

In short, partitioning can make what would otherwise be daunting, or in some cases unfeasible, operations as easy as they are in a small database.

Enhanced Statement Performance

The last general (potential) benefit of partitioning is in the area of enhanced statement (SELECT, INSERT, UPDATE, DELETE, MERGE) performance. We'll take a look at two classes of statements—those that modify information and those that just read information—and discuss what benefits we might expect from partitioning in each case.

Parallel DML

Statements that modify data in the database may have the potential to perform *parallel DML* (*PDML*). During PDML, Oracle uses many threads or processes to perform your INSERT, UPDATE, or DELETE instead of a single serial process. On a multi-CPU machine with plenty of I/O bandwidth, the potential increase in speed may be large for mass DML operations. In releases of Oracle prior to 9*i*, PDML required partitioning. If your tables were not partitioned, you could not perform these operations in parallel in the earlier releases. If the tables were partitioned, Oracle would assign a *maximum* degree of parallelism to the object, based on the number of physical partitions it had. This restriction was, for the most part, relaxed in Oracle9*i* and later with two notable exceptions. If the table you wish to perform PDML on has a bitmap index in place of a LOB column, then the table must be partitioned in order to have the operation take place in parallel, and the degree of parallelism will be restricted to the number of partitions. In general, though, you no longer need to partition to use PDML.

■**Note** We will cover parallel operations in more detail in Chapter 14.

Query Performance

In the area of strictly read query performance (SELECT statements), partitioning comes into play with two types of specialized operations:

- *Partition elimination*: Some partitions of data are not considered in the processing of the query. We have already seen an example of partition elimination.

- *Parallel operations*: Examples of this are parallel full table scans and parallel index range scans.

However, the benefit you can derive from these depends very much on the type of system you are using.

OLTP Systems

You should not look toward partitions as a way to massively improve query performance in an OLTP system. In fact, in a traditional OLTP system, you must apply partitioning with care so as to not *negatively* affect runtime performance. In a traditional OLTP system, most queries are expected to return virtually instantaneously, and most of the retrievals from the database are expected to be via very small index range scans. Therefore, the main performance benefits of partitioning listed previously would not come into play. Partition elimination is useful where you have full scans of large objects, because it allows you to avoid full scanning large pieces of an object. However, in an OLTP environment, *you are not full scanning* large objects (if you are, you have a serious design flaw). Even if you partition your indexes, any increase in performance achieved by scanning a smaller index will be miniscule—if you actually achieve an increase in speed at all. If some of your queries use an index *and* they cannot eliminate all but one partition from consideration, you may find your queries actually run slower after partitioning since you now have 5, 10, or 20 small indexes to probe, instead of one larger index. We will investigate this in much more detail shortly when we look at the types of partitioned indexes available to us.

Having said all this, there are opportunities to gain efficiency in an OLTP system with partitions. For example, they may be used to increase concurrency by decreasing contention. They can be used to spread out the modifications of a single table over many physical partitions. Instead of having a single table segment with a single index segment, you might have 20 table partitions and 20 index partitions. It could be like having 20 tables instead of 1, hence contention would be decreased for this shared resource during modifications.

As for parallel operations, as we'll investigate in more detail in the next chapter, you do not want to do a parallel query in an OLTP system. You would reserve your use of parallel operations for the DBA to perform rebuilds, create indexes, gather statistics, and so on. The fact is that in an OLTP system, your queries should already be characterized by very fast index accesses, and partitioning will not speed that up very much, if at all. This does not mean that you should avoid partitioning for OLTP; it means that you shouldn't expect partitioning to offer massive improvements in performance. Most OLTP applications are not able to take advantage of the times where partitioning is able to enhance query performance, but you can still benefit from the other two possible partitioning benefits; administrative ease and higher availability.

Data Warehouse Systems

In a data warehouse/decision-support system, partitioning is not only a great administrative tool, but also something that will speed up processing. For example, you may have a large table on which you need to perform an ad hoc query. You always do the ad hoc query by sales quarter, as each sales quarter contains hundreds of thousands of records and you have millions of online records. So, you want to query a relatively small slice of the entire data set, but it is not really feasible to index it based on the sales quarter. This index would point to hundreds of thousands of records, and doing the index range scan in this way would be terrible (refer to Chapter 11 for more details on this). A full table scan is called for to process many of your queries, but you end up having to scan millions of records, most of which won't apply to our query. Using an intelligent partitioning scheme, you can segregate the data by quarter such that when you query the data for any given quarter, you will full scan only that quarter's data. This is the best of all possible solutions.

In addition, in a data warehouse/decision-support system environment, parallel query is used frequently. Here, operations such as parallel index range scans or parallel fast full index scans are not only meaningful, but also beneficial to us. We want to maximize our use of all available resources, and parallel query is a way to do it. So, in this environment, partitioning stands a very good chance of speeding up processing.

Table Partitioning Schemes

There are currently four methods by which you can partition tables in Oracle:

- *Range partitioning*: You may specify ranges of data that should be stored together. For example, everything that has a timestamp within the month of Jan-2005 will be stored in partition 1, everything with a timestamp within Feb-2005 will be stored in partition 2, and so on. This is probably the most commonly used partitioning mechanism in Oracle.

- *Hash partitioning*: You saw this in the first example in this chapter. A column (or columns) has a hash function applied to it, and the row will be placed into a partition according to the value of this hash.

- *List partitioning*: You specify a discrete set of values, which determines the data that should be stored together. For example, you could specify that rows with a STATUS column value in ('A', 'M', 'Z') go into partition 1, those with a STATUS value in ('D', 'P', 'Q') go into partition 2, and so on.

- *Composite partitioning*: This is a combination of range and hash or range and list. It allows you to first apply range partitioning to some data, and then within that range have the final partition be chosen by hash or list.

In the following sections, we'll look at the benefits of each type of partitioning and at the differences between them. We'll also look at when to apply which schemes to different application types. This section is not intended to present a comprehensive demonstration of the syntax of partitioning and all of the available options. Rather, the examples are simple and illustrative, and designed to give you an overview of how partitioning works and how the different types of partitioning are designed to function.

■**Note** For full details on partitioning syntax, I refer you to either the *Oracle SQL Reference Guide* or to the *Oracle Administrator's Guide*. Additionally, the *Oracle Data Warehousing Guide* is an excellent source of information on the partitioning options and is a must-read for anyone planning to implement partitioning.

Range Partitioning

The first type we will look at is a range partitioned table. The following CREATE TABLE statement creates a range partitioned table using the column RANGE_KEY_COLUMN. All data with a RANGE_KEY_COLUMN *strictly less than* 01-JAN-2005 will be placed into the partition PART_1, and all data with a value *strictly less than* 01-JAN-2006 will go into partition PART_2. Any data not satisfying either of those conditions (e.g., a row with a RANGE_KEY_COLUMN value of 01-JAN-2007) will fail upon insertion, as it cannot be mapped to a partition:

```
ops$tkyte@ORA10GR1> CREATE TABLE range_example
  2  ( range_key_column date ,
  3    data             varchar2(20)
  4  )
  5  PARTITION BY RANGE (range_key_column)
```

```
 6  ( PARTITION part_1 VALUES LESS THAN
 7        (to_date('01/01/2005','dd/mm/yyyy')),
 8    PARTITION part_2 VALUES LESS THAN
 9        (to_date('01/01/2006','dd/mm/yyyy'))
10  )
11  /
Table created.
```

■Note We are using the date format DD/MM/YYYY in the CREATE TABLE to make this "international." If we used a format of DD-MON-YYYY, then the CREATE TABLE would fail with ORA-01843: not a valid month if the abbreviation of January was not Jan on your system. The NLS_LANGUAGE setting would affect this. I have used the three-character month abbreviation in the text and inserts, however, to avoid any ambiguity as to which component is the day and which is the month.

Figure 13-1 shows that Oracle will inspect the value of the RANGE_KEY_COLUMN and, based on that value, insert it into one of the two partitions.

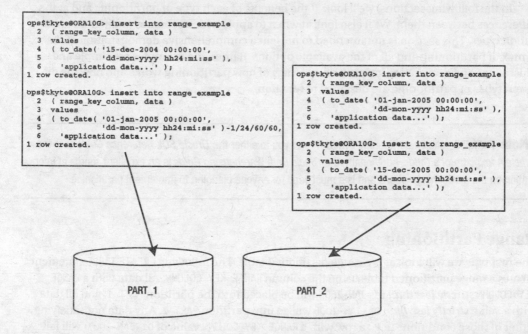

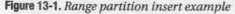

Figure 13-1. *Range partition insert example*

The rows inserted were specifically chosen with the goal of demonstrating that the partition range is strictly *less than* and not *less than or equal to*. We first insert the value 15-DEC-2004, which will definitely go into partition PART_1. We also insert a row with a date/time that is one second before 01-JAN-2005—that row will also will go into partition PART_1 since that is *less than* 01-JAN-2005. However, the next insert of midnight on 01-JAN-2005 goes into partition PART_2 because that date/time is not strictly less than the partition range boundary. The last row obviously belongs in partition PART_2 since it is less than the partition range boundary for PART_2.

We can confirm that this is the case by performing SELECT statements from the individual partitions:

```
ops$tkyte@ORA10G> select to_char(range_key_column,'dd-mon-yyyy hh24:mi:ss')
  2     from range_example partition (part_1);

TO_CHAR(RANGE_KEY_CO
--------------------
15-dec-2004 00:00:00
31-dec-2004 23:59:59

ops$tkyte@ORA10G> select to_char(range_key_column,'dd-mon-yyyy hh24:mi:ss')
  2     from range_example partition (part_2);

TO_CHAR(RANGE_KEY_CO
--------------------
01-jan-2005 00:00:00
15-dec-2005 00:00:00
```

You might be wondering what would happen if you inserted a date that fell outside of the upper bound. The answer is that Oracle will raise an error:

```
ops$tkyte@ORA10GR1> insert into range_example
  2  ( range_key_column, data )
  3  values
  4  ( to_date( '15/12/2007 00:00:00',
  5             'dd/mm/yyyy hh24:mi:ss' ),
  6    'application data...' );
insert into range_example
            *
ERROR at line 1:
ORA-14400: inserted partition key does not map to any partition
```

Suppose you want to segregate 2005 and 2006 dates into their separate partitions as we have, but you want all other dates to go into a third partition. With range partitioning, you can do this using the MAXVALUE clause, which looks like this:

```
ops$tkyte@ORA10GR1> CREATE TABLE range_example
  2  ( range_key_column date ,
  3    data            varchar2(20)
  4  )
  5  PARTITION BY RANGE (range_key_column)
  6  ( PARTITION part_1 VALUES LESS THAN
  7       (to_date('01/01/2005','dd/mm/yyyy')),
  8    PARTITION part_2 VALUES LESS THAN
```

```
 9          (to_date('01/01/2006','dd/mm/yyyy'))
10    PARTITION part_3 VALUES LESS THAN
11         (MAXVALUE)
12  )
13  /

Table created.
```

Now when you insert a row into that table, it will go into one of the three partitions—no row will be rejected, since partition PART_3 can take any value of RANGE_KEY_COLUMN that doesn't go into PART_1 or PART_2 (even null values of the RANGE_KEY_COLUMN will be inserted into this new partition).

Hash Partitioning

When *hash* partitioning a table, Oracle will apply a hash function to the partition key to determine in which of the N partitions the data should be placed. Oracle recommends that N be a number that is a power of 2 (2, 4, 8, 16, and so on) to achieve the best overall distribution, and we'll see shortly that this is absolutely good advice.

How Hash Partitioning Works

Hash partitioning is designed to achieve a good spread of data across many different devices (disks), or just to segregate data out into more manageable chunks. The hash key chosen for a table should be a column or set of columns that are unique, or at least have as many distinct values as possible to provide for a good spread of the rows across partitions. If you choose a column that has only four values, and you use two partitions, then all the rows could quite easily end up hashing *to the same partition*, obviating the goal of partitioning in the first place!

We will create a hash table with two partitions in this case. We will use a column named HASH_KEY_COLUMN as our partition key. Oracle will take the value in this column and determine the partition this row will be stored in by hashing that value:

```
ops$tkyte@ORA10G> CREATE TABLE hash_example
  2  ( hash_key_column   date,
  3    data              varchar2(20)
  4  )
  5  PARTITION BY HASH (hash_key_column)
  6  ( partition part_1 tablespace p1,
  7    partition part_2 tablespace p2
  8  )
  9  /
Table created.
```

Figure 13-2 shows that Oracle will inspect the value in the HASH_KEY_COLUMN, hash it, and determine which of the two partitions a given row will appear in:

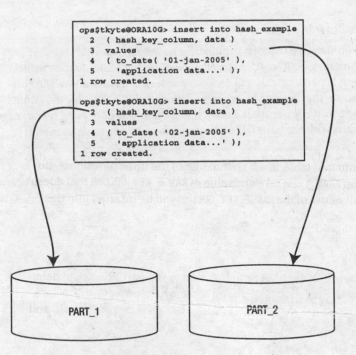

```
ops$tkyte@ORA10G> insert into hash_example
  2  ( hash_key_column, data )
  3  values
  4  ( to_date( '01-jan-2005' ),
  5    'application data...' );
1 row created.

ops$tkyte@ORA10G> insert into hash_example
  2  ( hash_key_column, data )
  3  values
  4  ( to_date( '02-jan-2005' ),
  5    'application data...' );
1 row created.
```

Figure 13-2. *Hash partition insert example*

As noted earlier, hash partitioning gives you no control over which partition a row ends up in. Oracle applies the hash function and the outcome of that hash determines where the row goes. If you want a specific row to go into partition PART_1 for whatever reason, you should *not*—in fact, you *cannot*—use hash partitioning. The row will go into whatever partition the hash function says to put it in. If you change the number of hash partitions, the data will be redistributed over all of the partitions (adding or removing a partition to a hash partitioned table will cause all of the data to be rewritten, as every row may now belong in a different partition).

Hash partitioning is most useful when you have a large table, such as the one shown in the "Reduced Administrative Burden" section, and you would like to "divide and conquer" it. Rather than manage one large table, you would like to have 8 or 16 smaller "tables" to manage. Hash partitioning is also useful to increase availability to some degree, as demonstrated in the "Increased Availability" section; the temporary loss of a single hash partition permits access to all of the remaining partitions. Some users may be affected, but there is a good chance that many will not be. Additionally, the unit of recovery is much smaller now. You do not have a single large table to restore and recover; you have a fraction of that table to recover. Lastly, hash partitioning is useful in high update contention environments, as mentioned in the "Enhanced Statement Performance" section when we talked about OLTP systems. Instead of having a single "hot" segment, we can hash partition a segment into 16 pieces, each of which is now receiving modifications.

Hash Partition Using Powers of Two

I mentioned earlier that the number of partitions should be a power of two. This is easily observed to be true. To demonstrate, we'll set up a stored procedure to automate the creation of a hash partitioned table with N partitions (N will be a parameter). This procedure will construct a dynamic query to retrieve the counts of rows by partition and then display the counts and a simple histogram of the counts by partition. Lastly, it will open this query and let us see the results. This procedure starts with the hash table creation. We will use a table named T:

```
ops$tkyte@ORA10G> create or replace
  2  procedure hash_proc
  3          ( p_nhash in number,
  4            p_cursor out sys_refcursor )
  5  authid current_user
  6  as
  7      l_text     long;
  8      l_template long :=
  9          'select $POS$ oc, ''p$POS$'' pname, count(*) cnt ' ||
 10          'from t partition ( $PNAME$ ) union all ';
 11  begin
 12      begin
 13          execute immediate 'drop table t';
 14      exception when others
 15          then null;
 16      end;
 17
 18      execute immediate '
 19      CREATE TABLE t ( id )
 20      partition by hash(id)
 21      partitions ' || p_nhash || '
 22      as
 23      select rownum
 24        from all_objects';
```

Next, we will dynamically construct a query to retrieve the count of rows by partition. It does this using the "template" query defined earlier. For each partition, we'll gather the count using the partition-extended table name and union all of the counts together:

```
 25
 26      for x in ( select partition_name pname,
 27                        PARTITION_POSITION pos
 28                   from user_tab_partitions
 29                  where table_name = 'T'
 30                  order by partition_position )
 31      loop
 32          l_text := l_text ||
 33                  replace(
 34                  replace(l_template,
```

```
35                              '$POS$', x.pos),
36                              '$PNAME$', x.pname );
37        end loop;
```

Now, we'll take that query and select out the partition position (PNAME) and the count of rows in that partition (CNT). Using RPAD, we'll construct a rather rudimentary but effective histogram:

```
38
39        open p_cursor for
40          'select pname, cnt,
41            substr( rpad(''*'',30*round( cnt/max(cnt)over(),2),''*''),1,30) hg
42            from (' || substr( l_text, 1, length(l_text)-11 ) || ')
43          order by oc';
44
45    end;
46  /
Procedure created.
```

If we run this with an input of 4, for four hash partitions, we would expect to see output similar to the following:

```
ops$tkyte@ORA10G> variable x refcursor
ops$tkyte@ORA10G> set autoprint on
ops$tkyte@ORA10G> exec hash_proc( 4, :x );
PL/SQL procedure successfully completed.

PN      CNT HG
-- ---------- ------------------------------
p1    12141 ******************************
p2    12178 ******************************
p3    12417 ******************************
p4    12105 ******************************
```

The simple histogram depicted shows a nice, even distribution of data over each of the four partitions. Each has close to the same number of rows in it. However, if we simply go from four to five hash partitions, we'll see the following:

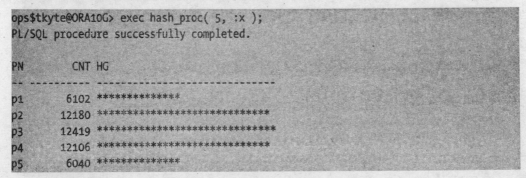

```
ops$tkyte@ORA10G> exec hash_proc( 5, :x );
PL/SQL procedure successfully completed.

PN      CNT HG
-- ---------- ------------------------------
p1     6102 ***************
p2    12180 ******************************
p3    12419 ******************************
p4    12106 ******************************
p5     6040 ***************
```

This histogram points out that the first and last partitions have just half as many rows as the interior partitions. The data is not very evenly distributed at all. We'll see the trend continue for six and seven hash partitions:

```
ops$tkyte@ORA10G> exec hash_proc( 6, :x );
PL/SQL procedure successfully completed.

PN          CNT HG
-- ---------- ------------------------------
p1         6104 **************
p2         6175 **************
p3        12420 ****************************
p4        12106 ****************************
p5         6040 **************
p6         6009 **************
6 rows selected.

ops$tkyte@ORA10G> exec hash_proc( 7, :x );
PL/SQL procedure successfully completed.

PN          CNT HG
-- ---------- ------------------------------
p1         6105 **************
p2         6176 **************
p3         6161 **************
p4        12106 ****************************
p5         6041 **************
p6         6010 **************
p7         6263 **************
7 rows selected.
```

As soon as we get back to a number of hash partitions that is a power of two, we achieve the goal of even distribution once again:

```
ops$tkyte@ORA10G> exec hash_proc( 8, :x );
PL/SQL procedure successfully completed.

PN          CNT HG
-- ---------- ------------------------------
p1         6106 ****************************
p2         6178 ****************************
p3         6163 ****************************
p4         6019 ****************************
p5         6042 ****************************
p6         6010 ****************************
p7         6264 ****************************
p8         6089 ****************************
8 rows selected.
```

If you continue this experiment up to 16 partitions, you would see the same effects for the ninth through the fifteenth partitions—a skewing of the data to the interior partitions, away from the edges, and then upon hitting the sixteenth partition you would see a flattening-out again. The same would be true again up to 32 partitions, and then 64, and so on. This example just points out the importance of using a power of two as the number of hash partitions.

List Partitioning

List partitioning was a new feature of Oracle9i Release 1. It provides the ability to specify in which partition a row will reside, based on discrete lists of values. It is often useful to be able to partition by some code, such as a state or region code. For example, you might want to pull together in a single partition all records for people in the states of Maine (ME), New Hampshire (NH), Vermont (VT), and Massachusetts (MA), since those states are located next to or near each other, and your application queries data by geographic region. Similarly, you might want to group together Connecticut (CT), Rhode Island (RI), and New York (NY).

You cannot use a range partition, since the range for the first partition would be ME through VT, and the second range would be CT through RI. Those ranges overlap. You cannot use hash partitioning since you cannot control which partition any given row goes into; the built-in hash function provided by Oracle does that.

With list partitioning, we can accomplish this custom partitioning scheme easily:

```
ops$tkyte@ORA10G> create table list_example
  2  ( state_cd   varchar2(2),
  3    data       varchar2(20)
  4  )
  5  partition by list(state_cd)
  6  ( partition part_1 values ( 'ME', 'NH', 'VT', 'MA' );
  7    partition part_2 values ( 'CT', 'RI', 'NY' )
  8  )
  9  /
Table created.
```

Figure 13-3 shows that Oracle will inspect the STATE_CD column and, based on its value, place the row into the correct partition.

As we saw for range partitioning, if we try to insert a value that isn't specified in the list partition, Oracle will raise an appropriate error back to the client application. In other words, a list partitioned table without a DEFAULT partition will implicitly impose a constraint much like a check constraint on the table:

```
ops$tkyte@ORA10G> insert into list_example values ( 'VA', 'data' );
insert into list_example values ( 'VA', 'data' )
            *
ERROR at line 1:
ORA-14400: inserted partition key does not map to any partition
```

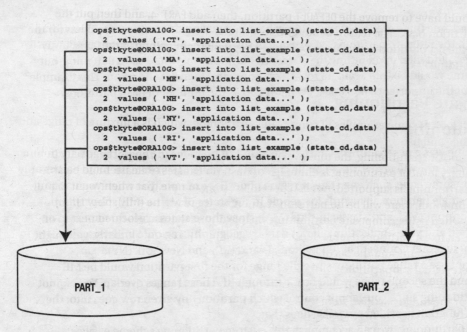

Figure 13-3. *List partition insert example*

If you want to segregate these seven states into their separate partitions, as we have, but have all remaining state codes (or, in fact, any other row that happens to be inserted that doesn't have one of these seven codes) go into a third partition, then we can use the VALUES (DEFAULT) clause. Here, we'll alter the table to add this partition (we could use this in the CREATE TABLE statement as well):

```
ops$tkyte@ORA10G> alter table list_example
  2  add partition
  3  part_3 values ( DEFAULT );
Table altered.

ops$tkyte@ORA10G> insert into list_example values ( 'VA', 'data' );
1 row created.
```

All values that are not explicitly in our list of values will go here. A word of caution on the use of DEFAULT: once a list partitioned table has a DEFAULT partition, you cannot add any more partitions to it:

```
ops$tkyte@ORA10G> alter table list_example
  2  add partition
  3  part_4 values( 'CA', 'NM' );
alter table list_example
        *
ERROR at line 1:
ORA-14323: cannot add partition when DEFAULT partition exists
```

We would have to remove the DEFAULT partition, then add PART_4, and then put the DEFAULT partition back. The reason behind this is that the DEFAULT partition could have had rows with the list partition key value of CA or NM—they would not belong in the DEFAULT partition after adding PART_4.

Composite Partitioning

Lastly, we'll look at some examples of composite partitioning, which is a mixture of range and hash or range and list.

In composite partitioning, the top-level partitioning scheme is *always* range partitioning. The secondary level of partitioning is either list or hash (in Oracle9*i* Release 1 and earlier only hash subpartitioning is supported, not list). It is interesting to note that when you use composite partitioning, there will be no partition segments—there will be only subpartition segments. When using composite partitioning, the partitions themselves do not have segments (much like a partitioned table doesn't have a segment). The data is physically stored in subpartition segments and the partition becomes a *logical container*, or a container that points to the actual subpartitions.

In our example, we'll look at a range-hash composite. Here we are using a different set of columns for the range partition from those used for the hash partition. This is not mandatory; we could use the same set of columns for both:

```
ops$tkyte@ORA10G> CREATE TABLE composite_example
  2  ( range_key_column   date,
  3    hash_key_column    int,
  4    data               varchar2(20)
  5  )
  6  PARTITION BY RANGE (range_key_column)
  7  subpartition by hash(hash_key_column) subpartitions 2
  8  (
  9  PARTITION part_1
 10      VALUES LESS THAN(to_date('01/01/2005','dd/mm/yyyy'))
 11      (subpartition part_1_sub_1,
 12       subpartition part_1_sub_2
 13      ),
 14  PARTITION part_2
 15      VALUES LESS THAN(to_date('01/01/2006','dd/mm/yyyy'))
 16      (subpartition part_2_sub_1,
 17       subpartition part_2_sub_2
 18      )
 19  )
 20  /
Table created.
```

In range-hash composite partitioning, Oracle will first apply the range partitioning rules to figure out which range the data falls into. Then it will apply the hash function to decide into which physical partition the data should finally be placed. This process is described in Figure 13-4.

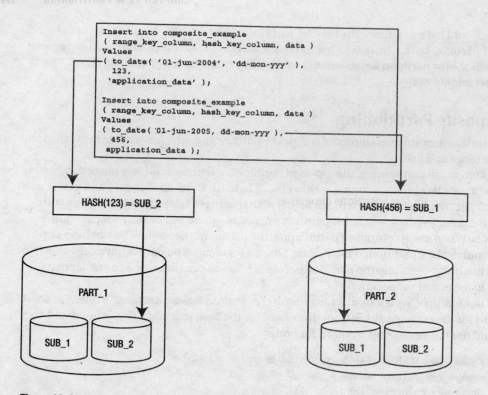

Figure 13-4. *Range-hash composite partition example*

So, composite partitioning gives you the ability to break up your data by range and, when a given range is considered too large or further partition elimination could be useful, to break it up further by hash or list. It is interesting to note that each range partition need not have the same number of subpartitions; for example, suppose you were range partitioning on a date column in support of data purging (to remove all old data rapidly and easily). In the year 2004, you had equal amounts of data in "odd" code numbers in the CODE_KEY_COLUMN and in "even" code numbers. But in 2005, you knew the number of records associated with the odd code number was more than double, and you wanted to have more subpartitions for the odd code values. You can achieve that rather easily just by defining more subpartitions:

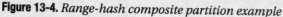

```
ops$tkyte@ORA10G> CREATE TABLE composite_range_list_example
  2  ( range_key_column   date,
  3    code_key_column    int,
  4    data               varchar2(20)
  5  )
  6  PARTITION BY RANGE (range_key_column)
  7  subpartition by list(code_key_column)
  8  (
  9  PARTITION part_1
 10      VALUES LESS THAN(to_date('01/01/2005','dd/mm/yyyy'))
 11      (subpartition part_1_sub_1 values( 1, 3, 5, 7 ),
 12       subpartition part_1_sub_2 values( 2, 4, 6, 8 )
 13      ),
```

```
14    PARTITION part_2
15        VALUES LESS THAN(to_date('01/01/2006','dd/mm/yyyy'))
16        (subpartition part_2_sub_1 values ( 1, 3 ),
17          subpartition part_2_sub_2 values ( 5, 7 ),
18          subpartition part_2_sub_3 values ( 2, 4, 6, 8 )
19        )
20    )
21    /
Table created.
```

Here you end up with five partitions altogether: two subpartitions for partition PART_1 and three for partition PART_2.

Row Movement

You might wonder what would happen if the column used to determine the partition is modified in any of the preceding partitioning schemes. There are two cases to consider:

- The modification would not cause a different partition to be used; the row would still belong in this partition. This is supported in all cases.

- The modification would cause the row to *move* across partitions. This is supported *if* row movement is enabled for the table; otherwise, an error will be raised.

We can observe these behaviors easily. In the previous example, we inserted a pair of rows into PART_1 of the RANGE_EXAMPLE table:

```
ops$tkyte@ORA10G> insert into range_example
  2  ( range_key_column, data )
  3  values
  4  ( to_date( '15-dec-2004 00:00:00',
  5             'dd-mon-yyyy hh24:mi:ss' ),
  6    'application data...' );
1 row created.

ops$tkyte@ORA10G> insert into range_example
  2  ( range_key_column, data )
  3  values
  4  ( to_date( '01-jan-2005 00:00:00',
  5             'dd-mon-yyyy hh24:mi:ss' )-1/24/60/60,
  6    'application data...' );
1 row created.

ops$tkyte@ORA10G> select * from range_example partition(part_1);

RANGE_KEY DATA
--------- --------------------
15-DEC-04 application data...
31-DEC-04 application data...
```

We take one of the rows and update the value in its RANGE_KEY_COLUMN such that it can remain in PART_1:

```
ops$tkyte@ORA10G> update range_example
  2      set range_key_column = trunc(range_key_column)
  3    where range_key_column =
  4      to_date( '31-dec-2004 23:59:59',
  5               'dd-mon-yyyy hh24:mi:ss' );
1 row updated.
```

As expected, this succeeds: the row remains in partition PART_1. Next, we update the RANGE_KEY_COLUMN to a value that would cause it to belong in PART_2:

```
ops$tkyte@ORA10G> update range_example
  2      set range_key_column = to_date('02-jan-2005','dd-mon-yyyy')
  3    where range_key_column = to_date('31-dec-2004','dd-mon-yyyy');
update range_example
       *
ERROR at line 1:
ORA-14402: updating partition key column would cause a partition change
```

That immediately raises an error, since we did not explicitly enable row movement. In Oracle8*i* and later releases, we can enable row movement on this table to allow the row to move from partition to partition.

▪**Note** The row movement functionality is not available on Oracle 8.0; you must delete the row and rein-sert it in that release.

You should be aware of a subtle side effect of doing this, however; namely that the ROWID of a row will change as the result of the update:

```
ops$tkyte@ORA10G> select rowid
  2    from range_example
  3    where range_key_column = to_date('31-dec-2004','dd-mon-yyyy');
ROWID
------------------
AAARmfAAKAAAAI+aAAB

ops$tkyte@ORA10G> alter table range_example
  2    enable row movement;
Table altered.

ops$tkyte@ORA10G> update range_example
  2      set range_key_column = to_date('02-jan-2005','dd-mon-yyyy')
  3    where range_key_column = to_date('31-dec-2004','dd-mon-yyyy');
1 row updated.
```

```
ops$tkyte@ORA10G> select rowid
  2     from range_example
  3    where range_key_column = to_date('02-jan-2005','dd-mon-yyyy');
ROWID
------------------
AAARmgAAKAAAI+iAAC
```

As long as you understand that the ROWID of the row will change on this update, enabling row movement will allow you to update partition keys.

■**Note** There are other cases where a ROWID can change as a result of an update. It can happen as a result of an update to the primary key of an IOT. The universal ROWID will change for that row, too. The Oracle 10*g* FLASHBACK TABLE command may also change the ROWID of rows, as might the Oracle 10*g* ALTER TABLE SHRINK command.

You need to understand that, internally, row movement is done as if you had, in fact, deleted the row and reinserted it. It will update every single index on this table, and delete the old entry and insert a new one. It will do the physical work of a DELETE plus an INSERT. However, it is considered an update by Oracle even though it physically deletes and inserts the row—therefore, it won't cause INSERT and DELETE triggers to fire, just the UPDATE triggers. Additionally, child tables that might prevent a DELETE due to a foreign key constraint won't. You do have to be prepared, however, for the extra work that will be performed; it is much more expensive than a normal UPDATE. Therefore, it would be a bad design decision to construct a system whereby the partition key was modified frequently and that modification would cause a partition movement.

Table Partitioning Schemes Wrap-Up

In general, range partitioning is useful when you have data that is logically segregated by some value(s). Time-based data immediately comes to the forefront as a classic example—partitioning by "Sales Quarter," "Fiscal Year," or "Month." Range partitioning is able to take advantage of partition elimination in many cases, including the use of exact equality and ranges (less than, greater than, between, and so on).

Hash partitioning is suitable for data that has no natural ranges by which you can partition. For example, if you had to load a table full of census-related data, there might not be an attribute by which it would make sense to range partition by. However, you would still like to take advantage of the administrative, performance, and availability enhancements offered by partitioning. Here, you would simply pick a unique or almost unique set of columns to hash on. This would achieve an even distribution of data across as many partitions as you'd like. Hash partitioned objects can take advantage of partition elimination when exact equality or IN (value, value, ...) is used, but not when ranges of data are used.

List partitioning is suitable for data that has a column with a discrete set of values, and partitioning by the column makes sense based on the way your application uses it (e.g., it easily permits partition elimination in queries). Classic examples would be a state or region code—or, in fact, many "code" type attributes in general.

Composite partitioning is useful when you have something logical by which you can range partition, but the resulting range partitions are still too large to manage effectively. You can apply the range partitioning and then further divide each range by a hash function or use lists to partition. This will allow you to spread out I/O requests across many disks in any given large partition. Additionally, you may achieve partition elimination at three levels now. If you query on the range partition key, Oracle is able to eliminate any range partitions that do not meet your criteria. If you add the hash or list key to your query, Oracle can eliminate the other hash or list partitions within that range. If you just query on the hash or list key (not using the range partition key), Oracle will query only those hash or list subpartitions that apply from each range partition.

It is recommended that, if there is something by which it makes sense to range partition your data, you should use that over hash or list partitioning. Hash and list partitioning add many of the salient benefits of partitioning, but they are not as useful as range partitioning when it comes to partition elimination. Using hash or list partitions within range partitions is advisable when the resulting range partitions are too large to manage, or when you want to use all PDML capabilities or parallel index scanning against a single range partition.

Partitioning Indexes

Indexes, like tables, may be partitioned. There are two possible methods to partition indexes:

- *Equipartition the index with the table*: This is also known as a *locally partitioned index*. For every table partition, there will be an index partition that indexes just that table partition. All of the entries in a given index partition point to a single table partition, and all of the rows in a single table partition are represented in a single index partition.

- *Partition the index by range*: This is also known as a *globally partitioned index*. Here the index is partitioned by range, or optionally in Oracle 10*g* by hash, and a single index partition may point to *any* (and all) table partitions.

Figure 13-5 demonstrates the difference between a local and a global index.

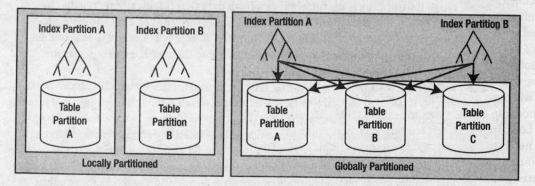

Figure 13-5. *Local and global index partitions*

In the case of a globally partitioned index, note that the number of index partitions may, in fact, be different from the number of table partitions.

Since global indexes may be partitioned by range or hash only, you must use local indexes if you wish to have a list or composite partitioned index. The local index will be partitioned using the same scheme as the underlying table.

■Note Hash partitioning of global indexes is a new feature in Oracle 10*g* Release 1 and later only. You may only globally partition by range in Oracle9*i* and before.

Local Indexes vs. Global Indexes

In my experience, most partition implementations in data warehouse systems use local indexes. In an OLTP system, global indexes are much more common, and we'll see why shortly—it has to do with the need to perform partition elimination on the index structures to maintain the same query response times after partitioning as before partitioning them.

■Note Over the last couple of years, it has become more common to see local indexes used in OLTP systems, as such systems have rapidly grown in size.

Local indexes have certain properties that make them the best choice for most data warehouse implementations. They support a more available environment (less downtime), since problems will be isolated to one range or hash of data. Since it can point to many table partitions, a global index, on the other hand, may become a point of failure, rendering all partitions inaccessible to certain queries.

Local indexes are more flexible when it comes to partition maintenance operations. If the DBA decides to move a table partition, only the associated local index partition needs to be rebuilt or maintained. With a global index, all index partitions must be rebuilt or maintained in real time. The same is true with sliding window implementations, where old data is aged out of the partition and new data is aged in. No local indexes will be in need of a rebuild, but all global indexes will be either rebuilt or maintained during the partition operation. In some cases, Oracle can take advantage of the fact that the index is locally partitioned with the table and will develop optimized query plans based on that. With global indexes, there is no such relationship between the index and table partitions.

Local indexes also facilitate a partition point-in-time recovery operation. If a single partition needs to be recovered to an earlier point in time than the rest of the table for some reason, all locally partitioned indexes can be recovered to that same point in time. All global indexes would need to be rebuilt on this object. This does not mean "avoid global indexes"—in fact, they are vitally important for performance reasons, as you'll learn shortly—you just need to be aware of the implications of using them.

Local Indexes

Oracle makes a distinction between the following two types of local indexes:

- *Local prefixed indexes*: These are indexes whereby the partition keys are on the leading edge of the index definition. For example, if a table is range partitioned on a column named LOAD_DATE, a local prefixed index on that table would have LOAD_DATE as the first column in its column list.

- *Local nonprefixed indexes*: These indexes do *not* have the partition key on the leading edge of their column list. The index may or may not contain the partition key columns.

Both types of indexes are able take advantage of partition elimination, both can support uniqueness (as long as the nonprefixed index includes the partition key), and so on. The fact is that a query that uses a local prefixed index will always *allow* for index partition elimination, whereas a query that uses a local nonprefixed index might not. This is why local nonprefixed indexes are said to be "slower" by some people—they do not *enforce* partition elimination (but they do support it).

There is nothing inherently better about a local prefixed index as opposed to a local non-prefixed index when that index is used as the initial path to the table in a query. What I mean by that is that if the query can start with "scan an index" as the first step, there isn't much difference between a prefixed and a nonprefixed index.

Partition Elimination Behavior

For the query that starts with an index access, whether or not it can eliminate partitions from consideration all really depends on the predicate in your query. A small example will help demonstrate this. The following code creates a table, PARTITIONED_TABLE, that is range partitioned on a numeric column A such that values less than two will be in partition PART_1 and values less than three will be in partition PART_2:

```
ops$tkyte@ORA10G> CREATE TABLE partitioned_table
  2  ( a int,
  3    b int,
  4    data char(20)
  5  )
  6  PARTITION BY RANGE (a)
  7  (
  8  PARTITION part_1 VALUES LESS THAN(2) tablespace p1,
  9  PARTITION part_2 VALUES LESS THAN(3) tablespace p2
 10  )
 11  /
Table created.
```

We then create both a local prefixed index, LOCAL_PREFIXED, and a local nonprefixed index, LOCAL_NONPREFIXED. Note that the nonprefixed index does not have A on the leading edge of its definition, which is what makes it a nonprefixed index:

```
ops$tkyte@ORA10G> create index local_prefixed on partitioned_table (a,b) local;
Index created.

ops$tkyte@ORA10G> create index local_nonprefixed on partitioned_table (b) local;
Index created.
```

Next, we'll insert some data into one partition and gather statistics:

```
ops$tkyte@ORA10G> insert into partitioned_table
  2  select mod(rownum-1,2)+1, rownum, 'x'
  3    from all_objects;
48967 rows created.

ops$tkyte@ORA10G> begin
  2      dbms_stats.gather_table_stats
  3      ( user,
  4       'PARTITIONED_TABLE',
  5        cascade=>TRUE );
  6  end;
  7  /
PL/SQL procedure successfully completed.
```

We take offline tablespace P2, which contains the PART_2 partition for both the tables and indexes:

```
ops$tkyte@ORA10G> alter tablespace p2 offline;
Tablespace altered.
```

Taking tablespace P2 offline will prevent Oracle from accessing those specific index partitions. It will be as if we had suffered "media failure," causing them to become unavailable. Now we'll query the table to see what index partitions are needed by different queries. This first query is written to permit the use of the local prefixed index:

```
ops$tkyte@ORA10G> select * from partitioned_table where a = 1 and b = 1;
         A          B DATA
---------- ---------- --------------------
         1          1 x
```

That query succeeded, and we can see why by reviewing the explain plan. We'll use the built-in package DBMS_XPLAN to see what partitions this query accesses. The PSTART (partition start) and PSTOP (partition stop) columns in the output show us exactly what partitions this query needs to have online and available in order to succeed:

```
ops$tkyte@ORA10G> delete from plan_table;
4 rows deleted.

ops$tkyte@ORA10G> explain plan for
  2  select * from partitioned_table where a = 1 and b = 1;
Explained.
```

```
ops$tkyte@ORA10G> select * from table(dbms_xplan.display);

PLAN_TABLE_OUTPUT
-------------------------------------------------------------------------------
| Operation                          | Name             | Rows | Pstart| Pstop |
-------------------------------------------------------------------------------
| SELECT STATEMENT                   |                  |    1 |       |       |
|  PARTITION RANGE SINGLE            |                  |    1 |    1  |    1  |
|   TABLE ACCESS BY LOCAL INDEX ROWID| PARTITIONED_TABLE|    1 |    1  |    1  |
|    INDEX RANGE SCAN                | LOCAL_PREFIXED   |    1 |    1  |    1  |
-------------------------------------------------------------------------------

Predicate Information (identified by operation id):
---------------------------------------------------
   3 - access("A"=1 AND "B"=1)
```

■**Note** The DBMS_XPLAN output has been edited to remove information that was not relevant, in order to permit the examples to fit on the printed page.

So, the query that uses LOCAL_PREFIXED succeeds. The optimizer was able to exclude PART_2 of LOCAL_PREFIXED from consideration because we specified A=1 in the query, and we can see clearly in the plan that PSTART and PSTOP are both equal to 1. Partition elimination kicked in for us. The second query fails, however:

```
ops$tkyte@ORA10G> select * from partitioned_table where b = 1;
ERROR:
ORA-00376: file 13 cannot be read at this time
ORA-01110: data file 13: '/home/ora10g/.../o1_mf_p2_1dzn8jwp_.dbf'
no rows selected
```

And using the same technique, we can see why:

```
ops$tkyte@ORA10G> delete from plan_table;
4 rows deleted.

ops$tkyte@ORA10G> explain plan for
  2  select * from partitioned_table where b = 1;
Explained.

ops$tkyte@ORA10G> select * from table(dbms_xplan.display);

PLAN_TABLE_OUTPUT
-------------------------------------------------------------------------------
| Operation                          | Name             | Rows | Pstart| Pstop |
-------------------------------------------------------------------------------
```

```
| SELECT STATEMENT                     |                   |  1 |      |      |
|  PARTITION RANGE ALL                 |                   |  1 |   1 |   2 |
|   TABLE ACCESS BY LOCAL INDEX ROWID| PARTITIONED_TABLE |  1 |   1 |   2 |
|    INDEX RANGE SCAN                  | LOCAL_NONPREFIXED |  1 |   1 |   2 |
-------------------------------------------------------------------------------

Predicate Information (identified by operation id):
-------------------------------------------------------
   3 - access("B"=1)
```

Here the optimizer was *not* able to remove PART_2 of LOCAL_NONPREFIXED from consideration—it needed to look in both the PART_1 and PART_2 partitions of the index to see if B=1 was in there. Herein lies a performance issue with local nonprefixed indexes: they do not *make* you use the partition key in the predicate as a prefixed index does. It is not that prefixed indexes are better; it's just that in order to use them, you must use a query that allows for partition elimination.

If we drop the LOCAL_PREFIXED index and rerun the original successful query as follows:

```
ops$tkyte@ORA10G> drop index local_prefixed;
Index dropped.

ops$tkyte@ORA10G> select * from partitioned_table where a = 1 and b = 1;
        A          B DATA
---------- ---------- --------------------
        1          1 x
```

It succeeds, but as we'll see, it used the same index that just a moment ago failed us. The plan shows that Oracle was able to employ partition elimination here—the predicate A=1 was enough information for the database to eliminate index partition PART_2 from consideration:

```
ops$tkyte@ORA10G> delete from plan_table;
4 rows deleted.

ops$tkyte@ORA10G> explain plan for
  2  select * from partitioned_table where a = 1 and b = 1;
Explained.

ops$tkyte@ORA10G> select * from table(dbms_xplan.display);
PLAN_TABLE_OUTPUT
--------------------------------------------------------------------------------
```

Operation	Name	Rows	Pstart	Pstop
SELECT STATEMENT		1		
PARTITION RANGE SINGLE		1	1	1
TABLE ACCESS BY LOCAL INDEX ROWID	PARTITIONED_TABLE	1	1	1
INDEX RANGE SCAN	LOCAL_NONPREFIXED	1	1	1

```
--------------------------------------------------------------------------------
```

```
Predicate Information (identified by operation id):
---------------------------------------------------
   2 - filter("A"=1)
   3 - access("B"=1)
```

Note the PSTART and PSTOP column values of 1 and 1. This proves that the optimizer is able to perform partition elimination even for nonprefixed local indexes.

If you frequently query the preceding table with the following queries:

```
select ... from partitioned_table where a = :a and b = :b;
select ... from partitioned_table where b = :b;
```

then you might consider using a local nonprefixed index on (b,a). That index would be useful for both of the preceding queries. The local prefixed index on (a,b) would be useful only for the first query.

The bottom line here is that you should not be afraid of nonprefixed indexes or consider them to be major performance inhibitors. If you have many queries that could benefit from a nonprefixed index as outlined previously, then you should consider using one. The main concern is to ensure that your queries contain predicates that allow for index partition elimination whenever possible. The use of prefixed local indexes enforces that consideration. The use of nonprefixed indexes does not. Consider also how the index will be used. If it will be used as the first step in a query plan, there are not many differences between the two types of indexes.

Local Indexes and Unique Constraints

To enforce uniqueness—and that includes a UNIQUE constraint or PRIMARY KEY constraints—your partitioning key *must be included in the constraint itself* if you want to use a local index to enforce the constraint. This is the largest limitation of a local index, in my opinion. Oracle enforces uniqueness only within an index partition—never across partitions. What this implies, for example, is that you cannot range partition on a TIMESTAMP field and have a primary key on the ID that is enforced using a locally partitioned index. Oracle will instead utilize a *global* index to enforce uniqueness.

In the next example, we will create a range partitioned table that is partitioned by a column named LOAD_TYPE, but has a primary key on the ID column. We can do that by executing the following CREATE TABLE statement in a schema that owns no other objects, so we can easily see exactly what objects are created by looking at every segment this user owns:

```
ops$tkyte@ORA10G> CREATE TABLE partitioned
  2  ( load_date date,
  3    id        int,
  4    constraint partitioned_pk primary key(id)
  5  )
  6  PARTITION BY RANGE (load_date)
  7  (
  8  PARTITION part_1 VALUES LESS THAN
  9  ( to_date('01/01/2000','dd/mm/yyyy') ) ,
 10  PARTITION part_2 VALUES LESS THAN
 11  ( to_date('01/01/2001','dd/mm/yyyy') )
```

```
12  .)
13  /
Table created.

ops$tkyte@ORA10G> select segment_name, partition_name, segment_type
  2    from user_segments;

SEGMENT_NAME    PARTITION_NAME   SEGMENT_TYPE
--------------  ---------------  -------------------
PARTITIONED     PART_1           TABLE PARTITION
PARTITIONED     PART_2           TABLE PARTITION
PARTITIONED_PK                   INDEX
```

The PARTITIONED_PK index is not even partitioned, let alone locally partitioned, and as we'll see, it cannot be locally partitioned. Even if we try to trick Oracle by realizing that a primary key can be enforced by a nonunique index as well as a unique index, we'll find that this approach will not work either:

```
ops$tkyte@ORA10G> CREATE TABLE partitioned
  2  ( timestamp date,
  3    id        int
  4  )
  5  PARTITION BY RANGE (timestamp)
  6  (
  7  PARTITION part_1 VALUES LESS THAN
  8  ( to_date('01-jan-2000','dd-mon-yyyy') ) ,
  9  PARTITION part_2 VALUES LESS THAN
 10  ( to_date('01-jan-2001','dd-mon-yyyy') )
 11  )
 12  /
Table created.

ops$tkyte@ORA10G> create index partitioned_idx
  2  on partitioned(id) local
  3  /
Index created.

ops$tkyte@ORA10G> select segment_name, partition_name, segment_type
  2    from user_segments;

SEGMENT_NAME    PARTITION_NAME   SEGMENT_TYPE
--------------  ---------------  -------------------
PARTITIONED     PART_1           TABLE PARTITION
PARTITIONED_IDX PART_2           INDEX PARTITION
PARTITIONED     PART_2           TABLE PARTITION
PARTITIONED_IDX PART_1           INDEX PARTITION
```

```
ops$tkyte@ORA10G> alter table partitioned
  2  add constraint
  3  partitioned_pk
  4  primary key(id)
  5  /
alter table partitioned
*
ERROR at line 1:
ORA-01408: such column list already indexed
```

Here, Oracle attempts to create a global index on ID, but finds that it cannot since an index already exists. The preceding statements would work if the index we created was not partitioned, as Oracle would have used that index to enforce the constraint.

The reasons why uniqueness cannot be enforced, unless the partition key is part of the constraint, are twofold. First, if Oracle allowed this, it would void most of the advantages of partitions. Availability and scalability would be lost, as each and every partition would always have to be *available* and *scanned* to do any inserts and updates. The more partitions you had, the less available the data would be. The more partitions you had, the more index partitions you would have to scan, and the less scalable partitions would become. Instead of providing availability and scalability, doing this would actually decrease both.

Additionally, Oracle would have to effectively *serialize* inserts and updates to this table at the transaction level. This is because if we add ID=1 to PART_1, Oracle would have to somehow *prevent* anyone else from adding ID=1 to PART_2. The only way to do this would be to prevent others from modifying index partition PART_2, since there isn't anything to really "lock" in that partition.

In an OLTP system, unique constraints must be system enforced (i.e., enforced by Oracle) to ensure the integrity of data. This implies that the logical model of your application will have an impact on the physical design. Uniqueness constraints will either drive the underlying table partitioning scheme, driving the choice of the partition keys, or point you toward the use of *global* indexes instead. We'll take a look at global indexes in more depth next.

Global Indexes

Global indexes are partitioned using a scheme that is different from that used in the underlying table. The table might be partitioned by a TIMESTAMP column into ten partitions, and a global index on that table could be partitioned into five partitions by the REGION column. Unlike local indexes, there is only one class of global index, and that is a *prefixed global index*. There is no support for a global index whose index key does not begin with the partitioning key *for that index*. That implies that whatever attribute(s) you use to partition the index will be on the leading edge of the index key itself.

Continuing on from our previous example, here is a quick example of the use of a global index. It shows that a global partitioned index can be used to enforce uniqueness for a primary key, so you can have partitioned indexes that enforce uniqueness, but do not include the partition key of TABLE. The following example creates a table partitioned by TIMESTAMP that has an index partitioned by ID:

```
ops$tkyte@ORA10G> CREATE TABLE partitioned
  2  ( timestamp date,
  3    id         int
  4  )
  5  PARTITION BY RANGE (timestamp)
  6  (
  7  PARTITION part_1 VALUES LESS THAN
  8  ( to_date('01-jan-2000','dd-mon-yyyy') ) ,
  9  PARTITION part_2 VALUES LESS THAN
 10  ( to_date('01-jan-2001','dd-mon-yyyy') )
 11  )
 12  /
Table created.

ops$tkyte@ORA10G> create index partitioned_index
  2   on partitioned(id)
  3   GLOBAL
  4   partition  by range(id)
  5   (
  6   partition part_1 values less than(1000),
  7   partition part_2 values less than (MAXVALUE)
  8   )
  9   /
Index created.
```

Note the use of MAXVALUE in this index. MAXVALUE can be used in any range partitioned table as well as in the index. It represents an "infinite upper bound" on the range. In our examples so far, we've used hard upper bounds on the ranges (values less than <*some value*>). However, a global index has a requirement that the highest partition (the last partition) must have a partition bound whose value is MAXVALUE. This ensures that all rows in the underlying table can be placed in the index.

Now, completing this example, we'll add our primary key to the table:

```
ops$tkyte@ORA10G> alter table partitioned add constraint
  2   partitioned_pk
  3   primary key(id)
  4   /
Table altered.
```

It is not evident from this code that Oracle is using the index we created to enforce the primary key (it is to me because I know that Oracle is using it), so we can prove it by simply trying to drop that index:

```
ops$tkyte@ORA10G> drop index partitioned_index;
drop index partitioned_index
           *
ERROR at line 1:
ORA-02429: cannot drop index used for enforcement of unique/primary key
```

To show that Oracle will not allow us to create a *non*prefixed global index, we only need try the following:

```
ops$tkyte@ORA10G> create index partitioned_index2
  2  on partitioned(timestamp,id)
  3  GLOBAL
  4  partition  by range(id)
  5  (
  6  partition part_1 values less than(1000),
  7  partition part_2 values less than (MAXVALUE)
  8  )
  9  /
partition  by range(id)
            *
ERROR at line 4:
ORA-14038: GLOBAL partitioned index must be prefixed
```

The error message is pretty clear. The global index *must* be prefixed. So, when would you use a global index? We'll take a look at two system types, data warehouse and OLTP, and see when they might apply.

Data Warehousing and Global Indexes

In the past, it used to be that data warehousing and global indexes were pretty much mutually exclusive. A data warehouse implies certain things, such as large amounts of data coming in and going out. Many data warehouses implement a sliding window approach to managing data—that is, drop the oldest partition of a table and add a new partition for the newly loaded data. In the past (Oracle8*i* and earlier), these systems would have avoided the use of global indexes for a very good reason: lack of availability. It used to be the case that most partition operations, such as dropping an old partition, would *invalidate* the global indexes, rendering them unusable until they were rebuilt. This could seriously compromise availability.

In the following sections, we'll take a look at what is meant by a *sliding window of data* and the *potential* impact of a global index on it. I stress the word "potential" because we'll also look at how we may get around this issue and how to understand what getting around the issue might imply.

Sliding Windows and Indexes

The following example implements a classic sliding window of data. In many implementations, data is added to a warehouse over time and the oldest data is aged out. Many times, this data is range partitioned by a date attribute, so that the oldest data is stored together in a single partition, and the newly loaded data is likewise stored together in a new partition. The monthly load process involves

- *Detaching the old data*: The oldest partition is either dropped or exchanged with an empty table (turning the oldest partition into a table) to permit archiving of the old data.

- *Loading and indexing of the new data*: The new data is loaded into a "work" table and indexed and validated.

- *Attaching the new data*: Once the new data is loaded and processed, the table it is in is exchanged with an empty partition in the partitioned table, turning this newly loaded data in a table into a partition of the larger partitioned table.

This process is repeated every month, or however often the load process is performed; it could be every day or every week. We will implement this very typical process in this section to show the impact of global partitioned indexes and demonstrate the options we have during partition operations to increase availability, allowing us to implement a sliding window of data and maintain continuous availability of data.

We'll process yearly data in this example and have fiscal years 2004 and 2005 loaded up. The table will be partitioned by the TIMESTAMP column, and it will have two indexes created on it—one is a locally partitioned index on the ID column, and the other is a global index (non-partitioned, in this case) on the TIMESTAMP column:

```
ops$tkyte@ORA10G> CREATE TABLE partitioned
  2  ( timestamp date,
  3    id         int
  4  )
  5  PARTITION BY RANGE (timestamp)
  6  (
  7  PARTITION fy_2004 VALUES LESS THAN
  8  ( to_date('01-jan-2005','dd-mon-yyyy') ) ,
  9  PARTITION fy_2005 VALUES LESS THAN
 10  ( to_date('01-jan-2006','dd-mon-yyyy') )
 11  )
 12  /
Table created.

ops$tkyte@ORA10G> insert into partitioned partition(fy_2004)
  2  select to_date('31-dec-2004','dd-mon-yyyy')-mod(rownum,360), object_id
  3  from all_objects
  4  /
48514 rows created.

ops$tkyte@ORA10G> insert into partitioned partition(fy_2005)
  2  select to_date('31-dec-2005','dd-mon-yyyy')-mod(rownum,360), object_id
  3  from all_objects
  4  /
48514 rows created.

ops$tkyte@ORA10G> create index partitioned_idx_local
  2  on partitioned(id)
  3  LOCAL
  4  /
Index created.
```

```
ops$tkyte@ORA10G> create index partitioned_idx_global
  2  on partitioned(timestamp)
  3  GLOBAL
  4  /
Index created.
```

This sets up our "warehouse" table. The data is partitioned by fiscal year and we have the last two years' worth of data online. This table has two indexes: one is LOCAL and the other is GLOBAL. Now it is the end of the year and we would like to do the following:

1. Remove the oldest fiscal year data. We do not want to lose this data forever; we just want to age it out and archive it.

2. Add the newest fiscal year data. It will take a while to load it, transform it, index it, and so on. We would like to do this work without impacting the availability of the current data, if at all possible.

The first step we might take would be to set up an empty table for fiscal year 2004 that looks just like the partitioned table. We'll use this table to exchange with the FY_2004 partition in the partitioned table, turning that partition into a table and in turn emptying out the partition in the partitioned table. The net effect is that the oldest data in the partitioned table will have been, in effect, removed after the exchange:

```
ops$tkyte@ORA10G> create table fy_2004 ( timestamp date, id int );
Table created.

ops$tkyte@ORA10G> create index fy_2004_idx on fy_2004(id)
  2  /
Index created.
```

We'll do the same to the new data to be loaded. We'll create and load a table that structurally looks like the existing partitioned table (but that is not itself partitioned):

```
ops$tkyte@ORA10G> create table fy_2006 ( timestamp date, id int );
Table created.

ops$tkyte@ORA10G> insert into fy_2006
  2  select to_date('31-dec-2006','dd-mon-yyyy')-mod(rownum,360), object_id
  3  from all_objects
  4  /
48521 rows created.

ops$tkyte@ORA10G> create index fy_2006_idx on fy_2006(id) nologging
  2  /
Index created.
```

We'll turn the current full partition into an empty partition and create a "full" table, with the FY_2004 data in it. Also, we've completed all of the work necessary to have the FY_2006 data ready to go. This would have involved verifying the data, transforming it—whatever complex tasks we need to undertake to get it ready.

Now we're ready to update the "live" data using an exchange partition:

```
ops$tkyte@ORA10G> alter table partitioned
  2  exchange partition fy_2004
  3  with table fy_2004
  4  including indexes
  5  without validation
  6  /
Table altered.

ops$tkyte@ORA10G> alter table partitioned
  2  drop partition fy_2004
  3  /
Table altered.
```

This is all we need to do to "age" the old data out. We turned the partition into a full table and the empty table into a partition. This was a simple data dictionary update. No large amount of I/O took place—it just happened. We can now export that FY_2004 table (perhaps using a transportable tablespace) out of our database for archival purposes. We could reattach it quickly if we ever needed to.

Next, we want to slide in the new data:

```
ops$tkyte@ORA10G> alter table partitioned
  2  add partition fy_2006
  3  values less than ( to_date('01-jan-2007','dd-mon-yyyy') )
  4  /
Table altered.

ops$tkyte@ORA10G> alter table partitioned
  2  exchange partition fy_2006
  3  with table fy_2006
  4  including indexes
  5  without validation
  6  /
Table altered.
```

Again, this was instantaneous; it was accomplished via simple data dictionary updates. Adding the empty partition took very little time to process. Then, we exchange the newly created empty partition with the full table, and the full table with the empty partition, and that operation is performed quickly as well. The new data is online.

Looking at our indexes, however, we'll find the following:

```
ops$tkyte@ORA10G> select index_name, status from user_indexes;

INDEX_NAME                      STATUS
------------------------------  --------
FY_2006_IDX                     VALID
FY_2004_IDX                     VALID
PARTITIONED_IDX_GLOBAL          UNUSABLE
PARTITIONED_IDX_LOCAL           N/A
```

The global index is, of course, unusable after this operation. Since each index partition can point to any table partition, *and* we just took away a partition and added a partition, that index is invalid. It has entries that point into the partition we dropped. It has *no* entries that point into the partition we just added. Any query that would make use of this index either will fail and not execute or, if we skip unusable indexes, the query's performance will be negatively impacted by not being able to use the index:

```
ops$tkyte@ORA10G> set autotrace on explain
ops$tkyte@ORA10G> select /*+ index( partitioned PARTITIONED_IDX_GLOBAL ) */ count(*)
  2  from partitioned
  3  where timestamp between sysdate-50 and sysdate;
select /*+ index( partitioned PARTITIONED_IDX_GLOBAL ) */ count(*)
*
ERROR at line 1:
ORA-01502: index 'OPS$TKYTE.PARTITIONED_IDX_GLOBAL' or partition
           of such index is in unusable state

ops$tkyte@ORA10G> select count(*)
  2  from partitioned
  3  where timestamp between sysdate-50 and sysdate;

  COUNT(*)
----------
      6750


Execution Plan
----------------------------------------------------------
   0      SELECT STATEMENT Optimizer=ALL_ROWS (Cost=59 Card=1 Bytes=9)
   1    0   SORT (AGGREGATE)
   2    1     FILTER
   3    2       PARTITION RANGE (ITERATOR) (Cost=59 Card=7234 Bytes=65106)
   4    3         TABLE ACCESS (FULL) OF 'PARTITIONED' (TABLE) (Cost=59 Card=7234

ops$tkyte@ORA10G> set autotrace off
```

So, our choices after performing this partition operation with global indexes are

- Skip the index, either transparently as Oracle 10g is doing in this example or by setting the session parameter SKIP_UNUSABLE_INDEXES=TRUE in 9i (Oracle 10g defaults this setting to TRUE). But then we lose the performance the index was giving us.

- Have the query receive an error, as it would in 9i unless SKIP_UNUSABLE_INDEXES were set to FALSE, and as would any query in 10g that explicitly requests to use a hint. We need to rebuild this index to make the data truly usable again.

The sliding window process, which so far has resulted in virtually no downtime, will now take a very long time to complete while we rebuild the global index. Runtime query performance of queries that relied on these indexes will be negatively affected during this time—either they will not run at all or they will run without the benefit of the index. All of the data must be scanned and the entire index reconstructed from the table data. If the table is many hundreds of gigabytes in size, this will take considerable resources.

"Live" Global Index Maintenance

Starting in Oracle9*i*, another option was added to partition maintenance: the ability to *maintain the global indexes* during the partition operation using the UPDATE GLOBAL INDEXES clause. This means that as you drop a partition, split a partition, perform whatever operation necessary on a partition, Oracle will perform the necessary modifications to the global index to keep it up to date. Since most partition operations will cause this global index invalidation to occur, this feature can be a boon to systems that need to provide continual access to the data. You'll find that you sacrifice the raw speed of the partition operation, but with the associated window of unavailability immediately afterward as you rebuild indexes, for a slower overall response time from the partition operation but coupled with 100 percent data availability. In short, if you have a data warehouse that cannot have downtime, but must support these common data warehouse techniques of sliding data in and out, then this feature is for you—but you must understand the implications.

Revisiting our previous example, if our partition operations had used the UPDATE GLOBAL INDEXES clause when relevant (in this example, it would not be needed on the ADD PARTITION statement since the newly added partition would not have any rows in it),

```
ops$tkyte@ORA10G> alter table partitioned
  2  exchange partition fy_2004
  3  with table fy_2004
  4  including indexes
  5  without validation
  6  UPDATE GLOBAL INDEXES
  7  /
Table altered.

ops$tkyte@ORA10G> alter table partitioned
  2  drop partition fy_2004
  3  UPDATE GLOBAL INDEXES
  4  /
Table altered.

ops$tkyte@ORA10G> alter table partitioned
  2  add partition fy_2006
  3  values less than ( to_date('01-jan-2007','dd-mon-yyyy') )
  4  /
Table altered.

ops$tkyte@ORA10G> alter table partitioned
  2  exchange partition fy_2006
  3  with table fy_2006
  4  including indexes
```

```
 5  without validation
 6  UPDATE GLOBAL INDEXES
 7  /
Table altered.
```

then we would have discovered the indexes to be perfectly valid and usable both *during* and *after* the operation:

```
ops$tkyte@ORA10G> select index_name, status from user_indexes;

INDEX_NAME                       STATUS
-------------------------------- --------

FY_2006_IDX                      VALID
FY_2004_IDX                      VALID
PARTITIONED_IDX_GLOBAL           VALID
PARTITIONED_IDX_LOCAL            N/A

6 rows selected.

ops$tkyte@ORA10G> set autotrace on explain
ops$tkyte@ORA10G> select count(*)
  2  from partitioned
  3  where timestamp between sysdate-50 and sysdate;

 COUNT(*)
----------
     6750

Execution Plan
----------------------------------------------------------
   0       SELECT STATEMENT Optimizer=ALL_ROWS (Cost=9 Card=1 Bytes=9)
   1    0    SORT (AGGREGATE)
   2    1      FILTER
   3    2        INDEX (RANGE SCAN) OF 'PARTITIONED_IDX_GLOBAL' (INDEX) (Cost=9...
```

But there is a tradeoff: we are performing the logical equivalent of INSERT and DELETE operations on the global index structures. When we drop a partition, we have to delete all of the global index entries that might be pointing to that partition. When we did the exchange of a table with a partition, we had to delete all of the global index entries pointing to the original data and then insert all of the new ones that we just slid in there. So the amount of work performed by the ALTER commands was significantly increased.

In fact, using runstats and a slightly modified version of the preceding example, we can measure the amount of "extra" work performed to maintain the global indexes during the partition operation. We'll slide out FY_2004 and slide in FY_2006 as before, adding in the requisite index rebuild. This will be the sliding window implementation that causes the data to become unavailable due to the need to rebuild the global indexes. We'll also then slide out FY_2005 and slide in FY_2007 using the UPDATE GLOBAL INDEXES clause, to emulate the sliding window implementation that provides for full data availability, even during the partition operations. In that manner, we can measure the same operations using the different techniques and compare them. Our expected outcome will be that the first approach will consume fewer database resources and, therefore, perform "faster" but will incur a measurable period of "downtime." The second approach, while consuming more resources and perhaps taking longer overall, will not incur downtime. As far as the end users are concerned, their ability to work never ceased. They might have been processing a bit slower (since we were competing with them for resources), but *they were still processing, and they never stopped.*

So, if we take the earlier example, but also create an empty FY_2005 table like FY_2004, and a full FY_2007 table like FY_2006, we can measure the differences between the index rebuild approaches, starting first with the "less available approach":

```
exec runStats_pkg.rs_start;

alter table partitioned exchange partition fy_2004
with table fy_2004 including indexes without validation;

alter table partitioned drop partition fy_2004;

alter table partitioned add partition fy_2006
values less than ( to_date('01-jan-2007','dd-mon-yyyy') );

alter table partitioned exchange partition fy_2006
with table fy_2006 including indexes without validation;

alter index partitioned_idx_global rebuild;

exec runStats_pkg.rs_middle;
```

Here is the highly available UPDATE GLOBAL INDEXES approach:

```
alter table partitioned exchange partition fy_2005
with table fy_2005 including indexes without validation
update global indexes;

alter table partitioned drop partition fy_2005
update global indexes;

alter table partitioned add partition fy_2007
values less than ( to_date('01-jan-2008','dd-mon-yyyy') );

alter table partitioned exchange partition fy_2007
with table fy_2007 including indexes without validation
update global indexes;

exec runStats_pkg.rs_stop;
```

We might observe the following:

```
ops$tkyte@ORA10G> exec runStats_pkg.rs_stop;
Run1 ran in 81 hsecs
Run2 ran in 94 hsecs
run 1 ran in 86.17% of the time

Name                             Run1        Run2         Diff
...
STAT...CPU used when call star     39          59           20
...
STAT...redo entries               938       3,340        2,402
STAT...db block gets            1,348       5,441        4,093
STAT...session logical reads    2,178       6,455        4,277
...
LATCH.cache buffers chains      5,675      27,695       22,020
...
STAT...table scan rows gotten  97,711     131,427       33,716
STAT...undo change vector size 35,100   3,404,056    3,368,956
STAT...redo size            2,694,172   6,197,988    3,503,816
```

The index rebuild approach did run faster, both as observed by the elapsed time and the CPU time. This fact has caused many a DBA to pause and say, "Hey, I don't want to use UPDATE GLOBAL INDEXES—it's slower." That is too simplistic of a view, however. What you need to remember is that while the operations overall took longer, processing on your system was not necessarily interrupted. Sure, you as the DBA might be looking at your screen for a longer period of time, but the really important work that takes place on your system was still taking place. What you need to do is see if this tradeoff makes sense for you. If you have an eight-hour maintenance window overnight in which to load new data, then by all means, use the rebuild approach if that makes sense. However, if you have a mandate to be available continuously, then the ability to maintain the global indexes will be crucial.

Looking at the redo generated by each approach, we can see that the UPDATE GLOBAL INDEXES generated considerably more—over 230 percent more—and we would expect that to only go up as we add more and more global indexes to the table. The redo generated by the UPDATE GLOBAL INDEXES is unavoidable and cannot be turned off via NOLOGGING, since the maintenance of the global indexes is not a complete rebuild of their structure but more of an incremental "maintenance." Additionally, since we are maintaining the live index structure, we must generate undo for that—in the event the partition operation fails, we must be prepared to put the index back the way it was. And remember, undo is protected by redo itself, so some of the redo you see generated is from the index updates and some is from the rollback. Add another global index or two and you would reasonably expect these numbers to increase.

So, UPDATE GLOBAL INDEXES is an option that allows you to trade off availability for resource consumption. If you have the need to provide continuous availability, it will be the option for you. But you will have to understand the ramifications and size other components of your system appropriately. Specifically, many data warehouses have been crafted over time to use bulk, direct path operations, bypassing undo generation and, when permitted, redo generation as well. Using UPDATE GLOBAL INDEXES cannot bypass either of those two elements. You'll need to examine the rules you used to size these components before using this feature, so you can assure yourself it can work on your system.

OLTP and Global Indexes

An OLTP system is characterized by the frequent occurrence of many small read and write transactions. In general, fast access to the row (or rows) you need is paramount. Data integrity is vital. Availability is also very important.

Global indexes make sense in many cases in OLTP systems. Table data can be partitioned by only one key—one set of columns. However, you may need to access the data in many different ways. You might partition EMPLOYEE data by LOCATION in the table, but you still need fast access to EMPLOYEE data by

- DEPARTMENT: Departments are geographically dispersed. There is no relationship between a department and a location.

- EMPLOYEE_ID: While an employee ID will determine a location, you don't want to have to search by EMPLOYEE_ID and LOCATION, hence partition elimination cannot take place on the index partitions. Also, EMPLOYEE_ID by itself must be *unique*.

- JOB_TITLE: There is no relationship between JOB_TITLE and LOCATION. All JOB_TITLE values may appear in any LOCATION.

There is a need to access the EMPLOYEE data by many different keys in different places in the application, and speed is paramount. In a data warehouse, we might just use locally partitioned indexes on these keys and use parallel index range scans to collect a large amount of data fast. In these cases, we don't necessarily need to use index partition elimination. In an OLTP system, however, we do need to use it. Parallel query is not appropriate for these systems; we need to provide the indexes appropriately. Therefore, we will need to make use of global indexes on certain fields.

The goals we need to meet are

- Fast access

- Data integrity

- Availability

Global indexes can accomplish these goals in an OLTP system. We will probably not be doing sliding windows, auditing aside for a moment. We will not be splitting partitions (unless we have a scheduled downtime), we will not be moving data, and so on. The operations we perform in a data warehouse are not done on a live OLTP system in general.

Here is a small example that shows how we can achieve the three goals just listed with global indexes. I am going to use simple, "single partition" global indexes, but the results would not be different with global indexes in multiple partitions (except for the fact that availability and manageability would *increase* as we added index partitions). We start with a table that is range partitioned by location, LOC, according to our rules, which places all LOC values less than 'C' into partition P1, those less than 'D' into partition P2, and so on:

```
ops$tkyte@ORA10G> create table emp
  2  (EMPNO            NUMBER(4) NOT NULL,
  3   ENAME            VARCHAR2(10),
  4   JOB              VARCHAR2(9),
  5   MGR              NUMBER(4),
  6   HIREDATE         DATE,
```

```
  7    SAL                  NUMBER(7,2),
  8    COMM                 NUMBER(7,2),
  9    DEPTNO               NUMBER(2) NOT NULL,
 10    LOC                  VARCHAR2(13) NOT NULL
 11  )
 12  partition by range(loc)
 13  (
 14  partition p1 values less than('C') tablespace p1,
 15  partition p2 values less than('D') tablespace p2,
 16  partition p3 values less than('N') tablespace p3,
 17  partition p4 values less than('Z') tablespace p4
 18  )
 19  /
Table created.
```

We alter the table to add a constraint on the primary key column:

```
ops$tkyte@ORA10G> alter table emp add constraint emp_pk
  2  primary key(empno)
  3  /
Table altered.
```

A side effect of this is that there exists a unique index on the EMPNO column. This shows we can support and enforce data integrity, one of our goals. Finally, we create two more global indexes on DEPTNO and JOB, to facilitate accessing records quickly by those attributes:

```
ops$tkyte@ORA10G> create index emp_job_idx on emp(job)
  2  GLOBAL
  3  /
Index created.

ops$tkyte@ORA10G> create index emp_dept_idx on emp(deptno)
  2  GLOBAL
  3  /
Index created.

ops$tkyte@ORA10G> insert into emp
  2  select e.*, d.loc
  3    from scott.emp e, scott.dept d
  4   where e.deptno = d.deptno
  5  /
14 rows created.
```

Now let's see what is in each partition:

```
ops$tkyte@ORA10G> break on pname skip 1
ops$tkyte@ORA10G> select 'p1' pname, empno, job, loc from emp partition(p1)
  2  union all
  3  select 'p2' pname, empno, job, loc from emp partition(p2)
  4  union all
```

```
  5  select 'p3' pname, empno, job, loc from emp partition(p3)
  6  union all
  7  select 'p4' pname, empno, job, loc from emp partition(p4)
  8  /

PN      EMPNO JOB        LOC
--  --------- --------- -------------
p2       7499 SALESMAN   CHICAGO
         7698 MANAGER    CHICAGO
         7654 SALESMAN   CHICAGO
         7900 CLERK      CHICAGO
         7844 SALESMAN   CHICAGO
         7521 SALESMAN   CHICAGO

p3       7369 CLERK      DALLAS
         7876 CLERK      DALLAS
         7902 ANALYST    DALLAS
         7788 ANALYST    DALLAS
         7566 MANAGER    DALLAS

p4       7782 MANAGER    NEW YORK
         7839 PRESIDENT  NEW YORK
         7934 CLERK      NEW YORK

14 rows selected.
```

This shows the distribution of data, by location, into the individual partitions. We can now review some query plans to see what we could expect performance-wise:

```
ops$tkyte@ORA10G> variable x varchar2(30);
ops$tkyte@ORA10G> begin
  2      dbms_stats.set_table_stats
  3      ( user, 'EMP', numrows=>100000, numblks => 10000 );
  4  end;
  5  /
PL/SQL procedure successfully completed.

ops$tkyte@ORA10G> delete from plan_table;
3 rows deleted.

ops$tkyte@ORA10G> explain plan for
  2  select empno, job, loc from emp where empno = :x;
Explained.

ops$tkyte@ORA10G> select * from table(dbms_xplan.display);
```

```
PLAN_TABLE_OUTPUT
--------------------------------------------------------------------------------
| Operation                          | Name   |Rows |Bytes|Pstart|Pstop|
--------------------------------------------------------------------------------
| SELECT STATEMENT                   |        |   1 |  27 |      |      |
|  TABLE ACCESS BY GLOBAL INDEX ROWID| EMP    |   1 |  27 |ROWID |ROWID |
|   INDEX UNIQUE SCAN                | EMP_PK |   1 |     |      |      |
--------------------------------------------------------------------------------
Predicate Information (identified by operation id):
--------------------------------------------------------------------------------
  2 - access("EMPNO"=TO_NUMBER(:X))
```

■Note The explain plan format has been edited to fit on the page. Columns in the report not relevant to the discussion have been omitted.

The plan here shows an INDEX UNIQUE SCAN of the nonpartitioned index EMP_PK that was created in support of our primary key. Then there is a TABLE ACCESS BY GLOBAL INDEX ROWID, with a PSTART and PSTOP of ROWID/ROWID, meaning that when we get the ROWID from the index, it will tell us precisely which index partition to read to get this row. This index access will be as effective as on a nonpartitioned table and perform the same amount of I/O to do so. It is just a simple, single index unique scan followed by a "get this row by ROWID." Now, let's look at one of the other global indexes, the one on JOB:

```
ops$tkyte@ORA10G> delete from plan_table;
3 rows deleted.

ops$tkyte@ORA10G> explain plan for
  2  select empno, job, loc from emp where job = :x;
Explained.

ops$tkyte@ORA10G> select * from table(dbms_xplan.display);

PLAN_TABLE_OUTPUT
--------------------------------------------------------------------------------
| Operation                          |Name       |Rows |Bytes|Pstart|Pstop|
--------------------------------------------------------------------------------
| SELECT STATEMENT                   |           |1000 |27000|      |      |
|  TABLE ACCESS BY GLOBAL INDEX ROWID|EMP        |1000 |27000|ROWID |ROWID |
|   INDEX RANGE SCAN                 |EMP_JOB_IDX| 400 |     |      |      |
--------------------------------------------------------------------------------
Predicate Information (identified by operation id):
--------------------------------------------------------------------------------
  2 - access("JOB"=:X)
```

Sure enough, we see a similar effect for the INDEX RANGE SCAN. Our indexes are used and can provide high-speed OLTP access to the underlying data. If they were partitioned, they would have to be prefixed and enforce index partition elimination; hence, they are scalable as well, meaning we can partition them and observe the same behavior. In a moment, we'll look at what would happen if we used LOCAL indexes only.

Lastly, let's look at the area of availability. The Oracle documentation claims that globally partitioned indexes make for "less available" data than locally partitioned indexes. I don't fully agree with this blanket characterization. I believe that in an OLTP system they are as highly available as a locally partitioned index. Consider the following:

```
ops$tkyte@ORA10G> alter tablespace p1 offline;
Tablespace altered.

ops$tkyte@ORA10G> alter tablespace p2 offline;
Tablespace altered.

ops$tkyte@ORA10G> alter tablespace p3 offline;
Tablespace altered.

ops$tkyte@ORA10G> select empno, job, loc from emp where empno = 7782;

     EMPNO JOB        LOC
---------- ---------- --------------
      7782 MANAGER    NEW YORK
```

Here, even though most of the underlying data is unavailable in the table, we can still gain access to any bit of data available via that index. As long as the EMPNO we want is in a tablespace that is available, and our GLOBAL index is available, our GLOBAL index works for us. On the other hand, if we *had* been using the "highly available" local index in the preceding case, we might have been prevented from accessing the data! This is a side effect of the fact that we partitioned on LOC but needed to query by EMPNO. We would have had to probe each local index partition and would have failed on the index partitions that were not available.

Other types of queries, however, will not (and cannot) function at this point in time:

```
ops$tkyte@ORA10G> select empno, job, loc from emp where job = 'CLERK';
select empno, job, loc from emp where job = 'CLERK'
                          *
ERROR at line 1:
ORA-00376: file 13 cannot be read at this time
ORA-01110: data file 13: '/home/ora10g/oradata/.../o1_mf_p2_1dzn8jwp_.dbf'
```

The CLERK data is in all of the partitions, and the fact that three of the tablespaces are offline does affect us. This is unavoidable unless we had partitioned on JOB, but then we would have had the same issues with queries that needed data by LOC. Anytime you need to access the data from many different "keys," you will have this issue. Oracle will give you the data whenever it can.

Note, however, that if the query can be answered from the index, avoiding the
TABLE ACCESS BY ROWID, the fact that the data is unavailable is not as meaningful:

```
ops$tkyte@ORA10G> select count(*) from emp where job = 'CLERK';

COUNT(*)
----------
         4
```

Since Oracle didn't need the table in this case, the fact that most of the partitions were
offline doesn't affect this query. As this type of optimization (i.e., answer the query using just
the index) is common in an OLTP system, there will be many applications that are not affected
by the data that is offline. All we need to do now is make the offline data available as fast as
possible (restore it and recover it).

Partitioning and Performance, Revisited

Many times I hear people say, "I'm very disappointed in partitioning. We partitioned our
largest table and *it went much slower*. So much for partitioning being a performance increasing feature."

Partitioning can do one of the following three things to overall query performance:

- Make your queries go faster

- Not impact the performance of your queries at all

- Make your queries go much slower and use many times the resources as the nonpartitioned implementation

In a data warehouse, with an understanding of the questions being asked of the data, the
first bullet point is very much achievable. Partitioning can positively impact queries that frequently full scan large database tables by eliminating large sections of data from consideration.
Suppose you have a table with 1 billion rows in it. There is a timestamp attribute. Your query
is going to retrieve one years' worth of data from this table (and it has ten years of data). Your
query uses a full table scan to retrieve this data. Had it been partitioned by this timestamp
entry—say, a partition per month—then you could have full scanned one-tenth the data
(assuming a uniform distribution of data over the years). Partition elimination would have
removed the other 90 percent of the data from consideration. Your query would likely run
faster.

Now, take a similar table in an OLTP system. You would never retrieve 10 percent of a
1 billion row table in that type of application. Therefore, the massive increase in speed seen
by the data warehouse just would not be achievable in a transactional system. You are not
doing the same sort of work, and the same possible improvements just are not realistic. Therefore, in general, in your OLTP system the first bullet point is not achievable, and you won't be
applying partitioning predominantly for increased performance. Increased availability—
absolutely. Administrative ease of use—very much so. But in an OLTP system, I say you have
to work hard to make sure you achieve the second point: that you do not impact the performance of your queries at all, negatively or positively. Many times, your goal is to apply
partitioning without affecting query response time.

On many occasions, I've seen that the implementation team will see they have a large table, say of 10 million rows. Now, 10 million sounds like an incredibly large number (and five or ten years ago, it would have been, but time changes all things). The team decides to partition the data. But in looking at the data, there are no logical attributes that make sense for RANGE partitioning. There are no sensible attributes for that. Likewise, LIST partitioning doesn't make sense. Nothing pops out of this table as being the "right thing" to partition by. So, the team opts for hash partitioning on the primary key, which just happens to be populated by an Oracle sequence number. It looks perfect, it is unique and easy to hash, and many queries are of the form SELECT * FROM T WHERE PRIMARY_KEY = :X.

But the problem is, there are many other queries against this object that are not of that form. For illustrative purposes, assume the table in question is really the ALL_OBJECTS dictionary view, and while internally many queries would be of the form WHERE OBJECT_ID = :X, the end users frequently have these requests of the application as well:

- Show me the details of SCOTT's EMP TABLE (WHERE OWNER = :O AND OBJECT_TYPE = :T ➥ AND OBJECT_NAME = :N).

- Show me all of the tables SCOTT owns (WHERE OWNER = :O AND OBJECT_TYPE = :T).

- Show me all of the objects SCOTT owns (WHERE OWNER = :O).

In support of those queries, you have an index on (OWNER,OBJECT_TYPE,OBJECT_NAME). But you also read that "local indexes are more available," and you would like to be more available regarding your system, so you implement with them. You end up re-creating your table like this, with 16 hash partitions:

```
ops$tkyte@ORA10G> create table t
  2  ( OWNER, OBJECT_NAME, SUBOBJECT_NAME, OBJECT_ID, DATA_OBJECT_ID,
  3    OBJECT_TYPE, CREATED, LAST_DDL_TIME, TIMESTAMP, STATUS,
  4    TEMPORARY, GENERATED, SECONDARY )
  5  partition by hash(object_id)
  6  partitions 16
  7  as
  8  select * from all_objects;
Table created.

ops$tkyte@ORA10G> create index t_idx
  2  on t(owner,object_type,object_name)
  3  LOCAL
  4  /
Index created.

ops$tkyte@ORA10G> begin
  2          dbms_stats.gather_table_stats
  3          ( user, 'T', cascade=>true);
  4  end;
  5  /
PL/SQL procedure successfully completed.
```

and you execute your typical OLTP queries you know you run frequently:

```
variable o varchar2(30)
variable t varchar2(30)
variable n varchar2(30)

exec :o := 'SCOTT'; :t := 'TABLE'; :n := 'EMP';

select *
  from t
 where owner = :o
   and object_type = :t
   and object_name = :n
/
select *
  from t
 where owner = :o
   and object_type = :t
/
select *
  from t
 where owner = :o
/
```

but you notice that when you run this with SQL_TRACE=TRUE and review the resulting TKPROF report the following performance characteristics:

```
select * from t where owner = :o and object_type = :t and object_name = :n

call     count     cpu     elapsed     disk     query     current     rows
------- ------   -------- ----------  ------- ---------  ---------- ----------
total       4     0.00       0.00        0        34          0          1

Rows     Row Source Operation
-------  -------------------------------------------------------
      1  PARTITION HASH ALL PARTITION: 1 16 (cr=34 pr=0 pw=0 time=359 us)
      1   TABLE ACCESS BY LOCAL INDEX ROWID T PARTITION: 1 16 (cr=34 pr=0
      1    INDEX RANGE SCAN T_IDX PARTITION: 1 16 (cr=33 pr=0 pw=0 time=250
```

You compare that to the same table, only with *no partitioning implemented*, and discover the following:

```
select * from t where owner = :o and object_type = :t and object_name = :n

call     count     cpu     elapsed     disk     query     current     rows
------- ------   -------- ----------  ------- ---------  ---------- ----------
total       4     0.00       0.00        0         5          0          1
```

```
Rows    Row Source Operation
-------  ------------------------------------------------
     1   TABLE ACCESS BY INDEX ROWID T (cr=5 pr=0 pw=0 time=62 us)
     1    INDEX RANGE SCAN T_IDX (cr=4 pr=0 pw=0 time=63 us)
```

You might immediately jump to the (erroneous) conclusion that partitioning causes a sevenfold increase in I/O: 5 query mode gets without partitioning and 34 with partitioning. If your system had an issue with high consistent gets (logical I/Os before), it is worse now. If it didn't have one before, it might well get one. The same thing can be observed for the other two queries. In the following, the first total line is for the partitioned table and the second is for the nonpartitioned table:

```
select * from t where owner =`:o and object_type = :t

call     count     cpu    elapsed      disk      query    current     rows
-------  ------  --------  ----------  ----------  ----------  ----------  ----------
total         5    0.01      0.01         0          47          0          16
total         5    0.00      0.00         0          16          0          16

select * from t where owner = :o

call     count     cpu    elapsed      disk      query    current     rows
-------  ------  --------  ----------  ----------  ----------  ----------  ----------
total         5    0.00      0.00         0          51          0          25
total         5    0.00      0.00         0          23          0          25
```

The queries each returned the same answer, but consumed 500 percent, 300 percent, or 200 percent of the I/Os to accomplish it—this is not good. The root cause? The index partitioning scheme. Notice in the preceding plan the partitions listed in the last line: 1 through 16.

```
     1   PARTITION HASH ALL PARTITION: 1 16 (cr=34 pr=0 pw=0 time=359 us)
     1    TABLE ACCESS BY LOCAL INDEX ROWID T PARTITION: 1 16 (cr=34 pr=0
     1     INDEX RANGE SCAN T_IDX PARTITION: 1 16 (cr=33 pr=0 pw=0 time=250
```

This query has to look at *each and every* index partition because entries for SCOTT may well be (in fact, probably are) in *each and every* index partition. The index is logically hash partitioned by OBJECT_ID, so any query that uses this index and does not also refer to the OBJECT_ID in the predicate must consider *every* index partition!

The solution here is to globally partition your index. For example, continuing with the same T_IDX example, we could choose to hash partition the index in Oracle 10*g*:

■**Note** Hash partitioning of indexes is a new Oracle 10*g* feature that is not available in Oracle9*i*. There are considerations to be taken into account with hash partitioned indexes regarding range scans, which we'll discuss later in this section.

```
ops$tkyte@ORA10G> create index t_idx
  2  on t(owner,object_type,object_name)
  3  global
  4  partition by hash(owner)
  5  partitions 16
  6  /
Index created.
```

Much like the hash partitioned tables we investigated earlier, Oracle will take the OWNER value, hash it to a partition between 1 and 16, and place the index entry in there. Now when we review the TKPROF information for these three queries again

call	count	cpu	elapsed	disk	query	current	rows
total	4	0.00	0.00	0	4	0	1
total	5	0.00	0.00	0	19	0	16
total	5	0.01	0.00	0	28	0	25

we can see we are much closer to the worked performed by the nonpartitioned table earlier—that is, we have not negatively impacted the work performed by our queries. It should be noted, however, that a hash partitioned index cannot be range scanned. In general, it is most suitable for exact equality (equals or in-lists). If you were to query WHERE OWNER > :X using the preceding index, it would not be able to perform a simple range scan using partition elimination—you would be back to inspecting all 16 hash partitions.

Does that mean that partitioning won't have any positive impact on OLTP performance? No, not entirely—you just have to look in a different place. In general, it will not positively impact the performance of your data retrieval in OLTP; rather, care has to be taken to ensure data retrieval isn't affected negatively. But for data modification in highly concurrent environments, partitioning may provide salient benefits.

Consider the preceding a rather simple example of a single table with a single index, and add into the mix a primary key. Without partitioning, there is, in fact, a single table: all insertions go into this single table. There is contention perhaps for the freelists on this table. Additionally, the primary key index on the OBJECT_ID column would be a heavy right-hand-side index, as we discussed in Chapter 11. Presumably it would be populated by a sequence; hence, all inserts would go after the rightmost block leading to buffer busy waits. Also, there would be a single index structure, T_IDX, for which people would be contending. So far, a lot of "single" items.

Enter partitioning. You hash partition the table by OBJECT_ID into 16 partitions. There are now 16 "tables" to contend for, and each table has one-sixteenth the number of users hitting it simultaneously. You locally partition the primary key index on OBJECT_ID into 16 partitions. You now have 16 "right-hand sides," and each index structure will receive one-sixteenth the workload it had before. And so on. That is, you can use partitioning in a highly concurrent environment to reduce contention, much like we used a reverse key index in Chapter 11 to reduce the buffer busy waits. However, you must be aware that the very process of partitioning out the data consumes more CPU itself than not having partitioning. That is, it takes more CPU to figure out where to put the data than it would if the data had but one place to go.

So, as with everything, before applying partitioning to a system to "increase performance," make sure you understand what that system *needs*. If your system is currently CPU bound, but that CPU usage is not due to contention and latch waits, introducing partitioning could make the problem worse, not better!

USING ORDER BY

This example brought to mind an unrelated but very important fact. When looking at hash partitioned indexes, we are faced with another case where the use of a index to retrieve data would *not* automatically retrieve the data sorted. Many people assume that if the query plan shows an index is used to retrieve the data, the data will be retrieved sorted. *This has never been true.* The only way we can retrieve data in any sort of sorted order is to use ORDER BY on the query. If your query does not contain an ORDER BY statement, you cannot make any assumptions about the sorted order of the data.

A quick example demonstrates this. We create a small table as a copy of ALL_USERS and create a hash partitioned index with four partitions on the USER_ID column:

```
ops$tkyte@ORA10G> create table t
  2  as
  3  select *
  4    from all_users
  5  /
Table created.

ops$tkyte@ORA10G> create index t_idx
  2  on t(user_id)
  3  global
  4  partition by hash(user_id)
  5  partitions 4
  6  /
Index created.
```

Now, we will query that table and use a hint to have Oracle use the index. Notice the ordering (actually, the lack of ordering) of the data:

```
ops$tkyte@ORA10G> set autotrace on explain
ops$tkyte@ORA10G> select /*+ index( t t_idx ) */ user_id
  2    from t
  3   where user_id > 0
  4  /

   USER_ID
----------
        11
        34
...
        81
       157
```

```
          19
          22
...
         139
         161
           5
          23
...
         163
         167
          35
          37
...
          75
         160
38 rows selected.

Execution Plan
----------------------------------------------------------
   0      SELECT STATEMENT Optimizer=ALL_ROWS (Cost=4 Card=38 Bytes=494)
   1    0   PARTITION HASH (ALL) (Cost=4 Card=38 Bytes=494)
   2    1     INDEX (RANGE SCAN) OF 'T_IDX' (INDEX) (Cost=4 Card=38 Bytes=494)

ops$tkyte@ORA10G> set autotrace off
```

So, even though Oracle used the index in a range scan, the data is obviously not sorted. In fact, you might observe a pattern in this data. There are "four sorted" results here: the ... replaces values that were increasing in value; and between the rows with USER_ID = 34 and 81, the values were increasing in the output. Then the row with USER_ID = 19 appeared. What we are observing is Oracle returning "sorted data" from each of the four hash partitions, one after the other.

This is just a warning that unless your query has an ORDER BY, you have no reason to anticipate the data being returned to you in any kind of sorted order whatsoever. (And no, GROUP BY doesn't have to sort either! There is no substitute for ORDER BY.)

Auditing and Segment Space Compression

Not too many years ago, U.S. government constraints such as those imposed by the HIPAA act (http://www.hhs.gov/ocr/hipaa) were not in place. Companies such as Enron were still in business, and another U.S. government requirement for Sarbanes-Oxley compliance did not exist. Back then, auditing was considered something that "we might do someday, maybe." Today, however, auditing is at the forefront, and many DBAs are challenged to retain online up to seven years of audit trail information for their financial, business, and health care databases.

Audit trail information is the one piece of data in your database that you might well insert but never retrieve during the normal course of operation. It is there predominantly as a forensic, after-the-fact trail of evidence. We need to have it, but from many perspectives, it is just something that sits on our disks and consumes space—lots and lots of space. And then every month or year or some other time interval, we have to purge or archive it. Auditing is something that if not properly designed from the beginning can kill you at the end. Seven years from now when you are faced with your first purge or archive of the old data is not when you want to be thinking about how to accomplish it. Unless you designed for it, getting that old information out is going to be painful.

Enter two technologies that make auditing not only bearable, but also pretty easy to manage and consume less space. These technologies are partitioning and segment space compression, as we discussed in Chapter 10. That second one might not be as obvious since segment space compression only works with large bulk operations like a direct path load, and audit trails are typically inserted into a row at a time, as events happen. The trick is to combine sliding window partitions with segment space compression.

Suppose we decide to partition the audit trail by month. During the first month of business, we just insert into the partitioned table; these inserts go in using the "conventional path," not a direct path, and hence are not compressed. Now, before the month ends, we'll add a new partition to the table to accommodate next month's auditing activity. Shortly after the beginning of next month, we will perform a large bulk operation on last month's audit trail—specifically, we'll use the ALTER TABLE command to move last month's partition, which will have the effect of compressing the data as well. If we, in fact, take this a step further, we could move this partition from a read-write tablespace, which it must have been in, into a tablespace that is normally read-only (and contains other partitions for this audit trail). In that fashion, we can back up that tablespace once a month, after we move the partition in there; ensure we have a good, clean, current readable copy of the tablespace; and then not back it up anymore that month. We might have these tablespaces for our audit trail:

- A current online, read-write tablespace that gets backed up like every other normal tablespace in our system. The audit trail information in this tablespace is not compressed, and it is constantly inserted into.

- A read-only tablespace containing "this year to date" audit trail partitions in a compressed format. At the beginning of each month, we make this tablespace read-write, move and compress last month's audit information into this tablespace, make it read-only again, and back it up.

- A series of tablespaces for last year, the year before, and so on. These are all read-only and might even be on slow, cheap media. In the event of a media failure, we just need to restore from backup. We would occasionally pick a year at random from our backup sets to ensure they are still restorable (tapes go bad sometimes).

In this fashion, we have made purging easy (i.e., drop a partition). We have made archiving easy, too—you could just transport a tablespace off and restore it later. We have reduced our space utilization by implementing compression. We have reduced our backup volumes, as in many systems, the single largest set of data is *audit trail data*. If you can remove some or all of that from your day-to-day backups, the difference will be measurable.

In short, audit trail requirements and partitioning are two things that go hand in hand, regardless of the underlying system type, be it data warehouse or OLTP.

Summary

Partitioning is extremely useful in scaling up large database objects in the database. This scaling is visible from the perspective of performance scaling, availability scaling, and administrative scaling. All three are extremely important to different people. The DBA is concerned with administrative scaling. The owners of the system are concerned with availability, because downtime is lost money, and anything that reduces downtime—or reduces the impact of downtime—boosts the payback for a system. The end users of the system are concerned with performance scaling. No one likes to use a slow system, after all.

We also looked at the fact that in an OLTP system, partitions may not increase performance, especially if applied improperly. Partitions can increase the performance of certain classes of queries, but those queries are generally not applied in an OLTP system. This point is important to understand, as many people associate partitioning with "free performance increase." This does not mean that partitions should *not* be used in OLTP systems—they do provide many other salient benefits in this environment—just don't expect a massive increase in throughput. Expect reduced downtime. Expect the same good performance (partitioning *will not* slow you down when applied appropriately). Expect easier manageability, which may lead to increased performance due to the fact that some maintenance operations are performed by the DBAs more frequently because they can be.

We investigated the various table-partitioning schemes offered by Oracle—range, hash, list, and composite—and talked about when they are most appropriately used. We spent the bulk of our time looking at partitioned indexes and examining the differences between prefixed and nonprefixed and local and global indexes. We investigated partition operations in data warehouses combined with global indexes, and the tradeoff between resource consumption and availability.

Over time, I see this feature becoming more relevant to a broader audience as the size and scale of database applications grow. The Internet and its database-hungry nature along with legislation requiring longer retention of audit data are leading to more and more extremely large collections of data, and partitioning is a natural tool to help manage that problem.

CHAPTER 14

■■■

Parallel Execution

*P*arallel execution, a feature of Oracle Enterprise Edition (it is not available in the Standard Edition), was first introduced in Oracle version 7.1.6 in 1994. It is the ability to physically break a large serial task (any DML, or DDL in general) into many smaller bits that may all be processed simultaneously. Parallel executions in Oracle mimic the real-life processes we see all of the time. Rarely would you expect to see a single individual build a house; it is far more common for many teams of people to work concurrently to rapidly assemble the house. In that way, certain operations can be divided into smaller tasks and performed concurrently. For example, the plumbing and electrical wiring can take place at the same time to reduce the total amount of time required for the job as a whole.

Parallel execution in Oracle follows much the same logic. It is often possible for Oracle to divide a certain large "job" into smaller parts and to perform each part concurrently. For example, if a full table scan of a large table is required, there is no reason why Oracle cannot have four parallel sessions, P001–P004, perform the full scan together, with each session reading a different portion of the table. If the data scanned by P001–P004 needs to be sorted, this could be carried out by four more parallel sessions, P005–P008, which could ultimately send the results to an overall coordinating session for the query.

Parallel execution is a tool that, when wielded properly, may increase the response time of certain operations by orders of magnitude. When it's wielded as a "fast = true" switch, the results are typically quite the opposite. In this chapter, the goal is not to explain precisely how parallel query is implemented in Oracle, the myriad combinations of plans that can result from parallel operations, and the like. I feel that much of that material is covered quite well in the *Oracle Administrator's Guide*, the *Oracle Concepts Guide* and, in particular, the *Oracle Data Warehousing Guide*. This chapter's goal is to give you an understanding of what class of problems parallel execution is and isn't appropriate for. Specifically, after looking at when to use parallel execution, we will cover the following:

- *Parallel query*: The ability to perform a single query using many operating system processes or threads. Oracle will find operations it can perform in parallel, such as full table scans or large sorts, and create a query plan to do so.

- *Parallel DML (PDML)*: This is very similar in nature to parallel query, but it is used in reference to performing modifications (INSERT, UPDATE, DELETE, and MERGE) using parallel processing. In this chapter, we'll look at PDML and discuss some of the inherent limitations associated with it.

- *Parallel DDL*: Parallel DDL is the ability of Oracle to perform large DDL operations in parallel. For example, an index rebuild, creation of a new index, loading of data, and reorganization of large tables may all use parallel processing. This, I believe, is the "sweet spot" for parallelism in the database, so we will focus most of the discussion on this topic.

- *Parallel recovery*: This is the ability of the database to perform instance or even media recovery in parallel in an attempt to reduce the time it takes to recover from failures.

- *Procedural parallelism*: This is the ability to run developed code in parallel. In this chapter, I'll discuss two approaches to this. In the first approach, Oracle runs our developed PL/SQL code in parallel in a fashion transparent to developers (developers are not developing parallel code; rather, Oracle is parallelizing their code for them transparently). The other approach is something I term "do-it-yourself parallelism," whereby the developed code is designed to be executed in parallel.

When to Use Parallel Execution

Parallel execution can be fantastic. It can allow you to take a process that executes over many hours or days and complete it in minutes. Breaking down a huge problem into small components may, in some cases, dramatically reduce the processing time. However, one underlying concept that will be useful to keep in mind while considering parallel execution is summarized by this very short quote from *Practical Oracle8i: Building Efficient Databases* (Addison-Wesley, 2001) by Jonathan Lewis:

> PARALLEL QUERY option is essentially nonscalable.

Parallel execution is essentially a nonscalable solution. It was designed to allow an individual user or a particular SQL statement to consume all resources of a database. If you have a feature that allows an individual to make use of everything that is available, and then you allow two individuals to use that feature, you'll have obvious contention issues. As the number of concurrent users on your system begins to overwhelm the number of resources you have (memory, CPU, and I/O), the ability to deploy parallel operations becomes questionable. If you have a four-CPU machine, for example, and on average you have 32 users executing queries simultaneously, then the odds are that you do *not* want to parallelize their operations. If you allowed each user to perform just a "parallel 2" query, then you would now have 64 concurrent operations taking place on a machine with only four CPUs. If the machine were not overwhelmed before parallel execution, it almost certainly would be now.

In short, parallel execution can also be a terrible idea. In many cases, the application of parallel processing will only lead to increased resource consumption, as parallel execution attempts to use *all available resources*. In a system where resources must be shared by many concurrent transactions, such as an OLTP system, you would likely observe *increased* response times due to this. Oracle avoids certain execution techniques that it can use efficiently in a serial execution plan and adopts execution paths such as full scans in the hope that by performing many pieces of the larger, bulk operation in parallel, it would be better than the serial plan. Parallel execution, when applied inappropriately, may be the cause of your performance problem, not the solution for it.

So, before applying parallel execution, you need the following two things to be true:

- You must have a very large task, such as the full scan of 50GB of data.

- You must have sufficient *available* resources. Before parallel full scanning 50GB of data, you would want to make sure that there is sufficient free CPU (to accommodate the parallel processes) as well as sufficient I/O. The 50GB should be spread over more than one physical disk to allow for many concurrent read requests to happen simultaneously, there should be sufficient I/O channels from the disk to the computer to retrieve the data from disk in parallel, and so on.

If you have a small task, as generally typified by the queries carried out in an OLTP system, or you have insufficient *available* resources, again as is typical in an OLTP system where CPU and I/O resources are often already used to their maximum, then parallel execution is not something you'll want to consider.

A Parallel Processing Analogy

I often use an analogy to describe parallel processing and why you need both a large task *and* sufficient free resources in the database. It goes like this: suppose you have two tasks to complete. The first is to write a one-page summary of a new product. The other is to write a ten-chapter comprehensive report, with each chapter being very much independent of the others. For example, consider this book. This chapter, "Parallel Execution," is very much separate and distinct from the chapter titled "Redo and Undo"—they did not have to be written sequentially.

How do you approach each task? Which one do you think would benefit from parallel processing?

One-Page Summary

In this analogy, the one-page summary you have been assigned is not a large task. You would either do it yourself or assign it to a single individual. Why? Because the amount of work required to "parallelize" this process would exceed the work needed just to write the paper yourself. You would have to sit down, figure out that there should be 12 paragraphs, determine that each paragraph is not dependent on the other paragraphs, hold a team meeting, pick 12 individuals, explain to them the problem and assign each person a paragraph, act as the coordinator and collect all of their paragraphs, sequence them into the right order, verify they are correct, and then print the report. This is all likely to take longer than it would to *just write the paper yourself, serially*. The overhead of managing a large group of people on a project of this scale will far outweigh any gains to be had from having the 12 paragraphs written in parallel.

The exact same principle applies to parallel execution in the database. If you have a job that takes seconds or less to complete serially, then the introduction of parallel execution and its associated managerial overhead will likely make the entire thing take longer.

Ten-Chapter Report

Now let's examine the second task. If you want that ten-chapter report fast—as fast as possible—the slowest way to accomplish it would be to assign all of the work to a single individual (trust me, I know—look at this book! Some days I wished there were 15 of me working on it).

Here you would hold the meeting, review the process, assign the work, act as the coordinator, collect the results, bind up the finished report, and deliver it. It would not have been done in one-tenth the time, but perhaps one-eighth or so. Again, I say this with the proviso that *you have sufficient free resources*. If you have a large staff that is currently not actually doing anything, then splitting up the work makes complete sense.

However, consider that as the manager, your staff is multitasking and they have a lot on their plates. In that case, you have to be careful with that big project. You need to be sure not to overwhelm your staff; you don't want to work them beyond the point of exhaustion. You can't delegate out more work than your resources (your people) can cope with, otherwise they'll quit. If your staff is already fully utilized, adding more work will cause all schedules to slip and all projects to be delayed.

Parallel execution in Oracle is very much the same. If you have a task that takes many minutes, hours, or days, then the introduction of parallel execution may be the thing that makes it run eight times faster. But then again, if you are already seriously low on resources (the overworked team of people), then the introduction of parallel execution would be something to avoid, as the system will become even more bogged down. While the Oracle server processes won't "quit" in protest, they could start running out of RAM and failing, or just suffer from such long waits for I/O or CPU as to make it appear as if they were doing no work whatsoever.

If you keep that in mind, remembering never to take an analogy to illogical extremes, you'll have the commonsense guiding rule to see if parallelism can be of some use. If you have a job that takes seconds, it is doubtful that parallel execution can be used to make it go faster—the converse would be more likely. If you are low on resources already (i.e., your resources are fully utilized), adding parallel execution would likely make things worse, not better. Parallel execution is excellent for when you have a really big job and plenty of excess capacity. In this chapter, we'll take a look at some of the ways we can exploit those resources.

Parallel Query

Parallel query allows a single SQL SELECT statement to be divided into many smaller queries, with each component query being run concurrently, and then the results from each combined to provide the final answer. For example, consider the following query:

```
big_table@ORA10G> select count(status) from big_table;
```

Using parallel query, this query could use some number of parallel sessions; break the BIG_TABLE into small, nonoverlapping slices; and ask each parallel session to read the table and count its section of rows. The parallel query coordinator for this session would then receive each of the aggregated counts from the individual parallel sessions and further aggregate them, returning the final answer to the client application. Graphically, it might look like Figure 14-1.

The P000, P001, P002, and P003 processes are known as *parallel execution servers*, sometimes also referred to as parallel query (PQ) slaves. Each of these parallel execution servers is a separate session connected as if it were a dedicated server process. Each one is responsible for scanning a nonoverlapping region of BIG_TABLE, aggregating their results subsets, and sending back their output to the coordinating server—the original session's server process—which will aggregate the subresults into the final answer.

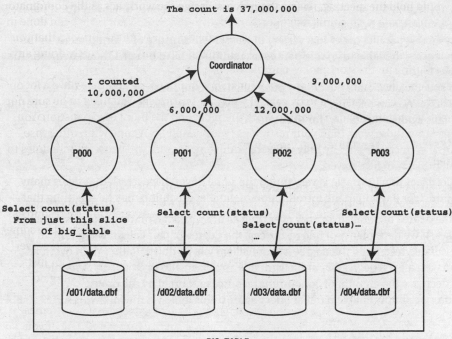

Figure 14-1. *Parallel select count (status) depiction*

We can see this in an explain plan. Using a BIG_TABLE with 10 million rows in it, we'll walk through enabling a parallel query for that table and discover how we can "see" parallel query in action. This example was performed on a four-CPU machine with default values for all parallel parameters; that is, this is an out-of-the-box installation where only necessary parameters were set, including SGA_TARGET (set to 1GB), CONTROL_FILES, DB_BLOCK_SIZE (set to 8KB), and PGA_AGGREGATE_TARGET (set to 512MB). Initially, we would expect to see the following plan:

```
big_table@ORA10GR1> explain plan for
  2  select count(status) from big_table;
Explained.

big_table@ORA10GR1> select * from table(dbms_xplan.display);

PLAN_TABLE_OUTPUT
-----------------------------------------
Plan hash value: 1287793122
-----------------------------------------------------------------------------
| Id  | Operation          | Name      | Rows|Bytes | Cost (%CPU)|Time      |
-----------------------------------------------------------------------------
|  0  | SELECT STATEMENT   |           |   1 |   17 | 32390   (2)|00:06:29  |
|  1  |  SORT AGGREGATE    |           |   1 |   17 |            |          |
|  2  |   TABLE ACCESS FULL| BIG_TABLE |  10M| 162M | 32390   (2)|00:06:29  |
-----------------------------------------------------------------------------
```

That is a typical *serial* plan. No parallelism is involved because we did not request parallel query to be enabled, and by default it will not be.

We may enable parallel query in a variety of ways, including use of a hint directly in the query or by altering the table to enable parallel execution paths to be considered (which is the option we use here).

We can specifically dictate the degree of parallelism to be considered in execution paths against this table. We can tell Oracle, "We would like you to use parallel degree 4 when creating execution plans against this table," for example:

```
big_table@ORA10GR1> alter table big_table parallel 4;
Table altered.
```

I prefer to just tell Oracle, "Please consider parallel execution, but you figure out the appropriate degree of parallelism based on the current system workload and the query itself." That is, let the degree of parallelism vary over time as the workload on the system increases and decreases. If we have plenty of free resources, the degree of parallelism will go up; in times of limited available resources, the degree of parallelism will go down. Rather than overload the machine with a fixed degree of parallelism, this approach allows Oracle to dynamically increase or decrease the amount of concurrent resources required by the query.

Therefore, we simply enable parallel query against this table via the following ALTER TABLE command:

```
big_table@ORA10GR1> alter table big_table parallel;
Table altered.
```

That is all there is to it—parallel query will now be considered for operations against this table. When we rerun the explain plan, this time we see the following:

```
big_table@ORA10GR1> explain plan for
  2  select count(status) from big_table;
Explained.

big_table@ORA10GR1> select * from table(dbms_xplan.display);

PLAN_TABLE_OUTPUT
------------------------------------------------------
Plan hash value: 1651916128

------------------------------------------------------------------------------
|Id | Operation            | Name     |Cost(%CPU)| TQ |IN-OUT|PQ Distrib |
------------------------------------------------------------------------------
|  0| SELECT STATEMENT     |          | 4465  (1)|      |      |           |
|  1|  SORT AGGREGATE      |          |          |      |      |           |
|  2|   PX COORDINATOR     |          |          |      |      |           |
|  3|    PX SEND QC (RANDOM) | :TQ10000 |          |Q1,00| P->S |QC (RAND)  |
|  4|     SORT AGGREGATE   |          |          |Q1,00| PCWP |           |
|  5|      PX BLOCK ITERATOR |        | 4465  (1)|Q1,00| PCWC |           |
|  6|       TABLE ACCESS FULL| BIG_TABLE| 4465  (1)|Q1,00| PCWP |           |
------------------------------------------------------------------------------
```

■Note The ROWS, BYTES, and TIME columns were removed from this plan output to allow it to fit on the page. The aggregate time for the query, however, was 00:00:54 as opposed to the previous estimate of 00:06:29 for the serial plan. Remember, these are *estimates*, not promises! Also, this is the plan output from Oracle 10*g*—the plan output from Oracle9*i* would have less detail (four steps instead of seven), but the net effect is identical.

If you read this plan from the bottom up, starting at ID=6, it shows the steps described in Figure 14-1. The full table scan would be split up into many "smaller scans" (step 5). Each of those would aggregate their COUNT(STATUS) values (step 4). These subresults would be transmitted to the parallel query coordinator (steps 2 and 3), which would aggregate these results further (step 1) and output the answer.

If you were to actually execute this query on a freshly started system (where no other parallel execution had been done), you might observe the following. Here we are using the Linux ps command to find processes that represent parallel query processes (we expect to find none), running the query with parallel execution enabled, and then looking for those processes again:

```
big_table@ORA10GR1> host  ps -auxww | grep '^ora10gr1.*ora_p00._ora10g'

big_table@ORA10GR1> select count(status) from big_table;

COUNT(STATUS)
-------------
    10000000

big_table@ORA10GR1> host  ps -auxww | grep '^ora10gr1.*ora_p00._ora10g'
ora10gr1  3411 35.5  0.5 1129068 12200 ?  S    13:27   0:02 ora_p000_ora10gr1
ora10gr1  3413 28.0  0.5 1129064 12196 ?  S    13:27   0:01 ora_p001_ora10gr1
ora10gr1  3415 26.0  0.5 1129064 12196 ?  S    13:27   0:01 ora_p002_ora10gr1
ora10gr1  3417 23.3  0.5 1129044 12212 ?  S    13:27   0:01 ora_p003_ora10gr1
ora10gr1  3419 19.5  0.5 1129040 12228 ?  S    13:27   0:01 ora_p004_ora10gr1
ora10gr1  3421 19.1  0.5 1129056 12188 ?  S    13:27   0:01 ora_p005_ora10gr1
ora10gr1  3423 19.0  0.5 1129056 12164 ?  S    13:27   0:01 ora_p006_ora10gr1
ora10gr1  3425 21.6  0.5 1129048 12204 ?  S    13:27   0:01 ora_p007_ora10gr1
```

As we can see, there are now eight parallel execution servers that have been started by Oracle. If we are curious enough to want to "watch" parallel query, we can easily do so using two sessions. In the session we will run the parallel query in, we'll start by determining our SID:

```
big_table@ORA10GR1> select sid from v$mystat where rownum = 1;

       SID
----------
       162
```

Now, in another session, we get this query ready to run:

```
ops$tkyte@ORA10GR1> select sid, qcsid, server#, degree
  2  from v$px_session
  3  where qcsid = 162
```

Shortly after starting the parallel query in the session with SID=162, we come back to this second session and run the query:

```
  4  /

       SID      QCSID    SERVER#     DEGREE
---------- ---------- ---------- ----------
       145        162          1          8
       150        162          2          8
       147        162          3          8
       151        162          4          8
       146        162          5          8
       152        162          6          8
       143        162          7          8
       144        162          8          8
       162        162
9 rows selected.
```

We see here that our parallel query session (SID=162) is the query coordinator SID (QCSID) for nine rows in this dynamic performance view. Our session is "coordinating" or controlling these parallel query resources now. We can see each has its own SID; in fact, each is a separate Oracle session and shows up as such in V$SESSION during the execution of our parallel query:

```
ops$tkyte@ORA10GR1> select sid, username, program
  2  from v$session
  3  where sid in ( select sid
  4                   from v$px_session
  5                  where qcsid = 162 )
  6  /
   SID USERNAME                       PROGRAM
------ ------------------------------ -------------------------------
   143 BIG_TABLE                      oracle@dellpe (P005)
   144 BIG_TABLE                      oracle@dellpe (P002)
   145 BIG_TABLE                      oracle@dellpe (P006)
   146 BIG_TABLE                      oracle@dellpe (P004)
   147 BIG_TABLE                      oracle@dellpe (P003)
   150 BIG_TABLE                      oracle@dellpe (P001)
   151 BIG_TABLE                      oracle@dellpe (P000)
   153 BIG_TABLE                      oracle@dellpe (P007)
   162 BIG_TABLE                      sqlplus@dellpe (TNS V1-V3)
9 rows selected.
```

■Note If a parallel execution is not occurring in your system, do not expect to see the parallel execution servers in V$SESSION. They will be in V$PROCESS, but will not have a session established unless they are being used. The parallel execution servers will be connected to the database, but will not have a session established. See Chapter 5 for details on the difference between a session and a connection.

In a nutshell, that is how parallel query—and, in fact, parallel execution in general—works. It entails a series of parallel execution servers working in tandem to produce subresults that are fed either to other parallel execution servers for further processing or to the coordinator for the parallel query.

In this particular example, as depicted, we had BIG_TABLE spread across four separate devices, in a single tablespace (a tablespace with four data files). When implementing parallel execution, it is generally "optimal" to have your data spread over as many physical devices as possible. You can achieve this in a number of ways:

- Using RAID striping across disks

- Using ASM, with its built-in striping

- Using partitioning to physically segregate BIG_TABLE over many disks

- Using multiple data files in a single tablespace, thus allowing Oracle to allocate extents for the BIG_TABLE segment in many files

In general, parallel execution works best when given access to as many resources (CPU, memory, and I/O) as possible. However, that is not to say that nothing can be gained from parallel query if the entire set of data were on a single disk, but you would perhaps not gain as much as would be gained using multiple disks. The reason you would likely gain some speed in response time, even when using a single disk, is that when a given parallel execution server is counting rows it is not reading them, and vice versa. So, two parallel execution servers may well be able to complete the counting of all rows in less time than a serial plan would.

Likewise, you can benefit from parallel query even on a single CPU machine. It is doubtful that a serial SELECT COUNT(*) would use 100 percent of the CPU on a single CPU machine—it would be spending part of its time performing (and waiting for) physical I/O to disk. Parallel query would allow you to fully utilize the resources (the CPU and I/O, in this case) on the machine, whatever those resources may be.

That final point brings us back to the earlier quote from *Practical Oracle8i: Building Efficient Databases*: parallel query is essentially nonscalable. If you allowed four sessions to simultaneously perform queries with two parallel execution servers on that single CPU machine, you would probably find their response times to be longer than if they just processed serially. The more processes clamoring for a scarce resource, the longer it will take to satisfy all requests.

And remember, parallel query requires two things to be true. First, you need to have a large task to perform—for example, a long-running query, the runtime of which is measured in minutes, hours, or days, not in seconds or subseconds. This implies that parallel query is not a solution to be applied in a typical OLTP system, where you are not performing long-running tasks. Enabling parallel execution on these systems is often disastrous. Second, you need ample free resources such as CPU, I/O, and memory. If you are lacking in any of these, then parallel query may well push your utilization of that resource over the edge, negatively impacting overall performance and runtime.

In the past, parallel query was considered mandatory for many data warehouses simply because in the past (say, in 1995) data warehouses were rare and typically had a very small, focused user base. Today in 2005, data warehouses are literally everywhere and support user communities that are as large as those found for many transactional systems. This means that you may well not have sufficient free resources at any given point in time to enable parallel query on these systems. That doesn't mean parallel execution in general is not useful in this case—it just might be more of a DBA tool, as we'll see in the section "Parallel DDL," rather than a parallel query tool.

Parallel DML

The Oracle documentation limits the scope of the term DML (PDML) to include only INSERT, UPDATE, DELETE, and MERGE (it does not include SELECT as normal DML does). During PDML, Oracle may use many parallel execution servers to perform your INSERT, UPDATE, DELETE, or MERGE instead of a single serial process. On a multi-CPU machine with plenty of I/O bandwidth, the potential increase in speed may be large for mass DML operations.

However, you should *not* look to PDML as a feature to speed up your OLTP-based applications. As stated previously, parallel operations are designed to fully and totally maximize the utilization of a machine. They are designed so that a single user can completely use all of the disks, CPU, and memory on the machine. In certain data warehouses (with lots of data and few users), this is something you may want to achieve. In an OLTP system (with a lot of users all doing short, fast transactions), you do not want to give a user the ability to fully take over the machine resources.

This sounds contradictory: we use parallel query to scale up, so how could it not be scalable? When applied to an OLTP system, the statement is quite accurate. Parallel query is not something that scales up as the number of concurrent users increases. Parallel query was designed to allow a single session to generate as much work as 100 concurrent sessions would. In our OLTP system, we really do not want a single user to generate the work of 100 users.

PDML is useful in a large data warehousing environment to facilitate bulk updates to massive amounts of data. The PDML operation is executed in much the same way as a distributed query would be executed by Oracle, with each parallel execution server acting like a process in a separate database instance. Each slice of the table is modified by a separate thread with its own independent transaction (and hence its own undo segment, hopefully). After they are all done, the equivalent of a fast 2PC is performed to commit the separate, independent transactions. Figure 14-2 depicts a parallel update using four parallel execution servers. Each of the parallel execution servers has its own independent transaction, in which either all are committed with the PDML coordinating session or none commit.

We can actually observe the fact that there are separate independent transactions created for the parallel execution servers. We'll use two sessions again, as before. In the session with SID=162, we explicitly enable parallel DML. PDML differs from parallel query in that regard; unless you explicitly ask for it, you will *not* get it.

```
big_table@ORA10GR1> alter session enable parallel dml;
Session altered.
```

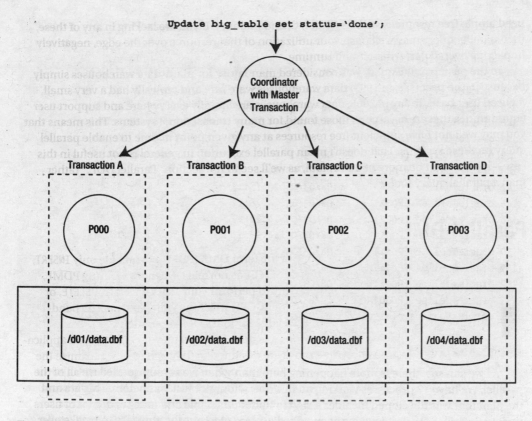

Figure 14-2. *Parallel update (PDML) depiction*

The fact that the table is "parallel" is not sufficient, as it was for parallel query. The reasoning behind the need to explicitly enable PDML in your session is the fact that PDML has certain limitations associated with it, which I list after this example.

In the same session, we do a bulk UPDATE that, because the table is "parallel enabled," will in fact be done in parallel:

```
big_table@ORA10GR1> update big_table set status = 'done';
```

In the other session, we'll join V$SESSION to V$TRANSACTION to show the active sessions for our PDML operation, as well as their independent transaction information:

```
ops$tkyte@ORA10GR1> select a.sid, a.program, b.start_time, b.used_ublk,
  2         b.xidusn ||'.'|| b.xidslot || '.' || b.xidsqn trans_id
  3    from v$session a, v$transaction b
  4   where a.taddr = b.addr
  5     and a.sid in ( select sid
  6                      from v$px_session
  7                     where qcsid = 162 )
  8   order by sid
  9  /
```

```
SID PROGRAM                START_TIME             USED_UBLK TRANS_ID
---- --------------------- ---------------------- --------- ------------
136 oracle@dellpe (P009)   08/03/05 14:28:17.          6256 18.9.37
137 oracle@dellpe (P013)   08/03/05 14:28:17           6369 21.39.225
138 oracle@dellpe (P015)   08/03/05 14:28:17           6799 24.16.1175
139 oracle@dellpe (P008)   08/03/05 14:28:17           6729 15.41.68
140 oracle@dellpe (P014)   08/03/05 14:28:17           6462 22.41.444
141 oracle@dellpe (P012)   08/03/05 14:28:17           6436 20.46.46
142 oracle@dellpe (P010)   08/03/05 14:28:17           6607 19.44.37
143 oracle@dellpe (P007)   08/03/05 14:28:17              1 17.12.46
144 oracle@dellpe (P006)   08/03/05 14:28:17              1 13.25.302
145 oracle@dellpe (P003)   08/03/05 14:28:17              1 1.21.1249
146 oracle@dellpe (P002)   08/03/05 14:28:17              1 14.42.49
147 oracle@dellpe (P005)   08/03/05 14:28:17              1 12.18.323
150 oracle@dellpe (P011)   08/03/05 14:28:17           6699 23.2.565
151 oracle@dellpe (P004)   08/03/05 14:28:17              1 16.26.46
152 oracle@dellpe (P001)   08/03/05 14:28:17              1 11.13.336
153 oracle@dellpe (P000)   08/03/05 14:28:17              1 2.29.1103
162 sqlplus@dellpe (TNS V1-V3) 08/03/05 14:25:46         2 3.13.2697

17 rows selected.
```

As we can see, there is more happening here than when we simply queried the table in parallel. We have 17 processes working on this operation, not just 9 as before. This is because the plan that was developed includes a step to update the table and independent steps to update the index entries. Looking at an edited explain plan output from DBMS_XPLAN (trailing columns were removed to permit the output to fit on the page), we see the following:

```
-------------------------------------------------
| Id | Operation            | Name      |
-------------------------------------------------
|  0 | UPDATE STATEMENT     |           |
|  1 |  PX COORDINATOR      |           |
|  2 |   PX SEND QC (RANDOM)| :TQ10001  |
|  3 |    INDEX MAINTENANCE | BIG_TABLE |
|  4 |     PX RECEIVE       |           |
|  5 |      PX SEND RANGE   | :TQ10000  |
|  6 |       UPDATE         | BIG_TABLE |
|  7 |        PX BLOCK ITERATOR |       |
|  8 |         TABLE ACCESS FULL| BIG_TABLE |
-------------------------------------------------
```

As a result of the pseudo-distributed implementation of PDML, certain limitations are associated with it:

- Triggers are not supported during a PDML operation. This is a reasonable limitation in my opinion, since triggers would tend to add a large amount of overhead to the update, and you are using PDML to go fast—the two features don't go together.

- There are certain declarative referential-integrity constraints that are not supported during the PDML, since each slice of the table is modified as a separate transaction in the separate session. Self-referential integrity is not supported, for example. Consider the deadlocks and other locking issues that would occur if it were supported.

- You cannot access the table you've modified with PDML until you commit or roll back.

- Advanced replication is not supported with PDML (because the implementation of advanced replication is trigger based).

- Deferred constraints (i.e., constraints that are in the deferred mode) are not supported.

- PDML may only be performed on tables that have bitmap indexes or LOB columns if the table is partitioned, and then the degree of parallelism would be capped at the number of partitions. You cannot parallelize an operation within partitions in this case, as each partition would get a single parallel execution server to operate on it.

- Distributed transactions are not supported when performing PDML.

- Clustered tables are not supported with PDML.

If you violate any of those restrictions, one of two things will happen: either the statement will be performed serially (no parallelism will be involved) or an error will be raised. For example, if you already performed the PDML against table T and then attempted to query table T before ending your transaction, then you will receive an error.

Parallel DDL

I believe that parallel DDL is the real "sweet spot" of Oracle's parallel technology. As we've discussed, parallel execution is generally not appropriate for OLTP systems. In fact, for many data warehouses, parallel query is becoming less and less of an option. It used to be that a data warehouse was built for a very small, focused user community—sometimes consisting of just one or two analysts. However, over the last decade I've watched them grow from small user communities to user communities of hundreds or thousands. Consider a data warehouse front-ended by a web-based application: it could be accessible to literally thousands or more users instantly.

But a DBA performing the large batch operations, perhaps during a maintenance window, is a different story. The DBA is still a single individual and he might have a huge machine with tons of computing resources available. The DBA has only "one thing to do": load this data, reorganize that table, rebuild that index. Without parallel execution, the DBA would be hard-pressed to really use the full capabilities of the hardware. With parallel execution, he can. The following SQL DDL commands permit "parallelization":

- CREATE INDEX: Multiple parallel execution servers can scan the table, sort the data, and write the sorted segments out to the index structure.

- CREATE TABLE AS SELECT: The query that executes the SELECT may be executed using parallel query, and the table load itself may be done in parallel.

- ALTER INDEX REBUILD: The index structure may be rebuilt in parallel.

- `ALTER TABLE MOVE`: A table may be moved in parallel.

- `ALTER TABLE SPLIT|COALESCE PARTITION`: The individual table partitions may be split or coalesced in parallel.

- `ALTER INDEX SPLIT PARTITION`: An index partition may be split in parallel.

The first four of these commands work for individual table/index partitions as well—that is, you may `MOVE` an individual partition of a table in parallel.

To me, parallel DDL is where the parallel execution in Oracle is of greatest measurable benefit. Sure, it can be used with parallel query to speed up certain long-running operations, but from a maintenance standpoint, and from an administration standpoint, parallel DDL is where the parallel operations affect us, DBAs and developers, the most. If you think of parallel query as being designed for the end user for the most part, then parallel DDL is designed for the DBA/developer.

Parallel DDL and Data Loading Using External Tables

One of my favorite new features in Oracle 9*i* is external tables, which are especially useful in the area of data loading. We'll cover data loading and external tables in some detail in the next chapter but, as a quick introduction, we'll take a brief look at these topics here to study the effects of parallel DDL on extent sizing and extent trimming.

External tables allow us to easily perform parallel direct path loads without thinking too hard about it. Oracle 7.1 gave us the ability to perform parallel direct path loads, whereby multiple sessions could write directly to the Oracle data files, bypassing the buffer cache entirely, bypassing undo for the table data, and perhaps even bypassing redo generation. This was accomplished via SQL*Loader. The DBA would have to script multiple SQL*Loader sessions, split the input data files to be loaded manually, determine the degree of parallelism, and coordinate all of the SQL*Loader processes. In short, it could be done, but it was hard.

With parallel DDL plus external tables, we have a parallel direct path load that is implemented via a simple `CREATE TABLE AS SELECT` or `INSERT /*+ APPEND */`. No more scripting, no more splitting of files, and no more coordinating the N number of scripts that would be running. In short, this combination provides pure ease of use, without a loss of performance.

Let's take a look at a simple example of this in action. We'll see shortly how to create an external table. We'll look at data loading with external tables in much more detail in the next chapter. For now, we'll use a "real" table to load another table from, much like many people do with staging tables in their data warehouse. The technique in short is as follows:

1. Use some extract, transform, load (ETL) tool to create input files.

2. Load these input files into staging tables.

3. Load a new table using queries against these staging tables.

We'll use the same `BIG_TABLE` from earlier, which is parallel-enabled and contains 10 million records. We're going to join this table to a second table, `USER_INFO`, which contains `OWNER`-related information from the `ALL_USERS` dictionary view. The goal is to denormalize this information into a flat structure.

We'll start by creating the USER_INFO table, enabling it for parallel operations, and then gathering statistics on it:

```
big_table@ORA10GR1> create table user_info as select * from all_users;
Table created.

big_table@ORA10GR1> alter table user_info parallel;
Table altered.

big_table@ORA10GR1> exec dbms_stats.gather_table_stats( user, 'USER_INFO' );
PL/SQL procedure successfully completed.
```

Now, we would like to parallel direct path load a new table with this information. The query we'll use is simply

```
create table new_table parallel
as
select a.*, b.user_id, b.created user_created
  from big_table a, user_info b
 where a.owner = b.username
```

The plan for that particular CREATE TABLE AS SELECT looked like this in Oracle 10*g*:

```
-------------------------------------------------------------------------
| Id | Operation                | Name      |  TQ  |IN-OUT| PQ Distrib |
-------------------------------------------------------------------------
|  0 | CREATE TABLE STATEMENT   |           |      |      |            |
|  1 |  PX COORDINATOR          |           |      |      |            |
|  2 |   PX SEND QC (RANDOM)     | :TQ10001  | Q1,01| P->S | QC (RAND)  |
|  3 |    LOAD AS SELECT         |           | Q1,01| PCWP |            |
|* 4 |     HASH JOIN            |           | Q1,01| PCWP |            |
|  5 |      PX RECEIVE          |           | Q1,01| PCWP |            |
|  6 |       PX SEND BROADCAST   | :TQ10000  | Q1,00| P->P | BROADCAST  |
|  7 |        PX BLOCK ITERATOR |           | Q1,00| PCWC |            |
|  8 |         TABLE ACCESS FULL| USER_INFO | Q1,00| PCWP |            |
|  9 |        PX BLOCK ITERATOR |           | Q1,01| PCWC |            |
| 10 |         TABLE ACCESS FULL | BIG_TABLE | Q1,01| PCWP |            |
-------------------------------------------------------------------------
```

If you look at the steps from 4 on down, that is the query (SELECT) component. The scan of BIG_TABLE and hash join to USER_INFO was performed in parallel, and each of the subresults was loaded into a portion of the table (step 3, the LOAD AS SELECT). After each of the parallel execution servers finishes its part of the join and load, it sends its results up to the query coordinator. In this case, the results simply indicated "success" or "failure," as the work had already been performed.

And that is all there is to it—parallel direct path loads made easy. The most important thing to consider with these operations is how space is used (or not used). Of particular importance is a side effect called *extent trimming*. I'd like to spend some time investigating that now.

Parallel DDL and Extent Trimming

Parallel DDL relies on direct path operations. That is, the data is not passed to the buffer cache to be written later; rather, an operation such as a CREATE TABLE AS SELECT will create new extents and write directly to them, and the data goes straight from the query to disk, in those newly allocated extents. Each parallel execution server performing its part of the CREATE ➥ TABLE AS SELECT will write to its own extent. The INSERT /*+ APPEND */ (a direct path insert) writes "above" a segment's HWM, and each parallel execution server will again write to its own set of extents, never sharing them with other parallel execution servers. Therefore, if you do a parallel CREATE TABLE AS SELECT and use four parallel execution servers to create the table, then you will have *at least* four extents—maybe more. But each of the parallel execution servers will allocate its own extent, write to it and, when it fills up, allocate another new extent. The parallel execution servers will never use an extent allocated by some other parallel execution server.

Figure 14-3 depicts this process. We have a CREATE TABLE NEW_TABLE AS SELECT being executed by four parallel execution servers. In the figure, each parallel execution server is represented by a different color (white, light gray, dark gray, or black). The boxes in the "disk drum" represent the extents that were created in some data file by this CREATE TABLE statement. Each extent is presented in one of the aforementioned four colors, for the simple reason that all of the data in any given extent was loaded by only one of the four parallel execution servers—P003 is depicted as having created and then loaded four of these extents. P000, on the other hand, is depicted as having five extents, and so on.

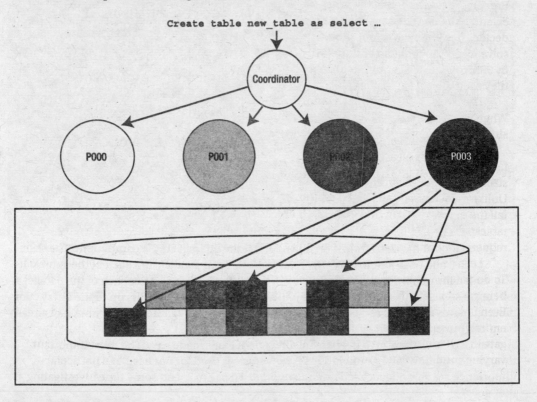

Figure 14-3. *Parallel DDL extent allocation depiction*

This sounds all right at first, but in a data warehouse environment, this can lead to "wastage" after a large load. Let's say you want to load 1,010MB of data (about 1GB), and you are using a tablespace with 100MB extents. You decide to use ten parallel execution servers to load this data. Each would start by allocating its own 100MB extent (there will be ten of them in all) and filling it up. Since each has 101MB of data to load, it would fill up its first extent and then proceed to allocate another 100MB extent, of which it would use 1MB. You now have 20 extents, 10 of which are full and 10 of which have 1MB each, and 990MB is "allocated but not used." This space could be used the next time you load, but right now you have 990MB of dead space. This is where extent trimming comes in. Oracle will attempt to take the last extent of each parallel execution server and "trim" it back to the smallest size possible.

Extent Trimming and Dictionary-Managed Tablespaces

If you are using legacy dictionary-managed tablespaces, then Oracle will be able to convert each of the 100MB extents that contain just 1MB of data into 1MB extents. Unfortunately, that would (in dictionary-managed tablespaces) tend to leave ten noncontiguous 99MB extents free, and since your allocation scheme was for 100MB extents, this 990MB of space would not be very useful! The next allocation of 100MB would likely *not* be able to use the existing space, since it would be 99MB of free space, followed by 1MB of allocated space, followed by 99MB of free space, and so on. We will not review the dictionary-managed approach further in this book.

Extent Trimming and Locally-Managed Tablespaces

Enter locally-managed tablespaces. Here we have two types: UNIFORM SIZE, whereby every extent in the tablespace is always precisely the same size, and AUTOALLOCATE, whereby Oracle decides how big each extent should be using an internal algorithm. Both of these approaches solve nicely the problem of the 99MB of free space, followed by 1MB of used space, followed by 99MB of free space, and so on, resulting in lots of free space that cannot be used. However, they each solve it very differently.

The UNIFORM SIZE approach obviates extent trimming from consideration all together. When you use UNIFORM SIZEs, Oracle cannot perform extent trimming. All extents are of that single size—none can be smaller (or larger) than that single size.

AUTOALLOCATE extents, on the other hand, do support extent trimming, but in an intelligent fashion. They use a few specific sizes of extents and have the ability to use space of different sizes—that is, the algorithm permits the use of all free space over time in the tablespace. Unlike the dictionary-managed tablespace, where if you request a 100MB extent, Oracle will fail the request if it can find only 99MB free extents (so close, yet so far), a locally-managed tablespace with AUTOALLOCATE extents can be more flexible. It may reduce the size of the request it was making in order to attempt to use all of the free space.

Let's now look at the differences between the two locally-managed tablespace approaches. To do that, we need a real-life example to work with. We'll set up an external table capable of being used in a parallel direct path load situation, which is something that we do frequently. Even if you are still using SQL*Loader to parallel direct path load data, this section applies entirely—you just have manual scripting to do to actually load the data. So, in order to investigate extent trimming, we need to set up our example load and then perform the loads under varying conditions and examine the results.

Setting Up

To get started, we need an external table. I've found time and time again that I have a legacy control file from SQL*Loader that I used to use to load data. One that looks like this, for example:

```
LOAD DATA
INFILE '/tmp/big_table.dat'
INTO TABLE big_table
REPLACE
FIELDS TERMINATED BY '|'
(
id ,owner ,object_name ,subobject_name ,object_id
,data_object_id ,object_type ,created ,last_ddl_time
,timestamp ,status ,temporary ,generated ,secondary
)
```

We can convert this *easily* into an external table definition using SQL*Loader itself:

```
$ sqlldr big_table/big_table big_table.ctl external_table=generate_only
SQL*Loader: Release 10.1.0.3.0 - Production on Mon Jul 11 14:16:20 2005
Copyright (c) 1982, 2004, Oracle.  All rights reserved.
```

Notice the parameter EXTERNAL_TABLE passed to SQL*Loader. It causes SQL*Loader in this case to not load data, but rather to generate a CREATE TABLE statement for us in the log file. This CREATE TABLE statement looked as follows (this is an abridged form; I've edited out repetitive elements to make the example smaller):

```
CREATE TABLE "SYS_SQLLDR_X_EXT_BIG_TABLE"
(
  "ID" NUMBER,
  ...
  "SECONDARY" VARCHAR2(1)
)
ORGANIZATION external
(
  TYPE oracle_loader
  DEFAULT DIRECTORY SYS_SQLLDR_XT_TMPDIR_00000
  ACCESS PARAMETERS
  (
    RECORDS DELIMITED BY NEWLINE CHARACTERSET WE8ISO8859P1
    BADFILE 'SYS_SQLLDR_XT_TMPDIR_00000':'big_table.bad'
    LOGFILE 'big_table.log_xt'
    READSIZE 1048576
    FIELDS TERMINATED BY "|" LDRTRIM
    REJECT ROWS WITH ALL NULL FIELDS
    (
      "ID" CHAR(255)
        TERMINATED BY "|",
      ....
    "SECONDARY" CHAR(255)
```

```
        TERMINATED BY "|"
    )
  )
  location
  (
    'big_table.dat'
  )
)REJECT LIMIT UNLIMITED
```

All we need to do is edit that a bit to name the external table the way we want; change the directories, perhaps; and so on:

```
ops$tkyte@ORA10GR1> create or replace directory my_dir as '/tmp/'
  2  /
Directory created.
```

And after that, all we need to do is actually create the table:

```
ops$tkyte@ORA10GR1> CREATE TABLE "BIG_TABLE_ET"
  2  (
  3    "ID" NUMBER,
...
 16    "SECONDARY" VARCHAR2(1)
 17  )
 18  ORGANIZATION external
 19  (
 20    TYPE oracle_loader
 21    DEFAULT DIRECTORY MY_DIR
 22    ACCESS PARAMETERS
 23    (
 24      RECORDS DELIMITED BY NEWLINE CHARACTERSET WE8ISO8859P1
 25      READSIZE 1048576
 26      FIELDS TERMINATED BY "|" LDRTRIM
 27      REJECT ROWS WITH ALL NULL FIELDS
 28    )
 29    location
 30    (
 31      'big_table.dat'
 32    )
 33  )REJECT LIMIT UNLIMITED
 34  /
Table created.
```

Then we make this table parallel enabled. This is the magic step—this is what will facilitate an easy parallel direct path load:

```
ops$tkyte@ORA10GR1> alter table big_table_et PARALLEL;
Table altered.
```

> **Note** The PARALLEL clause may also be used on the CREATE TABLE statement itself. Right after the REJECT LIMIT UNLIMITED, the keyword PARALLEL could have been added. I used the ALTER statement just to draw attention to the fact that the external table is, in fact, parallel enabled.

Extent Trimming with UNIFORM vs. AUTOALLOCATE Locally-Managed Tablespaces

That's all we need to do to set up the load component. Now, we would like to investigate how space is managed in a locally-managed tablespace (LMT) that uses UNIFORM extent sizes, compared to how space is managed in an LMT that AUTOALLOCATEs extents. In this case, we'll use 100MB extents. First we create LMT_UNIFORM, which uses uniform extent sizes:

```
ops$tkyte@ORA10GR1> create tablespace lmt_uniform
  2  datafile '/u03/ora10gr1/lmt_uniform.dbf' size 1048640K reuse
  3  autoextend on next 100m
  4  extent management local
  5  uniform size 100m;
Tablespace created.
```

Next, we create LMT_AUTO, which uses AUTOALLOCATE to determine extent sizes:

```
ops$tkyte@ORA10GR1> create tablespace lmt_auto
  2  datafile '/u03/ora10gr1/lmt_auto.dbf' size 1048640K reuse
  3  autoextend on next 100m
  4  extent management local
  5  autoallocate;
Tablespace created.
```

Each tablespace started with a 1GB data file (plus 64KB used by LMTs to manage the storage; it would be 128KB extra instead of 64KB if we were to use a 32KB blocksize). We permit these data files to autoextend 100MB at a time. We are going to load this file:

```
$ ls -lag big_table.dat
-rw-rw-r--  1 tkyte   1067107251 Jul 11 13:46 big_table.dat
```

which is a 10,000,000-record file. It was created using the big_table.sql script found in the "Setting Up" section at the beginning of this book and then unloaded using the flat.sql script available at http://asktom.oracle.com/~tkyte/flat/index.html. Next, we do a parallel direct path load of this file into each tablespace:

```
ops$tkyte@ORA10GR1> create table uniform_test
  2  parallel
  3  tablespace lmt_uniform
  4  as
  5  select * from big_table_et;
Table created.

ops$tkyte@ORA10GR1> create table autoallocate_test
  2  parallel
```

```
 3  tablespace lmt_auto
 4  as
 5  select * from big_table_et;
Table created.
```

On my system, which has four CPUs, these CREATE TABLE statements executed with eight parallel execution servers and one coordinator. I verified that was the case by querying one of the dynamic performance views related to parallel execution, V$PX_SESSION, while these statements were running:

```
sys@ORA10GR1> select sid, serial#, qcsid, qcserial#, degree
  2  from v$px_session;

     SID    SERIAL#    QCSID  QCSERIAL#    DEGREE
---------- ---------- ---------- ---------- ----------
     137        17       154        998         8
     139        13       154        998         8
     141        17       154        998         8
     150       945       154        998         8
     161       836       154        998         8
     138         8       154        998         8
     147        15       154        998         8
     143        41       154        998         8
     154       998       154

9 rows selected.
```

■Note In creating the UNIFORM_TEST and AUTOALLOCATE_TEST tables, we simply specified "parallel" on each table, with Oracle choosing the degree of parallelism. In this case, I was the sole user of the machine (all resources available) and Oracle defaulted it to 8 based on the number of CPUs (four) and the PARALLEL_THREADS_PER_CPU parameter setting, which defaults to 2.

The SID, SERIAL# are the identifiers of the parallel execution sessions, and the QCSID, QCSERIAL# is the identifier of the query coordinator of the parallel execution. So, with eight parallel execution sessions running, we would like to see how the space was used. A quick query against USER_SEGMENTS gives us a good idea:

```
ops$tkyte@ORA10GR1> select segment_name, blocks, extents
  2  from user_segments
  3  where segment_name in ( 'UNIFORM_TEST', 'AUTOALLOCATE_TEST' );

SEGMENT_NAME         BLOCKS     EXTENTS
---------------- ---------- ----------
UNIFORM_TEST         204800         16
AUTOALLOCATE_TEST    145592        714
```

Since we were using an 8KB blocksize, that shows a difference of about 462MB, or looking at it from ratio perspective, AUTOALLOCATE_TEST is about 70 percent the size of UNIFORM_TEST as far as allocated space goes. If we look at the actual used space,

```
ops$tkyte@ORA10GR1> exec show_space('UNIFORM_TEST' );
Free Blocks.............................        59,224
Total Blocks............................       204,800
Total Bytes.............................  1,677,721,600
Total MBytes............................         1,600
Unused Blocks...........................             0
Unused Bytes............................             0
Last Used Ext FileId....................             6
Last Used Ext BlockId...................             9
Last Used Block.........................        12,800
PL/SQL procedure successfully completed.

ops$tkyte@ORA10GR1> exec show_space('AUTOALLOCATE_TEST' );
Free Blocks.............................            16
Total Blocks............................       145,592
Total Bytes.............................  1,192,689,664
Total MBytes............................         1,137
Unused Blocks...........................             0
Unused Bytes............................             0
Last Used Ext FileId....................             8
Last Used Ext BlockId...................            41
Last Used Block.........................             8
PL/SQL procedure successfully completed.
```

■**Note** The SHOW_SPACE procedure is described in the "Setting Up" section at the beginning of this book.

---

we can see that if we take away the blocks on the freelist for UNIFORM_TEST—59,224 of them—the tables consume about the same amount of actual space, but the amount of space needed by the UNIFORM tablespace is considerably more. This is all due to the extent trimming that *did not* take place. It we look at UNIFORM_TEST, we see this clearly:

```
ops$tkyte@ORA10GR1> select segment_name, extent_id, blocks
  2  from user_extents where segment_name = 'UNIFORM_TEST';

SEGMENT_NAME       EXTENT_ID     BLOCKS
---------------   ----------   ----------
UNIFORM_TEST               0       12800
UNIFORM_TEST               1       12800
UNIFORM_TEST               2       12800
UNIFORM_TEST               3       12800
UNIFORM_TEST               4       12800
```

```
UNIFORM_TEST              5       12800
UNIFORM_TEST              6       12800
UNIFORM_TEST              7       12800
UNIFORM_TEST              8       12800
UNIFORM_TEST              9       12800
UNIFORM_TEST             10       12800
UNIFORM_TEST             11       12800
UNIFORM_TEST             12       12800
UNIFORM_TEST             13       12800
UNIFORM_TEST             14       12800
UNIFORM_TEST             15       12800

16 rows selected.
```

Each extent is 100MB in size. Now, it would be a waste of paper to list all 714 extents, so let's look at them in aggregate:

```
ops$tkyte@ORA10GR1> select segment_name, blocks, count(*)
  2  from user_extents
  3  where segment_name = 'AUTOALLOCATE_TEST'
  4  group by segment_name, blocks
  5  /

SEGMENT_NAME          BLOCKS    COUNT(*)
-----------------     -------   ----------
AUTOALLOCATE_TEST          8        128
AUTOALLOCATE_TEST        128        504
AUTOALLOCATE_TEST        240          1
AUTOALLOCATE_TEST        392          1
AUTOALLOCATE_TEST        512          1
AUTOALLOCATE_TEST        656          1
AUTOALLOCATE_TEST        752          5
AUTOALLOCATE_TEST        768          1
AUTOALLOCATE_TEST       1024         72

9 rows selected.
```

This generally fits in with how LMTs with AUTOALLOCATE are observed to allocate space. The 8, 128, and 1,024 block extents are "normal"; we will observe them all of the time with AUTOALLOCATE. The rest, however, are not "normal"; we do not usually observe them. They are due to the extent trimming that takes place. Some of the parallel execution servers finished their part of the load—they took their last 8MB (1,024 blocks) extent and trimmed it, resulting in a spare bit left over. One of the other parallel execution sessions, as it needed space, could use this spare bit. In turn, as these other parallel execution sessions finished processing their own loads, they would trim their last extent and leave spare bits of space.

Which approach should you use? If your goal is to direct path load in parallel as often as possible, I suggest AUTOALLOCATE as your extent management policy. Parallel direct path operations like this will not use use space under the object's HWM—the space on the freelist. Unless you do some conventional path inserts into these tables also, UNIFORM allocation will permanently have additional free space in it that it will never use. Unless you can size the extents for the UNIFORM LMT to be much smaller, you will see what I term excessive wastage over time—and remember that this space is associated with the segment and will be included in a full scan of the table.

To demonstrate this, let's do another parallel direct path load into these existing tables, using the same inputs:

```
ops$tkyte@ORA10GR1> alter session enable parallel dml;
Session altered.

ops$tkyte@ORA10GR1> insert /*+ append */ into UNIFORM_TEST
  2 select * from big_table_et;
10000000 rows created.

ops$tkyte@ORA10GR1> insert /*+ append */ into AUTOALLOCATE_TEST
  2 select * from big_table_et;
10000000 rows created.

ops$tkyte@ORA10GR1> commit;
Commit complete.
```

If we compare the space utilization of the two tables after that operation as follows:

```
ops$tkyte@ORA10GR1> exec show_space( 'UNIFORM_TEST' );
Free Blocks.............................        118,463
Total Blocks............................        409,600
Total Bytes.............................  3,355,443,200
Total MBytes............................          3,200
Unused Blocks...........................              0
Unused Bytes............................              0
Last Used Ext FileId....................              6
Last Used Ext BlockId...................        281,609
Last Used Block.........................         12,800

PL/SQL procedure successfully completed.

ops$tkyte@ORA10GR1> exec show_space( 'AUTOALLOCATE_TEST' );
Free Blocks.............................             48
Total Blocks............................        291,184
Total Bytes.............................  2,385,379,328
Total MBytes............................          2,274
Unused Blocks...........................              0
Unused Bytes............................              0
Last Used Ext FileId....................              8
Last Used Ext BlockId...................        140,025
Last Used Block.........................              8

PL/SQL procedure successfully completed.
```

we can see that as we load more and more data into the table UNIFORM_TEST using parallel direct path operations, the space utilization gets worse over time. We would want to use a significantly smaller uniform extent size or use the AUTOALLOCATE. The AUTOALLOCATE may well generate more extents over time, but the space utilization is superior due to the extent trimming that takes place.

Parallel Recovery

Another form of parallel execution in Oracle is the ability to perform parallel recovery. Parallel recovery may be performed at the instance level, perhaps by increasing the speed of a recovery that needs to be performed after a software, operating system, or general system failure. Parallel recovery may also be applied during media recovery (e.g., restoration from backups). It is not my goal to cover recovery-related topics in this book, so I'll just mention the existence of parallel recovery in passing. I recommend the following Oracle manuals for further reading on the topic:

- *Oracle Backup and Recovery Basics* for information regarding parallel media recovery

- *Oracle Performance Tuning Guide* for information regarding parallel instance recovery

Procedural Parallelism

I would like to discuss two types of procedural parallelism:

- Parallel pipelined functions, which is a feature of Oracle.

- "Do-it-yourself (DIY) parallelism," which is the application to your own applications of the same techniques that Oracle applies to parallel full table scans. DIY parallelism is more of a development technique than anything built into Oracle directly.

Many times you'll find that applications—typically batch processes—designed to execute serially will look something like the following procedure:

```
Create procedure process_data
As
Begin
For x in ( select * from some_table )
   Perform complex process on X
   Update some other table, or insert the record somewhere else
End loop
end
```

In this case, Oracle's parallel query or PDML won't help a bit (in fact, parallel execution of the SQL by Oracle here would likely only cause the database to consume more resources and take longer). If Oracle were to execute the simple SELECT * FROM SOME_TABLE in parallel, it would provide this algorithm no apparent increase in speed whatsoever. If Oracle were to perform in parallel the UPDATE or INSERT after the complex process, it would have no positive affect (it is a single-row UPDATE/INSERT, after all).

There is one obvious thing you could do here: use array processing for the UPDATE/INSERT after the complex process. However, that isn't going to give you a 50 percent reduction or more in runtime, and often that is what you are looking for. Don't get me wrong, you definitely want to implement array processing for the modifications here, but it won't make this process run two, three, four, or more times faster.

Now, suppose this process runs at night on a machine with four CPUs, and it is the only activity taking place. You have observed that only one CPU is partially used on this system, and the disk system is not being used very much at all. Further, this process is taking hours, and every day it takes a little longer as more data is added. You need to reduce the runtime by many times—it needs to run four or eight times faster—so incremental percentage increases will not be sufficient. What can you do?

There are two approaches you can take. One approach is to implement a parallel pipe-lined function, whereby Oracle will decide on appropriate degrees of parallelism (assuming you have opted for that, which is recommended). Oracle will create the sessions, coordinate them, and run them, very much like the previous example with parallel DDL where, by using CREATE TABLE AS SELECT OR INSERT /*+APPEND*/, Oracle fully automated parallel direct path loads for us. The other approach is DIY parallelism. We'll take a look at both approaches in the sections that follow.

Parallel Pipelined Functions

We'd like to take that very serial process PROCESS_DATA from earlier and have Oracle execute it in parallel for us. To accomplish this, we need to turn the routine "inside out." Instead of selecting rows from some table, processing them, and inserting them into another table, we will insert into another table the results of fetching some rows and processing them. We will remove the INSERT at the bottom of that loop and replace it in the code with a PIPE ROW clause. The PIPE ROW clause allows our PL/SQL routine to generate table data as its output, so we'll be able to SELECT from our PL/SQL process. The PL/SQL routine that used to procedurally process the data becomes a *table*, in effect, and the rows we fetch and process are the outputs. We've seen this many times throughout this book every time we've issued the following:

```
Select * from table(dbms_xplan.display);
```

That is a PL/SQL routine that reads the PLAN_TABLE; restructures the output, even to the extent of adding rows; and then outputs this data using PIPE ROW to send it back to the client. We're going to do the same thing here in effect, but we'll allow for it to be processed in parallel.

We're going to use two tables in this example: T1 and T2. T1 is the table we were reading previously, and T2 is the table we need to move this information into. Assume this is some sort of ETL process we run to take the transactional data from the day and convert it into reporting information for tomorrow. The two tables we'll use are as follows:

```
ops$tkyte-ORA10G> create table t1
  2  as
  3  select object_id id, object_name text
  4    from all_objects;
Table created.

ops$tkyte-ORA10G> begin
  2      dbms_stats.set_table_stats
```

```
3       ( user, 'T1', numrows=>10000000,numblks=>100000 );
4  end;
5  /
PL/SQL procedure successfully completed.

ops$tkyte-ORA10G> create table t2
2  as
3  select t1.*, 0 session_id
4    from t1
5   where 1=0;
Table created.
```

We used DBMS_STATS to "trick" the optimizer into thinking that there are 10,000,000 rows in that input table and that it consumes 100,000 database blocks. We want to simulate a big table here. The second table, T2, is simply a copy of the first table's structure with the addition of a SESSION_ID column. That column will be useful to actually "see" the parallelism that takes place.

Next, we need to set up object types for our pipelined function to return. The object type is simply a structural definition of the "output" of the procedure we are converting. In this case, it looks just like T2:

```
ops$tkyte-ORA10G> CREATE OR REPLACE TYPE t2_type
2  AS OBJECT (
3    id          number,
4    text        varchar2(30),
5    session_id number
6  )
7  /
Type created.

ops$tkyte-ORA10G> create or replace type t2_tab_type
2  as table of t2_type
3  /
Type created.
```

And now for the pipelined function, which is simply the original PROCESS_DATA procedure rewritten. The procedure is now a function that produces rows. It accepts as an input the data to process in a ref cursor. The function returns a T2_TAB_TYPE, the type we just created. It is a pipelined function that is PARALLEL_ENABLED. The partition clause we are using says to Oracle, "Partition, or slice up, the data by any means that work best. We don't need to make any assumptions about the order of the data."

You may also use hash or range partitioning on a specific column in the ref cursor. That would involve using a strongly typed ref cursor, so the compiler knows what columns are available. Hash partitioning would just send equal rows to each parallel execution server to process based on a hash of the column supplied. Range partitioning would send nonoverlapping ranges of data to each parallel execution server, based on the partitioning key. For example, if you range partitioned on ID, each parallel execution server might get ranges 1...1000, 1001...20000, 20001...30000, and so on (ID values in that range).

Here, we just want the data split up. How the data is split up is not relevant to our processing, so our definition looks like this:

```
ops$tkyte-ORA10G> create or replace
  2   function parallel_pipelined( l_cursor in sys_refcursor )
  3   return t2_tab_type
  4   pipelined
  5   parallel_enable ( partition l_cursor by any )
```

We'd like to be able to see what rows were processed by which parallel execution servers, so we'll declare a local variable L_SESSION_ID and initialize it from V$MYSTAT:

```
  6
  7   is
  8       l_session_id number;
  9       l_rec        t1%rowtype;
 10   begin
 11       select sid into l_session_id
 12         from v$mystat
 13        where rownum =1;
```

Now we are ready to process the data. We simply fetch out a row (or rows, as we could certainly use BULK COLLECT here to array process the ref cursor), perform our complex process on it, and pipe it out. When the ref cursor is exhausted of data, we close the cursor and return:

```
 14       loop
 15           fetch l_cursor into l_rec;
 16           exit when l_cursor%notfound;
 17           -- complex process here
 18           pipe row(t2_type(l_rec.id,l_rec.text,l_session_id));
 19       end loop;
 20       close l_cursor;
 21       return;
 22   end;
 23   /
Function created.
```

And that's it. We're ready to process the data in parallel, letting Oracle figure out based on the resources available what the most appropriate degree of parallelism is:

```
ops$tkyte-ORA10G> alter session enable parallel dml;
Session altered.

ops$tkyte-ORA10G> insert /*+ append */
  2   into t2(id,text,session_id)
  3   select *
  4   from table(parallel_pipelined
  5           (CURSOR(select /*+ parallel(t1) */ *
  6                     from t1 )
  7              ))
```

```
 8  /
48250 rows created.

ops$tkyte-ORA10G> commit;
Commit complete.
```

Just to see what happened here, we can query the newly inserted data out and group by
SESSION_ID to see first how many parallel execution servers were used, and second how many
rows each processed:

```
ops$tkyte-ORA10G> select session_id, count(*)
  2    from t2
  3    group by session_id;

SESSION_ID   COUNT(*)
----------   ----------
       241       8040
       246       8045
       253       8042
       254       8042
       258       8040
       260       8041
6 rows selected.
```

Apparently, we used six parallel execution servers for the SELECT component of this parallel operation, and each one processed about 8,040 records each.

As you can see, Oracle parallelized our process, but we underwent a fairly radical rewrite of our process. This is a long way from the original implementation. So, while Oracle can process our routine in parallel, we may well not have any routines that are coded to be parallelized. If a rather large rewrite of your procedure is not feasible, you may be interested in the next implementation: DIY parallelism.

Do-It-Yourself Parallelism

Say we have that same process as in the preceding section: the serial, simple procedure. We cannot afford a rather extensive rewrite of the implementation, but we would like to execute it in parallel. What can we do? My approach many times has been to use rowid ranges to break up the table into some number of ranges that don't overlap (yet completely cover the table).

This is very similar to how Oracle performs a parallel query conceptually. If you think of a full table scan, Oracle processes that by coming up with some method to break the table into many "small" tables, each of which is processed by a parallel execution server. We are going to do the same thing using rowid ranges. In early releases, Oracle's parallel implementation actually used rowid ranges itself.

We'll use a BIG_TABLE of 1,000,000 rows, as this technique works best on big tables with lots of extents, and the method I use for creating rowid ranges depends on extent boundaries. The more extents used, the better the data distribution. So, after creating the BIG_TABLE with 1,000,000 rows, we'll create T2 like this:

```
big_table-ORA10G> create table t2
  2  as
  3  select object_id id, object_name text, 0 session_id
  4    from big_table
  5  where 1=0;
Table created.
```

We are going to use the job queues built into the database to parallel process our procedure. We will schedule some number of jobs. Each job is our procedure slightly modified to just process the rows in a given rowid range.

■**Note** In Oracle 10*g*, you could use the scheduler for something this simple, but in order to make the example 9*i* compatible, we'll use the job queues here.

To efficiently support the job queues, we'll use a parameter table to pass inputs to our jobs:

```
big_table-ORA10G> create table job_parms
  2  ( job        number primary key,
  3    lo_rid  rowid,
  4    hi_rid  rowid
  5  )
  6  /
Table created.
```

This will allow us to just pass the job ID into our procedure, so it can query this table to get the rowid range it is to process. Now for our procedure. The code in **bold** is the new code we'll be adding:

```
big_table-ORA10G> create or replace
  2  procedure serial( p_job in number )
  3  is
  4      l_rec          job_parms%rowtype;
  5  begin
  6      select * into l_rec
  7        from job_parms
  8       where job = p_job;
  9
 10      for x in ( select object_id id, object_name text
 11                   from big_table
 12                  where rowid between l_rec.lo_rid
 13                                  and l_rec.hi_rid )
 14      loop
 15          -- complex process here
 16          insert into t2 (id, text, session_id )
 17          values ( x.id, x.text, p_job );
 18      end loop;
```

```
19
20      delete from job_parms where job = p_job;
21      commit;
22  end;
23  /
Procedure created.
```

As you can see, it is not a significant change. Most of the added code was simply to get our inputs and the rowid range to process. The only change to our *logic* was the addition of the predicate on lines 12 and 13.

Now let's schedule our job. We'll use a rather complex query using analytics to divide the table. The innermost query on lines 19 through 26 breaks the data into eight groups in this case. The first sum on line 22 is computing a running total of the sum of blocks; the second sum on line 23 is the total number of blocks. If we integer divide the running total by the desired "chunk size" (the total size divided by 8 in this case), we can create groups of files/blocks that cover about the same amount of data. The query on lines 8 through 28 finds the high and low file numbers and block numbers by GRP, and returns the distinct entries. It builds the inputs we can then send to DBMS_ROWID to create the rowids Oracle wants. We take that output and, using DBMS_JOB, submit a job to process the rowid range:

```
big_table-ORA10G> declare
 2          l_job number;
 3  begin
 4  for x in (
 5  select dbms_rowid.rowid_create
            ( 1, data_object_id, lo_fno, lo_block, 0 ) min_rid,
 6          dbms_rowid.rowid_create
            ( 1, data_object_id, hi_fno, hi_block, 10000 ) max_rid
 7     from (
 8  select distinct grp,
 9          first_value(relative_fno)
              over (partition by grp order by relative_fno, block_id
10            rows between unbounded preceding and unbounded following) lo_fno,
11          first_value(block_id   )
              over (partition by grp order by relative_fno, block_id
12            rows between unbounded preceding and unbounded following) lo_block,
13          last_value(relative_fno)
              over (partition by grp order by relative_fno, block_id
14            rows between unbounded preceding and unbounded following) hi_fno,
15          last_value(block_id+blocks-1)
              over (partition by grp order by relative_fno, block_id
16            rows between unbounded preceding and unbounded following) hi_block,
17          sum(blocks) over (partition by grp) sum_blocks
18     from (
19  select relative_fno,
20          block_id,
21          blocks,
22          trunc( (sum(blocks) over (order by relative_fno, block_id)-0.01) /
```

```
23                  (sum(blocks) over ()/8) ) grp
24    from dba_extents
25   where segment_name = upper('BIG_TABLE')
26     and owner = user order by block_id
27          )
28          ),
29          (select data_object_id
                from user_objects where object_name = upper('BIG_TABLE') )
30   )
31   loop
32          dbms_job.submit( l_job, 'serial(JOB);' );
33          insert into job_parms(job, lo_rid, hi_rid)
34          values ( l_job, x.min_rid, x.max_rid );
35   end loop;
36   end;
37   /
PL/SQL procedure successfully completed.
```

That PL/SQL block would have scheduled up to eight jobs for us (fewer if the table could not be broken in to eight pieces due to insufficient extents or size). We can see how many jobs were scheduled and what their inputs are as follows:

```
big_table-ORA10G> select * from job_parms;

    JOB LO_RID              HI_RID
---------- ------------------- -------------------
    172 AAAT7tAAEAAAAkpAAA AAAT7tAAEAAABQICcQ
    173 AAAT7tAAEAAABQJAAA AAAT7tAAEAAABwICcQ
    174 AAAT7tAAEAAABwJAAA AAAT7tAAEAAACUICcQ
    175 AAAT7tAAEAAACUJAAA AAAT7tAAEAAACoICcQ
    176 AAAT7tAAEAAACoJAAA AAAT7tAAEAAADMICcQ
    177 AAAT7tAAEAAADaJAAA AAAT7tAAEAAAD6ICcQ
    178 AAAT7tAAEAAAD6JAAA AAAT7tAAEAAAEaICcQ
    179 AAAT7tAAEAAAEaJAAA AAAT7tAAEAAAF4ICcQ
8 rows selected.

big_table-ORA10G> commit;
Commit complete.
```

That commit released our jobs for processing. We have JOB_QUEUE_PROCESSES set to 0 in the parameter file, so all eight started running and shortly finished. The results are as follows:

```
big_table-ORA10G> select session_id, count(*)
  2    from t2
  3    group by session_id;

SESSION_ID    COUNT(*)
---------- ----------
       172      130055
```

```
    173      130978
    174      130925
    175      129863
    176      106154
    177      140772
    178      140778
    179       90475
8 rows selected.
```

It's not as evenly distributed as the Oracle built-in parallelism in this case, but it's pretty good. If you recall, earlier you saw how many rows were processed by each parallel execution server and, using the built-in parallelism, the row counts were very close to each other (they were off only by one or two). Here we had a job that processed as few as 90,475 rows and one that processed as many as 140,778. Most of them processed about 130,000 rows in this case.

Suppose, however, that you do not want to use the rowid processing—perhaps the query is not as simple as SELECT * FROM T and involves joins and other constructs that make using the rowid impractical. You can use the primary key of some table instead. For example, say you want to break that same BIG_TABLE into ten pieces to be processed concurrently by primary key. You can do that easily using the NTILE built-in analytic function. The process is rather straightforward:

```
big_table-ORA10G> select nt, min(id), max(id), count(*)
  2    from (
  3  select id, ntile(10) over (order by id) nt
  4    from big_table
  5         )
  6  group by nt;

    NT    MIN(ID)    MAX(ID)    COUNT(*)
---------- ---------- ---------- ----------
     1          1     100000     100000
     2     100001     200000     100000
     3     200001     300000     100000
     4     300001     400000     100000
     5     400001     500000     100000
     6     500001     600000     100000
     7     600001     700000     100000
     8     700001     800000     100000
     9     800001     900000     100000
    10     900001    1000000     100000

10 rows selected.
```

Now you have ten nonoverlapping primary key ranges—all of nice, equal size—that you can use to implement the same DBMS_JOB technique as shown earlier to parallelize your process.

Summary

In this chapter, we explored the concept of parallel execution in Oracle. I started by presenting an analogy to help frame where and when parallel execution is applicable, namely when we have long-running statements or procedures and plenty of available resources.

Then we looked at how Oracle can employ parallelism. We started with parallel query and how Oracle can break large serial operations, such as a full scan, into smaller pieces that can run concurrently. We moved on to parallel DML (PDML) and covered the rather extensive list of restrictions that accompany it.

Then we looked at the sweet spot for parallel operations: parallel DDL. Parallel DDL is a tool for the DBA and developer alike to quickly perform those large maintenance operations typically done during off-peak times when resources are available. We briefly touched on the fact that Oracle provides parallel recovery before we moved on to discuss procedural parallelism. Here we saw two techniques for parallelizing our procedures: one where Oracle does it and the other where we do it ourselves.

If we're designing a process from scratch, we might well consider designing it to allow Oracle to parallelize it for us, as the future addition or reduction of resources would easily permit the degree of parallelism to vary. However, if we have existing code that needs to quickly be "fixed" to be parallel, we may opt for do-it-yourself (DIY) parallelism, which we covered by examining two techniques, rowid ranges and primary key ranges, both of which use DBMS_JOB to carry out the job in parallel in the background for us.

CHAPTER 15

■ ■ ■

Data Loading and Unloading

In this chapter, we will discuss data loading and unloading—in other words, how to get data *into* and *out of* an Oracle database. The main focus of the chapter is on the following bulk data loading tools:

- *SQL*Loader (pronounced "sequel loader")*: This is still a predominant method for loading data.

- *External tables*: This is a new feature with Oracle9*i* and above that permits access to operating system files as if they were database tables and, in Oracle 10*g* and above, even allows for the creation of operating system files as extracts of tables.

In the area of data unloading, we'll look at two techniques:

- *Flat file unload*: The flat file unloads will be custom developed implementations, but will provide you with a result that is portable to other types of systems (even a spreadsheet).

- *Data Pump unload*: Data Pump is a binary format proprietary to Oracle and is accessible via the Data Pump tool and external tables.

SQL*Loader

SQL*Loader (SQLLDR) is Oracle's high-speed, bulk data loader. It is an extremely useful tool used to get data into an Oracle database from a variety of flat file formats. SQLLDR can be used to load enormous amounts of data in an amazingly short period of time. It has two modes of operation:

- *Conventional path*: SQLLDR will employ SQL inserts on our behalf to load data.

- *Direct path*: SQLLDR does not use SQL in this mode; it formats database blocks directly.

The direct path load allows you to read data from a flat file and write it directly to formatted database blocks, bypassing the entire SQL engine, undo generation and, optionally, redo generation at the same time. Parallel direct path load is among the fastest ways to go from having no data to a fully loaded database.

We will not cover every single aspect of SQLLDR. For all of the details, refer to the *Oracle Utilities* manual, which dedicates seven chapters to SQLLDR in Oracle 10*g*. The fact that it is covered in seven chapters is notable, since every other utility, such as DBVERIFY, DBNEWID, and LogMiner get one chapter or less. For complete syntax and all of the options, I will refer you to the *Oracle Utilities* manual, as this chapter is intended to answer the "How do I . . .?" questions that a reference manual does not address.

It should be noted that the Oracle Call Interface (OCI) allows you to write your own direct path loader using C, with Oracle 8.1.6 Release 1 and onward. This is useful when the operation you want to perform is not feasible in SQLLDR, or when seamless integration with your application is desired. SQLLDR is a command-line tool (i.e., it's a separate program). It is not an API or anything that can be "called from PL/SQL," for example.

If you execute SQLLDR from the command line with no inputs, it gives you the following help:

```
[tkyte@desktop tkyte]$ sqlldr
SQL*Loader: Release 10.1.0.4.0 - Production on Sat Jul 16 10:32:28 2005
Copyright (c) 1982, 2004, Oracle.  All rights reserved.

Usage: SQLLDR keyword=value [,keyword=value,...]

Valid Keywords:
    userid -- ORACLE username/password
   control -- control file name
       log -- log file name
       bad -- bad file name
      data -- data file name
   discard -- discard file name
discardmax -- number of discards to allow      (Default all)
      skip -- number of logical records to skip   (Default 0)
      load -- number of logical records to load   (Default all)
    errors -- number of errors to allow         (Default 50)
      rows -- number of rows in conventional path bind array or
              between direct path data saves
              (Default: Conventional path 64, Direct path all)
  bindsize -- size of conventional path bind array in bytes  (Default 256000)
    silent -- suppress messages during run
              (header,feedback,errors,discards,partitions)
    direct -- use direct path                  (Default FALSE)
   parfile -- parameter file: name of file that contains parameter specifications
  parallel -- do parallel load                 (Default FALSE)
      file -- file to allocate extents from
skip_unusable_indexes -- disallow/allow unusable indexes or index partitions
                    (Default FALSE)
skip_index_maintenance -- do not maintain indexes, mark affected indexes as unusable
                    (Default FALSE)
commit_discontinued -- commit loaded rows when load is discontinued  (Default FALSE)
readsize -- size of read buffer (Default 1048576)
external_table -- use external table for load; NOT_USED, GENERATE_ONLY, EXECUTE
```

```
                 (Default NOT_USED)
columnarrayrows -- number of rows for direct path column array  (Default 5000)
streamsize -- size of direct path stream buffer in bytes  (Default 256000)
multithreading -- use multithreading in direct path
resumable -- enable or disable resumable for current session  (Default FALSE)
resumable_name -- text string to help identify resumable statement
resumable_timeout -- wait time (in seconds) for RESUMABLE  (Default 7200)
date_cache -- size (in entries) of date conversion cache  (Default 1000)
...
```

Rather than explain what each individual parameter technically means, I will point you to the *Oracle Utilities* manual, specifically Chapter 7 in the Oracle 10g *Utilities Guide* and Chapter 4 in the Oracle9i *Utilities Guide*. I will demonstrate the usage of a few of these parameters in this chapter.

To use SQLLDR, you will need a *control file*. A control file simply contains information describing the input data—its layout, datatypes, and so on—as well as information about the target table(s). The control file can even contain the data to load. In the following example, we'll build a simple control file in a step-by-step fashion, and I'll provide an explanation of the commands. (Note that the parenthetical numbers to the left in the code are *not* part of this control file; they are just there for reference.)

```
(1)   LOAD DATA
(2)   INFILE *
(3)   INTO TABLE DEPT
(4)   FIELDS TERMINATED BY ','
(5)   (DEPTNO, DNAME, LOC )
(6)   BEGINDATA
(7)   10,Sales,Virginia
(8)   20,Accounting,Virginia
(9)   30,Consulting,Virginia
(10)  40,Finance,Virginia
```

- LOAD DATA (1): This tells SQLLDR what to do (in this case, load data). The other thing SQLLDR can do is CONTINUE_LOAD, to resume a load. You would use this latter option only when continuing a multitable direct path load.

- INFILE * (2): This tells SQLLDR the data to be loaded is actually contained within the control file itself, as shown on lines 6 through 10. Alternatively, you could specify the name of another file that contains the data. You can override this INFILE statement using a command-line parameter if you wish. Be aware that *command-line options override control file settings*.

- INTO TABLE DEPT (3): This tells SQLLDR to which table you are loading data (in this case, the DEPT table).

- FIELDS TERMINATED BY ',' (4): This tells SQLLDR that the data will be in the form of comma-separated values. There are dozens of ways to describe the input data to SQLLDR; this is just one of the more common methods.

- (DEPTNO, DNAME, LOC) (5): This tells SQLLDR what columns you are loading, their order in the input data, and their datatypes. The datatypes are for the data in the *input* stream, not the datatypes in the database. In this case, they are defaulting to CHAR(255), which is sufficient.

- BEGINDATA (6): This tells SQLLDR you have finished describing the input data and that the very next lines, lines 7 to 10, are the actual data to be loaded into the DEPT table.

This is a control file in one of its most simple and common formats: to load delimited data into a table. We will take a look at some complex examples in this chapter, but this is a good one to get our feet wet with. To use this control file, which we will name demo1.ctl, all we need to do is create an empty DEPT table:

```
ops$tkyte@ORA10G> create table dept
  2  ( deptno  number(2) constraint dept_pk primary key,
  3    dname   varchar2(14),
  4    loc     varchar2(13)
  5  )
  6  /
Table created.
```

and run the following command:

```
[tkyte@desktop tkyte]$ sqlldr userid=/ control=demo1.ctl
SQL*Loader: Release 10.1.0.4.0 - Production on Sat Jul 16 10:59:06 2005
Copyright (c) 1982, 2004, Oracle.  All rights reserved.
Commit point reached - logical record count 4
```

If the table is not empty, we will receive an error message to the following effect:

```
SQLLDR-601: For INSERT option, table must be empty.  Error on table DEPT
```

This is because we allowed almost everything in the control file to default, and the default load option is INSERT (as opposed to APPEND, TRUNCATE, or REPLACE). To INSERT, SQLLDR assumes the table is empty. If we wanted to *add* records to the DEPT table, we could have specified APPEND, or to replace the data in the DEPT table, we could have used REPLACE or TRUNCATE. REPLACE uses a conventional DELETE statement; hence, if the table to be loaded into already contains many records, it could be quite slow to perform. TRUNCATE uses the TRUNCATE SQL command and is typically faster, as it does not have to physically remove each row.

Every load will generate a log file. The log file from our simple load looks like this:

```
SQL*Loader: Release 10.1.0.4.0 - Production on Sat Jul 16 10:59:06 2005
Copyright (c) 1982, 2004, Oracle.  All rights reserved.


Control File:   demo1.ctl
Data File:      demo1.ctl
  Bad File:     demo1.bad
  Discard File: none specified

 (Allow all discards)
```

```
Number to load: ALL
Number to skip: 0
Errors allowed: 50
Bind array:      64 rows, maximum of 256000 bytes
Continuation:    none specified
Path used:      Conventional

Table DEPT, loaded from every logical record.
Insert option in effect for this table: INSERT

   Column Name                    Position   Len  Term Encl Datatype
------------------------------- ---------- ----- ---- ---- ---------------------
DEPTNO                          FIRST       *    ,        CHARACTER
DNAME                           NEXT        *    ,        CHARACTER
LOC                             NEXT        *    ,        CHARACTER

Table DEPT:
  4 Rows successfully loaded.
  0 Rows not loaded due to data errors.
  0 Rows not loaded because all WHEN clauses were failed.
  0 Rows not loaded because all fields were null.

Space allocated for bind array:                 49536 bytes(64 rows)
Read   buffer bytes: 1048576

Total logical records skipped:          0
Total logical records read:             4
Total logical records rejected:         0
Total logical records discarded:        0

Run began on Sat Jul 16 10:59:06 2005
Run ended on Sat Jul 16 10:59:06 2005

Elapsed time was:      00:00:00.15
CPU time was:          00:00:00.03
```

The log file tells us about many of the aspects of our load. We can see the options we used (defaulted or otherwise). We can see how many records were read, how many loaded, and so on. The log file specifies the locations of all BAD and DISCARD files. It even tells us how long it took. The log file is crucial for verifying that the load was successful, as well as for diagnosing errors. If the loaded data resulted in SQL errors (i.e., the input data was "bad" and created records in the BAD file), these errors would be recorded here. The information in the log file is largely self-explanatory, so we will not spend any more time on it.

Loading Data with SQLLDR FAQs

We will now cover what I have found to be the most frequently asked questions with regard to loading data in an Oracle database using SQLLDR.

How Do I Load Delimited Data?

Delimited data, or data that is separated by some special character and perhaps enclosed in quotes, is the most popular data format for flat files today. On a mainframe, a fixed-length, fixed-format file would probably be the most recognized file format, but on UNIX and NT, delimited files are the norm. In this section, we will investigate the popular options used to load delimited data.

The most popular format for delimited data is the *comma-separated values* (*CSV*) format. In this file format, each field of data is separated from the next by a comma. Text strings can be enclosed within quotes, thus allowing for the string itself to contain commas. If the string must contain a quotation mark as well, the convention is to double up the quotation mark (in the following code we use "" in place of just "). A typical control file to load delimited data will look much like our first example earlier, but the FIELDS TERMINATED BY clause would generally be specified like this:

```
FIELDS TERMINATED BY ',' OPTIONALLY ENCLOSED BY '"'
```

It specifies that a comma separates the data fields, and that each field *might* be enclosed in double quotes. If we were to modify the bottom of this control file to be

```
FIELDS TERMINATED BY ',' OPTIONALLY ENCLOSED BY '"'
(DEPTNO, DNAME, LOC )
BEGINDATA
10,Sales,"Virginia,USA"
20,Accounting,"Va, ""USA"""
30,Consulting,Virginia
40,Finance,Virginia
```

when we run SQLLDR using this control file, the results will be as follows:

```
ops$tkyte@ORA10G> select * from dept;

    DEPTNO DNAME           LOC
---------- --------------- -------------
        10 Sales           Virginia,USA
        20 Accounting      Va, "USA"
        30 Consulting      Virginia
        40 Finance         Virginia
```

Notice the following in particular:

- Virginia,USA in department 10: This results from input data that was "Virginia,USA". This input data field had to be enclosed in quotes to retain the comma as part of the data. Otherwise, the comma would have been treated as the end-of-field marker, and Virginia would have been loaded without the USA text.

- Va, "USA": This resulted from input data that was "Va, ""USA""". SQLLDR counted the double occurrence of " as a single occurrence within the enclosed string. To load a string that contains the optional enclosure character, you must ensure the enclosure character is doubled up.

Another popular format is *tab-delimited data*, which is data separated by tabs rather than commas. There are two ways to load this data using the TERMINATED BY clause:

- TERMINATED BY X'09' (the tab character using hexadecimal format; in ASCII, 9 is a tab character)

- TERMINATED BY WHITESPACE

The two are very different in implementation, as the following shows. Using the DEPT table from earlier, we'll load using this control file:

```
LOAD DATA
INFILE *
INTO TABLE DEPT
REPLACE
FIELDS TERMINATED BY WHITESPACE
(DEPTNO, DNAME, LOC)
BEGINDATA
10 Sales Virginia
```

It is not readily visible on the page, but there are *two* tabs between each piece of data here. The data line is really

```
10\t\tSales\t\tVirginia
```

where the \t is the universally recognized tab escape sequence. When you use this control file with the TERMINATED BY WHITESPACE clause as shown previously, the resulting data in the table DEPT is

```
ops$tkyte@ORA10G> select * from dept;

    DEPTNO DNAME          LOC
---------- -------------- --------------
        10 Sales          Virginia
```

TERMINATED BY WHITESPACE parses the string by looking for the first occurrence of whitespace (tab, blank, or newline), and then it continues until it finds the next *non*-whitespace character. Hence, when it parsed the data, DEPTNO had 10 assigned to it, the two subsequent tabs were considered as whitespace, Sales was assigned to DNAME, and so on.

On the other hand, if you were to use FIELDS TERMINATED BY X'09', as the following modified control file does:

```
...
FIELDS TERMINATED BY X'09'
(DEPTNO, DNAME, LOC )
...
```

you would find DEPT loaded with the following data:

```
ops$tkyte@ORA10G> select * from dept;

    DEPTNO DNAME          LOC
---------- -------------- --------------
        10                Sales
```

Here, once SQLLDR encountered a tab, it output a value. Hence, 10 is assigned to DEPTNO, and DNAME gets NULL since there is no data between the first tab and the next occurrence of a tab. Sales gets assigned to LOC.

This is the intended behavior of TERMINATED BY WHITESPACE and TERMINATED BY <character>. Which is more appropriate to use will be dictated by the input data and how you need it to be interpreted.

Lastly, when loading delimited data such as this, it is very common to want to skip over various columns in the input record. For example, you might want to load fields 1, 3, and 5, skipping columns 2 and 4. To do this, SQLLDR provides the FILLER keyword. This allows you to map a column in an input record, but not put it into the database. For example, given the DEPT table and the last control file from earlier, we can modify the control file to load the data correctly (skipping over the tabs) using the FILLER keyword:

```
LOAD DATA
INFILE *
INTO TABLE DEPT
REPLACE
FIELDS TERMINATED BY x'09'
(DEPTNO, dummy1 filler, DNAME, dummy2 filler, LOC)
BEGINDATA
10      Sales       Virginia
```

The resulting DEPT table is now as follows:

```
ops$tkyte@ORA10G> select * from dept;

    DEPTNO DNAME          LOC
---------- -------------- --------------
        10 Sales          Virginia
```

How Do I Load Fixed Format Data?

Often, you have a flat file generated from some external system, and this file is a fixed-length file with positional data. For example, the NAME field is in bytes 1 to 10, the ADDRESS field is in bytes 11 to 35, and so on. We will look at how SQLLDR can import this kind of data for us.

This fixed-width, positional data is the optimal data format for SQLLDR to load. It will be the fastest way to process, as the input data stream is somewhat trivial to parse. SQLLDR will have stored fixed-byte offsets and lengths into data records, and extracting a given field is very simple. If you have an extremely large volume of data to load, converting it to a fixed position format is generally the best approach. The downside to a fixed-width file is, of course, that it can be much larger than a simple, delimited file format.

To load fixed-width positional data, you will use the POSITION keyword in the control file, for example:

```
LOAD DATA
INFILE *
INTO TABLE DEPT
REPLACE
( DEPTNO position(1:2),
  DNAME  position(3:16),
  LOC    position(17:29)
)
BEGINDATA
10Accounting    Virginia,USA
```

This control file does not employ the FIELDS TERMINATED BY clause; rather, it uses POSITION to tell SQLLDR where fields begin and end. Of interest with the POSITION clause is that we could use overlapping positions, and go back and forth in the record. For example, if we were to alter the DEPT table as follows:

```
ops$tkyte@ORA10G> alter table dept add entire_line varchar(29);
Table altered.
```

and then use the following control file:

```
LOAD DATA
INFILE *
INTO TABLE DEPT
REPLACE
( DEPTNO       position(1:2),
  DNAME        position(3:16),
  LOC          position(17:29),
  ENTIRE_LINE  position(1:29)
)
BEGINDATA
10Accounting    Virginia,USA
```

the field ENTIRE_LINE is defined as POSITION(1:29). It extracts its data from all 29 bytes of input data, whereas the other fields are substrings of the input data. The outcome of the this control file will be as follows:

```
ops$tkyte@ORA10G> select * from dept;

   DEPTNO DNAME          LOC           ENTIRE_LINE
---------- -------------- ------------- ------------------------------
       10 Accounting     Virginia,USA  10Accounting    Virginia,USA
```

When using POSITION, we can use relative or absolute offsets. In the preceding example, we used absolute offsets. We specifically denoted where fields begin and where they end. We could have written the preceding control file as follows:

```
LOAD DATA
INFILE *
INTO TABLE DEPT
REPLACE
( DEPTNO       position(1:2),
  DNAME        position(*:16),
  LOC          position(*:29),
  ENTIRE_LINE  position(1:29)
)
BEGINDATA
10Accounting     Virginia,USA
```

The * instructs the control file to pick up where the last field left off. Therefore (*:16) is just the same as (3:16) in this case. Notice that you can mix relative and absolute positions in the control file. Additionally, when using the * notation, you can add to the offset. For example, if DNAME started 2 bytes *after* the end of DEPTNO, we could have used (*+2:16). In this example, the effect would be identical to using (5:16).

The ending position in the POSITION clause must be the absolute column position where the data ends. At times, it can be easier to specify just the length of each field, especially if they are contiguous, as in the preceding example. In this fashion, we would just have to tell SQLLDR the record starts at byte 1, and then specify the length of each field. This will save us from having to compute start and stop byte offsets into the record, which can be hard at times. In order to do this, we'll leave off the ending position and instead specify the *length* of each field in the fixed-length record as follows:

```
LOAD DATA
INFILE *
INTO TABLE DEPT
REPLACE
( DEPTNO       position(1) char(2),
  DNAME        position(*) char(14),
  LOC          position(*) char(13),
  ENTIRE_LINE  position(1) char(29)
)
BEGINDATA
10Accounting     Virginia,USA
```

Here we had to tell SQLLDR only where the first field begins and its length. Each subsequent field starts where the last one left off and continues for a specified length. It is not until the last field that we have to specify a position again, since this field goes back to the beginning of the record.

How Do I Load Dates?

Loading dates using SQLLDR is fairly straightforward, but it seems to be a common point of confusion. You simply need to use the DATE data type in the control file and specify the date mask to be used. This date mask is the same mask you use with TO_CHAR and TO_DATE in the database. SQLLDR will apply this date mask to your data and load it for you.

For example, if we alter our DEPT table again:

```
ops$tkyte@ORA10G> alter table dept add last_updated date;
Table altered.
```

we can load it with the following control file:

```
LOAD DATA
INFILE *
INTO TABLE DEPT
REPLACE
FIELDS TERMINATED BY ','
(DEPTNO,
  DNAME,
  LOC,
  LAST_UPDATED date 'dd/mm/yyyy'
)
BEGINDATA
10,Sales,Virginia,1/5/2000
20,Accounting,Virginia,21/6/1999
30,Consulting,Virginia,5/1/2000
40,Finance,Virginia,15/3/2001
```

The resulting DEPT table will look like this:

```
ops$tkyte@ORA10G> select * from dept;

    DEPTNO DNAME          LOC             LAST_UPDA
---------- -------------- --------------- ---------
        10 Sales          Virginia        01-MAY-00
        20 Accounting     Virginia        21-JUN-99
        30 Consulting     Virginia        05-JAN-00
        40 Finance        Virginia        15-MAR-01
```

It is that easy. Just supply the format in the control file and SQLLDR will convert the date for us. In some cases, it might be appropriate to use a more powerful SQL function. For example, if your input file contains dates in many different formats: sometimes with the time component, sometimes without; sometimes in DD-MON-YYYY format; sometimes in DD/MM/YYYY format; and so on. You'll learn in the next section how to use functions in SQLLDR to overcome these challenges.

How Do I Load Data Using Functions?

In this section, you'll see how to refer to functions while loading data.

Using functions in SQLLDR is very easy once you understand how SQLLDR builds its INSERT statement. To have a function applied to a field in a SQLLDR script, simply add it to the control file in double quotes. For example, say you have the DEPT table from earlier, and you would like to make sure the data being loaded is in uppercase. You could use the following control file to load it:

```
LOAD DATA
INFILE *
INTO TABLE DEPT
REPLACE
FIELDS TERMINATED BY ','
(DEPTNO,
  DNAME         "upper(:dname)",
  LOC           "upper(:loc)",
  LAST_UPDATED date 'dd/mm/yyyy'
)
BEGINDATA
10,Sales,Virginia,1/5/2000
20,Accounting,Virginia,21/6/1999
30,Consulting,Virginia,5/1/2000
40,Finance,Virginia,15/3/2001
```

The resulting data in the database will be as follows:

```
ops$tkyte@ORA10G> select * from dept;

DEPTNO DNAME          LOC           ENTIRE_LINE                    LAST_UPDA
------ -------------- ------------- ------------------------------ ---------
    10 SALES          VIRGINIA                                     01-MAY-00
    20 ACCOUNTING     VIRGINIA                                     21-JUN-99
    30 CONSULTING     VIRGINIA                                     05-JAN-00
    40 FINANCE        VIRGINIA                                     15-MAR-01
```

Notice how you are able to easily uppercase the data just by applying the UPPER function to a bind variable. It should be noted that the SQL functions could refer to any of the columns, regardless of the column the function is actually applied to. This means that a column can be the result of a function on two or more of the other columns. For example, if you wanted to load the column ENTIRE_LINE, you could use the SQL concatenation operator. It is a little more involved than that, though, in this case. Right now, the input data set has four data elements in it. If you were to simply add ENTIRE_LINE to the control file like this:

```
LOAD DATA
INFILE *
INTO TABLE DEPT
REPLACE
FIELDS TERMINATED BY ','
(DEPTNO,
  DNAME         "upper(:dname)",
  LOC           "upper(:loc)",
  LAST_UPDATED date 'dd/mm/yyyy',
  ENTIRE_LINE   ":deptno||:dname||:loc||:last_updated"
)
BEGINDATA
```

```
10,Sales,Virginia,1/5/2000
20,Accounting,Virginia,21/6/1999
30,Consulting,Virginia,5/1/2000
40,Finance,Virginia,15/3/2001
```

you would find this error in your log file, for each input record:

```
Record 1: Rejected - Error on table DEPT, column ENTIRE_LINE.
Column not found before end of logical record (use TRAILING NULLCOLS)
```

Here, SQLLDR is telling you that it ran out of data in the record before it ran out of columns. The solution is easy in this case, and, in fact, SQLLDR even tells us what to do: use TRAILING NULLCOLS. This will have SQLLDR bind a NULL value in for that column if no data exists in the input record. In this case, adding TRAILING NULLCOLS will cause the bind variable :ENTIRE_LINE to be NULL. So, you retry with this control file:

```
LOAD DATA
INFILE *
INTO TABLE DEPT
REPLACE
FIELDS TERMINATED BY ','
TRAILING NULLCOLS
(DEPTNO,
  DNAME        "upper(:dname)",
  LOC          "upper(:loc)",
  LAST_UPDATED date 'dd/mm/yyyy',
  ENTIRE_LINE  ":deptno||:dname||:loc||:last_updated"
)
BEGINDATA
10,Sales,Virginia,1/5/2000
20,Accounting,Virginia,21/6/1999
30,Consulting,Virginia,5/1/2000
40,Finance,Virginia,15/3/2001
```

Now the data in the table is as follows:

```
ops$tkyte@ORA10G> select * from dept;

DEPTNO DNAME          LOC            ENTIRE_LINE                       LAST_UPDA
------ -------------- -------------- --------------------------------- ---------
    10 SALES          VIRGINIA       10SalesVirginia1/5/2000           01-MAY-00
    20 ACCOUNTING     VIRGINIA       20AccountingVirginia21/6/1999     21-JUN-99
    30 CONSULTING     VIRGINIA       30ConsultingVirginia5/1/2000      05-JAN-00
    40 FINANCE        VIRGINIA       40FinanceVirginia15/3/2001        15-MAR-01
```

What makes this feat possible is the way SQLLDR builds its INSERT statement. SQLLDR will look at the preceding and see the DEPTNO, DNAME, LOC, LAST_UPDATED, and ENTIRE_LINE columns in the control file. It will set up five bind variables named after these columns. Normally, in the absence of any functions, the INSERT statement it builds is simply

```
INSERT INTO DEPT ( DEPTNO, DNAME, LOC, LAST_UPDATED, ENTIRE_LINE )
VALUES ( :DEPTNO, :DNAME, :LOC, :LAST_UPDATED, :ENTIRE_LINE );
```

It would then parse the input stream, assigning the values to its bind variables, and then execute the statement. When you begin to use functions, SQLLDR incorporates them into its INSERT statement. In the preceding example, the INSERT statement SQLLDR builds will look like this:

```
INSERT INTO T (DEPTNO, DNAME, LOC, LAST_UPDATED, ENTIRE_LINE)
VALUES ( :DEPTNO, upper(:dname), upper(:loc), :last_updated,
         :deptno||:dname||:loc||:last_updated );
```

It then prepares and binds the inputs to this statement, and executes it. So, pretty much anything you can think of doing in SQL, you can incorporate into your SQLLDR scripts. With the addition of the CASE statement in SQL, doing this can be extremely powerful and easy. For example, say your input file could have dates in the following formats:

- HH24:MI:SS: Just a time; the date should default to SYSDATE.

- DD/MM/YYYY: Just a date; the time should default to midnight.

- HH24:MI:SS DD/MM/YYYY: The date and time are both explicitly supplied.

You could use a control file like this:

```
LOAD DATA
INFILE *
INTO TABLE DEPT
REPLACE
FIELDS TERMINATED BY ','
TRAILING NULLCOLS
(DEPTNO,
  DNAME          "upper(:dname)",
  LOC            "upper(:loc)",
  LAST_UPDATED
"case
 when length(:last_updated) > 9
 then to_date(:last_updated,'hh24:mi:ss dd/mm/yyyy')
 when instr(:last_updated,':') > 0
 then to_date(:last_updated,'hh24:mi:ss')
 else to_date(:last_updated,'dd/mm/yyyy')
 end"
)
BEGINDATA
10,Sales,Virginia,12:03:03 17/10/2005
20,Accounting,Virginia,02:23:54
30,Consulting,Virginia,01:24:00 21/10/2005
40,Finance,Virginia,17/8/2005
```

which results in the following:

```
ops$tkyte@ORA10G> alter session set nls_date_format = 'dd-mon-yyyy hh24:mi:ss';
Session altered.

ops$tkyte@ORA10G> select deptno, dname, loc, last_updated
  2  from dept;

    DEPTNO DNAME          LOC            LAST_UPDATED
---------- -------------- -------------- --------------------
        10 SALES          VIRGINIA       17-oct-2005 12:03:03
        20 ACCOUNTING     VIRGINIA       01-jul-2005 02:23:54
        30 CONSULTING     VIRGINIA       21-oct-2005 01:24:00
        40 FINANCE        VIRGINIA       17-aug-2005 00:00:00
```

Now, one of three date formats will be applied to the input character string (notice that you are *not* loading a DATE anymore; you are just loading a string). The CASE function will look at the length and the contents of the string to determine which of the masks it should use.

It is interesting to note that you can write your *own* functions to be called from SQLLDR. This is a straightforward application of the fact that PL/SQL can be called from SQL.

How Do I Load Data with Embedded Newlines?

This is something that has been problematic for SQLLDR historically: how to load free-form data that may include a newline in it. The newline character is the default end-of-line character to SQLLDR, and the ways around this did not offer much flexibility in the past. Fortunately, in Oracle 8.1.6 and later versions, we have some new options. The options for loading data with embedded newlines are now as follows:

- Load the data with some other character in the data that represents a newline (e.g., put the string \n in the text where a newline should appear) and use a SQL function to replace that text with a CHR(10) during load time.

- Use the FIX attribute on the INFILE directive, and load a fixed-length flat file.

- Use the VAR attribute on the INFILE directive, and load a variable-width file that uses a format such that the first few bytes of each line specify the length in bytes of the line to follow.

- Use the STR attribute on the INFILE directive to load a variable-width file with some sequence of characters that represents the end of line, as opposed to just the newline character representing this.

The following sections demonstrate each in turn.

Use a Character Other Than a Newline

This is an easy method if you have control over how the input data is produced. If it is easy enough to convert the data when creating the data file, this will work fine. The idea is to apply a SQL function to the data on the way into the database, replacing some string of characters with a newline. Let's add another column to our DEPT table:

```
ops$tkyte@ORA10G> alter table dept add comments varchar2(4000);
Table altered.
```

We'll use this column to load text into. An example control file with inline data could be as follows:

```
LOAD DATA
INFILE *
INTO TABLE DEPT
REPLACE
FIELDS TERMINATED BY ','
TRAILING NULLCOLS
(DEPTNO,
  DNAME        "upper(:dname)",
  LOC          "upper(:loc)",
  COMMENTS     "replace(:comments,'\\n',chr(10))"
)
BEGINDATA
10,Sales,Virginia,This is the Sales\nOffice in Virginia
20,Accounting,Virginia,This is the Accounting\nOffice in Virginia
30,Consulting,Virginia,This is the Consulting\nOffice in Virginia
40,Finance,Virginia,This is the Finance\nOffice in Virginia
```

Notice how in the call to replace we had to use \\n, not just \n. This is because \n is recognized by SQLLDR as a newline, and SQLLDR would have converted it into a newline, not a two-character string. When we execute SQLLDR with the preceding control file, the table DEPT is loaded with the following:

```
ops$tkyte@ORA10G> select deptno, dname, comments from dept;

    DEPTNO DNAME          COMMENTS
---------- -------------- --------------------------
        10 SALES          This is the Sales
                          Office in Virginia

        20 ACCOUNTING     This is the Accounting
                          Office in Virginia

        30 CONSULTING     This is the Consulting
                          Office in Virginia

        40 FINANCE        This is the Finance
                          Office in Virginia
```

Use the FIX Attribute

The FIX attribute is another method available to us. If we use this, the input data must appear in fixed-length records. Each record will be exactly the same number of bytes as any other record in the input data set. When using *positional* data, use of the FIX attribute is especially valid. These files are typically fixed-length input files to begin with. When using free-form delimited data, it is less likely that we will have a fixed-length file, as these files are generally of varying length (this is the entire point of delimited files: to make each line only as big as it needs to be).

When using the FIX attribute, we must use an INFILE clause, as this is an option to INFILE. Additionally, the data must be stored externally, not in the control file itself, using this option. So, assuming we have fixed-length input records, we can use a control file such as this:

```
LOAD DATA
INFILE demo.dat "fix 80"
INTO TABLE DEPT
REPLACE
FIELDS TERMINATED BY ','
TRAILING NULLCOLS
(DEPTNO,
  DNAME          "upper(:dname)",
  LOC            "upper(:loc)",
  COMMENTS
)
```

This file specifies an input data file that will have records that are 80 bytes each. *This includes the trailing newline* that may or may not be there. In this case, the newline is nothing special in the input data file. It is just another character to be loaded or not. This is the thing to understand: the newline at the end of the record (if present) will become part of the record. To fully understand this, we need a utility to dump the contents of a file on the screen so we can see what is really in there. Using UNIX (or any Linux variant), this is pretty easy to do with od, a program to dump files to the screen in octal and other formats. We'll use the following demo.dat file. Note that the first column in the following output is actually in octal (base 8), so the number 0000012 on the second line is in octal and represents the decimal number 10. That tells us what byte in the file we are looking at. I've formatted the output to show ten characters per line (using -w10), so 0, 12, 24, and 36 are really 0, 10, 20, and 30.

```
[tkyte@desktop tkyte]$ od -c -w10 -v demo.dat
0000000   1   0   ,   S   a   l   e   s   ,   V
0000012   i   r   g   i   n   i   a   ,   T   h
0000024   i   s       i   s       t   h   e
0000036   S   a   l   e   s  \n   O   f   f   i
0000050   c   e       i   n       V   i   r   g
0000062   i   n   i   a
0000074
0000106
0000120   2   0   ,   A   c   c   o   u   n   t
0000132   i   n   g   ,   V   i   r   g   i   n
0000144   i   a   ,   T   h   i   s       i   s
0000156       t   h   e       A   c   c   o   u
0000170   n   t   i   n   g  \n   O   f   f   i
0000202   c   e       i   n       V   i   r   g
0000214   i   n   i   a
```

```
0000226
0000240  3  0  ,  C  o  n  s  u  l  t
0000252  i  n  g  ,  V  i  r  g  i  n
0000264  i  a  ,  T  h  i  s     i  s
0000276     t  h  e     C  o  n  s  u
0000310  l  t  i  n  g  \n O  f  f  i
0000322  c  e     i  n     V  i  r  g
0000334  i  n  i  a
0000346
0000360  4  0  ,  F  i  n  a  n  c  e
0000372  ,  V  i  r  g  i  n  i  a  ,
0000404  T  h  i  s     i  s     t  h
0000416  e     F  i  n  a  n  c  e  \n
0000430  O  f  f  i  c  e     i  n
0000442  V  i  r  g  i  n  i  a
0000454
0000466
0000500
[tkyte@desktop tkyte]$
```

Notice that in this input file, the newlines (\n) are not there to indicate where the end of the record for SQLLDR is; rather, they are just data to be loaded in this case. SQLLDR is using the FIX width of 80 bytes to figure out how much data to read. In fact, if we look at the input data, the records for SQLLDR are not even terminated by \n in this input file. The character right before department 20's record is a space, not a newline.

Now that we know each and every record is 80 bytes long, we are ready to load it using the control file listed earlier with the FIX 80 clause. When we do so, we can see the following:

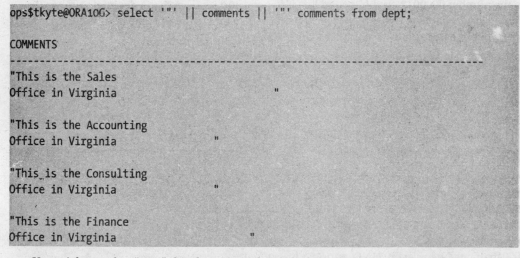

```
ops$tkyte@ORA10G> select '"' || comments || '"' comments from dept;

COMMENTS
--------------------------------------------------------------------------------
"This is the Sales
Office in Virginia                          "

"This is the Accounting
Office in Virginia               "

"This is the Consulting
Office in Virginia               "

"This is the Finance
Office in Virginia                     "
```

You might need to "trim" this data, since the trailing whitespace is preserved. You can do that in the control file, using the TRIM built-in SQL function.

A word of caution to those of you lucky enough to work on both Windows and UNIX: the end-of-line marker is different on these platforms. On UNIX, it is simply \n (CHR(10) in SQL). On Windows NT, is it \r\n (CHR(13)||CHR(10) in SQL). In general, if you use the FIX approach, make sure to *create and load* the file on a homogenous platform (UNIX and UNIX, or Windows and Windows).

Use the VAR Attribute

Another method of loading data with embedded newline characters is to use the VAR attribute. When using this format, each record will begin with some fixed number of bytes that represent the total length of the incoming record. Using this format, we can load variable-length records that contain embedded newlines, but only if we have a *record length field* at the beginning of *each and every* record. So, if we use a control file such as this:

```
LOAD DATA
INFILE demo.dat "var 3"
INTO TABLE DEPT
REPLACE
FIELDS TERMINATED BY ','
TRAILING NULLCOLS
(DEPTNO,
  DNAME         "upper(:dname)",
  LOC           "upper(:loc)",
  COMMENTS
)
```

then the VAR 3 says that the first 3 bytes of each input record will be the length of that input record. If we take a data file such as the following:

```
[tkyte@desktop tkyte]$ cat demo.dat
05510,Sales,Virginia,This is the Sales
Office in Virginia
06520,Accounting,Virginia,This is the Accounting
Office in Virginia
06530,Consulting,Virginia,This is the Consulting
Office in Virginia
05940,Finance,Virginia,This is the Finance
Office in Virginia
[tkyte@desktop tkyte]$
```

we can load it using that control file. In our input data file, we have four rows of data. The first row starts with 055, meaning that the next 55 bytes represent the first input record. These 55 bytes include the terminating newline after the word Virginia. The next row starts with 065. It has 65 bytes of text, and so on. Using this format data file, we can easily load our data with embedded newlines.

Again, if you are using UNIX and Windows (the preceding example was with UNIX, where a newline is one character long), you would have to adjust the length field for each record. On Windows, the preceding example's .dat file would have to have 56, 66, 66, and 60 as the length fields.

Use the STR Attribute

This is perhaps the most flexible method of loading data with embedded newlines. Using the STR attribute, we can specify a new end-of-line character (or sequence of characters). This allows us to create an input data file that has some special character at the end of each line—the newline is no longer "special."

I prefer to use a sequence of characters, typically some special marker, and then a newline. This makes it easy to see the end-of-line character when viewing the input data in a text editor or some utility, as each record still has a newline at the end of it. The STR attribute is specified in hexadecimal, and perhaps the easiest way to get the exact hexadecimal string we need is to use SQL and UTL_RAW to produce the hexadecimal string for us. For example, assuming we are on UNIX where the end-of-line marker is CHR(10) (linefeed) and our special marker character is a pipe symbol (|), we can write this:

```
ops$tkyte@ORA10G> select utl_raw.cast_to_raw( '|'||chr(10) ) from dual;

UTL_RAW.CAST_TO_RAW('|'||CHR(10))
-------------------------------------------------------------------------------
7C0A
```

which shows us that the STR we need to use on UNIX is X'7C0A'.

> ■**Note** On Windows, you would use UTL_RAW.CAST_TO_RAW('|'||chr(13)||chr(10)).

To use this, we might have a control file like this:

```
LOAD DATA
INFILE demo.dat "str X'7C0A'"
INTO TABLE DEPT
REPLACE
FIELDS TERMINATED BY ','
TRAILING NULLCOLS
(DEPTNO,
  DNAME          "upper(:dname)",
  LOC            "upper(:loc)",
  COMMENTS
)
```

So, if our input data looks like this:

```
[tkyte@desktop tkyte]$ cat demo.dat
10,Sales,Virginia,This is the Sales
Office in Virginia|
20,Accounting,Virginia,This is the Accounting
Office in Virginia|
30,Consulting,Virginia,This is the Consulting
```

```
Office in Virginia|
40,Finance,Virginia,This is the Finance
Office in Virginia|
[tkyte@desktop tkyte]$
```

where each record in the data file ends with a | \n, the previous control file will load it correctly.

Embedded Newlines Summary

We explored at least four ways to load data with embedded newlines in this section. In the upcoming section titled "Flat File Unload," we will use one of these techniques, the STR attribute, in a generic unload utility to avoid issues with regard to newlines in text.

Additionally, one thing to be very aware of—and I've mentioned it previously a couple of times—is that on Windows (all flavors), text files may end in \r\n (ASCII 13 + ASCII 10, carriage return/linefeed). Your control file will have to accommodate this: that \r is part of the record. The byte counts in the FIX and VAR, and the string used with STR must accommodate this. For example, if you took any of the previous .dat files that currently contain just \n in them and FTP-ed them to Windows using an ASCII transfer (the default), every \n would turn into \r\n. The same control file that just worked in UNIX would not be able to load the data anymore. This is something you must be aware of and take into consideration when setting up the control file.

How Do I Load LOBs?

We will now consider some methods for loading into LOBs. This is not a LONG or LONG RAW field, but rather the preferred datatypes of BLOB and CLOB. These datatypes were introduced in Oracle 8.0 and later, and they support a much richer interface/set of functionality than the legacy LONG and LONG RAW types, as discussed in Chapter 12.

We will investigate two methods for loading these fields: SQLLDR and PL/SQL. Others exist, such as Java streams, Pro*C, and OCI. We will begin working with the PL/SQL method of loading LOBs, and then we'll look at using SQLLDR to load them as well.

Loading a LOB via PL/SQL

The DBMS_LOB package has entry points called LoadFromFile, LoadBLOBFromFile, and LoadCLOBFromFile. These procedures allow us to use a BFILE (which can be used to read operating system files) to populate a BLOB or CLOB in the database. There is not a significant difference between the LoadFromFile and LoadBLOBFromFile routines, other than the latter returns OUT parameters that indicate how far into the BLOB column we have loaded data. The LoadCLOBFromFile routine, however, provides a significant feature: character set conversion. If you recall, in Chapter 12 we discussed some of the National Language Support (NLS) features of the Oracle database and the importance of character sets. LoadCLOBFromFile allows us to tell the database that the file it is about to load is in a character set different from the one the database is using, and that it should perform the required character set conversion. For example, you may have a UTF8-compatible database, but the files received to be loaded are encoded in the WE8ISO8859P1 character set, or vice versa. This function allows you to successfully load these files.

■Note For complete details on the procedures available in the DBMS_LOB package and their full set of inputs and outputs, please refer to the Oracle9*i Oracle Supplied Packages Guide* and the Oracle 10*g Oracle PL/SQL Packages and Types Reference*.

To use these procedures, we will need to create a DIRECTORY object in the database. This object will allow us to create BFILES (and open them) that point to a file existing on the file system that the database server has access to. This last phrase, "that the database server has access to," is a key point when using PL/SQL to load LOBs. The DBMS_LOB package executes entirely in the server. It can see only the file systems the server can see. It cannot, in particular, see your local file system if you are accessing Oracle over the network.

So we need to begin by creating a DIRECTORY object in the database. This is a straightforward process. We will create two directories for this example (note that these examples are executed in a UNIX environment; you will use the syntax for referring to directories that is appropriate for your operating system):

```
ops$tkyte@ORA10G> create or replace directory dir1  as '/tmp/';
Directory created.

ops$tkyte@ORA10G> create or replace directory "dir2" as '/tmp/';
Directory created.
```

■Note Oracle DIRECTORY objects are logical directories, meaning they are pointers to existing, physical directories in your operating system. The CREATE DIRECTORY command *does not* actually create a directory in the file system—you must perform that operation separately.

The user who performs this operation needs to have the CREATE ANY DIRECTORY privilege. The reason we create two directories is to demonstrate a common case-related ("case" as in uppercase versus lowercase characters) issue with regard to DIRECTORY objects. When Oracle created the first directory DIR1, it stored the object name in *uppercase* as it is the default. In the second example with dir2, it will have created the DIRECTORY object preserving the case we used in the name. The importance of this will be demonstrated shortly when we use the BFILE object.

Now, we want to load some data into either a BLOB or a CLOB. The method for doing so is rather easy, for example:

```
ops$tkyte@ORA10G> create table demo
  2  ( id        int primary key,
  3    theClob   clob
  4  )
  5  /
Table created.
```

```
ops$tkyte@ORA10G> host echo 'Hello World!' > /tmp/test.txt

ops$tkyte@ORA10G> declare
  2        l_clob    clob;
  3        l_bfile   bfile;
  4  begin
  5        insert into demo values ( 1, empty_clob() )
  6         returning theclob into l_clob;
  7
  8        l_bfile := bfilename( 'DIR1', 'test.txt' );
  9        dbms_lob.fileopen( l_bfile );
 10
 11        dbms_lob.loadfromfile( l_clob, l_bfile,
 12                          dbms_lob.getlength( l_bfile ) );
 13
 14        dbms_lob.fileclose( l_bfile );
 15  end;
 16  /
PL/SQL procedure successfully completed.

ops$tkyte@ORA10G> select dbms_lob.getlength(theClob), theClob from demo
  2  /
DBMS_LOB.GETLENGTH(THECLOB) THECLOB
--------------------------- ----------------
                         13 Hello World!
```

Walking through the preceding code we see

- On lines 5 and 6, we create a row in our table, set the CLOB to an EMPTY_CLOB(), and retrieve its value in one call. With the exception of temporary LOBs, LOBs "live" in the database—we cannot write to a LOB variable without having a pointer to either a temporary LOB or a LOB that is already in the database. An EMPTY_CLOB() is not a NULL CLOB; it is a valid non-NULL pointer to an empty structure. The other thing this did for us was to get a LOB locator, which points to data in a row that is locked. If we were to have selected this value out without locking the underlying row, our attempts to write to it would fail because LOBs must be locked prior to writing (unlike other structured data). By inserting the row, we have, of course, locked the row. If we were modifying an existing row instead of inserting, we would have used SELECT FOR UPDATE to retrieve and lock the row.

- On line 8, we create a BFILE object. Note how we use DIR1 in uppercase—this is key, as we will see in a moment. This is because we are passing to BFILENAME() the *name* of an object, not the object itself. Therefore, we must ensure the name matches the case Oracle has stored for this object.

- On line 9, we open the LOB. This will allow us to read it.

- On lines 11 and 12, we load the entire contents of the operating system file /tmp/ test.txt into the LOB locator we just inserted. We use DBMS_LOB.GETLENGTH() to tell the LOADFROMFILE() routine how many bytes of the BFILE to load (all of them).

- Lastly, on line 14, we close the BFILE we opened, and the CLOB is loaded.

If we had attempted to use dir1 instead of DIR1 in the preceding example, we would have encountered the following error:

```
ops$tkyte@ORA10G> declare
...
  6         returning theclob into l_clob;
  7
  8      l_bfile := bfilename( 'dir1', 'test.txt' );
  9      dbms_lob.fileopen( l_bfile );
...
 15  end;
 16  /
declare
*
ERROR at line 1:
ORA-22285: non-existent directory or file for FILEOPEN operation
ORA-06512: at "SYS.DBMS_LOB", line 523
ORA-06512: at line 9
```

This is because the directory dir1 does not exist—DIR1 does. If you prefer to use directory names in mixed case, you should use quoted identifiers when creating them as we did for dir2. This will allow you to write code as shown here:

```
ops$tkyte@ORA10G> declare
  2      l_clob    clob;
  3      l_bfile   bfile;
  4  begin
  5      insert into demo values ( 1, empty_clob() )
  6        returning theclob into l_clob;
  7
  8      l_bfile := bfilename( 'dir2', 'test.txt' );
  9      dbms_lob.fileopen( l_bfile );
 10
 11      dbms_lob.loadfromfile( l_clob, l_bfile,
 12                             dbms_lob.getlength( l_bfile ) );
 13
 14      dbms_lob.fileclose( l_bfile );
 15  end;
 16  /
PL/SQL procedure successfully completed.
```

There are methods other than the load from file routines by which you can populate a LOB using PL/SQL. Using DBMS_LOB and its supplied routines is by far the easiest if you are going to load the entire file. If you need to process the contents of the file while loading it, you may also use `DBMS_LOB.READ` on the `BFILE` to read the data. The use of `UTL_RAW.CAST_TO_VARCHAR2` is handy here if the data you are reading is in fact text, not `RAW`. You may then use `DBMS_LOB.WRITE` or `WRITEAPPEND` to place the data into a `CLOB` or `BLOB`.

Loading LOB Data via SQLLDR

We will now investigate how to load data into a LOB via SQLLDR. There is more than one method for doing this, but we will investigate the two most common methods:

- When the data is "inline" with the rest of the data.

- When the data is stored out of line, and the input data contains a file name to be loaded with the row. These are also known as *secondary data files* (*SDFs*) in SQLLDR terminology.

We will start with data that is inline.

Loading LOB Data That Is Inline   These LOBs will typically have newlines and other special characters embedded in them. Therefore, you will almost always use one of the four methods detailed in the "How Do I Load Data with Embedded Newlines?" section to load this data. Let's begin by modifying the DEPT table to have a CLOB instead of a big VARCHAR2 field for the COMMENTS column:

```
ops$tkyte@ORA10G> truncate table dept;
Table truncated.

ops$tkyte@ORA10G> alter table dept drop column comments;
Table altered.

ops$tkyte@ORA10G> alter table dept add comments clob;
Table altered.
```

For example, say we have a data file (demo.dat) that has the following contents:

```
10, Sales,Virginia,This is the Sales
Office in Virginia|
20,Accounting,Virginia,This is the Accounting
Office in Virginia|
30,Consulting,Virginia,This is the Consulting
Office in Virginia|
40,Finance,Virginia,"This is the Finance
Office in Virginia, it has embedded commas and is
much longer than the other comments field. If you
feel the need to add double quoted text in here like
this: ""You will need to double up those quotes!"" to
preserve them in the string. This field keeps going for up to
1000000 bytes (because of the control file definition I used)
or until we hit the magic end of record marker,
the | followed by an end of line - it is right here ->"|
```

Each record ends with a pipe symbol (|), followed by the end-of-line marker. The text for department 40 is much longer than the rest, with many newlines, embedded quotes, and commas. Given this data file, we can create a control file such as this:

```
LOAD DATA
INFILE demo.dat "str X'7C0A'"
INTO TABLE DEPT
REPLACE
FIELDS TERMINATED BY ',' OPTIONALLY ENCLOSED BY '"'
TRAILING NULLCOLS
(DEPTNO,
  DNAME        "upper(:dname)",
  LOC          "upper(:loc)",
  COMMENTS     char(1000000)
)
```

■**Note** This example is from UNIX, where the end-of-line marker is 1 byte, hence the STR setting in the preceding control file. On Windows, it would have to be '7C0D0A'.

To load the data file, we specify CHAR(1000000) on the column COMMENTS since SQLLDR defaults to CHAR(255) for any input field. The CHAR(1000000) will allow SQLLDR to handle up to 1,000,000 bytes of input text. You must set this to a value that is larger than any expected chunk of text in the input file. Reviewing the loaded data, we see the following:

```
ops$tkyte@ORA10G> select comments from dept;

COMMENTS
--------------------------------------------------------------------------------
This is the Consulting
Office in Virginia

This is the Finance
Office in Virginia, it has embedded commas and is
much longer than the other comments field. If you
feel the need to add double quoted text in here like
this: "You will need to double up those quotes!" to
preserve them in the string. This field keeps going for up to
1000000 bytes or until we hit the magic end of record marker,
the | followed by an end of line - it is right here ->

This is the Sales
Office in Virginia

This is the Accounting
Office in Virginia
```

The one thing to observe here is that the doubled-up quotes are no longer doubled up. SQLLDR removed the extra quotes we placed there.

Loading LOB Data That Is Out of Line A common scenario is to have a data file that contains the names of files to load into the LOBs, instead of having the LOB data mixed in with the structured data. This offers a greater degree of flexibility, as the data file given to SQLLDR does not have to use one of the four methods to get around having embedded newlines in the input data, as would frequently happen with large amounts of text or binary data. SQLLDR calls this type of additional data file a `LOBFILE`.

SQLLDR can also support the loading of a structured data file that points to another, single data file. We can tell SQLLDR how to parse LOB data from this other file, so that each row in the structured data gets loaded with a piece of it. I find this mode to be of limited use (I've never found a use for it myself to date), and I will not discuss it here. SQLLDR refers to these externally referenced files as *complex secondary data files*.

`LOBFILE`s are relatively simple data files aimed at facilitating LOB loading. The attribute that distinguishes `LOBFILE`s from the main data files is that in `LOBFILE`s, there is no concept of a record, hence *newlines never get in the way*. In `LOBFILE`s, the data is in any of the following formats:

- Fixed-length fields (e.g., load bytes 100 through 1.000 from the `LOBFILE`)

- Delimited fields (terminated by something or enclosed by something)

- Length/value pairs, a variable-length field

The most common of these types is the delimited fields—ones that are terminated by an end-of-file (EOF), in fact. Typically, you have a directory full of files you would like to load into LOB columns, and each file in its entirety will go into a `BLOB`. The `LOBFILE` statement with `TERMINATED BY EOF` is what you will use.

Say we have a directory full of files we would like to load into the database. We would like to load the `OWNER` of the file, the `TIME_STAMP` of the file, the `NAME` of the file, and the file itself. The table we would load into would be as follows:

```
ops$tkyte@ORA10G> create table lob_demo
  2  ( owner       varchar2(255),
  3    time_stamp  date,
  4    filename    varchar2(255),
  5    data        blob
  6  )
  7  /
Table created.
```

Using a simple `ls -l` on UNIX, and `dir /q /n` on Windows, and capturing that output, we can generate our input file and load it using a control file such as this on UNIX:

```
LOAD DATA
INFILE *
REPLACE
INTO TABLE LOB_DEMO
( owner          position(17:25),
```

```
    time_stamp    position(44:55) date "Mon DD HH24:MI",
    filename      position(57:100),
    data          LOBFILE(filename) TERMINATED BY EOF
)
BEGINDATA
-rw-r--r--    1 tkyte      tkyte       1220342 Jun 17 15:26 classes12.zip
-rw-rw-r--    1 tkyte      tkyte            10 Jul 16 16:38 foo.sql
-rw-rw-r--    1 tkyte      tkyte           751 Jul 16 16:36 t.ctl
-rw-rw-r--    1 tkyte      tkyte           491 Jul 16 16:38 testa.sql
-rw-rw-r--    1 tkyte      tkyte           283 Jul 16 16:38 testb.sql
-rw-rw-r--    1 tkyte      tkyte           231 Jul 16 16:38 test.sh
-rw-rw-r--    1 tkyte      tkyte           235 Apr 28 18:03 test.sql
-rw-rw-r--    1 tkyte      tkyte          1649 Jul 16 16:36 t.log
-rw-rw-r--    1 tkyte      tkyte          1292 Jul 16 16:38 uselast.sql
-rw-rw-r--    1 tkyte      tkyte           909 Jul 16 16:38 userbs.sql
```

Now, if we inspect the contents of the LOB_DEMO table after running SQLLDR, we will discover the following:

```
ops$tkyte@ORA10G> select owner, time_stamp, filename, dbms_lob.getlength(data)
  2  from lob_demo
  3  /

OWNER    TIME_STAM FILENAME        DBMS_LOB.GETLENGTH(DATA)
-------- --------- --------------- ------------------------
tkyte    17-JUN-05 classes12.zip                    1220342
tkyte    16-JUL-05 foo.sql                               10
tkyte    16-JUL-05 t.ctl                                875
tkyte    16-JUL-05 testa.sql                            491
tkyte    16-JUL-05 testb.sql                            283
tkyte    16-JUL-05 test.sh                              231
tkyte    28-APR-05 test.sql                             235
tkyte    16-JUL-05 t.log                                  0
tkyte    16-JUL-05 uselast.sql                         1292
tkyte    16-JUL-05 userbs.sql                           909

10 rows selected.
```

This works with CLOBs as well as BLOBs. Loading a directory of text files using SQLLDR in this fashion is easy.

Loading LOB Data into Object Columns Now that we know how to load into a simple table we have created ourselves, we might also find the need to load into a table that has a complex object type with a LOB in it. This happens most frequently when using the image capabilities. The image capabilities are implemented using a complex object type, ORDSYS.ORDIMAGE. We need to be able to tell SQLLDR how to load into this.

To load a LOB into an ORDIMAGE type column, we must understand a little more about the structure of the ORDIMAGE type. Using a table we want to load into, and a DESCRIBE on that table in SQL*Plus, we can discover that we have a column called IMAGE of type ORDSYS.ORDIMAGE, which we want to ultimately load into IMAGE.SOURCE.LOCALDATA. The following examples will work only if you have interMedia installed and configured; otherwise, the datatype ORDSYS.ORDIMAGE will be an unknown type:

```
ops$tkyte@ORA10G> create table image_load(
  2      id number,
  3      name varchar2(255),
  4      image ordsys.ordimage
  5  )
  6  /
Table created.

ops$tkyte@ORA10G> desc image_load
 Name                                    Null?    Type
 --------------------------------------- -------- -----------------------------
 ID                                               NUMBER
 NAME                                             VARCHAR2(255)
 IMAGE                                            ORDSYS.ORDIMAGE

ops$tkyte@ORA10G> desc ordsys.ordimage
 Name                                    Null?    Type
 --------------------------------------- -------- -----------------------------
 SOURCE                                           ORDSYS.ORDSOURCE
 HEIGHT                                           NUMBER(38)
 WIDTH                                            NUMBER(38)
 CONTENTLENGTH                                    NUMBER(38)
...

ops$tkyte@ORA10G> desc ordsys.ordsource
 Name                                    Null?    Type
 --------------------------------------- -------- -----------------------------
 LOCALDATA                                        BLOB
 SRCTYPE                                          VARCHAR2(4000)
 SRCLOCATION                                      VARCHAR2(4000)
...
```

> **Note** You could issue SET DESC DEPTH ALL or SET DESC DEPTH <n> in SQL*Plus to have the entire hierarchy displayed at once. Given that the output for the ORDSYS.ORDIMAGE would have been many pages long, I chose to do it piece by piece.

So a control file to load this might look like this:

```
LOAD DATA
INFILE *
INTO TABLE image_load
REPLACE
FIELDS TERMINATED BY ','
( ID,
  NAME,
  file_name FILLER,
  IMAGE column object
  (
    SOURCE column object
    (
      LOCALDATA LOBFILE (file_name) TERMINATED BY EOF
              NULLIF file_name = 'NONE'
    )
  )
)
BEGINDATA
1,icons,icons.gif
```

I have introduced two new constructs here:

- COLUMN OBJECT: This tells SQLLDR that this is not a column name; rather, it is part of a column name. It is not mapped to a field in the input file, but is used to build the correct object column reference to be used during the load. In the preceding file, we have two column object tags, one nested in the other. Therefore, the column name that will be used is IMAGE.SOURCE.LOCALDATA, as we need it to be. Note that we are not loading any of the other attributes of these two object types (e.g., IMAGE.HEIGHT, IMAGE.CONTENTLENGTH, and IMAGE.SOURCE.SRCTYPE). Shortly, we'll see how to get those populated.

- NULLIF FILE_NAME = 'NONE': This tells SQLLDR to load a NULL into the object column in the event that the field FILE_NAME contains the word NONE in it.

Once you have loaded an interMedia type, you will typically need to postprocess the loaded data using PL/SQL to have interMedia operate on it. For example, with the preceding data, you would probably want to run the following to have the properties for the image set up correctly:

```
begin
  for c in ( select * from image_load ) loop
    c.image.setproperties;
  end loop;
end;
/
```

SETPROPERTIES is an object method provided by the ORDSYS.ORDIMAGE type, which processes the image itself and updates the remaining attributes of the object with appropriate values.

How Do I Call SQLLDR from a Stored Procedure?

The short answer is that you can't do this. SQLLDR is not an API; it isn't something that is callable. SQLLDR is a command-line program. You can definitely write an external procedure in Java or C that runs SQLLDR, but that isn't the same as "calling" SQLLDR. The load will happen in another session, and it won't be subject to your transaction control. Additionally, you'll have to parse the resulting log file to determine if the load was successful or not, and how successful (i.e., how many rows got loaded before an error terminated the load) it may have been. Invoking SQLLDR from a stored procedure isn't something I recommend doing.

In the past, before Oracle9*i*, you might have implemented your own SQLLDR-like process. For example, the options could have been as follows:

- Write a mini-SQLLDR in PL/SQL. It can use either BFILES to read binary data or UTL_FILE to read text data to parse and load.

- Write a mini-SQLLDR in Java. This can be a little more sophisticated than a PL/SQL-based loader and can make use of the many available Java routines.

- Write a SQLLDR in C, and call it as an external procedure.

Fortunately, in Oracle9*i* and later, we have external tables that provide almost all of the functionality of SQLLDR and, additionally, can do many things SQLLDR cannot. We saw a quick example of external tables in the last chapter, where we used them to automate a parallel direct path load. We'll take a longer look at them in a moment. But first, I'd like to finish up our discussion of SQLLDR with some caveats.

SQLLDR Caveats

In this section, we will discuss some things to watch out for when using SQLLDR.

TRUNCATE Appears to Work Differently

The TRUNCATE option of SQLLDR might appear to work differently than TRUNCATE does in SQL*Plus, or any other tool. SQLLDR, working on the assumption you will be reloading the table with a similar amount of data, uses the extended form of TRUNCATE. Specifically, it issues the following:

```
truncate table t reuse storage
```

The REUSE STORAGE option does not release allocated extents—it just marks them as "free space." If this were not the desired outcome, you would truncate the table prior to executing SQLLDR.

SQLLDR Defaults to CHAR(255)

The default length of input fields is 255 characters. If your field is longer than this, you will receive an error message:

```
Record N: Rejected - Error on table T, column C.
Field in data file exceeds maximum length
```

This does not mean the data will not fit into the database column; rather, it indicates that SQLLDR was expecting 255 bytes or less of input data, and it received somewhat more than that. The solution is to simply use CHAR(N) in the control file, where N is big enough to accommodate the largest field length in the input file.

Command Line Overrides Control File

Many of the SQLLDR options may be either placed in the control file or used on the command line. For example, I can use INFILE FILENAME as well as SQLLDR ... DATA=FILENAME. The command line overrides any options in the control file. You cannot count on the options in a control file actually being used, as the person executing SQLLDR can override them.

SQLLDR Summary

In this section, we explored many areas of loading data. We covered the typical, everyday issues we will encounter: loading delimited files, loading fixed-length files, loading a directory full of image files, using functions on input data to transform the input, and so on. We did not cover massive data loads using the direct path loader in any detail; rather, we touched lightly on that subject. Our goal was to answer the questions that arise frequently with the use of SQLLDR and that affect the broadest audience.

External Tables

External tables were first introduced in Oracle9*i* Release 1. Put simply, they allow us to treat an operating system file as if it is a read-only database table. They are not intended to be a replacement for a "real" table, or to be used in place of a real table; rather, they are intended to be used as a tool to ease the loading and, in Oracle 10*g*, unloading of data.

When the external tables feature was first unveiled, I often referred to it as "the replacement for SQLLDR." This idea still holds true—*most* of the time. Having said this, you might wonder why we just spent so much time looking at SQLLDR. The reason is that SQLLDR has been around for a long time, and there are many, many legacy control files lying around. SQLLDR is still a commonly used tool; it is what many people know and have used. We are still in a period of transition from the use of SQLLDR to external tables, so SQLLDR is still very relevant.

What many DBAs don't realize is that their knowledge of SQLLDR control files is very readily transferable to the use of external tables. You'll discover, as we work through the examples in this part of the chapter, that external tables incorporate much of the SQLLDR syntax and many of the SQLLDR techniques.

SQLLDR should be chosen over external tables in the following three situations:

- You have to load data over a network—in other words, when the input file is not on the database server itself. One of the restrictions of external tables is that the input file must be accessible on the database server.

- Multiple users must *concurrently* work with the *same* external table processing different input files.

- You have to work with LOB types. External tables do not support LOBs.

With those three situations in mind, in general I strongly recommend using external tables for their extended capabilities. SQLLDR is a fairly simple tool that generates an INSERT statement and loads data. Its ability to use SQL is limited to calling SQL functions on a row-by-row basis. External tables open up the entire SQL set of functionality to data loading. Some of the key functionality features that external tables have over SQLLDR in my experience are as follows:

- The ability to use complex WHERE conditions to selectively load data. SQLLDR has a WHEN clause to select rows to load, but you are limited to using only AND expressions and expressions using equality—no ranges (greater than, less than), no OR expressions, no IS NULL, and so on.

- The ability to MERGE data. You can take an operating system file full of data and update existing database records from it.

- The ability to perform efficient code lookups. You can join an external table to other database tables as part of your load process.

- Easier multitable inserts using INSERT. Starting in Oracle9*i*, an INSERT statement can insert into one or *more* tables using complex WHEN conditions. While SQLLDR can load into multiple tables, it can be quite complex to formulate the syntax.

- A shallower learning curve for new developers. SQLLDR is "yet another tool" to learn, in addition to the programming language, the development tools, the SQL language, and so on. As long as a developer knows SQL, he can immediately apply that knowledge to bulk data loading, without having to learn a new tool (SQLLDR).

So, with that in mind, let's look at how to use external tables.

Setting Up External Tables

As a first simple demonstration of external tables, we'll rerun the previous SQLLDR example, which bulk loaded data into the DEPT table. Just to refresh your memory, the simple control file we used was as follows:

```
LOAD DATA
INFILE *
INTO TABLE DEPT
FIELDS TERMINATED BY ','
(DEPTNO, DNAME, LOC )
BEGINDATA
10,Sales,Virginia
20,Accounting,Virginia
30,Consulting,Virginia
40,Finance,Virginia
```

By far the easiest way to get started is to use this existing legacy control file to provide the definition of our external table. The following SQLLDR command will generate the CREATE TABLE statement for our external table:

```
[tkyte@desktop tkyte]$ sqlldr / demo1.ctl external_table=generate_only
SQL*Loader: Release 10.1.0.4.0 - Production on Sat Jul 16 17:34:51 2005
Copyright (c) 1982, 2004, Oracle.  All rights reserved.
[tkyte@desktop tkyte]$
```

The EXTERNAL_TABLE parameter has one of three values:

- NOT_USED: This is self-evident in meaning and is the default value.

- EXECUTE: This value means that SQLLDR will not generate a SQL INSERT statement and execute it; rather, it will create an external table and use a single bulk SQL statement to load it.

- GENERATE_ONLY: This value causes SQLLDR to not actually load any data, but only to generate the SQL DDL and DML statements it would have executed into the log file it creates.

■**Caution** DIRECT=TRUE overrides EXTERNAL_TABLE=GENERATE_ONLY. If you specify DIRECT=TRUE, the data will be loaded and no external table will be generated.

When using GENERATE_ONLY, we can see the following in the demo1.log file:

```
CREATE DIRECTORY statements needed for files
-----------------------------------------------------------------------
CREATE DIRECTORY SYS_SQLLDR_XT_TMPDIR_00000 AS '/home/tkyte'
```

We may or may not see a CREATE DIRECTORY statement in the log file. SQLLDR connects to the database during the external table script generation and queries the data dictionary to see if a suitable directory already exists. In this case, there was no suitable directory in place, so SQLLDR generated a CREATE DIRECTORY statement for us. Next, it generated the CREATE TABLE statement for our external table:

```
CREATE TABLE statement for external table:
-----------------------------------------------------------------------
CREATE TABLE "SYS_SQLLDR_X_EXT_DEPT"
(
  "DEPTNO" NUMBER(2),
  "DNAME" VARCHAR2(14),
  "LOC" VARCHAR2(13)
)
```

SQLLDR had logged into the database; that is how it knows the exact datatypes to be used in this external table definition (e.g., that DEPTNO is a NUMBER(2)). It picked them up right from the data dictionary. Next, we see the beginning of the external table definition:

```
ORGANIZATION external
(
  TYPE oracle_loader
  DEFAULT DIRECTORY SYS_SQLLDR_XT_TMPDIR_00000
```

The ORGANIZATION EXTERNAL clause tells Oracle this is not a "normal" table. We saw this clause before in Chapter 10 when we looked at IOTs. Currently there are three organization types: HEAP for a "normal" table, INDEX for an IOT, and EXTERNAL for an external table. The rest of the text starts to tell Oracle more about the external table. The ORACLE_LOADER type is one of two supported types (in Oracle9*i* it is the *only* supported type). The other type is ORACLE_ DATAPUMP, the proprietary Data Pump format used by Oracle in Oracle 10*g* and later. We will take a look at that type in a subsequent section on data unloading—it is a format that can be used to both load and unload data. An external table may be used both to create a Data Pump format file and to subsequently read it.

The very next section we encounter is the ACCESS PARAMETERS section of the external table. Here we describe to the database how to process the input file. As you look at this, you should notice the similarity to a SQLLDR control file; this is no accident. For the most part, SQLLDR and external tables use very similar syntax.

```
ACCESS PARAMETERS
(
  RECORDS DELIMITED BY NEWLINE CHARACTERSET WE8ISO8859P1
  BADFILE 'SYS_SQLLDR_XT_TMPDIR_00000':'demo1.bad'
  LOGFILE 'demo1.log_xt'
  READSIZE 1048576
  SKIP 7
  FIELDS TERMINATED BY "," OPTIONALLY ENCLOSED BY '"' LDRTRIM
  REJECT ROWS WITH ALL NULL FIELDS
  (
    "DEPTNO" CHAR(255)
      TERMINATED BY "," OPTIONALLY ENCLOSED BY '"',
    "DNAME" CHAR(255)
      TERMINATED BY "," OPTIONALLY ENCLOSED BY '"',
    "LOC" CHAR(255)
      TERMINATED BY "," OPTIONALLY ENCLOSED BY '"'
  )
)
```

These access parameters show how to set up an external table so that it processes files pretty much identically to the way SQLLDR would:

- RECORDS: Records are terminated by newlines by default, as they are for SQLLDR.

- BADFILE: There is a bad file (a file where records that fail processing are recorded to) set up in the directory we just created.

- LOGFILE: There is a log file that is equivalent to SQLLDR's log file set up in the current working directory.

- READSIZE: This is the default buffer used by Oracle to read the input data file. It is 1MB in this case. This memory comes from the PGA in dedicated server mode and the SGA in shared server mode, and it is used to buffer the information in the input data file for a session (refer to Chapter 4, where we discussed PGA and SGA memory). Keep that fact in mind if you're using shared servers: the memory is allocated from the SGA.

- SKIP 7: This determines how many records in the input file should be skipped. You might be asking, "Why 'skip 7'?" Well, we used INFILE * in this example; SKIP 7 is used to skip over the control file itself to get to the embedded data. If we did not use INFILE *, there would be no SKIP clause at all.

- FIELDS TERMINATED BY: This is just as we used in the control file itself. However, the external table did add LDRTRIM, which stands for *LoaDeR TRIM*. This is a trim mode that emulates the way in which SQLLDR trims data by default. Other options include LRTRIM, LTRIM, and RTRIM for left/right trimming of whitespace; and NOTRIM to preserve all leading/trailing whitespace.

- REJECT ROWS WITH ALL NULL FIELDS: This causes the external table to log to the bad file any entirely blank lines and to not load that row.

- *The column definitions themselves*: This is the metadata about the expected input data values. They are all character strings in the data file to be loaded, and they can be up to 255 characters in length (SQLLDR's default size), and terminated by , and optionally enclosed in quotes.

■**Note** For a comprehensive list of all options available to you when using external tables, review the *Oracle Utilities Guide* manual. This reference contains a section dedicated to external tables. The *Oracle SQL Reference Guide* manual provides the basic syntax, but not the details of the ACCESS PARAMETERS section.

Lastly, we get to the LOCATION section of the external table definition:

```
location
(
  'demo1.ctl'
)
) REJECT LIMIT UNLIMITED
```

That tells Oracle the name of the file to load, which is demo1.ctl in this case since we used INFILE * in the original control file. The next statement in the control file is the default INSERT that can be used to load the table from the external table itself:

```
INSERT statements used to load internal tables:
-------------------------------------------------------------------
INSERT /*+ append */ INTO DEPT
(
  DEPTNO,
  DNAME,
```

```
  LOC
)
SELECT
  "DEPTNO",
  "DNAME",
  "LOC"
FROM "SYS_SQLLDR_X_EXT_DEPT"
```

That would perform the logical equivalent of a direct path load if possible (assuming the APPEND hint may be obeyed; the existence of triggers or foreign key constraints may prevent the direct path operation from taking place).

Lastly, in the log file, we'll see statements that may be used to remove the objects SQLLDR would have us create after the load was complete:

```
statements to cleanup objects created by previous statements:
-------------------------------------------------------------------
DROP TABLE "SYS_SQLLDR_X_EXT_DEPT"
DROP DIRECTORY SYS_SQLLDR_XT_TMPDIR_00000
```

And that is it. If we take that log file and insert / where appropriate to make it a valid SQL*Plus script, then we should be ready to go—or not, depending on the permissions in place. For example, assuming the schema I log into has the CREATE ANY DIRECTORY privilege or READ access to an existing directory, I might observe the following:

```
ops$tkyte@ORA10G> INSERT /*+ append */ INTO DEPT
  2  (
  3     DEPTNO,
  4     DNAME,
  5     LOC
  6  )
  7  SELECT
  8     "DEPTNO",
  9     "DNAME",
 10     "LOC"
 11  FROM "SYS_SQLLDR_X_EXT_DEPT"
 12  /
INSERT /*+ append */ INTO DEPT
*
ERROR at line 1:
ORA-29913: error in executing ODCIEXTTABLEOPEN callout
ORA-29400: data cartridge error
KUP-04063: unable to open log file demo1.log_xt
OS error Permission denied
ORA-06512: at "SYS.ORACLE_LOADER", line 19
ORA-06512: at line 1
```

Well, that doesn't seem right at first. I'm logged into the operating system as TKYTE, the directory I'm logging into is /home/tkyte, and I own that directory, so I can certainly write to it (I created the SQLLDR log file there, after all!). What happened? The fact is that the external table code is running in the Oracle server software, in my dedicated or shared server. The process trying to read the input data file is the Oracle software owner, not my account. The process trying to create the log file is the Oracle software owner, not my account. Apparently, Oracle did not have the privilege required to write into my directory, and hence the attempted access of the external table failed. This is an important point. To read a table, the account under which the database is running (the Oracle software owner) must be able to do the following:

- *Read* the file we are pointing to. In UNIX, that means the Oracle software owner must have read and execute permissions on all directory paths leading to the file. In Windows, the Oracle software owner must be able to read that file.

- *Write* to the directories where the log file will be written to (or bypass the generation of the log file altogether, but this is not recommended in general). In fact, if the log file already exists, the Oracle software owner must be able to write to the existing file.

- *Write* to any of the bad files we have specified, just like the log file.

Returning to the example, the following command gives Oracle the ability to write into my directory:

```
ops$tkyte@ORA10G> host chmod a+rw .
```

Caution This command actually gives everyone the ability to write into my directory! This is just a demonstration; normally I would use a special directory perhaps owned by the Oracle software owner itself to do this.

Next, I rerun my INSERT statement:

```
ops$tkyte@ORA10G> l
  1  INSERT /*+ append */ INTO DEPT
  2  (
  3    DEPTNO,
  4    DNAME,
  5    LOC
  6  )
  7  SELECT
  8    "DEPTNO",
  9    "DNAME",
 10    "LOC"
 11* FROM "SYS_SQLLDR_X_EXT_DEPT"
ops$tkyte@ORA10G> /
4 rows created.

ops$tkyte@ORA10G> host ls -l demo1.log_xt
-rw-r--r--    1 ora10g   ora10g        578 Jul 17 10:45 demo1.log_xt
```

You can see that this time I accessed the file, I successfully loaded four rows, and the log file was created and, in fact, is owned by "Oracle," not by my operating system account.

Dealing with Errors

In a perfect world, there would be no errors. The data in the input file would be perfect, and it would all load correctly. That almost never happens. So, how can we track errors with this process?

The most common method is to use the BADFILE option. Here, Oracle will record all records that failed processing. For example, if our control file contained a record with DEPTNO 'ABC', that record would fail and end up in the bad file because 'ABC' cannot be converted into a number. We'll demonstrate this in the following example.

First, we add the following as the last line of demo1.ctl (this will add a line of data that cannot be loaded to our input):

```
ABC,XYZ,Hello
```

Next, we run the following command, to prove that the demo1.bad file does not exist yet:

```
ops$tkyte@ORA10G> host ls -l demo1.bad
ls: demo1.bad: No such file or directory
```

Then we query the external table to display the contents:

```
ops$tkyte@ORA10G> select * from SYS_SQLLDR_X_EXT_DEPT;

    DEPTNO DNAME           LOC
---------- --------------- -------------
        10 Sales           Virginia
        20 Accounting      Virginia
        30 Consulting      Virginia
        40 Finance         Virginia
```

Now we will find that the file exists and we can review its contents:

```
ops$tkyte@ORA10G> host ls -l demo1.bad
-rw-r--r--    1 ora10g   ora10g          14 Jul 17 10:53 demo1.bad

ops$tkyte@ORA10G> host cat demo1.bad
ABC,XYZ,Hello
```

But how can we programmatically inspect these bad records and the log that is generated? Fortunately, that is easy to do by using yet another external table. Suppose we set up this external table:

```
ops$tkyte@ORA10G> create table et_bad
  2  ( text1 varchar2(4000) ,
  3    text2 varchar2(4000) ,
  4    text3 varchar2(4000)
  5  )
  6  organization external
```

```
 7  (type oracle_loader
 8   default directory SYS_SQLLDR_XT_TMPDIR_00000
 9   access parameters
10   (
11     records delimited by newline
12     fields
13     missing field values are null
14     ( text1 position(1:4000),
15       text2 position(4001:8000),
16       text3 position(8001:12000)
17     )
18   )
19   location ('demo1.bad')
20  )
21  /
Table created.
```

This is just a table that can read any file without failing on a datatype error, as long as the lines in the file consist of fewer than 12,000 characters. If have more than 12,000 characters, then we can simply add more text columns to accommodate them.

We can clearly see the rejected records via a simple query:

```
ops$tkyte@ORA10G> select * from et_bad;

TEXT1           TEXT2            TEXT3
--------------- ---------------- ----------------
ABC,XYZ,Hello
```

A COUNT(*) could tell us how many records were rejected. Another external table created on the log file associated with this external table could tell us why the record was rejected. We would need to go one step further to make this a repeatable process, however. The reason is that the bad file is not "blanked" out if there were no errors in our use of the external table. So, if there were some preexisting bad file with data in it and our external table generated no errors, we would be misled into thinking there were errors.

I've taken three approaches in the past to resolve this issue:

- Use UTL_FILE and reset the bad file—truncate it, in effect, by simply opening it for write and closing it.

- Use UTL_FILE to rename any preexisting bad files, preserving their contents, but allowing us to create a new one.

- Incorporate the PID into the bad (and log) file names. We'll demonstrate this later in the "Multiuser Issues" section.

In that fashion, we'll be able to tell if the bad records in the bad file were generated by us just recently or if they were left over from some older version of the file itself and are not meaningful.

ALTER TABLE T PROJECT COLUMN REFERENCED | ALL

The COUNT(*) earlier in this section made me think about a new feature in Oracle 10*g*: the ability to optimize external table access by only accessing the fields in the external file that are referenced in the query. That is, if the external table is defined to have 100 number fields, but you select out only one of them, you can direct Oracle to bypass converting the other 99 strings into numbers. It sounds great, but it can cause a different number of rows to be returned from each query. Suppose the external table has 100 lines of data in it. All of the data for column C1 is "valid." and converts into a number. None of the data for column C2 is "valid," and it does not convert into a number. If you select C1 from that external table, you'll get 100 rows back. If you select C2 from that external table, you'll get 0 rows back.

You have to explicitly enable this optimization, and you should think about whether it is "safe" for you to use or not (only you know enough about your application and its processing to answer the question "Is it safe?"). Using the earlier example with the bad line of data added, we would expect to see the following output upon querying our external table:

```
ops$tkyte@ORA10G> select dname
  2    from SYS_SQLLDR_X_EXT_DEPT
  3  /

DNAME
---------------
Sales
Accounting
Consulting
Finance

ops$tkyte@ORA10G> select deptno
  2    from SYS_SQLLDR_X_EXT_DEPT
  3  /

    DEPTNO
----------
        10
        20
        30
        40
```

We know the "bad" record has been logged into the BADFILE. But if we simply ALTER the external table and tell Oracle to only "project" (process) the referenced columns, as follows:

```
ops$tkyte@ORA10G> alter table SYS_SQLLDR_X_EXT_DEPT
  2  project column referenced
  3  /

Table altered.
```

```
ops$tkyte@ORA10G> select dname
  2      from SYS_SQLLDR_X_EXT_DEPT
  3  /

DNAME
--------------
Sales
Accounting
Consulting
Finance
XYZ

ops$tkyte@ORA10G> select deptno
  2      from SYS_SQLLDR_X_EXT_DEPT
  3  /

    DEPTNO
----------
        10
        20
        30
        40
```

we get different numbers of rows from each query. The DNAME field was valid for every single record in the input file, but the DEPTNO column was not. If we do not retrieve the DEPTNO column, it does not fail the record—the resultset is materially changed.

Using an External Table to Load Different Files

A common need is to use an external table to load data from differently named files over a period of time. That is, this week we must load file1.dat, and next week it will be file2.dat, and so on. So far, we've been loading from a fixed file name, demo1.dat. What if we need subsequently to load from a second file, demo2.dat?

Fortunately, that is pretty easy to accommodate. The ALTER TABLE command may be used to repoint the location setting of the external table:

```
ops$tkyte@ORA10G> alter table SYS_SQLLDR_X_EXT_DEPT
  2  location( 'demo2.dat' );
Table altered.
```

And that would pretty much be it—the very next query of that external table would have it accessing the file demo2.dat.

Multiuser Issues

In the introduction to this section, I described three situations where external tables might not be as useful as SQLLDR. One of them was a specific multiuser issue. We just saw how to change the location of an external table—how to make it read from file 2 instead of file 1, and so on. The problem arises when multiple users each try to concurrently use that external table and have it point to different files for each session.

This cannot be done. The external table will point to a single file (or set of files) at any given time. If I log in and alter the table to point to file 1 and you do the same at about the same time, and then we both query that table, we'll both be processing the same file.

Generally, this issue is not one that you should encounter. External tables are not a replacement for "database tables"; they are a means to load data, and as such you would not use them on a daily basis as part of your application. They are generally a DBA or developer tool used to load information, either as a one-time event or on a recurring basis, as in a data warehouse load. If the DBA has ten files to load into the database using the same external table, she would *not* do them sequentially—that is, pointing the external file to file 1 and processing it, then file 2 and processing it, and so on. Rather, she would simply point the external table to *both files* and let the database process both of them:

```
ops$tkyte@ORA10G> alter table SYS_SQLLDR_X_EXT_DEPT
  2  location( 'file1.dat', 'file2.dat')
  3  /
Table altered.
```

If "parallel processing" is required, then the database already has the built-in ability to do this, as demonstrated in the last chapter.

So the only multiuser issue would be if two sessions both tried to alter the location at about the same time—and this is just a possibility to be aware of, not something I believe you'll actually run into very often.

Another multiuser consideration is that of the bad and log file names. What if you have many sessions concurrently looking at the same external table, or using parallel processing (which in some respects is a multiuser situation)? It would be nice to be able to segregate these files by session, and fortunately you can do that. You may incorporate the following special strings:

- %p: PID.

- %a: Parallel execution servers agent ID. The parallel execution servers have the numbers 001, 002, 003, and so on assigned to them.

In this fashion, each session will tend to generate its own bad and log files. For example, if you used the following BADFILE syntax in the CREATE TABLE from earlier:

```
RECORDS DELIMITED BY NEWLINE CHARACTERSET WE8ISO8859P1
BADFILE 'SYS_SQLLDR_XT_TMPDIR_00000':'demo1_%p.bad'
LOGFILE 'demo1.log_xt'
```

you would expect to find a file named similarly to the following:

```
$ ls *.bad
demo1_7108.bad
```

However, you still might have issues over lengthy periods of time. The PIDs will be reused on most operating systems. So the techniques outlined in dealing with errors may well still be relevant—you'll need to reset your bad file or rename it if it exists and if you determine this to be an issue.

External Tables Summary

In this section, we explored external tables. They are a new feature of Oracle9*i* and later that may, for the most part, replace SQLLDR. We investigated the quickest way to get going with external tables: the technique of using SQLLDR to convert the control files we have from past experiences. We demonstrated some techniques for detecting and handling errors via the bad files and, lastly, we explored some multiuser issues regarding external tables.

We are now ready to get into the last sections in this chapter, which deal with unloading data from the database.

Flat File Unload

One thing SQLLDR does not do, and that Oracle supplies no command-line tools for, is unload data in a format understandable by SQLLDR or other programs. This would be useful for moving data from system to system without using EXP/IMP or EXPDP/IMPDP (the new Data Pump replacements for EXP and IMP). Using EXP(DP)/IMP(DP) to move data from system to system works fine—as long as both systems are Oracle.

■**Note** HTML DB provides a data export feature as part of its SQL Workshop. You may export the information in a CSV format easily. This works well for a few megabytes of information, but it is not appropriate for many tens of megabytes or more.

We will develop a small PL/SQL utility that may be used to unload data on a server in a SQLLDR-friendly format. Also, equivalent tools for doing so in Pro*C and SQL*Plus are provided on the Ask Tom web site at http://asktom.oracle.com/~tkyte/flat/index.html. The PL/SQL utility will work fine in most small cases, but better performance will be had using Pro*C. Pro*C and SQL*Plus are also useful if you need the files to be generated on the client and not on the server, which is where PL/SQL will create them.

The specification of the package we will create is as follows:

```
ops$tkyte@ORA10G> create or replace package unloader
  2  AUTHID CURRENT_USER
  3  as
  4  /* Function run -- unloads data from any query into a file
  5                     and creates a control file to reload that
  6                     data into another table
  7
  8      p_query     = SQL query to "unload".  May be virtually any query.
  9      p_tname     = Table to load into.  Will be put into control file.
```

```
10      p_mode       = REPLACE|APPEND|TRUNCATE -- how to reload the data
11      p_dir        = directory we will write the ctl and dat file to.
12      p_filename   = name of file to write to.  I will add .ctl and .dat
13                     to this name
14      p_separator  = field delimiter.  I default this to a comma.
15      p_enclosure  = what each field will be wrapped in
16      p_terminator = end of line character.  We use this so we can unload
17                     and reload data with newlines in it.  I default to
18                     "|\n" (a pipe and a newline together) and "|\r\n" on NT.
19                     You need only to override this if you believe your
20                     data will have that sequence in it. I ALWAYS add the
21                     OS "end of line" marker to this sequence, you should not
22      */
23      function run( p_query      in varchar2,
24                    p_tname      in varchar2,
25                    p_mode       in varchar2 default 'REPLACE',
26                    p_dir        in varchar2,
27                    p_filename   in varchar2,
28                    p_separator  in varchar2 default ',',
29                    p_enclosure  in varchar2 default '"',
30                    p_terminator in varchar2 default '|' )
31      return number;
32 end;
33 /
Package created.
```

Note the use of AUTHID CURRENT_USER. This permits this package to be installed *once* in a database and used by anyone to unload data. All the person needs is SELECT privileges on the table(s) he wants to unload and EXECUTE privileges on this package. If we did not use AUTHID CURRENT_USER in this case, then the owner of this package would need direct SELECT privileges on all tables to be unloaded.

■**Note** The SQL will execute with the privileges of the invoker of this routine. However, all PL/SQL calls will run with the privileges of the *definer* of the called routine; therefore, the ability to use UTL_FILE to write to a directory is implicitly given to anyone with execute permission on this package.

The package body follows. We use UTL_FILE to write a control file and a data file. DBMS_SQL is used to dynamically process any query. We use one datatype in our queries: a VARCHAR2(4000). This implies we cannot use this method to unload LOBs, and that is true if the LOB is greater than 4,000 bytes. We can, however, use this to unload up to 4,000 bytes of any LOB using DBMS_LOB.SUBSTR. Additionally, since we are using a VARCHAR2 as the only output data type, we can handle RAWs up to 2,000 bytes in length (4,000 hexadecimal characters), which is sufficient for everything except LONG RAWs and LOBs. Additionally, any query that references a nonscalar attribute (a complex object type, nested table, and so on) will not work with this simple implementation. The following is a 90 percent solution, meaning it solves the problem 90 percent of the time.

```
ops$tkyte@ORA10G> create or replace package body unloader
  2  as
  3
  4
  5  g_theCursor    integer default dbms_sql.open_cursor;
  6  g_descTbl      dbms_sql.desc_tab;
  7  g_nl           varchar2(2) default chr(10);
  8
```

These are some global variables used in this package body. The global cursor is opened once, the first time we reference this package, and it will stay open until we log out. This avoids the overhead of getting a new cursor every time we call this package. The G_DESCTBL is a PL/SQL table that will hold the output of a DBMS_SQL.DESCRIBE call. G_NL is a newline character. We use this in strings that need to have newlines embedded in them. We do not need to adjust this for Windows—UTL_FILE will see the CHR(10) in the string of characters and automatically turn that into a carriage return/linefeed for us.

Next, we have a small convenience function used to convert a character to hexadecimal. It uses the built-in functions to do this:

```
  9
 10  function to_hex( p_str in varchar2 ) return varchar2
 11  is
 12  begin
 13      return to_char( ascii(p_str), 'fm0x' );
 14  end;
 15
```

Finally, we create one more convenience function, IS_WINDOWS, that returns TRUE or FALSE depending on if we are on the Windows platform, and therefore the end of line is a two-character string instead of the single character it is on most other platforms. We are using the built-in DBMS_UTILITY function, GET_PARAMETER_VALUE, which can be used to read almost any parameter. We retrieve the CONTROL_FILES parameter and look for the existence of a \ in it—if we find one, we are on Windows:

```
 16  function is_windows return boolean
 17  is
 18          l_cfiles varchar2(4000);
 19          l_dummy  number;
 20  begin
 21  if (dbms_utility.get_parameter_value( 'control_files', l_dummy, l_cfiles )>0)
 22  then
 23      return instr( l_cfiles, '\' ) > 0;
 24  else
 25      return FALSE;
 26  end if;
 27  end;
```

> **Note** The IS_WINDOWS function does rely on you using \ in your CONTROL_FILES parameter. Be aware that you may use /, but it would be highly unusual.

The following is a procedure to create a control file to reload the unloaded data, using the DESCRIBE table generated by DBMS_SQL.DESCRIBE_COLUMNS. It takes care of the operating system specifics for us, such as whether the operating system uses a carriage return/linefeed (this is used for the STR attribute):

```
28
29  procedure  dump_ctl( p_dir        in varchar2,
30                       p_filename   in varchar2,
31                       p_tname      in varchar2,
32                       p_mode       in varchar2,
33                       p_separator  in varchar2,
34                       p_enclosure  in varchar2,
35                       p_terminator in varchar2 )
36  is
37      l_output        utl_file.file_type;
38      l_sep           varchar2(5);
39      l_str           varchar2(5) := chr(10);
40
41  begin
42      if ( is_windows )
43      then
44          l_str := chr(13) || chr(10);
45      end if;
46
47      l_output := utl_file.fopen( p_dir, p_filename || '.ctl', 'w' );
48
49      utl_file.put_line( l_output, 'load data' );
50      utl_file.put_line( l_output, 'infile ''' ||
51                                    p_filename || '.dat'' "str x''' ||
52                                    utl_raw.cast_to_raw( p_terminator ||
53                                    l_str ) || '''"' );
54     .utl_file.put_line( l_output, 'into table ' || p_tname );
55      utl_file.put_line( l_output, p_mode );
56      utl_file.put_line( l_output, 'fields terminated by X''' ||
57                                    to_hex(p_separator) ||
58                                    ''' enclosed by X''' ||
59                                    to_hex(p_enclosure) || ''' ' );
60      utl_file.put_line( l_output, '(' );
61
62      for i in 1 .. g_descTbl.count
63      loop
64          if ( g_descTbl(i).col_type = 12 )
```

```
65              then
66                  utl_file.put( l_output, l_sep || g_descTbl(i).col_name ||
67                                      ' date ''ddmmyyyyhh24miss'' ');
68              else
69                  utl_file.put( l_output, l_sep || g_descTbl(i).col_name ||
70                                  ' char(' ||
71                                  to_char(g_descTbl(i).col_max_len*2) ||' )' );
72              end if;
73              l_sep := ','||g_nl ;
74          end loop;
75          utl_file.put_line( l_output, g_nl || ')' );
76          utl_file.fclose( l_output );
77  end;
78
```

Here is a simple function to return a quoted string using the chosen enclosure character. Notice how it not only encloses the character, but also doubles up the enclosure character if it exists in the string as well, so that they are preserved:

```
79  function quote(p_str in varchar2, p_enclosure in varchar2)
80          return varchar2
81  is
82  begin
83      return p_enclosure ||
84              replace( p_str, p_enclosure, p_enclosure||p_enclosure ) ||
85              p_enclosure;
86  end;
87
```

Next we have the main function, RUN. As it is fairly large, I'll comment on it as we go along:

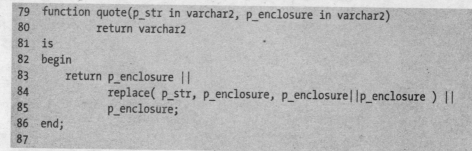

```
88  function run( p_query        in varchar2,
89              p_tname       in varchar2,
90              p_mode        in varchar2 default 'REPLACE',
91              p_dir         in varchar2,
92              p_filename    in varchar2,
93              p_separator   in varchar2 default ',',
94              p_enclosure   in varchar2 default '"',
95              p_terminator  in varchar2 default '|' ) return number
96  is
97      l_output          utl_file.file_type;
98      l_columnValue     varchar2(4000);
99      l_colCnt          number default 0;
100     l_separator       varchar2(10) default '';
101     l_cnt             number default 0;
102     l_line            long;
103     l_datefmt         varchar2(255);
104     l_descTbl         dbms_sql.desc_tab;
105 begin
```

We will save the NLS_DATE_FORMAT into a variable so we can change it to a format that preserves the date and time when dumping the data to disk. In this fashion, we will preserve the time component of a date. We then set up an exception block so that we can reset the NLS_DATE_FORMAT upon any error:

```
106     select value
107       into l_datefmt
108       from nls_session_parameters
109      where parameter = 'NLS_DATE_FORMAT';
110
111     /*
112        Set the date format to a big numeric string. Avoids
113        all NLS issues and saves both the time and date.
114     */
115     execute immediate
116        'alter session set nls_date_format=''ddmmyyyyhh24miss'' ';
117
118     /*
119        Set up an exception block so that in the event of any
120        error, we can at least reset the date format.
121     */
122     begin
```

Next we will parse and describe the query. The setting of G_DESCTBL to L_DESCTBL is done to "reset" the global table; otherwise, it might contain data from a previous DESCRIBE, in addition to data for the current query. Once we have done that, we call DUMP_CTL to actually create the control file:

```
123         /*
124            Parse and describe the query. We reset the
125            descTbl to an empty table so .count on it
126            will be reliable.
127         */
128         dbms_sql.parse( g_theCursor, p_query, dbms_sql.native );
129         g_descTbl := l_descTbl;
130         dbms_sql.describe_columns( g_theCursor, l_colCnt, g_descTbl );
131
132         /*
133            Create a control file to reload this data
134            into the desired table.
135         */
136         dump_ctl( p_dir, p_filename, p_tname, p_mode, p_separator,
137                            p_enclosure, p_terminator );
138
139         /*
140            Bind every single column to a varchar2(4000). We don't care
141            if we are fetching a number or a date or whatever.
142            Everything can be a string.
143         */
```

We are ready to dump the actual data out to disk. We begin by defining every column to be a VARCHAR2(4000) for fetching into. All NUMBERs, DATEs, RAWs—every type will be converted into VARCHAR2. Immediately after this, we execute the query to prepare for the fetching phase:

```
144        for i in 1 .. l_colCnt loop
145            dbms_sql.define_column( g_theCursor, i, l_columnValue, 4000);
146        end loop;
147
148        /*
149            Run the query - ignore the output of execute. It is only
150            valid when the DML is an insert/update or delete.
151        */
```

Now we open the data file for writing, fetch all of the rows from the query, and print it out to the data file:

```
152        l_cnt := dbms_sql.execute(g_theCursor);
153
154        /*
155            Open the file to write output to and then write the
156            delimited data to it.
157        */
158        l_output := utl_file.fopen( p_dir, p_filename || '.dat', 'w',
159                                    32760 );
160        loop
161            exit when ( dbms_sql.fetch_rows(g_theCursor) <= 0 );
162            l_separator := '';
163            l_line := null;
164            for i in 1 .. l_colCnt loop
165                dbms_sql.column_value( g_theCursor, i,
166                                       l_columnValue );
167                l_line := l_line || l_separator ||
168                          quote( l_columnValue, p_enclosure );
169                l_separator := p_separator;
170            end loop;
171            l_line := l_line || p_terminator;
172            utl_file.put_line( l_output, l_line );
173            l_cnt := l_cnt+1;
174        end loop;
175        utl_file.fclose( l_output );
176
```

Lastly, we set the date format back (and the exception block will do the same if any of the preceding code fails for any reason) to what it was and return:

```
177        /*
178            Now reset the date format and return the number of rows
179            written to the output file.
180        */
```

```
181         execute immediate
182             'alter session set nls_date_format=''' || l_datefmt || '''';
183         return l_cnt;
184  exception
185         /*
186             In the event of ANY error, reset the data format and
187             re-raise the error.
188         */
189         when others then
190             execute immediate
191             'alter session set nls_date_format=''' || l_datefmt || '''';
192             RAISE;
193     end;
194  end run;
195
196
197  end unloader;
198  /
Package body created.
```

To run this, we can simply use the following (note that the following does, of course, require that you have SELECT on SCOTT.EMP granted to one of your roles or to yourself directly):

```
ops$tkyte@ORA10G> set serveroutput on

ops$tkyte@ORA10G> create or replace directory my_dir as '/tmp';
Directory created.

ops$tkyte@ORA10G> declare
  2      l_rows   number;
  3  begin
  4      l_rows := unloader.run
  5          ( p_query      => 'select * from scott.emp order by empno',
  6            p_tname      => 'emp',
  7            p_mode       => 'replace',
  8            p_dir        => 'MY_DIR',
  9            p_filename   => 'emp',
 10            p_separator  => ',',
 11            p_enclosure  => '"',
 12            p_terminator => '~' );
 13
 14      dbms_output.put_line( to_char(l_rows) ||
 15                            ' rows extracted to ascii file' );
 16  end;
 17  /
14 rows extracted to ascii file
PL/SQL procedure successfully completed.
```

The control file that was generated by this shows the following (note that the numbers in parentheses in **bold** on the right are not actually in the file; they are solely for reference purposes):

```
load data                                              (1)
infile 'emp.dat' "str x'7E0A'"                         (2)
into table emp                                         (3)
replace                                                (4)
fields terminated by X'2c' enclosed by X'22'           (5)
(                                                      (6)
EMPNO char(44 ),                                       (7)
ENAME char(20 ),                                       (8)
JOB char(18 ),                                         (9)
MGR char(44 ),                                         (10)
HIREDATE date 'ddmmyyyyhh24miss' ,                     (11)
SAL char(44 ),                                         (12)
COMM char(44 ),                                        (13)
DEPTNO char(44 ),                                      (14)
)                                                      (15)
```

The things to note about this control file are as follows:

- Line (2): We use the STR feature of SQLLDR. We can specify what character or string is used to terminate a record. This allows us to load data with embedded newlines easily. The string x'7E0A' is simply a tilde followed by a newline.

- Line (5): We use our separator character and enclosure character. We do not use OPTIONALLY ENCLOSED BY, since we will be enclosing every single field after doubling any occurrence of the enclosure character in the raw data.

- Line (11): We use a large "numeric" date format. This does two things: it avoids any NLS issues with regard to the data, and it preserves the time component of the date field.

The raw data (.dat) file generated from the preceding code looks like this:

```
"7369","SMITH","CLERK","7902","17121980000000","800","","20"~
"7499","ALLEN","SALESMAN","7698","20021981000000","1600","300","30"~
"7521","WARD","SALESMAN","7698","22021981000000","1250","500","30"~
"7566","JONES","MANAGER","7839","02041981000000","2975","","20"~
"7654","MARTIN","SALESMAN","7698","28091981000000","1250","1400","30"~
"7698","BLAKE","MANAGER","7839","01051981000000","2850","","30"~
"7782","CLARK","MANAGER","7839","09061981000000","2450","","10"~
"7788","SCOTT","ANALYST","7566","19041987000000","3000","","20"~
"7839","KING","PRESIDENT","","17111981000000","5000","","10"~
"7844","TURNER","SALESMAN","7698","08091981000000","1500","0","30"~
"7876","ADAMS","CLERK","7788","23051987000000","1100","","20"~
"7900","JAMES","CLERK","7698","03121981000000","950","","30"~
"7902","FORD","ANALYST","7566","03121981000000","3000","","20"~
"7934","MILLER","CLERK","7782","23011982000000","1300","","10"~
```

Things to note in the .dat file are as follows:

- Each field is enclosed in our enclosure character.

- The DATEs are unloaded as large numbers.

- Each line of data in this file ends with a ~ as requested.

We can now reload this data easily using SQLLDR. You may add options to the SQLLDR command line as you see fit.

As stated previously, the logic of the unload package may be implemented in a variety of languages and tools. On the Ask Tom web site, you will find this example implemented not only in PL/SQL as here, but also in Pro*C and SQL*Plus scripts. Pro*C is the fastest implementation, and it always writes to the client workstation file system. PL/SQL is a good all-around implementation (there's no need to compile and install on client workstations), but it always writes to the server file system. SQL*Plus is a good middle ground, offering fair performance and the ability to write to the client file system.

Data Pump Unload

Oracle9*i* introduced external tables as a method to read external data into the database. Oracle 10*g* introduced the ability to go the other direction and use a CREATE TABLE statement to create external data, to unload data from the database. As of Oracle 10*g*, this data is extracted in a proprietary binary format known as *Data Pump format*, which is the same format the EXPDB and IMPDP tools provided by Oracle use to move data from database to database.

Using the external table unload is actually quite easy—as easy as a CREATE TABLE AS SELECT statement. To start, we need a DIRECTORY object:

```
ops$tkyte@ORA10GR1> create or replace directory tmp as '/tmp'
  2  /
Directory created.
```

Now we are ready to unload data to this directory using a simple SELECT statement, for example:

```
ops$tkyte@ORA10GR1> create table all_objects_unload
  2  organization external
  3  ( type oracle_datapump
  4    default directory TMP
  5    location( 'allobjects.dat' )
  6  )
  7  as
  8  select
  9  *
 10  from all_objects
 11  /
Table created.
```

I purposely chose the ALL_OBJECTS view, because it is a quite complex view with lots of joins and predicates. This example shows we can use this Data Pump unload technique to extract arbitrary data from our database. We could add predicates, or whatever we wanted, to extract a slice of data.

■**Note** This example shows we can use this Data Pump unload technique to extract arbitrary data from our database. Yes, that is repeated text. From a security perspective, this does make it rather easy for someone with access to the information to "take" the information elsewhere. You need to control access to the set of people who have the ability to create DIRECTORY objects and write to them, and who have the necessary access to the physical server to get the unloaded data.

The final step would be to copy allobjects.dat onto another server, perhaps a development machine for testing with, and extract the DDL to re-create this table over there:

```
ops$tkyte@ORA10GR1> select dbms_metadata.get_ddl( 'TABLE', 'ALL_OBJECTS_UNLOAD' )
  2      from dual;


DBMS_METADATA.GET_DDL('TABLE','ALL_OBJECTS_UNLOAD')
--------------------------------------------------------------------------------
  CREATE TABLE "OPS$TKYTE"."ALL_OBJECTS_UNLOAD"
   (    "OWNER" VARCHAR2(30),
        "OBJECT_NAME" VARCHAR2(30),
        "SUBOBJECT_NAME" VARCHAR2(30),
        "OBJECT_ID" NUMBER,
        "DATA_OBJECT_ID" NUMBER,
        "OBJECT_TYPE" VARCHAR2(19),
        "CREATED" DATE,
        "LAST_DDL_TIME" DATE,
        "TIMESTAMP" VARCHAR2(19),
        "STATUS" VARCHAR2(7),
        "TEMPORARY" VARCHAR2(1),
        "GENERATED" VARCHAR2(1),
        "SECONDARY" VARCHAR2(1)
   )
  ORGANIZATION EXTERNAL
   ( TYPE ORACLE_DATAPUMP
     DEFAULT DIRECTORY "TMP"

     LOCATION
      ( 'allobjects.dat'
      )
   )
```

This makes it rather easy to load this extract on another database, as it would simply be

```
SQL> insert /*+ append */ into some_table select * from all_objects_unload;
```

and you are done—the data is loaded.

Summary

In this chapter, we covered many of the ins and outs of data loading and unloading. We started with SQL*Loader (SQLLDR) and examined many of the basic techniques for loading delimited data, fixed-width data, LOBs, and the like. We discussed how this knowledge carries right over into external tables, a new feature in Oracle9*i* and later that is useful as a replacement for SQLLDR, but that still utilizes our SQLLDR skills.

Then we looked at the reverse process, data unloading, and how to get data out of the database in a format that other tools, such as spreadsheets or the like, may use. In the course of that discussion, we developed a PL/SQL utility to demonstrate the process—one that unloads data in a SQLLDR-friendly format, but could easily be modified to meet our needs.

Lastly, we looked at a new Oracle 10*g* feature, the external table unload, and the ability to easily create and move extracts of data from database to database.

Index